Human
Behavior

J.B. LIPPINCOTT COMPANY
Philadelphia

Human Behavior

An Introduction for Medical Students

Second Edition

Edited by

Alan Stoudemire, M.D.

Professor of Psychiatry
Director, Medical Student Education in Psychiatry
Department of Psychiatry and Behavioral Sciences
Emory University School of Medicine
Atlanta, Georgia

27 Contributors

Acquisitions Editor: Richard Winters
Sponsoring Editor: Jody Schott
Production Service: Chernow Editorial Services, Inc.
Indexer: Melanie Belkin
Cover Designer: Tom Jackson
Production Manager: Janet Greenwood
Production Coordinator: Mary Kinsella
Compositor: Circle Graphics
Printer/Binder: R.R. Donnelley & Sons, Crawfordsville

Second Edition

6   5   4   3

Library of Congress Cataloging-in-Publication Data

Human behavior: an introduction for medical students/edited by Alan
    Stoudemire; 27 contributors. – – 2nd ed.
        p.   cm.
    Companion v. to: Clinical psychiatry for medical students. c1994.
    Includes bibliographical references and index.
    ISBN 0-397-51337-2
    1. Clinical health psychology.   2. Physician and patient.
3. Psychology.   4. Human behavior.   I. Stoudemire, Alan.
II. Clinical psychiatry for medical students.
    [DNLM: 1. Behavior   2. Human Development. BF 121 H918 1994]
R726.7.H85 1994
616'.0019—dc20
DNLM/DLC
for Library of Congress   93-34437
                                                                            CIP

The authors and publisher have exerted every effort to ensure that drug selection and dosage set forth in this text are in accord with current recommendations and practice at the time of publication. However, in view of ongoing research, changes in government regulations, and the constant flow of information relating to drug therapy and drug reactions, the reader is urged to check the package insert for each drug for any change in indications and dosage and for added warnings and precautions. This is particularly important when the recommended agent is a new or infrequently employed drug.

Accompanying text:
Clinical Psychiatry for Medical Students, Second Edition
Edited by Alan Stoudemire, M.D.

This book is dedicated to my parents

Contributors

Bruce L. Ballard, M.D.

Associate Dean for Student Affairs and Equal Opportunity Programs
Associate Professor of Clinical Psychiatry
Cornell University Medical College
New York, New York

Miron Baron, M.D.

Professor of Clinical Psychiatry
Columbia University College of Physicians and Surgeons
New York, New York

Judith V. Becker, Ph.D.

Professor of Psychiatry and Psychology
University of Arizona College of Medicine
Tucson, Arizona

Peter J. Brown, Ph.D.

Professor of Anthropology
Associate Professor of Public Health
Emory University
Atlanta, Georgia

Steven A. Cohen-Cole, M.D.

Associate Professor of Psychiatry and Behavioral Sciences
Emory University School of Medicine
Atlanta, Georgia

Pamela G. Dorsett, Ph.D.

Adjunct Assistant Professor of Psychiatry and Behavioral Sciences
Emory University School of Medicine
Atlanta, Georgia

Mina K. Dulcan, M.D.

Osterman Professor of Child Psychiatry
Head, Department of Child Psychiatry
Children's Memorial Hospital
Professor of Psychiatry and Behavioral Sciences
Chief, Division of Child and Adolescent Psychiatry
Northwestern University Medical School
Chicago, Illinois

Dwight L. Evans, M.D.

Professor and Chairman of Psychiatry
Professor of Medicine and Neuroscience
University of Florida College of Medicine
Gainesville, Florida

Joan Fiore, Ph.D.

Adjunct Assistant Professor of Psychiatry and Behavioral Sciences
Emory University School of Medicine
Atlanta, Georgia

Robert N. Golden, M.D.

Associate Professor of Psychiatry
University of North Carolina School of Medicine
Chapel Hill, North Carolina

Stephen A. Green, M.D.

Clinical Professor of Psychiatry
Senior Scholar, Center for Clinical Bioethics
Georgetown University School of Medicine
Washington, DC

Jessica Gregg, M.A.

Department of Anthropology
Emory University
Atlanta, Georgia
Department of Anthropology
University of New Mexico
Albuquerque, New Mexico

John J. Haggerty, Jr., M.D.

Associate Professor of Psychiatry
University of North Carolina School of Medicine
Chapel Hill, North Carolina

John A. Hunter, Jr., Ph.D.

Research Associate Professor of Psychology
University of Arizona
Tucson, Arizona

Lawrence B. Inderbitzin, M.D.

Director, Emory Psychoanalytic Institute
Professor of Psychiatry and Behavioral Sciences
Emory University School of Medicine
Atlanta, Georgia

Mark E. James, M.D.

Assistant Professor of Psychiatry and Behavioral Sciences
Emory University School of Medicine
Atlanta, Georgia

Wayne Katon, M.D.

Professor of Psychiatry
Chief, Division of Consultation-Liaison Psychiatry
University of Washington School of Medicine
Seattle, Washington

Nancy L. Kriseman, L.C.S.W.

Licensed Clinical Social Worker
Private Practice
Atlanta, Georgia

Richard M. Levinson, Ph.D.

Associate Professor of Public Health
Emory University School of Public Health
Atlanta, Georgia

Cort A. Pedersen, M.D.

Associate Professor of Psychiatry
University of North Carolina School of Medicine
Chapel Hill, North Carolina

John M. Petitto, M.D.

Assistant Professor of Psychiatry
University of Florida College of Medicine
Gainesville, Florida

Susan B. Shelton, M.D., M.Ed.

Assistant Professor of Psychiatry and Behavioral Sciences
Emory University School of Medicine
Atlanta, Georgia

Alan Stoudemire, M.D.

Professor of Psychiatry and Behavioral Sciences
Emory University School of Medicine
Atlanta, Georgia

Troy L. Thompson II, M.D.

The Daniel Lieberman Professor and Chair
Department of Psychiatry and Human Behavior
Jefferson Medical College
Philadelphia, Pennsylvania

Bessel A. van der Kolk, M.D.

Associate Professor of Psychiatry
Harvard Medical School
Boston, Massachusetts

Edward A. Walker, M.D.

Assistant Professor of Psychiatry
University of Washington School of Medicine
Seattle, Washington

Thomas Wolman, M.D.

Clinical Assistant Professor of Psychiatry
University of Pennsylvania School of Medicine
Philadelphia, Pennsylvania

Foreword

It has become increasingly apparent during this era of health care reform that there is a pressing national priority to increase the knowledge of mental disease among all physicians, to implement the understanding of psychiatric treatments and interventions, and to improve the skills of the majority of physicians who will undertake these treatments. The National Institute of Mental Health estimates that sixty percent of the thirty-two million people with mental disease in the United States receive their treatment within the primary care sector entirely. In fact, only one in five with mental illness receives care from the core mental health professionals, with psychiatrists providing only a portion of that care. There is also growing awareness that many nonpsychiatric physicians lack the motivation, the interest, or the conceptual framework that would permit them to provide state-of-the-art treatment to their many patients suffering from mental disorders.

What has been missing in medical education in psychiatry is the excitement and enthusiasm that is so evident in *Human Behavior: An Introduction for Medical Students*, edited by Dr. Stoudemire. The conceptual model that is offered is not peculiar to the behavioral sciences. The biopsychosocial model, in fact, will eventually permeate all of medicine. Beginning with this context and moving through the lifecycle, the biological and psychological factors can be seen as the connecting links that support the scientific application of treatment approaches. This second edition ensures the continued availability of this most needed contribution to medical education and the eventual improvement of the medical care of the citizens of our nation.

Robert O. Pasnau, M.D.
Professor of Psychiatry
School of Medicine
University of California at Los Angeles
Los Angeles, California

Preface

The essence of being a physician is the ability to integrate excellent medical treatment with compassionate care of the patient. The primary emphasis, however, in medical training is devoted to assimilating a scientific knowledge base and practicing the technical aspects of medical diagnosis and treatment. Relatively little consistent attention is given to acquiring and developing the necessary knowledge and skills to understand and attend to the psychological and emotional needs of patients. With rapid advances in medical science, diagnostic technology, and medical therapeutics over the past 50 years, medical students have been literally crushed by the amount of scientific information they must assimilate. The amount of time and attention devoted to teaching students fundamental principles of human behavior and the psychological aspects of patient care are often given a relatively low priority. The information barrage that students are subjected to, as well as a widespread tendency to determine a specialty choice early in medical school, further contributes to a trend toward narrowness in the training of physicians. In addition, compared to the "hard data" of other scientific disciplines, psychiatry has often appeared diffuse, amorphous, and out of the mainstream of traditional medicine.

There has been an enormous increase in the scientific knowledge base for psychiatry in all of its facets: biological, psychological, and sociological. The biochemical basis for the major mental disorders is gradually being elucidated from studies of aberrant neurotransmitter and receptor activity and molecular genetics. This emerging scientific knowledge has had profound influences on the biological understanding of mental illness. In addition, the field of psychopharmacology has made remarkable advances in providing specific treatments for certain psychiatric illnesses such as psychotic, mood, and anxiety disorders. Advances in neuroradiographic and neuroendocrine probes of the central nervous system have also provided remarkable new ways of measuring biological parameters of normal and abnormal mental functioning. Moreover, while these biological advances may appear to have supplanted the importance of psychoanalytic theories and the perspectives of developmental psychology in psychiatric illness, a growing body of information indicates that certain types of developmental traumas, deprivations, and stresses may have a lasting impact on the central nervous system, leading to altered social behavior, dysfunctional interpersonal relationships, affective instability, and vulnerability to mental disorders. Hence, intriguing scientific evidence is accumulating that may potentially link psychological theories of behavior with neurobiology, enabling a true psychobiologic integration of the behavioral sciences. Where pertinent, this text will point toward trends in this psychobiological body of knowledge.

Throughout this text, the term *biopsychosocial model* will be used. In its essence, this theoretical model emphasizes the importance of understanding behavior and illness from a general systems perspective where multiple biological, psychological, and social systems interact and influence each other. To focus exclusively on a biological, psychosocial, or sociological area while neglecting the others leads to a narrow—and fundamentally mistaken—viewpoint. While in clinical situations necessity and urgency may lead the physician to focus on one given area initially (i.,e., attending to a patient's acute myocardial infarction in the emergency room), one must nevertheless not lose sight of the psychological aspects of the illness (the patient's fears and emotional reactions to the heart attack) the effects that the illness might have on other aspects of the patient's life (ability to work and financial affairs), behavioral risk factors that put that patient at risk (i.e., being overweight, smoking cigarettes) or stress that could have actually precipitated the myocardial infarction. Hence, this multidimensional biopsychosocial approach to patient care requires the physician to ultimately assess multiple aspects of the patients's condition in the diagnostic and treatment process.

It is upon the general premise of the biopsychosocial model that this book is based, and it is this viewpoint that forms the predominant theme of the text. The text itself is divided into five sections that address different aspects of a biopsychosocial understanding of human behavior.

The first chapter of the text begins with the cornerstone of the practice of medicine—the doctor–patient relationship. This chapter discusses contractual and psychologic aspects of the doctor–patient relationship framing this relationship within the context of the biopsychosocial model. The basic premises of the biopsychosocial model are discussed in detail in the following chapter, which emphasizes the abundance of scientific evidence to support the validity of the model. While Chapter 2 on the biopsychosocial model discusses at length sociological factors that influence vulnerability for outcome in medical disorders, the next chapter introduces psychological factors that affect medical conditions—with special attention given to the ramifications of stress on the neuroendocrine, immunologic, and cardiovascular systems. The final chapter in this introductory section completes the overview of the biopsychosocial model, examining cultural factors in the practice of medicine.

Section II presents in some detail the basic principles of two major schools of psychology: psychoanalytic and behavioral theory. The rationale in discussing these two perspectives is addressed in the introduction to the chapter on psychoanalytic psychology and involves a practical decision to cover principles in two major schools of thought in some detail, rather than covering multiple views in a superficial manner, which ultimately would be of little clinical use to the student. The important principles of psychoanalytic and behavioral theory are presented with emphasis on their practical importance for patient care.

In Section III, fundamentals of normal behavior are dealt with in a comprehensive manner from infancy to later life. This section begins with a discussion of normal human sexual development and provides a basic overview of the normal sexual response cycle. The following chapter on childhood and adolescent development forms a core conceptual framework for the entire text. The section also includes an excellent discussion of *adult* developmental cycles that extends to issues of death and dying. The importance of the family in development and adjusting to illness is also reviewed, as well as the physician's role in identifying and intervening in dysfunctional families. This section concludes with an intriguing discussion on one of the most important emerging areas in behavioral science, that is, the neurobiologic effects of developmental stresses and emotional trauma, which as noted above, may serve to integrate psychological and biological perspectives on behavior and mental illness.

Biological aspects of behavior are further discussed in Section IV, addressing two primary areas—neurobiology and behavioral genetics. These chapters present evidence for the biogenetic basis of human behavior, examining data derived from neuroanatomic, neurochemical, and genetic research that should intrigue and interest the most scientifically-oriented student.

The final chapter draws again upon the biopsychosocial model and attempts to integrate the principles discussed in previous chapters to demonstrate how they are useful and important in the care of patients. In this chapter, the specific types of emotional and psychological reactions that patients have to illness are discussed, as well as how they may be managed by physicians using the biopsychosocial model of medical care.

While this text briefly mentions and alludes to the significance of biological, psychological, and social factors in the development of psychiatric illness, specific psychopathological syndromes and the diagnosis and treatment of psychiatric disorders are not specifically addressed. Ideally, this text serves as the basis and entrée to the companion text *Clinical Psychiatry for Medical Students*, which addresses fundamental principles of clinical psychiatry—and also strives for an integrated approach to diagnosis and treatment of the major psychopathological syndromes in psychiatry.

As mentioned earlier in this introduction, the essence of the ideal physician is the ability to practice excellent medicine while attending to the psychological and emotional needs of the patient with compassion. This is certainly not a new concept in medicine and has been the ideal of the profession for centuries. Nowhere has this ethic been more eloquently summarized as in the classic 1927 essay by Dr. Francis Peabody entitled "The Care of the Patient":

Disease in man is never exactly the same as disease in an experimental animal, for in man the disease at once affects and is affected by what we call the emotional life. Thus, the physician who attempts to take care of patient while he neglects this factor is as unscientific as the investigator who neglects to control all the conditions that may affect his experiment. The good physician knows his patients through and through, and his knowledge is bought dearly. Time, sympathy and understanding must be lavishly dispensed, but the reward is to be found in that personal bond which forms the greatest satisfaction of the practice of medicine. One of the essential qualities of the clinician is interest in humanity, for the secret of the care of the patient is in caring for the patient.

Alan Stoudemire, M.D.

Acknowledgments

This text could not have been completed without the tireless dedication, loyalty, and effort of my administrative assistant, Lynda Mathews. Her contribution to this book is greatly appreciated.

Thanks are also extended to the students and faculty of Emory University School of Medicine as well as those of other medical schools. Their suggestions regarding the first edition of this text have, I hope, resulted in a more complete and refined second edition.

Recommended Textbooks

Diagnostic and Statistical Manual of Mental Disorders, 4th ed. Washington, DC. American Psychiatric Association, 1994.

> This is the "bible" of descriptive psychiatry. It contains epidemiological and descriptive data of the major psychiatric disorders.

Kaplan HI, Sadock BJ (eds): Comprehensive Textbook of Psychiatry, 6th ed, Vols 1 and 2. Baltimore, Williams & Wilkins, 1994

> This is an encyclopedic textbook that covers all areas of psychiatry. Detailed and comprehensive, it should be primarily used as a reference source.

Michels R (ed): Psychiatry, Vols 1–III. Philadelphia, JB Lippincott, 1993

> This is an excellent and comprehensive textbook of clinical psychiatry. Published in three volumes, the chapters are lucid, well edited, and are kept fresh by a subscription process that periodically updates the material.

Nicholi AM Jr (ed): New Harvard Guide to Psychiatry, 2nd ed. Cambridge, MA, Belknap Press of Harvard University Press, 1988

> This is an excellent overview of clinical psychiatry that is very readable and practical for a medical student audience. Chapters that are especially strong are those on the biological aspects of depression, the genetic aspects of schizophrenia, and the chapters on psychodynamic and psychoanalytic theory by Meissner, Vaillant, and Nemiah.

Stoudemire A, Fogel BS (eds): Psychiatric Care of the Medical Patient. New York, Oxford University Press, 1993

This comprehensive textbook is a detailed reference on the psychiatric disorders as encountered in medically ill patients. It contains detailed information regarding diagnosis, psychotherapy, and psychopharmacologic modifications that are required in treating psychiatric disorders in the medically ill.

Talbott J, Hales RE, Yudofsky S (eds): Textbook of Psychiatry, 2nd ed. Washington, DC, American Psychiatric Press, 1994

This is an excellent textbook of clinical psychiatry that is eminently readable and practical. The chapters will provide a somewhat more expanded discussion of the psychopathological syndromes contained in this text.

Contents

III Human Development Through the Lifecycle

IV Biological Basis of Behavior

V Clinical Applications

Index

I

The Biopsychosocial Model of Understanding Behavior in Health and Illness

Alan Stoudemire (ed). *Human Behavior: An Introduction for Medical Students,*
Second Edition. Copyright © 1994, 1990 by J. B. Lippincott Company.

1

The Doctor–Patient Relationship

Susan B. Shelton

The doctor–patient relationship is often considered the simplest of relationships, but, in fact, it is one of the most complicated. On the surface, it is the straightforward exchange between a medical expert and a person in need of care. On a deeper level, it is the interaction of two human beings dealing intimately with one another over issues of health, illness, and sometimes death. Unfortunately, this deeper level of interaction is often ignored.

As a medical student or new physician, you may want to maintain emotional distance from patients in order to deal with the enormous pressures of being a physician. Will you know enough to make the diagnosis and offer the right treatment? If the patient dies, will it be your fault? With so much to learn and so many expectations, it is hard to find the time and energy to worry about the nuances of the doctor–patient relationship.

It is tempting to believe that this relationship will automatically happen in a positive way or that it is just a matter of common sense. Most medical students pride themselves on their concern for and commitment to others. However, they may also bring to their profession an idealized if not naive view of themselves and of their relationships with future patients. This naïveté can lead to frustration and disappointment if it is not tempered with a realistic understanding of the intricate complexities of human personality and the many factors that may influence human behavior in the context of medical illness.

The purpose of both this chapter and text is to begin to examine the doctor–patient relationship in depth. In many respects, this entire text is devoted to understanding how human behavior is affected by medical illness, which will in turn affect the interaction between physician and patient. In this chapter we will focus on several aspects of the doctor–patient relationship including

- Use of the biopsychosocial model
- Empathic listening
- Styles of relating
- The concepts of transference, countertransference, and the real relationship
- Issues of compliance
- Difficult doctor–patient relationships

The following patient's story introduces many of the major issues to be addressed in this chapter, and it will serve as a reference point throughout this chapter.

A patient newly diagnosed with breast cancer expressed her needs and frustrations in a letter she wrote to her oncologist:

> I am writing this letter as a way to finally be heard by you.... At the time of our first meeting, when I told you I was glad to meet you and you countered my honest greeting with a sarcastic remark, "I know you are *not* glad to meet me," you made it perfectly clear that you saw yourself as the "bad guy" and that chemotherapy was going to be a "bad experience." In hindsight, I realize that the relationship you were offering, from the beginning, was never meant to be that of a supportive ally which I so desperately needed during this difficult, stress-filled treatment. Even the setting in which the chemotherapy was administered could never have been conducive to a calm, peaceful reaction....
>
> I am very angry for letting myself be intimidated by you. But I'm also angry and hurt by your impersonal, detached, and at times very rude treatment of me. I came to you anticipating truly professional, innovative, state-of-the-art care.... Care does not start and stop with the prescribing of drugs.... In addition to your medical opinion, I needed you to support me and encourage me through a very frightening journey. And you were not there for me.
>
> Due to a severe lack of sleep, continuing bladder inflammation problems, poor communication, and other physical and emotional effects of chemo, I gradually became exhausted and unable to cope with life in general, let alone chemo or cancer. You, as my primary physician doing chemotherapy, had a responsibility to remain informed about the results of the various examinations and procedures I was subjected to by doctors you referred me to. You also had a responsibility to communicate to me the impact their findings had on my treatment plan. Instead, I was left with the incredible hassle of trying to get in touch with them myself and relate their findings to my chemotherapy needs. This greatly added to the stress I was under.
>
> At our last visit, after talking with me for less than five minutes, you diagnosed me as severely depressed, referred me to a psychiatrist and suggested that Prozac might help. Then you turned your back on me while I was crying and walked out the door.

What this patient wanted and what most patients want from their physicians is to be heard, understood, and supported. Patients want a physician who will listen and respond to their individual concerns with empathy and respect. They want to know that their physician will respond to them when needed and will not abandon them in the midst of a chronic or terminal illness. As this woman expressed it, patients want a reliable "ally" who will be emotionally present as they cope with the uncertainty and pain of their diagnosis and treatment.

In order to provide this type of support, physicians must understand more than just the biological and medical aspects of a patient's illness.

BIOPSYCHOSOCIAL MODEL

To know a patient well, one must understand his or her world. As exemplified by the patient letter above, this understanding is not possible through the use of the biomedical model alone.

The *biomedical* model is defined as an approach to patient care in which only the biologic and medical aspects of a patient's illness are considered relevant information to be obtained. The model developed out of a prevalent misconception that one can focus on the disease entity without considering the person who has the disease (Cassell, 1991). Not included in this model are the patient's psychological experience and social environment. These omitted factors can have a major impact on a patient's susceptibility to illness and on illness outcome.

In contrast, the *biopsychosocial* model is a comprehensive approach to patient care in which all major aspects of a patient's life are explored (biological, psychological, and social). When done well, this approach enables the physician to provide more effective treatment. This topic will be fully addressed in Chapter 2 by Drs. Cohen-Cole and Levinson as well as in Chapter 14 by Dr. Green. However, one example may help to illustrate the point.

The oncologist mentioned earlier used the biomedical model in his approach to patient care. He focused on the disease process and pharmacotherapy needed to treat that disease. If he had used the biopsychosocial model, he would have understood the patient's story that follows.

A CASE STUDY

JL was a woman in her mid-30s who discovered a lump in her left breast during a routine breast exam. She was a conscientious woman who tried to take care of her health in the same way she took care of her life—through careful planning and control. She saw herself as self-reliant and in charge of what happened to her.

She developed these attributes as a child. She identified with a very controlled and controlling mother and received little emotional support from either parent during times of crisis. When she had a problem or suffered a loss, her mother's advice was always to "get over it."

As an adult she saw herself as someone who asked for and received little support from others. She was a devoted mother, active in church and social activities, and had recently made a decision to return to work. Despite a troubled marriage, she felt optimistic about her life.

Her physician assured her that her lump was a cyst, and a mammogram seemed to confirm this. However, attempts to drain the "cyst" were unsuccessful. A difficult biopsy revealed an unsuspected cancer, and the patient underwent a mastectomy. She remained "very strong" throughout these procedures but felt little support from those around her, including her husband. The patient subsequently went to an oncologist for chemotherapy, and it was in this setting that her "strength" finally gave way.

If the oncologist working with JL had understood more about the patient's social situation and emotional makeup, he would have realized that she was a woman who was struggling with issues of control and an unspoken need for support. JL had spent her life believing that one could control situations by doing "the right thing" (e.g., doing routine breast exams) and by being self-sufficient. Overwhelmed by her illness, her attempts at control failed her. A physician who recognized these elements in her life would have been able to give her some sense of control by fully discussing options, assisting her in the decision-making process, and assuring her through action that someone was in charge of her situation and effectively coordinating her care. By recognizing the patient's limited support system, the physician could have provided more personalized care by taking the time to listen to her concerns.

EMPATHIC LISTENING

There is an active component to effective listening that involves the ability to empathize with patients.

Empathy is the ability to momentarily experience the feelings of another, i.e., to put oneself in another person's place. It is not the same as "feeling sorry" for a patient (sympathy) or offering reassurance. It involves attempts to understand the meaning of an illness by viewing that illness through the eyes of the patient.

In medical school there is an emphasis on learning to ask the right questions in the right way to arrive at the correct diagnosis. Physicians have too much to do and too little time. They are encouraged to get to the essence of the problem as rapidly as possible. New physicians worry that they will fail to ask the one question that holds the key to the diagnosis. They may feel they are wasting precious time when the patient insists on discussing his own agenda. Often physicians will need to redirect patients, but how and when they do this is an art. Sometimes letting patients talk will be the shortest route to understanding their illness, and it is the shared understanding that will lead to effective treatment.

There are several major goals in a medical interview. The most obvious one is to obtain needed information about the patient and his illness (data collection). A second goal is to provide emotional support. Less obvious, but equally important, is the goal of establishing a working relationship between the physician and the patient. To establish this relationship physicians must do more than ask the right questions; they must accurately hear the answers and listen for the patient's themes. They must understand what most concerns the patient even if this is not the doctor's primary concern. Physicians must then communicate this understanding through words and action. A sample dialogue may help clarify how one listens empathically.

JL said to her physician,

> I am frustrated with all of the disjointed care I am getting. No one is telling me what is going on with my body. First I have one reaction and then another, and no one seems to be aware of what anyone else is doing to me. I can't sleep, I'm exhausted; and I keep having one problem after another.

An unempathic response and essentially the response the patient received is the following:

> It's clear you are not handling your illness very well right now. I think you are depressed. I think you need to see a psychiatrist and try Prozac, which might help.

A response that tries to understand the patient's point of view is the following:

> You have had a number of side effects from the chemo, and they haven't cleared up as readily as I would have liked. You seem understandably frustrated with how things are going, including perhaps being frustrated with me for not being able to spend more time discussing reports from all the subspecialists you have seen lately. Let me tell you what I know about right now, and as soon as I get the rest of the reports I will call you, and we'll meet again to go over them.
>
> You look and seem exhausted and you're telling me you haven't been sleeping. Let's figure out what we can do to help you get the sleep you need in the short run. I also wonder how you are coping with all you've been through. You tell me you don't have much support at home, and I would think about seeing someone to talk to—like a psychiatrist. I recommend that frequently to people newly diagnosed with cancer, and it often helps. Let me know if you're interested in that, and I'll get you a good referral.

What this second exchange did was directly address the concerns of the patient in a nondefensive way and in the physician's own words to see if they matched the patient's perceptions of the problem. It also attempted to resolve the patient's frustration by indicating the physician was ready to take charge of the case in a personal way.

Empathic listening is essential in establishing a solid therapeutic alliance between physician and patient, and without this alliance little effective treatment can be provided.

Equally important in establishing this alliance is the way in which the physician relates to the patient.

STYLES OF RELATING

Physicians have varying approaches to patient care in terms of

1. the quality of the interaction, e.g., warmth vs. detachment,
2. the nature of the communication, e.g., who does most of the talking, and
3. the decision-making process, e.g., who makes the decisions.

These factors can intermix in a number of ways, and different authors have used different designations for physicians' styles (Emanuel and Emanuel, 1992; Frankel, 1987; Kaplan and Sadock, 1991; Underwood and Owen, 1985). More important than the particular designations are the concepts that underlie them. See Table 1–1 for a summary of the categories described below.

The Paternalistic or Autocratic Style

The stereotypical image of the physician in the early 1900s was of a warm father figure who comforted the patient and gave advice (Book, 1991). With the explosion of scientific and medical knowledge in the mid-1990s, this style evolved into a more technical and often detached scientific approach to patient care in which the focus of the physician shifted from the patient to the disease.

Physicians who use the autocratic style may be warm or aloof depending on their personalities. They provide information to the patient to the extent that they feel this is necessary or helpful. They typically dominate and control the interview process and

Table 1–1 **Physician Styles**

THE PATERNALISTIC OR AUTOCRATIC STYLE
• May be warm or detached.
• Decisions are made primarily by the physician.
• Information is provided to the patient from the physician. The physician is dominant in the interview process.

THE SHARED DECISION-MAKING STYLE
• Interaction is typically warm.
• Decisions are shared based on expertise of each participant.
• Information is shared. The physician asks more questions and is less dominant in the interview.

THE CONSUMER-BASED STYLE
• Interaction may be warm or detached.
• Decisions are made primarily by the patient.
• Information is provided based on patient questions. The patient may dominate the interview process.

will ask fewer open-ended questions and fewer questions in general than their more egalitarian colleagues. They make most or all decisions regarding patient care.

The critically ill patient requiring emergency procedures will do best with the physician who takes charge of the situation and makes the decisions necessary to save the patient's life. There are also some patients who relate best to this style in general. These may be patients who feel overwhelmed by their illness, are in crisis, or feel reassured by a strong authority figure who tells them what to do (LeBaron et al, 1985).

The Shared Decision-Making Style

Many physicians find the autocratic role uncomfortable or unhelpful to their patients. They may use a more interactive approach in which both the physician and the patient bring their particular expertise into the interview process. The physician brings knowledge of the disease, treatment options, and possible outcomes. The patient brings personal experience with the illness, priorities, and specific concerns. Together they work toward a consensus regarding treatment.

The interaction between physician and patient is typically warm and empathic (although again this depends upon the personalities of physician and patient). The communication is less dominated by the physician, who is more likely to ask questions including those which focus on psychosocial concerns. This is the style of communication the patient is most likely to perceive positively (Bertakis, et al, 1991; Buller and Buller, 1987).

The Consumer-Based Style

This third style coincides with the current "corporate" phase of medical care (Book, 1991). Using this approach, options are described by the physician and decisions are left in the hands of the patient or others who will be paying the bills. This is most frequently, but not exclusively, seen in situations that do not involve serious illness. For example, the patient who wants plastic surgery to correct a perceived flaw may be left ultimately to make the choice about what is to be done.

The interaction will often be cordial and businesslike, and communication may be dominated by the patient. The physician is there essentially to answer questions.

Some physicians can readily shift their approach among these styles depending upon the patient's needs or the situation. They recognize the patient who needs to be actively involved in decision making and the one who would be overwhelmed by such involvement. They also recognize situations that require an autocratic approach versus those which do not.

Other physicians are less flexible. They have one approach to patient care and expect patients to adapt to them. If the patient is not satisfied with the physician's style, he may find another doctor who is more compatible. JL provides a fairly typical example of this solution. The oncologist's style was detached and autocratic. The patient wanted a physician who was warm, engaged, and would share the decision-making process with her. Because of this mismatch, the patient sought treatment elsewhere.

Sometimes, however, the mismatch may persist. This may be particularly true for indigent patients, patients who are easily intimidated, or patients in rural communities. Such patients may feel they have no options except to stay with their doctor or drop out of treatment altogether.

The Unethical Relationship

There is a fourth type of relationship between physician and patient that may overlap with any of the three styles previously mentioned. Whenever a physician uses a patient for his or her own end, an unethical relationship exists (Fromm-Reichman, 1950). This patient exploitation may be subtle or blatant. It is sometimes outside the physician's conscious awareness and may involve transference and countertransference feelings, which will be discussed in the next section of this text. It is often done with the "consent" of the patient. For example, a physician may get a patient to agree to a sexual relationship. This remains an unethical arrangement because it has occurred in the context of the doctor–patient relationship (Nicholi, 1988).

The physician has a special obligation toward patients that involves trust, confidentiality, competence, and responsibility. It is not an equal relationship. A doctor who is found wanting in any of these four areas can be held accountable. Patients come to their physicians expecting them to honor this code of ethics, and it is the physician's responsibility to maintain appropriate professional boundaries no matter what the patient does. When in doubt regarding an evolving relationship with a patient, physicians are encouraged to seek formal or informal consultation from colleagues to clarify what may be happening and what is needed to maintain appropriate professional conduct.

TRANSFERENCE, COUNTERTRANSFERENCE, AND THE REAL RELATIONSHIP

Individuals view one another through distorted lenses that have to do with past experience and early encounters. The more intense the relationship the more likely it is to evoke feelings related to past relationships. This is called transference. In effect, the patients are "transferring" feelings toward others in their life onto the physician. If an individual has grown up perceiving people around him as unhelpful or even harmful, it should not be surprising the physician is viewed in much the same way.

Physicians may also have intense and sometimes distorted emotional responses to patients. These responses may be the result of the patient's attitude toward the physician, e.g., an adoring patient may elicit a sense of exaggerated concern on the part of the physician or a hostile and demeaning patient may elicit an angry and defensive response from the physician. The physician may also respond to a patient based on the physician's history, e.g., an older man may elicit a deferential approach in a physician who had a much-loved father; a young woman may evoke a protective stance in a physician who helped raise younger siblings. These feelings can be broadly defined as countertransference feelings. In simple terms these are emotional reactions to the patient that often involve the physician's past experience.

Transference and countertransference are technical psychoanalytic terms that will be defined in more detail in Chapter 5 by Drs. Inderbitzin and James. As noted above, they are the emotional responses between patient and physician that are influenced by unconscious factors related to past relationships. They usually surprise the physician with their intensity. Most physicians are disconcerted when the patient they are trying to help appears angry, seductive, or distrustful. They may be equally appalled when they discover there is a patient whom they particularly dislike or one who makes them feel especially inadequate. A typical response to these unpleasant feelings is to try to deny or ignore them. While this may seem like a reasonable approach, it is one that can lead to more trouble in the long run. Doctors who are unwilling to recognize and understand their dislike for certain patients may instead try to avoid them. This will certainly compromise the relationship and ultimately the care provided.

In addition to transference and countertransference feelings, the nature of the *real* relationship will also have an impact on behavior. Friction can occur between doctor and patient when either or both have difficult personality traits. Problems arise when physicians are rigid, overly controlling, or have an inordinate desire to be "worshipped" or idealized by others. Physicians wishing for or expecting worship from patients find it particularly difficult to tolerate patients' anger. The oncologist working with JL is a case in point. From the patient's description this was a physician who was rigid and aloof. It is likely that the patient displaced some of her anger about the illness and the lack of certainty about her prognosis onto the physician. This may have been poorly tolerated by the physician, who then literally turned his back on her and sent her to a psychiatrist to get medicated.

It is also likely there were more classic transference and countertransference elements in this relationship. The patient viewed important figures from the past as unhelpful and unsupportive. This may have contributed to the intensity of her reaction to this physician. We know nothing about the physician's history and can only speculate about possible countertransference reactions. Because of his personal history, did this physician feel the patient's questions and requests were challenges to his authority and competence? Did he have a need to remain distant from patients who might subsequently die despite his best efforts?

Transference and countertransference feelings always exist between patients and physicians although they may vary in intensity. They are inherently neither good nor bad. The feelings themselves do not cause harm even when they are "negative" ones such as anger, hatred, or fear. When recognized and examined, these feelings can be a source of much useful and positive information. Harm can occur when they are ignored or denied. Physicians who cannot consciously acknowledge their dislike for certain patients may inadvertently and unconsciously harm them by dismissing them or by aggressively treating them with unnecessary tests, procedures, etc. When physicians can recognize these negative (and positive) feelings, they can explore their source through self-reflection and sometimes consultation with colleagues. Once they understand the meaning of the feelings, they can respond appropriately and consciously in a way that will ultimately be more therapeutic for the patient.

ISSUES OF COMPLIANCE

The ultimate goal of any interaction between physician and patient is to ensure that effective treatment is provided. This leads directly to the issue of compliance with treatment recommendations.

Poor compliance is a major problem in medical practice. It can be minimized or exacerbated by physician interventions and by the quality of the doctor–patient relationship (Fuller and Gross, 1990). As many as 50% of patients do not comply with treatment. One study showed that one-third of patients complied with all treatment recommendations, one-third complied with some recommendations, and one-third were completely noncompliant (Sackett and Haynes, 1976). These figures do not change significantly with increasing severity of illness.

The statistics are demoralizing; they suggest that a correct diagnosis and treatment strategy is only half the battle. Far more complicated is the effort to get patients to comply with recommended treatment. It is easy to become frustrated with patients who do not comply with recommendations—the obese patient, for example, who will not lose weight or the smoker who will not quit. More dramatic are those patients who do not make important life changes after significant events, such as the patient who cannot slow down after a myocardial infarction.

Change is a difficult proposition for everyone. The doctor who has had a serious illness or even a minor one will be in the best position to understand how difficult compliance can sometimes be. The simplest example of noncompliance might be the need for a full course of antibiotic medication to treat streptococcal pharyngitis. Every medical student knows the importance of this, and most can acknowledge how difficult it was for them to stick to the regimen without forgetting one or more doses.

The most effective approach to the problem of noncompliance is to look at factors that may impede compliance and those that seem to enhance it (Stoudemire and Thompson, 1983). The factors are numerous and patient-specific, but they can be categorized (see Table 1–2).

Factors Related to Noncompliance

1. *The patient may not feel bad.* Patients have a hard time taking their antihypertensive medications because they don't feel ill. Likewise, the patient being treated for an acute infection may stop taking medication as soon as symptoms are relieved.
2. *The patient may wish to deny the illness.* Taking medication or following some other treatment regimen is a reminder of the illness. A simple solution is to become noncompliant.
3. *The patient may not understand the rationale for the treatment or how the medication is to be taken.* This is particularly possible if the patient and physician do not communicate well.
4. *The patient may find the treatment regimen too difficult or disruptive to follow (Stone, 1979).* One patient reported that several different physicians were treating her and she was asked to take 12 different medications throughout the day.

Table 1–2 **Factors Affecting Compliance**

FACTORS THAT IMPEDE COMPLIANCE
1. Low level of subjective distress.
2. Denial of illness.
3. Poor communication between physician and patient.
4. Complex regimens.
5. Treatment that is embarrassing or humiliating.
6. Outside factors that make compliance difficult.
7. Patient's perception that it is beneficial to remain ill.
8. Side effects that are significant for the patient.

FACTORS THAT ENHANCE COMPLIANCE
1. Good rapport between physician and patient.
2. Simple regimens.
3. Clear instructions that patient can repeat back to physician.
4. Positive feedback for adherence.
5. Increased level of distress.
6. Decreased waiting room time.
7. Increased time with physician.

5. *The patient may feel embarrassed or humiliated by the treatment recommended.* This may be particularly true for young people who do not want to be seen as sick by their peers. They may find it difficult to take medications at school and therefore become noncompliant or "forget" to take their medications during the day.

6. *The patient's family, work pressures, or other outside factors may limit compliance.* For example, the woman in a high-pressure executive position may find it impossible to comply with her physician's advice that she cut back on her work hours. Family members may refuse to acknowledge illness in a relative, or they may give advice that contradicts that of the physician.

7. *The patient may perceive that he benefits from being ill.* He may get additional attention from family members, more time off work, etc. He may, on a conscious or unconscious level, wish to remain ill and therefore be noncompliant.

8. *The patient may be noncompliant because of side effects from the medication.* If the medication makes patients feel worse, it is likely they will stop taking it.

There are undoubtedly other factors which contribute to poor compliance. A patient may let his physician know what they are if he is asked about them in a nonpunitive and nonjudgmental way. However, often physicians will need to ask repeatedly about compliance problems, especially those related to personal embarrassment or denial of illness.

Factors That Enhance Compliance

1. *Good rapport with the physician.* Patients who believe that their physician understands them and is interested in their wel-

fare are far more likely to comply with the recommendations. It is also undoubtedly true that such a relationship will foster improved communication and greater mutual understanding. Shared priorities and styles of communicating enhance compliance.

2. *Simplifying treatment regimens.* Patients will have a far easier time with once-a-day dosing whenever this is possible, with fewer pills and with a regimen that is easy to remember, e.g., taking medications at bedtime (Porter, 1969).

3. *Clear and simple instructions.* Physicians give directions regarding medication, but they do not always check to see what has been understood. Patients retain information better when it is presented at the beginning of a session rather than at the end (Ley, 1972). It is often useful to write down instructions if the patient can read and to ask the patient to repeat the instructions. Misconceptions and misunderstandings can be readily cleared up if patients are asked to tell their physician what they understand about their illness and treatment regimen (Fuller and Gross, 1990).

4. *Positive feedback.* Compliance improves when patients are encouraged and praised for the progress they are making.

5. *Increased level of subjective distress.* Patients who feel bad tend to be compliant (Olson et al, 1985). Physicians can help patients understand the consequences of noncompliance by increasing their awareness of the disease and its impact on them.

6. *Decreased waiting room time.* While many physicians say there is little they can do about how long patients wait, it is well worth the effort to look at ways to make an office more efficient from a patient's perspective (Kaplan and Sadock, 1991).

7. *Increased time spent with the patient.* Good time-management practices can increase the amount of time physicians have to spend with their patients.

Probably the single most important way to increase compliance will be to identify the specific reasons why a particular patient finds it difficult to adhere to treatment. A useful approach to fostering compliance is to examine factors systematically as they relate to the patient, the medical regimen, the spouse and family, and the doctor–patient relationship. See Table 1–3 (reprinted from Stoudemire and Thompson, 1983) for specific questions to ask in examining each category.

DIFFICULT DOCTOR–PATIENT RELATIONSHIPS

This final section of the chapter focuses on particularly troubling aspects of patient care. These are the situations or types of patients that many physicians find especially frustrating or difficult to manage.

Table 1–3 **Fostering Compliance**

PATIENT FACTORS
1. Have the basic nature of the illness, rationale for treatment, benefits of compliance, and hazards of noncompliance been explained to and understood by the patient?
2. Does the patient appear appropriately concerned about the illness and motivated for treatment? (If not, why?)
3. Have major psychiatric syndromes been ruled out?
4. Can the patient recite the name of the medication and when and how to take it?

THE MEDICAL REGIMEN
1. Is the regimen as simple as possible in terms of the number of pills and the number of daily doses?
2. Are doses arranged around daily self-care rituals (at meals, at bedtime)?
3. Have frequent side effects been anticipated and explained in terms that will not frighten the patient?

THE SPOUSE AND FAMILY
1. Does the spouse or other support figure understand the illness and the need for medication? Will they support compliance?

THE DOCTOR–PATIENT RELATIONSHIP
1. Has continuity of care been established?
2. Has good rapport been established with the patient? (If not, why?)

(Reprinted with permission from Stoudemire and Thompson [1983])

Difficult situations arise both in hospital and outpatient settings. Some of these difficulties relate to the situation itself, such as the patient who dies suddenly, leaving a bewildered and angry family behind. Others relate to the personality of the patient and how that personality style is affected by illness, such as the patient with obsessive-compulsive traits who finds himself in the hospital with a myocardial infarction. Still others may relate to vulnerable areas for the physician, such as the physician who finds it personally threatening to work with a dying patient. While the list of possibilities is endless, certain situations arise more frequently than others.

The Dying Patient

For many physicians, treating the dying patient is a particularly painful and difficult task. Physicians typically see themselves as healers; they make people well. When patients don't get well, and it is clear they will die despite every attempt to save them, many physicians see this as a personal failure. Their response may be denial or more commonly abandonment. They may distance themselves from their dying patients in order to preserve their image as omnipotent healers. They may also wish to spare themselves the pain of losing someone they have come to know and the pain of facing their own vulnerability, i.e., their own death. If the feelings can be acknowledged and understood, then they do not lead to abandonment of the patient.

Work with a dying patient can be a source of enormous personal growth for both patient and physician. There is no formula for the process. However, patients will tell their physician what they need if the physician is willing to listen. In this situation it is the patient who is the guide. What most patients want to know is that their physician will support them to the end and will listen and accommodate to their needs. Each patient will have a unique set of concerns about dying—for some it will be the possible pain involved, for others the focus may be on unfinished business or loved ones who will be left behind. Still others may see it as a release from suffering. An example may help to highlight several issues.

A CASE STUDY

DM was a young man in his early 20s with AIDS. He had become severely depressed when he first learned he was HIV positive a few years earlier. He recovered from this depression and resumed his normal lifestyle, which included a relatively monogamous but often stormy relationship with a lover who was also HIV positive. The patient came to see a psychiatrist after his second prolonged hospitalization, presumably to work on his relationship with his lover. He was finding it difficult to remain monogamous at the same time that he valued and needed his lover's support. His concerns about dying, which he alluded to infrequently, were related to pain and disfigurement.

Most of his work in therapy dealt with living rather than dying. The patient focused on straightening out his relationships with others and in finding pleasure and support in these relationships. When his final illness came, he struggled with it for some time, often feeling frustrated with his primary physician when treatment was painful or unsuccessful. These moments of frustration were short-lived, however. For the most part he saw his physician as present and concerned. He used his psychiatrist to check out his feelings and his decisions regarding his care. Eventually he chose to go home to die, which he did after several days. He did this with unexpected grace after spending a good day with his family and lover.

This case illustrates a number of important issues. Patients who are dying are still very much concerned with life. There may be a transition point in the process of dying, but until that moment is reached, a patient's concerns are mostly about living. In some cases denial may help patients go on living. This does not mean the physician withholds information. It is vital to be honest with the patient, although it is important to find out first what the patient knows or suspects about his illness. Most patients are aware of how ill they are and often know they are dying (Burrows, 1991). For many, it is a relief when someone is willing to talk to them about it.

Another important point related to this example is that people die in their own way. The adage "People die the way they live" is not always true. The patient in the example was a fragile, anxious person who often felt overwhelmed by minor difficulties. However, this is not how he reacted at the end of his life. Instead, he found the strength and acceptance that allowed him to die peacefully.

Dealing with death and the dying patient is discussed at some length in Chapter 10 by Drs. Wolman and Thompson.

The Seductive Patient

Patients often idealize their physicians. Sometimes this may take the form of an erotic or sexualized transference; patients may decide they are in love with their physician. These can be very powerful emotions that may both flatter and disturb the physician. They may elicit a variety of countertransference feelings from uneasiness to sexual arousal to the feeling that this particular patient is, in fact, very special and in need of extra attention. Again, it is not the feelings themselves that cause trouble; it is what the physician *does* with the feelings that matter. By understanding that the source of the feelings is the patient's need to idealize the physician and to test the boundaries of their relationship, physicians may be better able to mitigate their own reactions. Many patients will be quite provocative with their caregivers. Erotic or provocative behavior will have a number of patient-specific meanings.

Physicians who are honest with themselves acknowledge that they may also have erotic feelings about some patients. Ethical obligations prohibit acting on these feelings, but they do not and cannot prohibit having the feelings themselves.

It is unfortunate that medical school typically does so little to help physicians deal with these often intense emotional responses. Talking to responsible colleagues is one way to sort out the feelings. A formal or informal psychiatric consultation can often help physicians deal more effectively with seductive patients. In rare circumstances it may be necessary to transfer a patient to the care of another physician if it appears objective treatment of the patient is no longer possible. It is also easier for physicians to deal with these feelings when they have fulfilling lives outside the office (Fromm-Reichman, 1950).

The "Hateful" Patient

There are certain patients that most physicians find hard to treat (Groves, 1978). Often these are patients who are demanding and dissatisfied with treatment. They tend to blame their physician and others around them for their illness. They may alternate between overidealizing their physicians and demeaning them. Physicians should feel wary when patients tell them they're the first doctor who ever understood them. It is likely that these patients will have unrealistic expectations and that they will subsequently devalue and demean their physicians. Doctors tend to pass these patients along to their colleagues as "interesting cases." This is sometimes unfair to all concerned. Such patients can often benefit from an invested professional approach that maintains clear boundaries. These patients can also benefit from psychotherapy, although they frequently resist this form of treatment. A single example may serve as a template for the type of patient who tends to push physicians to their limit.

A CASE STUDY

A young woman was in the hospital with an asthma attack. She managed to stir up the ward by being demanding, childlike, and uncooperative. She considered some nurses to be "good staff" and others to be "bad staff." The same was true with her physicians. The "good staff" tended to reciprocate by viewing her as an unfortunate young woman who was being unfairly judged by other staff members. The "bad staff" saw the patient as manipulative, time consuming, and ungrateful. Physicians tended to share these diverse opinions depending on whether they were the "good" or "bad" doctor. A psychiatrist was called in to help settle the staff who began to bicker among themselves. The primary physician asked the psychiatrist to "help with the management" of the patient.

In the psychiatric literature, this type of patient would probably be called a "borderline" personality disorder. These patients can generate a remarkable amount of turmoil. They have very contradictory views of themselves and others and tend to dump their inner turmoil into the world around them. What the psychiatrist did in this particular case was to get the staff to begin talking to one another. Their composite view of this patient was far more accurate than any particular view one staff member held. The psychiatrist recommended that the patient have one primary nurse and one primary physician with whom she was to discuss all of her concerns about care. This limited her ability to separate people into camps. Other staff were told to channel the young woman's concerns to the primary nurse and doctor. These individuals coordinated their information to avoid a split between the good doctor/bad nurse or vice versa. The patient remained difficult and demanding, but the staff were better able to function in her best interest because they were no longer caught up in her projections and turmoil.

The Patient with a Thousand Symptoms

These patients tax a physician as much or more than the difficult patient just described. They appear to be invested in remaining ill. These are the patients who have multiple complaints that do not add up to a single disease picture. They often receive various diagnostic procedures to no avail. They may doctor-shop or continue to come to the same physician despite their ostensible dissatisfaction that the doctor is unable to cure them. Doctors often respond to these patients with frustration and anger. Sometimes they respond aggressively by ordering unnecessary tests or performing unneeded procedures. It is not unusual for such patients to list ten or more procedures they have had for which there was only sketchy justification.

There are several important points to make about this type of patient. These patients turn up frequently in general outpatient practice, accounting for 5 to 10% of patients seen (Folks et al, 1994). Their need to be ill is often unconscious and their symptoms are real to them and not a fabrication. In addition, even somatizing patients, i.e., patients who translate emotional problems into physical symptoms, can develop genuine physical problems. Doctors need to be alert to this possibility at the same time that they refrain from unnecessary procedures. These patients do best when they are seen frequently by one personal physician on a long-term basis. These are patients who should be seen monthly whether or not they have a problem. Often this contact can eliminate the need to create a major health crisis to obtain the longed-for attention. These patients are difficult to treat in psychotherapy despite the fact that their problems have an emotional base. The best approach is one that combines frequent visits to a primary physician with adjunctive psychotherapy if the patient can tolerate it. The focus of the medical approach is on management rather than cure (Folks et al, 1994).

The Patient in the Hospital Setting

Unlike the type of patient just described, there are many other patients who function well in the outpatient setting; they only become problematic when hospitalized or when faced with a severe or debilitating illness.

Hospitals tend to rob patients of their sense of dignity and personal control. Even the most benevolent hospital has a schedule that is not the patient's schedule. Patients also feel out of control because there is something wrong with their body. It is difficult if not impossible to maintain a sense of autonomy in a hospital setting. In general patients become more childlike when hospitalized. How specific patients deal with hospitalization depends upon their personality style. Patients with rigid personalities and an obsessional style may be overwhelmed by the perceived loss of control. They may become argumentative, noncompliant, or deny that they have a problem in the first place. If this type of patient has a myocardial infarction, he may want to resume a full schedule of work while still in the hospital. Alternatively, patients who tend to be dependent may become completely submissive and helpless. The paranoid individual may become increasingly distrustful, demanding second opinions and threatening lawsuits.

Patients will use the same styles they used to cope with the world when in good health, but they may do it with less flexibility. They may look like exaggerated versions of themselves. The empathic physician can help lower the level of distress for these patients and improve their functioning by responding to their particular needs and fears (Nardo, 1987). If patients are allowed to maintain some control over their lives in the hospital, they will respond better emotionally.

The Mentally Disturbed Patient

There are many patients requiring medical care who suffer from severe emotional illnesses. Some emotional illnesses may be related to the medical condition itself, such as depression from hypothyroidism or depression related to a chronic and debilitating illness. Other conditions will be unrelated to the medical problem but may significantly interfere with medical care received. The patient who suffers from untreated paranoid schizophrenia may have a difficult time trusting the physician enough to allow treatment.

Often physicians are frightened of the patient who is mentally disturbed. Most patients with serious mental illness can be successfully treated; they may not be cured and they may relapse, but this is not different from any patient with a chronic illness. Physicians should treat such patients in the same way they treat all other patients— with concern and respect.

Sometimes physicians err in the opposite direction. They may fail to recognize serious emotional illness when it exists or fail to refer a patient for psychiatric follow-up when this is clearly indicated. The more exposure physicians have to mentally ill patients the more readily they will recognize those who need psychiatric care and the more comfortable they will be in their work with them.

It is always appropriate to ask a psychiatric colleague for a formal or informal consultation regarding a patient who appears to have emotional difficulties.

SUMMARY

Every medical student knows that the decision to become a physician involves enormous commitment and dedication. The learning process is unending. Part of this process involves a willingness to learn about oneself and one's patients. It is the human interaction that will ultimately be a major source of much pleasure and some frustration to the physician. The relationship the physician has with each patient serves as a cornerstone for that patient's successful treatment. The rest of this book will lay the groundwork for understanding human behavior, which is essential for establishing an effective and successful doctor–patient relationship.

ANNOTATED BIBLIOGRAPHY

Cassell, EJ: The Nature of Suffering and the Goals of Medicine, New York, Oxford University Press, 1991

Scholarly, well-written treatise on the need to shift the focus of medicine from the disease model to the sick person who is suffering. "Bodies do not suffer, people do."

Emmanuel E, Emmanuel L: Four models of the physician–patient relationship, JAMA 267(16): 2221–2226, 1992

The authors identify four types of relationships (the paternalistic, informative, interpretive, and deliberative models) and discuss the values and limitations of each. Of equal or more interest are the letters in response to this article. See Rennie D, Dan BB (eds): Letters. JAMA 268(11): 1410–1413, 1992

Fuller MG, Gross RT: Adherence to medical regimes in Behavior and Medicine. Edited by Wedding D. St Louis, Mosby Year Book, 1990

Comprehensive chapter that focuses on all aspects of patient compliance.

Groves, JE: Taking care of the hateful patient. N Engl J Med 298(16): 883–887, 1978

This article is a classic which discusses countertransference feelings in practical terms and offers useful suggestions for working with difficult patients. Includes "dependent clingers," "entitled demanders," "manipulative help rejecters," and "self-destructive deniers."

Nardo, MJ: The personality in the medical setting: a psychodynamic understanding in Psychiatry Vol 2. Edited by Michaels R. New York, Basic Books, 1987

Well-written and practical guide to working with different personality types in the hospital setting. Includes compulsive, histrionic, depressive-masochistic, borderline, narcissistic, and paranoid personalities.

REFERENCES

Bertakis, KD, Roter D, Putnam SM: The relationship of physician medical interview style to patient satisfaction. J Fam Practice 32(2):175–181, 1991

Book HE: Is empathy cost efficient? Am J Psychotherapy 45(1):21–30, 1991

Buller MK, Buller DB: Physicians' communications style and patient satisfaction. Health Soc Behav 28:375–388, 1987

Burrows A: A piece of my mind: The man who didn't know he had cancer. JAMA 266(18):2550, 1991

Cassell EJ: The Nature of Suffering and the Goals of Medicine. New York, Oxford University Press, 1991

Emanuel E, Emanuel L: Four models of the physician–patient relationship. JAMA 267(16):2221–2226, 1992

Folks DG, Ford CV, Houck CA: Somatoform disorders, factitious disorders, and malingering. In Stoudemire A (ed): Clinical Psychiatry for Medical Students, 2nd ed. Philadelphia, Lippincott, 1994

Frankel BL: The physician–patient relationship. In Wiener JM (ed): Behavioral Science. New York, John Wiley & Sons, 1987

Fromm-Reichman F: The psychiatrist's part in the doctor–patient relationship. In Principles of Intensive Psychotherapy. Chicago, The University of Chicago Press, 1950

Fuller MG, Gross RT: Adherence to medical regimens. In Wedding D (ed): Behavior and Medicine. St. Louis, Mosby Year Book, 1990

Groves, JE: Taking care of the hateful patient. N Engl J Med 298(16):883–887, 1978

Kaplan HI, Sadock BJ: The doctor–patient relationship. In Synopsis of Psychiatry, 6th ed. Baltimore, Williams & Wilkins, 1991

LeBaron S, Reyher J, Stack JM: Paternalistic vs egalitarian physician styles: The treatment of patients in crisis. Family Practice 21(1):56–62, 1985

Ley P: Primary, rated importance and recall of medical information. J Health Soc Behav 13:311–317, 1972

Nardo MJ: The personality in the medical setting: A psychodynamic understanding In Michaels R (ed): Psychiatry. New York, Basic Books, 1987

Nicholi AM: The therapist–patient relationship. In Nicholi AM (ed): The Harvard Guide to Modern Psychiatry. Cambridge, Harvard University Press, 1988

Olson RA, Zimmerman JL, de la Roche SR: Medical adherence in pediatric populations In Zeiner AR, Bendell P, Walker CE (eds): Health Psychology: Treatment and Research Issues. New York, Plenum Press, 1985

Porter AM: Drug defaulting in general practice. Br Med J 1:218–222, 1969

Rennie D, Dan BB (eds): Letters: Models of the physician–patient relationship. JAMA 268(11):1410–1413, 1992

Sackett DL, Haynes RB: Compliance with Therapeutic Regimens. Baltimore, Johns Hopkins, 1976

Stone GC: Patient compliance and the role of the expert. J Soc Issues 35:34–59, 1979

Stoudemire A, Thompson TL: Medication noncompliance: Systematic approaches to evaluation and intervention. Gen Hosp Psychiatry 5:233–239, 1983

Underwood P, Owen A: Styles of doctoring and models of health. Australian Fam Physician 14(7):658–662, 1985

Alan Stoudemire (ed). *Human Behavior: An Introduction for Medical Students*, Second Edition. Copyright © 1994, 1990 by J. B. Lippincott Company.

2 *The Biopsychosocial Model in Medical Practice*

Steven A. Cohen-Cole
and Richard M. Levinson

In Chapter 1, Dr. Shelton introduced the concept of the biopsychosocial model in medicine and discussed it in the context of the doctor–patient relationship. In this chapter, this model is discussed in a more expanded manner.

The following four postulates set forth the broad outlines of the biopsychosocial model of illness, which forms the underlying philosophy of this textbook.

1. Most illness, whether physical or psychiatric, is influenced and determined by biological, psychological, and social phenomena.
2. Biological, psychological, and social variables influence the predisposition, onset, course, and outcome of most illnesses.
3. Physicians who are able to evaluate the relationships of biological, psychological, and social variables in their patients' illnesses will be able to develop more effective therapeutic interventions and to achieve better patient outcomes.
4. To evaluate and manage medical problems adequately, physicians must be able to establish and maintain therapeutic doctor-patient relationships with many different types of patients.

Each chapter in this text will present a different perspective based on these four postulates. This book will provide students with practical approaches to integrating these variables in patient care. This chapter presents empirical and clinical data that support the four postulates described above, along with suggestions to help future physicians use this approach in the care of their patients.

WHY SHOULD PHYSICIANS STUDY EMOTIONS, BEHAVIOR, OR SOCIAL PROCESSES?

Many medical students may wonder what a course in human behavior really has to do with their future practice of medicine. They may feel that they have come to medical school to learn about disease: how to diagnose and treat ailments of the body. Such students may think that, while humanistic medicine (i.e., "caring for" and being "nice" or "understanding" to patients) is an important part of medical practice, the principles of a humanistic approach to medical practice are intuitive, self-evident, more or less "common sense," and cannot or do not need to be "taught." In addition, many practicing clinicians and students acknowledge that patients with psychiatric problems often come to physicians for help, but they feel that such patients can be referred elsewhere for help with their psychiatric problems and that medical practice should focus on physical illnesses.

This view of disease and medical practice, which many physicians endorse, has been described as the "biomedical model of illness" (Engel, 1977). It argues that psychological and social variables are of secondary importance in illness and the treatment process and that physician's major efforts should be primarily, if not exclusively, focused on the biological aspects of physical illnesses.

Focusing exclusively on biological aspects overlooks great variations in how people feel—how they experience the disease. After reviewing surveys of health in the U.S., Barsky (1988) reported a paradox of health status in America. He noted that although there have been substantial improvements in the objective health status of the population, with increased life expectancy and a decline in mortality rates, people report higher rates of disability, symptoms, and general dissatisfaction with their health. Some of the increases in self-reported illness or disability could be associated with the success of medicine in sustaining the lives of persons who live with chronic health problems. Yet Barsky believes that some of the deterioration in reported health is associated with a lower tolerance of symptoms accompanied by a greater inclination to attribute uncomfortable feelings, such as lower back pain, to an "illness." Discomforts that were previously tolerated and overlooked are more likely to be defined as health problems requiring medical treatment. Thus, how patients perceive and understand their feelings as the presence of disease may have much to do with variations in the actual reported health status of the population. To be effective, physicians must take into consideration how patients subjectively experience and understand their own "illnesses."

Therefore, this text disputes the position of a purist interpretation of the "biomedical" model and advocates an integrated approach to patient care by use of a "biopsychosocial model of illness." This view endorses a multidimensional or systems approach to the practice of medicine and conceptualizes illness and illness outcomes as determined by multiple interacting biological, psychological, and social variables.

The biopsychosocial model maintains that emotional, behavioral, and social processes are implicated in the development, course, and outcome of illness. Medical students need to learn basic principles of psychosocial assessment and intervention to be able to practice this type of clinical medicine and to be able to provide adequate and comprehensive care for their patients. Physicians who can integrate the psychologic and social variables in their patients' illnesses will generally be able to develop more effective clinical interventions that will lead to better treatment outcome.

A body of research indicates that patient satisfaction with physician visits is based primarily on the psychosocial dimensions of care. If patients perceive that their doctors care about them, show concern, and seem understanding, they are more satisfied and evaluate the quality of medical care more positively. On average, this "emotional" dimension appears more influential than the physician's technical competence in patients' assessment of the quality of their care (Ben-Sira, 1976). Even the satisfaction of patients who visit physicians with a primary interest in receiving procedures or medications is more influenced by the psychosocial aspects of the care received (such as counseling or education) than by the technical services (Brody et al, 1989). Therefore, physicians who endorse a biopsychosocial approach to medical practice will generally have better relationships with their patients, and will find the practice of medicine less stressful and more personally fulfilling.

After the following case study, this chapter will then cover a wide range of topics related to biopsychosocial medicine including:

1. Psychological and social factors related to the predisposition, onset, course, and outcome of physical illness;
2. The use of psychosocial treatments for physical illness;
3. A review of psychobiological mechanisms that might mediate between psychosocial processes and biological effects;
4. Recent findings in psychiatric epidemiology, particularly as they relate to the general practice of medicine;
5. Sociocultural influences on illness and illness behavior;
6. The applicability of the biopsychosocial model to traditional psychiatric illnesses.

The following case study will provide a basis to begin a discussion of biopsychosocial assessment and treatment. The case will be presented, and a model biopsychosocial formulation will be developed along with multidimensional treatment recommendations.

A CASE STUDY

Mr. RF is a 47-year-old married male with a 60-pack-year history of cigarette smoking (i.e., two packs a day for 30 years), who has a 5-year history of laryngeal cancer. He received several neck surgeries 5 years ago and now reports that his life has "never been the same" since that time. Physical problems include difficulty talking and swallowing, with unpredictable and uncontrollable episodes of coughing and vomiting. These episodes are extremely embarrassing to him and have led him to restrict his activities. He does not want to go out anymore and does not want to socialize with friends or family.

He and his wife report that he has been depressed for 5 years, but that the depression has gotten much worse in the last year or so. He does not want to do anything and derives almost no pleasure in living. He has frequent crying spells and has great difficulty sleeping at night. He usually can fall asleep without too much trouble, but often awakens in the middle of the night and cannot fall back asleep. He feels sad most of the time and feels that life is a burden. He often feels that he would prefer to be dead than to live in his current situation, but he says that he would not consider suicide. His appetite is poor, although he has not lost weight. He reports "no energy" and very low self-esteem. He is guilty about what he has done to his family as a result of this illness and blames himself for the illness because of his heavy smoking history. He has trouble making decisions and reports trouble concentrating, as exemplified in his difficulty keeping his mind on books, television programs, or conversations.

He reports a sudden cessation of sexual activity since his diagnosis of cancer. He has no libido and feels unattractive to his wife. He and his wife report the almost total absence of physical intimacy in their relationship during the last 5 years. They do not hug each other anymore. There is little overt conflict, and the patient feels grateful to his wife and feels that they have become "closer" since his illness. His wife, however, is very tearful in discussing the impact of the illness on her life. She feels guilty and responsible for her husband, but does not want to have to restrict her own life unreasonably. She feels that she has retained the ability to enjoy life and that if her husband cannot be motivated to go out, she has the right to go out without him. She spends time with her children and other friends.

Mr. RF and his wife are both worried about finances. Since his operations and his trouble talking, he has been unable to continue his work as a real estate agent. He has been denied Social Security disability payments. His wife works in retail sales, but her income is not sufficient to cover their household expenses, including the costs of their two children, a girl aged 14 and a boy aged 10. They are having trouble meeting the mortgage payments on their house, and they may need to sell the house and move into an apartment.

In addition, the patient is extremely worried about the impact of his illness on his children, especially because his own father died of lung cancer when the patient was 12. His mother, in addition, suffered from depressive illnesses, with two psychiatric hospitalizations for this problem.

He was referred for psychiatric evaluation. His internist felt that he was suffering from a rather severe depression and that his overall quality of life was more impaired than would be expected from the effect of the cancer itself.

CASE FORMULATION

Biological Variables

The biological variables are obviously the chief precipitants of Mr. RF's deteriorating condition. The cancer had a devastating impact on his life. He suffered from several difficult surgeries, and, after these surgeries, he could no longer function as well as he had previously.

Some new physical symptoms have been troublesome. His talking has become more dysarthric (slurred with poor enunciation). He has lost sensation on part of his tongue, and his coughing has become much worse. He is in the process of a new neurologic evaluation to determine whether he is suffering from a recurrence of his cancer. He has just learned that he is also suffering from hypothyroidism secondary to neck radiation for the cancer.

The hypothyroid condition can itself cause a secondary mood disorder, which mimics major depression (O'Shanick et al, 1987). Similarly, the patient has been on the antihypertensive beta blocker, propranolol, which has also been implicated in mood disturbances (Hall et al, 1980). In addition, the patient's mother suffered from depressive illness. This family history suggests a biologically transmitted genetic predisposition to depression (see Chapter 13 by Dr. Baron on genetic vulnerability to psychiatric illness).

Psychological Variables

Mr. RF's psychological character traits play a prominent role in his current problems. He has always been a rather controlled, orderly person who has depended on his intellect and a thorough, rational approach to problems to help him cope with life's vicissitudes. He always disdained emotionality and felt that most of life's difficulties could be overcome if sufficient effort was put into working out practical solutions. He spent a great deal of effort organizing his work and his private life in order to arrange his affairs to be as predictable as possible. This personality style has been referred to as the "obsessive style" (Mackinnon and Michels, 1971) (see Chapter 5 by Drs. Inderbitzen and James for a discussion of ego defenses and personality style).

The cancer, by itself, presented a major threat not only to his life, but, by its very nature, to the predictability and certainty of his future. For a patient with an obsessive style of coping, the vagaries of cancer treatment and outcome present particularly troubling stresses. In addition, the patient's difficulty with eating and talking, as well as his unpredictable vomiting, compromised his control of his social circumstances and led to extremely embarrassing situations.

One episode on a trip to visit family was particularly disturbing. While eating dinner in an elegant restaurant, he suddenly and unpredictably vomited. This episode was so distressing to him, that he now phobically avoids all social situations. His depressive symptomatology has become much worse since then. The hopelessness, anhedonia (i.e., inability to experience interest or pleasure), and fatigue have gotten worse since then. He refuses almost all activities.

In addition to these difficulties, the patient is extremely guilty about his cigarette smoking and blames himself for his illness and the deleterious effect it is having on his family. He worries about the psychological impact of the cancer on his children, especially if he should die from the disease. He cannot stop thinking about the death of his own father when he was young, and he is sad for himself and for his children at the same time.

Social Variables

The social variables are also prominent in this case. First of all, the loss of the patient's income has had a very negative impact on the family. Worries about finances have introduced new stresses into the family, and they are facing the loss of their home. The loss of the job has also had a negative impact on the patient's self-esteem in that he is no longer able to fulfill the "manly" role of "breadwinner" for the family.

In addition, the patient has cut himself off from several important sources of social support that might contribute positively to his current quality of life. Because of extreme vulnerability to social embarrassment, the patient does not see friends or children as much as previously. He may go for weeks without any outside contacts.

His withdrawal has had very negative effects on his wife, and this has also affected their marital relationship. There is no more sexual intimacy. His wife is tearful in discussing this and the fact that there is no more physical contact (including hugging) of any kind in their marriage. As we discussed this, the patient said that it is very hard for him to express emotional issues and added that he feels very unlovable in his present condition.

Biopsychosocial Formulation

The biopsychosocial formulation must evaluate and integrate the impact of different variables on the clinical problem. The patient is clearly suffering from "major depression," which is itself a biopsychosocial illness. Neurochemical, endocrine, and neurophysiologic alterations are all part of this illness syndrome. Mr. RF's obsessive personality style makes adaptation to illness difficult because good coping with cancer requires some ability to live with uncertainty as well as adequate self-esteem to cope with potentially embarrassing situations. His loss of his father at an early age may, in fact, predispose him to future depressive illness (see Chapter 11 by Dr. van der Kolk for a discussion of developmental trauma as predisposing factors for future anxiety and depression).

His marriage and social contacts are also threatened by his illness and his response to the illness. The possibility of a recurrence of the malignancy presents a new challenge to a very unstable psychological and social equilibrium.

It would be misleading, however, as well as dangerous to conclude that Mr. RF has "good reasons" to be depressed. He certainly has many good reasons to be "sad," but the syndrome of major depression does not uniformly result from significant physical illness or any severe stress. While the prevalence of psychiatric disorders is considerably higher in patients with chronic physical illness than in the general population (lifetime prevalence of 42% compared to 33%) (Wells et al, 1988), the majority of patients with terminal cancer do not, in fact, develop major depressive syndromes (Cohen-Cole and Stoudemire, 1987). Major depression is associated with physiological and neurovegetative changes that occur in only a subset of individuals with severe physical illness (Cassem, 1988). When physical illness is complicated by a major depression, it should be vigorously recognized and treated. As Cassem (1988) has pointed out, "depression is a dread complication of physical illness." Physicians who suggest that patients may have "good reasons" to be depressed may do their patients a disservice because the incorrect assumption that depression is "normal" may lead to an acceptance of the syndrome without obtaining proper and effective treatment.

Biopsychosocial Management

Biopsychosocial management requires the integration of different therapeutic strategies along all three relevant dimensions.

Biological Interventions

Biological intervention for the cancer evaluation must proceed rapidly and without delay. The depression must be treated similarly. First of all, the patient must receive appropriate thyroid replacement therapy. It is possible that this intervention may make a major difference in the patient's symptoms of depression. Similarly, the physician should consider substituting another antihypertensive for the propranolol, which might be exacerbating his depression. (Chapter 12 by Dr. Pedersen and colleagues discusses the biological influences on behavior, including mood regulation.)

If the patient does not respond rapidly to thyroid replacement or substitution of antihypertensives, biological intervention for the major depression must be initiated. An antidepressant medication, such as doxepin or fluoxetine, should be prescribed to address the disruption in the patient's neurobiologic mood regulating and stress response system, and the drug should be monitored closely for effectiveness and side effects (Cohen-Cole and Stoudemire, 1987).

Psychological Interventions

Psychological intervention is just as important. Several different forms of psychotherapy for major depression, including interpersonal and cognitive approaches, have been demonstrated to be as effective as pharmacotherapy. The short-term interpersonal approach would focus on the difficulties the patient has experienced in making the transition from his role as breadwinner to the "sick role." The interpersonal approach would also focus on the new stresses on the marriage because of the cancer (see Chapter 10 by Drs. Wolman and Thompson on adult lifecycles and the stressful effects of illness on the family).

In contrast, a cognitive approach would emphasize the unrealistic expectations Mr. RF places on himself in the face of the devastating illness and help him maintain his self-esteem in spite of his new need to be more dependent on others (see Chapters 5 and 6 for a general overview of psychodynamic and behavioral/learning principles in psychotherapy).

Formal psychotherapy would definitely be indicated for Mr. RF, but many such patients will not accept this form of treatment. They may believe that the need for psychotherapy points to a character "defect," and they defend themselves against this view by refusing psychotherapy. Other patients refuse psychotherapy because of the expense involved.

Primary physicians can help such patients accept formal psychotherapy by legitimizing the process of therapy. Physicians can point out that depression is indeed a medical illness that can be helped by expert treatment, including psychotherapy as well as mediations. Physicians can also help patients accept psychiatric referral by offering to collaborate with the treating psychotherapist and to remain in contact with the patient during the treatment. It is also often helpful to discuss examples of other patients with similar problems who have benefited from psychiatric referral.

Is there anything that the primary care physician can do with depressed cancer patients who do not accept psychiatric referral? There is, in fact, a great deal that can be done (see Chapter 14 by Dr. Green on basic approaches to the psychological care of patients). As discussed in Chapter 1, a solid interpersonal relationship must be established and maintained. This involves the use of good communication skills. *Careful listening* is essential, along with allowing the patient the opportunity to ventilate his/her feelings. Patients must be given *adequate opportunities to ask questions* as well. *Empathic comments*, which reflect the patient's feelings, can be quite helpful (e.g., "It is clear that you are especially worried about the impact that your illness may have on your children"). *Legitimizing* these feelings is also reassuring to patients (e.g., "I can certainly understand why you would find it so hard to think about the effect of your illness on your children"). Offering direct statements of support (e.g., "I will do what I can to help") as well as statements of partnership ("Let's try to work on this problem together") also can have a significant impact on the patient's ability to cope. Lastly, *respectful comments that praise* the patient for actual coping efforts that have succeeded are usually very comforting (e.g., "I am really impressed with how well you managed to cope with your children's fears last week") (Cohen-Cole and Bird, 1986a).

The most important communication skill is the *flexibility* required to observe the patient's response to different interventions and the ability and willingness to try interventions that will work for each patient. Some patients require more active support, while others prefer quiet listening. Physicians can learn these different approaches if they observe their patients closely and demonstrate the willingness to listen to their needs.

With respect to Mr. RF, physicians can help such obsessive patients by giving them as much control over their treatment as possible. Providing adequate detailed information is essential, and questions must be answered directly and as specifically as possible. Commenting directly on the difficulty of loss of control is usually perceived as empathic by obsessive or worry-prone patients (e.g., "I can certainly understand why this unpredictable illness is so particularly stressful to you, since you have always been able to manage your affairs in an orderly, predictable way").

Similarly, obsessive patients usually are frightened and resistant to becoming dependent on anyone. Sometimes if this fear is acknowledged, physicians can help their patients by indicating that sometimes accepting dependency takes unusual strength (e.g., "I know that it is hard to have to depend on someone else to provide for your basic needs, but I want you to realize that it takes particular strength and courage to be able to ask for and accept help that you, in fact, really do need. You actually can do your friends and family a favor by accepting the help that they really do want to offer").

This patient may be reexperiencing the grief he suffered as a child as well as anticipatory grief over his own possible death. (Chapter 14 discusses in some detail the "grief model" of coping with illness, which relates directly to the type of supportive psychotherapy that the primary care physician may be able to provide.)

Social Interventions

Social intervention in this case is crucial. Vocational rehabilitation might be helpful in finding some productive employment for the patient. Social workers might help the patient find ways to appeal the Social Security decisions, and, if necessary, legal assistance could be considered to appeal disability decisions.

Mr. RF's marriage is quite stressed. There is loneliness for him and his wife, and they have not been able to talk to each other about their needs. A decrease in sexual activity is common after cancer diagnoses, but this decrease need not herald the end of all physical intimacy (e.g., hugging). Mr. RF and his wife need the opportunity to talk to each other about their needs. A primary care physician can be very helpful in this regard, simply by bringing up issues of intimacy and sexual relationships for open discussion. More open communication and ventilation of feelings are often sufficient to help resolve such problems. In more complicated cases, referral for sexual therapy can be essential (see Chapter 7 on human sexuality by Drs. Becker and Hunter).

The children are probably quite anxious themselves and may be suffering from psychological distress or even a psychiatric disorder. Every effort should be made to have them seen by the primary physician or by someone with special skills on the healthcare team. If indicated, individual or family therapy for the children may be important (see Chapter 8 by Dr. Dulcan on how children cope with illness).

Mrs. F has her own feelings of guilt, responsibility, and resentment, which have an impact on the overall quality of life of the couple as well as the family. She could benefit from a chance to explore and work through some of these feelings, either with the primary physician or with a psychotherapist.

Summary

Many of the interventions suggested above for the adequate management of Mr. RF involve sophisticated and extensive psychosocial interventions. In order for physicians to be able to provide this type of comprehensive patient care, they must develop the knowledge and skill necessary in the course of their medical training.

The psychosocial interventions described above do, in fact, require more time than a mechanical and narrowly biological or "purely medical" approach, but they do not require the intensity or time demands of formal psychotherapy. Increasingly, time is a very costly commodity for physicians because reimbursements from insurers compensate less well for patient visits than for performing diagnostic or surgical procedures (Eisenberg, 1992). It should be remembered, however, that patients with chronic illness return to primary physicians many times and that a great deal can be accomplished through short, supportive appointments spaced over longer periods of time.

Thus, in addition to the prescription of antidepressants, the adequate treatment of this patient necessitates numerous other psychological and social interventions. The physician who is interested and sufficiently well trained to provide this comprehensive care can function efficiently and effectively in this role. Physicians should make it clear to such patients that a consultation with a psychiatrist may be necessary but would not disrupt their general medical care. In making a psychiatric or other mental health referral, the primary physician should always indicate willingness and interest in staying involved in the care of the patient.

The prognosis for Mr. RF to obtain improved functioning and improved quality of life is quite good, assuming the patient complies with these multimodal treatment interventions.

THE BIOPSYCHOSOCIAL MODEL IN MEDICAL PRACTICE

Just as the biopsychosocial model of illness helps us understand and effectively treat patients like Mr. RF, who have concurrent major *psychiatric* disorders that are complicating their primary physical condition, the biopsychosocial approach is just as helpful for *medical patients*. In other words, evaluation and management of psychological and social variables are critical in the care of the physically ill, *even if there is no major clinically significant psychiatric disorder present.* The following section will discuss the ways in which psychosocial variables have been shown to be significant in the predisposition, onset, course, and outcome of physical illness. Psychosocial interventions that lead to improved physical outcome and the psychobiologic mechanisms by which some of these influences may operate will also be cited. The section will conclude with suggestions for the practice of clinical medicine.

Psychological and Behavioral Predisposition to Physical Illness

There are many psychological, behavioral, and social variables that play a role in the development of physical illness. In fact, lifestyle and personal habits, such as tobacco use, alcohol and drug abuse, overeating, poor nutrition, lack of exercise, and so forth account together for about 70% of all illness and death in the United States (Houpt et al, 1980). Obesity, for example, is related to heart disease, diabetes, and hypertension. Nicotine addiction from tobacco smoking is directly associated with lung cancer, emphysema, and coronary artery disease. Alcohol is related to cirrhosis of the liver, gastric ulcers, dementia, and half of the yearly fatal traffic accidents in the U.S. The financial costs of these behaviorally related illnesses are staggering: the direct costs alone were approximately $250 billion in 1983 (70% of a healthcare expenditure of $355 billion) (Kamerow et al, 1986). This figure does not even include an estimate of the indirect costs (e.g., lost productivity).

Personality factors have also been thought to be predisposing factors to certain physical illnesses. Probably the best known is the so-called Type A behavior pattern and its relationship to coronary artery disease. Coronary artery disease is now the leading cause of death in this country, and any knowledge about predisposing or other risk factors should help us design appropriate interventions. Type A individuals feel under relentless pressure of time and are usually under a competitive and hostile strain with other people. Such persons are usually quite serious and ambitious in their work. They often find it hard to relax and to enjoy interpersonal pleasures. In general, Type A individuals walk and eat rapidly, hurry others along in conversation, speak with a very strong emphasis, clench their hands and teeth, try to do two things at once, and experience great time pressure (Friedman, 1969).

Early studies found that people with strong Type A behavior patterns have two times the incidence of coronary artery disease compared with persons without this pattern (Type B individuals). Similarly, once someone experienced a heart attack, the presence of the Type A behavioral pattern was associated with five times the likelihood of experiencing a second heart attack. Furthermore, the presence of Type A behavior was associated with two times the likelihood of a heart attack being fatal (Rosenman et al, 1975).

There has been extensive controversy about the validity of the Type A behavior pattern and its hypothesized association with coronary artery disease. Some recent studies have failed to demonstrate the expected results (Ragland and Brand, 1988). Current conceptualization of the Type A behavior pattern now focuses more specifically on the dimensions of suspiciousness and hostility (Williams et al, 1980).

A major intervention study based on the Type A construct has recently lent some support to its validity. A 5-year controlled study examined the effects on cardiac recurrence of an elaborate stress-management intervention focused on reducing the strength of the Type A behavior pattern. At the end of the follow-up period, the recurrence rate for nonfatal infarcts in the intervention group was approximately half of that in the other groups. Moreover, within the treatment group itself, the rates of recurrence were lowest among those with the greatest reduction in Type A behaviors (Friedman et al, 1984). In general, despite recent skepticism, some elements of the Type A construct seem to describe a robust and persisting relationship to coronary artery disease and may still be considered as a possible risk factor for this disease (Dimsdale, 1988). The Type A personality and its possible relationship to cardiovascular disease is also discussed in Chapter 3 by Drs. Walker and Katon.

Onset of Illness

The most common psychosocial variable associated with illness onset has to do with the sometimes illusive concept of "stress." Everyone "knows" that stress is related to disease; the stress-illness connection is widespread in popular mythology and the media. The concept of stress provides the philosophic linkage between the mind and the body. It is a fascinating, controversial, and pervasive concept in medical care today.

Stress concepts are controversial because they are sometimes very loosely defined and oversimplified. Exaggerated claims that stress causes all illness in a rather straightforward, mechanistic manner have led to skepticism. However, careful definitions and well-designed research have led to some remarkable findings about the relationship of stress and illness.

Generally speaking, the term *stress* has been used to describe emotional distress, the situational conditions that appear to provoke such distress, or both. For the purposes of clarity in this chapter, "stress" will denote the subjective state of distress, and the conditions that provoke this arousal will be termed "stressors." In order for conditions to cause subjective stress, they generally must tax the adaptive capacity of the person.

Holmes and Rahe (1967) postulated that major events in a person's life requiring change of any kind, whether positive or negative, would require adaptive efforts and readjustment of the organism. They argued that these effects can be cumulative and that the more readjustment required by the person, the more likely the person would be to develop physical illnesses. Holmes and Rahe (1967) developed the Social Readjustment Rating Scale to measure the impact of cumulative life events on the person (Table 2–1). As can be seen, a number associated with hypothesized readjustment is assigned to each of 43 different but common life events. The higher the number, the more readjustment is usually required after the event. While there have been many methodologic criticisms of this instrument, hundreds of subsequent investigators using better instruments have also demonstrated an association between life event "scores" and future development of physical illnesses (i.e., the higher the current life events scores, the more likely persons have been to develop physical illnesses in the future [Cohen, 1981]). The psychobiological mechanisms through which life events or stressors can lead to illness are just beginning to be clarified and will be reviewed in a subsequent section.

Table 2–1 **Social Readjustment Rating Scale**

RANK	LIFE EVENT	VALUE
1	Death of spouse	100
2	Divorce	73
3	Marital separation	65
4	Jail term	63
5	Death of close family member	53
6	Personal injury or illness	50
7	Marriage	47
8	Fired at work	46
9	Marital reconciliation	45
10	Retirement	44
11	Change in health of family member	40
12	Pregnancy	39
13	Sex difficulties	39
14	Gain of new family member	39
15	Business readjustment	38
17	Death of close friend	36
18	Change to different line of work	36
19	Change in number of arguments	35
23	Child leaving home	29
24	Trouble with in-laws	29
25	Outstanding personal achievement	28
27	Begin or end school	26
29	Revision of personal habits	24
31	Change in work hours or conditions	20
32	Change in residence	20
33	Change in school	20
36	Change in social activities	18
39	Change in family get togethers	16
43	Minor violation of the law	11

(Adapted from Holmes TH, Rahe RH: The social readjustment rating scale. J Psychosom Res 11:213–218, 1967)

A study conducted in Britain found strong evidence for a link between stress and the common cold (Cohen et al, 1991). Healthy men and women volunteers were given nasal drops containing a low infectious dose of 1 of 5 respiratory viruses resembling those commonly transmitted person-to-person in producing illnesses. Two days before and 7 days after exposure, the subjects were quarantined to apartments and examined daily by physicians for evidence of respiratory infections such as signs and symptoms (e.g., sneezing, watery eyes, nasal stuffiness, sinus pain, sore throat, cough and sputum), number of facial tissues used, and a serum sample. Prior to the exposure, subjects completed a series of measures of stress or stressful events in their lives over the past months. The investigators found that higher levels of stress were associated with a greater likelihood of viral infections and severity of cold symptoms. The findings suggest that stress compromises the immune system so that people are more vulnerable to viral infections.

Animal research has also been very illuminating in helping us understand the relationship of stressors to illness. A very large literature provides convincing data that a variety of stressors to animals (crowding, maternal separation, isolation, cold, immersion in water, electric shocks, rotation stress, and so forth) lead to increased incidence of hypertension, heart disease, ulcers, and decreased resistance to microbes, x-rays, and transplanted tumor cells (Ader, 1981; Cassel, 1974; Weiner, 1977; Weiner et al, 1981). Psychobiological mechanisms leading to disease vulnerability are discussed in detail in Chapter 11.

There are several lines of investigation linking stress and mortality. One of the most replicable findings about stressful life events has demonstrated the risk of grief. Widows and widowers suffer a significantly increased risk of dying in the year after the death of their spouses (Middleton and Raphael, 1987). A study published in the *New England Journal of Medicine* demonstrates that psychological stress among patients with cardiac disease is associated with silent myocardial ischemia and ventricular dysfunction. This strongly suggests that stress is related to undesirable cardiac events and possibly cardiac death (Rozanski et al, 1988). Sudden cardiac death is often precipitated by emotional distress (Dimsdale, 1988). Psychological factors that affect vulnerability to medical illness, including a detailed discussion of the concept of "stress," are discussed in more detail in the following chapter.

Lack of social support also seems to be related to the occurrence of illness. One elegant epidemiologic study demonstrated in a prospective fashion that persons with low social support suffered from a significantly increased mortality 5 years later. This proved to be true even after controlling for the effects of smoking, health status, healthcare behavior, and all other health-related variables known to the investigators (Berkman and Syme, 1979).

Epidemiological studies of community populations in the U.S., Finland, and Germany found that social isolation is associated with two or three times the risk of mortality compared to those who are well integrated into their communities (House et al, 1988). For example, in the 1950s researchers noted that residents of Roseto, Pennsylvania, had unusually low rates of mortality associated with heart disease. On closer investigation, they found a close-knit homogeneous community of Italian Americans whose families immigrated to the U.S. in the 1880s. Evidence suggested that the high levels of social integration served to protect the community from heart disease leading to myocardial infarctions (Bruhn and Wolf, 1979). Interestingly, more recent studies (Egolf et al, 1992) found the "Roseto Effect" to have diminished as Roseto became "Americanized." Rates of myocardial infarctions for men and women in Roseto have reached those of comparable age and sex in neighboring towns as close family ties and the community cohesiveness of their town has eroded. With proportionately fewer adults in the U.S. likely to have close community ties, supportive family relationships, or links through participation in voluntary organizations, vulnerability to various kinds of stressors and stress-related illnesses may increase.

Influence of Psychosocial Variables on the Course and Outcome of Illness

Numerous psychosocial variables have been shown to relate to the course and outcome of physical illnesses. In particular, an accumulation of significant life events can herald poor outcome. Social support in some circumstances has been shown to buffer the deleterious impact of high life events. A particularly ominous circumstance, then, is the combination of high life events without adequate social support to buffer these experiences. These two variables, particularly in combination, have been shown in numerous studies to predict poor outcome of physical illnesses.

High stress (as measured by the presence of many significant life events) and low social support was associated with four times the subsequent risk of death in patients with myocardial infarctions. This order of magnitude was identical to the relative risk associated with other cardiac complications such as arrhythmias, congestive heart failure, and so forth (Ruberman et al, 1984).

Similarly, obstetric patients with high life events scores and low social support have three times the rate of pregnancy complications (Nuckolls et al, 1972). Asthmatic patients experiencing high degrees of stressful life events and low social support are more likely to be using high-dose steroid treatments (de Araujo et al, 1972).

Psychosocial Interventions Make a Difference in the Outcome of Physical Illness

The research indicating that psychosocial variables have an impact on illness predisposition, onset, course, and outcome becomes particularly important when it comes to the point of designing interventions. Prediction, by itself, has an importance in medical care, but psychosocial interventions that can be shown to improve the prognosis of physical illness might be able to lower morbidity and mortality.

Numerous studies indicate that psychosocial interventions do indeed affect health outcomes in a positive direction. A metaanalysis of 34 controlled studies examining the effects of a supportive, educational, or psychotherapeutic intervention on patients after myocardial infarctions or surgery demonstrated that such interventions were associated with improved physical outcome (less pain, temperature, infection, and so forth) as well as improved emotional outcome (less anxiety and depression). Furthermore, experimental subjects receiving the supportive interventions were discharged an average of 2 days earlier than control subjects (Mumford et al, 1982).

The study of cardiac patients with Type A behavior, discussed above, showed that behavioral intervention could halve the likelihood of experiencing future infarctions (Friedman et al, 1984). Providing a supportive companion to women in labor resulted in one-half the complications compared with randomized control patients who did not receive this companionship. In addition, the women with the supportive companions achieved better bonding with their infants (Sosa et al, 1980).

Psychiatric treatment in patients with chronic physical illnesses, such as hypertension, diabetes and chronic respiratory illnesses has been shown to be associated with lower overall medical costs (Mumford et al, 1984). Psychiatric care has also be shown to have an "offset effect," lessening the use of medical services by patients. In a 5-year study of patients in a large health maintenance organization, Hankin et al (1983) found that providing psychiatric care to patients with mental health problems *significantly reduced* their use of nonpsychiatric care, especially their use of primary care medical services.

In addition, formal psychotherapy has been found effective in improving the outcome of patients with a wide range of physical illnesses (Cohen-Cole et al, 1986). For example, in a classic study, Spiegel and colleagues (1989) randomly assigned 50 women with metastatic breast cancer to therapeutic support groups that met over the period of one year, with 36 women of comparable medical status assigned to routine care as a control group. The support groups were intended to reduce feelings of social isolation and help women cope with their disease and its impact on their lives. There was considerable evidence that the groups were appreciated by the participants because they improved the quality of life. The investigators also found that women randomly assigned to the therapy also *lived longer*. Looking back 10 years since the onset of the study, women in the therapy group lived a mean of 36.6 months whereas the mean survival of the control group was only 18.9 months.

Psychobiological Mechanisms

How does stress lead to illness? How does low support lead to poor physical outcome? How does psychosocial intervention improve physical outcome?

Most of the mechanisms through which psychosocial variables exert their specific effects on illness processes cannot yet be elaborated in molecular detail. However, many psychoendocrine, psychoneurologic, and psychoimmunologic pathways are beginning to be discovered and described.

The hypothalamus recognizes threatening circumstances and responds with the secretion of releasing factors, such as corticotropin releasing factor (CRF), which activate the anterior pituitary gland to release hormones, like adrenocorticotropic hormone (ACTH), which, in turn, act on the adrenal gland to stimulate the production of cortisol. Cortisol has widespread bodily effects, including effects on glucose utilization, metabolism, blood flow to large muscles, and so forth. Cortisol, in addition, suppresses many immune functions.

Selye (1976) was one of the early investigators to hypothesize the mechanism of hyperadrenal function as a mediator of the relationship between stress and disease. Other endocrine activation also seems stress related. Studies have demonstrated that prolactin, growth hormone, thyroid hormone, and androgens also increase with subjective stress (Sachar, 1980) (see also Chapter 3).

The autonomic nervous system is also implicated in the axis between stress and physical problems. Hypothalamic recognition of danger is the originator of the mechanism. Hypothalamic stimulation activates the autonomic nervous system with the elaboration of epinephrine and norepinephrine, which have widespread bodily effects including increased heart rate, blood pressure, and respiration. Such mechanisms may be related to the development of hypertension and related illnesses.

In addition to endocrine and nervous system responses, psychoimmunologic relationships may be implicated in the connection between psychosocial variables and illness outcomes. Grieving widows and widowers have been shown to have impaired lymphocyte responses to nonspecific mitogens. Persons under stress also show impaired natural killer cell activity (Dorian and Garfinkel, 1987). Numerous animal studies show the same associations linking stress with impaired immunity and increased illness outcomes (Dorian and Garfinkel, 1987). These mechanisms will be discussed in more detail in the following chapter.

Implications for the Practice of Medicine: Interveiwing Skills

The importance of psychological and social variables in medical practice requires that physicians develop the knowledge and skills necessary to integrate these factors into general patient care. The skills necessary for this integration are complex and cannot be fully covered in this short introductory textbook.

The most important skill is the ability of the physician to communicate well with the patient. As discussed in Chapter 1, the doctor–patient relationship is the foundation of excellence in clinical medicine, and the interview is the building block of good relationships. Unfortunately, there is reason to believe that the general interviewing skills of physicians in practice are inadequate. One recent study demonstrated that physicians tended to interrupt their patients within the first *18* seconds of the interview. Patients did not get to tell their own stories, and physicians did not obtain an understanding of all the most important problems of their patients (Beckman and Frankel, 1984). Other studies have shown that the empathic skills that students demonstrate in their early years of training tend to diminish as they advance in their education (Maguire and Rutter, 1976). Physicians do not educate their patients well, and 50% of patients do not follow physicians' recommendations (Meichenbaum and Turk, 1987). It is likely that physicians with better educational and motivational skills would lead to better-informed patients who would adhere better to treatment recommendations. Such training has, in fact, been shown to lead to better patient outcome (Cohen-Cole and Bird, 1986b).

There are three basic functions to the medical interview:

1. To collect relevant data to develop and test hypotheses about illnesses.
2. To develop and maintain therapeutic relationships with patients.
3. To educate and motivate patients to adhere to treatment recommendations (Bird and Cohen-Cole, 1990).

Each of these interviewing functions is best served by specific skills in communicating with patients. While these cannot be reviewed here, they are discussed in detail elsewhere, and medical students can get the opportunity to learn these skills in other settings (Cohen-Cole, 1991; Lipkin et al, in press).

The development of adequate interviewing skill is only the beginning of what is required to be able to integrate psychologic and social variables in medical practice. Physicians must also develop the disposition to collect relevant data concerning specific variables. For example, physicians should learn to ask patients about recent life stresses and levels of social support. Negative health habits, such as smoking, drinking, poor dietary habits, not wearing seat belts, and so forth, should be evaluated, and efforts should be made to educate patients and motivate them to change. Relevant knowledge of psychological processes should be mastered. Possible psychosocial treatment interventions should be learned and implemented where relevant. The task for physicians is large and complex. This text provides a starting point in this important process and students are referred to standard textbooks on medical interviewing for more detail (Cohen-Cole, 1991).

EPIDEMIOLOGY OF PSYCHIATRIC DISORDERS IN GENERAL MEDICAL PRACTICE

Psychiatric Disorders in the Community

As discussed above, physicians need general psychosocial knowledge and assessment skills to be able to evaluate and appropriately manage relevant psychologic and social variables in patients with *physical* disorders. However, it is important for medical students to realize that similar skills are also needed for the recognition and management of overt *psychiatric* disorders that present in the general medical sector.

Almost 30 million Americans suffer from mental disorders, alcohol abuse, or other substance abuse in any 6-month period of time. These illnesses cause untold suffering, as well as enormous morbidity and mortality. The financial costs are staggering. The direct and indirect costs of these illnesses were estimated to be $218 *billion* in 1983. Mortality from alcohol and drug abuse, substance abuse–related accidents, and suicides related to other mental disorders all account for 108,000 deaths per year (Kamerow et al, 1986).

Patients with mental disorders tend to be high attenders of general medical clinics. These patients use about *twice* as many general healthcare resources as those without mental disorders. Interestingly, these general healthcare costs can be reduced by proper treatment for their substance abuse or mental disorder (Mumford et al, 1984).

The recently completed "Epidemiologic Catchment Area Study" (ECA) provides data from a household survey of 20,000 persons in five sites across the United States. About 20% of Americans have suffered from a clinically significant and diagnosable mental disorder in the preceding year. Over one-third (32%) of Americans have suffered from a mental disorder at some time in their lives. Phobias have the highest lifetime prevalence, followed by mood disorders (major depression and dysthymia) and alcohol abuse/dependence. Tables 2–2, 2–3, and 2–4 show the different prevalence rates of major mental disorders by social background characteristics (Robins et al, 1991).

It is interesting to note that anxiety and depressive disorders are much more common in women and that substance abuse is more common among men. Overall, the total prevalence of mental disorders is about the same in men as in women, although women are much more likely to seek help for their problems than are men. Another important finding is that, contrary to expectations, mental disorders *do not* increase with age. In fact, they seem to decrease after the age of 65. The "baby boom" generation now seems to be suffering from a dramatically increased prevalence of mood disorders in particular (Robins et al, 1991).

Table 2–2 **Selected Findings from the Epidemiologic Catchment Area Study**

	PREVALENCE (%)	
DISORDER	Lifetime	1 Year
Any disorder*	32.2	20.0
Schizophrenia	1.5	1.0
Mania	0.8	0.6
Major depression	6.4	3.7
Dysthymia	3.3	5.4
Alcohol abuse/dependence	13.8	6.3
Phobia	14.3	8.8
Somatization disorder	0.1	0.1
Antisocial personality	2.6	1.2

* *Note:* The ECA study systematically underestimates the true prevalence of mental disorders because the survey instrument (the "Diagnostic Interview Scale") did not include a number of important psychiatric disorders including posttraumatic stress disorder, somatoform pain disorder, hypochondriasis, conversion disorder, psychological factors affecting physical condition, and all personality disorders other than antisocial personality.
(Data from Robins L, Regier D (eds): Psychiatric Disorders in America: The Epidemiologic Catchment Area Study. Free Press. New York. 1991)

Table 2–3 **Selected Lifetime Prevalence by Sex**

	PREVALENCE (%)	
DISORDER	Male	Female
Any disorder	36.0	30.0
Major depression	2.6	7.0
Agoraphobia	3.2	7.9
Alcohol abuse	23.8	4.8
Antisocial personality	4.5	0.8

Table 2–4 **Selected Lifetime Prevalence by Age**

	PREVALENCE (%)			
DIAGNOSIS	**18–29 yr**	**30–44 yr**	**45–64 yr**	**65+ yr**
Major depression	5.0	7.5	4.0	1.4
Alcohol abuse/dependence	33.5	33.4	24.3	15.0

Besides the ECA study, there have been many other epidemiologic studies of psychiatric disorders, comparing prevalence in rural versus urban settings and in primitive versus more-advanced societies. These studies were undertaken to test the hypothesis that civilization and industrialization may be associated with increased rates of mental illness. While there are some small differences, the most impressive finding of cross-cultural epidemiology has been the result that the prevalence of major mental disorders appears to be fairly stable across international boundaries (industrialized/nonindustrialized) as well as urban/rural boundaries (Murphy JM, 1988). There are some important exceptions, however, to these crosscultural universals in the prevalence of the major mental disorders: schizophrenia is slightly *more* common in lower socioeconomic classes (in the U.S.) and *less* common in less-developed societies; schizophrenia tends to have a better outcome in less-developed societies; economic and social instability are both associated with higher rates and poorer outcome of mental illness; bipolar disorder is slightly more prevalent in more socially advantaged classes; depression is somewhat more common in urban areas; depression is more likely to occur in relatively powerless women, without emotional support and no outside employment (Kleinman, 1988; Boyd and Weissman, 1988; Murphy and Helzer, 1988).

As Brown, Ballard, and Gregg note in Chapter 4, the presentation of both physical and mental illness symptoms may vary in different cultures. For example, Kleinman and Kleinman (1985) describe how symptoms of mental disturbances are described as somatic complaints in Asian cultures far more than among Westerners. Depressed patients often report a variety of diffuse and changeable physical symptoms such as vague aches and pains, feeling tired all over, dizziness and palpitations, and deny feeling depressed when asked. When Lau et al (1983) studied 213 cases of depression in Hong Kong, they found 96% of the patients presenting their symptoms as physical complaints including headache, insomnia, feverishness, cough, and lower back pain. Kleinman (1980) notes that the languages spoken in China and Taiwan have few words referring to psychological states. Perhaps because Americans with little education also lack a psychological "vocabulary of discomfort," Kleinman finds that they, too, tend to present symptoms of mental disorders in somatic terms more than better-educated persons (Kleinman and Kleinman, 1985). This characteristic of describing feelings and mood states in physical terms has been called "somatothymia" by Stoudemire (1991).

Although extreme mental disturbances such as psychotic depression, schizophrenia, and bipolar disorder are recognized throughout the world, they have different names and the expression of symptomatic behaviors varies. For example, a schizophrenic in a tribal society may say that his behavior is controlled by powerful sorcerers and witches whereas his counterpart in the West might claim to be controlled by Martians or electrical impulses (Helman, 1990).

Locals generally differentiate "normal" controlled behaviors motivated by belief systems or rituals from similar behaviors that are not motivated by the sociocultural context and therefore labelled as "abnormal" and "pathological" (Helman, 1990). Edgerton (1977) reported a consensus among laypersons in four East African cultures that actions such as violent conduct, wandering around naked, talking nonsense, and sleeping and hiding in the bush—as long as they occurred "without reason"—are indicators of "madness."

Some disorders unique to other cultures share the symptoms of mental disorders with different labels in our own society. *Susto* (or "magical fright") is common throughout Latin America and among Hispanics in the Southwestern U.S. As Rubel (1977) described it, *susto* is based on the belief that an individual is composed of a physical body and of souls or spirits that can become detached from the body and wander freely. The loss of soul or spirit is believed to occur when someone is sleeping and dreaming or when one is shocked, frightened, or very surprised. The clinical presentations of *susto* are restlessness during sleep, loss of appetite, and lack of interest in dress or personal hygiene. Epidemiological studies of *susto* find that it is commonly preceded by a series of life stresses, including those that lead individuals to feel that they cannot meet the social expectations of their family or social group. Healing is carried out by a *curandero* who devises various strategies for coaxing or entreating the soul or spirit to rejoin the body (Rubel, 1977).

Psychiatric diseases therefore exist and are recognized as abnormal or pathological in most societies. The experience of the disorder—or illness—may vary, as will the understanding of its causes or etiology. Cultural influences and provincial belief systems as they affect definitions of disease, illness, and illness "behaviors" will be discussed in more detail in Chapter 4.

Epidemiology of Psychiatric Disorders in Primary Care

A significant proportion—an estimated 41% to 63%—of all mental health visits are made to *primary care* physicians rather than to mental health specialists (Mechanic, 1989). Several recent studies (including the ECA study) confirm that one in every four general medical patients (25%) have a major psychiatric illness. It has been found that 6% to 10% of medical patients meet criteria for major depression and 3% to 6% meet criteria for panic disorder. At least 10% of all medical patients are likely to have an alcohol problem (Kessler et al, 1985; Von Korff et al, 1987). Among hospitalized medical-surgical patients, those patients with psychiatric problems had significantly longer lengths of hospital stays (19 compared with 9 days) (Fulop et al, 1987). More than half of all these patients will *never* get help for their mental illnesses from mental health specialists. Their only chance for appropriate care will be from their primary care physician (Shulman et al, 1985).

Are these patients being appropriately recognized and treated by their primary physicians? The answer is an unequivocal *no*!

Several studies that examined the ability of physicians to detect psychiatric disorders have concurred with the finding that only 10% to 50% (at the most) of major psychiatric disorders were detected. One study of major depression in the community determined that only 17% of patients with major depression were treated with an antidepressant medication, but over half were taking sedative hypnotic agents such as benzodiazepines for insomnia and other nonspecific complaints (prescribed in most cases by their primary care physician) (Weissman et al, 1981). Only 8% of panic disorder patients were adequately treated. One study in Boston found that *none* of the patients who were diagnosed independently as meeting psychiatric criteria for alcohol abuse were recognized by the primary care physician (Borus et al, 1988). Of those patients seen by primary care physicians, relatively few are referred for specialty care. Patients also consistently underreport personal distress to their physicians (Eisenberg, 1992). Most people who commit suicide visit their primary physician in the month before they actually kill themselves. Their psychological distress is rarely recognized (Murphy GE, 1988).

Why is so much mental illness missed in the primary care sector? These problems result from a combination of factors that relate to both the patient and the doctor. First of all, patients do not usually go to their doctor complaining of a mental illness. They usually present with somatic complaints that require a high level of suspicion as well as diagnostic expertise on the part of the physician to diagnose accurately. Many patients also do not want to believe that they may be suffering from a mental disorder. Finally, physicians must be able to educate patients skillfully concerning the current psychobiologic understanding of mental illness in order to get them to accept proper treatment.

From the physician's point of view, psychiatric diagnoses are often missed because of time constraints, as well as limited knowledge and skills and lack of disposition to recognize such disorders (Cohen-Cole et al, 1982). Mental health training of primary care physicians is woefully inadequate. Residents in internal medicine receive an average of 8 hours over 3 years of residency training in the management of mental disorders. This is true despite the fact that these problems occur in 25% of their patients (Strain et al, 1985). Family practice residents receive more than this, but almost no mental health training from psychiatrists (Goldberg et al, 1985).

Primary care physicians can increase their awareness of psychiatric illnesses and use this information to improve their quality of care. Physicians can communicate their interest and a willingness to listen—a cue many depressed people feel is lacking—thereby inhibiting the expression of their distress. This may alert the physician to potential suicide risks, encourage more supportive behavior, and, if needed, lead to referral for specialty care. In this way, the doctor–patient relationship may enhance the quality of patient care (Mechanic, 1989).

Psychiatric illnesses are among the most common and troubling disorders in the country and represent the major problem of 25% of all medical patients. Surveys of practicing physicians indicate that they feel undertrained in recognizing and treating these disorders. Current research indicates that physicians underrecognize psychiatric problems. The need for further education is clear.

SOCIAL EPIDEMIOLOGY AND ILLNESS BEHAVIOR: SOCIOCULTURAL INFLUENCES ON DISEASE, MEDICAL UTILIZATION, AND OTHER ILLNESS-RELATED BEHAVIORS

Social Epidemiology

Further arguments for the biopsychosocial model can be made from the standpoint of social epidemiology. Social epidemiology represents the field of study of relationships between social groupings and patterns of illness. Four variables—age, sex, race, and socioeconomic variables—have been studied most intensively.

Age Factors

Physical Disorders. The incidence of illness is affected by age. In childhood the majority of illnesses are acute infections and exanthemas, the latter being reduced with vaccinations against the measles and rubella. The incidence of acute illness declines rapidly in adolescence and more gradually in old age while chronic diseases increase in prevalence (Susser et al, 1985). Eighty-six percent of persons over age 65 have one or more chronic medical conditions, most commonly arthritis, hypertension, and heart disease. Hearing impairments, diabetes, cataracts, and varicose veins are also common ailments of the elderly (Cockerham, 1992a).

Life expectancy has increased dramatically. In 1900, an American could expect to live to age 47; present life expectancy is more than 70 years. Life expectancy at age 65 increased only 2 years between 1900 and 1950 (11.9 to 13.9 years). Between 1950 and the mid-1980s, life expectancy at age 65 increased 3.8 years for women and 1.6 years for men, with overall mortality rates falling 29% in that period. Most of the decline was due to heart and cerebrovascular disease strokes (Estes and Lee, 1986).

The overall decline in mortality, associated with declines in infant mortality and mortality associated with infectious diseases, accompanied by declining fertility rates, accounts for an increasing proportion of the population over age 65. In 1900, persons over age 65 were only 4% of the population; by 1987 they represented 12.3% of the population (or 29.8 million people). By 2050, 20% of the population is expected to be over the age of 65 (Cockerham, 1992a).

Mental Disorders. Age is also associated with the prevalence of mental impairments. Psychiatric disorders typically begin when people are young, the median age at first symptoms being only 16 (the average age of the U.S. population is 40). Ninety percent of those developing mental disorders in their lifetimes exhibit symptoms by age 38, with the exception of cognitive impairment disorders (such as Alzheimer's Disease), which increase in frequency much later in life, especially after age 70. Particular disorders differ in their median age at onset. For symptoms of antisocial personality, the median age is 8 years; for phobias, age 10; somatization disorders, age 15; drug abuse, age 18; and schizophrenia and manic episodes, age 19. The median age for the onset of obsessive compulsive disorders is 20 years; alcohol abuse/dependence, age 21; panic disorder, age 23; and major depression, age 25 (Robins et al, 1991).

Adolescence is an important period for the development of many disorders, and most symptoms begin between the ages of 15 and 29 (Burke, 1990). The ECA studies suggest that the prevalence of depression, drug abuse, and alcohol dependence have been increasing among younger age groups over the past 40 years (Burke et al, 1991). Klerman (1976) hypothesized that western societies were entering an "Age of Melancholy" characterized by changing family structures and increased urbanization, which has resulted in greater problems in mental health among adolescents and young adults.

Gender Factors

Physical Disorders. As long as vital statistics have been available in the U.S., men have shown higher rates of mortality than women, but women have exhibited higher rates of morbidity and health services use (Verbrugge, 1985). Although women tend to report more morbidity, men tend to suffer a greater prevalence of life-threatening chronic diseases or behavioral and environmental risks. At all ages, males exceed female death rates for heart disease, cancer, cerebrovascular accidents, and pneumonia, along with homicides, suicides, and accidental injuries (Cockerham, 1992a). Although the more frequent symptoms of women are generally minor, in later life women also die from the same diseases as men. For example, coronary heart disease is the leading cause of death for women after the age of 66, whereas it is the greatest killer of men after age 39. As Verbrugge notes (1985 : 163), "Men and women essentially suffer the same types of problems; what distinguishes the sexes is the frequency of those problems and the pace of death."

Differences in age-specific mortality are reflected in life expectancy. (Table 2–5) In 1988, the average life expectancy at birth for white females in the U.S. was 78.9 years compared to 72.3 for white males. For black females life expectancy was 73.4 years compared to 64.9 years for black males. A greater proportion of females than males survive at every age. For example, the chances of fetal death during the prenatal stage are approximately 12% greater among males and 130% greater for males during the neonatal (newborn) stage (Cockerham, 1992a).

Table 2–5 **Average Number of Years of Life Expectancy in the United States by Race and Sex, Since 1900**

YEAR	WHITE MALES	WHITE FEMALES	BLACK MALES	BLACK FEMALES
1900	46.6	48.7	32.5*	33.5*
1950	66.5	72.2	58.9	62.7
1960	67.4	74.1	60.7	65.9
1970	68.0	75.6	60.0	68.3
1980	70.7	78.1	63.8	72.5
1987	72.2	78.9	65.2	73.6
1988	72.3	78.9	64.9	73.4

(National Center for Health Statistics, 1991)
* Includes all nonwhites.

Table 2–6 details age-adjusted rates for causes of death adjusted to sex and race, in the U.S. Some of the gender differences in mortality are associated with lifestyles associated with sex roles in western cultures. Expectations of aggression among males appear to be associated with greater rates of death and injury among adolescent men from accidents and violence. Men are also more likely to be employed in high-risk occupations and are more likely to use alcohol and other drugs and to experience health consequences as a result (Cockerham, 1992a).

Figure 2–1 presents the leading causes of death for adults aged 25 to 64, but does not denote gender differences. Verbrugge (1985), however, has suggested that men and women may be moving toward greater equality in mortality rates as lifestyles change for women. For example, rates of cigarette smoking and alcohol consumption among women have been approaching that of men, and women are entering the labor force in occupations that have been dominated by men. Lung cancer, the eighth leading cause of death for women in 1960, became the leading cause of death for women in 1986, exceeding breast cancer.

As noted, women report higher rates of morbidity and utilize health services more than men, even when reproductive health symptoms and services are excluded (Cockerham, 1992a; Cleary et al, 1982; Verbrugge, 1985). Women have higher morbidity from acute and nonfatal chronic conditions. Excesses are especially large (twofold or more) for varicose veins, frequent constipation, gallbladder conditions, chronic enteritis and colitis, corns and bunions, thyroid conditions, anemias, migraines, and chronic urinary diseases. Also more common among women are hypertensive disease, hemorrhoids, chronic bronchitis, chronic sinusitis, diverticula of the intestine, arthritis, and synovitis/bursitis/tenosynovitis (Verbrugge, 1985).

Women also restrict their activities for health problems more then men—about 25% more days per year and 40% more days in bed per year, on average. Between the

Table 2–6 Age-Adjusted Death Rates for Selected Causes of Death, According to Sex and Race, United States, 1988*

	WHITE MALES	WHITE FEMALES	BLACK MALES	BLACK FEMALES
All causes	664.2	384.4	1,037.8	593.1
Heart disease	220.5	114.2	286.2	181.1
Cerebrovascular diseases	30.0	25.5	57.8	46.6
Cancer	157.6	110.1	227.0	131.2
Pulmonary disease	27.8	14.5	26.0	10.0
Pneumonia and influenza	18.0	10.7	28.0	13.4
Liver disease and cirrhosis	12.1	5.0	20.7	9.3
Diabetes	9.6	8.4	19.8	22.1
Accidents	49.9	18.8	69.0	22.2
Suicide	19.8	5.1	11.8	2.4
Homicide	7.7	2.8	58.2	12.7
AIDS	9.9	0.7	31.6	6.2

(National Center for Health Statistics, 1991)
*Deaths per 100,000 resident population.

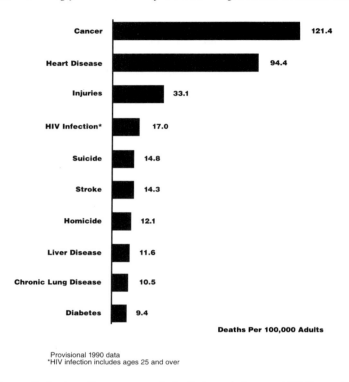

Provisional 1990 data
*HIV infection includes ages 25 and over

Figure 2–1. *Leading causes of death for adults aged 25 through 64. (Centers for Disease Control, National Center for Health Statistics)*

ages of 17 and 44, women have twice the number of physician visits and hospital stays as men do (excluding reproductive-related problems, the gap is 30%). Women obtain substantially more prescription medications than men, especially psychotropic drugs (Verbrugge, 1985).

Considerable research has explored the reasons for higher rates of morbidity among women than men. A portion of the difference may be an artifact of reporting behavior. Some speculate that women are more sensitive to body discomforts as a result of childhood socialization while men repress their reporting as they adhere to a cultural norm of stoicism. Further, women are more often interviewed in home surveys on health status and may underreport the symptoms of their spouses relative to their own (Verbrugge, 1985).

The bulk of the research, however, suggests the differences in morbidity are not merely artifactual but are real and associated with social role demands. In American society, the combined demands on women as caregivers, spouses, and employees apparently exceed those on men and, in some cases such as employment, the rewards are fewer (Bird and Fremont, 1991). Women also perceive themselves as having less control in making decisions that affect their lives than men (Rosenfeld, 1989). The excessive role demands, lower rewards, and lack of control contribute to chronic stress, which is associated with a greater incidence and prevalence of symptoms.

When role demands are comparable for men and women in studies, there are little or no differences in morbidity between men and women. In one study, when role demands were statistically controlled, or held constant, the morbidity for men exceeded that of women (Bird and Fremont, 1991).

Marital status interacts with gender in its association with both morbidity and mortality rates. Mortality rates among the married are less than those of comparable ages who are single due to divorce, separation, widowhood, or never having married. Only a small portion of the difference is accounted for by selection, such that healthier persons are more likely to marry. The bulk of the difference is caused by mortality associated with the use of legal, but harmful, substances (e.g., lung cancer with smoking or cirrhosis of the liver with excessive alcohol use), with intentional or unintentional injuries (homicides, automobile accidents, suicides), and with conditions requiring prolonged care (tuberculosis, diabetes). Marriage has a significant impact on mortality rates for men, but there is hardly any effect on the health of women (Gove, 1973).

The greater impact of marriage on the mortality of men probably occurs because the lifestyles of single men pose greater health risks than those of women. The lives of men change more dramatically with marriage. Evidence in support of this hypothesis was reported by Umberson (1987), who found changes in a variety of health-risk behaviors for men with marriage and even more with parenthood. Changes in the behavior of women with marriage and parenthood were minimal. In this culture, marriage provides men with caregivers—the traditional role of wives—and also acts as a form of social control. Women appear not to derive such health benefits from marriage in America (Umberson, 1987).

Mental Disorders. For mental disorders the picture is different. The ECA studies mentioned earlier indicate that, contrary to previous research reporting of greater levels of mental illness for women than men, more men than women report mental disorders during their lifetimes (36% as opposed to 30%). Males have excess amounts of alcohol abuse and antisocial personality whereas females have higher rates of somatization, obsessive-compulsive, and major depressive disorders (Robins and Regier, 1991; Link and Dohrenwend, 1989). Community studies focusing more generally on mood disorders or depression scales find women with considerably more symptoms of mental disorders than men (Kessler, 1989). Although some of the gender differences have been attributed to reporting styles of men and women, the bulk of the research and the ECA studies suggest the differences for specific disorders are real.

As with general morbidity, research attributes some of the differences in psychiatric disorders to social roles and experiences. Women reportedly experience greater chronic stress from their social roles, making them more vulnerable to stressful life events and contributing directly to symptoms of depression (Kessler, 1989). In general, married women employed outside the home enjoy better mental health than those remaining at home as housewives (Cockerham, 1992b). Additional research shows that the mental health benefits of employment are less for women when the family is very dependent on their income or when women are also expected to perform the full range of family roles. Thus, working class or single parents receive fewer mental health benefits from working than middle class women (Kessler and McLeod, 1984; Ross et al, 1983). Some (Thoits, 1987) attribute the greater vulnerability of women to depression to having less control over many situations or fewer resources with which to make decisions about their lives.

Rates of mental disorder are especially high among separated, divorced, and never-married men and women compared to those who are married. The never-married have much higher rates of drug abuse and higher rates of schizophrenia, bipolar disorder, alcohol dependency, and antisocial personality. Mental health can be both a cause and effect of marital status, since social competence is required for stable relationships. Widowhood is not necessarily associated with greater levels of psychiatric disorder, except that associated with bereavement (Robins and Regier, 1991).

Social support associated with marriage may function to protect some from stressful life events and therefore resist the onset of mental disorders. A study of depression in London (Brown and Harris, 1978) found that of women suffering comparable stressful life events, those who did not have a supportive, intimate relationship with their husbands were more likely to experience symptoms of depression. Although both women and men appear to derive mental health benefits from marriage, the advantages for men exceed those for women (Cockerham, 1992b). This may explain why women do not suffer as much as men from marital dissolutions. Women also adjust to spousal death better than men and adjust as well, if not better, to divorce (Kessler, 1989).

Race

Physical Disorders. Racial or ethnic groups manifest great differences in mortality and morbidity. Asian Americans have the best health quality levels followed closely by that of whites, but blacks are especially disadvantaged relative to these groups. Black infants have had nearly twice the mortality rates as whites and, although the rates have diminished, the gaps between races persist (Cockerham, 1992a).

In the U.S., blacks have a higher prevalence than whites of most life-threatening illnesses such as AIDS, cancer, heart disease, and hypertension (Polednak, 1989). Although blacks comprise 12% of the population, they are 20% of diagnosed hypertensives. Between the ages of 25 and 44, hypertension kills black males 15 times more frequently than it does white males. The ratio of white to black females dying in the same age category is 17 to 1. Homicide is the leading cause of death for black men between the ages of 15 and 24 (Cockerham, 1992a).

Differences are reflected in life expectancies. In 1988 the average life expectancy of black males at birth was 64.9 years, 7.4 years less than white males (72.3 years) and 14 years less than white females (78.9 years) (Cockerham, 1992a). In Harlem, an area of New York City with a predominantly black population, a black male is less likely to survive to the age of 40 than a male in Bangladesh, one of the poorest nations in the world (McCord and Freeman, 1990).

Part of the race and ethnic differences are accounted for by quality of life, availability resources, and behavior. Blacks are more likely to smoke and drink alcohol excessively and have high cholesterol, excess weight, and diabetes (Otten et al, 1990). The problems are compounded by poor access to health services.

Relative to non-Hispanic whites, Hispanics also have a disadvantaged health status with more diabetes, tuberculosis, hypertension, lung cancer, alcoholism, and deaths from cirrhosis of the liver and homicide. They also experience disproportionate numbers of AIDS cases but experience lower mortality rates associated with heart disease and most forms of cancer. Hispanics are not a homogeneous population and among them in the U.S., Cubans have the best health status, followed by Mexican Americans and Puerto Ricans (Cockerham, 1992a).

Native Americans, including American Indians and native Alaskans, have improved their overall health status over the past 40 years. American Indians still have a high mortality rate associated with diabetes. For example, the Pima Indians have rates that are 10 to 15 times higher than the general American population.

Much of the differences between ethnic or racial group are confounded by social class. Several minorities such as blacks, Hispanics, and Native Americans are disproportionately from lower socioeconomic class backgrounds, which are also associated with higher morbidity and mortality rates.

Mental Disorders. The ECA studies find that blacks have higher rates of overall mental disorders than whites or Hispanics. Among older persons, blacks have higher rates of cognitive impairment and somatization. Blacks do not have higher rates of antisocial personality or drug and alcohol abuse. Their overrepresentation in institutionalized populations for these conditions relates to a greater likelihood of vulnerability to criminal activity and prosecution associated with symptoms of the these disorders (Robins and Regier, 1991).

Native Americans have rates of alcoholism 2 to 3 times higher than the general population and, relatedly, injuries and deaths associated with automobile accidents. Suicide rates are 20% higher than the general population, particularly among Native American youth (Cockerham, 1992b).

Hispanic Americans are underrepresented in treatment populations of the mentally ill which may be partially associated with language barriers to institutional care (Aneshensel et al, 1991). Some studies of Hispanics report that the Mexican-American culture contains supportive elements, particularly family and kinship ties, that reduce vulnerability to mental disorders (Mirowsky and Ross, 1984). Similarly, kinship and community ties may partially account for the low rates of mental disorder among Asian Americans (Cockerham, 1992b).

Again, some of the differences in prevalence of mental disorders between ethnic groups may be accounted for by social class. Studies investigating overall rates of mental illness in communities that control for (or hold constant) social class found that differences between the ethnic groups were significantly reduced or they disappeared (Warheit et al, 1975; Thomas and Hughes, 1986). Therefore, we next consider the relationship of social class to health.

Social Class

Physical Disorders. Social class, whether indicated by income, occupational prestige, or educational attainment, is associated with health status. Persons from lower social class backgrounds have higher rates of morbidity, mortality, and disability than those of higher social classes (Dutton, 1986; Dutton and Levine, 1989).

Part of the association may be caused by the inadequate access to health services by persons with low incomes. Yet even in societies with universal access to services, social class is associated with mortality and morbidity (Reid, 1989). A remarkable 10-year study of 17,530 British men between the ages of 40 and 64, all employed by the civil service, found associations between civil service rank and health status. The highest-ranking administrators had the lowest death rates and the lowest-status unskilled workers had the highest likelihood of death, most of it associated with coronary heart disease (Marmot et al, 1984).

Some of the class-related differences may be associated with conditions of life and risk behaviors such as smoking, obesity, lack of intentional exercise, drug and alcohol use, and diet. Some unhealthy behaviors may represent adaptations or methods for coping with difficult life conditions associated with having few material or social resources. The physical or environmental conditions of low-income populations contain a high risk of harm from violence, unemployment, crowding, poor housing, social isolation, and stress, etc. (Dutton, 1986; Bunker et al, 1989).

Ironically, coronary heart disease, traditionally associated with affluence and a higher incidence in wealthier countries, is more common among low-income populations (Cockerham, 1992a). In the U.S., the incidence of coronary heart disease has been declining over the past 25 years. The advantages are disproportionately shared by persons of higher social class backgrounds, seemingly associated with healthier lifestyles and social and physical environments (Polednak, 1989; Stamler, 1985).

Mental Disorders. As with physical health, mental health is also directly associated with social class. The ECA study found that the least educated had the highest rates of mental disorders. The prevalence of mental disorders were also associated with other indicators of lower social class such as being welfare recipients, having unskilled jobs or not being employed. The unemployed had at least double the rate of every major mental disorder except drug abuse. Bipolar disorder, schizophrenia, and panic disorder were particularly overrepresented among both unemployed and unskilled workers (Robins and Regier, 1991).

Of the various indicators of social class, education appears most associated with mental disorders in women and income levels in men (Kessler, 1980). By categories of mental illness, schizophrenia clearly appears associated with lower social class along with most other disorders, whereas anxiety and bipolar mood disorders are apparently more prevalent in higher social classes (Link and Dohrenwend, 1989).

One of the classic studies interviewed adults in the Midtown Manhattan area of New York City in nearly 2,000 randomly selected households. Using standard instruments designed to tap a range of mental pathology, they found greater proportions of impaired persons with lower incomes. The authors argued that lower social status created pathology as a result of life conditions, but social status also increased the vulnerability of those exposed to stressors. Given similar levels of stress, persons from the lower social classes would be more likely to develop mental symptoms (Langner and Michael, 1963).

Attempts to untangle why social class is associated with mental disorders, particularly schizophrenia, have offered several explanations. The "social causation" interpretation argues that deprivation produces more psychopathology (Kohn, 1972). Somewhat related is the argument that lower social class conditions undermine coping capacity or resources that make populations more vulnerable to mental illness (Kessler and Cleary, 1980).

A second explanation, "social selection," reverses the causal direction. It argues that persons who are mentally impaired may be selected into the lower social classes because of failures in life. An inability to achieve in occupations, education, or both causes individuals to "drift" down into the lowest social classes. A related version of this explanation is that persons predisposed genetically to schizophrenia disproportionately come from lower social class origins and they also fail to be upwardly mobile in social class through achievements in life (Kohn, 1972).

Evidence supports both explanations for schizophrenia (Dohrenwend et al, 1992). Yet neither alone fully explains the association between class and mental disorder.

Utilization and Related Illness Behaviors

Definitions

In order to more fully understand the importance of human behavior in medical practice, it is important to distinguish among the concepts of "disease," "illness," and "illness behavior." *Disease* refers to a disturbance in physiologic functioning of the organism. Such a disturbance can occur without the person's awareness. *Illness* refers to a state of poor health recognized by the person and usually treated by an expert. *Illness behavior* refers to the ways people respond to bodily indications and to the perceptions, values, attitudes, and interpretations that lead people to behave in particular ways in reference to their bodies (Kleinman et al, 1978).

From these definitions, it should be clear that disease and illness are not the same. Many patients may have "silent" disease. There may be some physiological disruption of which they are not aware. Similarly, there are many people who have *illnesses* but who have no evidence of physiological *disease*. Finally, the behaviors of persons may vary greatly according to whether or not they perceive themselves as ill and to their attitudes and values about how they should behave because of the presence of illness. As noted earlier, cultural influences are what constitutes "illness" and the determinants of variations in "illness behavior" are discussed in more detail in Chapter 4.

Physicians must deal as much with illness and illness behaviors as they do with disease itself. Physicians who understand something about cultural, social class, and personality differences in illness behavior will be able to provide more effective medical care. Patterns of illness behavior often make a great impact on the physical outcome of disease.

Decision Time: An Example of the Impact of Health Attitudes on Utilization and Outcome of Disease Processes

Deaths from myocardial infarction represent the number one killer of adult males from the ages of 30 to 60. Fifty percent of patients with myocardial infarction die before they ever reach a hospital (DiMatteo and Friedman, 1982). There is a great deal of variation, however, in the amount of time it takes such patients to reach the hospital. Fifty-six percent arrive within 4 hours after the onset of symptoms, 28% arrive within 4 to 14 hours after the onset of symptoms, and 16% arrive more than 14 hours after the onset of symptoms. Transportation issues only relate to about 10% of these cases. There are other factors that must be invoked to explain these great differences in how different persons respond to the initial awareness of chest discomfort. These variables account for the differences in decision time (DiMatteo and Friedman, 1982).

There are three general sets of factors that help explain differences in decision time.

Background Factors. Social class, age, sex, and ethnicity all have an impact on decision time. Persons of lower social class are less likely to seek medical help quickly. This may have to do with rather objective access and financial issues: They are less able to afford care, they may have more difficulty finding transportation, they may not feel as well treated, and so forth.

Older patients are less likely to go for help quickly, and older females, in particular, are less likely to seek help quickly for symptoms of chest discomfort. This may relate more to the fact that females are less likely to think of cardiac events as explaining their chest symptoms than are men. Ethnic differences account for a great deal of variation in decision time. People of British descent have been trained to be more stoic about pain, and they are much less likely to seek help rapidly for symptoms of chest discomfort. Such differences can account for a great deal of the variations in decision times and can account for many of the variations in the lethality of the heart attack itself (DiMatteo and Friedman, 1982).

Psychological Processes. Psychological issues are extremely important in determining the response time of the person to physical symptoms. Patients must make a "cognitive appraisal" of the meaning of their perceived symptoms and then make judgments about what to do about it. Many persons misinterpret their initial cardiac symptoms. In fact, 70% of persons who first experience the pain of cardiac ischemia originally consider the pain to result from abdominal indigestion or some source other than cardiac.

The psychological defense of *denial* can play an important part in decision time. Mechanisms of defense are psychological processes that enable persons to avoid the anxiety of facing certain issues. The defense mechanisms operate at an unconscious level, so that the persons are truly unaware of their operation. Denial is one very powerful mechanism through which the awareness of certain anxiety-provoking issues can be minimized or unrecognized. Because heart attacks are so terribly overwhelming, many persons do not want to face the anxiety of coping with this reality. The persons who are able to maintain steadfast denial for long periods of time after the onset of cardiac symptoms are the ones most likely to experience long decision times and are at more risk from the cardiac death before reaching the hospital (DiMatteo and Friedman, 1982). (The concept of denial is discussed from the psychodynamic perspective in both Chapters 5 and 14.)

Social Variables. The social context or situation of the patient also plays an important role in the amount of decision time it takes from the first awareness of chest discomfort to the arrival in the hospital for care. The day of the week seems to play a role as well. Persons are more likely to arrive at the hospital sooner if the pain episode occurs during the week, rather than on the weekend. Similarly, if the pain occurs at work, persons are more likely to seek care rapidly. It seems as if persons value their weekends and time at home and do not want to use this time in seeking medical help.

The presence of a spouse is also important. When the chest discomfort occurs in the presence of a spouse, the person is much more likely to get to medical help sooner. It seems much easier for persons to delay getting help if they are alone at the time the symptoms first occur.

In general, these variables—background, individual psychology or personality, and social variables—help determine the amount of time that a person takes from the time of first perception of chest discomfort to the time he/she decides to seek medical care. The seven most important variables all fall within these three categories:

1. Presence of the symptoms themselves.
2. Recognition of the symptoms.
3. Amount of social or physical disability.
4. Perceived seriousness.
5. Extent of cultural "stoicism."
6. Amount of relevant information or medical knowledge.
7. Availability of sources of help.

These variables all contribute to the patient's decision time before going to the hospital. The most important of these variables are psychosocial in nature and account for a great deal of the ultimate variation in survival. For example, the mortality of "early" arrivals is about 10% compared with the mortality of late arrivals, which is about 27% (DiMatteo and Friedman, 1982).

Demographic, Cultural, and Sociopsychological Variables Related to Utilization

The same type of variables that are related to the decision time to seek medical attention for chest pain symptoms are related to healthcare utilization in general. Some term the behavior associated with defining symptoms and taking action "illness behavior."

Age and Gender. The findings for age and gender are fairly consistent. Utilization of health services is greatest among the elderly and the very young. Some of the more socially isolated elderly may seek medical care as a means of social contact and look forward to visiting their doctors for that purpose.

As noted, women utilize health services more than men. On average, they report more symptoms, make more physician visits, have more prescription drug use, and have higher rates of hospitalization, even correcting for maternity or reproductive health problems (Cockerham, 1992a).

In part, the greater utilization of services by women is associated with higher rates of morbidity. Evidence supports several additional explanations for greater use of health services by women. Women may be more sensitive to body discomforts as a result of childhood socialization when they were encouraged to express their discomfort and seek help. Boys, on the other hand, are discouraged from expressing pain or discomfort and are more likely to be rewarded for stoic behavior. Women are more apt to label their symptoms as physical illnesses and assess injuries as more serious and requiring care. As principal caregivers for their children and elderly parents, women become more knowledgeable about health and illness and are more accustomed to consulting with physicians through their care of others. More flexible schedules, at least for women who are not employed outside the household, may allow greater use of health services. Women also are more likely than men to have regular physicians, another factor associated with greater use of physicians (Verbrugge, 1985).

Ethnicity and Social Class. Utilization of health services is influenced by ethnicity and social class background. The bulk of the differences in ethnicity is accounted for by social class, minorities being disproportionately from lower social class backgrounds.

The availability of Medicare for persons 65 years of age and older and Medicaid for some with low incomes has increased the capacity of people to contact physicians. By the mid-1980s, persons with low incomes had as many contacts with physicians per year as those with high incomes. This pattern does not indicate equity in access to care because with higher morbidity low-income persons actually needed to see physicians even more. Among those in need of care, low-income persons still received medical attention less often than higher-income persons (Dutton, 1986).

Access to care has actually deteriorated further throughout the 1980s, particularly for those with low incomes (Freeman et al, 1987). Currently, an estimated 32 to 37 million Americans lack any form of health insurance and rely primarily on overburdened public facilities, when available, for their care. Even in countries with national systems providing universal access to health services, persons from lower social class backgrounds have lower utilization rates (Cockerham, 1992a). Those from deprived backgrounds use fewer health services because they are less likely to recognize symptoms as requiring medical attention, lack transportation or the capacity to leave jobs to seek medical attention, find the facilities they attend to be rather unpleasant, and because they are more alienated from service delivery systems and bureaucracies (Dutton, 1978).

Ethnicity accounts for differences in utilization because varying cultural beliefs account for how diseases are understood, how symptoms are defined, and the perceptions of appropriate sources of care. (Chapter 4 describes some of these variations in more detail.)

Some groups, such as rural Mexican Americans in the Southwest, are suspicious of modern medical care and avoid seeking care until symptoms become very severe. Because their theories of disease etiology do not fit the conventional biomedical model, Mexican Americans are likely to seek care from more familiar traditional healers such as a *curandero* (Cockerham, 1992a). Scott (1978) has described the diversity of services used in the Miami, Florida, area by Bahamian, Cuban, Haitian, Puerto Rican, and southern U.S. black populations. She finds, consistent with most studies, that the majority of these populations utilize a dual system of healing, patronizing a variety of lay and spiritual healers along with modern medical practitioners. Often the modern Western practitioner is sought to treat the symptoms, while the traditional healer is expected to address the "real" causes of the illness—why the patient was somehow "selected" for disease, disability, or harm. Thus, some patients entering the office of a physician will already be under the care and treatment of a traditional healer.

Folk beliefs about the causes and treatments of illness are pervasive. Gillick (1985) points out that the way many educated, middle-class Americans think about the causes and cures of illness is alien to that of physicians. She describes a variety of "commonsense" models about the way educated populations understand how the body functions and beliefs about vitamin deficiency, disease resistance, stress, and the causes of infectious diseases—most of them rather inaccurate. Each belief has led to popular treatments or preventive activities that are not helpful from a biomedical perspective.

A recent survey (Eisenberg et al, 1993) revealed that 34% of all Americans used "unconventional" therapies in the past year and annual visits to practitioners providing unconventional therapies exceeded the number of annual visits to primary care physicians. Most (83%) using unconventional therapies also sought treatment from medical doctors but three-fourths of them did not disclose the use of unconventional therapies to their doctors. Persons using unconventional therapies represented the full range of social class and ethnicity, but the usage was more prevalent among better educated, wealthier Americans. Gillick (1985) echoes others doing cross-cultural research on health in advising physicians to elicit their patients' theories and understanding of disease in order to be more effective in giving advice and fostering adherence to recommended therapies.

Social Networks. When people experience symptoms, they generally first describe their feelings to family, friends, and others before seeking care. Thus, patients act on symptoms with the reactions, advice, and guidance of laypersons in a social network. By the time patients enter a physician's care, they have proceeded through a "lay referral system" that has helped to define the appropriate response (Friedson, 1960).

If the social network is tightly integrated, such as a stable, multigenerational, culturally homogeneous community, the attitudes and beliefs of the social network will be very influential. If they are suspicious of Western healers, as with some rural Mexican Americans in the Southwest, patients will not seek care from the Western healer except as a last resort. If the tightly knit community is very accepting of modern medical care, such as Mormons in Salt Lake City, Utah (Geertsen et al, 1975), patients will readily seek care.

Social–Psychological Factors in Utilization. As discussed above in relation to decision time, individual psychological factors play an important role in healthcare utilization. Unconscious denial of the significance of physical symptoms can delay lifesaving medical intervention until it is too late.

In addition to the importance of mechanisms of psychological defense, individual health beliefs will exert an impact of eventual utilization of medical resources. In order for individuals to seek care, they must first decide that the symptoms represent an "illness." This usually depends on the amount of pain or discomfort they are experiencing and the amount of impairment in role functioning caused by the symptoms. Other symptoms or changes in the biological state of the organism might also be seen as important depending on the knowledge of the person and the implications of these changes for future activities.

In addition to defining the symptoms as indicative of illness, the person must also believe that there is something that can be done for the symptoms by a physician.

Even then, the individual may not visit the physician if it is seen as too expensive, too painful or unpleasant, or too inconvenient.

Thus, decisions about medical utilization are made within the context of ethnic, social network, and social class matrices and modified by social–psychological factors that weigh benefits and costs of treatment with an individual's personal health beliefs (Cockerham, 1978; DiMatteo and Friedman, 1982).

These same sociocultural variables apply to a patient's ability to accept or reject or adapt to the *sick role* (described below) and also have a great deal to do with the patient's ability or desire to adhere to the treatment recommendations made by the physician. The issue of adherence to medical regimens is central to the overall outcome of medical care because most patients cannot be expected to recover from or avoid future disease complications unless they follow physicians' recommendations. Unfortunately, rates of nonadherence are extremely high: Hundreds of studies support the finding that about 50% of physicians' recommendations are *not* followed by their patients. This nonadherence cannot be explained by low education, low social class, or low intelligence. Ethnic, social network, social class, and health beliefs all seem more important (Meichenbaum and Turk, 1987).

In addition, other psychosocial factors are also critical, in particular the nature of the relationship between the doctor and the patient and the educational skills of the physician (Meichenbaum and Turk, 1987). This is yet another area where the communication skills of the physician are crucial to determining the illness outcome of the patient (Cohen-Cole and Bird, 1986b).

The Sick Role
Illness has a well-defined role in our society, and being sick is associated with a relatively clear set of obligations and responsibilities that were first described by the sociologist Talcott Parsons (1951). In Western societies, our social norms or expectations award the sick with two rights in exchange for two obligations.

The first "right" is that sick persons are exempted from normal social activities. For example, people are not expected to work, or work as effectively, at their jobs and may be excused from meeting deadlines. The second right is that they are not blamed for their conditions; the sick are not held responsible for having an illness. In exchange, patients are expected to define their conditions as undesirable and not resign themselves to the illness. The second related expectation is for patients to cooperate with physicians in attempting to get well.

Drawing on the "sick role" perspective generates some insights into the social nature of health and illness. For example, some conditions in our society are not fully accorded the status of sickness. Alcohol- and drug-dependent persons are sometimes not viewed as "sick," perhaps because they are seen as resigning themselves to a condition rather than cooperating to get well and, hence, are held responsible for their condition (Chalfant and Kurtz, 1971). Similarly, persons with AIDS may be viewed as responsible for their conditions and thought by some to deserve punishment rather than treatment.

A corresponding dynamic is the push by some groups to have their behaviors viewed or understood as medical conditions. Some (Conrad and Schneider, 1980; Barsky, 1988) describe the "medicalization" of various behaviors or conditions in Western societies. For example, organized groups have been promoting the labeling of gamblers, alcoholics, and hyperactive children as "sick" rather than "bad" since the behaviors are attributed to an underlying illness rather than to willful behaviors.

Patients who do not cooperate with their treatment or who do not respond as expected to medical treatment may be viewed negatively by the medical profession. Labels such as "crock," "troll," and "gomer" are used to characterize these patients who do not fit into the sick role model (Leiderman and Grisso, 1985). Once patients get labeled in this manner, physicians often feel less obligated to follow through on the rest of their own responsibilities and obligations for taking care of the patients (Cohen-Cole and Freidman, 1983).

Although the sick role concept may offer some insights into understanding how society responds to those with illnesses, it does not offer a good description of many health problems. The norms of absolving persons of responsibility for their illnesses may be less apparent as we learn more about the causes of chronic conditions. As people recognize that diet, exercise, smoking, alcohol consumption, and other factors are associated with the onset of chronic conditions, there may be a shift to seeing the ill as responsible and, perhaps, punitive actions will be taken. Proposals to increase insurance premiums for smokers or add taxes on alcohol and cigarettes to be used for medical services are illustrative. Negative feelings of the general public or health workers toward persons with AIDS may, in part, reflect blaming sick individuals for the behavior that led to the health condition. The shift suggests a move away from the sick role toward "blaming the victim" on the part of some.

The sick role, in expecting patients not to be resigned to a condition and collaborate actively with a physician in treatment, also may be inappropriate for some disorders. It applies less well to chronic conditions such as hypertension or diabetes and for chronic degenerative or terminal conditions. It also overlooks those actively engaged in self care, seeking care from a variety of nonphysician healers, or the culturally diverse ways people understand and react to their symptoms.

THE BIOPSYCHOSOCIAL MODEL FOR PSYCHIATRIC PATIENTS

This chapter has reviewed the many ways that patients with physical illnesses need to be seen in a biopsychosocial context in order to understand their needs and to care for them adequately. Conversely, the same biopsychosocial perspective needs to be followed for patients with primary psychiatric disorders and *no other clear physical illnesses*. It is becoming increasing clear that many, and perhaps most major psychiatric disorders are characterized by genetic vulnerability and biological dysfunction (see Chapters 12 and 13). In others, the biologic dysfunction can be linked to early environmental deprivations or stresses (see Chapter 11). Finally, biological treatments have been shown to be remarkably effective for treating many psychiatric disorders and for returning disabled patients to active functioning.

While biological psychiatry has made great strides in the last few decades, it is crucial to note that psychological and social variables are also critical in the etiology and treatment of psychiatric disorders, even for those disorders with primarily biological underpinnings. Social variables can predict course and outcome of many disorders and psychosocial interventions can have profound effects on the outcome of psychiatric disorders.

Thus, *it should be clear that psychiatric disorders are not qualitatively different from any other medical illness.* They are, in fact, *medical illnesses* just like any other medical illness. The historic disjunction between the mind and the body is no longer relevant for modern medicine. Biological, psychological, and social variables are crucial for determining the etiology, onset, course, and outcome of all illness. This is just as true for illnesses with primarily physical symptoms as well as for illnesses with primarily mental or behavioral symptoms.

SUMMARY

This chapter has presented and described the biopsychosocial model of illness, along with clinical and research findings that support its applicability to patients with physical as well as psychiatric symptoms. Physicians need to learn to integrate a wide variety of psychological and social data into their work with patients in order to provide adequate and comprehensive care. In fact, when medical care has been expanded to include this biopsychosocial perspective, patient outcome, as well as patient and physician satisfaction, has been shown to improve.

The remainder of this textbook provides a broad template for physicians to practice more integrated clinical medicine, according to these well-documented biological, psychological, and social principles.

ANNOTATED BIBLIOGRAPHY

Balint M: The Doctor, His Patient and the Illness. New York, International University Press, 1957

    A classic text that discusses the role of the primary care physician in the management of psychological problems of general medical patients.

Cassel J: Psychosocial processes and "stress": Theoretical formulation. Int J Health Serv 4:471–481, 1974

    This paper represents an elegant integration of research findings related to stress and makes a very sophisticated theoretic argument about the illness process as it relates to stressful situations.

Cohen-Cole SA: The Medical Interview: The Three-Function Approach. St Louis, C. V. Mosby, 1991

    This text provides a basic overview of the medical interview, appropriate for medical students and primary care physicians.

DiMatteo RM, Friedman HS: Social Psychology and Medicine. Cambridge, Oelgeschlager, Gunn, and Hain, 1982

    This excellent text covers a wide range of issues related to social and psychological issues in general medical practice.

Stoudemire A, Fogel B (eds): Psychiatric Care of the Medical Patient. New York, Oxford University Press, 1993

    This text represents the "state of the art" of psychiatric issues in medical disorders. Sophisticated and up to date.

Usdin G, Lewis JM (eds): Psychiatry in General Medical Practice. New York, McGraw-Hill, 1979

This excellent source book for primary care physicians contains numerous articles on many illnesses. Good discussions of doctor–patient relationship issues throughout. It is a little dated on psychopharmacology, however.

Weiner, H: Psychobiology and Human Disease. New York, Elsevier, 1977

This book documents in exhaustive detail the research findings that demonstrate psychological and social contributions to the predisposition, onset, course, and outcome of seven physical illnesses. Weiner also synthesizes current psychobiological understanding of these etiologic relationships.

REFERENCES

Ader R (ed): Psychoneuroimmunology. New York, Academic Press, 1981

Aneshensel CS, Rutter CM, Lachenbruch PA: Social structure, stress, and mental health: Competing conceptual and analytical models. Am Sociological Rev 56:166–178, 1991

Barsky AJ: The paradox of health. N Engl J Med 318:414–418, 1988

Beckman HB, Frankel RM: The effect of physician behavior on the collection of data. Ann Intern Med 101:692–696, 1984

Ben-Sira Z: The function of the professional's affective behavior in client satisfaction: A revised approach to social interaction theory. J Health Soc Behav 17:3–11, 1976

Berkman LF, Syme SL: Social networks, host resistance, and mortality: A nine year follow-up of Alameda County residents. Am J Epidemiol 109:186–204, 1979

Bird CE, Fremont AM: Gender, time use, and health. J Health Soc Behav 32:114–129, 1991

Bird S, Cohen-Cole SA: The 'three function model' of the medical interview: An educational device. In Hale M (ed.): Models of Teaching Consultation-Liaison Psychiatry, Basel, Switzerland, Karger, 1990.

Borus JF, Howes MJ, Devins NP et al: Primary health care providers' recognition and diagnosis of mental disorders in their patients. Gen Hosp Psychiatry 10:317–321, 1988

Boyd JH, Weissman MM: Epidemiology of major affective disorders. In Michels R, Cavenar JO, Cooper AM et al (eds): Psychiatry, revised edition—1988, Vol 3. Philadelphia, JB Lippincott, 1988

Brody DS, Miller SM, Lerman CR, et al: The relationship between patients' satisfaction with their physicians and perceptions about interventions they desired and received. Med Care 27:1027–1035, 1989

Brown GW, Harris T: Social Origins of Depression: A Study of Psychiatric Disorders in Women. New York, The Free Press, 1978

Bruhn JG, Wolf S: The Roseto Story: An Anatomy of Health. Norman, OK, University of Oklahoma Press, 1979

Bunker JP, Gomby DS, Kehrer BH (eds): Pathways to Health: The Role of Social Factors. Menlo Park, CA, Henry J. Kaiser Foundation, 1989

Burke KC, Burke JD, Regier DA, Rae DS: Age at onset of selected mental disorders in five community populations. Arch Gen Psychiatry 47:511–518, 1990

Burke KC, Burke JD, Rae DS, Regier DA: Comparing age at onset of major depression and other psychiatric disorders by birth cohorts in five U.S. community populations. Arch Gen Psychiatry 48:789–795, 1991

Cassel J: Psychosocial processes and "stress": Theoretical formulation. Int J Health Serv 4:471–481, 1974

Cassem N: Depression secondary to physical illness. In Frances AJ, Hales RE (eds): Review of Psychiatry, Vol 7. Washington, APA Press, 1988

Chalfant HP, Kurtz R: Alcoholics and the sick role: Assessments by social workers. J Health Soc Behav 12:66–72, 1971

Cleary PD, Mechanic D, Greenley JR: Sex differences in medical care utilization: An empirical investigation. J Health Soc Behav 23:106–119, 1982

Cockerham WC: Medical Sociology, 5th ed. Englewood Cliffs, NJ, Prentice-Hall, 1992a

Cockerham WC: Sociology of Mental Disorder 3rd ed. Englewood Cliffs, NJ, Prentice-Hall, 1992b

Cohen F: Stress and bodily illness. Psychiatr Clin North Am 4:269–286, 1981

Cohen S, Tyrrell DAJ, Smith AP: Psychological stress and susceptibility to the common cold. N Engl J Med 325:606–611, 1991

Cohen-Cole SA: The Medical Interview: The Three-Function Approach. St Louis, CV Mosby, 1991

Cohen-Cole SA: Interviewing the cardiac patient. I. A practical guide for assessing quality of life. Quality of Life and Cardiovascular Care 2:7–12, 1985

Cohen-Cole SA: On teaching the new (and old) psychobiology. In Friedman C, Purcell EF (eds): The New Biology and Medical Education. New York, Josiah Macy Foundation, 1983

Cohen-Cole SA, Bird J: Interviewing the cardiac patient. II. A practical guide for helping patients cope with their emotions. Quality of Life and Cardiovascular Care 3:53–65, 1986a

Cohen-Cole SA, Bird J: Interviewing the cardiac patient. III. A practical guide to educate patients and to promote cooperation with treatment. Quality of Life and Cardiovascular Care 3:101–112, 1986b

Cohen-Cole SA, Bird J, Freeman A et al: An oral examination of the psychiatric knowledge of medical housestaff: Assessment of needs and evaluation baseline. Gen Hosp Psychiatry 4:103–111, 1982

Cohen-Cole SA, Friedman CP: The language problem: Integration of psychosocial variables into routine medical care. Psychosomatics 24:54–57, 1983

Cohen-Cole SA, Pincus A, Stoudemire A et al: Recent research developments in consultation-liaison psychiatry. Gen Hosp Psychiatry 8:316–329, 1986

Cohen-Cole SA, Stoudemire A: Major depression and physical illness: Special considerations in diagnosis and biological treatment. Psychiatr Clin North Am 10:1–17, 1987

Conrad P, Schneider JW: Deviance and Medicalization: From Badness to Sickness. St. Louis, Mosby, 1980

de Araujo G, Dudley DL, Van Asdel PP, Jr: Psychosocial assets and severity of chronic asthma. J Allergy Clin Immunol 50:257–261, 1972

DiMatteo RM, Friedman HS: Social Psychology and Medicine. Cambridge, MA, Oelgeschlager, Gunn, and Hain, 1982

Dimsdale J, Ruberman W, Carleton R et al: Sudden cardiac death: Stress and cardiac arrhythmias. Circulation 76(Suppl 1): 1198–1201, 1987

Dimsdale, JE: Research links between psychiatry and cardiology: Hypertension, Type A behavior, sudden death, and the physiology of emotional arousal. Gen Hosp Psychiatry 10:328–338, 1988

Dohrenwend BP, Levav I, Shrout PE et al: Socioeconomic status and psychiatric disorders: The causation-selection issue. Science 255:946–952, 1992

Dorian B, Garfinkel PE: Stress, immunity, and illness: A review. Psychol Med 17:393–407, 1987

Dutton DB: Explaining the low use of health services by the poor: Costs, attitudes, or delivery systems? Am Sociological Rev 43:348–368, 1978

Dutton DB: Social class, health, and illness. In Aiken LH, Mechanic D (eds): Applications of Social Science to Clinical Medicine and Health Policy. New Brunswick, NJ, Rutgers University Press, 1986, pp. 31–62

Dutton DB, Levine S: Overview, critique, and reformulation. In Bunker JP, Gomby DS, Kehrer BH (eds): Pathways to Health: The Role of Social Factors. Menlo Park, CA, Henry J Kaiser Foundation, 1989, pp. 29–69

Edgerton RB: Conceptions of psychosis in four East African societies. In Landy D (ed): Culture, Disease and Healing: Studies in Medical Anthropology. New York, Macmillan, 1977, pp. 358–367

Egolf B, Lasker J, Wolf S et al: The Roseto effect: A 50-year comparison of mortality rates. Am J Public Health 82:1089–1092

Eisenberg DM, Kessler RC, Foster C et al: Unconventional medicine in the United States. N Engl J Med 328:246–252, 1993

Eisenberg L: Treating depression and anxiety in primary care. N Engl J Med 326:1080–1084, 1992

Engel G: The need for a new medical model: A challenge for biomedicine. Science 196:129–136, 1977

Estes CL, Lee PR: Health problems and policy issues of old age. In Aiken LH, Mechanic D (eds): Applications of Social Science to Clinical Medicine and Health Policy. New Brunswick, NJ, Rutgers University Press, 1986, pp. 335–355

Freeman HE, Blendon RJ, Aiken LH et al: Americans report on their access to care. Health Affairs 6:6–18, 1987

Freidson E: Client control and medical practice. Am J Sociology 65:374–382, 1960

Friedman M: Pathogenesis of Coronary Artery Disease. New York, McGraw-Hill, 1969

Friedman M, Thoresen CE, Gill JJ, et al: Alteration of Type A behavior and reduction in cardiac recurrences in post-myocardial infarction patients. Am Heart J 108:237–248, 1984

Fulop G, Strain JJ, Vita J et al: Impact of psychiatric comorbidity on length of hospital stay for medical/surgical patients: A preliminary report. Am J Psychiatry 144:878–882, 1987

Geertsen R, Klauber MR, Rindflesh M et al: A re-examination of Suchman's views on social factors in health care utilization. J Health Soc Behav 16:226–237, 1975

Gillick MR: Common-sense models of health and disease. N Engl J Med 313:700–703, 1985

Goldberg RJ, Novack DH, Fulton JP et al: A survey of psychiatry and behavioral science curriculum in primary care residency training. J Psychiatric Education, 9:3–11, 1985

Gove WR, Tudor JF: Adult sex roles and mental illness. Am J Sociology 78:812–835, 1973

Greenley JR, Mechanic D, Cleary PD: Seeking help for psychological problems: A replication and extension. Med Care 25:1113–1128, 1987

Hall RCW, Stickney SK, Gardner ER: Behavioral toxicity of nonpsychiatric drugs. In Hall R (ed): Psychiatric Presentation of Medical Illness: Somatopsychic Disorders. New York, SP Medical and Scientific Books, 1980, pp. 337–353

Hankin JR, Kessler LG, Goldberg ID et al: A longitudinal study of offset in the use of nonpsychiatric services following specialized mental health care. Med Care 21:1099–1110, 1983

Helman CG: Culture, Health, and Illness. London, Wright, 1990

Holmes H, Rahe RH: The social readjustment rating scale. J Psychosom Res 11:213–218, 1967

Houpt JL, Orleans CS, George LK et al: The role of psychiatric and behavioral factors in the practice of medicine. Am J Psychiatry 137:37–47, 1980

House JS, Landis KR, Umberson D: Social relationships and health. Science 241:540–545, 1988

James M, Cohen-Cole SA: Major depression: Recent perspectives. Emory University Journal of Medicine, 3:110–119, 1989

Kamerow DB, Pincus HA, Macdonald DI: Alcohol abuse, other drug abuse, and mental disorders in medical practice. JAMA 255:2054–2057, 1986

Kessler LG, Cleary PD, Burke JD Jr: Psychiatric disorders in primary care: Results of a follow-up study. Arch Gen Psychiatry 42:583–587, 1985

Kessler RC: Sociology and psychiatry. In Kaplan HI, Sadock BJ (eds): Comprehensive Textbook of Psychiatry, vol. 1, 5th ed. Baltimore, Williams & Wilkins, 1989, pp. 299–301

Kessler RC, Cleary PD: Social class and psychological distress. Am Sociological Rev 45:463–478, 1980

Kessler RC, McLeod JD: Sex differences in vulnerability to undesirable life events. Am Sociological Rev 49:620–631, 1984

Kleinman A: Patients and Healers in the Context of Culture. Berkeley, CA, University of California Press, 1980

Kleinman A: Rethinking Psychiatry: From Cultural Category to Personal Experience. New York, The Free Press, 1988

Kleinman A, Eisenberg L, Good B: Culture, illness, and care. Ann Intern Med 88:251–258, 1978

Kleinman A, Kleinman J: Culture and care. In Kleinman A, Good B (eds): Culture and Depression. Berkeley, CA, University of California Press, 1985, pp. 429–490

Klerman G: Age and clinical depression: Today's youth in the twenty-first century. J Gerontol 31:318–323, 1976

Kohn ML: Class, family, and schizophrenia: A formulation. Soc Forces 50:295–304, 1972

Langner T, Michael S: Life Stress and Mental Health: The Midtown Manhattan Study. London, The Free Press of Glencoe, 1963

Lau BWK, Kung NYT, Chung JTC: How depressive illness presents in Hong Kong. Practitioner 227:112–114, 1983

Leiderman DB, Grisso J: The gomer phenomenon. J Health Soc Behav 26:222–232, 1985

Link BG, Dohrenwend BP: The epidemiology of mental disorders. In Freeman HE, Levine S (eds): Handbook of Medical Sociology, 3rd ed. Englewood Cliffs, NJ, Prentice-Hall, 1989, pp. 102–127

Lipkin M, Putnam S, and Lazare A (eds) The Medical Interview, Springer-Verlag, New York, in press.

MacKinnon RA, Michels R: The Psychiatric Interview in Clinical Practice. Philadelphia, WB Saunders, 1971

Maguire GP, Rutter DR: Training medical students to communicate. In Bennett AE (ed): Communication Between Doctors and Patients. London, Oxford University Press, 1976

Marmot MG, Shipley MJ, Rose G: Inequalities in death: Specific explanations of a general pattern. Lancet 83:1003–1006, 1984

McCord C, Freeman HP: Excess mortality in Harlem. N Engl J Med 322:173–177, 1990

Mechanic D: Mental Health and Social Policy, 3rd ed. Englewood Cliffs, NJ, Prentice Hall, 1989

Meichenbaum D, Turk DC: Facilitating Treatment Adherence: A Practitioner's Guidebook. New York, Plenum Press, 1987

Middleton W, Raphael B: Bereavement: State of the art and state of the science. Psychiatr Clin North Am 10:329–345, 1987

Mirowsky J, Ross CE: Mexican culture and its emotional contradictions. J Health Soc Behav 25:2–13, 1984

Mumford E, Schlesinger H, Glass G: The effects of psychological intervention on recovery from surgery and heart attacks: An analysis of the literature. Am J Public Health 72:141–151, 1982

Mumford E, Schlesinger HJ, Glass GV et al: New look at evidence about reduced cost of medical utilization following mental health treatment. Am J Psychiatry 141:1145–1158, 1984

Murphy GE: Suicide and attempted suicide. In Michels R, Cavenar JO, Cooper AM et al (eds): Psychiatry, revised edition—1988, Vol 1. Philadelphia, JB Lippincott, 1988

Murphy JM: Cross-cultural psychiatry. In Michels R, Cavenar JO, Cooper AM et al (eds): Psychiatry, revised edition—1988, Vol 3. Philadelphia, JB Lippincott, 1988

Murphy JM, Helzer JE: Epidemiology of schizophrenia in adulthood. In Michels R, Cavenar JO, Cooper AM et al (eds): Psychiatry, revised edition—1988, Vol 3. Philadelphia, JB Lippincott, 1988

Nuckolls CB, Cassel J, Kaplan BH: Psychosocial assets, life crises and the prognosis of pregnancy. Am J Epidemiol 95:431–441, 1972

O'Shanick GJ, Gardner DF, Kornstein SG: Endocrine disorders. In Stoudemire A, Fogel BS (eds): Principles of Medical Psychiatry. Orlando, Grune & Stratton, 1987

Otten MW, Teutsch SM, Williamson DF, Marks JS: The effect of known risk factors on the excess mortality of black adults in the United States. JAMA 268:845–850, 1990

Parsons T: The Social System. New York, The Free Press, 1951

Polednak AP: Racial and Ethnic Differences in Disease. New York, Oxford University Press, 1989

Ragland D, Brand R: Type A behavior and coronary heart disease case-fatality. N Engl J Med 318:65–69, 1988

Regier DA, Boyd SH, Burke JD Jr et al: One month prevalence of mental disorders in the United States. Arch Gen Psychiatry 45:977–986, 1988

Reid I: Social Class Differences in Britain, 3rd ed. Glasgow, UK, Fontana Press, 1989

Robins LN, Locke BZ, Regier DA: An overview of psychiatric disorders in America. In Robins LN, Regier DA (eds): Psychiatric Disorders in America: The Epidemiologic Catchment Area Study. New York, The Free Press, 1991, pp. 328–366

Robins LN, Regier DA (eds): Psychiatric Disorders in America: The Epidemiologic Catchment Area Study. New York, The Free Press, 1991

Rosenfeld S: The effects of women's employment: Personal control and sex differences in mental health. J Health Soc Behav 30:77–91, 1989

Rosenman R, Brand R, Jenkins C et al: Coronary heart disease in the Western Collaborative Group Study: Final followup experience of 8 and a half years. JAMA 233:872–877, 1975

Ross CE, Mirowsky J, Ulbrich P: Distress and the traditional female role: A comparison of Mexicans and Anglos. Am J Sociology 89:670–682, 1983

Rozanski A, Bairey N, Krantz D et al: Mental stress and the induction of silent myocardial ischemia in patients with coronary artery disease. N Engl J Med 318:1005–1012, 1988

Rubel A: The epidemiology of folk illness: susto in Hispanic America. In Landy D (ed): Culture, Disease and Healing: Studies in Medical Anthropology. New York, Macmillan, 1977, pp. 119–128

Ruberman W, Weinblatt E, Goldberg J et al: Psychosocial influences on mortality after myocardial infarction. N Engl J Med 311:552–559, 1984

Sachar EJ: Advances in Psychoneuroendocrinology. Psychiatr Clin North Am. Philadelphia, WB Saunders, 1980

Scott CS: Health and healing practices among five ethnic groups in Miami, Florida. In Bauwens EE (ed): The Anthropology of Health. St. Louis, MO, Mosby, 1978, pp. 61–70

Selye H: The Stress of Life, rev ed. New York, McGraw-Hill, 1976

Shulman RA, Kramer PD, Mitchel JB: The hidden mental health network: Treatment of mental illness by nonpsychiatric physicians. Arch Gen Psychiatry 42:89–94, 1985

Sosa R, Kennell J, Klaus M et al: The effect of a supportive companion on perinatal problems, length of labor, and mother-infant interaction. N Engl J Med 303:597–600, 1980

Spiegel D, Kraemer HC, Bloom JR et al: Effect of psychosocial treatment on survival of patients with metastatic breast cancer. Lancet 2:888–891, 1989

Stamler J: Coronary heart disease: Doing the "right things." N Engl J Med 312:1053–1055, 1985

Stoudemire A: Somatothymia: Parts I and II. Psychosomatics 32:365–381, 1991

Strain J, Pincus HA, Houpt JL et al: Models of mental health training for primary care physicians. Psychosom Med. 47:95–110, 1985

Susser MW, Watson W, Hopper K: Sociology in Medicine, 3rd ed. New York, Oxford University Press, 1985

Thoits PA: Gender and marital status differences in control and distress: Common stress versus unique stress explanations. J Health Soc Behav 28:7–22, 1987

Thomas ME, Hughes M: The continuing significance of race: A study of race, class, and quality of life in America, 1972–1985. Am Sociological Rev 51:830–841, 1986

Umberson D: Family status and health behaviors: Social control as a dimension of social integration. J Health Soc Behav 28:306–319, 1987

Verbrugge LM: Gender and health: An update on hypotheses and evidence. J Health Soc Behav 26:156–182, 1985

Von Korff M, Shapiro S, Burke JD et al: Anxiety and depression in a primary care clinic. Arch Gen Psychiatry 44:152–156, 1987

Warheit GJ, Holzer CE, Avery SA: Race and mental illness: An epidemiologic update. J Health Soc Behav 16:243–256, 1975

Weiner H: Psychobiology and Human Disease. New York, Elsevier North-Holland, 1977

Weiner H, Hofer MA, Stunkard AJ (eds): Brain, Behavior, and Bodily Disease. New York, Raven Press, 1981

Weissman MM, Myers JK, Thompson WD: Depression and its treatment in a US urban community 1975–1976. Arch Gen Psychiatry 38:417–421, 1981

Wells KB, Golding JM, Burnam M: Psychiatric disorder in a sample of the general population with and without chronic medical conditions. Am J Psychiatry 145:976–981, 1988

Williams R, Haney T, Lee K et al: Type A behavior, hostility, and coronary atherosclerosis. Psychosom Med 42:539–549, 1980

Alan Stoudemire (ed). *Human Behavior: An Introduction for Medical Students*,
Second Edition. Copyright © 1994, 1990 by J. B. Lippincott Company.

3 *Psychological Factors Affecting Medical Conditions and Stress Responses*

Edward A. Walker and
Wayne J. Katon

In keeping with this text's emphasis on the biopsychosocial model, we now consider in somewhat more detail how psychological variables may interact with social factors and biological systems in the pathogenesis of disease and illness. In that regard, the concept of "stress"—whether it is considered in relationship to biological, psychological, or social systems—is critical. Although the concept of stress is difficult to define, it is an ubiquitous if not unavoidable component of life. While most people have an intuitive belief that "too much of it" makes them ill, only in the last two decades have methodologically sophisticated studies firmly established a link between stress and medical illness. This research has elucidated several important concepts:

1. Stressful life events are correlated with increased risk of becoming medically ill.
2. Some stressors can be perceived *positively* and others *negatively*, and this perception is mediated by cognitive "coping" mechanisms.
3. Maladaptive ways of coping with stress such as smoking, alcohol, and substance abuse may alter susceptibility to illness.
4. A strong network of social support seems to buffer a patient from the effects of stress.
5. The central nervous, endocrine, and immune systems appear to have numerous interconnections.
6. An individual's response to physical and psychological illness depends on both genetic and acquired (developmental and learning) factors.

The Diagnostic and Statistical Manual of Mental Disorders (DSM-IV) (APA 1994) provides the category of "Psychological Factors Affecting Medical Condition" (PFAMC) to indicate the influence of psychological processes on the initiation or exacerbation of physical disease (Table 3–1). The category can be used to describe conditions that in the past have been deemed to have a "psychosomatic" or "psycho-physiological" component, and may include such conditions as tension headache, diabetes, angina pectoris, painful menstruation, obesity, gastric ulcer, rheumatoid arthritis, asthma, ulcerative colitis, and many others. In each case environmental factors must be temporally related to the onset or worsening of the disease.

This chapter will examine the evidence concerning the role of psychological and psychosocial variables in altering individual susceptibility to disease processes. Although biological and genetic factors play a primary role in disease onset, the development of disease is a multifactorial process involving a complex interplay between the environment and humans as psychobiological organisms. We will review the historical

---

Table 3–1 **Diagnostic Criteria for 316: Psychological Factors Affecting Medical Condition (PFAMC)***

A. The presence of a general medical condition (coded on Axis III)
B. Psychological factors adversely affect the general medical condition in one of the following ways:
  (1) The factors have influenced the course of the medical condition as shown by a close temporal association between the psychological factors and the development or exacerbation of, or delayed recovery from, the general medical condition.
  (2) The factors interfere with the treatment of the general medical condition.
  (3) The factors constitute additional health risks for the individual.
  (4) Stress-related physiologic responses precipitate or exacerbate symptoms of the general medical condition.

Choose name based on the nature of the psychological factors (if more than one factor is present, indicate the most prominent):
  Mental Disorder Affecting Medical Condition (e.g., an Axis I disorder such as Major Depressive Disorder delaying recovery from a myocardial infarction)
  Psychological Symptoms Affecting Medical Condition (e.g., depressive symptoms delaying recovery from surgery; anxiety exacerbating asthma)
  Personality Traits or Coping Style Affecting Medical Condition (e.g., pathological denial of the need for surgery in a patient with cancer; hostile, pressured behavior contributing to cardiovascular disease)
  Maladaptive Health Behaviors Affecting Medical Condition (e.g., non-compliance with medication or diet; overeating; lack of exercise; unsafe sex)
  Stress related Physiological Response Affecting Medical Condition (e.g., stress-related exacerbations of chest pain, hypertension, arrhthmia, or tension headache)
  Other or Unspecified Psychological Factors Affecting Medical Condition (e.g., interpersonal, cultural, religious)

*Adapted from DSM-IV (APA 1994)

development of the mind-body relationship, the evidence linking stress to disease modulation, and the physiological connections between mind and body, namely the autonomic nervous system, the neuroendocrine system, and the immune system.

A CASE STUDY

Mr. R is a 30-year-old white male who presented to his physician with a 2-month history of abdominal bloating and epigastric pain. Over the preceding 14 days he had noticed increasing fatigue, passed several black, tarry stools, and had been having trouble running his business as a fence builder due to lack of energy. He had a family history of peptic ulcer disease. On physical exam he was found to be quite pale and had epigastric pain to palpation and tachycardia. On lab exam he was found to have guaiac positive stool and a low hematocrit. The patient was admitted to the hospital where a duodenal ulcer was diagnosed. He made a rapid recovery on cimetidine despite refusing blood transfusion because of religious beliefs (he was a Jehovah's Witness).

Many stressful events were noted in the months prior to admission. The patient had undergone a traumatic divorce, and he and his wife shared joint custody of their two children. Despite the divorce, however, the patient employed his wife in his business. In addition, he discovered 1 year prior to admission that his wife had embezzled $12,000 from his business and that he was already several thousand dollars in debt to the Internal Revenue Service.

The patient was raised in a family with little emotional support and a distant critical father. He worked very hard to win his father's affection but was constantly frustrated. His style of coping with stress based on this family experience was to trust few people, to work hard, and to rely only on himself and perhaps his wife. He perceived his wife's embezzlement as a disaster both financially and emotionally and felt he no longer could trust anyone. He fired his staff of workers and increased his own work load to 12 to 14 hours a day, 7 days a week to handle the threat and anxiety of potential bankruptcy. Thus he coped by withdrawing from people, relying even less on others, working harder, and trying to deny his pain and anger towards his wife. He began to feel progressively worn out approximately 6 months prior to admission and admitted to depressed mood, anxiety, insomnia, decreased energy, and at times feelings of hopelessness. He developed a clinical depression as his coping mechanisms were overwhelmed. Nevertheless, he continued to work hard and approximately 2 months prior to admission began to experience abdominal pain. He admitted, however, to distrusting doctors ("they're only out to rob you"), and therefore waited until he could "barely drag" himself to work to come into the clinic, again using coping mechanisms of denial and minimization toward his physical condition.

Because illness onset is multifactorial in origin (see Fig. 3–1), treatment must be targeted specifically at biological, psychological, and social

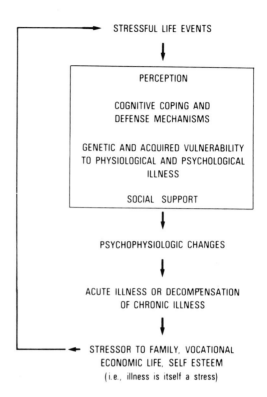

Figure 3-1. *Model of illness onset.*

problems. For instance, the family physician treated this patient's peptic ulcer with cimetidine and antacids. When attempts at counseling him regarding his depression, anxiety, and rigid personality traits were not successful, the patient eventually accepted his doctor's recommendation to get psychiatric help. In psychotherapy the patient gained insight into his behavior and used his illness experience as a chance for growth. He began to take more recreational time off from work, ultimately hired help for his business, and was able to get a bank loan to stabilize his business. At a 6-month follow-up he was asymptomatic and felt he was coping with interpersonal and family problems better than he had prior to his illness.

THE HISTORICAL DEVELOPMENT OF THE MIND-BODY RELATIONSHIP

Our current concepts of mind and body are the products of a long evolutionary process that naturally followed the sociocultural, scientific, and philosophical trends of each historical period. Our early ancestors confronted many of the same diseases we know of today without the aid of a scientific method or the knowledge of anatomy, physiology, and behavior that we take for granted in modern medicine. Theological explanations were frequently invoked, such as possession by evil spirits, and rituals were employed to rid the body of evil influences. The powerful attraction of these early beliefs as explanatory models is apparent in their continued appeal to many people in an otherwise scientific twentieth-century society.

The ancient Greek physicians developed the beginnings of a rational approach to our understanding of disease and how it affects mind and body. Although they discriminated between *soma* (body) and *psyche* (soul), this distinction was often blurred. Hippocrates believed that many diseases and mental states were caused by emotions, or passions as they were known, and theorized a mind-body physiology based on combinations of four basic humors (yellow bile, black bile, phlegm, and blood) with the four basic elements (air, earth, fire, and water). Various combinations of these building blocks produced different diseases and mental states. The physical manifestations of such mental states as fear and anger were hard to ignore, and when strong emotions precipitated symptoms such as chest pain or death it provided "evidence" for the physical potency of the passions.

A major conceptual change occurred in the seventeenth century as causality, observation, and measurement were given new emphasis as the desire to understand the structure of the universe and its component parts increased. Against the background of this new scientific method, René Descartes advanced his philosophy of distinguishing the thinking mind (*res cogitans*) from the physical body (*res extensa*), a division that fundamentally changed the way physicians thought about the mind and body. Descartes' theory, misinterpreted for centuries as a rigid dualism, formed the basis for contemporary misunderstandings about the nature of mind and body. The heritage of this conceptual confusion is seen in the thinking of many modern physicians who seek to divide "organic" from "psychological" disease and who speak of "psychiatric overlays" on physical conditions, as if, by removing the "overlay," the patient would return to a state of pure organic disease.

Current theories of mind-body interaction were most markedly influenced in the late nineteenth century by Sigmund Freud and his contemporaries. Freud, originally a neurologist seeking to find a scientifically unified theory of biology and behavior, became interested in patients with somatic symptoms in whom no physical pathology could be found. These patients, known as "hysterics," were problematic to his physician colleagues who tried various remedies without results. His followers began to postulate the existence of specific personality types and later unconscious psychodynamic conflicts and attitudes as the causes of specific physiological conditions.

This belief that stress and psychological conflict could not only *influence* but actually *produce* specific physical diseases became a focus of many of these physicians. Several of these clinicians, most notably Franz Alexander, formulated theories involving particular diseases that would result from specific psychological conflicts and defenses, the so-called *specificity theory* of psychosomatic disorders. Thus, the chronic suppression of emotional tension would lead to discharge in autonomic nervous system pathways causing structural change in specific tissues and organs. The so-called organic neuroses (essential hypertension, bronchial asthma, neurodermatitis, ulcerative colitis, peptic ulcer, rheumatoid arthritis, and thyrotoxicosis) became the classic paradigms of psychosomatic illness of this new school with the idea that they were each caused by a specific type of psychopathology.

Experimental evidence has never supported this degree of specificity, and the theory is no longer widely held. One of the important enduring contributions of this specificity theory, however, is the finding that the Type A behavior pattern (TABP)—characterized by time urgency, achievement striving, and hostility—is a risk factor for coronary artery disease (CAD). Recent critiques of TABP have found that not all the Type A personality characteristics are equally associated with this increased risk, but that *hostility, cynicism* and *antagonistic relationships* appear to be most strongly correlated with vulnerability to CAD (Koskenvuo et al, 1988; Goldstein and Niaura, 1992; Niaura and Goldstein, 1992).

The early promise of psychiatric research in providing specific connections between mind and body gradually fell into disrepute as the fragile research underpinnings by and large did not stand the test of time. There were many exceptions to this such as Pavlov's studies on conditioned reflexes, Cannon's work on the fight-or-flight response, Wolff's studies of gastric acid secretion, and Selye's work on stress and cortisol. But with the tremendous technological specialty thrust of medicine much of this psychosomatic framework fell into disregard. Medicine was taught as the study of physiological "organic" illness and psychiatry as the study of psychological illness. A patient's illness was worked up biomedically, and when an organic etiology was not found the patient could then be referred to a psychiatrist.

This dualistic view of mind and body was built on a model of the physical universe that employed the linear cause-and-effect rules of classical mechanics. During the mid-twentieth century a new model of causality was developed in the ideas of von Bertilanffy and Bateson who saw the universe from a systems perspective: that systems have self-regulating, homeostatic properties that create a circular cause-effect. All living things depend on this type of *homeostatic equilibrium*, nesting systems within systems to maintain life.

Noting this complexity of living things, George Engel (1977), an internist with training in psychoanalysis, proposed the *biopsychosocial model* as a paradigm for explaining the multiple ways in which an organism's physical health could be modified not only by physical pathogens, but by learning, cultural norms, and mental processes. Similar to the psychobiological theories of psychiatrist Adolf Meyer, Engel promoted a model of disease not simply as a reductionistic chain of physical events, but more as a complex summation of organic, psychological, and social variables, each capable of exerting profound effects on the outcome of disease. Although patients might intuitively grasp the connections between mind, body, and stress, many contemporary physicians continue to maintain an archaic, reductionistic philosophy that sacrifices common sense for the sake of "scientific" biomedical method.

The lesson from history is that the challenge for contemporary medical students will be to master the technical biomedical aspects of medical treatment without sacrificing the psychological, social, and environmental factors that are an important part of holistic patient care. This may seem to be an enormous burden early in medical school as a tremendous weight is put on memorization of large amounts of factual information; however, practicing physicians draw heavily on their knowledge of behavior, stress, and mind-body interactions to devise practical, effective treatment plans that help their patients cope with medical illness. (The biopsychosocial model is also discussed in Chapter 1 by Dr. Shelton, in Chapter 2 by Drs. Cohen-Cole and Levinson, and in Chapter 14 by Dr. Green.)

WHAT IS STRESS AND HOW DOES IT INFLUENCE DISEASE?

The concept of "stress" was originally imported from physics by Hans Selye to describe the actions of forces against an object in equilibrium. With reference to behavior it has been used to refer to: (1) an aversive stimulus event, (2) a specific physiological or psychological response, or (3) a special type of transaction between the person and the environment (Cohen, 1981). Confusion is avoided if each of these is considered separately. We will distinguish *stressors* (or stressful life events) from the *psychological state of stress* (feelings of threat, harm, or loss) and from *stress responses* (or physiological, psychological, or social levels).

Stressors are defined as those life events that induce *change in routine*, the *persistence of positive or negative environmental conditions*, or specific types of *situations of monotony* where no change has occurred when change may have been expected (i.e., not getting an anticipated promotion at work).

Although there has been a growing awareness of the ability of stress to influence morbidity and mortality since the mid-nineteenth century, it was not until the 1950s that well-designed studies investigated this relationship. In a pioneering prospective study of pulmonary tuberculosis patients, Holmes (1961) found that the predictors of recovery were psychosocial assets such as strong family ties, steady employment, adequate income and job satisfaction, regular recreation, frequent social participation, flexibility and reliability, and realistic goals. He soon moved from the study of predictors of recovery to predictors of illness onset.

As previously mentioned in Chapter 2, based on this experience Holmes and Rahe (1967) developed the Schedule of Recent Life Events (SRE) to allow quantitative definition of life crises. The SRE (Table 3–2) is a checklist of 43 events requiring various degrees of adaptation (e.g., losses, childbirth, catastrophe, success). Each life change is assigned a particular number of life-change units (LCUs) (death of a spouse, for example, is rated at 100 LCUs), and within a particular time period the individual accumulates an LCU score. Holmes and Rahe found a nearly linear relationship between LCU scores and the number of illnesses experienced, with the highest correlation in the 6 months following these life events. Thus, the more LCUs an individual accumulated the more likely he was to experience illness of all kinds in a subsequent 2-year period.

In later retrospective studies Holmes and Rahe found that 30% to 35% of individuals with low life-change scores (in the range of 100) developed an illness, 50% of the people in the intermediate range (200 LCU range) developed an illness, and 80% of those in the high range (300 LCUs) developed an illness in the subsequent 2-year period. In prospective studies a very similar picture emerged; about 80% of the people in the high-risk group got sick, about 50% of the people in the medium-risk group got sick, and about 30% of the people in the low-risk group got sick. Since then

Table 3–2 **The Social Readjustment Rating Scale**

LIFE EVENT	MEAN VALUE
Death of a spouse	100
Divorce	73
Marital separation	65
Jail term	63
Death of a close family member	63
Personal injury or illness	53
Marriage	50
Fired at work	47
Marital reconciliation	45
Retirement	45
Change in health of family member	44
Pregnancy	40
Sex difficulties	39
Gain of new family member	39
Business readjustment	39
Change in financial state	38
Death of a close friend	37
Change to different line of work	36
Change in number of arguments with spouse	35
Foreclosure of mortgage or loan	30
Change in responsibilities at work	29
Son or daughter leaving home	29
Trouble with in-laws	29
Outstanding personal achievement	28
Spouse began or stopped work	26
Begin or end school	26
Change in living conditions	25
Revision of personal habits	24
Trouble with boss	23
Change in work hours or conditions	20
Change in residence	20
Change in schools	20
Change in recreation	19
Change in church activities	19
Change in social activities	18
Change in sleeping habits	16
Change in number or family get-togethers	15
Change in eating habits	15
Vacation	13
Christmas	12
Minor violations of the law	11

several studies have validated this relationship between life changes and the onset of a number of psychiatric, medical, and surgical diseases.

Across all cultures death of a spouse is consistently rated as the most significant life change correlated with increased morbidity and mortality. Numerous studies have shown during the first 6 months following bereavement there is a significant increase in death and illness of the surviving spouse, especially widowers, compared to ex-pected rates for age (Raphael, 1987). Emerging evidence that this involves a process of alteration of immune system function is addressed later in the chapter.

Although most investigators now agree that there is a statistical correlation between life-change scores and the development of illness, the correlations are relatively low, i.e., life-change units are probably only one of the variables involved. While most researchers agree that stress-induced illness may be caused by chronic physiological arousal, the final response to stress may be mediated by several factors that can either buffer or intensify the stressor. These are the person's (1) perception or *cognitive appraisal* of the events, (2) *coping* or defense mechanisms, (3) *social support* systems, and (4) the degree of *genetic vulnerability*. We shall look at each of these factors in more detail.

Cognitive Appraisal of Life-Change Events

Events that are stressful to one person may not be for another. Thus, if a person has adequate resources to meet a challenge or does not believe danger exists, a stress reaction may not occur. Lazarus has pointed out that a stimulus can evoke a stress reaction by psychophysiological means only if it is interpreted by the individual as *harmful or threatening* so that coping processes are brought into play to minimize potential harm (Lazarus, 1977). The LCU methodology of Holmes and Rahe made no attempt to separate negative or positive life events, yet there is evidence they may have different physiological consequences. For example, although cortisol, catechol-amines, and growth hormone rise after negative life events, only catecholamines show a rise after events of a pleasurable nature (Rose, 1980). Further, undesirable life events are stronger predictors of disease outcomes (Vinokur, 1975). Rahe, recognizing the impact of perception of life change, has modified the SRE so that in recent prospective studies subjects now not only list their life changes but score their own LCUs subjectively according to the degree of life adjustment needed to handle the event.

Hinkle et al (1958) also found that episodes of illness are not randomly distrib-uted among the population. They found in several large populations that 25% of the people experienced 50% of the illness episodes over a 20-year period. These illnesses often appeared in a cluster during people's lives, and the clusters of illness episodes were most apt to occur when the individuals perceived that they were having difficulty adapting to the environment.

Coping and Defense Mechanisms

Coping is defined by the dictionary as struggling or contending. It describes behavior involving special physical and emotional energy and attention that is re-quired to deal with some difficult circumstances. Lazarus (1977) defined two types of coping or self-regulation of a perceived stress. One that he calls *direct-action* occurs when the person tries to alter or master the troubled interaction with the environment as when he attempts to demolish, avoid, or flee the harmful agent, or to prepare somehow to meet the danger. Thus if a student faced with an important and potentially threatening examination spends the anticipatory interval immersed in preparation, he is engaged in a direct-action form of coping. This sense of mastery and readiness, regardless of whether or not it is realistic, mitigates the stress reaction prior to the time when the threat must be faced.

A second coping mechanism called *palliation* occurs when direct action is too costly to undertake or when the person is unable to manage successfully the environmental transaction. Such modes of control include ego defenses (i.e., denial, rationalization), taking tranquilizers, alcohol, sleeping pills, or engaging in a variety of techniques like muscle relaxation, jogging, yoga, etc. These palliative forms of coping are focused on possible ways of reducing the affective, visceral, or motor disturbances that are distressing the person as opposed to attempts to master the environmental transaction on which the stress reaction depends. This decrease in distressing symptoms may enable individuals to think more clearly and problem-solve or even confront situations they would normally avoid.

Numerous studies have shown that the way an individual copes may reduce physiological arousal in the face of stressful events. For example, patients with myocardial infarction who adopt the use of an appropriate amount of denial and minimization as major ways of coping with their anxiety about death and disability have fewer potentially fatal arrhythmias. (Freeman, 1987). It is also known that patients whose coping ability has become overwhelmed are prone to the development of mental illnesses like depression, anxiety attacks, or psychosis and subsequently have two to four times the prevalence of medical illness (Hankin, 1979). Patients who inherit or acquire (through traumatic early childhood experience) susceptibility to mental illness under stress are also more likely to develop medical illness.

Social Support

Recent research evidence suggests that those who have social supports are protected in crisis from a variety of pathological states (Bebbington, 1987). It is thought that supports buffer the individual from the potentially negative effects of crisis and can facilitate coping and adaptation. Patients with social supports and assets may live longer and have a lower incidence of somatic illness as well as more positive mental health. Studies of marital and health status consistently reveal that those who are married have lower mortality rates than those who are single, widowed, or divorced (Ortmeyer, 1974). These risks are consistently higher for men than women and seem to decline with age (see also Chapter 2).

Medalie and Goldbourt (1976) in a prospective study of 10,000 adult men found seven risk factors (anxiety, severe family problems, age, total serum cholesterol, systolic or diastolic blood pressure, certain electrocardiographic abnormalities, and diabetes mellitus) associated with the development of new angina pectoris. They found that the husband's subjective perception of a high degree of love and support from his wife reduced the risk of angina pectoris even in the presence of high-risk factors. Similarly, in a large prospective study of men after myocardial infarction, Ruberman et al (1984) found that socially isolated men with high life stress had four times the risk of cardiac death compared with their low stress, nonisolated counterparts. Thus, life stress, loss of control, and job strain can combine with decreased social support to increase the risk for morbidity and mortality from CAD (Goldstein and Niaura, 1992; Niaura and Goldstein, 1992).

Lack of family support has also been shown to influence the incidence of streptococcal pharyngeal infections. Meyer and Haggerty (1962) prospectively studied 76 families for a 1-year period with systematic throat cultures for hemolytic streptococci. Acute or chronic family stressors appeared to influence not only whether an individual became ill following colonization but also the degree of postinfection immune titers.

Brown et al (1978) studied the incidence of major depressive disorder in 458 women who had been exposed to stressful life events. Women with high degrees of stress and little support had four times the rate of depression than women with equal degrees of stress but much support. They concluded that a confiding, intimate relationship with a spouse buffered the person from the effects of high amounts of stress.

Finally, the long-term influence of childhood developmental stressors has been shown to be important in modifying the pathogenesis of disease. In Chapter 11 on behavioral and psychobiological effects of developmental trauma, Dr. van der Kolk outlines a model of how early abuse (presence of a negative factor) and neglect (absence of a positive factor) can cause lasting changes in homeostasis and physiologic reactivity to disease. Thus, particular traumatic events during critical periods of CNS development can lead to an irreversible failure to achieve developmental milestones due to reduced CNS plasticity. Although we are just beginning to understand the specific neurological deficits, they appear to be both on anatomical and neurochemical levels, suggesting that social support has a direct effect on the expression of biological structure.

Biological Predisposition to Stress-Induced Illness

Another component in the multifactorial causation of onset of illness is the patient's health and organ susceptibility to illness. We have already alluded to biological and learned predispositions to mental illness. Many patients also have diseases like angina pectoris, duodenal ulcers, and juvenile onset diabetes mellitus. Stress may play a contributing role in causation especially in the first two illnesses, but there is no doubt that once the disease is present, symptoms of these disorders can be exacerbated by stress. That is, once end-organ damage has occurred the patient is more likely to respond to stressful events with an exacerbation of chronic illness symptoms, despite a prior history of adequate coping with an identical stressor. On the other hand, some patients exhibit a biological "hardiness," sometimes called *resilience*, that appears to protect them from stress-induced physical pathology.

Acute stressors appear to be greater risk factors for sudden cardiac death for individuals who already have some form of heart pathology, usually ischemic heart disease (Lown, 1980). Similarly, acutely stressful life events may not necessarily predispose individuals to schizophrenia; however, they are associated with exacerbation or precipitation of an episode of the illness in some vulnerable individuals (Bebbington, 1987).

PSYCHOPHYSIOLOGICAL PATHWAYS

Evidence has been presented that stressful life events are important factors in the onset of illness. But what are the pathways and mechanisms that mediate the body's reaction to stress? Recently, many of the pathways of this stress response have been illuminated, and the hypothalamus appears to act as a central mediator for the coordinated regulation of the autonomic nervous, immune, and neuroendocrine systems (see Fig. 3–2). This phylogenetically ancient part of the brain integrates cortical (cognitive), limbic (emotional), and autonomic (visceral) inputs, and controls many of the neural and endocrine systems required for both homeostasis and rapid adaptation. The affected tissues and organs complete the cycle by feeding back to the higher initiating and regulating centers. The hypothalamus, therefore, appears to be the locus where psychological stress may be converted into physiological function. While

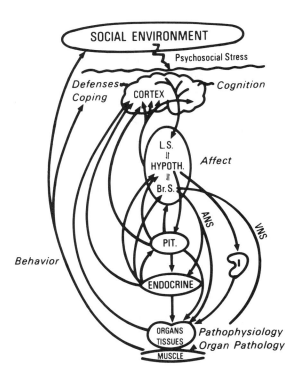

Figure 3–2. *Psychophysiological pathways of the stress response. (Reproduced with permission from Reiser MF: The psychophysiology of stress and coping. In: Psychophysiology—Report Number 1. Philadelphia: SmithKline, 1980)*

L.S.=Limbic System
Br.S.=Brain Stem
HYPOTH.=Hypothalamus
PIT.=Pituitary
ANS=Autonomic Nervous System
VNS=Voluntary Nervous System
I=Immune System

neuroendocrine mechanisms in the regulation of mood and behavior are discussed in detail in Chapter 12 by Dr. Pedersen and colleagues, this section focuses on stress-related factors involved in neuroendocrine and immune systems.

The hypothalamus contains the nuclei of the autonomic nervous system, which are grouped into two divisions, the sympathetic and parasympathetic, that innervate the viscera and many hormone-secreting cells. For example, the pancreatic insulin cells are directly contacted both by sympathetic and parasympathetic nerves that respectively suppress and stimulate insulin secretion (Sterling, 1981).

The brain also influences the body's hormones by means of its own chemical messengers. Some act directly on peripheral tissues; others act on peripheral hormone-secreting cells. Still others act on the pituitary, which controls both peripheral tissues and endocrine organs. The balance of corticotropin-releasing hormone (CRF) in the hypothalamus and norepinephrine (NE) in the brainstem locus ceruleus modulates both the tone of the autonomic nervous system as well as the production of adrenocorticotropic hormone (ACTH), which subsequently regulates serum levels of cortisol, a principal hormone in the stress response. Both the cellular and humoral arms of the immune system also appear to be under the control of the brain through these hormones.

What is the reason for having these central controls since there are local self-regulating controls of physiological homeostasis (blood pressure, serum glucose level, etc.)? Neural controls permit hormonal and organ changes to occur in anticipation of changes in local feedback systems; such anticipatory changes then can reduce the size and length of metabolic fluctuations. Additionally, most processes in the body cannot be kept constant and must vary by the demands of the environment on the organism. Blood pressure must be able to vary with changes in demands (i.e., sudden fright, sexual intercourse, taking a test). If the only controls over blood pressure were local then it would be impossible to have such adaptive changes in blood pressure because every deviation from the "normal" would be automatically corrected (Sterling, 1981).

BROAD PATTERNS OF NEUROENDOCRINE AND NEUROIMMUNE RESPONSE

Probably as a result of the experience of our primitive ancestors, we have evolved a complex but efficient energy management system that flexibly reacts to changes in our environment. Our nervous, endocrine, and immune systems have two basic states of readiness, one vegetative and reparative, the other highly responsive to impending or actual danger. The evolutionary value of both of these states is obvious in a hostile, unpredictable environment, but our primordial physiology, designed for coping with episodic, intense stress may be ill-equipped to deal with modern life with its chronic, variable level stressors.

These hormonal, autonomic, and immune system changes are under central nervous system control via an elaborate network of cell groups found in and around the hypothalamus that have the role of maintaining a flexible homeostasis. Kiely (1974) has labeled these reciprocally balanced components the *ergotropic* and *trophotropic* systems.

The Ergotropic System

The *ergotropic system* integrates functions that prepare the individual for positive action. It is characterized by alerting, arousal, excitement, increased skeletal muscle tone, and sympathetic nervous system activity and the release of catabolic hormone products. It is similar to Cannon's description of the fight-or-flight responses, but includes many changes in sympathetic nervous system discharge as well as neuroendocrine and behavioral parameters (see Table 3–3).

This system must quickly mobilize energy to deal with unexpected environmental demands. Complex molecules are broken down into component parts such as free fatty acids and glucose that can be rapidly converted into energy. Reproductive and reparative processes are slowed. The thymus shrinks and the levels of antibodies and white cells in the blood fall. Increased cardiac output and blood pressure speed extra blood to the tissues. Flow to the heart, muscle, and brain must be maintained or increased, but flow to the gut, kidney, and skin is decreased because the blood is needed elsewhere (Sterling, 1981).

Cannon, in the early part of the century, noted that during arousal as in preparation for fight-or-flight there was not only an increase in blood pressure but also a change in blood flow. More blood was delivered to the heart and skeletal muscle and less to the skin, gut, and kidneys. Later, Selye showed that cortisol is also secreted during arousal and makes an important contribution to this mobilization. Several other behaviorally activating hormones also increase during arousal with corresponding decreases in hormones whose functions include energy storage, growth, renewal, repair, and maintenance of surveillance against infectious agents and the body's own malignant cells.

The Trophotropic System

The *trophotropic system* reverses this ergotropic process and integrates systems that promote withdrawal and conservation of energy: raising the stimulus barrier to perceptual input, decreasing skeletal muscle tone and, increasing parasympathetic nervous function and the circulation of anabolic hormones. This system is turned on by relaxation or lack of perceived threat.

Table 3–3 **Characteristics of the Ergotropic and Trophotropic Systems**

	ERGOTROPIC	**TROPHOTROPIC**
Predominant Autonomic Nervous System Branch	sympathetic	parasympathetic
Blood Flow	brain and muscle	gut, kidney, and skin
Skeletal Muscle	increased tone	decreased tone
Immune function	decreased	increased
Reproductive function	decreased	increased
Metabolism	catabolic	anabolic

The anabolic hormones promote energy storage, growth, renewal, repair, and maintenance of surveillance against infectious agents and the body's own malignant cells. In the anabolic state the body stores energy or glycogen, fat, and protein by polymerization of glucose, fatty acids, and amino acids. Bone is replaced by reabsorption and redeposition of calcium salts. Wounds are healed by production of new cells and by extracellular deposition of proteins. The immune system is maintained by continuous cell and antibody production in the bone marrow, lymphoid tissue, and thymus.

These two systems have reciprocal activity and are maintained in a flexible balance. With mild to moderate degrees of excitation of the ergotropic system there is a corresponding degree of inhibition of the trophotropic system and vice versa. Therefore mild to moderate arousal turns on the catabolic hormones of the sympathetic system and inhibits parasympathetic discharge with its anabolic hormones. At moderate to high degrees of trophotropic or ergotropic activation the facilitory effects are more sharply increased and reciprocal inhibition of the opposite system is maximal. Thus, in moderate to high levels of arousal, the level of ergotropic tuning is very high and trophotropic responsivity becomes nil. At this level of arousal an ergotropic response may be elicited by a stimulus that normally would produce a trophotropic response. An example here is having a difficult day at work and coming home irritable and uptight and kicking the affectionate cat or "snapping" at the spouse or children.

Finally, at maximal degrees of arousal both the ergotropic and trophotropic systems discharge simultaneously (Kiely, 1974). A clinical example is the state of anxiety wherein a variety of skeletal, visceral, and psychic disturbances effect simultaneous discharge of both systems. Flooding of the cerebral cortex by afferents from both systems may be experienced as dread; weak knees may coexist with tremulous hands, representing skeletal muscle tone effects of the mixed ergotropic and trophotropic system discharge. Simultaneous activation of sympathetic and parasympathetic divisions may be expressed as sweating, tachycardia, nausea, vomiting, and bowel and bladder hyperactivity.

In summary, accompanying the shift from relaxation to arousal there is a shift in a whole pattern of hormonal secretions, accompanied by an increase in sympathetic nervous system discharge. The endocrine pattern in arousal promotes the mobilization of energy at the expense of maintenance and repair processes. The catabolic processes are accompanied by auxiliary mobilization of the renovascular system for conservation of salts and water. All of these shifts are initiated by the brain via control over the autonomic and endocrine systems.

For a person to remain healthy, however, these periods of arousal must be balanced by periods of relaxation in order to replenish the resources exhausted by catabolism. Without this, there would be no repair of accumulated damage, no vigilance against pathogens. In some patients stress may become chronic as coping mechanisms are overwhelmed and the patient develops a psychiatric illness such as depression or anxiety attacks, physical illness, or both.

PSYCHONEUROIMMUNOLOGY

There is an increasing body of evidence that the central nervous system, the endocrine system, and the immune system may have multiple bidirectional interconnections that allow mutual modulation and feedback (Stein, 1986). Since the coining of the term *psychoneuroimmunology* in 1964 by Ader, there have been numerous studies of the relationship between the immune system and stress, psychiatric illness, and environmental factors. Although these data are as yet inconclusive, strong patterns have emerged that suggest a coherent theory of CNS-immune system interaction.

One of the most impressive examples of this linkage has been the investigations of the ability of the immune system to be *classically conditioned* (Ader, 1975) (see Chapter 6 by Dr. Dorsett on behavioral concepts). For example, in experiments repeatedly "pairing" oral saccharin with cyclophosphamide (an immunosuppressant), significant immunosuppression can be demonstrated upon presentation of the saccharin stimulus *alone*. This is important because it involves a purely behavioral stimulus engaging the immune response with a noxious effect.

In a double-blind study (Smith and McDaniel, 1983) subjects were repeatedly skin tested with tuberculin antigen on one arm and saline on the other. After 5 trials the syringes were reversed and marked diminishment or absence of reaction was noticed where the saline was expected by the subject. Upon explanation of the identity of the test substances the previously vigorous response was obtained. Whether this was due to conditioning or cognitive set, the influence of higher cortical centers in modulation of the response is evident.

Kiecolt-Glaser (Kennedy, 1988) in three separate controlled studies examined the immunologic function of 75 first-year medical students during final examinations, 38 recently separated or divorced women, and 34 relatives chronically caring for Alzheimer disease patients. She observed similar quantitative and qualitative changes in immune cells in these three groups of acutely and chronically stressed individuals, including decreases in percentages of T-helper cells, decreased numbers and function of natural killer (NK) cells, and changes in herpes virus latency. Psychological variables including loneliness, attachment, and depression were related to the decrements in immunologic surveillance.

Both humoral and cell mediated immunity seem to be modulated by stress. Stress has been reported to influence the courses of certain illnesses such as asthma, strep throat and arthritis that involve B-cell systems, but the more robust findings involve T-cell mechanisms (Stein, 1986). The importance of T-cell regulation of the entire immunologic response has been recently underscored with the epidemic of AIDS. Studies have shown that stressors such as death of a spouse, sleep deprivation, and inability to escape from chronic physical threat can alter T-cell regulatory patterns and response to mitogens. The protective effects of coping seem to prevent this alteration. Rats exposed to a tail shock paradigm (over which they had no control) showed markedly diminished T-cell mitogen response compared with a second group of rats who were able to control the termination of the shock. This difference existed despite the fact that they received an equal total amount of shock (Stein, 1986).

The current state-of-the-art research in psychoneuroimmunology shows it to be in its infancy. Many substances such as cortisol, growth hormone, substance P, endorphins, opioids, and somatostatin have been shown to be immunomodulators. Innervation of the thymus, spleen, and lymph nodes has suggested possible direct CNS effects, and the continued study of the immune cell surface has demonstrated receptors for adrenergic and cholinergic neurotransmitters (Stein, 1986). Solomon (1987) has proposed more than 30 "postulates" of immune-endocrine-CNS interaction analogous to Koch's postulates of infectious disease. Yet, despite the relatively small amount of data in this area, preliminary controlled studies are increasingly implicating stress in the modulation of the immune system. Correspondingly, behavioral strategies that decrease the influence of stressors continue to show promise in the repair and strengthening of the immune system (Kiecolt-Glaser, 1992). As our understanding of this complex system increases it can only add to the continued unraveling of the mystery of stress and disease. Chapter 11 discusses the scientific evidence that traumatic stress early in life can neurobiologically alter the individual's neuroimmune system.

TREATMENT STRATEGIES

Although a thorough discussion of treatment approaches is beyond the scope of this chapter, the application of certain general principles can be useful. The overall strategy is a careful understanding of the potency of the biopsychosocial model as both a diagnostic aid and treatment guide. The biopsychosocial model is, in reality, an integrated alliance of three major heuristic models: biomedical, psychological, and social-behavioral. While the treatment plan needs to reflect the physician's understanding of the mutual interdependence of these approaches, for the sake of evaluation and planning they can be usefully separated. This involves making a biomedical diagnosis, a psychological diagnosis, and a social-behavioral diagnosis followed by a treatment plan for each.

Let us take, for example, the case of a 29-year-old woman with chronic strep throat and a major depression. From a *biomedical* standpoint, the following observations arise:

Biomedical data:

1. Neurovegetative symptoms secondary to hypothalamic dysregulation.
2. Decreased immunologic surveillance.
3. Poor nutritional status.

Biomedical diagnoses:

1. Major depression.
2. Streptococcal pharyngitis.
3. Impaired nutrition.

Biomedical treatment:

1. Antidepressant therapy.
2. Antibiotic therapy.
3. Dietary counseling.

Next, the *social-behavioral* viewpoint:

Social-behavioral data:

1. Husband physically beats patient.
2. Cigarette smoking.
3. Drinks too much alcohol.

Social-behavioral diagnoses:

1. Physical abuse by spouse.
2. Nicotine abuse.
3. Alcohol abuse.
4. Maladaptive coping.

Social-behavioral treatment:

1. Referral to women's shelter.
2. Behavior modification plan to reduce and stop smoking.
3. Alcoholics Anonymous referral.
4. Supportive counseling by M.D. to suggest new ways of coping.

Finally, the *psychological* aspect:

Psychological data:

1. Patient repeatedly chooses to return to abusive partner.
2. Adult child of alcoholic parents.

Psychological diagnoses:

1. History of childhood abuse by father.
2. ACOA (adult child of alcoholic) syndrome.

Psychological treatment:

1. Referral for insight-oriented psychotherapy.
2. Education about ACOA syndrome.
3. Referral to ACOA group.

By combining the distinctive viewpoints afforded by the model, an integrated treatment plan emerges that accounts for many aspects of the patient's functioning. The prescription of an antidepressant may be less effective in the face of continued physical assault, just as progress in insight-oriented psychotherapy would be hampered by the cognitive slowing typical of pharmacologically untreated major depression. Not all aspects of this plan would be immediately implemented in the first visit; however, the longitudinal perspective of primary care allows a gradual unfolding of this strategy over time, thus allowing patients to proceed at their own pace.

SUMMARY

Disease onset appears to be multifactorial. Over the past century we have learned a great deal about the biological components of susceptibility to illness, yet it has been only in the last 20 to 30 years that we have rigorously examined the psychosocial factors. We no longer view the psychosocial problems as causative of disease but rather as important factors in altering susceptibility to illness. The challenge to future physicians is to integrate this biopsychosocial view of patients into diagnosis and treatment in a pragmatic and compassionate manner.

ANNOTATED BIBLIOGRAPHY

Vitaliano PP, Maiuro RD, Russo J et al: A biopsychosocial model of medical student distress. J Beh Medicine 11:311–331, 1988

> An excellent overview of the stress and coping of medical students, illuminating many of the concepts in this chapter.

Engel GL: The clinical application of the biopsychosocial model. Am J Psychiatry 137:535–544, 1980

> One of the best illustrations of the biopsychosocial model comparing the management of a myocardial infarction patient using the biomedical and biopsychosocial models.

Kiecolt-Glaser JK, Glaser R: Psychoneuroimmunology: Can psychological interventions modulate immunity? J Consult Clin Psychology 60:569–575, 1992

> An excellent summary of recent research concerning behavioral modification of immune system activity.

Lipowski, ZJ: Psychosomatic medicine: past and present. Can J Psychiatry 31:2–21, 1986

> A historical overview of the development of the concept of "psychosomatic" including a summary of current and future research trends.

Chrousos GP, Gold PW: The concepts of stress and stress system disorders. JAMA 267:1244–1252, 1992

> A timely scholarly review of "what's new" in the physiology of the stress response, aimed at clinicians.

Kennedy S, Kiecolt-Glaser JK, Glaser R: Immunological consequences of acute and chronic stressors: Mediating role of interpersonal relationships. Br J Med Psychology 61:77–85, 1988

> A thorough review of social support and its modulating effect on the production of medical illness.

Sternberg EM et al: The stress response and the regulation of inflammatory disease. Ann Intern Med 117:854–866, 1992

> This review is a well-written, concise summary of recent developments with respect to behavioral influences on immune system function.

Stoudemire A, Hales RE: Psychological and behavioral factors affecting medical conditions and DSM-IV: An overview. Psychosomatics 32:5–13, 1992

> The introduction to a 12-part series of scholarly reviews used in revising the DSM-IV criteria for Psychological Factors Affecting Medical Condition.

REFERENCES

Ader R, Cohen N: Behaviorally conditioned immunosuppression. Psychosom Med 37:333, 1975

American Psychiatric Association: Diagnostic and Statistical Manual, 4th ed. Washington, DC, American Psychiatric Association, 1994

Bebbington PE: Psychosocial Etiology of Schizophrenia and Affective Disorders. In Michels R, Cavenar JO (eds): Psychiatry. Philadelphia, J.B. Lippincott, 1987

Brown GW, Harris T: Social Origins of Depression. London, Tavistock, 1978

Cohen F: Stress and bodily illness. Psychiat Clin N Amer, 4:269–286, 1981

Engel GL: The need for a new medical model: A challenge for biomedicine. Science 196:129–136, 1977

Freeman AM, Folks DG: Psychiatric Aspects of Cardiovascular Disease. In Michels R, Cavenar JO (eds): Psychiatry. Philadelphia, J.B. Lippincott, 1987

Goldstein MG, Niaura R: Psychological factors affecting physical condition: Cardiovascular disease literature review. Part I. Psychosomatics 33:134–145, 1992

Hankin J, Oktary JS: Mental Disorder and Primary Care: An Analytic Review of the Literature. U.S. Department of Health, Education and Welfare, AHEW Publication No. (ADM) 78–661. U.S. Government Printing Office, Washington, D.C., 1979

Hinkle LE, Wolff HG: Etiologic investigations of the relationships between illness, life experiences and the social environment. Ann Intern Med 49:1373–1388, 1958

Holmes T, Joffe JR, Ketchan JW, Sheehy TF: Experimental study of prognosis. J Psychosom Res 5:235–252, 1961

Holmes TH, Rahe RH: The social readjustment rating scale. J Psychosom Res 11:213–218, 1967

Kennedy S, Kiecolt-Glaser JK, Glaser R: Immunological consequences of acute and chronic stressors: Mediating roles of interpersonal relationships. Br J Med Psychology 61:77–85, 1988

Kiecolt-Glaser JK, Glaser R: Psychoneuroimmunology: Can psychological interventions modulate immunity? J Consult Clin Psychology 60:569–575, 1992

Kiely WF: From the symbolic stimulus to the pathophysiological response: Neurophysiological mechanisms. Int J Psychiatr Med 5:517–529, 1974

Koskenvuo M, Kaprio J, Rose RJ et al: Hostility as a risk factor for mortality and ischemic heart disease in men. Psychosom Med 50:330–334, 1988

Lazarus RS: Psychological Stress and Coping in Adaptation and Illness. In Lipowski ZJ, Lipsitt DR, Whybrow PC (eds): Psychosomatic Medicine. New York, Oxford University Press, 1977

Lown B, Desilva RA, Reich P et al: Psychophysiologic factors in sudden cardiac death. Am J Psychiatry 137:1325–1335, 1980

Medalie JH, Goldbourt U: Angina pectoris among 10,000 men. Am J Med 60:910, 1976

Niaura R, Goldstein MG: Psychological factors affecting physical condition: Cardiovascular disease literature review. Part II. Psychosomatics 33:146–155, 1992

Meyer RJ, Haggerty RJ: Streptococcal infections in families: Factors affecting individual susceptibility. Pediatrics 29:539–549, 1962

Ortmeyer CF: Variations in Mortality, Morbidity and Health Care by Marital Status. In Erhardt CF, Berlin JE (eds): Mortality and Morbidity in the United States. Cambridge, Harvard University Press, 1974

Raphael B, Middleton W: Current state of research in the field of bereavement. Isr J Psychiatry Relat Sci 24:5–32, 1987

Rose RM: Endocrine responses to stressful psychological events. Psychiat Clin N Amer 3(2):251–276, 1980

Ruberman W, Weinblatt E, Goldberg JD et al: Psychosocial influences on mortality after myocardial infarction. N Engl J Med 311:552–559, 1984

Smith RG, McDaniel SM: Psychologically mediated effect on the delayed hypersensitivity reaction to tuberculin in humans. Psychosom Med 45:65–70, 1983

Solomon GF: Psychoneuroimmunology: Interactions between central nervous system and immune system. J Neuroscience Res 18:1–9, 1987

Stein M, Schleifer SJ, Keller SE: Brain, Behavior and Immune Process. In Michels R, Cavenar JO (eds): Psychiatry. Philadelphia, J.B. Lippincott, 1987

Sterling P, Eyer J: Biological basis of stress-related mortality. Soc Sci Med 15E:3–42, 1981

Vinokur A, Selzer ML: Desirable versus undesirable life events: Their relationship to stress and mental distress. J Persp Soc Psychol 32:329–337, 1975

Alan Stoudemire (ed). *Human Behavior: An Introduction for Medical Students,*
Second Edition. Copyright © 1994, 1990 by J. B. Lippincott Company.

4 Culture, Ethnicity, and the Practice of Medicine

Peter J. Brown, Bruce Ballard, and Jessica Gregg

*Disease and its treatment are only in the abstract purely biologic
processes. Actually, such facts as whether a person gets sick at all, what
kind of disease he acquires and what kind of treatment he receives
largely depend upon social factors.*

Erwin Ackerknecht

Culture is the fundamental source of the diversity in thought and behavior
among different human groups. If you were to travel around the world, you would
undoubtedly be struck by the cultural diversity you found—in food, architecture,
religious beliefs, ideas about sex and marriage, and so on—and those differences
would make the trip exciting and fun. But such cultural variation represents a
challenge to the physician, because ideas about the etiology of illness and what to do
when a person is ill also vary with culture. This chapter argues that sensitivity to
cultural variation has practical benefits for the effective delivery of healthcare. To a
large degree, this argument builds upon the biopsychosocial model introduced in
Chapter 1 by Dr. Shelton and Chapter 2 by Drs. Cohen-Cole and Levinson, particularly
in terms of social variation in illness behavior.

Special consideration of the impact of culture and ethnicity on behavior is
warranted because of the simple, but often unrecognized, fact that the United States is
one of the most culturally heterogeneous nations. The ethnic diversity of patients who
may come into a major metropolitan hospital is remarkable. We are a nation of
immigrants, irrespective of a national ideology (the "melting pot" myth) that mini-

mizes the importance of ethnic and class differences. Clinical training is the first time many medical students must regularly interact with people whose backgrounds are very different from their own. In the context of healthcare, a strict application of a biomedical model of disease also minimizes the importance of social diversity, because all cases (like all Americans) are expected to be alike.

But differences based on ethnicity or class are not simply "noise" that can be ignored. From an epidemiologic standpoint, ethnicity and class are clearly related to lifestyle patterns such as diet, smoking or stress, as major causes of morbidity and mortality. As described in Chapter 2, basic elements of a patient's interaction with the medical system—for example, the interpretation of symptoms, the decision to seek care, or even the manner in which pain is experienced and reported—are largely determined by learned social and cultural factors. Social science research suggests that patient noncompliance often arises from an incongruence between the patient's view of what is going on and the physician's view. There is a danger of *ethnocentrism* when one simply "explains away" noncompliance in terms of the personality of the patient. Understanding the patient's point of view and effectively communicating with patients from different cultural backgrounds represent a central challenge to the practice of medicine today.

In this chapter we stress the importance of two fundamental and related concepts that must be applied to the understanding of patients and their illness behaviors: culture and ethnicity. The first part of the chapter outlines some conceptual underpinnings of medical anthropology. We show that culturally prescribed behaviors shape epidemiological risk. We also argue that cultural beliefs are central to socially constructed definitions of health and disease. In other words, culture provides definitions of what is normal or healthy, while it also provides explanations of how and why people get sick. The second half of the chapter focuses on ethnicity, briefly describing the range of cultural beliefs about health and illness found in major ethnic groups in the United States. Sensitivity to variation in cultural beliefs can improve the serious problem of patient compliance. The chapter concludes with practical suggestions for improving cross-cultural communication between physicians and their patients.

THE FUNDAMENTAL CONCEPT OF CULTURE

Human societies, unlike those of other animals, are distinguished by *Culture*—learned patterns of thought and behavior. The ability to adapt through the nonbiological mechanism of culture is the primary reason for the remarkable success of our species. Culture is transmitted from one generation to the next through the symbolic communication of language. It includes not only directly observable behaviors like patterns of diet and social organization but also ideologic components including beliefs and values. As such, culture provides a context of *meaning* to individuals. Both cultural behaviors and beliefs can have important adaptive functions.

Anthropologists believe that the thousands of cultural variations in the world today reflect adaptations to local environmental conditions and all are evolutionarily derived from the original human lifestyle of hunting and gathering. Of course, cultural variation is constrained by some of the biological universals of behavior that predate the evolution of culture. There are not many universals of culture, but some, like the incest taboo, appear to be best explained in terms of sociobiological theory (Wilson, 1978).

One useful model of culture, seen in Figure 4–1, divides culture into three mutually dependent layers. The material foundation of a cultural system is the economic mode of production, which includes the technology and the population size that the productive economy allows and requires. Contingent on the first layer is the system of social organization, which includes kinship and marriage practices, politics, and status differentiation. Contingent upon the social structure is the ideology or belief system, including ideas, beliefs, and values, both secular and sacred. Most anthropologists believe that the ideology is an extremely important part of culture, in part because it rationalizes and reinforces the economy and social structure. Ideology enables people to make sense of their world and to share their common world view. A culture is an integrated system: a change in one part causes changes in the other layers. The materialist model indicates that the direction of causal change is from the bottom layer upward (the thicker arrows in Figure 4–1). An economic change has drastic implications for population size, social organization, and associated beliefs. On the other hand, most people *within* a society tend to explain things from the top down.

One important universal in human cultures is that all societies have ethnomedical systems that attempt to combat the inevitability of disease and death. All medical systems include, at a minimum, three logically coherent elements: (1) a theory of the etiology of illness, (2) techniques for the diagnosis of illness, and (3) methods for appropriate therapy. In many societies, it is difficult to distinguish between the ethnomedical and religious systems. For a physician practicing in a multiethnic context, it is important to be aware of these preexisting medical beliefs and to avoid the fallacy of seeing patients as "empty vessels" waiting to be filled with biomedical knowledge (Polgar, 1963).

Culture Shapes Epidemiological Risk

Disease is never randomly distributed—either within or between societies. The kinds of diseases we are exposed to (and will die from) depend on the kind of culture we live in and our particular role within society. Economic production systems can change particular ecological settings to increase or decrease the risk of contracting a

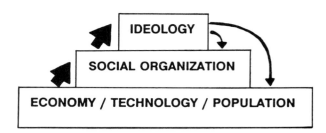

Figure 4–1. *A materialist model of culture.*

particular disease. People living in small hunting and gathering bands have different health risks from peasant farmers using irrigation or urbanites working in an industrial setting.

Brown and Inhorn (1990) have described a wide variety of infectious diseases where the epidemiological distribution of the disease is largely determined by particular cultural behaviors. For example, the slow virus *kuru* has been found only among the Fore tribe of the highlands of Papua New Guinea. It is hypothesized that the transmission of this virus was due to ritualized mortuary behaviors including cannibalism of the brains of infected individuals. Less dramatic cultural behaviors have been linked to diseases such as malaria, shistosomiasis, echinococcosis, and sexually transmitted diseases. Larson (1989) demonstrates how labor migration and patrilineal kinship systems in central Africa put women at high risk for contracting AIDS. The culture of sexuality in Brazil, examined by Parker (1987), adds to the problem of sexually transmitted diseases because of high cultural value placed on different sexual behaviors, including anal intercourse.

The most common causes of death in affluent societies like the United States, the cardiovascular diseases, are also shaped by cultural traditions of high-fat diets, little exercise, and high-stress working conditions. Such epidemiological risks are linked not only to cultural traditions but more importantly to social class.

Culture Provides Explanatory Models of Illness

Medical anthropologists sometimes distinguish between *disease* and *illness*. Disease refers to the objective clinical signs and pathophysiologic process that can result in a recognized diagnostic label from the *International Classification of Disease* (ICD) or from the *Diagnostic and Statistical Manual* (DSM). Illness refers to individuals' perceptions of being "not well" so that they act upon those perceptions. Although illness refers to a subjective experience, physicians should recognize that it is no less "real" than disease. Of course there can be disease without "illness," as in hypertension, and illness without "disease," as in the common case of a patient who complains of not feeling well but for whom no physical abnormality can be identified.

Ethnomedical systems provide both a categorization scheme for illnesses and, more importantly, explanations for their cause (Fabrega, 1974). From a cross-cultural perspective, Foster (1976) distinguished between *personalistic* and *naturalistic* medical systems based on the predominant orientation of their etiologic theory. This distinction is summarized in Table 4–1, although in complex societies like our own, elements of both types coexist. In personalistic systems, illness is thought to be the result of supernatural forces aimed at the patient for a particular reason, either through sorcery or spirit possession or because of a breach of taboo. In these systems, diagnosis and therapy largely involve shamanistic trance and ritual, aimed at correcting and counteracting the supernatural causes of illness; therapy is thought to be effective largely because of the belief of the patient in the power of the curer. Naturalistic ethnomedical systems, which include the traditional medicine of complex civilizations (India, China, Greece), are based on a principle of balance between elements of the body. Diagnosis based on the examination of symptoms and therapy involves the adjustment of humors to re-create the body's natural balance and health.

Table 4–1 **Typology of Ethnomedical Systems**

	PERSONALISTIC	**NATURALISTIC**
Causation	Active agent	Equilibrium loss
Illness	Special case of misfortune	Unrelated to other misfortune
Religion/magic	Intimately tied to illness	Unrelated to illness
Prevention	Positive action	Avoidance
Responsibility	Beyond patient control	Resides in patient
Societies	"Primitive" bands/tribes	State ancient "great traditions"

(Adapted from Foster GM: Disease etiologies in non-Western medical systems. Am Anth 78:773–782, 1976)

A widely dispersed concept in naturalistic systems is the hot/cold theory of disease (discussed below for Hispanic patients).

In the context of modern medical care it is more important for a clinician to be able to elicit the patient's "explanatory model" of illness (Kleinman 1988) rather than to memorize details of an ethnomedical belief system. *An explanatory model (EM) for disease is an individual's personal interpretation of disease.* As such, an EM allows a person to understand the causes, consequences, and prognosis of an illness experience; an EM can give meaning to life-threatening conditions. As lay explanations, EMs often differ from biomedical explanations for disease, and this disparity between belief systems may underlie problems with communication and noncompliance between patients and healers. When physicians recognize and acknowledge alternative explanatory models, then they have the ability to identify both areas of potential treatment noncompliance and areas where the belief systems converge and can reinforce appropriate therapy (Snow, 1993; Chrisman and Maretzki, 1982).

While lay explanatory models show significant individual variation, research indicates that ethnicity is an extremely important factor (Harwood, 1981). A patient's explanatory model can be learned through a few additional questions asked during the taking of a patient's history. Kleinman and colleagues (1978) have suggested eight questions (listed in Table 4–2) for eliciting such information. Some patients may view the physician as the ultimate expert on diagnosis and treatment and find these questions inappropriate. However, these questions are very useful for understanding why a particular patient with a particular constellation of symptoms is seeking medical care. Asking such questions in a clinical interaction can get important social and cultural concerns "on the table" for discussion.

Culture Defines Normality

Cultural behaviors and beliefs are usually learned in childhood and they are often deeply held and seldom questioned by adults, who pass their "obvious" knowledge and habits to their offspring. In this regard, cultural beliefs and values are largely unconscious factors in the motivation of individual behaviors. Cultural beliefs define

Table 4–2 **Questions for Eliciting a
Patient's Explanatory Model of Illness**

1. What do you think has caused your problem?
2. Why do you think it started when it did?
3. What do you think your sickness does to you? How does it work?
4. How bad [severe] do you think your illness is? Do you think it will last a
   long time, or will it be better soon, in your opinion?
5. What kind of treatment would you like to have?
6. What are the most important results you hope to get from treatment?
7. What are the chief problems your illness has caused you?
8. What do you fear most about your sickness?

(Adapted from Kleinman A, Eisenberg L, Good B. Culture, illness and care. Ann Intern
Med 88:251–258, 1978)

"what is normal" and therefore constrain the choices of behaviors available to an
individual.

Members of all societies are *ethnocentric* in that they use their own arbitrary
beliefs and values to judge people from another culture. What is considered "normal"
and "abnormal," acceptable and unacceptable, moral and immoral interpersonal
behavior varies from culture to culture and even within subcultures of society.
Anthropologists have long observed that cultural patterns—including definitions of
normal behavior—are generally "in fit" with local environmental conditions. In other
words, culture has adaptive value.

For example, Favazza (1985) contrasts the cultural patterns of two tribes in
highland Papua New Guinea, the Enga and the Fore, in terms of sexuality, marriage,
and mourning practices (see also Brown, 1978). The Enga, on one hand, face chronic
overpopulation, and their cultural patterns function to limit population growth. The
Enga have a taboo against premarital sex: a broad incest taboo in the patrilineal line,
limiting available marriage partners; a high value placed on celibacy; and rules that
prohibit the marriage of males less than age 30. Widows are strangled upon the death
of a husband, and infanticide is practiced. It is reported that death was not considered
a great cause for community anguish. In contrast, the Fore tribe, who live in an area of
underpopulation, have cultural patterns that may function to increase fertility, including liberal degrees of sexual experimentation, tribal ceremonies with erotic elements,
encouragement of early marriage, and the inheritance of widows by the dead husband's male relatives. In contrast with the Enga, the Fore reportedly suffer considerable anguish over the death of one of their members. Hence, what is considered normal
or ethical in terms of behavioral standards is relative to cultural and ecological
contexts.

Understanding a patient's cultural norms is particularly important in the context
of mental illness because what is considered a mental disorder should represent a
significant deviation from local standards of expected behavior (Cockerham, 1986).
Hence, societies vary as to what falls out of the realm of "normal" behavior and
becomes "abnormal"—the latter often being labeled as some form of psychiatric or

mental illness. There is little doubt that social labels of abnormality can function as mechanisms of social control (Szaz, 1974), even as political tools to control dissidents. This idea, however, has been subject to controversy. There appear to be boundaries on the relative range within which societies define normality. Cross-cultural studies of the objective characteristics of "crazy" behavior, in societies as diverse as the Eskimo and the Yoruba of Nigeria, have been shown to be remarkably similar (Konner, 1989; Murphy, 1976) suggesting that some psychiatric illnesses (including schizophrenia) may be universal.

Certain cultures have special manifestations of mental illness or aberrant behavior that have been described as "culture-bound syndromes" (Favazza, 1985; Simons and Hughes, 1985). The idea is that some mental illnesses are inextricably linked to a particular cultural context. There has been considerable debate concerning some of these culturally limited disorders, and it now appears that the general pattern may fit within DSM categories, although the content of symptoms must be culturally interpreted.

Classic examples of these "culture-bound syndromes" include the conditions *koro latah*, and *amok*. Initially described in Southeast Asia (but also reported in Nigeria and the United States), koro is described as the perception that the penis is shrinking and retracting into the abdomen. A man with koro fears that death will occur once the penis has sunk all the way into his abdomen. Panic accompanies the experience of koro, and epidemics of this syndrome have been reported in India, Thailand, and Singapore. *Latah*, found in Malaysia, involves an elaborated startle reflex during which startled individuals say obscene things or their attention can be captured so that their behavior temporarily matches that of the person who startled them. Women who are latah are sometimes startled many times a day, primarily for the entertainment of on-lookers. *Amok* ("running amok") is a syndrome first reported in Malaya and characterized by a period of brooding followed by extreme violence and homicidal attacks, ending with exhaustion and amnesia; this pattern has also been labeled the sudden mass assault taxon. Episodes of behavior resembling all three syndromes have been reported in other areas of the world, and it now appears likely that these are "culturally constructed" rather than culturally limited. Although these syndromes sound bizarre, one would note that most standards for health and illness are also culturally constructed and dependent on the observer's own frame of reference and expectations. Indeed, it was not long ago that homosexuality was diagnosed as a mental illness in the United States. This is true for medical as well as mental health problems. In the social context where their prevalence is high, malaria, pinta, diarrhea, and kwashiorkor have all been described and treated in particular cultures as "normal" (Brown and Inhorn, 1990).

Culture Affects Personality Development

Anthropologists have examined the relationship between cultural practices, particularly early childhood experiences, and later adult personality. This area of inquiry, begun in the 1930s and heavily influenced by psychoanalytic theory, led to descriptions of "national character," some of which had weaknesses of stereotyping. Cross-cultural comparative studies show a covariance between a society's environmental circumstances and subsistence ecology, which, in turn, constrain the social learning contexts of childhood, adolescence, and ultimately adult personality. Such a "modal personality" is ultimately reflected in the art, ritual, and religion of the society. For example, John and Beatrice Whiting (1975) have demonstrated how "husband–wife intimacy" (including sleeping arrangements and paternal involvement with children) is correlated with the degree to which a society is involved in war or its preparations.

The essential contribution of cultural factors to child development relates to the socialization and learning environment of the child (Favazza, 1985; Konner, 1989). That environment includes techniques of discipline, stressors the child may be exposed to, initiation rituals, behavioral expectations of the child, and skills of the parents and other caretakers. Children develop into adults, having had much of their values and standards of behavior transmitted to them by the family. The behavior and personality of the individuals along with the values inculcated by the family are absorbed from the cultural milieu and, thus, at least partially, determine how the individual interacts with society.

Until recently it was generally accepted that culturally determined child-rearing practices affect adult personality development in three ways. First, excessive child-hood deprivations predispose people to adult psychopathology; second, the sharing of childcare responsibilities by the mother may be beneficial; and third, conflicts within a family concerning love and hate and dependence and independence are more impor-tant than conflicts about toilet training or sexual behavior (Favazza, 1985, p 250). A problem with this area of research is the absence of any cross-culturally valid definitions of the independent variable (i.e., deprivations) or the dependent variables (i.e., psychopathology). Despite the tremendous variety of child-rearing practices throughout the world, including cultures characterized by physical abuse (Scheper-Hughes, 1987) and institutionalized homosexuality in initiation rituals (Konner, 1989), a central conclusion from cross-cultural research must be that most children grow up to be relatively well-adjusted adults.

Cross-cultural research on child development has forced the reconsideration of important concepts in psychiatry and psychology such as the universality of the childhood Oedipus complex (which, according to Malinowski [1927] does not fit the social dynamics of a matrilineal society like the Trobriands) or the universality of social stress related to sexuality in adolescence (which, according to Mead [1928], did not fit a permissive society like Samoa). In recent years both of these classic examples have been questioned (the Oedipus case by Spiro [1982] and the Samoa case by Freeman [1983]). Indeed, the entire model of early childhood influences on adult psychologic features has been seriously questioned in the work of Kagan (see Konner, 1989).

Nevertheless, there is little doubt that certain cultural and socioeconomic contexts may engender increased psychopathology as well as medical disease. Enor-mous stress is placed on people when social processes change rapidly or situations are created where people are subjected to situations that they have little or no ability to control. For example, in a classic study, Kardiner and Ovesey emphasized the impact of oppression and discrimination on the personality development of American blacks. They stated:

The result of the continuous frustrations in childhood is to create a personality devoid of confidence in human relations, of an eternal vigilance and distrust of others. This is a purely defensive maneuver which purports to protect the individual against the repeatedly traumatic effects of disappointment and frustration. He must operate on the assumption that the world is hostile. (Kardiner and Ovesey, 1951, p 308).

The study was notable for its identification of the impact of social discrimination on personality development in certain individuals. Yet the observations may have overemphasized psychopathological findings while not adequately recognizing the adaptive strength of blacks to social oppression.

In a different context, in rural Western Ireland, Scheper-Hughes (1979) has described the cultural setting for the unusually high prevalence of serious mental illness, particularly schizophrenia. Economic stresses in the region are severe and have resulted in female emigration and depopulation. The traditional pattern of land inheritance is linked to markedly delayed marriage ages for men and high rates of celibacy. The culture displays an ethos of severe sexual repression, as well as ridicule and scapegoating of children. In the historic past, the Irish tolerated eccentrics, including people who had visions, but today there is little such tolerance; this has resulted in high rates of hospitalization. Scheper-Hughes argues that these conditions contribute to the region's high prevalence of schizophrenia, as well as the specific symbolic themes in which disturbed thought patterns are presented by Irish patients.

CULTURE AND MEDICAL CARE

Ethnicity, Social Class, and Medical Care

In complex societies like our own, *ethnicity* is a fundamental source of cultural diversity and, for the medical practitioner, of potential misunderstanding. The concept of ethnicity has three fundamental aspects: (1) it establishes ties by reference to common origins, (2) it implies that members of the collectivity share particular patterns of behavior and interpersonal interaction, and (3) it implies that ethnic groups participate with one another in a larger social system (Harwood, 1981).

It is important to emphasize that this is a discussion of ethnicity rather than "race." The idea of race has been abandoned by nearly all biological anthropologists and human biologists. Race is a common and politically powerful social concept but has no practical utility in biological studies. Indeed, there is genetic and phenotypic variation between human populations, but these differences simply cannot be forced into discrete or relevant categories; the idea of race is simply folk-biology. In a powerful recent analysis Hahn (1992) has shown that the use of race in health statistics is full of politically relevant contradictions devoid of biological validity and falsely implies that health differentials stemming from class or ethnic inequalities actually have a genetic basis. Importantly, in comprehensive analyses of sociomedical problems such as infant mortality, it is social class that has the strongest explanatory power.

It is useful to remember that there is much variation in the degree to which members of ethnic groups share cultural standards or publicly express their ethnicity.

Indeed, the concept of ethnicity brings with it a serious danger of *stereotyping*, the mistaken notion that all members of another group are alike. Even among recent immigrants there is much cultural variation based on regional, educational, and class differences in the country of origin. The length of time a person has been in the United States, his or her socioeconomic milieu, and the language spoken at home all make cultural stereotyping a dangerous enterprise.

It is important, nevertheless, that practitioners become culturally sensitized to the *range* of cultural beliefs and behaviors present in the ethnic groups they serve. This information can be clinically valuable in a medical setting, for example, in terms of interpreting a patient's complaints. In a classic study, Zborowski (1952) described ethnic variation in attitudes toward pain and cultural standards for communicating about their pain. Whereas both Jewish and Italian-American patients were described as having an "emotional" response to pain, the Italian Americans in the sample were more concerned with the immediate relief from pain while Jewish patients were anxious about the implications of the pain in terms of the future health and welfare of the family. On the other hand, "WASP" patients reflected a cultural belief that it was "no use" to complain about pain and preferred to describe or report the experience. Patients from this cultural background attempt to avoid being a "nuisance" in the hospital setting, thinking of themselves as part of a team. A serious report of pain from this group, because it is based on different cultural standards about interpersonal communication of unpleasant things, must also be evaluated differently. Recently, Bates (1992, 1993) has completed methodologically rigorous studies of pain and ethnicity focusing on Puerto Rican Americans, WASPs, and African Americans, that demonstrate the influence of ethnicity on the actual perception of pain as well as rules about communicating distress.

The experience of pain can only be communicated to the physician through the patient and his cultural beliefs and standards. The physician must be aware of both the danger of stereotyping and individual variation, and the characteristic health beliefs and behaviors of ethnic groups. The multicultural diversity created by the large number of African-American and Hispanic patients already present in the United States, as well as recent immigrants from Caribbean countries, Central America, and Southeast Asia has increased the importance of physicians evaluating the role of sociocultural factors that may influence disease vulnerability, attitudes toward illness and medical treatment, and, for our purposes, manifestations of presumed mental illness. With this in mind, a brief summary of some ethnic minorities in the United States is appropriate. (For more detailed discussions see Clark 1983; on general clinical issues, see Barker, 1992; Galanti, 1991; Harwood, 1981; or Spector, 1985; and Gaw, 1982 and 1992, for psychiatric disorders.)

African-American Culture

African Americans comprise a very heterogeneous social category. Yet, as a group, they have been historically distinct, suffering from slavery in the past and recurring racism to the present time. Thus, while it is important to avoid the danger of stereotyping, it is also important to recognize that historical pressures and racism affect the culture of all African Americans. As Bell Hooks notes, "there is a radical difference between a repudiation of the idea that there is a black 'essence' and recognition of the way black identity has been specifically constituted in the experience of exile and struggle" (1990).

African-American religion and healing developed simultaneously as slaves attempted to create both meaning for their suffering and the methods to alleviate it. The life-view in which African-American medicine operated considered the universe a hostile place where the forces of good and evil, God and Satan, struggled for control in both the natural realm of man and God and in the unnatural realm of sorcery and the devil (Matthews, 1987). Within this universe, illnesses may have natural or unnatural causes. Natural events occur according to the laws of God and nature, and may therefore be explained as resulting from extreme behaviors that upset the balance of nature (such as too much drinking or eating) or as the result of God's will, perhaps as punishment for sinful behavior. Unnatural events are supernatural, caused by the devil or some other force of evil, and are therefore unpredictable, and are both caused and cured by magic (Snow, 1983, p 821). This categorization and interpretation of disease provided illnesses with context and meaning, thus making them more tolerable.

Given that African Americans continue to struggle with racism and social inequity, it is perhaps not surprising that many elements of this meaning-providing system continue to exist in African-American culture. Recent ethnographic studies of the health beliefs and practices of urban, lower-class African Americans include several observations useful for clinicians (Snow, 1983, 1993; Mathews, 1987; Flaskerund and Rush, 1989; Heurtin-Roberts and Reisin, 1990). Illnesses continue to be categorized as "natural" and "unnatural." Unnatural causes of illness include "hexes" (voodoo, hoodoo, rootwork) and satanic influence. The hex can cause a variety of symptoms, particularly gastrointestinal problems, and is often thought to be the malign work of a close relative or friend. The idea of hex can be a predominant theme in the presentation of psychiatric cases. Jordan reports that a belief in the power of the hex has led some African Americans to use voodoo for therapy (Jordan, 1975). Snow reports that many African Americans believe medical doctors cannot help in the case of a hex, and patients seek the care of traditional religious healers with the power to cure them (Snow, 1993). Unless belief in rootwork is identified as part of the patient's presentation by the evaluating physician, extensive medical and psychiatric evaluation may prove to be frustrating. In general, however, African Americans rely almost entirely on orthodox biomedicine for their care (Jackson, 1981).

Importantly, biomedical definitions are frequently integrated into traditional belief systems, creating conditions with similar names but different perceived etiologies and cures, which may contribute to serious (and potentially dangerous) miscommunication between physicians and African-American patients. This is especially true for those illnesses considered "natural." For instance, an extremely important concern for those who believe in the traditional African-American model is the condition of the blood. Healthy blood is "at rest" or "quiet" (Heurtin-Roberts and Reisin, 1990), and illness results when blood begins rising in the body toward the head. Two conditions, "high-blood" and "high-pertension" may result. High-blood is the result of too much or too-thick blood. Excessive blood slowly rises toward the head and "works on the heart too hard" (Heurtin-Roberts and Reisin, 1990). The condition is thought to be hereditary but is believed to be exacerbated by rich diets and red meat. It is treated with medically prescribed anti-hypertensive drugs and vinegar bitters or epsom salts, which should "thin out" the blood (Snow, 1993; Heurtin-Roberts and Reisin, 1990).

"High-pertension" is perceived as a more acute condition than high-blood. In an individual suffering from high-blood, the blood stays elevated, slowly damaging the heart. High-pertension, on the other hand, causes the blood to shoot up suddenly to the head, often causing immediate death. Like high-blood, high-pertension is also considered the result of excessively thick blood, but the rapid ascendance of the blood to the head (as opposed to the moderately elevated condition of blood in high-blood) is produced by acute anxiety or nervousness. Treatment for high-pertension stresses the importance of relaxation and rarely includes medication, though tranquilizing pills are perceived as somewhat effective. Changes in diet and weight loss are considered ineffective treatments (Snow, 1983; Heurtin-Roberts and Reisin, 1990). Physicians treating African-American patients with hypertension need to remain cognizant of these folk models in order to avoid confusion and severe miscommunication in treatment.

At the same time, in working with African-American patients from higher social classes who have accepted current biomedical approaches to disease, it is important for the physician to recognize that there can be circumstances of racism and discrimination in the work environment that increase job stress. This can be an aspect of the current culture of African Americans. These stress factors would be important if one is treating hypertension in a patient from that background, since such stress might influence the response to treatment.

Where folk models overlap with physician models of illness, clinicians may find an important ally in folk models for the prevention and treatment of disease. For instance, Flaskerund and Rush (1989) note that low-income African-American women in Los Angeles have integrated AIDS into their traditional beliefs about illness and healing practices. Defining AIDS as a "natural" illness, the women advised that to prevent the disease a person must live moderately, refrain from excessive sexual activity, eat right, and keep clean. The authors note that AIDS prevention programs among these women, then, should focus less exclusively on using condoms and not sharing needles, and should broaden to more frequently include advice on the importance of monogamy to a moderate lifestyle (Flaskerund and Rush, 1989).

In addition, the long history of racism in the United States has left some African Americans suspicious of advanced biomedical explanations of disease. In the case of AIDS, there are some African Americans who, when made aware of the increasingly endemic incidence of AIDS in inner city African-American communities, reject current information on transmission because of a belief that the appearance of this disease is part of a conspiracy or plot to destroy African Americans. These patients will not readily accept the concept of a virally transmitted disease that requires epidemiologic control through changes in behavior. Unless the physician maintains some cognizance of this, education efforts connecting AIDS transmission to intravenous drug use and unprotected sexual contact may, in certain instances, fall on deaf ears.

Hispanic-American Cultures

The Spanish-speaking population of the United States is made up of a variety of ethnic groups, including people with cultural roots in Puerto Rico, Mexico, and Cuba, as well as both Indian and Mestizo groups of Latin America. The cultural heterogeneity within this category is significant and important, yet there are several key commonalities. First are the obvious problems of language and problems of communication, which can be particularly critical in a healthcare setting. Other commonalities include general conditions of poverty and migration-associated stress; a cultural emphasis on the extended family; interactional norms linked with notions of respect and modesty for women; and some basic philosophic premises about the relationship of body and mind. The health beliefs and behaviors of these groups have been the subject of much social scientific research (Bauwens and Spicer, 1977; Schreiber and Homiak, 1981).

In respect to Mexican Americans, Murillo (1972) notes that there is no specific Mexican-American family type but thousands of different families depending on regional, historic, political, socioeconomic, and acculturation factors. The Spanish language may or may not be spoken in the home. For example, some Mexican Americans have very little familiarity with Spanish, while others are bilingual and deal with differing nuances of communication, depending on the language being used. With the mixture of European, Spanish, and Indian influences, Mexican Americans may have a range of religious beliefs; therefore it may be erroneous to assume, for example, that a patient is unduly influenced by Catholicism.

Research on the folk medical beliefs of all Hispanic groups indicates that both natural and supernatural causes of illness are thought to operate. Natural causes include drafts (*mal aire*), fallen fontanelle in children (*mollera caida*), intestinal obstruction (*empacho*), but most importantly an imbalance of hot and cold elements (see Pachter, 1993 for the most comprehensive treatment of this subject). The hot/cold theory of disease is based on traditional Hippocratic beliefs of four humors (the moist/dry distinction is essentially ignored in these folk beliefs). Illnesses, foods, and remedies are classified in the hot/cold system in terms of their essential character; illnesses represent either an excess or surfeit of hot or cold humors. Therefore a cure, in this cultural conception, involves readjusting the body's humors to recreate a healthy balance. Harwood (1971, 1981) has shown that for Puerto Rican patients, the hot/cold theory can present problems of compliance when, for example, a "hot" illness like rheumatic fever is treated with a "hot" remedy like antibiotics. From the patient's perspective such an incongruence may defy their own cultural logic. Harwood shows, however, that the "principle of neutralization" in which the "hot" nature of an antibiotic can be balanced by taking the pill with a "cool" substance, like fruit juice or tea, can resolve the cultural incongruence and improve results (see Harwood, 1981, for detailed clinical suggestions). It is important to remember, however, that Puerto Rican and other Hispanic patients vary in the degree to which they give credence to the folk model, and, therefore, the clinician must try to determine, for individual patients, whether this folk conceptualization may affect treatment outcome.

Because of language problems, there may be mislabeling of some symptoms as "psychotic" in Hispanic patients, especially in patients who present with pseudohallucinations or the syndrome of *ataque* (also called Puerto Rican syndrome; see Harwood, 1977). The ataque syndrome includes anxiety, hyperventilation, and occasional behavior resembling a seizure disorder; it is usually transient (Pachter, 1993).

According to Harwood, the belief system of *espiritismo* (spiritism) is a common feature of Puerto Rican health culture in the Northeast. Espiritismo is a belief based on the reality and power of spirit possession, communication through mediums, and removal of harmful influences by spiritist specialists. It is practiced in neighborhood *centros*, which resemble a "clinic" with mediums and assistants. Patients are reported to present with a variety of somatic and anxiety-related symptoms, including nightmares and mood disturbances. The "therapy" of the patients is conducted by the medium, who communicates with a spirit who essentially conducts an exploratory psychotherapeutic interview with the patient to determine areas of emotional pain and conflict. Various types of malevolent spirits, which may possess the body, can control the patient. Harwood's work (1977) shows that spiritists provide valuable mental health services to this underserved community and that their work can be successfully integrated with the biomedical approach.

Mention should also be made of the mental health conditions of *susto* (soul loss, or magical fright) and *nervios* (nerves). The symptoms of susto are similar to those of depression, although the condition is thought to be the result of the inadvertent separation of the soul from the body. The ritual cures of *curanderos* have been shown to relieve symptoms (Rubel et al, 1984). Hispanic ideas of curing appear to be linked to several philosophic premises (Table 4–3).

While the concept of good and evil spirits occupying and controlling one's body and behavior may sound primitive, it is quite similar to commonly held beliefs about spiritual life prevalent in Christianity and that persist in many fundamentalist and "mainstream" Christians. Even psychoanalysis employs concepts of "good and bad objects" that are "introjected" or "internalized" intrapsychically from one's environment. Moreover, classic psychoanalysis has its own ritualistic aspects; techniques of therapy are thus heavily influenced by cultural factors.

Other Ethnic Groups

Cultural summaries of health beliefs and behaviors relevant for clinical care are available for a wide variety of ethnic groups, including Chinese, Haitians, Italians, and

Table 4–3 **Latino Philosophic Premises about Health and Curing**

1. Illness can result from strong emotional states.
2. Illness can be caused by being out of balance with the environment.
3. Patients can be the innocent victims of malevolent forces.
4. The body and soul are separable.
5. Cure requires participation of the entire family.
6. The natural world cannot be distinguished from the supernatural.
7. Sickness of a member can bring a family closer.
8. A healer should be open and treat you with respect.

(Adapted from Maduro R: Curanderismo and Latino views of disease and curing. West J Med 139:64–71, 1983)

Navajos (Harwood, 1981); Filipinos, Japanese, Southeast Asians, Jamaicans, Pacific Islanders, Middle Easterners, Soviet Jews, and Alaskan Eskimos (Clark, 1983); and Chinese Americans, Afghan refugees, East Indians, Iranians, Korean Americans, Laotian refugees, Ethiopians, Russian emigrés, and seasonal farm workers (Barker, 1992). Spector (1985) and Bauwens and Spicer (1977) provide similar discussions for lower-income whites.

Of particular note is Kleinman's (1980) work on traditional Chinese culture, aimed at understanding how cultural beliefs influence the experience of illness and the patient role. He has shown a general reticence of the Chinese to verbalize distressful affect and a tendency of anxiety and depression to be manifested in predominantly physical or somatic symptoms. The extent to which these characteristics appear in Chinese Americans, including the effect of acculturation, is not clear. This same tendency to "somatize" dysphoric feeling states and for psychiatric disorders to present with predominantly physical symptoms is extremely common in primary care medical settings in the United States in both Caucasian and African-American patients.

Biomedical Culture

Clearly, it is important for physicians to understand the cultural models of disease held by their patient populations. It is also important that physicians and their patients recognize that biomedicine (medicine as it is practiced in hospitals, universities, and clinics in most industrialized nations) itself forms a subculture containing culture-specific values, beliefs, and practices. Patient-physician interactions may in fact be viewed as cross-cultural communication, with each participant struggling to understand the worldview of the other.

Though practitioners and patients of biomedicine often tend to regard this system as based purely in scientific fact and therefore as beyond or above culture, anthropologists studying biomedicine have made it clear that the system is as much a product of a particular cultural milieu as are other types of healing. They do not argue that biomedical notions of anatomy, physiology, and disease etiology are only applicable to individuals and populations in particular cultural systems. Rather, they emphasize that the environment in which biomedical ideas and practices are generated influences both the type of idea that is generated and the ways in which that idea is eventually implemented.

The influence of culture on biomedicine may be explored in two ways: (1) by examining the social and historical context in which biomedicine has developed and (2) by examining the influence of specific cultural contexts on the biomedicine subculture. Most historians trace the origins of biomedicine to the philosophy of René Descartes, which was previously discussed in Chapter 3. Descartes postulated a possible separation of the mental and the social worlds from the physical body, although Descartes' theories have been interpreted in a simplistic manner. The "dualism" attributed to Descartes was an intrinsic concept in Greek philosophy dating to Socrates and Plato and involved metaphysical, not scientific, concepts. Nevertheless, mind-body dualism permeated much of Western thought and formed an essential component of traditional biomedical theory (Scheper-Hughes and Lock, 1987) in which diseases afflict the bounded, physical body, and therefore the body alone is the focus of the therapeutic encounter (see also Chapter 2). Social and mental disorders are considered outside the realm of biomedicine (Rhodes, 1990; Scheper-Hughes and Lock, 1987). Critics argue that Cartesian thinking in biomedicine leads to an unfortunate reluctance on the part of physicians to adopt a more integrated approach to illness, one which understands disease as the product of a mind-body-society interaction. They contend that an understanding of illness as a product of social environment and mental state as well as the product of biological malfunction would allow physicians the ability to more fully comprehend the causes and consequences of illness (Cousins, 1979; Scheper-Hughes and Lock, 1978; Finkler 1991; Cassell, 1991).

Even as biomedicine can be understood as a distinct system that developed out of a specific cultural historical context, it can also be analyzed as several varied systems, each uniquely affected by a different cultural context. For instance, it is possible to make distinctions between biomedical cultures in France, England, and the United States (Hunt, 1992). Physicians in England and the United States, diagnosing and treating heart conditions, differ markedly in their assessment of the need for patients to undergo heart surgery. French physicians are unique in prescribing lactobacillus from yogurt cultures in conjunction with prescriptions for antibiotics in order to counteract stomach upset from those medicines. No other biomedical system does this (Hunt, 1992).

In Finkler's study of biomedicine in Mexico City, the author notes that while biomedicine in Mexico "is practiced along the lines of a worldwide biomedical model that focuses on the body and its anatomical lesions and depends chiefly on pharmacological treatments" (Finkler, 1991), individual physicians combine biomedical understandings with traditional folk understanding to explain sickness. Thus, common folk conditions such as *nervios* and *susto* (traditionally believed to be caused by anger, anxiety and/or fright, and to result in numerous symptoms such as jabbing pains in the heart, trembling, tiredness, insomnia, and headaches) were often translated by the physicians in Finkler's study into organic dysfunctions. The author explains that "physicians frequently diagnose patients with problems of the spine. Their emphasis on the spinal column may reflect a reinterpretation of nerves as a dysfunction of the nervous system that is lodged in the spine and that causes a nerve sickness" (Finkler, 1991, p 80). Here, then, culture clearly influences how physicians interpret symptoms and how illnesses are addressed in the biomedical system.

Several analysts have noted that in the United States the North American emphases on the individual and on technology give rise to a biomedical culture that is more focused on treatment than on alleviation of suffering. Suffering is experienced by *persons*, not simply by bodies (Cassell, 1991). Increasing reliance on advanced technology, however, focuses physician efforts more narrowly on the body and away from the sufferer and his or her subjective needs.

Farmer and Kleinman illustrate this point through a study of the AIDS-related deaths of two individuals, Anita in Haiti and Robert in Boston. Having suffered from AIDS for two years, Robert entered the hospital after being barred from air travel home to Chicago because of his medical condition. Weary of treatment, Robert made clear to the hospital staff that he did not want any more invasive care. At most, he wanted enough care to enable him to board an airplane, and if that was not possible he requested that he just be "kept clean." Instead, he was given a feeding tube, an endoscopy, and a CT scan of the neck, and he died a few hours after receiving the last procedure.

Anita died in Haiti. She was given almost no medical care and died in the house of her godmother, who refused to take her to the clinic:

> Why should we take her there ... She will not recover from this disease. She will have to endure the heat and humiliation of the clinic. She will not find a cool place to lie down. What she might find is a pill or an injection to make her feel more comfortable for a short time. I can do better than that ... for some people a decent death is as important as a decent life. (Farmer and Kleinman, 1989)

In a culture where advanced technology is scarce and therefore rarely perceived as the solution to most problems and where social ties are perceived as more important than individual autonomy, Anita's life was not extended through technological advances, but neither was her suffering deepened by social isolation and invasive and ultimately useless therapy. The point the authors make here is not that technology is bad or that biomedicine as practiced in the United States is wrong. Rather, they argue that North Americans have allowed cultural biases toward technology and treatment of the individual to permeate notions of healing to the extent that physicians often ignore other equally vital and much more elemental aspects of healing.

DISCUSSION

Social and cultural factors are essential for understanding human behavior because they provide both context and meaning for action. Human thought and behavior encompasses such diversity between social groups because of culture. In childhood, all people learn their social group's beliefs about health, illness, and what to do when sick. Because such beliefs can influence the interpretation of symptoms and effective communication between the patient and physician, they are very important.

Learned cultural behaviors, for example, in diet or notions of "ideal body type," can influence the social epidemiologic distribution of disease. Higher prevalence of disease in minority ethnic groups, however, is better understood in terms of social class than culture itself. The social stresses of poverty have a large impact on physical and mental health.

In most social situations, stereotyping is used to distance ethnic groups by creating barriers of misunderstanding between them. Physicians and other healthcare personnel must recognize the impact of their own sociocultural backgrounds on attitudes, perceptions, and prejudices that they may have toward persons of social, educational, ethnic, cultural, and lifestyle backgrounds different from their own. Physicians must be able to listen to the patient as well as respond in an empathic and nonjudgmental manner. It is also valuable to remember that the medical community itself has a culture—a set of values and beliefs about health and illness—which can simply be foreign and poorly understood by patients.

It is important to know and understand the cultural background of patients in both medical and psychiatric practice. Failure to do so will complicate understanding the patient's symptoms, making a correct diagnosis, and planning and communicating an effective treatment plan. Errors that may occur include stereotypic labeling of minority patients, drawing premature conclusions regarding the patient based on the patient's ethnic group and cultural and socioeconomic background, and failure to use interpreters when major language and cultural barriers exist between physician and patient (Favazza, 1985).

Suggestions for Improved Cross-Cultural Communication

If a physician is regularly dealing with patients from an ethnic group different from his or her own, it is valuable to be aware of the *range* of health beliefs and practices of that group; readings listed below contain coherent summaries. A multicultural clinical setting provides additional challenges to the practitioner. Berlin and Fowkes (1983) suggest the mnemonic *LEARN* (Table 4–4) to improve cross-cultural communication in the clinical setting. The first suggestion is the most important—*listen* to the patient's perception of the problem. This can be done by eliciting the patient's "explanatory model" through the questions indicated in Table 4–2. Research on patient satisfaction with physician consultation indicates that active verbal interaction, particularly the time spent listening to the patient, was the strongest predictor of satisfaction (Korsch and Negrete, 1972). When physicians explain their view of a patient's problem, it is important to use terms that can be understood. The acknowledgment of possible differences between the patient's and physician's views needs to be accomplished in such a manner that the patient's ideas are not demeaned but, rather, treated with respect. Such mutual respect, coming from both sides of a cultural boundary, can lead to a treatment plan that is acceptable to both patient and physician.

Table 4–4 LEARN: A Guideline for Improved Communication

L	Listen with sympathy and understanding to the patient's perception of the problem.
E	Explain your perceptions of the problem.
A	Acknowledge and discuss differences and similarities.
R	Recommend treatment.
N	Negotiate an agreement.

(Adapted from Berlin EO, Fowkes WC: A teaching framework for cross-cultural health care. West J Med 139:130–134, 1983)

ANNOTATED BIBLIOGRAPHY

Barker JC: Cross-cultural medicine: A decade later. West J Med 157: 1992

This special issue summarizes cultural information and clinical problems on sixteen ethnic groups in northern California, including recent political refugees.

Clark, MM: Cross-cultural medicine. West J Med 139: 1983

This special edited issue contains excellent summaries on the health beliefs and behaviors of twelve different ethnic groups, as well as more theoretic summaries of issues surrounding culture and medicine.

Gaw A: Cross-Cultural Psychiatry. Boston, John Wright-PSG, 1982

This book includes papers by a number of writers, elucidating aspects of psychiatry as applied to minority groups in the United States. It is useful for acquiring some general background information that is important in the clinical assessment of patients.

Harwood A: Ethnicity and Health Care. Cambridge, Harvard University Press, 1981

An excellent collection of articles on major ethnic groups and their demographic and social epidemiologic characteristics and health beliefs. The article by Jackson on lower-class urban blacks is particularly recommended.

REFERENCES

Acosta FX, Yamamoto J, Evans LA: Effective Psychotherapy for Low Income and Minority Patients. New York, Plenum Press, 1982

Bates MS, Edwards WT, Anderson, KO: Pain. J Intl Association Study Pain 52(1):101–112, 1993

Bates MS, Edwards WT: Ethnicity and disease. Int J Population Differences Disease Patterns 2(1):63–83, 1992

Bauwens E and Spicer EH: Ethnic Medicine in the Southwest. Tucson, University of Arizona Press, 1977

Berlin EO, Fowkes WC: A teaching framework for cross-cultural health care. West J Med 139:130–134, 1983

Bradshaw WH: Training psychiatrists for working with blacks in basic residency programs. Am J Psychiatry 135:1520–1524, 1978

Brown P: Highland Peoples of New Guinea. Cambridge, Cambridge University Press, 1978

Brown P, Inhorn M: Disease, ecology and human behavior. In Johnson TM, Sargent CF (eds): Medical Anthropology: A Handbook of Theory and Methods. New York, Greenwood Press, 1990

Cassell EJ: The Nature of Suffering and the Goals of Medicine. New York, Oxford University Press, 1991

Chrisman NJ, Maretzki TW: Clinically Applied Anthropology: Anthropologists in Health Science Settings. Dordrecht, Reidel Publishing Company, 1982

Clark, MM: Cross-cultural medicine. West J Med 139: 1983

Clark MM: Cross-cultural medicine: A decade later. Western J Med 157(3), 1992

Cockerham WC: Medical Sociology, 3rd ed. Englewood Cliffs, NJ, Prentice Hall, 1986

Cousins N: Anatomy of an Illness as Perceived by the Patient. New York, Bantam Books, 1979

Eisenberg L, Kleinman A: The Relevance of Social Science for Medicine. Dordrecht, Reidel Publishing Company, 1981

Fabrega H: Disease and Social Behavior: An Interdisciplinary Perspective. Boston, MIT Press, 1974

Farmer P, Kleinman A: AIDS as Human Suffering. Daedalus Spring, 1989

Favazza AE: Anthropology and Psychiatry. In Kaplan HI, Sadock BJ (eds): Comprehensive Textbook of Psychiatry, 4th ed. Baltimore/London, Williams & Wilkins, 1985

Finkler K: Physicians at Work, Patients in Pain: Biomedical Practice and Patient Response in Mexico. Boulder, CO, Westview Press, 1991

Flaskerund JH, Rush CE: AIDS and traditional health beliefs and practices of black women. Nursing Res 38(4):210–215, 1989

Foster GM: Disease etiologies in non-Western medical systems. Am Anth 78:773–782, 1976

Freeman D: Margaret Mead and Samoa. Cambridge, Harvard University Press, 1983

Galanti G: Caring for Patients from Different Cultures: Case Studies from American Hospitals. Philadelphia, University of Pennsylvania Press, 1991

Gaw A: Chinese Americans. In Gaw A (ed): Cross-Cultural Psychiatry. Boston, John Wright-PSG, 1982

Gaw A, Ed. Culture, Ethnicity, and Mental Illness. Washington, DC, American Psychiatric Press, 1992

Hahn RA: The state of federal health statistics on racial and ethnic groups. JAMA 267(2):268–271, 1992

Harwood A: The hot-cold theory of disease: Implications for the treatment of Puerto Rican patients. JAMA 216:1153–1158, 1971

Harwood A: Rx—Spiritist as Needed: A Study of a Puerto-Rican Mental Health Resource. New York, Wiley, 1977

Harwood A: Ethnicity and Medical Care. Cambridge, Harvard University Press, 1981

Heurtin-Roberts S, Reisin E: Folk Models of Hypertension among Black Women. In Coreil J, Mull JD (eds): Anthropology and Primary Health Care. Boulder, CO, Westview Press, 1990

Hooks B: Yearning: Race, Gender, and Cultural Politics. Boston, South End Press, 1990

Hunt GJ: Social and Cultural Aspects of Health, Illness, and Treatment. In Goldman HH (ed): Review of General Psychiatry, 3rd ed. Norwalk, CT, Appleton and Lange, 1992

Jackson JJ: Urban Black Americans. In Harwood A (ed): Ethnicity and Medical Care. Cambridge, Harvard University Press, 1981

Johnson TM, Sargent CF (eds): Medical Anthropology: Contemporary Theory and Method. New York, Praeger, 1990

Jordan WC: Voodoo Medicine. In Williams RA (ed): Textbook of Black-Related Diseases. New York, McGraw-Hill, 1975

Kardiner A, Ovesey L: The Mark of Oppression. Cleveland, World Publishing, 1951

Kleinman A: Patients and Healers in the Context of Culture. Berkeley, University of California Press, 1980

Kleinman A: Rethinking Psychiatry: From Cultural Category to Personal Experience. New York, The Free Press, 1988

Kleinman A: The Illness Narratives. New York, Basic Books, 1988

Kleinman A, Eisenberg L, Good B: Culture, illness and care. Ann Intern Med 88:251–258, 1978

Konner M: Anthropology and Psychiatry. In Kaplan HI, Sadock BJ (eds): Comprehensive Textbook of Psychiatry, 5th ed. Baltimore, Williams & Wilkins, 1989

Korsch BM, Negrete VF: Doctor–patient communication. Sci Am 227(2):66–74, 1972

Larson A: Social context of human immunodeficiency virus transmission in Africa: Historical and cultural bases of East and Central African sexual relations. Rev Infect Dis 11:716–731, 1989

Leighton AH: Relevant generic issues. In Gaw A (ed): Cross-Cultural Psychiatry. Boston, John Wright-PSG, 1982

Maduro R: Curanderismo and Latino views of disease and curing. West J Med 139:64–71, 1983

Malinowski B: Sex and Repression in Savage Society. London, Routledge and Kegan Paul, 1927

Mathews H: Rootwork: Description of an ethnomedical system in the American South. Southern Med J 80(7):885–891, 1987

Mead M: Coming of Age in Samoa. New York, Morrow, 1928

Murillo N: The Mexican-American family. In Wagner NN, Haug MJ (eds): Chicanos: Social and Psychological Perspectives. St Louis, CV Mosby, 1972

Murphy JM: Psychiatric labeling in cross-cultural perspective. Science 191:1019–1028, 1976

Pachter LM: Latino folk illness. Med Anthropology 15(2), 1993

Parker R: Acquired immunodeficiency syndrome in urban Brazil. Med Anthropology Q 1:155–175, 1987

Polednak AP: Host Factors in Disease: Age, Sex, Race, and Ethnic Group. Springfield, MA, CC Thomas, 1987

Polgar S: Health Action in Cross-Cultural Perspective. In Freeman HE, Levine S, Reader LG (eds): Handbook of Medical Scoiology. Englewood Cliffs, NJ, Prentice Hall, 1963

Rhodes LA: Studying Biomedicine as a Cultural System. In Johnson TM, Sargent CF (eds): Medical Anthropology: Contemporary Theory and Method. New York, Praeger, 1990

Rubel AJ, O'Nell CW, Collado-Ardon R: Susto, A Folk Illness. Berkeley, University of California Press, 1984

Scheper-Hughes N: Saints, Scholars and Schizophrenics. Berkeley, University of California Press, 1979

Scheper-Hughes N: Child Survival: Anthropological Perspectives on the Treatment and Maltreatment of Children. Dordrecht, Reidel Publishing Company, 1987

Scheper-Hughes N, Lock M: The mindful body: A prolegomenon to future work in medical anthropology. Med Anthropology Q 1(1):6–41, 1987

Schreiber JM, Homiak JP: Mexican Americans. In Harwood A (ed): Ethnicity and Medical Care. Cambridge, Harvard University Press, 1981

Simons RC, Hughes CC: Culture-Bound Syndromes: Folk Illnesses of Psychiatric and Anthropological Interest. Dordrecht, Reidel Publishing Company, 1985

Snow L: Traditional health beliefs and practices among lower class black Americans. West J Med 139:16–24, 1983

Snow LF: Walkin' Over Medicine. Boulder, CO, Westview Press, 1993

Spector RE: Cultural Diversity in Health and Illness. Norwalk, CT, Appleton-Century-Crofts, 1985

Spiro M: Oedipus in the Trobriands. Chicago, University of Chicago Press, 1982

Spurlock J: Black Americans. In Gaw A (ed): Cross-Cultural Psychiatry. Boston, John Wright-PSG, 1982

Spurlock J, Lawrence LE: The black child. In Noshpitz JD (ed): Basic Handbook of Child Psychiatry. New York, Basic Books, 1979

Szaz TS: The Myth of Mental Illness. New York, Harper & Row, 1974

Whiting JW, Whiting BB: Children of Six Cultures: A Psychocultural Analysis. Cambridge, Harvard University Press, 1975

Wilson EO: On Human Nature. Cambridge, Harvard University Press, 1978

Zborowski M: Cultural components in response to pain. J Soc Issues 8:16–30, 1952

Zola IK: Structural constraints in the doctor–patient relationship: The case of non-compliance. In Eisberg L, Kleinman A (eds): The Relevance of Social Science for Medicine. Dordrecht, Reidel Publishing Company, 1981

II Major Psychological Theories of Human Behavior

Alan Stoudemire (ed). *Human Behavior: An Introduction for Medical Students,* Second Edition. Copyright © 1994, 1990 by J. B. Lippincott Company.

5 *Psychoanalytic Psychology*

Lawrence B. Inderbitzin and Mark E. James

Chapters 5 and 6 focus on several major psychological approaches that have been developed to understand human behavior. This chapter examines *psychoanalytic* theory, and Chapter 6 by Dr. Dorsett explores *behavioral/learning* schools of psychology. The decision to present only these two major branches of psychology is based on (1) the practical limitations of space imposed by the length of this book; (2) the goal of focusing on the *essential* principles of understanding human behavior; (3) the fact that psychoanalytic and behavioral/learning approaches to behavior are fundamental in understanding other schools of psychology; and (4) the fact that these theories have received the most widespread application in understanding and managing the problems of psychiatric and medical patients.

Important psychological concepts derived from other theories, however, are discussed and integrated into other chapters in the text. For example, the cognitive psychology of Jean Piaget is discussed in Chapter 8 by Dr. Dulcan, family systems theory is discussed in Chapter 9 by Dr. Fiore, the life cycle developmental theory of Erik Erikson is discussed in Chapter 11 by Dr. van der Kolk, and theories of attachment behavior are elaborated in Chapter 10 by Drs. Wolman and Thompson. Therefore, while Chapters 5 and 6 present the two most widely used *fundamental* theories for understanding human behavior, other important concepts are integrated throughout the text, emphasizing the importance of reading this text as a whole rather than in parts.

For a more thorough introduction to psychoanalytic concepts, the introductory texts by Brenner, Nemiah, Engel, and Malan are recommended (see Annotated Bibliography). Readers are referred to standard comprehensive textbooks of psychiatry for information regarding contributions to understanding human behavior by individuals such as Allport, Maslow, Lewin, Adler, Rank, Klein, Reich, Horney, Sullivan, Fairbairn, Balint, and Winnicott. We begin now with a comprehensive discussion of psychoanalytic theory.

PSYCHOANALYTIC THEORY

There are three fundamental aspects to psychoanalytic psychology: (1) a *method of investigation* of the mind; (2) a *general theory* of human behavior; and (3) a *method of treatment* for certain psychological disorders. This chapter discusses basic concepts primarily related to the latter two. Psychoanalysis grew from medical roots and was begun and initially developed by neurologist Sigmund Freud. From its beginning, psychoanalysis was oriented toward seeking the *origins* of psychological disturbances and understanding how the biologically endowed infant developed in interaction with the environment. Contrary to popular belief, Freud emphasized the importance and interplay of *both* biological and environmental influences throughout his writings (1905, 1916–1917), a view that is consistent with the general bio-psychosocial philosophy of this text.

While psychoanalytic concepts facilitate a comprehensive approach to under-standing personality, they also have many practical applications in understanding the emotional reactions of patients during the stress of physical illness. For example, under the stress of physical illness, some patients will "regress" to more childlike behavior and have intense emotional reactions directed toward their physicians that often require specific interventions. The following case study demonstrates some of these principles.

A CASE STUDY

A 45-year-old woman was hospitalized for the evaluation of pelvic pain. She was eventually diagnosed with ovarian cancer in an early stage, and her physicians felt she was a good candidate for surgery. As the di-agnosis and nature of her illness were explained, she listened quietly with a passive, bland facial expression. When asked if she had any ques-tions, she said simply that there must have been a mistake "during all the testing," and that she was sure she did not have cancer because she could "just feel" that she did not. Over the next 24 hours, she began to insist that there would have been a clear message from "the Lord" di-rectly to her if such a serious illness were present and that she could not allow surgical treatment for "something that isn't there anyway." She had been a religious woman in a traditional manner all her life and had not spoken of such direct communications from God in the past. She had no history of psychiatric illness and was described by her husband as "very strong and always in control of her emotions."

Her primary physician had several interviews with her over the next 2 days, listening patiently as she expressed her certainty that everything was "ok" and no treatment was needed. Without argument or confronta-

tion, the physician calmly repeated his diagnostic impressions and rec-
ommendations at the close of each meeting. On one occasion, the patient
became slightly tearful as she was assuring the physician that there had
been an error in the tests. The physician remarked that it would be very
frightening, in any case, to be told that one had cancer and needed an
operation. The woman cried more deeply and apologized for "acting like
a baby." As she felt permission to cry and to be afraid, she sobbed with
the physician and then with her family as she began to agree that the
evaluation had been carefully performed and the appropriate treatment
should begin.

In the face of the extreme stress of learning she had cancer, this pa-
tient had regressed to a more primitive level of functioning. Her defen-
sive denial was not characteristic of her previous personality style and
represented her effort to maintain her sense of strength and emotional
control. To acknowledge illness and fear was to "act like a baby" and
might have felt like risking the loss of the love of her family members
around whom she was always strong and in control. The physician was
empathic and respectful of his patient's psychologic needs and conflicts.
He tried to understand the feelings behind the patient's defenses, and he
allowed the patient to maintain her defensive posture and resulting
equilibrium until she felt safe and supported enough to accept the pain-
ful current reality.

As will be seen in the subsequent sections of this chapter, certain psychoanalytic concepts such as regression, defenses, ego strength, and transference can assist and deepen an understanding of the patient's behavior and facilitate the most effective way of helping a patient such as this through the course of an illness (see Table 5–1).

FUNDAMENTAL CONCEPTS

In developing psychoanalysis, Freud's methodology was essentially empiric. Because his theories were influenced by the science of his time (Helmholtz School), it is easily overlooked that the fundamental concepts are firmly rooted in clinical observations. In any scientific theory there is an interrelationship between the various hypotheses and concepts, with some being more basic and better established than others. In psychoanalytic theory, its various components are sometimes referred to as "points of view" (Rapaport, 1960).

The concept of *psychic determinism* provides the orienting attitude and groundwork on which everything else in psychoanalytic theory rests. It means that *all psychological events are determined by antecedent ones and that nothing occurs by chance in mental life.* The *unconscious or topographic point of view,* like psychic determinism, is so well established that these two hypotheses have been described as "established laws of the mind" (Brenner, 1974, p 2). The term *uncon-scious* means *unnoticeable* and refers to mental processes and content that are

(text continues on page 113)

Table 5–1 **Glossary of Key Concepts**

Adaptive point of view

The human organism has evolved to adapt to external reality; the ego has developed as an internal regulator of behavior and as an "organ" of adaptation.

Anal

This psychosexual stage occurs from 18 months to 3 years, during which anal sphincter control evolves and the child is aware of bowel function; pleasure is attained from anal and rectal stimulation through defecation and retention of feces; at this time, the child is involved with issues of mastery and autonomy, and conflicts emerge between obedience and defiance.

Character (personality) disorder

A disturbance of the personality involving habitual inflexibility of patterns of behavior without significant subjective discomfort; behavior is *ego-syntonic* in that the patient views it as appropriate, reasonable, and justified; yet the outcome of such behavior often results in problems for the patient.

Compromise formation

Activity or product of the functioning of the ego that balances the gratification of drives with the opposition against such gratification; although the instinctual drives and their associated unconscious wishes continually push for expression, this is opposed by the adaptation of the person to reality and by inner standards and morals; the ego allows for the gratification of drives in a disguised, substitute, or partial form, which is consciously unrecognizable as such; most mental events are the product of compromise formation; those that come to attention clinically are referred to as neurotic symptoms.

Conscious

Mental processes consisting of the ordinary stream of thoughts and emotions, which are actively experienced as they occur; these obey rational, secondary process logic; used as a noun or adjective.

Countertransference

The feelings and attitudes of the therapist toward the patient, which may arise from activation of conflicts from the therapist's own past, or which may be a result of the patient's projections onto the therapist; countertransference may negatively impact the therapeutic approach toward the patient or may provide a source of data about unconscious processes occurring in the patient.

Defense mechanisms

Specific unconscious mental methods used by the ego to protect against the danger of conscious awareness of repressed drives or wishes associated with the real or imagined punishments of childhood.

Developmental point of view

Behavior is a product of both intrinsic factors and interaction of the person with the environment, but these change in an expectable sequence during the course of development; all behaviors form a continuum dating back to earliest infancy, and most symptoms relate to past experience during development.

Dynamic-motivational point of view

Psychoanalysis explains human behavior and mental phenomena as being motivated by goal-directed forces (wishes or needs inherent in the nature of humans), which may be in opposition to one another, resulting in conflicts and compromise formations.

Dynamic unconscious

The processes and contents of the "system unconscious" held out of conscious awareness by the action of repression; they strive for discharge but are abhorrent or threatening morally, so this resulting conflict causes anxiety; if the repression fails, neurotic symptoms may result.

(continued)

Table 5–1 *(continued)*

Ego

In Freud's structural model, it is the agency of the mind that mediates between id drives, external reality, and the prohibitions of the superego, working to facilitate maximal gratification while simultaneously adapting to external and internal moral standards; its complex set of functions includes reality testing, regulation of drives, relationships with other people and mental representations of others, thought processes (organizing perceptions, forming conclusions, remembering, concentrating, learning, judgment, and so forth), defense mechanisms, autonomous functions (perception, motor function, intention, intelligence, language), and synthetic, integrating, and organizing functions.

Ego-ideal

Subgroup of superego functions that includes goals, ideals, and standards of exemplary achievement; it serves to regulate mood, behavior, and self-esteem through the generation of affects or shame.

Empathy

A special way of knowing or perceiving the emotional psychological state of another; one person momentarily shares the quality of feelings possessed by another person.

Free association

The method of operation by the patient in psychoanalysis in which he or she thinks freely and reports everything that comes to mind without the usual selectiveness used in conventional discourse.

Id

In Freud's structural model, unconscious collection of drives, urges, and wishes that continually push for complete gratification despite reality.

Insight

The subjective experiential knowledge of formerly unconscious pathogenic mental content and conflicts that occurs during the process of psychoanalysis and is accompanied by adaptive behavioral changes.

Instinctual drives

Innate inner stimuli that motivate the organism toward gratification, usually through another person; the two basic instinctual drives are the *sexual* and the *aggressive*.

Interpretation

Therapeutic intervention by the analyst to assist the patient to become aware of inner mental conflicts and ideas that had been excluded from consciousness, with the goal of accomplishing self-knowledge and symptomatic improvement.

Latency

This stage lasts from approximately age 5 to 12; the sexual drives and conflicts are less apparent as the major activities of this time period are learning and other socially approved channels of gratification; this is a period of considerable development of the ego.

Metapsychology

A highly abstract conceptual framework for organizing, systematizing, and orienting clinical data.

Neurosis

A mental disturbance involving abnormalities of thought, behavior, attitudes, and emotions; classic neuroses include hysteria, obsessions, phobias, and depression; the symptoms of neurosis are *ego-dystonic* (i.e., they are recognized by the patients as abnormal and alien to the self).

Object

A person or thing through which instinctual needs can be gratified or expressed; the inner mental schemas that conceptualize other persons are referred to as *object representations;* the area of study that explores the relationship of the self to inner objects is the theory of *object relations;* some include interpersonal relations in this definition.

(continued)

Table 5–1 *(continued)*

Oral

The psychosexual phase during the first 18 months of life during which the mouth, lips, and tongue are the major source of sensual pleasure; because the infant is dependent on the mother during this stage, optimal development allows the infant to acquire a sense of trust and a sense that the world is safe and needs will be met.

Phallic–oedipal

The psychosexual stage occurring between the ages of 3 and 6; this phase begins as the penis or clitoris becomes the major source of sensual pleasure; the child develops an intense desire to possess exclusively the parent of the opposite sex and to eliminate the perceived rival other parent; the jealous conflict of a triangular relationship, with attendant fantasies related to castration, leads eventually to identification with the parents and the development of the superego.

Pleasure–unpleasure principle

The tendency of the mind to work toward achieving pleasure and avoiding unpleasure; according to Freud, this serves to reduce the amount of drive tension or mental stimulation, because pleasure represents a discharge of mental energy, and unpleasure represents an increase in undischarged mental energy.

Preconscious

In Freud's topographic model, psychic material not occurring as "deeply" in the mind as conscious or unconscious material; can be experienced consciously through attention.

Primary process

Type of thought occurring in the unconscious, characterized by irrationality, wishfulness, and domination by emotions and instinctual drives; the logic of primary process uses mechanisms seen in dreams such as displacement, condensation, and symbolization.

Psychic determinism

All psychologic events in the present are influenced and shaped by past experiences; nothing in mental life occurs solely by chance.

Repetition compulsion

The tendency to repeat periodically the same, usually painful, experience; this is also referred to as the "neurosis of destiny"; because repetition compulsion is closely linked historically and conceptually with Freud's idea of death instinct, the more recent term "compulsion to repeat" may be preferable.

Resistance

The automatic opposition to free association that is activated to protect against the emergence of awareness of inner unconscious conflicts.

Secondary process

Rational, logical, controlled thinking that characterizes the ordinary conscious stream of thought.

Stages of psychosexual development

(See *oral, anal,* and *phallic*—the three stages.) Regular sequence of development of the instinctual drives; the expression of drives centers on and is organized around specific sensual anatomical regions (oral, anal, and phallic), which change in pleasurable emphasis in a specific inborn order as the infant grows and develops; multiple other developmental phenomena occur during these stages and are interwoven with the psychosexual phenomena during each phase. (See Fig. 5–1).

Structural model

Freud's later model (following topographic model) of psychic functioning, which categorizes three mental structures (see *ego, id,* and *superego*) defined as collections of psychological processes and functions.

(continued)

Table 5–1   *(continued)*

Superego

In Freud's structural model, the group of mental functions that represent morals, standards (see also *ego-ideal*), prohibitions, and conscience, and generate the affects of guilt and shame; it is acquired through internalization of parental figures through identification.

Therapeutic alliance

The rational, nonneurotic, conscious relationship between patient and doctor based on the mutual agreement to work together for the patient's benefit.

Topographic model

Freud's first model (the structural model followed) of psychic functioning, which classifies three "regions" (see *conscious, preconscious,* and *unconscious*) of mental operations in terms of their relationship to consciousness.

Transference

The unconscious displacement of feelings, attitudes, and expectations from important persons in the patient's childhood to current relationships.

Unconscious

Everything in the mind outside of normal conscious awareness; processes here are irrational, obey primary process logic, and may be revealed through dreams, a slip of the tongue (parapraxis), or free associations.

---

significant and important in determining behavior but of which the person is *unaware. Unconscious* is used in psychoanalysis both as an adjective and a noun, and the latter refers to a portion of the mind sometimes called the *dynamic unconscious,* which contains drives, feelings, and ideas held out of conscious awareness by countering forces.

Freud's first theory of the mind and of intrapsychic conflict was the *topographic model* in which the mind was divided into *conscious, unconscious* (repressed), and *preconscious* (the preconscious being capable of becoming conscious under directed attention). The *conscious* province of the mind was governed primarily by what was referred to as *secondary process* (rational, logical thinking). The unconscious, on the other hand, was governed by different laws referred to as *primary process*—irrational thought processes that defy Aristotelian logic and are closely linked to emotional states; primary process includes the type of symbolic thought that characteristically occurs in dreams.

Freud (1900) wrote *The Interpretation of Dreams* within the framework of the topographic model, which subsequently (Freud, 1923) became subordinate to the *structural model* (discussed later). Freud's monumental discoveries about the meaning of dreams also served to confirm the significant findings from his earlier research with hysteria, such as the importance of the unconscious, the instinctual drives, and the influence of past developmental experiences on the present. His understanding of dreams led to the formulation of a new general psychology.

Dreams

In respect to dream theory, current evidence indicates that dreams serve a variety of purposes, including activation of brain circuitry to maintain the functional integrity of dendritic and synaptic connections, storage of memories, and the integration of data about new life experiences with preexisting cognitive and emotional response patterns (Winson, 1985). According to psychoanalytic theory, one of the most important functions of dreaming is the expression, fulfillment, or gratification of unconscious infantile wishes or impulses in a disguised or difficult to recognize form. Put simply, the dream is a coded message and *represents a wish fulfillment.*

On awakening, the dream that is consciously remembered is referred to as the *manifest dream.* It is never what it seems to be, but rather, is a product of the action of dream activity on the *latent dream content,* which consists of unconscious infantile urges, wishes, and conflicts. The dream is also shaped by one's ongoing daily concerns, known as the *day residue,* and by any physical sensations occurring during sleep, such as discomfort or noise.

The mental activity that transforms the latent dream content into the manifest dream is referred to as the *dream work.* Unconscious impulses, memories, day residue, and physical sensations are reworked, disguised, and distorted during the dream work by specific mechanisms described by Freud. *Condensation* is the process by which a large amount of unconscious material is combined and expressed in a single event or image in the manifest dream. Often one thing in the manifest dream represents the simultaneous expression of multiple unconscious urges, conflicts, or thoughts and feelings. *Displacement* is the mechanism that disguises the meaning of the dream by changing the object toward which the impulse is directed or the person to whom the feeling is attached. This results in the strange or illogical quality of dream imagery. The emotional charge belonging to an important latent idea is transferred to a more neutral or innocuous manifest image. Foreground material in the *manifest* dream may then represent less significant *latent* content, whereas some of the lesser events in the manifest dream may be associated with more important latent content. *Symbolism* is the mechanism by which an unconscious idea is represented metaphorically in the manifest dream by something else. Finally, in the *dream work,* the various distorted themes and images are woven into a relatively coherent story line, a process known as *secondary elaboration.*

In psychoanalysis, dream analysis can lead to insights about defensive processes and resistances, the state of the transference, and important childhood events in addition to unconscious instinctual strivings (wishes). In early psychoanalytic history, dreams were considered *the* "royal road to the unconscious," in contrast to the current view that dreams are *one* important and unique source of data for analysis.

A CASE STUDY

A young man in psychotherapy had often described the anger he felt as a child toward his mother, and a dream helped to provide a better understanding of this anger. He depicted his mother as self-centered, inhibited, and depressed. He suspected she was sexually frigid with his father. In recent sessions he felt envious of his psychiatrist. He reported a dream: "I was in a hospital and realized I was an intern. I was wheeling a woman on a gurney. She was supposed to have a complicated operation but it's like she was going to die anyway. She looked like my friend's mother. Then I was in my parents' basement where my father

*had a workshop, and the woman was lying on the workbench. I was sup-
posed to perform the operation but didn't know what to do. I put a big
pill into her mouth. Then I woke up. I felt anxious."*

*He noted that certain aspects of the woman in the dream also re-
minded him of his mother. He began talking for the first time about a
wish he had had throughout much of his life—that he could somehow
make his mother feel better, make her happier, so she would love him
and respond to him. The psychiatrist made a mental note of the oedipal
wish also expressed in the dream, of the patient operating on his mother
on his father's workbench, and its similarity to his replacing his father
in the parental bed. Toward the end of the session the patient stated, "I'd
like to bring her here so you could cure her, but there's something about
the idea of her lying on your couch that makes me angry."*

The Dynamic Point of View

The description of the unconscious and the topographic model continues with
the *dynamic or motivational point of view*. Freud's belief that behavior is in part
determined by *wishes* or *needs* ("instinctual drives" in psychoanalytic theory) that
are biologically derived was based on two familiar observations: (1) that behavior is
not always triggered by external stimulation but often occurs without it, as though
spontaneously; and (2) behavior, in general, may be observed to have causally determined goal-directed components (Rapaport, 1960, p 48).

Experienced as an inner pressure, the instinctual drives in Freud's theory aim
toward satisfaction, guided by the compass of "the pleasure-unpleasure principle
leading toward activities that provide gratification and away from those that provide
pain" (Cooper et al, 1989, p 2). Instinctual drives require something (usually termed
object in psychoanalytic theory) through which or in regard to which they can achieve
their aims, and the coordination between drive and object are now assumed to be
guaranteed by evolution (i.e., the infant's need to nurse at the mother's breast).

It is important to note that the instinctual drives of humans differ significantly
from the instincts of other animals. *"Instincts" refers to innate, biologically inherited propensities to respond in stereotypic ways that have individual or species
survival value.* Certain complex behaviors of animals, such as mating rituals and
migrations of birds, have survival value and are *unlearned*. The instinctual drives of
humans, while they may have great compelling force, do not always *necessarily* have
survival value. In addition, because of intelligence factors, humans have a great
capacity for learning and problem solving (an *ego* capacity in psychoanalytic terms)
that, coupled with a long and complex process of social and emotional development,
leads to extensive plasticity and adaptability.

Two basic drives are most often emphasized by psychoanalysts, the *sexual* and
the *aggressive*. Although Freud defined sexual in a broad way, equating it with
sensual or pleasurable (1905), the term sexual drive has continued to be *erroneously*
used as a synonym for sex and/or for sexual intercourse. In most of the manifestations
of the drives that we can observe, the sexual and the aggressive components are
intermingled. Although part of our constitutional endowment, the instinctual drives

undergo a complex development (psychosexual development) and will be described later in conjunction with the *developmental point of view*.

The ***adaptive point of view*** in psychoanalytic theory refers to external reality as a source of stimuli, and this thesis has undergone greater change in psychoanalytic psychology than any other (Rapaport, 1960). Of central importance are the contributions of Hartmann (1939, 1948, 1958). The human organism from this point of view is considered to be a product of evolution and is born preadapted to reality. The ego develops as an internal regulator of behavior and becomes the human's "organ of adaptation." Reality and adaptation "are the matrix of all behavior" (Rapaport, 1960, pp 60–61).

The ***developmental hypothesis***, or the *genetic point of view* (the term *genetic* referring here to a process of development—not in the sense of cell biology) was implicit even in Freud's earliest work. From this point of view, every behavior is the product of two basic interacting factors: (1) intrinsic forces, which are *antecedent* to and *independent* of experience; and (2) *experiential* factors, which are based on learning or other forms of environmental influence. In this conception, all behaviors are part of a continuum extending back to earliest infancy. Furthermore, development is not a straight line process forward but rather occurs in a series of progressions and regressions. The clinically important concepts of regression and fixation are interrelated and are intrinsic aspects of the developmental hypothesis.

Regression, mentioned earlier as a frequent behavioral reaction observed in patients during the stress of both physical and psychiatric illness, refers to the *turning back* from a more mature pattern of behavior to a more immature or childlike state of feeling and thinking. The process of regression often serves a self-protective or defensive purpose. The following case history is illustrative of this process.

A CASE STUDY

A 55-year-old university professor was transferred to the oncology unit after being diagnosed with colon cancer. After surgery that resulted in a colostomy, he became increasingly withdrawn and uncommunicative. He told his physician that he was certain his wife of 30 years no longer loved him, and he wondered if she would continue to visit. He became apathetic and uninvolved in his treatment, even though his physicians were optimistic about his prognosis. He began to depend on the nurses for bathing and feeding, acting as if he were physically incapable of managing himself. A formerly proud, independent, and dignified man, his behavior became more dependent and helpless. He complained, whined, and became angry when his demands were not immediately met.

This patient "regressed" to an earlier mode of functioning in reaction to the diagnosis of cancer. Such regression of ego functioning is often associated with the development of depression, increased dependency needs, and preoccupation with the fears characteristic of early childhood. In this case, the patient subsequently revealed that he experienced his surgery not only as a mutilation of his body but was ashamed and embarrassed by the loss of control of his bowels imposed by the colos-

tomy. He also felt helpless, afraid, and had an intense need to be cared for, but hated these feelings of dependency at the same time.

The concept of *fixation* refers to an arrest or failure in the developmental process. There is a tendency for areas of development that are not fully mastered to retain a component of continued or unresolved emphasis in the person's behavior that plays a role in later personality functioning. The concepts of fixation and regression are strongly linked to each other because under stress there is a tendency of patients to *regress* to stages of developmental immaturity in which they may be *fixated*. In Freud's thinking, the degree of *regression* was determined in part by the level of the patient's developmental immaturity or "point of fixation" in psychosexual development. These ideas were central in his thinking about the etiology of neurosis. The following elaboration of the developmental hypothesis will help to clarify these concepts further.

PSYCHOSEXUAL DEVELOPMENT

Based on evidence from adult and childhood analyses as well as child observations, Freud postulated an inborn developmental sequence of *psychosexual stages* according to which areas of the body progressively achieved primacy in regard to certain pleasurable sensations and activities. He termed these modes of functioning *oral, anal,* and *phallic*. Under normal circumstances Freud postulated that there is a more or less orderly progression from one "zone" to the next, with each phase merging into the next as psychosexual development proceeds. However, conflicts at any stage of development could result in fixation and regression to an earlier unmastered developmental phase.

The *oral stage* of psychosexual development in this theory occurs approximately during the first year and a half of life. During this stage, the mouth, lips, and tongue are the primary areas of pleasurable sensations and gratification; and the majority of the child's activities and relationships to others occur principally through the oral cavity and mucosa. The prototype of oral pleasure is the baby nursing at the breast. This is a period of absolute dependence on the mother for nourishment, pleasurable sensation, and a secure atmosphere. A sense of trust should develop that the world is a safe place and that the child's basic needs will be met.

Evidence of difficulties encountered during the oral period of development are sometimes revealed in the personalities of adults, especially during times of stress, as in the following case.

A CASE STUDY

A 30-year-old woman was followed as an outpatient in a general medical practice. She tended to be unusually clinging and dependent on the physician for reassurance, although she recognized that she was basically physically healthy. She was extremely sensitive to the slightest delay and sometimes remarked that her physician was not "warm

enough," never gave her enough time, and probably "really didn't care."
She often made demands for medication and had a tendency to become
dependent on tranquilizers and sleeping pills. In expressing her need
for a secure, consistent, and dependable caretaker, she was both clinging
and needy but, at the same time, was unable to trust her physician, and
was silently resentful toward him. Exploration of her early family life
revealed evidence of a cold, inconsistent, and neglectful mother who gave
little emotional nurturance to her children, leaving them with unmet
yearnings to be cared for, nurtured, and protected.

Such personality traits and modes of interpersonal behavior may result from fixation at and/or regression to the oral phase of development. This period of infancy is marked by feelings of helplessness, dependency, and need for nurturance and protection. Children who are neglected, deprived, or abused, either physically or emotionally during this period of development may experience a lifelong unmet intense "hunger" for love and may feel a sense of insecurity accompanied by a basic mistrust of others; they often both expect and fear that they will be hurt or rejected in interpersonal relationships. These difficulties with trust, attachment, and commitment may be complicated by a sense that they are unlovable or not worthwhile. When unmet needs of love, mixed with fear of rejection and feelings of anger, frustration, low self-esteem, and depression become intrinsic parts of the personality makeup, there are often also difficulties establishing stable adult relationships. This stage of development is also discussed in the context of attachment theory in Chapters 8 and 9 and Eriksonian psychosocial theory in Chapter 10. The neurobiological effects of developmental trauma in this phase of development are discussed in Chapter 11.

The *anal stage*, which Freud termed *sadistic–anal* to emphasize the importance of the *aggressive* drive in this stage, occurs from about *18 months to 3 years*. The anal and rectal mucosa, as well as the feces themselves, are a main source of both pleasurable and unpleasurable sensations, which become a focus of the child's interest. During this period, anal sphincter control develops, and the child acquires a sense of mastery and autonomy. Struggles for control often ensue as the child has more freedom to produce or withhold bowel movements. The child simultaneously begins to experience some degree of independence and a new sense of control over other aspects of life.

Developmental issues at this stage are marked by struggles over control versus lack of control, obedience versus defiance, protest versus submission, and giving versus withholding, leading to the unfortunate labeling of this period as the "terrible twos." The frequent use of the word "no" is not necessarily a sign of defiance and stubbornness but a way of the child to assert his or her own needs and wishes, resist unwanted intrusion of the parents, and protect self-interests independent of the wishes of the parents. It is a time when the child is testing his or her assertion, aggression, and independence, and represents an effort to exert some degree of independent control. Problems during this stage of development are often associated with family environments that are strict, rigid, overly controlling, critical, and emotionally constricted. Children's early attempts at expressing anger and assertiveness are sometimes responded to with severe criticism and punishment in such settings, resulting in the perception that certain emotions are bad, dangerous, or unacceptable. The resentment and frustrations of being unable to express their own angry feelings are then repressed and may require rigid personality defenses to maintain a sense of control. Such persons as adults may appear to be emotionally rigid, aloof, and constrained, and have difficulties expressing affectionate as well as angry feelings. In psychiatric terminology these traits are characteristic of *obsessive–compulsive* personalities.

A critical, demanding, perfectionistic family atmosphere may contribute to smoldering resentment. This situation, combined with a fear of expressing their feelings, makes the core problem of obsessive-compulsive patients one of unresolved anger and fear of both punishment and loss of the parent's love and approval. Attempts to gain parental love by achieving and being "perfect" may become a driving force in the personality. Hence, the person's self-esteem becomes overly dependent on productivity and approval from external sources. The following is illustrative.

A CASE STUDY

A 40-year-old businessman was admitted to the hospital for evaluation of abdominal pain. He was polite, but his manner was formal, tense, controlled, and emotionally distant. While undergoing diagnostic procedures, he appeared constantly indecisive, demanding a thorough and logical explanation for each step in the diagnostic process. He was stubborn at times and submitted slowly and reluctantly to the most routine recommendations and requests. He experienced the medical workup as an issue of control and as being "forced" into something he did not want to do.

This patient's behavior indicated a central conflict reflecting ambivalence over the childhood issue, "Should I obey or say 'no'?" If the physician respects this sort of patient's need for control and independence and provides careful detailed explanations, "power struggles" and treatment failures can often be avoided.

According to Freud, the *phallic*, or the *phallic–oedipal* stage, is next to occur and extends from about age 3 to age 6. The leading organ of pleasure during this stage is the phallus (the penis for the boy and the clitoris for the girl), and masturbatory stimulation results in pleasure that more closely approaches the usual sense of the word "sexual" (see also Chapters 7 and 8).

Freud considered the *Oedipus complex*, which occurs during this stage of development, to be of central importance in both normal and pathologic psychologic development. The central defining features of the Oedipus complex relate to the attitude of the child toward the parent of the opposite sex. From the little boy's perspective, he wishes to possess mother exclusively and eliminate father; from the little girl's perspective, the wish is to eliminate mother and take her place with father. In order to fully understand and appreciate the Oedipus complex and its decisive influence on subsequent development and functioning, several factors need to be further emphasized.

By the age of 4 or 5, the child has reached a level of development of conceptual thinking characterized by a *qualitative* as well as a *quantitative* difference in perceptual and cognitive capacities. Children are able to fantasize and to recognize within themselves the existence of feelings of love, hate, jealousy, and fear, much as they occur in later life. Furthermore, they are able to perceive their parents not only in terms of their sexual differences but also in terms of the parents having some kind of relationship including a sexual one, from which the child is excluded. This *triangular* relationship is characteristic of the oedipal phase and differentiates it from the "preoedipal" child's relationships, which are predominantly dyadic or "two-wayed." In addition, the intensity of the feelings associated with the Oedipus complex is comparable to the most passionate love affair in adult life. The child's situation may be further complicated by the fact that the jealously hated rival—the parent of the same sex—is also someone who is loved. Wishes to eliminate the feared and hated rival may result in intense fears of punishment for these hostile wishes but also the threat of the loss of the parent's love.

As the little boy enters the oedipal phase, his primary attachment is already to his mother, and his developing mental fantasy life begins to center on wanting to possess her exclusively in some sexual way, which is still poorly defined in his mind. The stirrings within him are expressed in wishes such as to look at her, touch her, and marry her. He may show increasing jealousy and hostility toward his father, who is viewed as a rival for mother's affections, that culminate in wishes to get rid of father in some way. Resultant fears that father will find out about his wishes and retaliate by punishing him, possibly by even castrating him, combined with his wishes to maintain his loving relationship with his father, lead him to renounce his wishes for mother and to strengthen his *identification* with father. It is as if the little boy says to himself, "I can't have Mommy, so I'll give up my wishes for her and grow up to be like Daddy and marry someone like Mommy."

The situation with the little girl is more complicated and also extremely controversial. Freud (1925) thought that the little girl's first "phallic" impulses were directed toward the mother just like the little boy's and that her attention was focused on her clitoris much like the little boy's is focused on his penis. Thus, the little girl's oedipal phase *begins* with masculine strivings. When the little girl discovers the little boy's penis, she feels that her clitoris is "inferior" and experiences this as a "narcissistic injury," a degrading humiliation that leads both to "penis envy" and a blaming of her mother for the plight. According to classic Freudian theory, this leads to a relinquishing of mother as the primary source of love and a turning to the father in hopes that he will provide her with a penis or a baby as a substitute. In the little girl's mind, her mother now becomes the jealous rival. Freud (1925, p 256) thought, *"Whereas in boys the Oedipus complex is destroyed by the castration complex, in girls it is made possible and led up to by the castration complex."* The oedipal dynamics of girls tend to be repressed relatively less than the oedipal conflict of boys, possibly due to the relatively lesser quantity of anxiety over the threat of genital damage in comparison to boys. Hence girls continue during development to be more noticeably attached to their fathers and more openly in conflict with their mothers. Freudian theory holds that threats of punishment, loss of love, or the fantasy of genital damage by the father's penis normally contribute to repression and resolution of this conflict.

Freud believed, then, that feminine identification is a developmental by-product of a primary sense of *genital inferiority*, and that *penis envy*, the discontent with one's own genitals and the desire to possess a penis or other masculine qualities, persists unconsciously as a core determinant of personality in women. This theory emphasized only what the little girl does not have rather than what she does have. Although many psychoanalysts have reported findings from selected patients that tended to confirm Freud's view of female sexual development, others such as Stoller (1968, 1976), Blum (1976), and Kleeman (1976) have reported evidence of a girl's *primary femininity* as had been proposed much earlier by Horney (1926), Jones (1927), and Fenichel (1945). Current theory derived from clinical work and observation of children (Chehrazi, 1986) indicates that early in development girls recognize and form mental representations of their genitals and experience them in a positive and pleasurable way. Identifying with the mother and expressing wishes for a baby occur prior to the oedipal conflict. (Additionally, a boy may also experience a sense of genital inferiority as he recognizes in fantasy that "his penis is much too small for his mother's genital and [he] reacts with the dread of his own inadequacy, of being dejected and derided" [Horney, 1932].)

The recognition of anatomical differences is an important event for both sexes. Some girls may experience curiosity and envy for the penis as a transient phase specific reaction, which is normally worked through and resolved. Derivatives relating to conflicts at this stage of development have been observed to reemerge in some women in the context of regression, neurosis, or narcissistic character pathology, and is evidenced by hostile rivalry toward men with feelings of inadequacy and sexual dysfunction. Freud also suggested that the development of the superego, which occurs as a consequence of resolving the Oedipus complex, is inadequate in women. However, this component of his theory has been discarded, and, in contemporary theory, the female superego is not inferior to the male counterpart but differs in content. Obviously, these theories of female development have incited controversy and severe criticism.

Resolution of the Oedipal Stage

Eventually, for both boys and girls, reality dictates that an exclusive relationship with the parent of the opposite sex is not possible, resulting in the so-called oedipal defeat. Sexual identity becomes crystallized as identifications with the parent of the same sex are solidified. The wish to possess the parent of the opposite sex and the intensely competitive feelings toward the parent of the same sex become repressed. A variety of possible traumas during this period (such as disturbed family interactions; emotional, physical, or sexual abuse; loss of a parent; and illnesses and operations) may contribute to neurotic pathology.

Disturbances in development prior to the oedipal stage often distort the oedipal situations. For example, if a girl has a cold, unavailable, or rejecting mother, she may turn to the father prematurely and intensely for nurturance and support, resulting in an overly sexualized attachment to him in the oedipal period. Anger toward the unempathic or emotionally rejecting mother may persist with an inner core of unmet needs for love and acceptance. In an effort to get father's attention and compete with mother, the prototypical theatrical, dramatic, attention-seeking, seductive "little girl" routine may become a persistent and ingrained personality trait. While these persons may be "seductive" in a sense, the behavior relates unconsciously to the use of their femininity and sexual attractiveness to gain love and attention to compensate for the frustrating relationship with their mother. Hence, adult sexualized relationships have as a fundamental goal securing maternal nurturance and closeness.

In boys, another variant of the oedipal conflict results when a cold, rejecting, or unavailable father provides an untenable model for identification. The boy, therefore, becomes intensely involved with mother and also identifies predominantly with her, leading to the so-called effeminate male or male hysteric. Special problems may result if the father is demeaning, humiliating, or abusive, thereby compounding the sense of anger and frustration in the child through further injuries to his sense of self-esteem. Hence, little boys who are subjected to intense teasing, criticism, and humiliation by their fathers (where the father is competitive with their son for the wife's attention) may develop painful self-doubts about their basic masculinity, adequacy, and competence. The hypermasculine "macho" personality sometimes represents an attempt to compensate for and deny traumatic shame and humiliation experienced during the phallic-oedipal stage of psychosexual development. These persons are recognized in adulthood as always needing to prove their masculinity in various types of hyperaggressive, hypersexual, and risk-taking behaviors.

One classic example of behavior that indicates unresolved oedipal issues in both adult men and women is the repetitive pattern of becoming intensely attracted to persons of the opposite sex whom they "cannot have" or who are in some way unavailable or inappropriate. This is a repetition of the effort to competitively secure love of the unavailable parent of the opposite sex, which was never resolved. The typical dilemma for such persons is that, even if they are eventually able to secure the love of their longed-for romantic object, they may soon lose interest and move on to another "conquest" in an effort to again win love, approval, and affirmation of their self-worth.

There are many other variations on the oedipal theme. Personality characteristics that are often evidence of unresolved oedipal-related issues in adults include intense concerns over competitiveness, envy, rivalry, jealousy with underlying feelings of insecurity, excessive guilt, and conflicts about success.

Massive trauma in psychosexual development can occur if children are subjected to overt sexual molestation, abuse, or incest, or if the parent is covertly and overtly sexually seductive with the child. While sexual abuse was once thought to be a rare event, it has been estimated that as many as 10% to 25% of female children may have been subjected to some form of sexual abuse, with alcoholism in the family being a primary risk factor. While a discussion of the pervasive impact that sexual abuse may have on children's psychosexual development and their later interpersonal and sexual relationships is beyond the scope of this text, one may say that the effects are often devastating and cause lasting problems if psychotherapeutic treatment is not received.

THE DEVELOPMENT OF THE EGO AND THE STRUCTURAL MODEL

We now turn from the subject of the stages of psychosexual development to the concept of the *ego*. In Freud's earliest work, the term *ego* stood for the person, self, or consciousness, which, in turn, was equated with "the dominant mass of ideas" (Freud, 1893–1895, p 116). *Defenses* or *ego defense mechanisms* were associated with consciousness, and the unconscious was used to refer to that part of the mind in which unacceptable wishes, feelings, and ideas were sequestered from conscious awareness.

As Freud developed his psychoanalytic techniques with an increasing emphasis on free association, and his clinical experience expanded, he observed that psychologic defenses against forbidden or painful unconscious material were also unconscious. Furthermore, he recognized that self-punitive tendencies could also be outside of awareness (such as unconscious sense of guilt). These and other observations led to Freud's elaboration of the *structural model* in 1923. "Structure" is not being referred to here in a physical or anatomic sense; in psychoanalytic theory mental structures are defined as those determiners of behavior whose rate of change is slow; therefore, they have a relatively stable, enduring, or permanent quality. The structures of the structural model are *hypothetic constructs* that are defined by their psychological functions in mental life. The three major components of the structural model are the *id, ego*, and *superego*, which are discussed below.

The *id* is closely tied to biological endowment and is considered the source of motivation (instinctual drives). Wishes are considered to be derived from the drives. The id functions unconsciously and in accordance with the *pleasure principle;* that is, it strives for immediate and complete gratification without regard for reality.

The *superego*, which also functions in a largely unconscious manner, includes the moral values, standards, and prohibitions that are internalized in the course of development. The superego or conscience prohibits and is punitive (i.e., by guilt). The superego also includes the *ego ideal*, which embodies the goals and aspirations of the person and is important in the regulation of self-esteem and mood. It originates during early development to compensate for the loss of primary narcissism and is modified during subsequent developmental phases as the idealized qualities of significant others are internalized. Although major internalization of the ego ideal occurs as the oedipal conflict is resolved, this structure reaches its definitive quality during late adolescence (Blos, 1974).

Some analysts consider the ego ideal to be a substructure of the ego rather than the superego, and others think it is an altogether separate mental structure. One major function of the ego ideal is protection against narcissistic injury (damage to self-esteem) because a person can compare his or her thoughts and behavior against internal standards rather than with idealized others. Pathology of the ego ideal contributes to disorders of self-esteem regulation as observed in patients with narcissistic personality disorder and depression (Bibring, 1953; Reich, 1960). Conflict of the ego with the superego can produce the emotions of guilt and/or shame.

Although most analysts agree that the superego as an autonomous, structured, functional entity is established in conjunction with the resolution of the Oedipus complex, its development does not begin or end at this point. The superego is developmentally closely linked to the ego, and both agencies evolve through processes known as *identification* and *internalization*. The external prohibitions and restraints of the parents are transformed into internal regulators by the child because of fear of punishment and need for the parent's love (to offend or displease the parent would bring about rejection). Thus, precursors to the superego begin during the anal stage of development, if not even earlier, and are evidenced by a change from pleasure in messiness and rebellion to pride in cleanliness and control. The postoedipal (approximately ages 6 to 8—early latency) superego is characteristically harsh and severe but not fully reliable in controlling behavior. This severity of superego tends to decrease in late latency (ages 8 to 12). Further transformation in the superego based on new identifications with peers and cultural standards during adolescence result in more autonomy and the ability to make one's own decisions and regulate self-esteem internally. Hence, one begins to make choices based more on one's own value judgment and moral standards rather than being controlled by the dictates of the internalized parental superego developed during childhood. The ego's functions include those that relate to reality (i.e., reality testing and adaptation to reality), regulation of drives and feelings, defensive reactions, relationships to other people, intellectual synthesis and integration, and autonomous activities (perception, cognition, and motility, and so forth). All of these functions undergo a gradual development beginning in infancy. Although some of the ego's functions are conscious, many are unconscious. No sharp line can be drawn between id and ego; they exist on a continuum and cannot be separated except in situations of conflict (Freud A, 1966).

A CASE STUDY

A young married man presented at his doctor's office with symptoms of a urinary tract infection (UTI). Physical examination and laboratory studies verified the diagnosis of a UTI, which responded well to antibiotic therapy. He returned later, however, complaining of unusual sensations in his penis and said that he was certain he had AIDS. Additional testing, including HIV serology, was negative. He insisted that despite the test results he must have AIDS. He complained that he had low energy, felt amotivated, had lost his appetite, and couldn't sleep. As the medical interview continued, he noted that he was feeling depressed and worried. About eight weeks prior to the interview, he had attended a bachelor's party for his best friend at a local establishment where nude dancers performed. He left rather intoxicated and sexually aroused. On the way home he solicited a prostitute to perform oral sex on him. Afterward he immediately felt guilty and ashamed and lapsed into despair. He tortured himself with how he could do such a thing to his wife and young son. During the following weeks he kept secret what had happened but ruminated constantly how "dirty, depraved, and disgusting" he was. Later, when he developed dysuria, he somehow knew he was doomed and had contracted AIDS.

He was referred to a psychiatrist who prescribed antidepressant medication and a course of psychoanalytically oriented psychotherapy. During the psychotherapeutic work it became evident that he set very high standards for himself as a husband and father. He often longed for the freedom of his high school days, but he resolved not to think about it and dedicated himself to his family responsibilities. He had a very strict conscience and often felt guilty in many spheres of his life. He came to realize that believing he had AIDS was in essence a form of self-punishment by which he sentenced himself to death for the "sexual crime" he had committed. His subsequent therapy revealed and highlighted the interaction of the psychic agencies id, ego, superego, and ego ideal in his acute conflicts. He was eventually able to view his sexual indiscretion in a more realistic light, and although he harbored regret and took responsibility for his actions, he realized that his obsession with HIV reflected an unconscious wish for punishment that was out of proportion to his actual behavior.

THE ROLE OF ANXIETY
IN PSYCHOANALYTIC THEORY

In conjunction with the structural theory, Freud described the *central role of anxiety* in mental conflict in another of his major works, *Inhibitions, Symptoms, and Anxiety* (1926). The concept of anxiety is inextricably linked to his theories of neurosis. In two classic psychoanalytic case studies ("Little Hans" and the "Wolf Man"), he recognized that anxiety causes repression (forcing of ideas and feelings into the unconscious) and related the development of anxiety to *four typical danger situations*, each characteristic of a particular stage of development. Freud postulated that when more stimuli occur than can be adequately mastered by the immature ego, the situation becomes traumatic for the child, and anxiety develops.

The first danger situation is loss of the nurturing or caretaking parent, the primary "object" of the child's dependency and love (*loss of the object*). In this situation, the fear is loss of or abandonment by the mother. The next danger situation is fear of the *loss of the parent's love*. By the third or fourth year, the fear is loss of the penis or *castration* in the boy and the analogous fear of *genital damage* in the girl. The fourth danger, according to Freud, occurs in conjunction with the resolution of the Oedipus complex and is the fear of disapproval or punishment by the superego (*guilt*).

An additional aspect of Freud's theory of anxiety is the ego's ability to *anticipate* a danger situation and actively produce a small alerting amount of anxiety, which he called *signal anxiety*. Other feelings, such as depression, can also function in a warning capacity. This signal not only warns of danger but initiates psychologic defensive activities to regulate, control, and ward off the threat from conscious awareness and protect against further disturbing feelings.

THE MECHANISMS OF DEFENSE

In the structural theory, intrapsychic conflict and anxiety are central. According to the *principle of multiple function*, all behavior serves several functions, is responsive to many pressures, or is a solution for many tasks. Thus, for the psychoanalyst, no behavior is *only* what it manifestly seems to be. Instinctual drives, defenses, unpleasurable affects (including guilt from the superego) are the components of psychic conflict that combine to form what Brenner has referred to as *"compromise formations"* (Brenner, 1982). All compromise formations are over-determined (i.e., more than one wish or defense is represented simultaneously in all behaviors).

Ego *mechanisms of defense* are various automatic, involuntary, unconsciously instituted psychological activities that are activated in response to signals of anxiety or other unpleasurable feelings. The phenomenon of *repression* is considered the primary ego defense, and Anna Freud (1936) in her influential book, *The Ego and Mechanisms of Defense*, describes other mechanisms of defense used by the ego, such as identification, isolation of affect, reaction formation, regression, undoing, projection, reversal, turning against the self, and sublimation (Table 5–2). She also notes defenses are often mistakenly equated with psychopathology even though they are a necessary and adaptive aspect of personality development and functioning. The term *defense mechanisms* can be misleading because there are no special ego functions that serve *only* purposes of defense, and any aspect of ego function can be used for defensive purposes (Brenner, 1982).

As previously noted, signal anxiety alerts the ego to a conflictual situation that may lead to a danger situation or a combination of danger situations. The term *defense* indicates the ego's opposition to other components of the conflict, such as unacceptable wishes, painful affects, or self-punitive impulses. The ego's action may be conscious or unconscious and may result in observable behavior or in an inhibition and/or absence of expected behavior. It is important to remember that the ego may defend against a wide range of painful affects, such as depression, guilt, or shame, and that both the objects of defense and the defensive actions are numerous and diverse. For example, one feeling can be used to defend against another, such as an angry contempt of someone to ward off a sense of admiration and envy. Denial may be directed at an aspect of internal reality such as sexual longing or at an external reality such as the death of a loved one. The complex nature of conflict and the principle of multiple function described earlier make it impossible to categorize defenses completely.

Defenses develop in an approximate chronology, and empiric studies demonstrate that defensive styles correlate with independent measures of mental health and certain diagnostic categories (Vaillant, 1986). This has led to systems of classifying defenses (immature, neurotic, and mature) that tend to be oversimplified and perhaps misleading. The most mature person uses "immature" defense at times and vice versa (see Table 5–2). If defenses that are "normal" in early childhood, like denial, projection, and splitting, persist into later years, severe psychopathology may result, such as that seen in patients with borderline personality disorder discussed later in this chapter.

THEORY OF NEUROSIS

The psychoanalytic theory of neurosis is grounded in the structural model. The basic tenet of the structural theory of neurosis is that intrapsychic conflict leads to *compromise* among the agencies of the mind. The extent to which the compromise is

Table 5-2 **Defense Mechanisms**

Delusional projection
Frank delusions about external reality, usually of a persecutory type.

Denial (psychotic)
Denial of external reality.

Distortion
Grossly reshaping external reality to suit inner needs.

Projection
Attributing one's own unacknowledged feelings to others.

Schizoid fantasy
Tendency to use fantasy, autistic retreat, and imaginary relationships for the purpose of conflict resolution and gratification.

Hypochondriasis
The transformation of reproach toward others arising from bereavement, loneliness, or unacceptable aggressive impulses into first self-reproach and then complaints of pain, somatic illness, and neurasthenia.

Passive–aggressive behavior
Aggression toward others expressed indirectly and ineffectively through passivity.

Acting out
Direct expression of an unconscious wish or impulse in order to avoid being conscious of the affect or the ideation that accompanies it.

Dissociation
Temporary but drastic modification of the integration of consciousness or memory, or of one's character or sense of personal identity, to avoid emotional distress.

Repression
Seemingly inexplicable naïveté, memory lapse, or failure to acknowledge input from a selected sense organ.

Displacement
The redirection of conflicted feelings toward a relatively less important object than the person or situation arousing the feelings.

Reaction formation
Conscious affect and/or behavior that is diametrically opposed to an unacceptable instinctual (id) impulse.

Intellectualization
Thinking about instinctual wishes in formal, bland terms that leave the associated affect unconscious.

Altruism
Vicarious but constructive and instinctually gratifying service to others.

Humor
Overt expression of feelings without individual discomfort or immobilization and without unpleasant effect on others.

Suppression
The capacity to hold all components of a conflict in mind and then to postpone action, emotional response, or worrying.

Anticipation
Realistic anticipation of or planning for future inner discomfort.

Sublimation
Indirect or attenuated expression of instincts without adverse consequences or marked loss of pleasure.

(Adapted from Vaillant GE (ed): Empirical Studies of Ego Mechanisms of Defense, pp 105–117. Washington DC, American Psychiatric Press, 1986) "neurotic" is determined by the degree of anxiety or other painful affect involved and the amount of maladaptive behavior entailed.

Any time the ego is confronted with impulses that, if gratified, would lead to psychic danger, the ego signals a conflict. It allows a small discharge of anxiety to initiate defenses against the threatening impulse and accommodates to the pressure of the drives, superego, and external reality with a compromise. It is the success of such compromises in terms of feelings and behavior that determines the health and stability of the person. Ideally, anxiety should be experienced primarily in its *signal function* (i.e., as an appropriate signal to possible danger), and the person's conduct should afford pleasure while being generally acceptable to others. A defense against an impulse can also help satisfy the impulse in a more acceptable way (e.g., displacement or sublimation). In cases of pathologic guilt, the aggressive drive may be involved in superego acts of self-punishment. Every compromise has aspects of drive satisfaction, moral values, and accommodation to reality.

In what is known as a *symptom neurosis*, the compromise is felt as painful and maladaptive, and although the person may feel unable to alter the pattern, there is conscious acknowledgment of suffering and motivation to change. In *character neuroses*, the situation is somewhat different. The essence of character is in the repetitive and incessant use of certain defenses that gives the person a particular "stamp." Although character traits and defenses may be rigid and automatic, they often are relatively comfortable to the person and are termed *ego-syntonic*, indicating that they are not a source of distress. For these reasons, conflicts stemming from maladaptive character defenses may be more difficult to treat, and efforts to change such mechanisms are met with a great deal of resistance. From the patient's point of view, these characteristic compromises are familiar and sensible and may be described as "part of the way I am." The reasons for interpersonal conflicts are externalized and are believed to be due to the faults of others. An important insight from the study of character is the need to transform such defenses into *ego-dystonic* experiences with a subsequent motivation to change.

OBJECT RELATIONS THEORY OF DEVELOPMENT

The term *object* first appeared in psychoanalytic theory as an essential aspect of the definition of drive. Freud defined the term *object* as the thing toward which a drive is directed, and there could be no drives without objects. The term is often used to describe real people existing as a part of external reality, as well as images of those people within the mind. A multiplicity of object relations theories have evolved, and there are great differences, even among object relations theorists, as to how the term *object* or *object relations theory* should be defined.

In this presentation, we distinguish interpersonal relations, which refer to relationships with people in the real world, from internalized object relations, which is our main focus. The child's earliest experiences have dyadic (self-object) features even before there is clear differentiation between the self and object.

We have chosen to present the work of Spitz and Mahler to illustrate how the earliest structures of the psychic apparatus are built up during specific stages of development through the process of internalization of object relations. Their work is strongly empirically based and consistent with the important clinical and theoretic contributions of Jacobson and Kernberg. It must be remembered, however, that there are other, very different approaches to object relations theories, such as those of Klein, Fairbairn, Guntrip, Balint, and Winnicott.

Rene Spitz (1965) was probably the first major psychoanalytic investigator who used direct observations of the early mother–child relationships to study the development of object relations. (The term *object relations* in psychoanalytic terms usually refers to the relationship of the infant to anything other than him- or herself, which is at least initially the mother, then father, and later other "objects" of the person's attention and desire.)

Although Spitz was not the first investigator to note the smile of the infant that appears at around 6 weeks, he placed it in the context of social significance and considered it the *first organizer* of the psychic structure (Spitz, 1965). Spitz believed that during the first few weeks of life, neonates lived in a relatively undifferentiated, disconnected state, primarily perceiving only internal stimuli and little beyond their own bodies. This phase of development between birth and about 1 month of age was described similarly by Mahler, who called this period the *normal autistic phase* (Mahler et al, 1975). The mother's attuned responses to the child's needs are provided in such a way as to promote a sense of safety and to protect the infant from any excessive internal and external stimulation, stress, or discomfort.

Awareness of something other than oneself—initially the mother—who satisfies one's needs begins at about the second month of life, the beginning of the phase called *normal symbiosis*. As a result of the mother's helpful ministrations, infants begin to retain mental representations of her associated with reduction of tension and with pleasurable sensations such as satiety and cuddling. The infant's perception of mother, however, is still only fragmentary and not clearly differentiated from his or her own sense of self. It was postulated that infant and mother identities "share a common boundary" and sense of fusion or merger (symbiosis). The term *part-object* was used to designate that, at this time, the mother is only "partly" recognized in terms of her nurturing and/or frustrating functions, which could at times be perceived by the infant as inconsistent. "Good-mother" representations become associated with the all-fulfilling, nurturing, and pleasurable aspects of mother, and "bad-mother" representations become associated with aspects of mother that may be frustrating or do not meet the infant's demands for immediate gratification or are punitive or rejecting. Ideally, the child would integrate these separate aspects and responses of mother into a coherent unified mental representation so that the child realizes that one and the same mother can be both gratifying but occasionally frustrating as well. In addition, the child would also realize that seemingly conflicting emotions (anger and love) could be felt toward the same person at alternating times or that these two emotions could be experienced simultaneously (ambivalence).

The two earliest stages of relative nondifferentiation between infant and mother (normal autism and normal symbiosis) end at about 5 months in this model of development, and the formal phase of *separation–individuation* proper begins (Mahler et al, 1975; see Table 5–3 and Fig. 5–1).

Table 5–3 **The Separation–Individuation Process**

PHASE/AGE	COMMENT
Normal autistic (Birth–1 month)	No differentiation of inside versus outside, "me" versus "not me." Experience of need-satisfying activities of mother blend with the experience of needs themselves. Establishment of physiological homeostatic equilibrium in new postpartum conditions.
Normal symbiotic (1 month–5 months)	Increased attention and interest in outside world. Dawning awareness of mother and establishment of specific bond with her (or primary caretaker). Specific smiling response.
Subphases	
A. Differentiation (5 months–7 months)	Increasing manual, tactile exploration of mother's face. Efforts to push back to take a look at mother. Comparison of mother with "other," familiar and unfamiliar (comparative scanning). Curiosity and wonder about external world with frequent "checking back to mother." Development of stranger anxiety.
B. Practicing (7 months–16 months)	"Early" practicing period with motility away from mother by crawling, climbing, and righting self. Practicing period "proper" heralded by free, upright locomotion. Rapid development of autonomous ego functions in close proximity to mother. Active exploration of environment with mother as "home base" and frequent trips back to her for "emotional refueling." Development of separation anxiety. Beginning of representational intelligence and first level of self-identity.
C. Rapprochement (16 months–24 months)	Toddler more aware of loss of "ideal sense of self" when separated from mother. Experience of separateness as relative helplessness. Efforts made to regain union with mother by bringing and sharing objects with her, seeking attention and "wooing." Wish to be helped and soothed by mother immediately when needed while simultaneously wishing to retain autonomy and self-control (ambitendency). Frequent "no-win" situations for mother as she tries to foster autonomy and also provide safety and assistance for child.
D. Object constancy (24 months–36 months)	Establishment of self-representation as predominantly positive in spite of child's imperfections and limitations. Internal representation of mother as basically "good" and reliable, even though occasionally frustrating and disappointing. Recognition of mother as a separate person with wishes and preferences of her own. Increasing tolerance of separations and more trusting of adult substitutes. Continued development of a variety of ego functions allowing greater frustration tolerance, understanding of limits, and ability to obey simple rules for personal safety.

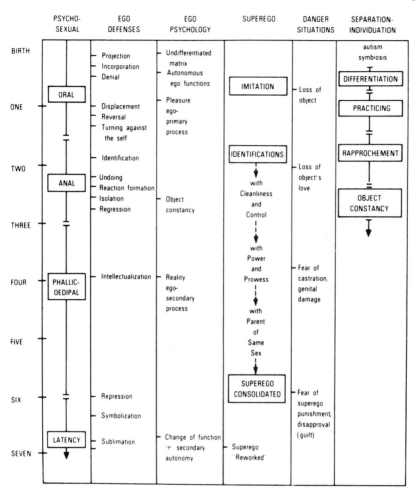

Figure 5–1. *Parallel lines of human development.*

The period of 6 to 36 months is a critical stage of development when a discrete self-concept and identity are developed based on a sense of awareness of separateness from mother. Patients with so-called *borderline* personality disorders have been associated with major developmental difficulties at this stage of development.

There are four *subphases* of separation–individuation. The first is called *differentiation* (5 to 7 months). It is heralded by the tendency of the increasingly alert child to push himself or herself back from the usual position of molding to the mother's shoulder and "take a look." This early deployment of physical measures to "push back" from mother and scan and explore her visually is labeled the *hatching process.*

Practicing, the second subphase, encompasses a period of 7 to 16 months. It is evidenced by a dramatic maturation of motor function. The child can now crawl and explore and exhibits the joy of discovery. Toddlers at this stage feel omnipotent and oblivious to harm as they experience a "love affair with the world." Children during this phase often become so absorbed in and delighted with their activities that they are oblivious to mother, only occasionally needing to return to her for "refueling" and reassurance that she is consistently there to protect and nurture them as the need arises.

Rapprochement is the third phase of separation–individuation. It extends from about 16 months until 18 to 24 months. Mother is no longer taken for granted by the child. The child's increased awareness of being separate and having her own limitations in meeting all the child's needs threatens the child with a traumatic loss of self-esteem. For example, if the child is upset, hurt, or unable to carry out a task, he or she may be torn between wishes to be near mother and be comforted by her and a compulsion to move away from her and function independently. There may be periods of increased irritability and an increase in stranger and separation anxiety during this time. Mahler (1975) referred to the rapprochement period as a "crisis" because of the deep ambivalence and conflict within the toddler about dependence–independence issues. The mother, at this time, is confronted with frequent "no-win" situations. The resolution of this phase depends in large part on her ability to allow the child sufficient separation and autonomy while still being flexibly available for support "on demand." Difficulties in negotiating this period of great vulnerability have been associated with serious personality problems in adults. The following example illustrates the rapprochement phase.

A CASE STUDY

A 20-month-old boy was admitted to the pediatric unit for an asthma attack. This was his fourth admission in 5 months, and it was evident that there were problems with his taking medication at home. The mother felt that her son had become "impossible to handle." She stated, "He wants to take the medicine himself but he spills it, and when I try to help he resists and spits it out." The nurses observed that the mother quickly limited the child's appropriate explorations of the ward and was overly protective, and the child was frequently seen trying to free himself from her "hugs."

In this characteristic rapprochement phase conflict of separation–individuation, the mother needed to be supported in her efforts to do things for her son that he could not safely do alone, while also loosening the restraints on his explorations, curiosity, and attempts at independence.

In the third year of life, the fourth and final subphase unfolds, and the child ideally obtains what is known as *object constancy*. A secure sense of self is developed with differentiation between the self and a stable mental representation of the mother who can be seen as a distinct person with wishes and preferences of her own and experienced as "good" even when she is frustrating or disappointing.

The term *object constancy* has been used in two different ways, which has led to some confusion. In the cognitive sense, the term has been used to refer to the capacity to maintain a stable inner image of a person even when the person is not present. This use is derived from Jean Piaget's (see Chapter 8) concept of "object permanence" and is a prerequisite for the establishment of object constancy. Object constancy, which should solidify during the third year of life, refers to the ability to maintain an inner image or representation of the mother, the thought of which enables the child to experience a sense of safety, comfort, and love even in the mother's absence. Problems in the adult personality stemming from difficulties in attaining "object constancy" during separation–individuation are exemplified by the following case.

A CASE STUDY

A 25-year-old man was admitted to intensive care after taking an overdose. When he was alert, he described taking the pills "on impulse" after a fight with his girlfriend precipitated by her wish to leave him. His history revealed a pattern of self-destructive actions, particularly after frustrations and disappointments in close relationships. His relationships were usually stormy and chaotic, with frequent outbursts or rage when he felt rejected or disappointed by the other person. Although the young man saw people frequently and had a number of superficial friends, none of the relationships endured, and he usually felt painfully empty and depressed when alone. He was intolerant of the shortcomings of others and the inevitable disappointments in human relationships. He appeared to be unable to maintain an idea of another person as basically "good" when he felt that his needs were not being totally met. His emotional reactions to such frustrations alternated between rage and despair, and, characteristically, his aggression became directed toward himself in a self-destructive manner.

In medical settings, persons of this sort often oscillate between idealizing and devaluing their physicians, depending on how thoroughly they feel their needs are being met at any given moment. It can be very difficult for the physician who is feeling unfairly attacked by an ungrateful patient to avoid responding by retaliating, by becoming angry, or by rejecting the patient. Some physicians will acquiesce to unreasonable demands to avoid feeling guilty in response to provocations, thereby avoiding the full blast of the patient's anger. The general pattern of alternating between idealization and devaluation of others is a general characteristic of borderline personalities. Separation–individuation theory will again be discussed in Chapters 8 and 10.

SELF THEORY AND THE DEVELOPMENT OF THE SELF

Another psychological theory that has developed out of the general framework of the psychoanalytic tradition is *self psychology*. It offers some important insights into certain aspects of personality development. The primary focus of self psychology as elucidated by Kohut (1971) is on the development and psychopathology of the core sense of self. Kohut defined and used the terms *self* and *narcissism* in a way that differed from other psychoanalysts. He considered the self to be a psychic structure, but not one of the "agencies" of the mind such as the ego or superego as described by Freud.

In attempting to understand patients with narcissistic personality disorders, Kohut observed and described specific kinds of psychological reactions, known as *transferences*, that emerged during his treatment of such patients. First, he described an "idealizing" transference that corresponds to the patient's image of the idealized parent; second, he described a "mirroring transference" that represents a component of the patient's own self-aggrandized image. Developmentally, Kohut postulated that the child's "grandiose" sense of self is the equivalent of "I am perfect; look at me"; the idealized image of the parent is "You are perfect, and I am a part of you." From these two structures, Kohut postulated a *separate developmental line* for the development of one's sense of "self." For example, the grandiosity, sense of invincibility, and exhibitionism often seen in children (hence, the popularity of and identification with "super hero" cartoon characters) are the forerunners of initiative, ambition, and healthy self-esteem in the adult when developmental disturbances do not seriously interfere.

Kohut placed great emphasis on the need for the mother to be *empathic* with the child for the development of a healthy sense of self. The mother must provide "mirroring" or approving responses of pleasure and excitement to the child's exhibitionism and prevent sudden severe traumatic disappointments when the inevitable frustrations of reality are met and children painfully realize their own limitations. Thus he emphasized the mother's functions as a necessary regulator, modulator, and protector of the child's self-esteem through empathic responsiveness. The failure of the mother to help the child attenuate the infantile grandiosity and transform it into a realistic and healthy sense of self-esteem leads to pathology of the self as evidenced by a retention of grandiosity in the adult.

Persons with narcissistic personalities may display an air of arrogant grandiosity and entitlement. Their lives are a desperate search for power, attention, or money to shore up their sense of self and their basic sense of value. Patients with narcissistic personality disorders are often characterized by egocentricity, self-importance, grandiosity, selfishness, and arrogance in varying degrees. They tend to relate to other people in an exploitive manner and use others primarily to embellish or meet their own needs.

Kohut considered the development of the self as *the* central issue in psychic development and thought the sexual and aggressive drives, so crucial in classic Freudian theory, were by-products of disturbed development of the self. His theory of psychopathology emphasizes defects in the development of self rather than intrapsychic conflicts. Classic Freudian analytic approaches based on resolving intrapsychic conflict are not necessarily incompatible with Kohut's emphasis on empathy and healing of the self in the therapeutic process. Empathy on the part of the therapist has always been an intrinsic part of traditional psychoanalytic treatment. Kohut's contributions not only emphasize the importance of empathy, but also focus attention on narcissistic psychopathology and personality types who are considered unlikely to benefit from traditional psychoanalytic approaches.

A CASE STUDY

A middle-aged woman came for an appointment with her doctor, whom she described as "the best specialist in town." Her doctor actually found her annoying as she often spoke disparagingly of others and tended to prolong appointments with seemingly endless descriptions of her bodily functions. Because of a busy schedule, the doctor cut her appointment short and laughed uncomfortably when she protested. She looked hurt but composed herself and walked stiffly out of the office. Two days later she called for an urgent appointment for a severe headache, backache, and several other symptoms. She complained that her body was "falling apart," and she appeared enraged. Physical examination was essentially unremarkable. On further conversation, she described feeling humiliated at her last appointment. She drove home, yelled at her husband, cursed her doctor for being "a jerk," and sat for hours in front of the TV "feeling dead." These feelings persisted and her aches and pains escalated, so she again called to see her doctor. Since her physician knew something about psychological theories of narcissism, she realized on further reflection that her hurried manner and laughter with the patient had been received as a failure of empathy and a severe injury to the patient's self-esteem, causing a state of self-fragmentation experienced as emotional and physical "coming-apart." When she conveyed this awareness to the patient in a caring and empathic manner, the patient immediately felt remarkably better.

PSYCHOANALYTIC THEORY AND THE PHYSICIAN–PATIENT RELATIONSHIP

Now that the basic concepts in psychoanalytic theory have been reviewed, how may they be practically helpful in clinical medicine? One may begin to address this question by examining the nature of the physician–patient relationship, which was discussed in Chapter 1.

The therapeutic importance of the relationship between the physician and patient has been known and emphasized throughout recorded medical history. Hippocrates insisted that the physician know the patient "as an individual and [know] all the relevant circumstances of his life" (Hutchins, 1952, p 117). However, the remarkable technologic advances in medicine, which have greatly increased our knowledge about diseases, make it easy to forget that for each patient the experience of illness is different, depending on the person's specific circumstances.

Psychoanalysts, beginning with Freud, considered the physician–patient relationship to be a subject for explicit study. As introduced in Chapter 1 by Dr. Shelton, the phenomenon of *transference* is an essential and extremely valuable concept that explains various aspects of the physician–patient relationship that may appear to be inexplicable and unreasonable. The term *transference* is defined as unconsciously applying feelings, attitudes, and expectations from important persons in one's *past* to people in one's *current* life. Freud first learned about the role of transference in the psychoanalytic situation in a manner that would be ultimately helpful for all practicing physicians in caring for their patients. His singular focus on the interesting psychopathology of his patient Dora (1905), led to his overlooking an important aspect of the physician–patient relationship, the *transference*, aspects of which were subsequently responsible for failure of her treatment. Freud described it this way: "Owing to the readiness with which Dora put one part of the pathogenic material at my disposal during the treatment, I neglected the precaution of looking out for the first signs of *transference*, which was being prepared in connection with another part of the same material—a part of which I was in ignorance. . . . In this way the transference took me unawares, and because of the unknown quantity in me, which reminded Dora of Herr K., she took her revenge *on me* as she wanted to take her revenge *on him*, and *deserted me* as she believed herself to have been *deceived and deserted by him*" (Freud, 1905, pp 118–119). Freud failed to recognize a particularly painful and problematic aspect of a past relationship that Dora transferred onto and repeated with Freud during the treatment. This led Dora to reject Freud as a therapist as once she had been rejected by Herr K. and thus the treatment failed.

Transference reactions stem from early childhood experiences with the parents and include a broad range of dependent, sexual, and aggressive feelings and wishes. Transference occurs, to some extent, in all human relationships and forms the substrate for one's emotional reactions to other people throughout life. Transference often develops with special intensity between patient and physician due to the dependency on the physician that often develops in the context of painful and anxiety-provoking medical illness. Transference feelings may lead to childlike expectations for the physician to protect and nurture the patient back to health as would a parent.

Freud divided transference into positive and negative (hostile) types and further subdivided positive transference into an "unobjectionable" positive transference and the "erotic" transference. Negative transference and erotic transference function as resistances to the psychoanalytic treatment process. However, the "unobjectionable" positive transference was considered by Freud to be necessary and especially useful in the physician–patient relationship (Freud, 1911–1913, p 139).

Countertransference refers to the displacement *onto the patient by the therapist or physician* of feelings, wishes, and attitudes derived from the therapist's or the physician's own early childhood experiences. Hence, countertransference may be thought of as the physician's own transference to the patient.

It is not uncommon for patients to have or develop transferences to their physicians, and the vast majority of such reactions are positive if patients are capable of basic trust in other people and are capable of forming a cooperative relationship with the physician. Evidence of problematic (negative) transference reactions are evidenced by patients who appear unreasonably suspicious, hostile, litigious, antagonistic, provocative, excessively dependent or clinging, or sexually seductive. Hence, a mistrustful patient may have been traumatized or hurt in early stages of life when especially vulnerable to a person on whom he or she sought help or were dependent—usually a parent figure. This mistrust and anger can be transferred onto the physician because the patient may react to the physician (unconsciously) in a similar manner. Problematic erotic transferences can also seriously disrupt the doctor–patient relationship.

Likewise, physicians may suddenly experience intense, seemingly inappropriate reactions to patients—either hostile, affectionate, or sexual—if the patient comes to represent a conflicted significant figure from their own life. Awareness that such reactions on either the patient's or physician's part may be complicating the physician–patient relationship should give rise to self-inspection on the part of the physician and possibly a psychiatric consultation (formal or informal) to gain an objective view of the situation. Problematic transference reactions in the medical setting are usually most pronounced when patients are severely regressed under the stress of a medical illness or the patient (or physician) has evidence of a preexisting personality disorder. Transference and countertransference reactions have been discussed in Chapter 1, especially in regard to distinguishing unconscious versus "realistic" emotional interactions between doctor and patient.

The Treatment Alliance

Another aspect of the physician–patient relationship derived from psychoanalytic therapy applicable to the medical setting is the *treatment alliance*, which is also referred to as the therapeutic alliance or working alliance. In general, these terms all refer to the rational, conflict-free, conscious relationship between the patient and physician, which is based on their agreement to work together for the patient's benefit. It is probably based in part on the existence of a positive transference.

In general, an attitude of concern, respect, honesty, and courtesy combined with empathy and protection of privacy and confidentiality will foster a positive relationship in any physician–patient relationship. Studies indicating why therapist/physician–patient relationships fail have tended to confirm this observation. If the physician is able to convey a genuine interest in being helpful to the patient, and there is a congruence between the patient's own current, crucial interests and the interests of the physician, the treatment, medical or psychiatric, is most likely to continue on a positive track and not be prematurely interrupted by the patient (Inderbitzin, 1990; Nicholi, 1978). (See also Chapter 1.)

Illness, and especially hospitalization, tend to create a situation of *forced dependency* and certain types of regressive behavior in patients, which may pose a threat to the physician–patient relationship and the ongoing treatment. The specific nature of the patient's reaction in such instances is determined by a variety of factors, including the circumstances of the current situation (such as the nature and severity of the illness), the current state of the physician–patient relationship, and previous experiences with caretakers in similar situations. A major determinant, however, is the nature of the underlying personality structure of both the patient and physician.

The applications of psychoanalytic concepts and psychodynamic-based therapy in the care of the medically ill patient are discussed further in Chapter 14 by Dr. Green.

PSYCHOANALYSIS AND PSYCHOANALYTIC PSYCHOTHERAPY

Psychoanalytically oriented psychotherapy is a method of treatment based on psychoanalytic theory and technique and is the most widely practiced form of psychotherapy in the United States (Henry et al, 1973; Parloff, 1979). It is most often described in terms of comparisons and contrasts with its parent discipline, classic Freudian psychoanalysis. As described first by Freud (1911–1913), psychoanalysis is the treatment of choice for patients who suffer from chronic symptoms or characterologic problems reflecting intrapsychic conflict, developmental arrests or deviations, and/or structural deficits not inconsistent with growth potential. Psychoanalysis is particularly preferable over other treatment methods if chronic symptoms have not improved or are not likely to improve with briefer, less intense forms of psychotherapy. Furthermore, if some other treatment would provide temporary relief but with high risk of recurrence of the chronic symptoms, psychoanalysis should be considered. In addition to these criteria for psychoanalysis, patients must also fulfill certain criteria for analyzability, which include the capacity to form a treatment relationship, maintain it in the face of a therapeutic regression, and then ultimately relinquish it.

The overall goal of psychoanalysis is to foster the greatest change in personality structure that is possible. Psychotherapeutic goals vary widely, but an overall goal is the resolution of symptoms and some degree of behavioral change. Patients suffering from acute symptoms, even if they reflect evidence of intrapsychic conflict, are treated more appropriately with psychotherapy than psychoanalysis, unless the symptoms are embedded in a rigid character structure, or there is evidence of developmental distortions or arrested development. The psychoanalytic treatment situation is designed in such a way as to intensify the transference relationship and center the patient's infantile neurotic conflicts around the person of the analyst. Although this may occur also in other forms of treatment, *it is not an aim* of routine psychotherapy; some psychotherapies, such as brief psychotherapy, are designed to minimize transference manifestations. Patients who show evidence of not being able to distinguish between transference reactions to the analyst and reality should, in general, be treated by psychotherapeutic rather than psychoanalytic methods. In psychoanalytic technique, the analyst tries to avoid becoming a model for the patient and uses interventions primarily intended to promote insight. The psychotherapist, however, sometimes deliberately tries to provide a model for the patient and offers suggestions and other supportive measures.

Psychoanalysis requires four to five sessions per week, use of the couch, and is open-ended with a usual duration of at least 3 years. The technique of free association is central to the methodology of classic psychoanalysis (Kris, 1989). The psychoanalytic situation is structured in such a way (including the analyst's neutrality and relative personal anonymity) to foster a temporary therapeutic regression, allowing intrapsychic conflicts to be observed by analyst and patient. The analytic situation is, in a sense, artificially contrived to enable patients to reexperience and remember in the here and now as much of their painful and problematic past as is possible and to bring past experiences to the conscious surface where insight can be used for change. In his or her interventions, the psychoanalyst is guided primarily by the manifestations of transference and resistance (Freud, 1914), and *interpretation* is the primary technique applied to gain insight and foster change in the intrapsychic balance.

Modifications of classic psychoanalytic technique and the development of other psychoanalytically oriented psychotherapies resulted from efforts to shorten psychoanalytic treatment and adapt it to a wider range of patients, including those too disturbed to tolerate classic psychoanalysis. Insight-oriented (expressive) psychotherapy and so-called supportive psychotherapy are not dichotomous methods of treatment. Supportive elements exist even in the most insight-oriented classic psychoanalysis, and, at times, interpretations, which are usually thought of as an expressive therapeutic technique, can be the most effective supportive intervention. Books by Luborsky (1984) and Werman (1987) emphasize that supportive and expressive therapies exist on a continuum, and these authors illustrate the flexible application of psychoanalytic concepts to different kinds of patients with various types of goals and at different stages of treatment.

Psychoanalytic psychotherapy (dynamic psychotherapy), including psychoanalysis, has been shown to be effective for a wide variety of problems and disorders (Bergin and Lambert, 1978; Luborsky et al, 1975; Smith et al, 1980, Wallerstein, 1986; and Bachrach, 1991). Results of efficacy studies of psychoanalytic psychotherapy demonstrate target symptom improvement rates of 86% to 92%, and that this is maintained at 7-year follow-up (Luborsky et al, 1988; Crits-Christoph, 1992). Nevertheless, there are many unanswered questions and remaining problems. We need to learn much more about what therapy, administered by what therapist, is effective for which patients with what conditions as well as the differences in outcomes between brief dynamic psychotherapy and longer term treatments such as psychoanalysis (Luborsky, 1984). Like any other effective treatment in medicine, psychotherapy has the potential of causing great harm as well as much benefit to patients. It is essential that an experienced clinician who is knowledgeable about both psychopathology and various treatment modalities perform a careful diagnostic evaluation and assess the need for medical and neurologic evaluation and the possible need for psychopharmacological agents before any form of psychotherapy is recommended. Many authors, such as Levine (1952) and Malan (1979), have emphasized the crucial role of diagnosis and have described diagnostic evaluation processes that begin with a clinical psychiatric diagnosis but necessarily go far beyond that. Such a diagnostic process always includes a psychodynamic understanding of the conflicts within the patient and between the patient and his environment, as well as how these conflicts developed out of the patient's past. Study of the precipitating factors of the present illness are particularly useful in this endeavor. Furthermore, it is necessary to know about the patient's strengths and highest level of functioning, weaknesses and most severe disturbances, and the balance between the two. Only the clinician who is able to grasp empathically the patient's inner world and way of being in the world is able to prescribe effectively. Many of the principles and practices of psychotherapy that are especially helpful in understanding and helping patients with emotional difficulties in coping with medical illness are discussed in Chapter 14. Students interested in a more detailed discussion regarding contrasts between psychodynamic therapy, psychoanalysis, and other forms of psychotherapy are referred to a detailed discussion of the same in the accompanying text. (See reference to Ursano, Silberman, and Diaz, 1994.)

ANNOTATED BIBLIOGRAPHY

Brenner C: The Mind in Conflict. Madison, CT, International Universities Press, 1982

> In this work, Brenner elaborates on the theory of psychic conflict—how infantile wishes come into conflict and lead to various compromise formations. Along the way he reviews his own revisions of important psychoanalytic concepts.

Brenner C: An Elementary Textbook of Psychoanalysis, rev ed. New York, International Universities Press, 1973

> This book is a widely recommended and thoroughly comprehensive introduction to the fundamental concepts of classic psychoanalytic theory. Brenner discusses the fundamental hypotheses, the drives, psychosexual stages of development, the topographic and structural models, ego functioning, object relations, parapraxes, wit, dreams, psychopathology, and psychic conflict.

Engel G: Psychological Development in Health and Disease. Philadelphia, WB Saunders, 1962

> This is a distillation of George Engel's thinking about human psychologic functioning derived from many years of teaching medical students and residents. The development of the psychic apparatus is described as resulting from the interaction of biological, psychological, and social processes. Engel also discusses how psychologic adaptations affect body functions in health and disease. The first half of the book delineates the stages of development in considerable detail; the second half presents a unified concept of health and disease, explaining the role of psychological processes in medical and psychiatric illnesses.

Freud A: (1936). The Ego and the Mechanisms of Defense, rev ed. New York, International Universities Press, 1966

> This classic work by Anna Freud, originally published in 1936, advanced the theory of the role and functioning of the ego. It examines various ego defense mechanisms, including how and why they operate, and is illustrated with many clinical examples from the author's psychotherapeutic work with children.

Greenberg JR, Mitchell SA: Object Relations in Psychoanalytic Theory. Cambridge MA, Harvard University Press, 1983

> This scholarly work provides a detailed, comprehensive description of various theories of object relations, including those of Freud, Sullivan, Klein, Fairbairn, Winnicott, Guntrip, Hartmann, Mahler, Jacobson, Kernberg, Kohut, Sandler, and others. The authors contrast and compare theories based on a drive/structure model and those based on a relational/structure model.

Levy S: Principles of Interpretation. New York, Jason Aronson, 1984

> This book is concerned with the technical theory of interpretation used in psychoanalytically oriented psychotherapy. Levy describes how the interviewer or therapist listens to the productions of the patient, and then formulates and verbalizes interventions that best facilitate the therapeutic process. Many clinical vignettes illustrate the technical points described.

MacKinnon R, Michels R: The Psychiatric Interview in Clinical Practice. Philadelphia, WB Saunders, 1971

> The authors provide a discussion of basic principles of the psychodynamic interview, then focus on how these are applied in the interviewing and psychotherapy of patients with specific types of psychopathology. Their discussions describe the core psychodynamic issues present in these patients, how these will manifest in the interview, and how the interviewer can therapeutically intervene.

Malan D: Individual Psychotherapy and the Science of Psychodynamics. London, Butterworths, 1979

> Malan describes the principles and techniques of intensive psychotherapy, beginning with basic psychoanalytic principles. He stresses the observational data and the psychodynamic formulations that can be generated to explain the data and test the hypotheses. This book is structured around many illustrative case examples and explains a method of brief psychotherapy as well as long-term therapy. The theoretic orientation of the author includes attention to object relations and the role of the vicissitudes of infantile experience in shaping adult psychopathology.

Nemiah J: Foundations of Psychopathology. New York, Oxford University Press, 1961

> This book reviews the basic concepts of psychoanalysis, then provides an explanation of the psychodynamic bases of various types of psychopathology. It is strongly empiric in its approach, and the concepts are richly illustrated with many clinical cases, which clearly demonstrate the applicability of psychoanalytic principles in the management of medical and psychiatric patients. One especially useful element is the emphasis on the role of fantasy in mental life.

Ursano RJ, Silberman EK, Diaz A: The Psychotherapies: Basic Theoretical Principles and Techniques. In Stoudemire A (ed): Clinical Psychiatry for Medical Students, 2nd ed. Philadelphia, Lippincott, 1994

> An excellent overview of the various types of psychotherapies, giving theoretical basis for each as well as clinical indications.

Waelder R: Basic Theory of Psychoanalysis. New York, International Universities Press, 1960

> The author reviews many fundamental concepts of psychoanalysis, with elaboration on the topics of the sexual and aggressive instincts, anxiety, ego psychology, and basic principles of psychotherapy. Waelder effectively addresses many of the criticisms that have been leveled at psychoanalysis over the years.

Zetzel E, Meissner W: Basic Concepts of Psychoanalytic Psychiatry. New York, Basic Books, 1973

> This book reviews psychoanalytic theory, including discussions of anxiety, repression, developmental theory, primary and secondary process, narcissism, ego functions and development, object relations, identity formation, neurosis, and therapy. Like most of the books on this list, it evolved out of years of teaching these principles to residents and medical students.

REFERENCES

Bachrach H, Galatzer-Levy R, Skolnikoff A, Waldron S: On the efficacy of psychoanalysis. J Am Psychoanal Assoc 39:871–916, 1991

Bergin A, Lambert M: The evaluation of therapeutic outcomes. In Garfield S, Bergin A (eds): Handbook of Psychotherapy and Behavioral Change: An Empirical Analysis. New York, John Wiley & Sons, 1978

Bibring E: The mechanism of depression. In Greenacre P (ed): Affective Disorders. New York, International Universities Press, 1953

Blos P: The genealogy of the ego ideal. Psychoanal Study Child 29:43–88, 1974

Blum G: Masochism, the ego ideal, and the psychology of women. J Am Psychoanal Assoc 24(Suppl):157–191, 1976

Brenner C: The Mind in Conflict. New York, International Universities Press, 1982

Brenner C: An Elementary Textbook of Psychoanalysis, rev ed. New York, Doubleday, 1974

Chehrazi S: Female psychology: A review. J Am Psychoanal Assoc 34:141–162, 1986

Cooper A, Francis A, Sacks M: The Psychoanalytic Model. In Michels R, Cavenar J, Cooper A et al (eds): Psychiatry, vol 1. Revised New York, Basic Books; Philadelphia, JB Lippincott, 1989

Crits-Christoph P: The efficacy of brief dynamic psychotherapy: A meta-analysis. Am J Psychiatry 149:151–158, 1992

Erikson E: Configurations in play—clinical notes. Psychoanal Q 6:139–214, 1937

Fenichel O: The Psychoanalytic Theory of Neurosis. New York, W.W. Norton, 1945

Freud A: (1936). The Ego and the Mechanisms of Defense, rev ed. New York, International Universities Press, 1966

Freud S: Inhibitions, Symptoms and Anxiety. SE 20, 1926

Freud S: Some Psychical Consequences of the Anatomical Distinction Between the Sexes. SE19, 1925

Freud S: The Ego and the Id. SE19, 1923

Freud S: General Theory of the Neuroses. SE16, 1916–1917

Freud S: On the history of the psycho-analytic movement. SE14, 1914.

Freud, S. Papers on Technique. SE12, 1911–1913

Freud S: Fragment of an Analysis of a Case of Hysteria. SE7, 1905

Freud S: The Interpretation of Dreams. SE4 & 5, 1900

Freud S: Studies on Hysteria. SE2, 1893–1895

Hartmann H: (1939). Ego Psychology and the Problem of Adaptation New York, International Universities Press, 1958

Hartmann H: The mutual influences in the development of the ego and id. Psychoanal Study Child 7:9–30, 1952

Hartmann H: Comments on the psychoanalytic theory of instinctual drives. Psychoanal Q 17:368–388, 1948

Hartmann H, Kris E, Loewenstein R: Comments on the formation of psychic structure. Psychoanal Study Child 2:11–38, 1946

Henry W, Sims J, Spray S: Public and Private Lives of Psychotherapists. San Francisco, Jossey-Bass, 1973

Horney K: The dread of women: Observations on a specific difference in the dread felt by men and women respectively for the opposite sex. Intl J Psycho-analysis 13:348–360, 1932

Horney K: The flight from womanhood: The masculinity complex in women as viewed by men and women. Intl J Psycho-Analysis 7:324–339, 1926.

Hutchins R (ed): Great Books of the Western World. Chicago, University of Chicago Press, 1952

Inderbitzin L: Treatment alliance in acute schizophrenia. In Levy S, Ninan P (eds): Schizophrenia: Treatment of the Acute Psychotic Episode. Washington, DC, American Psychiatric Press, 1990

Jones E: The early development of female sexuality. In Papers on Psycho-Analysis. London, Balliere, Tindall and Cox, 1948

Kleeman J: Freud's views on early female sexuality in the light of direct child observation. J Am Psychoanal Assoc 24 (Suppl):3–28, 1976

Kohut H: Analysis of the Self. New York, International Universities Press, 1971

Kris A: Psychoanalysis and psychoanalytic psychotherapy. In Michels R, Cavenar J, Cooper A et al (eds): Psychiatry, vol 1. Revised New York, Basic Books; Philadelphia, JB Lippincott, 1989

Levine M: Principles of psychiatric treatment. In Alexander F (ed): Dynamic Psychiatry. Chicago, University of Chicago Press, 1952

Luborsky L: Principles of Psychoanalytic Psychotherapy. New York, Basic Books, 1984

Luborsky L, Crits-Christoph P, Mintz J, Auerbach A: Who Will Benefit from Psychotherapy? Predicting Therapeutic Outcomes. New York, Basic Books, 1988

Luborsky L, Singer B, Luborsky L: Comparative studies of psychotherapies: Is it true that "Everybody has won and all must have prizes"? Arch Gen Psychiatry 32:995–1008, 1975

Mahler M, Pine F, Bergman A: The Psychological Birth of the Human Infant. New York, Basic Books, 1975

Malan D: Individual Psychotherapy and the Science of Psychodynamics. Boston, Butterworths, 1979

Nicholi A: The therapist-patient relationship. In Nicholi A (ed): The Harvard Guide to Modern Psychiatry. Cambridge, The Belknap Press of Harvard University Press, 1978

Parloff MB: Can psychotherapy research guide the policymaker? A little knowledge may be a dangerous thing. Am Psychol 34:296–306, 1979

Rapaport D: The Structure of Psychoanalytic Theory. Psychological Issues 2(2). New York, International Universities Press, 1960

Rapaport D: A historical survey of psychoanalytic ego psychology. Introduction in Erikson E: Identity and the Life Cycle. Psychological Issues 1(1). New York, International Universities Press, 1959

Reich A: Pathologic forms of self-esteem regulation. Psychoanal Study Child 15:215–232, 1960

Smith M, Glas G, Miller T: The Benefits of Psychotherapy. Baltimore, Johns Hopkins Press, 1980

Spitz R: The First Year of Life. New York, International Universities Press, 1965

Stoller R: Primary femininity. J Am Psychoanal Assoc 24 (Suppl):59–78, 1976

Stoller R: Sex and Gender. New York, Science House, 1968

Ursano RJ, Silberman EK, Diaz A: The Psychotherapies: Basic Theoretical Principles and Techniques. In Stoudemire A (ed): Clinical Psychiatry for Medical Students, 2nd edn. Philadelphia, Lippincott, 1994.

Vaillant G: Empirical Studies of Ego Mechanisms of Defense. Washington, DC, American Psychiatric Press, 1986

Wallerstein R: Forty-two Lives in Treatment: A Study of Psychoanalysis and Psychotherapy. New York, The Guilford Press, 1986

Werman D: The Practice of Supportive Psychotherapy. New York, Brunner/Mazel, 1987

Winson J: Brain and Psyche: The Biology of the Unconscious. New York, Vintage Books, 1985

6

Behavioral and Social Learning Psychology

Pamela G. Dorsett

The preceding chapter was an overview of the basic principles of psychoanalytic psychology and its application to the care of patients. In this chapter, the contributions of behavioral theory will be discussed. While the concluding section of this chapter compares psychoanalytic with behavioral theory and therapy, no attempt will be made necessarily to reconcile or integrate psychoanalytic and behavioral theory, although serious efforts have been made to do so (Marmor and Woods, 1980). It is the position of this text that both perspectives have value and clinical importance in understanding human behavior. The two approaches are presented recognizing that appreciation of diverse models may facilitate selection and the integrated use of the most appropriate techniques for each patient's given needs.

CHARACTERISTICS OF BEHAVIORAL THEORY

The philosophy of the science of human behavior called behaviorism has evolved from a rich albeit brief history. There are several basic characteristics and assumptions common to most positions within what is known as *behavioral psychology*.

First, the subject matter for study is *objectively measurable behavior*, particularly relationships between behavior and other verifiable events. Behaviors may be external and directly observable like social interactions, or internal such as emotions and cognitions. Physiological responses are internal events that can be monitored through instrumentation.

A second characteristic of behavioral psychology is a commitment to *experimentation* and the *empirical method*. Behavior is defined objectively and in such a way that it can be measured reliably. The nature of the relationships between behavior and variables such as environmental events are explored, described, and analyzed by means of experiments using methodology similar to that employed in the study of the natural sciences. Through experimentation, general laws or principles of behavior can be discovered such that behavior can be predicted and controlled.

Third, *learning* is emphasized. Further, it is assumed that adaptive and maladaptive behaviors are acquired in basically the same ways. The behavioral perspective rejects the notion of traits and underlying processes (e.g., conflicts) in explaining behavior. Personality development, whether "normal" or "abnormal," is seen as the result of the unique contributions of learning experiences and genetic endowment. Maladaptive behavior that is not learned can be affected by learning principles, and significant environmental factors can be changed to alter this behavior. As such, the behavioral view is optimistic regarding change.

Many figures have made significant contributions to the behavioral movement. An overview is presented in Table 6–1 and several key figures and their respective contributions are discussed in more detail in the sections which follow. (See Kazdin [1978] for a complete history of the behavioral psychology movement.)

CLASSICAL OR RESPONDENT CONDITIONING

Ivan Pavlov (1849–1936) and two other neurophysiologists in Russia, Ivan Sechenov (1829–1905) and Vladimir Bechterev (1857–1927), played significant roles in promoting application of the experimental method to the study of psychological phenomena and formulating the principles of classical or respondent conditioning (Table 6–2). Pavlov studied digestion and developed a surgical technique that made it possible to obtain secretions directly from the glands and, therefore, to observe and measure the secretions outside the animal's body. He had already begun to direct his research toward elucidation of the variables affecting the acquisition and elimination of "psychic secretions" (i.e., gastric secretions elicited by stimuli such as the sight of food rather than by direct physical stimulation) when he received the Nobel Prize in 1904 for his work in digestion. His initial attempts to explain the secretions on the basis of "expectancies" were not productive, so he set about the task of analyzing the nature of the responses and their relationship to other events.

Pavlov found that by repeatedly pairing a stimulus that elicited the salivation reflex, the previously neutral stimulus would also elicit a reflexive-type response. For example, a tone would not elicit salivation. However, if the tone was presented with food for several conditioning trials, then, when presented alone, the tone did elicit salivation. In this paradigm, the food is called an *unconditioned stimulus* (UCS), and the response it elicits is called an *unconditioned response* (UCR) or reflex. The tone, a previously neutral stimulus that comes to elicit salivation through conditioning or pairing with the UCS, is called a *conditioned stimulus* (CS). The response it elicits is a *conditioned response* (CR).

Table 6–1 **Major Contributions to the Behavioral Movement**

Ivan Sechenov (1829–1905)	Proposed that behavior was reflexive to external stimuli and advocated the use of experimental methodology for the study of behavior.
Vladimir Bechterev (1857–1927)	Focused on aversive stimuli and reflexes with humans and other species. Attempted to apply principles of reflexology to psychiatric disorders. Advocated objectivism, empiricism, and experimentation in psychology.
Ivan Pavlov (1849–1936)	Formulated principles of classical (respondent) conditioning. Advocated objectivism, empiricism, and experimentation in psychology.
John B. Watson (1878–1958)	Advocated objectivism, empiricism, and experimentation in psychology with observable behavior as the subject matter. Publicized the behavioral position. "Father of Behaviorism." Extended application of the classical conditioning model to the development of emotions in humans.
Edward L. Thorndike (1874–1949)	Studied patterns of behavior in trial-and-error learning. Formulated the Law of Effect and emphasized the consequences of behavior.
Edward C. Tolman (1896–1961)	Maintained that behavior is purposive and referred to subjective states in accounting for behavior. Proposed that reinforcement serves as information and not to strengthen behavior directly.
B. F. Skinner (1904–1991)	Shifted focus of explanations for behavior from stimuli to consequences. Formulated principles of operant conditioning. Advocated a methodology for studying behavior called the experimental analysis of behavior. Presented the radical behaviorism position. Helped distinguish operant and respondent (classical) conditioning. Had great impact on the development of behavior modification.
Joseph Wolpe (1915–)	Employed an animal model to study the development of emotional reactions and ways of treating such problems. Developed treatment techniques based on the principle of reciprocal inhibition. Techniques generated research and contributed to the development of behavior therapy.
Albert Bandura (1925–)	Emphasized reciprocal determinism and cognitive and self-regulatory processes. Elucidated variables affecting observational learning.

Table 6–2 **Classical or Respondent Conditioning**

TERM	DEFINITION	EXAMPLE
Unconditioned stimulus (UCS)	Elicits an unconditioned response or reflex.	Blast of air into eye causes eye blink.
Unconditioned response (UCR)	Reflex elicited by an unconditioned stimulus.	Eye blink in response to blast of air.
Conditioned stimulus (CS)	Previously neutral stimulus that comes to elicit an unconditioned response through pairings with an unconditioned stimulus.	Tone presented immediately before blast of air into eye. Tone alone comes to elicit eye blink.
Conditioned response (CR)	Response elicited by the conditioned stimulus.	Eye blink in response to tone.
Discrimination	The conditioned response is elicited by some stimuli similar to the conditioned stimulus but not by others.	Tones of a particular frequency range elicit the eye blink but others do not.
Generalization	Stimuli similar to the conditioned stimulus elicit the conditioned response.	Tones most similar to the original one elicit the eye blink.
Extinction	Conditioned stimulus loses the power to elicit the conditioned response by no longer being paired with the unconditioned stimulus.	After repeated presentations of the tone without the blast of air, the tone alone no longer elicits the eye blink.

Pavlov determined that the CS loses its power to elicit a CR if it is no longer paired with the UCS, a process called *extinction*. After some period of time has elapsed following extinction, the presentation of the CS may again temporarily elicit the CR. This phenomenon is called *spontaneous recovery*.

In his work, Pavlov demonstrated that, once a CS had been established, similar stimuli also elicited the CR, a phenomenon called *generalization*. Tones of similar though different frequencies, for example, elicited a salivation response. However, if *different* tones were presented *without* being followed by the food and only *one* tone was paired with the UCS, then only *one stimulus* elicited the CR. This is the process of *discrimination*.

A very practical clinical example of this phenomenon may be observed in patients receiving chemotherapy for cancer. Anticipatory nausea and vomiting in cancer patients receiving chemotherapy can be explained by *respondent condition-ing*. The UCS is the chemotherapy agent that produces nausea and vomiting, the UCR's, as side effects. Various neutral stimuli such as the smell of the hospital or sight of the treatment room become associated with the UCS. After several pairings, the neutral stimuli become CS's and elicit nausea and vomiting—the CR's. Generalization may occur, whereby more and more stimuli become CS's. Theoretically, extinction of the CR's could require visits to the hospital after completion of chemotherapy in order to expose the patient to CS's without additional pairings with the UCS. This is not a practical intervention and, fortunately, there is an effective alternative treatment for conditioned nausea and vomiting, relaxation, which will be discussed later in the chapter.

Respondent Conditioning and the Development of Emotions

From a behavioral perspective, classical or respondent conditioning is the basis for the emotional responses we have to events, objects, situations or people. John B. Watson (1878–1958) extended application of the model to study the development of emotions in humans.

Watson believed that all learning occurred according to the principles of respondent conditioning, including emotions, which he saw as physiological responses to observable stimuli. He and his assistant experimentally demonstrated that a phobia could be developed by means of respondent conditioning (Watson and Rayner, 1920). In a classic experiment, a 9-month-old named Albert was presented with a white rat and initially showed no indications of fear but rather approached and touched the animal. The child was then presented with the rat as a metal bar was banged loudly, resulting in a startle response. After several conditioning trials, Albert cried at the sight of the rat and would not approach or touch the rat. Additionally, the fear *generalized* to other similar, white furry objects, such as a rabbit, a dog, a fur coat, and a ball of white wool. Unfortunately, Albert's mother left the hospital before Watson could decondition Albert's fear.

Although such an experiment would not be conducted today because of obvious ethical problems, it remains a classic study. It demonstrated that an emotional response and related maladaptive behavior, in this case a phobia, could be acquired through a relatively simple learning process rather than being the result of underlying processes and conflicts that can be neither observed nor studied experimentally.

Conditioned emotional responses (CER's) can be positive or negative depend-ing on the nature of the UCS and the CS and the individual's conditioning history. Albert's fear of white furry objects is an example of a conditioned aversive emotional response. Hearing the voice of one's lover, on the other hand, may elicit pleasurable emotional responses. When dealing with conditioned aversive emotional responses, individuals can engage in avoidance behavior so the CER's do not extinguish. That is, the person avoids pairing the negative CS with a neutral event and extinction cannot occur. Consequently, conditioned aversive emotional responses and avoidance behav-ior can continue indefinitely. Consider the individual who grows up in a home where his parents have explosive, angry outbursts that terrify him. Throughout life, the person may not only avoid confrontations with others who might get angry with him, but he also avoids confronting his own anger because it is frightening. Continuing avoidance of situations in which he might encounter angry people prevents extinction of the conditioned aversive emotional responses, notably his fear.

In order to understand avoidance behavior and how it is learned, the model formulated by B. F. Skinner and called *operant conditioning*, must be considered.

OPERANT CONDITIONING

B. F. Skinner (1904–1991) wrote extensively about the philosophy of science he called *radical behaviorism* (e.g., Skinner, 1953; 1974). This philosophy recognizes private events such as cognitions and emotions as important but also defines these experiences as behaviors that are affected, as are observable behaviors, by environmental events. Private events do not cause other behaviors, according to Skinner; private events are behaviors explained by environmental contingencies. ("Contingencies" refer to the interrelationships among behaviors, antecedents, and consequences.)

Skinner studied discrete and easily measured behavior of the individual subject intensively over time. He designed his own apparatus and recording devices. The "Skinner box" consists of a soundproofed box with a lever and food magazine. Depressing the lever closes a circuit, which automatically records the number of times the lever pressing brought about the delivery of food. The lever press response facilitates investigation of variables and their relationships to behavior. For example, by manipulating the behavioral requirements for delivering food, Skinner could observe reliable, distinctive patterns of behavior specific to the particular contingencies implemented. The methodology he advocated for studying behavior is called the *experimental analysis of behavior*.

Skinner shifted the focus of explanations for behavior to consequences and a type of conditioning he called *operant*. He developed a program of research in *operant conditioning* that resulted in the formulation of basic principles that govern behavior and the extension of these principles, discovered in the animal laboratory, to applications to human behavior.

In operant conditioning, an animal or person "operates" on the environment and produces a change, a consequence for the behavior. As such, the organism is viewed as *active*. In respondent conditioning the subject is passive because responses are *elicited* by stimuli. An operant is *emitted* in the presence of certain stimuli and produces *consequences* that affect the future probability of the behavior. For example, a food-deprived rat in an operant chamber ("Skinner box") depresses a lever, which results in delivery of a food pellet. The animal's response (the lever press) produces a change in its environment—the response closes the circuit and food is delivered. The rat learns that delivery of food is *contingent* (i.e., dependent) on the occurrence of the lever press, which will affect the likelihood of the response occurring again. In the case of respondent conditioning, presentation of the CS produces a CR; it is the *stimulus* that controls the behavior.

Consequences are defined in terms of their effect on behavior. If the effect is to *strengthen* or *increase* behavior, the event is *reinforcing*. When the behavior is *decreased* or *weakened* by the event, it is *punishing* (Table 6–3).

Table 6–3 **Operant Conditioning—Consequences**

TERM	DEFINITION	EXAMPLE
Positive reinforcement	Increasing the probability of a behavior by presenting a positive reinforcer following occurrence of the behavior.	Patient is praised for adhering to diet restriction 1 week and continues to do so for a second week.
Negative reinforcement	Increasing the probability of a behavior by terminating or avoiding an aversive event or the loss of a positive reinforcer following the occurrence of the behavior.	Patient adheres to diet and exercise regimen in order to discontinue daily insulin.
Positive punishment	Decreasing the probability of a behavior by presenting a punisher following occurrence of the behavior.	Patient is reprimanded for smoking and stops for several days.
Negative punishment	Decreasing the probability of a behavior by removing a positive reinforcer or the opportunity for positive reinforcement following occurrence of the behavior.	Patient is not seen for an appointment when he/she arrives more than 15 minutes late, and frequency of tardiness decreases.
Extinction	Decreasing/eliminating a behavior by discontinuing reinforcement that maintained the behavior.	Excessive patient requests for mood-altering medications are decreased by refusing to comply with such requests.

The critical feature of the consequence is not whether it is judged to be "pleasant" or "unpleasant." *It is the effect of the consequences on behavior that is important.* Assume that two different patients, for example, experience the same physiological effects when they take a particular narcotic analgesic. However, one patient may take the medication only once and discard it and another may overuse the medication. The behavior of taking the medication is reinforced or strengthened by the effects of the drug in one case and the same medication effect may *punish* or weaken the behavior in another patient.

Consider as well the typical elementary school classroom. Within a class of 20–30 students, some will work quietly for long periods without misbehaving to avoid being scolded by the teacher. Other pupils in the class engage in frequent disruptive behavior because it functions to consistently produce teacher attention, albeit negative (negative attention). In the latter case scolding actually *reinforces* misbehavior (increases the likelihood of recurrence). These children may receive little teacher attention, and *negative* attention may be better than none at all.

Reinforcement

Reinforcement refers to the procedure of increasing the probability of a behavior occurring by the *contingent* delivery of a reinforcing event that follows the behavior. The event that strengthens the behavior is called a *reinforcer*.

Reinforcers may be *positive* or *negative* depending on whether the consequence entails the presentation or removal of some event. For example, one patient may take medication as ordered because doing so is associated with either improved physical status or attention and praise from family members and the physician. The behavior of taking the medication is *positively reinforced* in this case. Another patient may comply with the physician's order because taking the medication results in the termination or avoidance of unpleasant physical symptoms. In this situation, compliant behavior is *negatively reinforced*. Behavior that is strengthened because it avoids contact with an aversive event is called *avoidance behavior*. When the behavior results in termination or removal of the aversive event, it is referred to as *escape behavior*. Some patients may stop taking the medication once their symptoms have ceased and only resume the regimen when unpleasant effects reoccur.

There are several different types of reinforcers. The reinforcing properties of *primary reinforcers* seem to be more biologically based rather than being dependent on learning. Examples include food, sex, and water. Other types of reinforcers acquire their reinforcing properties through pairing with other established reinforcers. These are called *conditioned reinforcers*. An example of a conditioned reinforcer is praise, which is frequently paired with other reinforcers. *Generalized reinforcers* are events that acquire and maintain their reinforcer effectiveness through pairing with many other reinforcers. Money, for example, can be exchanged for numerous and diverse objects, events, and so forth, which are reinforcing for the person. Money would cease to be reinforcing if it were no longer paired with other reinforcers. Conditioned and generalized reinforcers can be particularly useful in bridging the time between occurrence of a behavior and delivery of more powerful, but delayed, reinforcers. For example, receiving a letter of acceptance for a manuscript with positive feedback may function to strengthen writing behavior.

Tokens are a special type of generalized reinforcer that can be exchanged for various objects, events, and so forth, called *backup reinforcers*. They allow for behavior to be immediately reinforced. Token systems have been effectively implemented and used in schools, prisons, and institutions for the mentally retarded (Kazdin, 1977). Economic principles are employed in setting up these systems.

Several factors influence reinforcer effectiveness. First, the reinforcer must be presented *contingently*. That is, it should be delivered *contingent on the occurrence of desirable behavior*. Second, the most effective procedure is *immediate presentation* of the reinforcer after the behavior has occurred. Third, it is important to consider the difficulty of performing the behavior, how much behavior is required, and the amount of the reinforcer. Although the general rule is "more reinforcer means greater effectiveness," too much reinforcer can result in *satiation* or a *decrease* in reinforcer effectiveness. Generally, the greater the deprivation or limits on contact with the reinforcer, the more effective the reinforcer will be for altering behavior.

Developing New Behavior

Contingencies of reinforcement can strengthen behaviors once they occur. However, particular skills may either not be in the person's repertoire or the desired behavior may just not occur at all. In such cases there are no opportunities to reinforce the response. The starting point is to identify behavior that is already occurring that resembles the desired behavior and to reinforce it. The behavioral requirement for reinforcer delivery is gradually increased as the behavior becomes more similar to the target behavior. Dissimilar behaviors are extinguished. This is the process of *differential reinforcement* and the result is *response differentiation*. The procedure of differentially reinforcing closer and closer approximations to the final target behavior is called the *method of successive approximations*. Completely new behavior is produced through *shaping*.

Complex behaviors or skills, whether desirable or undesirable, are often developed originally from simple behaviors through the process of shaping, such as learning to play an instrument.

Shaping was an essential component of an intervention to teach toileting behaviors to a 5-year-old child. (Functional encopresis is an elimination disorder (DSM-IV; APA 1994) in which the individual defecates in inappropriate places. Sometimes stool is passed involuntarily because the person retains feces.)

A CASE STUDY

An eight-year-old boy was referred for psychological intervention by his pediatric gastroenterologist because of primary functional encopresis. He had never had a consistent period of continence, and his parents requested help for overflow incontinence secondary to functional fecal retention. The child was chronically constipated, retaining stool for a week or more at a time, and causing considerable discomfort and a distended abdomen. Evacuation with enemas was usually necessary. Laxatives were of minimal assistance since he fought to hold back bowel movements brought about by these agents. He had a history of parental criticism and punishment for soiling in his clothes. The youngster refused to sit on a toilet or potty chair at the time the family presented for treatment.

Power struggles between the child and his parents were well entrenched and included but were not limited to toileting. Parent-training was implemented first with an emphasis on increasing positive consequences for any appropriate behaviors, minimizing aversive controls, and eliminating punishers for soiling. A reinforcement system to shape toileting behaviors was first applied at preschool. He earned praise and access to a "surprise bag" of small tangible reinforcers at school by sitting, even for a few seconds initially, on the toilet in the classroom after lunch. The duration of time required to sit on the toilet to earn praise and a trinket was gradually increased. Then the requirement included having a bowel movement, small at first, and then larger to earn the reinforcer. Within ten weekdays he was sitting on the toilet and having bowel movements with no soiling at school. After two additional weeks the program was implemented at home and he began having regular bowel movements there as well. The "surprise bag" was replaced by a token system and over time, he more and more frequently "forgot" to ask

for his tokens. He verbalized pride in his clean clothes and "flat tummy,"
felt better physically and was no longer teased by his classmates for
"smelling bad," to name but a few of the naturally occurring reinforcers
that maintained the child's toileting behaviors after tangible rewards
were faded.

Imitation

Obviously all new skills do not require shaping. We acquire a great deal of complex behavior by observing others and imitating their behaviors. *Modeling* is a very powerful means of learning new behavior.

Albert Bandura's classic studies demonstrated very clearly that children can learn behaviors by observing others (Bandura et al, 1963). Modeling has been successfully employed to reduce fear and anxiety in children and adults. A filmed model was used by Jay, Elliott, Katz, and Siegel (1987) as a component in a cognitive-behavioral program to reduce distress of pediatric oncology patients undergoing bone marrow aspirations and lumbar punctures. The children observed a videotape of another oncology patient successfully using coping techniques during the invasive medical procedures. The treatment "package," which also included breathing, distraction, rehearsal, and reinforcement, was more effective than oral diazepam (Valium), an anxiety suppression medication, in decreasing behavioral distress during the procedures.

Characteristics of the model as well as the consequences of the behavior for the model affect the likelihood of imitation by an observer. Imitative behaviors can become intrinsically reinforcing. The young ballet dancer diligently practices barre exercises such as the *grand battement en avant* so as to "match" the method of the teacher. Performance of the behavior itself is reinforcing. Further discussion of observational learning is presented within the context of social learning theory.

Extinction

In *extinction*, the reinforcer that has maintained a response no longer follows the behavior and the behavior decreases and is eliminated. Once the response no longer occurs, we say that it has been *extinguished.*

Francis (1988) described a child with obsessive–compulsive disorder with an extinction procedure. The 11-year-old obsessively worried about dying and also engaged in compulsive reassurance-seeking questions. Parents were instructed to withhold their responses and change the conversation when the youngster asked questions seeking reassurance. Francis reported elimination of the behavior within six days using extinction.

Chronic pain patients may complain excessively about physical discomfort for which there is no medical cure. Such complaints are frequently maintained, at least in part, by the attention and sympathy they evoke from others. The behavior may be decreased by withholding attention and sympathy when complaining occurs (an extinction procedure) and also socially reinforcing the patient's talk about any subject other than pain (e.g., the weather, how well he or she feels, recent activities, and so forth) with attention and praise.

It is typical to see a *temporary increase* in the intensity, rate, or duration of a behavior when an extinction procedure has been implemented. Emotional behavior intensifies as well, particularly initially. In the case described above, for example, patient complaints would increase at first in intensity and frequency. The patient might become louder, more emotional, and engage in additional nonverbal pain behaviors as well. The time it takes for the behavior to be eliminated depends on the schedule of reinforcement that has maintained the behavior.

Schedules of Reinforcement

The *schedule of reinforcement* is the rule that specifies the time and response requirements for a reinforcer to be delivered. The rate and pattern of the behavior as it is maintained and/or extinguished are determined by the schedule. When there is only one schedule operating in a situation, it is called a *simple schedule*. Such schedules can be *continuous* or *intermittent*.

Continuous reinforcement (CRF) means that every occurrence of the behavior is immediately reinforced. If a behavior is reinforced intermittently, some occurrences will not be reinforced. When establishing new behaviors it is important to reinforce continuously at first. As the behavior is strengthened, the frequency of reinforcement is gradually decreased. The reinforcement program described earlier for the youngster with encopresis included changing the schedule of reinforcement from continuous to intermittent once the target behavior occurred consistently. The frequency of reinforcement was gradually decreased over time.

If a response has been reinforced continuously, then it will extinguish more rapidly than if it has been reinforced on an intermittent basis. Behaviors maintained by intermittent schedules are said to be more *resistant to extinction*. It is easier to discriminate that extinction has begun when every occurrence of the behavior has previously resulted in reinforcement.

A common problem for many new parents is dealing with infant cries at bedtime. The sound of a child crying is distressing to most people, and they will engage in behaviors to terminate the sound (escape behavior that is negatively reinforced for the adult). If crying at bedtime is reinforced quickly and consistently by picking up the baby and, perhaps, rocking it to sleep, it will be easier to extinguish the crying behavior than if the parents let the child cry for relatively longer periods on occasion and then take it from the crib. In the latter case, it is more difficult to discriminate that extinction is occurring. Going to a crying child to check that it is all right (or even to comfort the child briefly) *without removing it from the crib* will not typically reinforce the crying.

Children with chronic or recurrent pain problems may escalate pain complaints when parents respond inconsistently to these behaviors (McGrath, 1990). The same behavior on the part of the child is dealt with differently by the parents on varying occasions. For example, the child may complain of abdominal pain and be taken to school in tears one day only to be allowed on another occasion to stay home with a parent. The intermittent schedule teaches the child to intensify the severity of the complaints and other pain behaviors. These behaviors will also be more difficult to extinguish.

Punishment

We have already discussed the extinction procedure as one way to eliminate behavior. However, it is not always possible to identify the reinforcer(s) maintaining a behavior nor is it always feasible to control reinforcement for some behaviors. For example, a teacher is more likely to ignore misbehavior of a school-age child than are his or her peers. *In order to extinguish a response, any reinforcer maintaining the behavior must be consistently withheld.* There are also situations in which extinction of a particular behavior would be dangerous or unethical. For example, attention may be the reinforcer maintaining self-injurious behavior in a mentally retarded child. However, the child could seriously injure himself or herself if allowed to self-abuse while attention was withheld. Extinction can also be fairly lengthy at times, particularly if the behavior has been maintained on an intermittent schedule of reinforcement. In such cases, it may be more appropriate to use procedures that rapidly suppress behavior.

A *punisher* is an event that decreases the behavior it follows. *Positive punishment* entails the contingent presentation of an event immediately after the occurrence of the behavior with a resulting decrease in the probability of that behavior. *Negative punishment* consists of the contingent removal of a positive reinforcer or the opportunity to have access to freely available positive reinforcers when a behavior occurs, again with a resultant reduction in the future occurrence of the response. Contingent ignoring, restriction of privileges or possessions, and time out from reinforcement are all examples of negative punishment. A simple example of positive punishment is criticism for tardiness to one's job. Negative punishment for this behavior might be losing part of one's wages for the time missed from work (or losing one's job).

We may inadvertently punish adaptive behavior. For example, well-meaning parents may tell their child with a chronic pain problem to stop doing certain activities.

Time out from reinforcement is frequently used as a punisher for child misbehaviors and merits further discussion. The technique includes components of extinction and punishment. *Time out* requires a limited period (usually one minute per year of age for the child) of no access to freely available reinforcers or of the opportunity to earn reinforcers. Although children are frequently removed to a specific place devoid of materials to play with or things to do, one can also ignore all behavior for a comparable time period without changing the surroundings.

Sometimes parents send their children to their rooms as punishment and find that it does not suppress the inappropriate behavior. Closer analysis typically reveals that the room provides ready and undisturbed access to an array of positive reinforcers ranging from video games and books to music. Besides, such a practice can establish the room as a negative CS, which can then elicit conditioned aversive emotional responses. This is not a situation conducive to uneventful bedtimes and sleeping through the night in one's own room.

As is the case for reinforcers, there are also different types of punishers. *Primary punishers* do not require association with other punishers to be effective, although effectiveness is diminished through adaptation. *Conditioned punishers* must be paired with other punishers to be effective. Threats of punishment, for example, may deter behavior but only if followed by delivery of the punisher if the behavior is performed. *Generalized punishers*, such as social disapproval, are associated with many other punishers.

There are several factors that influence the effectiveness of punishment and are essential to consider. First, *it is necessary to reinforce appropriate behavior that is incompatible with the undesired response*. Punishment does not teach *appropriate* behavior; it is a procedure that often rapidly, but only temporarily, suppresses undesirable behavior. Once punishment is terminated, a previously punished behavior will reoccur unless an appropriate positive alternative is learned and rewarded.

Second, *the punisher should be contingent on occurrence of the behavior and should be delivered immediately*. Delayed consequences, such as punishing a young child at home for behavior that occurred at school or the use of noncontingent positive or negative punishment are not likely to be effective in changing behavior.

Third, *the person should be deprived with respect to the punisher*. Frequent use of punishers will decrease their effectiveness and result in emotional behavior. There are data indicating, for example, that excessive aversive consequences and noncontingent reinforcement are employed by parents of children with conduct disorders (Snyder, 1977). The children learn aggressive behavior through *modeling* and are also taught that there is no relationship between their behavior and consequences. The necessity of frequent administration over time is a good indication that a consequence is not working to reduce a behavior. Using the same consequence for all misbehaviors, whether positive or negative punishment, diminishes effectiveness. An additional consideration here is that the intensity of the punisher often increases as frequency of administration increases. A *habituation effect* occurs over time with greater negative side effects and dimished effectiveness.

Fourth, *behavior that is being punished should not also be reinforced*. If punishment is paired with reinforcement, the procedure will, in all likelihood, not result in a decrease in behavior. For example, someone may frequently criticize another person's behavior and then immediately try to make amends with displays of physical affection. The punisher may actually become a discriminative stimulus for positive reinforcement and not function to decrease the offensive behavior being criticized.

Problems with the Use of Negative Controls

Although respondent (Pavlovian) and operant (Skinnerian) conditioning have been discussed separately in this chapter, in reality, the processes are interactive and probably inseparable (Baldwin and Baldwin, 1981). Many of the problems of using negative means of influencing behavior such as punishment and negative reinforcement relate to the interplay of respondent and operant conditioning, including the development of aversive emotional responses. Baldwin and Baldwin (1981) emphasize the use of positive reinforcement over negative reinforcement or punishment.

They maintain that presenting others with aversive stimuli, as one does with negative reinforcement such as nagging or criticism, diminishes positive social interactions and, through conditioning, makes the desired behavior an aversive CS. The person learns to dislike the behavior. For example, if nagging and criticism are used by a child's parents to get the youngster to clean his or her room, the child will probably learn to dislike cleaning because of the association of cleaning with aversive stimuli. One might also observe emotional behaviors associated with the onset of the aversive stimulation, as in the case of the child who starts to stamp, yell, or cry when told to clean his or her room. The alternative, more effective, strategy is to *positively reinforce* behavior.

Baldwin and Baldwin (1981) recommend minimizing application of punishment, particularly when alternative methods are available, because of several negative effects of using punishment:

The punishing agent often models aggressive behavior, verbally or physically. Severe criticism or ridicule and/or physical punishment teaches the recipient that aggression is an acceptable means of dealing with people. The individual may not aggress against the punishing agent but is more likely to engage in verbally or physically aggressive behavior with peers, especially if male (Bandura and Walters, 1959; Bandura, 1973; Hoffman, 1960, cited in Baldwin and Baldwin, 1981). It is especially counterproductive to punish aggression with aggression. People who use negative punishment procedures (e.g., restriction of privileges, time out from reinforcement) may also apply positive punishers such as criticism or being physically "rough" with a child en route to the time-out area.

Punishment generates emotional behavior and more intense verbal or physical activity. In response to aversive stimulation, a youngster may cry, an adult may threaten, or either may hit depending on the situation. Again, violence is more likely to be directed toward peers, a pattern that, when initiated during childhood, can continue through the adult years, such as the spouse who hits his wife when angry. Application of negative punishment procedures can produce emotional responses as well, such as the child who cries when taken to sit in the corner, the teenager who slams the door and talks back when restricted for the weekend, and the spouse who shouts and storms out of the house in response to the other's refusal to attend or talk.

People learn to avoid punishment and also the punishing agent. Behaviors that avoid punishment are negatively reinforced and are usually undesirable responses. For example, people learn what they can do so as not to get "caught" again for a previously punished behavior. Sometimes this is lying about engaging in a behavior and, when lying is punished, Baldwin and Baldwin (1981) suggest the person learns how to be a better liar. Children may "lose" or "forget" to deliver less-than-satisfactory report cards or notes from teachers about misbehavior to their parents. The adolescent who is prohibited from seeing certain friends or is restricted from all privileges for weeks at a time, refines a repertoire of deceptive behavior in order to continue to see friends and engage in activities. When punishment is used frequently or is severe, the recipient may also learn to avoid the punishing agent, thus diminishing the opportunities for the agent to either punish or reinforce other behavior.

Negative emotional responses are conditioned when aversive controls are used. Stimuli present in the situation when punishment is delivered can become conditioned aversive stimuli and elicit negative responses including "anxiety, shame, guilt, or bad feelings about [oneself]" (Baldwin and Baldwin, 1981, p 266). As more stimuli elicit the negative CER's, the effects generalize to the point that some individuals' functioning is impaired by symptoms of anxiety or other distress. People also engage in behaviors to avoid negative CER's. For example, children who have experienced little reinforcement and much criticism and other punishers by parents and teachers for academic or behavioral difficulties at school usually say they "hate" school and frequently drop out once they reach legal age to do so.

Response suppression produced by punishment can generalize to other behaviors. The individual's behavioral repertoire can be generally inhibited if punishment is employed for many behaviors. Baldwin and Baldwin (1981) indicate that although severe generalized response suppression is rare, shyness, a milder form, is more common.

Antecedents

So far we have discussed the importance of consequences for operant behavior. The *antecedents* of behavior are also significant variables in explaining behavior (Table 6–4). People behave in the presence of certain stimuli or stimulus situations.

We learn to engage in different behaviors depending on the situation. This is accomplished by means of *discrimination training:* in the presence of some stimuli a particular behavior is *reinforced* and in the presence of different stimuli the behavior is *extinguished.* A small child may learn, for example, that one parent ignores tantrums while the other gives the child what he or she wants and, therefore, will *reinforce* the tantrum. The parent who reinforces the tantrums becomes a *discriminative stimulus* (S^D) for tantrums (i.e., the presence of this parent signals that reinforcement is forthcoming if the behavior does occur). The other parent is associated with nonreinforcement of tantrums and is called an S^Δ (S-delta) if the behavior occurs less frequently in his or her presence than in the presence of the S^D. When the tantrum is more likely to occur in the presence of the S^D than in its absence, we say that *stimulus control* over the tantrum behavior has been established. The behavior is called *discriminated behavior.*

In clinical medicine, a person with a chronic pain problem may be observed to emit more pain behaviors when another person is present to observe and respond to the behaviors than when no one is near or when someone who does not attend to the pain behavior is present. In this situation, there is stimulus control over the pain behavior. (However, this does not mean that the patient is intentionally or consciously behaving in such a way. One need not necessarily be aware of the contingencies in order for one's behavior to be affected by them.)

In order to facilitate the development of discriminated behavior, two stimuli are sometimes presented together. One stimulus is then gradually removed or *faded* so the other controls the response. For example, modeling may be initially paired with verbal instructions but faded over time.

It is frequently desirable for a behavior to occur in the presence of different and/ or novel stimuli or situations. Such an occurrence is called *generalization.* This is accomplished by *generalization training,* which entails reinforcement of the behavior in the presence of other stimuli until all members of a stimulus class are associated

Table 6–4 **Operant Conditioning—Antecedents**

TERM	DEFINITION	EXAMPLE
Discrimination training	In the presence of certain stimuli or stimulus situations, a behavior is reinforced, and, in the presence of others, the behavior is extinguished.	A medical student gets credit for labeling an event that increases the behavior it follows a "reinforcer" but not for labeling it anything else.
Discriminative stimulus (S^D_I)	Signals that reinforcement is forthcoming if the behavior occurs in its presence.	Giving a correct definition in response to the question "What is a positive reinforcer?" results in credit for a correct answer.
S^Δ	Signals that reinforcement is not forthcoming if the behavior occurs in its presence.	Giving the definition for a punisher in response to the question "What is a positive reinforcer?" results in no credit for the answer.
Discriminated behavior	Behavior that is more likely to occur in the presence of the S^D than in its absence.	Giving the definition for positive reinforcer is more likely to occur when asked "What is a positive reinforcer?" than when some other question is asked.
Stimulus control	Achieved for a behavior when it is more likely to occur in the presence of the S^D than in its absence.	The question comes to control the response of the definition.
Fading	Stimulus is gradually removed or faded so that another stimulus presented with it will control the response.	Initially a verbal prompt may be required to facilitate the response of giving the definition but is gradually removed so that the question only controls the response.
Generalization	Behavior occurs in the presence of different and/or novel stimuli or stimulus situations.	Given one example of a positive reinforcer, the student is able to identify others.

with occurrence of the behavior. For example, a person may be working to improve his or her assertiveness skills and begins practicing with one family member. The person practices with more and more family members until eventually he or she is responding assertively with the group (or stimulus class) of family members.

THE PRINCIPLE OF RECIPROCAL INHIBITION

Joseph Wolpe employed an animal model to study the development of emotional reactions or "experimental neuroses" and ways of treating such problems once acquired. Cats were shocked while in cages and sometimes as they approached food.

The "experimental neuroses" consisted of behaviors indicative of anxiety associated with the cage and lack of feeding behavior despite severe food deprivation. The behaviors generalized to similar situations and were more intense in situations that more closely resembled the experimental cage, room, and so forth. Wolpe reasoned that since feeding behavior had been inhibited by anxiety, then anxiety might be inhibited by eating. Wolpe subsequently reduced the "neurotic symptoms" in the cats by inducing feeding in the original room or in rooms that resembled the original room. Once the cat fed in the original room without signs of anxiety, it was placed in the cage as well. Wolpe considered the "neurosis" eliminated once the cat ate in the experimental cage without indications of anxiety. He maintained that the animal could not be fearful or anxious and feed simultaneously. That is, anxiety and feeding are *reciprocally inhibiting*, the occurrence of one inhibits the other.

Wolpe extended the treatment procedures based on laboratory work with animals to applications with humans. He developed an abbreviated version of Jacobson's (1938) progressive muscle relaxation procedure and initially employed relaxation to inhibit anxiety and fear in the presence of actual anxiety-provoking stimuli. Basically, he sought a method more convenient than gradual in vivo (real life) exposure and decided to try imagined scenes. *Systematic desensitization*, as he called it, entails pairing deep muscle relaxation with imaginal scenes in a graded fashion from the least to most anxiety provoking. The responses to anxiety-provoking stimuli are "reconditioned" with relaxation, replacing or "inhibiting" the anxiety. Wolpe also used assertive responses and sexual arousal to inhibit anxiety.

Wolpe's work constituted a bridge between animal experimentation in the laboratory and the development of treatment procedures for human problems. Behavioral techniques developed by Wolpe, such as systematic desensitization, were based on the principle of reciprocal inhibition formulated from experiments. Much research was generated from his work, particularly related to systematic desensitization, and this contributed significantly to the development of behavior therapy.

SOCIAL LEARNING OR SOCIAL COGNITIVE THEORY

The foremost theorist and researcher in the area of social learning is Albert Bandura. He agrees with Skinner that behavior is influenced by contingencies, but he emphasizes cognitive processes such as expectancies and the effects of these processes on the behavior of the person and the environment. Bandura (1986) relabeled *social learning* theory and called it *social cognitive* theory, indicating that as his theoretical approach developed, its scope broadened and extended beyond learning mechanisms alone.

The major principle of social cognitive theory is *triadic reciprocal determinism*, which refers to the mutually causal relationship between *behavior, personal factors*, and *environmental events*. Cognitive capabilities, such as the use of symbols, make it possible for people to process thoughts, communicate with one another, anticipate consequences, and learn by observing others. Individuals are therefore able to motivate themselves and engage in self-directed behavior, including self-evaluation and regulation.

Bandura's conceptualization of causation as the interaction of environmental, behavioral, and personal factors may be illustrated with a discussion of several major contributions of social learning or social cognitive theory—modeling, self-regulation, and self-efficacy.

Modeling

Learning that occurs by observing others and the consequences of their behavior is highly efficient. The survival value of such a process is obvious when compared to trial-and-error learning. For example, acquisition of very complex behaviors, such as driving a car and social skills, are facilitated by observing others.

Modeling is a means by which knowledge, skills, and rules can be learned and represented symbolically. As such, there are a number of functions that modeling can serve with regard to learning and these may operate concurrently in a given situation.

1. A new pattern of behavior can be acquired by observing how to combine component behaviors in a different way. For example, dancers have a repertoire of movements and skills that are combined in various ways with each new choreography they learn. Surgical residents learn to apply techniques in specific ways for the type of surgery they are performing by observing the most experienced surgeons.

2. Bandura (1986) also maintains that modeling can function to inhibit or disinhibit performance of behaviors that are part of the individual's repertoire. For example, students may be inhibited from volunteering to answer questions in a particular class because they have observed the instructor consistently find fault with others' answers. Disinhibition can be facilitated by observing, for example, a model who copes in a difficult situation and is successful. Interventions designed to help children manage the discomfort and fear associated with invasive medical procedures, such as bone marrow aspirations and lumbar punctures, include a coping model component (e.g., Jay, Elliott, Katz, and Siegel, 1987).

3. Modeling can facilitate occurrence of or "induce" appropriate behavior that is already part of the person's repertoire. For example, some people may not give money to a homeless person until they observe someone else do so or they may volunteer to perform certain tasks only after others have first offered their services. Bandura (1986) calls this a *response-cueing* function.

4. The attention of the observer can be directed to certain stimuli or situations by the model's behavior, thus making the observer more likely to perform the behavior in the presence of these cues. For example, some people may snack at a party, even if they are

not hungry, because their attention is drawn to the food by the sight of others eating.

5. Finally, Bandura (1986) maintains that modeling can influence occurrences of emotional responses and anticipatory arousal in situations where a model has displayed emotions. Children, for example, can learn to be fearful of situations such as thunderstorms by observing an anxious parent during such events.

According to Bandura (1977), modeling is mediated by a number of component processes. First, one must attend to the model or modeling stimulus in order for observational learning to occur. There are several aspects of the attentional processes. Both characteristics of the observer and the model affect what will actually be observed. For example, models who are more attractive or pleasing to the observer are more likely to be observed than those without these characteristics. With respect to observer characteristics, the person must have, for example, adequate sensory capacities for attending.

Second, the person must remember the observed behavior by means of retention processes. These include, for example, symbolic coding or having verbal labels or descriptions for the behavior. Symbolic (mental) or motor rehearsal are additional processes that may be employed to retain what was observed.

Motor reproduction processes have to do with reproducing the information retained into specific behavior. The physical capabilities of the observer, for example, determine whether the observed behavior can be performed.

Finally, motivational processes determine if the observed behavior will be performed. The processes include, for example, vicarious reinforcement or reinforcement observed for the model's behavior. Bandura posits that individuals who see the model's behavior reinforced will likely expect that their own matching or imitative behavior will also be followed by such consequences. Other motivational processes include the nature of self-evaluation and feedback and self-reinforcement.

Bandura's contributions in the area of observational learning are highly significant. As indicated earlier, his classic studies demonstrated very clearly that children learn aggressive behavior from observing aggressive models (Bandura et al, 1963). Subsequent research has shown that one of the best predictors of aggressive behavior in children is aggressive behavior by the parents (Pfeffer et al, 1983).

Self-regulation

Self-direction is an important aspect of Bandura's social cognitive theory. The capability to regulate one's behavior entails multiple skills. There are three processes involved in self-regulation according to Bandura (1986): *self-observation, self-evaluation*, and *self-reaction*. This section includes descriptions of the processes and possible dysfunctions related to depression.

Self-observation or Monitoring

In order to obtain information to establish standards of behavior and to judge current behavior relative to these standards, one must observe relevant dimensions of one's behavior with some regularity and accuracy. Self-monitoring is influenced by attentional processes, self-perception, and symbolic representation of information obtained. Dysfunction in this process can be related to a self-perpetuating cycle of depressed mood that adversely affects the way experiences are monitored and processed, and this faulty processing further exacerbates the individual's depressed mood. Bandura (1986) suggests that depressed persons *negatively distort* their perceptions and recollections of events. For example, such individuals may take an important examination and recall more about what they did not know on the test than what they were able to answer. This distorted recollection of the event adversely affects their mood, and they begin to recall other experiences that reflect negatively on their competence.

Judgment or Self-evaluation

This process entails evaluation of behavior in relation to internalized personal standards and other points of reference such as peers or a normative group as well as consideration of the value of the performance. Furthermore, Bandura (1986) indicates that it is important to take into account the causal attributions of the individual with respect to success and failure. Dysfunction in any or all of these subprocesses may be related to depressed mood. The individuals described above negatively appraise their performances either in relation to peers, a normative group, or their own standards and attributes the failure to lack of ability rather than situational factors. Further, these individuals devalue their accomplishments in relation to others.

Self-reaction

The third process in self-regulation is self-reaction, which directs and motivates behavior. Individuals can evaluate their behavior positively or negatively and reward or punish the performance. Depressed persons are less likely to positively evaluate and reward an activity and more likely to severely punish than nondepressed persons, according to Bandura (1986). Repeated negative self-reaction is associated with depressed mood.

It can be adaptive to modify standards and other subprocesses of self-regulation. Consider the case of a 20-year-old college student and musician with a chronic pain problem subsequent to injury in an automobile accident.

A CASE STUDY

The patient was a sophomore music student when he was "rear-ended" in a motor vehicle accident. He did not suffer major injury but was left with chronic neck and shoulder pain associated with whiplash some months after the accident. He was an accomplished cellist who was accustomed to practicing 3–4 hours each day. He was also an exceptional student who expected to earn As in all of his college classes. After the accident, the patient experienced difficulty in studying for extended periods as well as in sitting for exams because of the strain on his neck and shoulder muscles and the resulting pain. Most attempts to play the cello were followed by significant increases in pain. He was not willing to practice his instrument for only a few minutes on alternating days as his physical therapist advised, and he could not accept less than excellent grades in his courses. He became increasingly depressed and withdrawn, and his pain problem continued to worsen.

Subsequent to his accident, the young man was not able to perform academically or musically according to previous standards. Nevertheless, he continued to apply these standards and to evaluate his performance in reference to them. The result was that he consistently fell short, producing negative and punishing self-reactions and multiple adverse effects, including distorted self-monitoring over time. The patient experienced a sense of failure, self-deprecation, greater physical pain, and depressed mood. He devalued what he was able to accomplish within his limitations and participated in fewer and fewer activities as his depression intensified.

Self-efficacy

Bandura defines the concept of self-efficacy in the following way:

Perceived self-efficacy is defined as people's judgments of their capabilities to organize and execute courses of action required to attain designated types of performances. It is concerned not with the skills one has but with judgments of what one can do with whatever skills one possesses. (Bandura, 1986, p 391)

It is Bandura's contention that it is not sufficient that individuals have skills to behave competently; it is also necessary that they have perceived self-efficacy with regard to these skills. People may expect a particular consequence for a behavior (outcome expectation) and have the behavior in their repertoire but not engage in the activity because they judge themselves as deficient in that situation. The greater one's self-efficacy, the more likely it is for the person to persist in the face of difficulty.

According to Bandura (1986), there are four sources of information regarding self-efficacy:

1. *Success experiences* increase self-efficacy and failures decrease appraisals of efficacy. If self-efficacy is strong, occasional failures are more likely to be attributed to situational factors rather than to lack of ability. Bandura also maintains that self-efficacy generalizes to similar situations.
2. *Vicarious experiences* in which others are observed to be capable can facilitate self-efficacy, particularly when the individual lacks information about how to evaluate his or her competence in the situation.
3. *Verbal persuasion* can be a source of information about self-efficacy when the person already has some confidence in his or her capabilities in the situation. When the person then tries and succeeds, self-efficacy is further strengthened.

4. *Physiological state* gives the individual information about susceptibility to failure. The absence of signs of autonomic arousal is associated with greater likelihood of success. A negative cycle of
physiological arousal, negative thoughts, and greater arousal can be
set into motion.

The concept of self-efficacy is useful from Bandura's perspective in understanding anxiety disorders. He says that expectations regarding outcome and efficacy cause
fear and avoidance rather than fear causing avoidance behavior. For example, patients
with social phobias may consistently avoid situations that require speaking in front of
groups of persons. They may experience numerous physiological signs of anxiety in
such situations that intensify their embarrassment and self-consciousness and cause
them to further doubt their abilities to speak coherently in front of others. Individuals
have expectations about what they would say, how they would say it, and possible
consequences (outcome) as well as an expectation about whether they could do what
they know how to do (efficacy). From Bandura's viewpoint, experiencing success will
increase efficacy and decrease avoidance and fear. Verbal persuasion is less likely to be
effective in such a situation.

Turk, Rudy, and Sorkin (1992) relate the concept of self-efficacy to coping with
chronic pain. They make the case that the strength of the patient's self-efficacy for
coping with pain affects the likelihood of the person engaging in coping behaviors and
persisting in the face of difficulty. Setting the patient up to succeed with gradual
increases in activities and pacing facilitates development of realistic expectancies and,
consequently, occurrences of coping behaviors. The authors also suggest that avoidance behaviors are mediated by expectancies about pain. Avoidance of activities
persists because the patient believes that performance of the behavior(s) will cause
pain, and the expectation is not changed because consequences are avoided and not
experienced. Individuals are assisted so that they engage in activities associated with
less pain than expected and, through repeated experiences of this type, expectancies
are modified to become more realistic and adaptive.

CLINICAL APPLICATIONS: COGNITIVE
AND BEHAVIORAL THERAPIES

Behavior therapy or modification entails the application of laboratory-based
psychological principles for changing behavior. A great deal of research has been and
continues to be generated in evaluation of treatment techniques derived from principles of operant and respondent conditioning. It is also important to note that these
procedures are applied in an individualized fashion and that treatment may consist of
multiple interventions. Furthermore, an appreciation of the underlying principles of
any behavioral treatment is essential to ensure the technique is applied appropriately
and efficaciously.

The term *cognitive-behavioral therapy* frequently refers to treatment "packages" (or protocols) that include a number of component procedures. Some of these
components may be called "behavioral" such as exposure, relaxation, contingency
management, social skills training, or biofeedback. Others are described as "cognitive"

because they address factors such as expectancies, self-talk, perceptions, interpretations, self-efficacy, and the like.

Interventions that are intended to modify cognitions usually include behavioral methods such as self-monitoring, rehearsal, or exposure. Historically, studies have not clearly shown that cognitions are altered because of the "cognitive" techniques employed or that changes in behavior were due to alterations in cognitions. However, researchers in the field are enthusiastically engaged in treatment comparison studies and component analyses of behavioral and cognitive-behavioral intervention packages for multiple problem areas.

It is beyond the scope of this chapter to review and/or compare cognitive-behavioral and behavioral therapies for psychiatric or medical disorders. This section however, includes brief presentations of the following: (1) the cognitive or cognitive-behavioral therapies of Meichenbaum, Beck, and Ellis; (2) descriptions/definitions of a sample of therapy techniques and a case study illustration of the application of some of these techniques to treat obsessive–compulsive disorder; (3) behavior therapy applications within behavioral medicine and a case study illustration of the applications of behavior therapy for a health-related problem; and (4) applications of behavior therapy for prevention of illness and disease.

Cognitive Behavior Modification

Meichenbaum (1977) maintains that the same principles that govern observable behavior can also be applied to modify private events, such as cognitions. By altering cognitions such as "self-talk," behavior and emotions can also be changed. Meichenbaum developed two procedures that emphasize the role of self-talk in facilitating behavior change. *Self-instructional Training* entails identification of maladaptive thoughts; that is, individuals learn what they say to themselves in situations identified as problematic (e.g., speaking in front of groups of people). Then, the therapist models appropriate self-instructions, positive self-talk, and self-reinforcement for handling the situation successfully. Finally, the person practices, first self-instructing aloud and then silently, and the therapist gives feedback. According to a recent review of cognitive therapy for anxiety disorders by Oakely and Padesky (1990), additional research is needed to evaluate Self-instructional Training.

Stress Inoculation Training focuses on the acquisition of coping skills that can be applied across different situations. According to Meichenbaum (1977), training includes three phases, the first of which is educational. The patient learns about the relationship between maladaptive patterns of thinking and emotions and behavior. Second, coping self-talk is rehearsed for each step of dealing with a stressor, including preparing for it, confronting and handling the stressor, coping with being overwhelmed by the event, and praising oneself for handling the situation. Finally, the skills are applied in vivo.

Rational-emotive Therapy (RET)

Ellis (1962) identifies faulty cognitions as the basis for people's distress. *Rational-emotive Therapy* (RET) focuses on directly changing patterns of thinking and is based on the assumption that one's interpretation or perception of events produces emotional consequences. In other words, it is not the event itself that causes a person to experience emotions of anxiety, happiness, or fear, but his or her beliefs about the event. Ellis discusses the relationship in terms of an "ABC" model where A is the event, B is the belief about the event, and C is the emotional consequence. Ordinarily, people think their emotions are caused by events but, according to Ellis, they are the result of either rational or irrational beliefs about the situation. Therapy involves disputation of the irrational beliefs. However, Ellis (1979, cited by Oakley and Padesky, 1990) indicates that RET includes many techniques, including numerous behavioral procedures. This makes it difficult to evaluate the effectiveness of RET. The reader is referred to reviews by Haaga and Davison (1989) and Lyons and Woods (1991). The latter review consists of a meta-analysis of outcome studies. The authors only cautiously conclude that RET is an effective treatment due to significant methodological problems of the studies reviewed.

Beck's Cognitive Therapy

Beck (1967, 1976) proposes a model for conceptualizing and treating anxiety, depression, and other disorders that is based on the premise, similar to Ellis's, that it is the individual's perception or interpretation of events that causes emotional distress. With regard to depression, Beck (1967) suggests that as a child the person forms a "negative self-schema" that is characterized by a kind of theme, such as abandonment or criticism, depending on the nature of childhood experiences. Individuals view themselves, the environment, and the future negatively because of the self-schema. When adults have experiences similar to painful childhood experiences, they process the information in ways that are consistent with the negative self-schema (e.g., as abandonment) and feel depressed. The cognitive errors in processing information function to sustain the depression (Thorpe and Olson, 1990).

Cognitive themes and information-processing errors also apply in anxiety disorders (Beck, 1976). Oakley and Padesky (1990) suggest that once the person judges a situation as dangerous, the entire system is affected—including autonomic arousal, behavior, emotions, and cognitions—and the changes are self-sustaining. A similar scenario also occurs with depression.

Cognitive therapy focuses on the themes of negative self-schemata, but not initially. At first, therapy centers on helping the patient see the relationship between cognitions, emotions, and behaviors through self-monitoring. Behavioral tasks are assigned as "experiments" to have the patient "test out" beliefs about himself or herself against "reality" and, for depressed patients, for activation. As therapy continues, there is more emphasis on evaluating maladaptive thoughts and on "testing" their validity until the person directly confronts the theme of their negative self-schema and works to change it.

Oakley and Padesky's (1990) review includes an excellent description of the application of cognitive therapy for anxiety disorders. The author's conclusion regarding the effectiveness of Beck's cognitive therapy for anxiety disorders is that it is a "promising approach" but larger, more methodologically sound studies are needed to draw firmer conclusions regarding efficacy. Hollon, Shelton, and Loosen (1991) reviewed studies comparing cognitive therapy with pharmacotherapy for depression and reached similar conclusions. They indicated that cognitive therapy has not been well established as an alternative to pharmacotherapy for depression because of the limitations of current research.

THERAPY TECHNIQUES

1. *Contingency management* entails application of the principles of reinforcement and punishment to change behavior, such as increasing compliance with medical treatment or parental requests or decreasing unhealthy or maladaptive behaviors (i.e., overeating, smoking, or physical aggression). Token systems have been implemented to increase medical treatment compliance (Dapcich-Miura and Hovell, 1979).

2. *Parent training* (e.g., Forehand and McMahon, 1982; Patterson and Guillion, 1976) consists of instruction in contingency management skills including how to (1) identify specific behaviors to change; (2) increase positive interactions with the child and decrease commands and criticisms; (3) provide positive reinforcers such as praise, affection, and tokens for desirable behavior; (4) extinguish negative attention-getting behaviors; (5) use time out or *response cost* for inappropriate behaviors. Response cost is a punishment procedure whereby points or tokens are taken away contingent upon occurrences of particular behaviors.

3. Contingencies can be mutually agreed upon and written down in the form of contracts. The *contingency contract* specifies behaviors and their consequences in explicit detail and is most effective when negotiated with all parties having input and agreeing on the contingencies. Taylor and associates (1980), for example, decreased a patient's unnecessary overuse of medical services by making visits to two health professionals contingent on not seeing others without permission.

4. *Social skills training* entails systematic instruction and training in an area of communication using behavioral principles. Global skill areas such as assertiveness or conversational skills are broken down into specific, teachable units of behavior. The social skills training model consists of: (1) describing the specific behavior to be learned along with a rationale for its acquisition; (2) modeling the behavior; (3) having the person practice the skill by role-playing; and (4) giving feedback for the performance. The steps are repeated until each skill is mastered. Chaney (1989) suggests, for example, that training in "drink refusal" for alcoholics is useful as one component of in-patient treatment. The inclusion of intensive social skills training as part of in-patient treatment for adult schizophrenics resulted in a number of im-

provements including shorter hospitalization and fewer relapses posttreatment (Liberman, Mueser, and Wallace, 1986).

5. *Exposure to fear-provoking stimuli* is the treatment of choice for many anxiety disorders. Table 6–5 includes the disorders for which exposure is the primary intervention or a major component of treatment as concluded by authors of recent reviews of the areas. The procedure can be accomplished in a number of ways. *Gradual in vivo exposure* may be self-paced or arranged by a therapist. An anxiety hierarchy is developed that consists of identifying fear-inducing situations for the person and then quantifying each of these in terms of how much distress the patient experiences (or imagines he or she would experience) if actually in the situation. Typically, the items are quantified by rating "subjective units of distress" (SUDS) on a scale of zero to one hundred. The situations are arranged in the hierarchy, and exposure begins with the least fear-provoking situation. Once the patient experiences minimal to no anxiety in this situation, the next one is faced and so on, until the person can handle the most difficult situations for himself or herself. An example of an anxiety hierarchy for gradual exposure for treatment of a driving phobia is illustrated in Table 6–6.

6. *Systematic desensitization* is basically gradual imaginal exposure. There are occasions when patient anxiety is so severe that treatment with in vivo exposure is preceded by systematic desensitization. For example, a homebound agoraphobic may not be able to venture from the safety of the house at all. Gradual imaginal exposure decreases anxiety and fear sufficiently to make it possible to initiate gradual in vivo exposure.

7. *Imaginal flooding* entails indirect exposure in an abrupt and prolonged fashion. The patient is instructed to imagine the anxi-

Table 6–5 **Applications of Exposure as a Primary Treatment Component for Anxiety Disorders**

ANXIETY DISORDER	INTERVENTION	REVIEW
Agoraphobia	In vivo exposure	Craske, Rapee, and Barlow, 1992
Obsessive–compulsive disorder	In vivo exposure with response prevention	Stanley, 1992
Posttraumatic stress disorder	In vivo or imaginal exposure (plus stress management with combat veterans)	Keane, Gerardi, Quinn, and Litz, 1992
Simple phobia	Exposure	Borden, 1992
Social phobia	Exposure	Turner, Beidel, and Townsley, 1992

Table 6–6 **Sample Anxiety Hierarchy for a Patient with a Driving Phobia**

100 SUDS	Sitting in traffic on a bridge over a body of water by myself
95 SUDS	Crossing a body of water over a bridge by myself with no traffic in sight
90 SUDS	Sitting in traffic on a bridge over a body of water with someone with me in the car
85 SUDS	Sitting in traffic on a bridge by myself with cars lined up as far as I can see
80 SUDS	Sitting on the expressway by myself with cars backed up as far as I can see
75 SUDS	Sitting in traffic on a bridge with someone with me with cars lined up as far as I can see
70 SUDS	Sitting on the expressway with someone with me with cars lined up as far as I can see
65 SUDS	Driving over a bridge on the expressway by myself in stop-and-go traffic
60 SUDS	Driving on the expressway by myself in stop-and-go traffic
55 SUDS	Driving over a bridge on the expressway with someone with me in stop-and-go traffic
50 SUDS	Driving on the expressway with someone with me in stop-and-go traffic
45 SUDS	Driving over a bridge on the expressway by myself with no traffic in sight
40 SUDS	Driving on the expressway by myself with no traffic in sight
35 SUDS	Driving on surface streets by myself and stopping in a long line of traffic
30 SUDS	Driving on surface streets by myself in stop-and-go traffic
25 SUDS	Driving on surface streets with someone and stopping in a long line of traffic
20 SUDS	Driving on surface streets by myself in stop-and-go traffic
15 SUDS	Driving on surface streets by myself and stopping at a traffic light and not being the first car in the line
10 SUDS	Driving on surface streets by myself and stopping at a traffic light and being the first car in the line
5 SUDS	Driving on a familiar stretch of road that is mildly congested but has no traffic lights
0 SUDS	Driving on a familiar stretch of road that has no traffic lights and very little traffic

ety-provoking scenario by the therapist and continues to do so until there is significant reduction in anxiety. Self-report, overt behavior, and physiological responses (e.g., pulse rate and blood pressure) are assessed to evaluate level of anxiety. Imaginal flooding has been employed for treatment of posttraumatic stress disorder associated, for example, with combat experiences (Keane et al, 1992).

Flooding in vivo consists of abrupt, prolonged exposure to the fear-producing stimuli. The patient is accompanied to the situation, as in the case of agoraphobia, or may be presented the stimuli in the office by a therapist. The person stays in the situation until there is a significant reduction in anxiety. The procedure is repeated until the anxiety is eliminated.

There is not a single theory proposed about how exposure works to reduce anxiety. One explanation is that escape and avoidance behaviors as well as anxiety are extinguished because exposure to the situations does not result in aversive consequences. Bandura (1977) suggests that exposure functions to increase self-efficacy, which results in diminished anxiety and additional efforts on the part of the patient to perform such behaviors.

8. *Response prevention* consists of not allowing the patient to engage in behaviors, such as compulsive rituals, that serve an anxiety-reductive function. For example, a compulsive handwasher would not be allowed to wash. The rationale is that performance of the ritual, as in the case of obsessive–compulsive disorder, is negatively reinforced because it terminates or avoids anxiety. The avoidance behavior is extinguished.

The behavioral treatment of choice for obsessive–compulsive disorder is a combination of response prevention and exposure (Foa et al, 1980). Parameters to consider in implementing the intervention include moderate levels of anxiety generated in frequent sessions with short time periods separating sessions (Stanley, 1992).

9. *Relaxation techniques* can be employed as a treatment component for diverse problems such as anticipatory nausea and vomiting associated with cancer chemotherapy, chronic pain, and insomnia, as well as an adjunct to other treatments for stress reduction, hypertension, and anxiety. Some researchers have suggested that patient anxiety may potentiate conditioned responses in chemotherapy (Andrykowski and Redd, 1987; Burish and Carey, 1986) and acquisition and application of relaxation skills can alleviate or even prevent development of anticipatory nausea and vomiting (Burish, Carey, Krozely, and Greco, 1987). *Progressive muscle relaxation* (or PMR) (Jacobson, 1938) entails learning to deeply relax the muscles of the body by systematically tensing each of several muscle groups and abruptly releasing the tension. This helps increase awareness of the differences in the sensations of tension and relaxation and also how to produce relaxation. Eventually patients are able to induce a state of deep relaxation without the tension-release cycles. *Diaphragmatic breathing*, which typically consists of instruction in how to use one's diaphragm to breath more deeply and slowly, and *imagery or visualization techniques* can also be employed to induce relaxation or deepen a relaxed state produced by PMR. Relaxation exercises have applicability across a wide range of psychiatric and medical problems from managing chronic pain to helping prevent reoccurrences of herpes (Burnette et al, 1991).

10. *Biofeedback* is a tool to promote self-regulation of physiological responses such as heart rate, blood pressure, brain waves, body temperature, penile erections, and muscle activity. Electrical signals from the particular response are measured, amplified, and then converted to visual or auditory information for the patient. This objective, observable feedback about a particular system or function of the body helps the patient learn how to exert control over the response.

In the area of chronic pain, biofeedback is useful for promoting relaxation as well as for reactivating muscles that have not been used because of the association of movement of those muscles with pain. Other examples of clinical applications include electromyographic (EMG) biofeedback for neuromuscular recovery in cardiovascular accident patients and for fecal incontinence caused by sphincter weakness.

11. *Cognitive restructuring* refers to alterations in patterns of thinking and may include the methods of Ellis, Meichenbaum, Beck, or others. For example, a patient's belief that he or she must be perfect in order to be worthwhile, might be challenged by logical argument as well as completion of assignments in which they purposely perform a task or behavior less than perfectly.

12. *Problem-solving skills training* involves instruction in the use of a model consisting of several steps: (1) define the problem; (2) brainstorm possible solutions; (3) evaluate solutions and implement one; and (4) evaluate the solution implemented. Training can be especially useful for individuals who behave impulsively.

13. *Stress-management training* is frequently based on Meichenbaum's Stress Inoculation Training and includes educational, rehearsal, and application phases. During the educational phase, the patients learn about their individual responses to stress, sources of stress, and means of avoiding or coping with stressors. Time management and assertiveness are ways to avoid stress. Relaxation skills training, positive self-talk, and problem solving are examples of coping skills. In the rehearsal phase the patients practice the skills and then actually apply them.

The following case illustrates application of several interventions for treatment of obsessive–compulsive disorder (OCD) and related problems.

A CASE STUDY

At age 32 when she presented for behavioral treatment, the patient had suffered from severe OCD symptoms for approximately five years. She was overwhelmed with obsessions and compulsions that were primarily related to an intense fear of hurting others. This included fears of hitting someone with her car or poisoning them. She repeatedly checked any foodstuffs she came into close proximity with and refused to cook food that others were to eat. It was very difficult for her to drive because if she hit a bump of any kind she obsessed about whether she had hit a person. She then checked and rechecked by going around the block, listening for sirens, even listening to the news about a person being injured by a hit-and-run driver. In addition to behavioral rituals, the patient repeated prayers and other thoughts obsessively. She was very tense and distressed and extremely unassertive. A "people pleaser" who neither wanted to hurt nor offend others by telling them how she felt, refusing their requests, or asking them to change their behavior, the patient often felt devalued by others and out of control of her life.

Treatment consisted of exposure and response prevention for obsessions and compulsions and related avoidance behavior (such as not touching others' food or cooking for them), therapist support and reinforcement, stress management, and assertiveness training. Exposure and response prevention were implemented in the areas of handling food and driving with therapist assistance. The patient was also given behavioral assignments between sessions. With respect to poisoning others, exposure first entailed the therapist bringing food to the session and having the client pick it up and hand it to the therapist who then ate it. The task was made more difficult by putting the food in another room and requesting that she bring it into the therapist's office without being watched. Then the therapist placed a bottle of cleanser near the food and the patient was instructed to get the food and bring it to another room without supervision. Over time, the client brought packaged foods and then foods she prepared. Eventually she was able to have the food and a household cleanser on the seat of her car at the same time. Assignments also included taking food to work to share with co-workers and cooking for family and friends.

In addition to working on obsessions and compulsions about poisoning others, exposure and response prevention were employed to decrease anxiety and rituals related to driving and hitting people. The therapist rode with the client in her car around increasingly more populated areas and in parking lots with speed breakers. She was not allowed to circle back to check when she hit a bump or curb and was not permitted to check the rearview mirror more than once. Between-session assignments most often consisted of practicing exposure and not performing rituals for situations she had already succeeded with during recent and previous sessions.

The patient participated in assertiveness training that focused on appropriate expression of emotions (positive and negative), refusing requests, and making requests for behavior change. A social skills training model was employed to teach specific nonverbal and verbal component behaviors that included the following: (1) make eye contact; (2) speak in a normal conversation volume; (3) use "I" statements, such as "I feel angry when you make unreasonable requests of me"; (4) say no to the request and offer an alternative, if appropriate (for example, "I cannot come over at lunch today to take you to the store, Mom, but I can do it after work or on Saturday"); and (5) request behavior change of others, when appropriate. For example, "I know you are upset, but I would appreciate your not yelling at me. It makes me feel angry, too." Generalization of effects was facilitated with behavioral assignments to practice specific skills, initially in less threatening situations and eventually in more difficult ones.

Stress management consisted of relaxation skills training, Meichenbaum's steps for Stress Inoculation Training, and positive self-instruction and problem solving. The patient practiced all of the techniques and also learned how to praise and reward herself for effort as well as accomplishment.

The patient was very compliant with treatment and within six months of the initiation of treatment reported a 75% reduction in obsessions and compulsions and significantly improved mood. Symptoms increased during periods of stress but she learned to recognize these times, use stress management, coping, and problem-solving skills and to acknowledge that the temporary exacerbation did not mean total relapse. The patient cooked for others, drove through areas with many pedestrians without checking, and re-established many activities she had enjoyed prior to onset of severe OCD symptoms. She participated in less and less frequent therapy sessions to receive support and assistance with structuring tasks. By the end of one year, she came in every one to two months for follow-up visits.

BEHAVIORAL MEDICINE

Behavioral medicine involves the application of behavior principles and technology to medical or health-related problems. Behavior therapy is useful for treating numerous health-related problems and some of these are listed along with sample interventions in Table 6–7.

The following case study is an example of application of a treatment protocol for tension headaches in a young woman.

Table 6–7 **Examples of Clinical Applications of Behavior Therapy to Health-Related Problems**

HEALTH-RELATED PROBLEM	TECHNIQUES
Anorexia Nervosa	Contingency management, cognitive restructuring, family therapy
Bulimia Nervosa	Exposure with response prevention, cognitive restructuring
Chronic Pain	Contingency management, relaxation, stress management, biofeedback, shaping
Encopresis	Contingency management, biofeedback
Epilepsy	Symptom-contingent relaxation
Headache	Relaxation, biofeedback
Insomnia	Stimulus control, sleep restriction
Irritable Bowel Syndrome	Relaxation/stress management, hypnosis
Muscular Rehabilitation	Biofeedback
Raynaud's Disease	Biofeedback

A CASE STUDY

The patient is a 17-year-old college freshman who lives with her parents and 12-year-old brother. She had weekly tension headaches that could last for a few hours or 1–2 days. The patient worried constantly about her appearance, grades, getting a good job, and what her peers and teachers thought of her. All of her classmates and instructors knew about her headaches and greeted her with questions about them. Her family members planned their own activities around how she was feeling and would cancel or postpone family outings if she was not feeling well so they could help her. Because she constantly worried, the patient's family and friends frequently reassured her, telling her to not be so serious and to "take it easy." Her younger brother assumed most of her household responsibilities, and her parents tried to protect her from knowing about their stressors.

Multiple behavioral interventions were appropriate for the young woman. Relaxation skills training and other stress-management techniques were taught to her, and she was referred for physical therapy. Her irrational beliefs about herself, including perfectionism, were challenged within sessions, and she was also given less-than-perfect behavior assignments to complete. She was requested to monitor her headaches, including antecedents and consequences. Family responses to the patient's pain were an important part of the intervention. Family members were instructed to continue with their plans even if the patient was not feeling well and to encourage her to perform household tasks and recreational activities even when she did not feel well. Further, they were taught how to ignore her complaints of physical discomfort and to attend and praise efforts to cope with her headaches or to prevent them by engaging in relaxation and/or physical therapy exercises.

The patient reported significant reductions in headache intensity and frequency and benefits of relaxation exercises after six weeks of treatment. Further reduction was noted in relation to altered patterns of responding by family members. She also increased leisure activities and reported increased abilities to cope with her discomfort and other problems.

PREVENTION OF ILLNESS AND DISEASE

In addition to treatment of medical problems, behavioral interventions are also useful in primary, secondary, and tertiary prevention of disease and injury as discussed by Oyama and Andrasik (1992). The authors suggest that healthy behaviors can be strengthened and unhealthy ones decreased with the use of behavioral techniques.

Primary prevention includes interventions to prevent onset of illness or injury. For example, Kelly et al (1989) designed a cognitive-behavioral protocol with educational and social skills training components to reduce high-risk sexual behaviors associated with AIDS. Behavioral interventions such as contingency management, modeling, and practice are also useful in preventing child injuries in the home and in automobiles (Roberts, Fanurik, and Layfield, 1987). Oyama and Andrasik (1992) cite the work of Flay and associates (Flay, d'Avernas, Best, Kersell, and Ryan, 1983; Flay, Ryan, Best, Brown, Kersell, d'Avernas, and Zanna, 1985) on the Waterloo Smoking Prevention Project for preteens and teenagers.

Compliance with medical treatment and preparation for hospitalization and/or medical procedures are examples of secondary prevention goals of promoting healthy behaviors after an illness has been diagnosed. Newly diagnosed diabetics, for example, must learn how to check their blood glucose levels and administer insulin as well as adhere to particular dietary restrictions. Applicable behavioral strategies to promote such behaviors are behavioral rehearsal, reinforcement, and problem solving (Oyama and Andrasik, 1992).

There is a good deal of empirical support for the benefits of preparing patients for hospitalization or invasive medical procedures. In recent years, behavioral researchers have developed and evaluated interventions designed to provide such preparation in order to reduce the stress associated with the experience and enhance recovery (Anderson, 1987; Ludwick-Rosenthal and Neufeld, 1988). For example, Oyama and Andrasik (1992) indicate that preparation for coronary artery bypass graft surgery often consists of provision of information about the procedure, recovery and postoperative experience, as well as training in relaxation techniques. Intervention packages have been shown to be effective in decreasing behavioral distress of pediatric oncology patients undergoing bone marrow aspirations and lumbar punctures (Jay et al, 1987) and venipunctures (Manne, Redd, Jacobsen, Gorfinkle, Schorr, and Rapkin, 1990).

COMPARISONS OF THE BEHAVIORAL AND PSYCHOANALYTIC MODELS

A comparison of behavioral and psychoanalytic models for explaining and changing human behavior yields multiple differences (Table 6–8). There is, however, at least one similarity of these two diverse schools of thought, namely *determinism*. Psychoanalysts and behaviorists both posit *causes* for behavior that do not include the notion of free will.

At this point, the two approaches diverge. Major differences have to do with the nature of the causes, the significance of behavior itself, and the focus of interventions to produce change. Psychoanalytic theory proposes that behavior is symbolic of underlying, intrapsychic processes and that neurotic behavior is a symptom of unconscious conflict. The focus of treatment is, therefore, primarily directed towards understanding the underlying processes rather than on the behavior or symptoms. Early experiences are highly significant from a psychoanalytic perspective in which treatment entails bringing unconscious material and conflicts into consciousness.

The behavioral position is that the behavior of the individual is the focus of treatment. Behavior is seen as being determined, not by intrapsychic processes, but by reinforcement history, current contingencies, and genetic endowment. Observable

Table 6–8 **The Behavioral and Psychoanalytic Models**

BEHAVIORAL MODEL	PSYCHOANALYTIC MODEL
1. Behavior is determined by current contingencies, reinforcement history, and genetic endowment.	Behavior is determined by intrapsychic processes.
2. Problem behavior is the focus of study and treatment.	Behavior is interpreted as a symbol of intrapsychic processes and neurotic symptoms of unconscious conflict. The underlying conflict is the focus of treatment.
3. Contemporary variables, such as contingencies of reinforcement, are the focus of the analysis.	Historical variables, such as childhood experiences, are the focus of the analysis.
4. Treatment entails application of principles of operant and/or classical conditioning.	Treatment consists of bringing unconscious conflicts into consciousness.
5. Objective observation, measurement, and experimentation are the methods employed. The focus is on observable behavior and environmental events (antecedents and consequences).	Subjective methods of interpretation of behavior and inference regarding unobservable events (e.g., intrapsychic processes) are employed.
6. Theory is based on experimentation.	Theory is predominantly based on case histories.
7. Tenets can be formulated into testable hypotheses and evaluated through experimentation.	Many tenets cannot be formulated into testable hypotheses to be evaluated through experimentation.

environmental events such as antecedents and consequences, the current contingencies, are analyzed. As such, the behavioral approach emphasizes contemporary rather than historical factors in explaining and changing behavior. Behavioral interventions consist of applying principles of operant and/or classical conditioning to change the behavior itself.

There are also significant differences in the two models from the standpoint of methodology. Psychoanalysis is subjective, and the focus as well as the mechanisms of change are largely unobservable. Inference and interpretation are employed by the therapist. Additionally, psychoanalytic theory was developed from case histories, and tenets of the theory are quite difficult to evaluate empirically and validate.

The behavioral approach, on the other hand, is objective and based on the empirical method. Behavioral theory has been formulated and tested by means of experimentation. Also, the approach entails a commitment to empirical evaluation of behavioral treatment interventions.

CRITICISMS OF THE BEHAVIORAL MODEL

One criticism of the behavioral model is that explanations for human behavior are oversimplified and ignore emotions and cognitions. There are two aspects of the response to such criticism. First, simple principles established in the animal laboratory can be employed to account for complex behaviors. Current applications of behavior therapy are often comprehensive and address multiple problems of the person. The second issue raised in this criticism is related to the role of private events in explaining behavior. Although all behaviorists do not ascribe a causal role to internal events in explaining behavior, few deny that thoughts and feelings are important and should be considered. Behavioral, physiological, cognitive, and emotional factors may all be dealt with in treatment depending on the nature of the primary problem. Treatment of posttraumatic stress disorder (Fairbank and Keane, 1982), for example, entails assessment of behavioral, physiological, and self-report indices of fear or anxiety.

A second criticism is based on an assumption that if the person's behavior is determined by principles of operant or respondent conditioning, then the person is passive and does not himself or herself affect the environment. While this may apply in the case of respondent conditioning, in operant conditioning the person operates on the environment and produces a change. There is, therefore, an interactive relationship with the surroundings, not a passive one.

Some critics maintain that changes produced by behavioral procedures are not maintained over time or do not generalize to the natural environment. This is an important issue for all psychological interventions, regardless of theoretical perspective. Maintenance and generalization are aspects of treatment outcome that are addressed in evaluations of behavioral interventions. These data show better results for some types of interventions than others. For example, follow-up data for behavioral treatment of agoraphobia are generally more impressive than the maintenance of weight loss produced by behavioral intervention.

A fourth issue raised by critics of behavioral approaches is that of "symptom substitution." The notion is that elimination of a problem behavior or "symptom," without dealing with the underlying cause, will result in the reappearance of the behavior or the development of another problem behavior (i.e., one symptom will be substituted for another if the intrapsychic conflict is not resolved). The concept is based on assumptions about the nature of maladaptive behavior and inferences regarding unobservable processes that stem largely from psychoanalytic theory and its basis in a "closed hydraulic system" model of psychic energy. It is difficult to investigate symptom substitution empirically due to the lack of specificity by those who propose the argument regarding the nature of the symptoms, the conditions under which it is likely to occur, or the length of time posttreatment that elapses prior to appearance of the "substitute" symptom (Bandura, 1969). Research does not support the argument for symptom substitution. There are situations in which a behavior may be only temporarily suppressed as in the case of punishment for a response without reinforcement for a desirable incompatible behavior. This does not mean that symptom substitution has occurred. It can mean that empirically derived and validated procedures have not been properly implemented.

A related criticism of a behavioral approach by some is that it is superficial and does not focus on promoting insight and self-understanding. From a behavioral perspective, the focus is on changing behavior, setting specific goals that can be objectively defined and assessed. The difficulty in setting similar goals involving insight or self-understanding are apparent. Moreover, behavior change does not necessarily follow insight regarding the causes of the behavior. Self-understanding may, however, be a collateral of behavior change.

Many criticisms are actually misconceptions about behaviorism and behavioral interventions, and some are briefly summarized (and corrected) in Table 6–9. More complete discussions of misconceptions and criticisms can be found about radical behaviorism in Skinner's (1974) *About Behaviorism* and about behavior therapy in Bellack and Hersen (1980) or Wolpe and Wolpe (1988).

CONTRIBUTIONS OF THE BEHAVIORAL APPROACH

Contributions of the behavioral model are primarily related to the major features of the approach, namely objectivity, commitment to experimentation and the empirical method, and an emphasis on learning and environmental contributions to behavior. These features of the approach are important for both clinical practice and research.

The behavioral approach entails formulation of specific, individualized goals for treatment, which consist of objectively defined and measurable behaviors. Treatment focuses on current conditions and is also described objectively and precisely so as to allow for reporting and replication by others. Progress toward treatment goals and

Table 6–9 **Misconceptions about Behaviorism and Behavior Therapy**

MISCONCEPTION	CORRECTION
1. Genetic endowment is ignored in accounting for behavior.	Behavior is explained in terms of current contingencies, reinforcement history, *and* genetic endowment.
2. Individual uniqueness is not considered.	Although principles of behavior are applicable for all persons, the specific contingencies in effect and the learning history are unique for each individual. These factors must be considered for each person. Also, intensive, systematic study of the person over time has been promoted and used by behaviorists as an experimental methodology.
3. The approach is mechanistic and dehumanizing, and behavior therapists are cold and not empathic.	The approach is objective and systematic. The goals are humanistic and include alleviation of human suffering. Research suggests that behavior therapists display warmth and empathy comparable to therapists with different orientations (Sloane et al, 1975).
4. Behavioral techniques are appropriate for only some groups (e.g., children, the mentally retarded) and for very circumscribed problems (e.g., phobias).	Behavioral principles apply across groups and problem behaviors. Research indicates that some treatment procedures are more effective than others for specific problem behaviors or disorders.

evaluation of the intervention involve measurement of target behaviors during base-line, treatment, and follow-up periods. Such features of the model are particularly significant from the standpoint of accountability in clinical practice as well as the practical utility of specificity in formulating treatment goals and objectivity in assessing progress toward these goals.

Behavior therapy is self-evaluative; empirical demonstration of the effectiveness and identification of the limits of interventions are a commitment of the field. Intensive study of the individual allows for investigation of the types of problems and persons for whom a particular intervention is most effective. Important aspects of treatment effectiveness such as maintenance of effects over time and generalization to other situations and behaviors are evaluated, and clinical research efforts are increasingly focused on programming and facilitating positive outcomes in these areas. This commitment to evaluation increases the likelihood that the individual patient receives the most appropriate and effective treatment and that the body of knowledge about interventions will continue to grow.

Interventions are often implemented and effectiveness is assessed in the person's natural environment. Because paraprofessionals and nonprofessionals can be trained to implement programs designed by professionals expert in the behavioral approach, the feasibility and cost-effectiveness of intervening in the natural environment are enhanced. This, in turn, enhances generalization and maintenance. Behavior therapy techniques are frequently less time consuming and less expensive than other approaches and are as effective or more effective than most of these.

ANNOTATED BIBLIOGRAPHY

Baldwin JD, Baldwin JI: Behavior Principles in Everyday Life. Englewood Cliffs, NJ, Prentice-Hall, 1981

   This is an excellent resource for information about operant and respondent conditioning with many examples of applications of behavioral principles to day-to-day living.

Bandura A: Social Foundations of Thought and Action: A Social Cognitive Theory. Englewood Cliffs, NJ, Prentice-Hall, 1986

   Social cognitive theory is presented in this source with detailed presentations of observational learning, self-efficacy, and relevance of the theoretical approach for conceptualizing psychiatric disorders such as depression and anxiety.

Barlow DH (ed): Clinical Handbook of Psychological Disorders. New York, Guilford Press, 1985

   The purpose of this edited handbook is to provide professionals with illustrations of how to implement behaviorally oriented interventions for a number of disorders such as agoraphobia, depression, obesity, and sexual dysfunction.

Barlow DH: Anxiety and Its Disorders. New York, Guilford Press, 1988

   The author presents an integrated account of anxiety and the evaluation of treatment approaches.

Gentry WD (ed): Handbook of Behavioral Medicine. New York, Guilford Press, 1984

   This edited handbook is especially useful for learning more about medical and health-related applications of behavioral interventions.

Hatch JP, Fisher JG, Rugh JD (eds): Biofeedback: Studies in Clinical Efficacy. New York, Plenum Press, 1987

   Clinical applications and current research in the area of biofeedback are presented. Examples of some of the problems addressed are gastrointestinal disorders, Raynaud's syndrome, chronic pain, and hypertension.

Kazdin AE: History of Behavior Modification: Experimental Foundations of Contemporary Research. Baltimore, MD, University Park Press, 1978

> Kazdin's presentation of the history of behavior modification is thorough, organized, and readable. A great deal of information about key figures of the behavioral movement and their respective contributions is available in the book.

Kratochwill TR, Morris RJ (eds): The Practice of Child Therapy, 2nd ed. New York, Pergamon Press, 1991

> Readers interested in more information about behavioral applications for diverse problems of children and adolescents may find this a useful resource.

Marmor J, Woods JM: The Interface between Psychodynamic and Behavioral Therapies. New York, Plenum Medical Books, 1980

> The authors discuss how behavior therapy can be integrated or used in parallel with psychodynamically oriented approaches.

Skinner BF: About Behaviorism. New York, Vintage Books, 1974

> Skinner presents a lucid, interesting discussion of the philosophy of science called radical behaviorism and addresses numerous misconceptions about radical behaviorism and the experimental analysis of behavior.

Skinner BF: Science and Human Behavior. New York, The Free Press, 1953

> Skinner's discussion of punishment in this book is worthwhile reading. He argues cogently against the use of punishment and for a number of alternative strategies to decrease undesirable behavior.

Thorpe GL, Olson SL: Behavior Therapy: Concepts, Procedures and Applications. Boston, Allyn and Bacon, 1990

> This text provides a good overview of behavior therapy including theoretical underpinnings and applications to various disorders.

Tunks E, Bellisimo A: Behavioral Medicine: Concepts and Procedures. New York, Pergamon Press, 1991

> The authors present a practical, readable guide to clinical applications within behavioral medicine.

Turner SM, Calhoun KS, Adams HE (eds): Handbook of Clinical Behavior Therapy. New York, John Wiley & Sons, 1992

> Readers interested in descriptions of behavior therapy applications and reviews of the research regarding efficacy for numerous clinical problems will find this a useful text.

REFERENCES

American Psychiatric Association: Diagnostic and Statistical Manual of Mental Disorders, 4th ed. Washington, DC, American Psychiatric Association, 1994

Andeson EA: Preoperative preparation for cardiac surgery facilitates recovery, reduces psychological distress and reduces the incidence of acute postoperative hypertension. Consult Clin Psychol 55:513–520, 1987

Andrykowski MA, Redd WH: Longitudinal analysis of the development of anticipatory nausea. J Consult Clin Psychol 55:36–41, 1987

Baldwin JD, Baldwin JI: Behavior Principles in Everyday Life. Englewood Cliffs, NJ, Prentice-Hall, 1981

Bandura A: Social Foundations of Thought and Action: A Social Cognitive Theory. Englewood Cliffs, NJ, Prentice-Hall, 1986

Bandura A: Social Learning Theory. Englewood Cliffs, NJ, Prentice-Hall, 1977

Bandura A: Aggression: A Social Learning Analysis. Englewood Cliffs, NJ, Prentice-Hall, 1973

Bandura A: Principles of Behavior Modification. New York, Holt, Rinehart and Winston, 1969

Bandura A, Ross D, Ross S: Imitation of film-mediated aggressive models. J Ab Soc Psychol 66:3–11, 1963

Bandura A, Walters RH: Adolescent Aggression. New York, Ronald, 1959

Beck AT: Cognitive Therapy and the Emotional Disorders. New York, International Universities Press, 1976

Beck AT: Depression: Clinical, Experimental and Theoretical Aspects. New York, Harper & Row, 1967

Bellack AS, Hersen M: Introduction to Clinical Psychology. New York, Oxford University Press, 1980

Borden, JW: Behavioral Treatment of Social Phobia. In Turner SM, Calhoun KS, Adams HE (eds): Handbook of Clinical Behavior Therapy. New York, John Wiley & Sons, 1992

Burish TG, Carey MP: Conditioned aversive responses in cancer chemotherapy patients: Theoretical and developmental analysis. J Consult Clin Psychol 54:593–600, 1986

Burish TG, Carey MP, Krozely MG, Greco FA: Conditioned side effects induced by cancer chemotherapy: Prevention through behavioral treatment. J Consult Clin Psychol 55:42–48, 1987

Burnette, MM, Koehn KA, Kenyon-Jump R, Hutton K, Stark C: Control of genital herpes recurrences using progressive muscle relaxation. Behav Therapy 22:237–247, 1991

Chaney EF: Social Skills Training. In Hester RK, Miller WR (eds): Handbook of Alcoholism Treatment Approaches: Effective Alternatives. New York, Pergamon, 1989

Craske MG, Rapee RM, Barlow DH: Cognitive-Behavioral Treatment of Panic Disorder, Agoraphobia and Generalized Anxiety Disorder. In Turner SM, Calhoun KS, Adams HE (eds): Handbook of Clinical Behavior Therapy. New York, John Wiley & Sons, 1992

Dapcich-Miura E, Hovell MF: Contingency management of adherence to a complex medical regimen in an elderly heart patient. Behav Therapy 10: 193–201, 1979

Ellis A: On Joseph Wolpe's espousal of cognitive behavior therapy. Am Psychol 34:98–99, 1979

Ellis A: Reason and Emotion in Psychotherapy. New York, Lyle Stuart, 1962

Fairbank JA, Keane TM: Flooding for combat-related stress disorders: Assessment of anxiety reduction across traumatic memories. Behav Therapy 13:499–510, 1982

Flay BR, d'Avernas JR, Best A, Kersell MW, Ryan BA: Cigarette Smoking: Why Young People Do It and Ways of Preventing It. In McGrath PJ, Firestone P (eds): Pediatric and Adolescent Behavioral Medicine: Issues in Treatment, Vol 10. New York, Springer, 1983

Flay BR, Ryan KB, Best JA, Brown K, Kersell MW, d'Avernas JR, Zanna MP: Are social-psychological smoking prevention programs effective: The Waterloo study. J Behav Med 8:37–59, 1985

Foa EB, Steketee G, Milby JB: Differential effects of exposure and response prevention in obsessive–compulsive washers. J Consult Clin Psychol 48:71–79, 1980

Forehand R, McMahon RJ: Helping the Noncompliant Child: A Clinician's Guide to Parent Training. New York, Guilford Press, 1982

Francis G: Childhood obsessive–compulsive disorder: Extinction of compulsive reassurance-seeking. J Anxiety Disorders 2:361–366, 1988

Haaga DAF, Davison GC: Outcome Studies of Rational-emotive Therapy. In Bernard ME, DiGiuseppe R (eds): Inside Rational-emotive Therapy: A Critical Appraisal of the Theory and Therapy of Albert Ellis. New York, Academic Press, 1989

Hoffman ML: Power assertion by the parent and its impact on the child. Child Dev 31:129–143, 1960

Hollon SD, Shelton RC, Loosen PT: Cognitive therapy and pharmacotherapy for depression. J Consult Clin Psych 59:88–99, 1991

Jacobson E: Progressive Relaxation. Chicago, University of Chicago Press, 1938

Jay SM, Elliott CH, Katz E, Siegel SE: Cognitive-behavioral and pharmacologic interventions for children's distress during painful medical procedures. J Consult and Clin Psychol 55:860–865, 1987

Kazdin AE: History of Behavior Modification: Experimental Foundations of Contemporary Research. Baltimore, University Park Press, 1978

Kazdin AE: The Token Economy. New York, Plenum, 1977

Keane TM, Gerardi RJ, Quinn SJ, Litz BT: Behavioral Treatment of Post-traumatic Stress Disorder. In Turner SM, Calhoun KS, Adams HE (eds): Handbook of Clinical Behavior Therapy. New York: John Wiley & Sons, 1992

Kelly JA, St. Lawrence JS, Hood HV, Brasfield TL: Behavioral intervention to reduce AIDS risk activities. J Consult Clin Psychol 57:60–67, 1989

Liberman RP, Mueser KT, Wallace CJ: Social skills training for schizophrenic individuals at risk for relapse. Am J Psychiatry 143:523–526, 1986

Ludwick-Rosenthal R, Neufeld RWJ: Stress management during noxious medical procedures: An evaluative review of outcome studies. Psychol Bull 104:326–342, 1988

Lyons LC, Woods PJ: The efficacy of rational-emotive therapy: A quantitative review of the outcome research. Clin Psychol Rev 11:357–369, 1991

McGrath PA: Pain in Children: Nature, Assessment and Treatment. New York, Guilford Press, 1991

Manne SL, Redd WH, Jacobsen PB, Gorfinkle K, Schorr O, Rapkin B: Behavioral intervention to reduce child and parent distress during venipuncture. J Consult Clin Psychol 58:565–572, 1990

Marmor J, Woods JM: The Interface Between Psychodynamic and Behavioral Therapies. New York: Plenum Medical Books, 1980

Meichenbaum DH: Cognitive Behavior Modification. New York, Plenum, 1977

Oakley ME, Padesky CA: Cognitive Therapy for Anxiety Disorders. In Hersen M, Eisler RM, Miller PM (eds): Progress in Behavior Modification, Vol. 25. Newbury Park, CA, Sage Publications, 1990

Oyama O, Andrasik F: Behavioral Strategies in the Prevention of Disease. In Turner SM, Calhoun KS, Adams HE (eds): Handbook of Clinical Behavior Therapy. New York, John Wiley & Sons, 1992

Patterson GR, Guillion ME: Living with Children: New Methods for Parents and Teachers, rev ed. Champaign, IL, Research Press, 1976

Pfeffer C, Plutchik R, Mizruchi M: Predictors of assaultiveness in latency age children. Am J Psychiatry 140:31–34, 1983

Roberts MC, Fanurik D, Layfield DA: Behavioral approaches to the prevention of childhood injuries. Special issue: Children's injuries: Prevention and public policy. J Soc Issues 43:105–118, 1987

Skinner BF: About Behaviorism. New York, Vintage Books, 1974

Skinner BF: Science and Human Behavior. New York, The Free Press, 1953

Sloane RB, Staples FR, Cristol AH et al: Psychotherapy Versus Behavior Therapy. Cambridge, Harvard University Press, 1975

Snyder JJ: Reinforcement and analysis of interaction in problem and nonproblem families. J Ab Child Psychol 86:528–535, 1977

Stanley MA: Obsessive–Compulsive Disorder. In Turner SM, Calhoun KS, Adams HE (eds): Handbook of Clinical Behavior Therapy. New York, John Wiley & Sons, 1992

Taylor CB, Pfenninger JL, Candelaria T: The use of treatment contracts to reduce medical costs of a difficult patient. J Behav Therapy Experimental Psychiatry 11:77–82, 1980

Thorpe GL, Olson SL: Behavior Therapy: Concepts, Procedures and Applications. Boston, Allyn and Bacon, 1990

Turk DC, Rudy TE, Sorkin BA: Chronic Pain: Behavioral Conceptualizations and Interventions. In Turner SM, Calhoun KS, Adams HE (eds): Handbook of Clinical Behavior Therapy. New York, John Wiley & Sons, 1992

Turner SM, Beidel DC, Townsley RM: Behavioral Treatment of Social Phobia. In Turner SM, Calhoun KS, Adams HE (eds): Handbook of Clinical Behavior Therapy. New York, John Wiley & Sons, 1992

Watson JB, Rayner R: Conditioned emotional reactions. J Experimental Psychol 3:1–14, 1920

Wolpe J, Wolpe D: Life Without Fear: Anxiety and Its Cure. Oakland, CA, New Harbinger Publications, 1988

III Human Development Through the Lifecycle

Alan Stoudemire (ed). *Human Behavior: An Introduction for Medical Students,*
Second Edition. Copyright © 1994, 1990 by J. B. Lippincott Company.

7 Human Sexual Development and Physiology

Judith V. Becker and
John A. Hunter, Jr.

Because human life begins with procreative activity, it may be appropriate that this section on normal human development begins with an overview of human sexuality. Human sexuality is an integral part of life from birth until death and concerns about sexuality are an issue throughout the lifecycle. Many factors can affect sexual development and sexual functioning, such as genetic endowment, biological factors, interpersonal development, and cultural background. Consequently, physicians should be knowledgeable about human sexuality from a variety of perspectives—including biological, psychological, cultural, and behavioral. Physicians are often called on to advise patients regarding sexual matters and assess sexual dysfunction in almost all areas of medical and surgical practice.

Clinicians universally report that the majority of patients seen in clinic or hospital settings are uncomfortable discussing issues related to sexuality. Patients tend to rely on physicians and other healthcare professionals to broach the subject first. It is important that the physician be aware of and sensitive to the patient's reticence, but it is equally important that physicians be aware of *their own* relative comfort or discomfort in assessing matters of sexuality in their patients. A solid understanding of all aspects of sexual development and physiology will facilitate the clinician's skills in their regard and decrease whatever anxiety physicians themselves may experience dealing with the sexual problems of their patients. This chapter covers basic aspects of human sexuality, including genetic and hormonal factors in determination of genital gender expression, an overview of basic developmental considerations, and the normal human sexual response cycle. Other developmental, biological, and cultural factors as they affect the expression of human sexual behavior are discussed in other chapters of this text. This chapter provides a basic introductory overview of sexuality. Human sexuality and human sexual development are also discussed by Dr. Dulcan in Chapter 8. Hormonal influences on sexual behavior are discussed by Dr. Pedersen and his colleagues in Chapter 12.

SEXUAL HISTORY INTERVIEW

There are several available physician guides to sexual history taking (see Fagan and Schmidt, 1994). Table 7–1 outlines pertinent areas of inquiry. These interviews should be comprehensive and detailed enough to allow for accurate and reliable diagnosis of common medical conditions that patients experience. The physician, however, should be aware that at least as important as the content of the interview is the process by which the physician conducts it.

Given the long-existing cultural prohibitions against open and frank discussion of sexuality in our society, most individuals find such subject matter embarrassing and anxiety provoking. Patient related reluctance to identify sexual problems can sometimes be unwittingly compounded by the physician's own inhibitions and inner

Table 7–1 **Basic Sexual History (modified to age of patient and clinical circumstances)**

Introductory comments about why the interview is being conducted and its routine or special nature given the clinical situation at hand; reassurance about confidentiality
Open-ended question, to give the patient an opportunity to voice any areas of special worry or concern regarding this part of the interview or sexual concerns in general
Source of information about sex in growing up
Attitudes of the parents toward sex
Age of onset of puberty
Age of menarche and menstrual history in women
Age of first intense romantic or sexually oriented relationship
History of childhood molestation or incest
History of venereal diseases
Attitudes about masturbation and frequency
Age of first intercourse; number of partners
General pattern of attraction to person of the opposite or same sex; general patterns of heterosexuality or homosexuality
Abortions, miscarriages, pregnancies; complications of pregnancies
Method(s) of birth control
Frequency of current sexual activity
Physical discomfort with sexual activity:
  Men: Problem with arousal or achieving and maintaining erection, ejaculation control; ability to achieve orgasm; physical comfort with intercourse
  Women: Problems with arousal, lubrication, achieving orgasm, physical comfort with intercourse
Conflicts in relationship, or marriage over sexual matters: frequency, methods of birth control, sexual dysfunction
Medications or illness that seem to affect negatively sexual desire or functioning
Issues regarding decision to avoid or achieve conception and have children
Risk factors for AIDS or other concerns regarding this disease

conflicts. Physicians encounter myriad human conditions that not only require technical understanding but that can evoke emotional reactions as well (i.e., pregnant
teenagers, HIV positive patients, etc.). It is important that physicians acknowledge
that they are is not immune from such psychological reactions or personal biases and
seek to explore with the help of peers and colleagues their own value and belief
systems as they relate to sexuality and sexual behavior. This personal exploration can
lead to greater professional sensitivity and acumen, including patient populations that
the physician may simply need to refer elsewhere for professional care or consultation
(see discussion of special populations).

Of utmost importance to the gathering of sexual history data is the establishment of an atmosphere of relative patient comfort and confidence. Such interviews
should be conducted in private, and the physician should inquire if there are issues
that the patient prefers to remain confidential from family or spouse. The physician
should be sensitive to the patient's potential embarrassment and anxieties and
attempt to convey a nonjudgmental and concerned attitude toward expressed problems. The physician's own body posture and facial gestures can be cues to the patient
about the acceptability of the subject matter, and a warm smile and gentle nodding of
the head can be comforting and reassuring. Contrastingly, the avoidance of eye
contact or stern inflection by the physician can convey disapproval or give indication
that this is a subject that is best not discussed. The physician should be aware that it is
common that patients, especially adolescents, are ignorant of technical terminology
for various anatomical and physiological functions, and may need to express their
concerns utilizing lay terminology. While physicians can help the patient correctly
label or describe such functions, they should be sensitive to patients' potential
embarrassment and not present information in a pedantic or stilted manner. The
extent to which the physician is able to establish good rapport with the patient and
serve as a source of information and reassurance will largely determine whether the
patient will continue to seek out the physician when concerns arise in the future.

Patients should be reassured that sexual history questions are a confidential,
routine part of the medical interview and given the opportunity to voice any general
concerns or questions regarding their sexual life in an open-ended manner before the
structured interviewed questions are asked. Depending on the response to this open-
ended question, the clinician might then ask questions about the areas listed in Table 7–1
in a systematic manner. Patients should be reassured that if there are areas they would
rather not talk about for any particular reason, that certain questions can be deferred to a
later date. Likewise, if patients are uncomfortable with discussing particular topics,
physicians may ask about the nature of their concern. The interview should be modified
according to the age of the patient and general clinical circumstances; some areas may be
explored in some depth while others may not be clinically relevant.

SEXUAL DEVELOPMENT

Prenatal

Of the 23 pairs of chromosomes in each cell in the human body, one pair, the sex
chromosomes, is responsible for sexual development. The genetic sex of a person is
established at conception. The sperm cell contributes either an x or y chromosome,

and the ovum contributes an x chromosome. The outcome of the pairing of chromosomes in the majority of cases is either female (xx) or male (xy). Chromosomal abnormalities can occur, however, and involve either the loss or addition of a chromosome (Table 7–2). For example, when an additional chromosome is added (xxy), the resulting pattern is Klinefelter's syndrome, the most common sex chromosome disorder. Such individuals develop a male body type; during adolescence, sexual development may be delayed because of a testosterone deficiency. The characteristics of Klinefelter's are apparent by adulthood with atrophic testes and infertility (Kolodny et al, 1979). The xyy genetic pattern is another variation, which has on occasion been associated with impulsive and aggressive behavioral problems.

The absence of a chromosome, such as in Turner's syndrome (xo), produces a female body type and external genitalia; however, ovaries are absent. Short stature and amenorrhea characterize this disorder. Females born with an xxx pattern have diminished fertility.

During the first 6 weeks of life, male and female embryos appear identical; the as yet undifferentiated pair of gonads will differentiate to become either ovaries or testes. If the y chromosome is present in the embryo, the gonads will differentiate into testes. A substance referred to as the H-Y antigen is responsible for this transformation. In the absence of the y chromosome or H-Y antigen, the gonads develop into ovaries.

If the gonads differentiate into testes, fetal androgen (testosterone) is secreted and male genitalia (epididymus, vas deferens, ejaculatory ducts, penis, and scrotum) develop. In the absence of fetal androgen, female genitalia (fallopian tubes, uterus, clitoris, and vagina) develop.

If fetal androgen is present in the body of a genetic female (adrenogenital syndrome), the effect is that the external genitalia are masculinized. In some cases, the clitoris is enlarged. In others, there is a fully developed penis and scrotal sac (minus the testes). If in a genetic male androgen is missing or androgen receptors are defective (androgen insensitivity syndrome), female genitalia will develop.

Table 7–2 **Summary of Chromosomal Abnormalities in Sex Differentiation**

DISORDER	CHROMOSOMAL PATTERN	PHYSIOLOGIC–BEHAVIORAL CHARACTERISTICS
Klinefelter's syndrome	47, XXY	Sexual development may be delayed because of testosterone deficiency. Atrophic testes and infertility.
Turner's syndrome	45, XO XYY	Short stature, amenorrhea, ovaries absent. Occasionally associated with impulsivity and aggressive behavioral patterns.
Female adrenogenital syndrome	46, XX	Excessive fetal androgen present and external genitalia masculinized. Tomboyishness in childhood.
Androgen insensitivity syndrome	46, XY	Genetically male, however, androgen receptors defective, consequently, external female genitalia develop. Raised as females.

Sexual Development in the Infant and Young Child

The level of sex hormones in the blood stream of neonates is relatively high for both boys and girls during the first few weeks of life, as the infant adjusts from dependence on the mother to autonomous functioning. These levels typically subside more quickly in females than males, but are at prepubertal levels in both sexes by the end of the first year. During the first year of life males show higher levels of testosterone and luteinizing hormone (LH), while females show greater levels of follicular stimulating hormone (FSH) (Higham, 1980).

Upon birth, sexual development and differentiation, which have been controlled in utero by genetic and hormonal factors, are then subject to both social and cultural influences (Money and Ehrhardt, 1972). During the first year of life, the child experiences pair bonding. The infant's needs are to be nourished, touched, and held. Because it is usually the mother who primarily meets these needs, the first bond of attachment is to her. The "oral" stage of infant development includes not only the sucking and swallowing reflexes that achieve nourishment but all aspects of bodily contact, including cuddling and touching (Higham, 1980). (See also Chapter 5 by Drs. Inderbitzen and James for psychoanalytic perspectives.)

Male and female children manifest behavioral differences in the first few years of life. Maccoby and Jacklin (1974), in review of research on sex differences, conclude that males and females differ in four primary areas: (1) girls have greater verbal ability; (2) boys have greater visual-spatial and (3) mathematic abilities; and (4) boys are more aggressive. These authors note that biologic factors may be implicated in aggression, while the sex differences observed in the other three areas are influenced by social pressure. (Biological and hormonal factors in development in human behavior are discussed at some length in Chapter 12.)

Males and females appear to possess at birth certain neurosensory response capacities associated with later sexual functioning. Male infants frequently exhibit erections during the first few weeks after birth, and female infants may have the capacity for vaginal lubrication. Genital touching or genitopelvic stimulation appears to be relatively common in both males and females during the first year of life, and orgasms have been observed in infants of both sexes before the age of 6 months (Martinson, 1980; Kinsey, Pomeroy, and Martin 1948; Bakwin, 1974).

Several investigators (Spitz, 1949; Kolodny et al, 1979) have made distinctions between the more reflective genital play of infants and the volitional and more cognitively driven masturbatory behavior of older youths and adults. However, genital stimulation and sexual responsiveness is a phenomenon that appears relatively early in life and is observable in young children. Male and female children touch and explore their genitals as early as 6 to 12 months of age. It has been estimated that 32% of males 2 to 12 months of age, and 57% of those 2 to 5 years have the capacity to achieve an orgasm (Martinson, 1980). Researchers agree it is critical that infants be assigned a gender status in accord with their external genital status because gender identity is imprinted during the first 24 to 36 months of life and, once established, is highly resistant to change. In the majority of cases, gender status is assigned at birth; the physician at delivery observes the genitalia and announces the sex. In those cases where individuals are born with ambiguous genitalia or a defect in the sex organs, there may be a delay in assigning gender status. Parental counseling is imperative to facilitate the assigning of gender status in ambiguous anatomical cases.

Developmentally, by age 3 and sometimes earlier, children develop an awareness of gender identity. Gender identity is typically followed by establishment of sex-role preferences during the preschool and latency years, and finally sexual preference (orientation) by puberty (Zucker and Green, 1992). Modeling and reinforcement of sex roles occurs within the family environment and to some extent may be influenced by cultural and social factors. Gender disturbances can occur early in life. Girls appear to be less susceptible to gender disorders than are boys. For example, the ratio of males to females applying for transsexual surgery is four to one. Furthermore, males are more likely to develop paraphilias. Paraphilias are characterized by sexual fantasies or arousal to sexual objects or behaviors that are not considered normative. For example, arousal or sexual urges involving nonhuman objects, children, or nonconsenting partners, suffering or humiliation (pedophilia, sadism, fetish, exhibitionism). There is evidence to suggest that gender disturbances in children can be linked to early developmental trauma and dysfunctional families (Meyer and Dupkin, 1985).

Sexual interest is displayed during early childhood. Affectionate behavior in children, including hugging, touching, and kissing, can be observed by age 2. Three-year-olds have been shown to evidence an awareness of genital differences. By age 4, children may begin to exhibit some sexual play ("show and tell" or "doctor and nurse" games). Four-year-olds also show an interest in learning where babies come from and how they get into or out of their mothers. Also at age 4, children begin to show the need for privacy in dressing habits and bathroom behavior. However, they continue to be curious about their own bodies and the bathroom behaviors of others.

At age 5, children become more modest about exposing their bodies and, in general, are more self-contained. Six-year-olds display a greater awareness and interest in sex differences. The 6-year-old may also use slang vocabulary and joke about elimination functions. By age 7, children feel more self-conscious about their bodies and body exposure.

The middle (prepubertal) years of childhood have historically been labeled "latency" because it was believed that the sex drive was suppressed. However, more recent studies of childhood sexuality contradict this belief. Kinsey et al (1953) reported that sex play with peers occurred equally in opposite sex playmates. Furthermore, the number of girls and boys who had experienced orgasm showed a gradual increase in the prepubertal years. Latency also appears to often be a period of intensified romantic interests. Although there is considerable variation in individuals and cultural groups across the country, many prepubertal youths begin dating and engage in kissing and fondling. In some youths, this may involve more intense sexual foreplay or actual intercourse prior to adolescence.

Puberty

Puberty is a period marked by profound anatomical and physiological changes in males and females. These changes are catalyzed by increases in the production of androgens in males, and estrogens in females. In females, the adrenals and maturing ovaries account for the increases in estrogen production. These hormonal increases stimulate bodily changes in females that include the widening of the hips and the softening of the skin and the development of secondary sexual characteristics (i.e., breasts, labia, and clitoral growth; the emergence of axillary and pubic hair). Internal sexual structures, including the uterus and vaginal canal, also grow and mature during this period. Menses typically follows the initiation of breast development by a year or two and usually begins between the ages of 11 and 13. Endocrine changes that occur during the normal menstrual cycle are seen in Fig. 7–1.

Puberty generally begins later in boys than girls and may occur in a more irregular fashion (Diamond and Diamond, 1986). Fat deposits on the chest and abdomen precede muscular development and are accompanied by growth of the testes, scrotum, and penis. The prostate and seminal vesicles also develop and enlarge

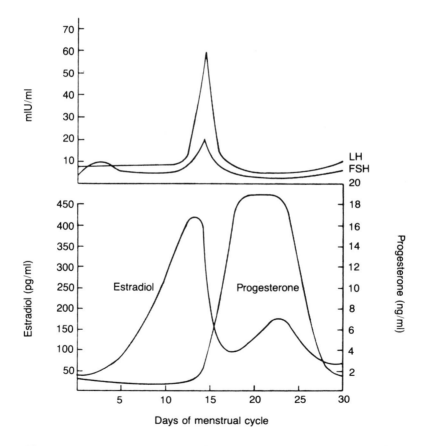

Figure 7–1. *Hormone changes during a typical menstrual cycle. (Reproduced with permission from Benson RC (ed): Current Obstetric and Gynecologic Diagnosis and Treatment, 3rd ed. Copyright 1980 by Lange Medical Publications, Los Altos, CA)*

during this period. The maturation of the testes result in increased testosterone production, which promotes long-bone growth in addition to sexual changes.

Both males and females experience growth in height and weight. In general, boys experience a growth spurt about two years later than girls. There is wide variation in the timing of pubertal events, related to genetic as well as environmental factors (Tanner, 1975). For girls, breast budding may begin any where from age 8 to age 13; the onset of menarche usually occurs between the ages of 10 and 16.5. For boys, penile and testicular growth begins between the ages of 10.5 and 14.5 (Marshall and Tanner, 1969, 1970).

In Western societies there has been a decrease in the age of onset of puberty. Over the past 150 years, the age of onset menarche has dropped from age 17 to 13 (Tanner, 1975). This is probably related to complex changes in nutrition, social conditions, and public health (Meyer-Bahlburg, 1980). Although adolescents become capable of reproduction during puberty, the adolescent girl's first couple of menstrual cycles may not involve ovulation. For male adolescents, ejaculation may occur before sperm are viable. This period of sterility in adolescent males and females is variable in length.

The physiological events that occur during puberty can extend over a period of three to four years in females and longer in males. Adolescence represents a critical period of transition between childhood and adulthood and marks major psychological as well as physiological changes. Adolescents struggle to develop a sense of identity during this time period (Erickson, 1963), and the physiological changes that they experience can create considerable anxiety and confusion. These feelings may be accentuated both by cognitive developmental changes occurring during this period (i.e., egocentrism as discussed by Piaget, 1977) as well as a greater sense of alienation from parents. Many young adolescents are ignorant of the meaning of the changes they are experiencing, yet uncomfortable in asking parents for help.

The physician can be a source of guidance and comfort to young adolescents. For girls, the onset of puberty may mark the first pelvic exam and represent an opportunity for education about the changes that they are experiencing. As adolescents are frequently too embarrassed to ask questions about these issues directly, the physician can spontaneously provide relevant information with the simple explanation that it is one of his or her responsibilities to review such matters (Diamond and Diamond, 1986). Common concerns of girls include the rate of development of their breasts, confusion about the length of their menstrual cycle, the timing of ovulation, and the variable nature of the menstrual flow, and a lack of understanding as to their internal and external sexual anatomy. Questions may also present regarding sexual arousal and observed vaginal wetting as well as the nature of other vaginal discharges. Boys often manifest concerns about penis size and development and the unevenness of bodily changes and growth (i.e., feet grow before other body parts, etc.). The occurrence of nocturnal emissions can also be a source of concern to young males. As discussed later in this chapter, youths in our society are in need of education regarding birth control and the prevention of sexually transmitted diseases.

During the period of adolescence, males and females may engage in self-stimulatory sexual behavior as well as sexual behavior with their peers. Masturbation to orgasm occurs more frequently in males than females. Hunt (1974) reported that

63% of the males in his study sample had masturbated to orgasm by age 13, compared to 33% of the female sample. Hunt also reported that adolescents masturbate at an earlier age than reported by the Kinsey studies. Hunt (1974) found that 93% of males and 63% of females masturbate at some time in their lives. The frequency of masturbation during adolescence is greater than at any other time during the life span for males and may occur several times per day. The psychological and cognitive maturational changes that accompany physiological change during adolescence bring a new meaning to masturbatory behavior in adolescents. No longer is such behavior viewed as simply a physiological outlet for tensions, but it is also considered a mental rehearsal of sexual behavior in the form of sexual fantasies. As such, masturbatory fantasy and behavior can be a step toward the development of sexual identity, sexual preference, and the emerging capacity for sexual intimacy (Weinstein and Rosen, 1991). Even though masturbation is a common practice and potentially serves many developmental needs, it is often a source of embarrassment and guilt.

Sex play, including mutual masturbation, may occur during prepuberty and puberty. About 10% of boys and 5% of girls engage in sexual relations with a same sex peer during adolescence, although very few (only 3% of boys and fewer girls) engage in committed homosexual relationships (Chilman, 1983).

Adolescents today engage in intercourse at an earlier age and more frequently than did previous generations of adolescents. Seventeen percent of boys and 5% of girls age 15 reported having had intercourse at least once; by age 19, 45% to 69% of the females, and 56% to 81% of males have had intercourse (Zelnik, Kantner, and Ford, 1981; Darling, Davidson, and Passarello, 1992; National Research Council, 1987). These frequencies vary when race, education, and socioeconomic status are examined. Generally, the age at first intercourse is lower, and the rates of youth engaging in nonmarital intercourse are higher, in lower socioeconomic and minority adolescent populations (i.e., 41.4% of African-American females have had intercourse by age 15, contrasted with 18.3% of white females) (Zelnik, Kantner, and Ford, 1981). Both males and females tend to engage in first intercourse with older partners (Darling, Davidson, and Passarello, 1992).

Of considerable concern are emerging data indicating that the majority of juveniles who first engage in intercourse do not utilize any form of contraception or protection from sexually transmitted diseases. It has been estimated that only 37% to 44% of females and 33% to 43% of males use a contraceptive during their first sexual experience (Darling et al, 1992). The most commonly provided explanation for having unprotected sex for females is that the experience was unplanned. Males cite the lack of availability of a contraceptive as their most frequent explanation, followed by they were intoxicated, "too excited," or that use of a contraceptive was "not their problem" (Darling et al, 1992, p 99). The problem of teenage pregnancy is discussed later in this chapter.

The context of sexual activity and its psychological meaning may be different for adolescent males and females. Females are more likely than males to report that their first sexual experience was in the context of a committed relationship and was an attempt to achieve interpersonal intimacy. Males appear to be slower in evolving toward engaging in relational sexual intimacy than females and more prone in their early developmental years to be motivated by achievement of status, inquisitiveness, and sexual arousal (Weinstein and Rosen, 1991). As a result of the interplay of physical and psychological factors, females are more likely than males to report that their first sexual experience was aversive. In one study, more than 72% of surveyed females reported that they experienced moderate to severe pain during their first intercourse. This experience of pain appeared to be associated with a number of variables, including a lack of physical maturity, conventional attitudes toward sexuality, and unhappiness with the experience and their partners. Adolescent females are also more likely than adolescent males to report feeling exploited during their first intercourse and less physiologically and psychologically satisfied (Weis, 1985; Darling et al, 1992).

The comprehensiveness and complexity of changes that adolescents experience create special vulnerabilities and needs. Because adolescence is a period of sexual maturation, the adolescent may have concerns about his or her changing body and sexual drive. Adolescents often face sexual issues related to masturbation, sexual anatomy, sexual identity, premarital sex, contraception, pregnancy, abortion, and sexually transmitted diseases, including AIDS. For adolescents to resolve these issues successfully, they need to have a knowledgeable, caring, and supportive adult available to listen and provide guidance. The role of the physician is particularly critical because the physician may be the person the adolescent seeks out for assistance with these issues. Consequently, it is important that the physician be nonjudgmental. If, for ethical reasons, the physician feels that he/she cannot be nonjudgmental in regard to some issue (e.g., abortion, contraception), then a referral should be made to other individuals or agencies. In Chapter 8 developmental aspects of human sexuality from infancy through adolescence are discussed further.

Adulthood

Once individuals reach adulthood, they are faced with a plethora of choices in every aspect of life, including marriage, childbearing, and lifestyle. Sexual conflicts and problems may arise during this period, often brought on by pressure to conform to peer influence and societal and sexual norms. Individuals may experience problems with pair bonding. For some people, infertility may present a problem; for others pregnancy may put a stress on their sexual relationship. The presence of a child or children may reduce the time couples have to spend alone with each other. It is crucial that couples be able to communicate with one another to solve any problems that may arise.

Middle age is a period during which persons begin to adapt to the aging process. For some people, this period is one of liberation (children leave home, more time for leisure activities); others experience feelings of anxiety and despair. Sexually, physiological changes are seen in both men and women. For women, menopause is brought about as a result of lower levels of sex hormones. As the ovaries age, circulatory levels of estrogen and progesterone gradually decrease. Age of menopause can vary from the late 30s to late 50s. As a result of lowered hormonal levels, a number of changes occur. The vaginal wall, labia majora, uterus, and fallopian tubes shrink, and the reduction of vaginal lubrication in the expansion of the vagina can make intercourse uncomfortable. Estrogen replacement can be used to treat these problems if medically safe. Postmenopausal women, however, do not typically experience significant decreases in their levels of sexual desire or their capacity for orgasm. Sexual interest in women is linked to an interplay of both biological and psychological factors. Biologically, sexual interest is possibly more dependent on the adrenal production of androgens than ovarian production of estrogens. The adrenal production of sex hormones does not appear to significantly diminish with age (Kane, Lipton, and Ewing, 1969). Furthermore, there is no evidence of reduced clitoral sensitivity with age. Psychologically, many factors affect a woman's desire for continued sexual activity postmenopause, including issues of self-esteem, a history of having enjoyed sex, and the availability of an interested and emotionally suitable partner. There is no evidence of increased psychiatric morbidity during the menopause (such as depression) contrary to popular belief, although flushing, "hot flashes," and some degree of transient emotional lability may be seen because of fluctuation of estrogen levels.

Physiological changes also occur in males. However, these changes in endocrine and reproduction functions are more gradual and occur somewhat later than in women. Androgen levels, which are relatively constant after puberty, show a gradual decline until the mid-40s when they drop to 55% to 60% of what they were earlier. By age 65, levels are 30% of what they were at age 30 (Silny, 1980). As the male ages, a number of behavioral changes in sexuality occur. Penile erection is slower, the erectile refractory period following ejaculation increases, morning erections and nocturnal emissions occur less frequently, and there is a decline in ejaculation force and amount of ejaculate (Silny, 1980). Although the male sexual response appears to be more affected by age than the female's, most males remain sexually active throughout middle age.

The Elderly

The capacity for sexual enjoyment is present at all ages as is the need for love and intimacy. Persons who are in good health and have willing and cooperative sexual partners can continue active sex lives until their 90s or older. It is almost a universal phenomenon among physicians to assume that old people are not interested in sex, are generally sexually inactive, or believe that it is not necessary to inquire about sexual matters in the elderly. To the contrary, there are numerous sexual issues in elderly males and females that can be addressed by the physician. Kinsey's studies showed that 94% of males and 84% of females were still sexually active by age 60 (Kinsey, Pomeroy, and Martin, 1948). However, advancing age brings on a number of physiological changes that can cause embarrassment and lead toward premature withdrawal from sexual activities. In males, androgen levels continue to decrease past age 65 and are only 10% to 15% of the levels during puberty in 75-year-olds. Their testicles seem smaller compared to younger men's, and they experience less penile tumescence. Thresholds for sexual arousal also appear to increase with age. However, complete erectile impotence does not appear prominent in men until age 75 or older (Silny, 1980).

The number of sperm found in the ejaculate of men decreases with age, but rarely ceases altogether and typically remains at a sufficient level to permit fertilization throughout the life span. The prostate gland does tend to increase in size in men as they get older, which can result in troubling symptoms (i.e., frequent urination, seepage of urine, etc.) and impaired sexual function. This is an area where physician counsel and treatment can often be very helpful.

As previously discussed, age does not appear to impair sexual capacity in women to the extent that it affects males. Women remain clitorically responsive throughout the life span and can be multiorgasmic at an advanced age (Silny, 1980). Unlike males, there appears to be very little change in their refractory period after orgasm (one minute or less). However, women also face major sexual issues in advanced age, including the scarcity of sexual partners. This problem is accentuated by the generally longer life span of women and the greater extent to which the male sexual response is diminished by age. Physician sensitivity to the emotional and physical issues associated with sexuality in the elderly is greatly needed. (See also Chapter 10 by Drs. Wolman and Thompson.)

SPECIAL PATIENT POPULATIONS

Teenage Pregnancy

The rise of adolescent pregnancy rates in this country is alarming. These rates have risen steadily over the past 20 to 30 years, along with birth rates for unmarried teenage mothers (22.4/1000 to 40.6/1000 between 1970 and 1989) (Diamond and Diamond, 1986; Bowler et al, 1992). It has been estimated that 10% of all female adolescents report being pregnant at least once (Sorenson, 1973), and that there are at least 700,000 adolescent pregnancies each year. These teen pregnancies result in approximately 300,000 abortions, 200,000 out-of-marriage births, 100,000 marriages, and 100,000 miscarriages (Crooks, 1980; Zelnik et al, 1981). The birth rate of minority teenagers is up to five times higher than for white teenagers (Bowler et al, 1992). Because of the relative biological immaturity of adolescent females and possibly other more subtle factors (i.e., less adequate prenatal care, etc.), pregnancy complications are four to five times higher for adolescent females (Crooks, 1980; Zelnik et al, 1981). Aside from physical complications, there are a plethora of psychological issues that face teenage parents.

There is a marked need for birth control counseling for sexually active teenagers, and support services for pregnant teenagers. Up to 50% of sexually active teenagers report that they did not feel comfortable discussing contraceptive use with their parents, and most do not use contraceptives during their first year of coital experiences (Chilman, 1983; Zelnik et al, 1981). Pregnant teenagers require not only emotional support but also help in objectively exploring options of abortion, adoption, marriage, and single parenthood. Teenagers report that support programs provide practical assistance, peer support, a more positive sense of self, and a feeling of being understood (McCullough and Scherman, 1991). Physician involvement is needed in the direct provision of these services and in their planning and development.

Homosexual Patients

It is estimated that there are at least 20 million homosexual persons living in the United States today, comprising approximately 10% of the total population (Caulkins, 1981). Gay men and lesbian women face innumerable social, psychological, and health-related issues and concerns. Because of societal prejudices and discrimination, they have often been denied access to basic services, including health care. Homosexual men and women who do seek out physicians are often uncomfortable in confiding to their physician the nature of their sexual orientation. The absence of such identification may hinder accurate diagnosis and proper counseling and medical treatment.

Sexually active gay men, in particular, encounter a number of risks and special health concerns. The rise in cases of AIDS in the United States in gay and other high-risk populations is a matter of national concern (see discussion on treatment of HIV-positive patients). Their health care needs may extend beyond what is normally provided to heterosexual individuals (i.e., genital, oropharyngeal and rectal cultures; periodic HIV testing, etc.) and cannot be adequately met unless they are afforded a physician-patient relationship based upon respect, acceptance, and understanding (Caulkins, 1981). Physicians must explore their own personal feelings as they relate to the treatment of homosexual patients. To the extent that the physician's personal beliefs engender emotional discomfort or disdain for homosexual individuals, ethics dictate that he or she should make referrals to other treatment providers.

HIV-Positive Patients

The number of HIV-positive individuals continues to increase each year in this country, with AIDS representing a health threat to not only homosexuals, but also to heterosexuals, females as well as males, and youths as well as older adults. Given this rise in incidence, the chances of the physician encountering an HIV-positive patient is significantly enhanced. This phenomenon presents the physician with medical issues of proper diagnosis and treatment and psychological issues related to patient care and feelings of personal safety and comfort.

No longer is risk of HIV infection limited to populations of gay men or intravenous drug users. An alarming number of adolescents and young adults appear to be at risk. As discussed by Bowler et al (1992), the number of AIDS cases in adolescents and young adults increased 53% between the end of 1988 and 1990, and AIDS is now the seventh leading cause of death in the 15 to 24-year-old age group. Many young adults with the AIDS syndrome are presumed to have become infected during adolescence, given the several years of "incubation" typically seen before the onset of AIDS symptoms. African Americans and Hispanics are disproportionally represented in both adolescent and adult groups. Although males are generally at greater risk than females in all age groups, this difference is considerably diminished in the adolescent population (10 : 1 male to female ratio in adults; 3 : 1 in adolescents). The greater risk for female adolescents may be the result of several factors, including the high incidence of unprotected sex in adolescence, apparently higher rates of engaging in anal intercourse, particularly among some urban minority youths, and perhaps greater physiological vulnerability to infections (see Bowler et al, 1992).

It is imperative that physicians feel comfortable addressing the risk of HIV infection with their patients, particularly with those from populations that are at highest risk for contracting it. It is oftentimes an issue with which the patient may be concerned, but too embarrassed to inquire about. Physicians need to provide information to their patients in an open and candid manner and also with a sensitivity to the complexity of the emotional issues involved. Those physicians who treat AIDS patients need to be able to provide these individuals with not only the best medical treatment available, but also the delivery of these services in the context of an emotionally supportive relationship. Physicians must show understanding and empathy for their patients, regardless of the manner in which the individual contracted the disease. As with other emotionally laden issues, the physician must first explore his or her own personal values and areas of emotional sensitivity. To the extent that the physician's own beliefs conflict with those of the patient, or the patient's condition creates significant emotional discomfort or vulnerability that cannot be resolved, the physician should consider a referral to another healthcare provider.

Impact of Life Events on Sexuality

Persons at any age may undergo a life experience that can affect their sexual functioning. It is important that physicians be aware of these events; they include: sexual assault, illness, trauma (spinal cord injuries), surgical procedures (mastectomy, hysterectomy, enterostomy), medication (antihypertensives, psychotropics), and sexually transmitted diseases (HIV infection, herpes, and so forth). The effects of medical illness on sexual functioning may be reviewed elsewhere (Fagan and Schmidt, 1993).

HUMAN SEXUAL RESPONSE

Human sexual response represents a complex interaction of the nervous, vascular, and endocrine systems, which interact to produce sexual desire, arousal, and orgasm. In order to understand the sexual response cycle, it is necessary to have an understanding of its anatomical and physiological determinants.

Male Genital Anatomy

Male sexual anatomy consists of external organs (the penis, scrotum, and testes) and internal organs (the prostate, vas deferens, seminal vesicles, and Cowper's glands).

The penis consists of the glans penis, corona, corpora cavernosa, and corpus spongiosum (which also contains the urethra). The corpora spongiosum and cavernosa contain erectile tissue. The corpora cavernosa diverge at the base of the penis to form the crura, which are attached to the pelvic bone (Figs. 7–2 & 7–3).

The testes are located within the scrotum. The principal functions of the testes are sperm production and production of testosterone. Sperm are produced within the seminiferous tubules.

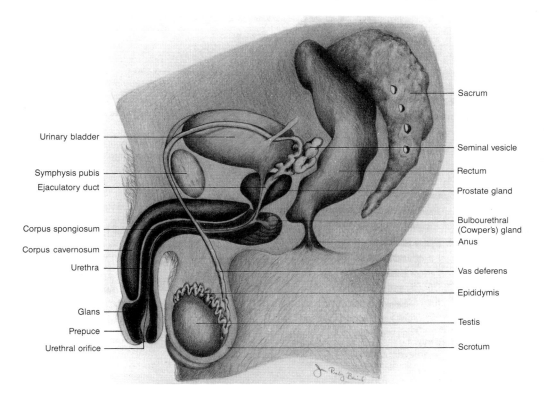

Figure 7–2. *Internal side view of the male reproductive system.*

Female Genital Anatomy

As in the male, the female sexual anatomy consists of external organs, including the mons, labia, clitoris, the perineum, and the internal organs, which consist of the vagina, cervix, uterus, ovaries, and fallopian tubes. The mons is the area of fatty tissue and hair that covers the pubic bone. From the bottom of the mons extend the labia majora, which merge with the perineum. Within the labia majora are the labia minora. The labia minora enclose the clitoris, urethral opening, and vaginal opening (Figs. 7–4 and 7–5).

The clitoris, which consists of the glans and shaft, is covered by the clitoral hood. The clitoral shaft, like the penis, contains the corpora cavernosa and the corpus spongiosum. The base of the shaft forms the crura, which are attached to the pelvic bone. The perineum is the area between the posterior boundary of the labia and the anus.

The vagina has been described as a "potential space." The vagina has the capacity to contract and expand and is lined with squamous epithelium cells, which are responsible for vaginal lubrication. At the top of the vagina is the cervix, which is a passageway between the vagina and uterus. The uterus is a muscular structure

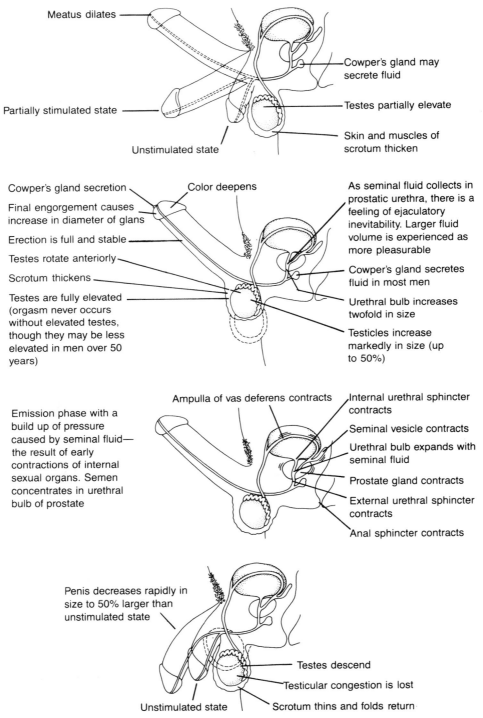

Meatus dilates

Cowper's gland may secrete fluid

Partially stimulated state

Testes partially elevate

Unstimulated state

Skin and muscles of scrotum thicken

Cowper's gland secretion

Color deepens

Final engorgement causes increase in diameter of glans

Erection is full and stable

Testes rotate anteriorly

Scrotum thickens

Testes are fully elevated (orgasm never occurs without elevated testes, though they may be less elevated in men over 50 years)

As seminal fluid collects in prostatic urethra, there is a feeling of ejaculatory inevitability. Larger fluid volume is experienced as more pleasurable

Cowper's gland secretes fluid in most men

Urethral bulb increases twofold in size

Testicles increase markedly in size (up to 50%)

Ampulla of vas deferens contracts

Internal urethral sphincter contracts

Emission phase with a build up of pressure caused by seminal fluid— the result of early contractions of internal sexual organs. Semen concentrates in urethral bulb of prostate

Seminal vesicle contracts

Urethral bulb expands with seminal fluid

Prostate gland contracts

External urethral sphincter contracts

Anal sphincter contracts

Penis decreases rapidly in size to 50% larger than unstimulated state

Testes descend

Testicular congestion is lost

Unstimulated state

Scrotum thins and folds return

Figure 7–3. *External and internal changes in the male sexual response cycle.*

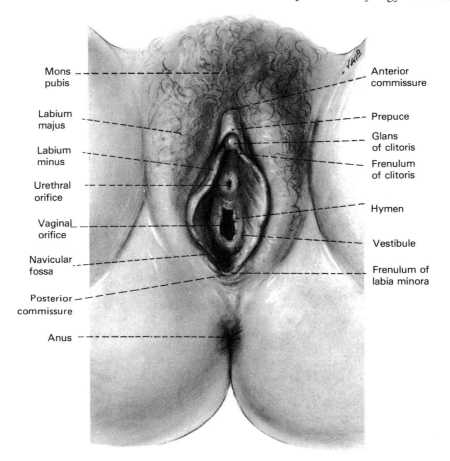

Mons pubis

Labium majus

Labium minus

Urethral orifice

Vaginal orifice

Navicular fossa

Posterior commissure

Anus

Anterior commissure

Prepuce

Glans of clitoris

Frenulum of clitoris

Hymen

Vestibule

Frenulum of labia minora

Figure 7–4. *The vulva. (Reprinted with permission from Danforth DN, Scott JR: Obstetrics and Gynecology, 5th ed. Philadelphia, JB Lippincott, 1986)*

comprised of three layers. The ovaries are located on either side of the uterus. The ovaries secrete the hormones progesterone and estrogen and release ova, which are transported from the ovary to the uterus by the fallopian tubes.

Human Sexual Physiology

Sexual response is not limited to the functions of the genitalia. To fully understand sexual response, the role of sexual stimuli and the response of the nervous system must also be examined.

Weiss (1972) suggests that sexual stimuli can be divided into two categories: reflexogenic (direct tactile stimulation of erogenous zones) and psychogenic (thoughts,

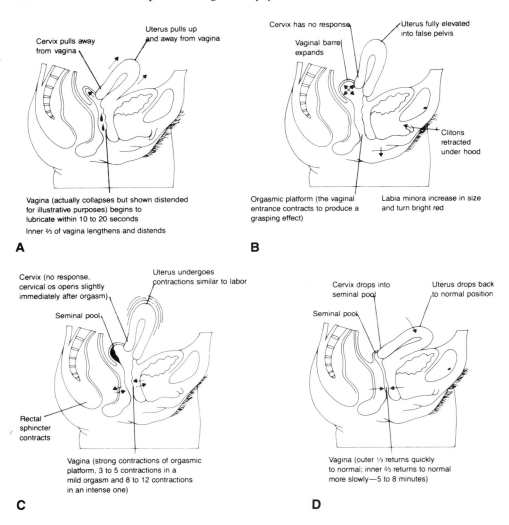

Figure 7–5. *Internal changes in female sexual response cycle. (A) Excitement stage, (B) plateau stage, (C) orgasm stage, and (D) resolution stage. (Reprinted with permission from Reeder JR, Martin LL: Maternity Nursing, 16th ed. Philadelphia, JB Lippincott, 1987)*

images, fantasies, sights, smells, sounds, tastes, and so forth). The source of sexual stimulation in many instances is a combination of both. There is tremendous variability in what serves as sexual stimulation for people. Learning and conditioning play a major role in determining what a particular person will find arousing.

The nervous system serves as the communication system to the body to facilitate the sexual response. In this interaction both the central nervous system and the peripheral nervous system are involved. When a person is exposed to sexual stimuli, a message is sent from the brain or spinal cord through the peripheral nervous system (to either the autonomic or somatic branches). Stimulation of the somatic branch is responsible for the muscle tension that occurs during sexual stimulation. Stimulation by the autonomic nervous system is responsible for penile erection and vaginal lubrication.

The autonomic nervous system has two branches, the parasympathetic and sympathetic. These two branches are seen as antagonistic, in that the parasympathetic branch releases acetylcholine and is dominant during periods of relaxation, whereas the sympathetic branch releases adrenaline and noradrenaline and responds during periods of stress. These systems work in concert during sexual arousal. The *parasympathetic* nervous system is responsible for the expansion of the arterial blood vessels and the concomitant erection of the penis in males and vaginal lubrication in females. As arousal increases, the sympathetic nervous system plays a greater role, as evidenced by an increase in heart rate and blood pressure. Ejaculation is triggered by discharge of the sympathetic branch. This discharge creates an imbalance in the autonomic nervous system and is compensated by the release of acetylcholine from the parasympathetic branch. With this release comes the sensation of relaxation and warmth after orgasm (Rosen and Rosen, 1981) in both men and women.

As mentioned previously, sexual experience can vary tremendously from individual to individual. Responses to sexual stimulation can be influenced by a number of factors. Byrne and Byrne (1977) describe three components that serve to influence a person's response to sexual stimulation; these are informational, emotional, and imaginal. The *informational* component represents a person's beliefs and expectations regarding sexuality. The *emotional* component consists of perceptions and feelings about sexual stimuli. For example, a person may experience happiness, joy, anxiety, or guilt in response to sexual stimuli. The *imaginal* component refers to the images or fantasies a person experiences when faced with sexual stimuli.

The endocrine system plays a crucial role in sexual response. The hormones responsible for sexual and reproductive functions are produced by the endocrine glands under the supervision of the hypothalamus. The hypothalmus is responsible for sending messages to the autonomic nervous system as well as regulating hormone levels. The endocrine glands involved in sexual functioning include the anterior pituitary, adrenal glands, and gonads (testes or ovaries). The sexual hormones secreted by the anterior pituitary include follicle-stimulating hormone (FSH), luteinizing hormone (LH), and prolactin. These hormones, called gonadotropins, stimulate the gonads to produce hormones. Estrogen and progesterone are produced and secreted by the ovaries, testosterone by the testes. Prolactin is responsible for progesterone production and the stimulation of the mammary glands to produce milk after childbirth.

The role of the vascular system is equally as important. In the male, penile erection is achieved through vascular engorgement of erectile tissue in the cavernosa and spongy corpora of the penis. There is controversy, however, over the specific neurovascular mechanisms involved. There is also controversy over the role nervous mechanisms and arteriovenous shunts play in the control of tumescence.

In females, data suggest that precapillary arterial dilation accompanies the early phases of vasocongestion and shift to arterialized blood flow, and increased venous output occurs as arousal increases (Wagner and Ottesen, 1980).

The Sexual Response Cycle

A number of models of the sexual response cycle have been proposed, ranging from a two-stage model to a four-stage model. Ellis (1906) proposed a two-stage model, which involved the processes of tumescence and detumescence. Kaplan (1979) describes a three-stage model including *desire*, produced by activation of a specific neural system in the brain, *excitement*, produced by reflex dilatation of blood vessels, and *orgasm*, reflex contractions of certain genital muscles.

Masters and Johnson (1966), based on their psychophysiological laboratory studies, describe a four-stage model. The four stages are *excitement, plateau, orgasm,* and *resolution* (Fig. 7–6).

Excitement is characterized by the onset of sexual feelings. During this stage, blood pressure and heart rate increase, breathing becomes faster and deeper, and skin "mottling" occurs. In males, erection is experienced, the scrotum thickens, the scrotal sac flattens, and the testes begin to elevate. In females, the breasts begin to swell, nipples become erect, and vaginal lubrication occurs. Some women experience vasocongestion of the clitoris. The uterus enlarges and begins to rise from the pelvic floor. The vagina begins to enlarge.

The *plateau* stage is characterized by a more advanced state of arousal. The penis is distended, and the testicles have thickened and elevated. Reflex contraction of the cremasteric muscles cause the testes to move upward toward the body. The testes may increase as much as 50% from their basal size.

Females experience a marked vasocongestion of the outer third of the vagina during the plateau stage. Masters and Johnson have labeled this the *orgasmic platform*. The vasocongestion causes the labia minora to become larger and thicker, and it may change in color to dark red or purple. During the plateau stage, the uterus has ascended from the pelvic floor.

Orgasm is a reflex brought about by the vasocongestion and myotonia that occur during arousal. The buildup of muscle tension during sexual arousal is a major factor in triggering the orgasmic response. In the male, ejaculation occurs. During the first stage (emission) of ejaculation, semen is moved to the urethra. Masters and Johnson have labeled the sensations that occur during the emission phase as the period of "ejaculatory inevitability." The ejaculatory phase (expulsion) is characterized by semen being expelled from the urethra. The contractions of the bulbocavernosus muscles create the expulsion. Following ejaculation the male experiences a refractory period (a certain length of time must elapse before he can ejaculate again). The length of the refractory period varies from male to male. In general, it is correlated with age, in that the older the person, the longer the refractory period.

For the female, orgasm is characterized by rhythmic contractions of the perineal, bulbar, and pubococcygeal muscles, and the muscles of the perineal floor. Females do not experience a refractory period, and thus multiple orgasms are possible within a relatively short period of time.

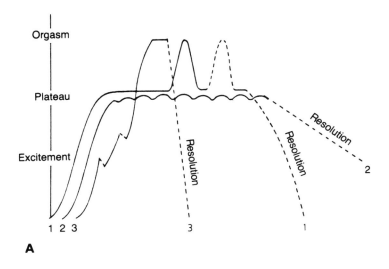

A

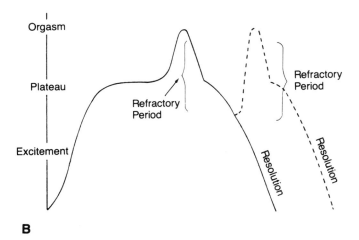

B

Figure 7–6. *The sexual response cycle.* **A:** *Three representative variations of female sexual response.* Pattern 1 *shows multiple orgasm;* pattern 2 *shows arousal that reaches the plateau level without going on to orgasm (note that resolution occurs very slowly); and* pattern 3 *shows several brief drops in the excitement phase followed by an even more rapid resolution phase.* **B:** *The most typical pattern of male sexual response. The dotted line shows one possible variation: a second orgasm and ejaculation occurring after the refractory period is over. Numerous other variations are possible, including patterns that would match 2 and 3 of the female response cycle. (Masters WH, Johnson VE: Human Sexual Response. Boston, Little, Brown & Co., 1966. © 1966 by William H. Masters and Virginia E. Johnson)*

The final stage, *resolution*, is characterized by the body returning to its basal state.

Rosen and Beck (1988), commenting on these various models, note that, while it is important to formulate and specify sexual arousal in terms of a model, the existing models are incomplete and potentially biased. These authors further propose that the three- and four-stage models are little more than elaborations of the biphasic model. Further research addressing the key psychophysiological concepts is necessary. As noted in Figure 7–6, multiple patterns of sexual response may occur particularly in women. About 5% to 10% of women may rarely or never experience orgasm, yet experience marked sexual pleasure during sexual activity. Most women usually require direct clitoral, noncoital stimulation (i.e., by manual or oral methods) to achieve orgasm during sexual activity.

DISCUSSION

The overview that has been presented relates to sexual functioning in an intact individual. Sexual dysfunctions occur when there are disruptions in the psychological, physiological, or anatomical processes involved in the process. It is important for physicians to be aware that sexual problems can arise in both heterosexual and homosexual relationships. The physician should not assume that the patient is in a heterosexual relationship. When taking a sexual history, use the phrase "sexual partner" so that the patient is free to disclose, if she or he chooses, whether the partner or partners are male, female, or both. It is important in providing good patient care that physicians be aware of their own attitudes regarding sexuality and sexual preference and are nonjudgmental in providing services to patients whose sexual preference is different from their own.

A discussion of the specific types of sexual dysfunction and their treatments is beyond the scope of this chapter, and is discussed in the companion text to this volume on clinical psychiatry (Fagen & Schmidt, 1994).

It should be emphasized, however, that sexual concerns and dysfunction occur quite commonly in the general population, especially in the context of medical illness. Physicians have an essential educational and therapeutic role in helping patients with sexual matters, and, therefore, the importance of a sound knowledge for physicians in both normal and abnormal sexual functioning cannot be overemphasized.

Finally, it should be emphasized again that sexuality must always be understood and assessed in the context of each individual patient's psychological, physical, and social matrix. The approach to assessing a patient's sexual functioning or dysfunctioning will be determined by the patient's developmental stage; age; social situation; sexual orientation and preferences; medical status; and cultural, religious, and ethical considerations. In an era when sexual behavior and attitudes toward sex have undergone profound changes in all areas of society—including the healthcare sector—special challenges are presented for physicians in providing medical care, education, counseling, and treatment for their patients.

The techniques and format for taking a medically oriented sexual history from a patient have been briefly reviewed. Additional guidance is provided elsewhere (Fagan and Schmidt, 1994). Table 7–1, however, lists the essential areas that should be covered in this type of interview, whether it is taken as a separate examination or part of a comprehensive medical history. Of equal importance as *what* is asked is *how* the interview is conducted. For more information about sexual assessment and indications for referral for sexual dysfunction therapy, see Fagan and Schmidt, 1994. For more details regarding sexual development, physiology, the diagnosis and treatment of specific sexual dysfunctions, see selected articles in the Annotated Bibliography.

ANNOTATED BIBLIOGRAPHY

Becker JV, Kavoussi RJ: Sexual Disorders. In Talbott J, Hales R, Yudofsky S (eds): Textbook of Psychiatry. Washington DC, American Psychiatric Press, 1987

> An overview of sexuality and sexual dysfunction from the standpoint of clinical psychiatry.

Fagan PJ, Schmidt CW: Psychosexual Disorders. In Stoudemire A (ed): Clinical Psychiatry for Medical Students. 2nd ed. Philadelphia, JB Lippincott, 1994

Fagan PJ, Schmidt CW: Sexual dysfunction in the medically ill. In Stoudemire A, Fogel BS (eds): Psychiatric Care of the Medical Patient, New York, Oxford University Press, 1993

> Excellent overview chapters for medical students of basic approaches to assessing and treating sexual dysfunctions most commonly encountered in general medical practice.

LoPiccolo J, Stock WE: Treatment of sexual dysfunction. J Consult Clin Psychol 54:158–167, 1986

> Presents a review of current knowledge on treatment of sexual dysfunctions.

Masters WH, Johnson VE, Kolodny RC: Human sexuality. Boston, Little, Brown & Co, 1982

> Good introductory level text on topic of human sexuality.

Money J, Ehrhardt A: Man and Woman, Boy and Girl. Baltimore, Johns Hopkins Press, 1974

> Comprehensive presentation of the differentiation and dimorphism of gender identity from conception to maturity.

REFERENCES

Bakwin H: Erotic feelings in infants and young children. Medical Aspects of Human Sexuality 8:200–215, 1974

Bowler S, Sheon A R, D'Angelo LJ, Vermund SH: HIV and AIDS among adolescents in the United States: Increasing risk in the 1990s. J Adolescence 15:345–371, 1992

Byrne D, Byrne L: Exploring Human Sexuality. New York, Thomas Crowell, 1977

Caulkins S: The male homosexual client. Issues in Health Care Women 3:321–340, 1981

Chilman CS: The development of adolescent sexuality. J Res Dev Ed 16:17–25, 1983

Crooks R: Our Sexuality. Benjamin/Cummings Publishing Co, Menlo Park CA, 1980

Darling CA, Davidson JK, Passarello LC: The mystique of first intercourse among college youth: The role of partners, contraceptive practices, and psychological reactions. J Youth Adolescence 21:97–118, 1992

Diamond M, Diamond GH: Adolescent sexuality: Biosocial aspects and intervention strategies. J Soc Work and Human Sex 5:3–13, 1986

Ellis H: Studies in the Psychology of Sex. New York, Random House, 1906

Erikson E: Childhood and Society. New York, WW Norton and Co, 1963

Fagan PJ, Schmidt CW Jr: Sexual Dysfunction in the medically ill. In Stoudemire A, Fogel BS (Eds.) Psychiatric Care of the Medical Patient. New York, Oxford University Press, 1993

Fagan PJ, Schmidt CW: Psychosexual Disorders. In Stoudemire A (ed): Clinical Psychiatry for Medical Students, 2nd ed. Philadelphia, JB Lippincott, 1994

Higham E: Sexuality in the infant and neonate: Birth to two years. In Wolman BB, Money J (eds): Handbook of Human Sexuality, pp 16–27. Englewood Cliffs, NJ, Prentice-Hall, 1980

Hunt M: Sexual Behavior in the 70s. New York, Dell, 1974

Kane FJ, Lipton MA, Ewing JA: Hormonal influences in female sexual response. Arch Gen Psychiatry 20:202–209, 1969

Kaplan HS: Disorders of Sexual Desire. New York, Bruner/Mazel, 1979

Kinsey AC, Pomeroy WB, Martin CE: Sexual Behavior in the Human Male. Philadelphia, WB Saunders, 1948

Kinsey AC, Pomeroy WB, Martin CE et al: Sexual Behavior in the Human Female. Philadelphia, WB Saunders, 1953

Kolodny RC, Masters WH, Johnson VE: Textbook of Sexual Medicine. Boston, Little, Brown & Co, 1979

Maccoby E, Jacklin C: The Psychology of Sex Differences. Stanford, CA, Stanford University Press, 1974

Marshall WA, Tanner JM: Variations in the patterns of pubertal changes in boys. Arch Dis Child 45:13–23, 1970

Marshall WA, Tanner JM: Variations in patterns of pubertal changes in girls. Arch Dis Child 44:291–303, 1969

Martinson FM: Childhood Sexuality. In Wolman BB and Money J (eds): Handbook of Human Sexuality, pp 29–53. Englewood Cliffs, NJ, Prentice-Hall, 1980

Masters WH, Johnson VE: Human Sexual Response. Boston, Little Brown & Co, 1966

McCullough M, and Scherman A: Adolescent pregnancy: Contributing factors and strategies for prevention. Adolescence 26:809–816, 1991

Meyer JK, Dupkin C: Gender disturbance in children. Bull Menninger Clin 49:236–269, 1985

Meyer-Bahlburg H: Sexuality in Early Adolescence. In Wolman BB, Money J (eds): Handbook of Human Sexuality, pp 62–82. Englewood Cliffs, NJ, Prentice-Hall, 1980

Money J, Erhardt A: Man and Woman, Boy and Girl. Baltimore, Johns Hopkins University Press, 1972

National Research Council: Risking the Future. Washington, DC, National Academy Press, 1987

Piaget J: The Development of Thought: Equilibration of Cognitive Structures. New York, Viking Press, 1977

Rosen RC, Beck JG: Patterns of Sexual Arousal. New York, Guilford Press, 1988

Rosen R, Rosen LR: Human Sexuality. New York, Alfred A. Knopf, 1981

Silny AJ: Sexuality and Aging. In Wolman BB, Money J (eds): Handbook of Human Sexuality, pp 124–146. Englewood Cliffs, NJ, Prentice-Hall, 1980

Sorenson R: Adolescent Sexuality in Contemporary America. New York, World Publishing, 1973

Spitz RA: Autoerotism: some empirical findings and hypotheses on three of its manifestations in the first year of life. In Spitz RA (ed): The Psychoanalytic Study of the Child, pp 85–120. New York, International Universities Press, 1949

Tanner JM: Growth and Endocrinology of the Adolescent. In Gardner LI (ed): Endocrine and Genetic Diseases of Childhood and Adolescence, pp 14–64. Philadelphia, WB Saunders, 1975

Wagner G, Ottesen B: Vaginal blood flow during sexual stimulation. Obstet Gynecol 56:621–624, 1980

Weinstein E, and Rosen E: The development of adolescent sexual intimacy: Implications for counselling. Adolescence 26:331–339, 1991

Weis DL: The experience of pain during women's first sexual intercourse: Cultural mythology about female sexual initiation. Arch Sex Behav 14:421–437, 1985

Weiss HD: The physiology of human erection. Ann Intern Med 76:793–799, 1972

Zelnik MD, Kantner JF, Ford K: Sex and Pregnancy in Adolescence. Beverly Hills CA, Sage Publications, 1981

Zucker KJ, Green R: Psychosexual disorders in children and adolescents. J Child Psychol Psychiatry 33:107–151, 1992

Alan Stoudemire (ed). *Human Behavior: An Introduction for Medical Students,*
Second Edition. Copyright © 1994, 1990 by J. B. Lippincott Company.

8

Childhood and Adolescent Development

Mina K. Dulcan

This chapter reviews the basic principles and theories of normal human development from conception through adolescence. Significant milestones in physical, cognitive, language, emotional, and social growth are covered. In the discussion that follows, roughly 20 years of development are divided into prenatal, infant (the first year), toddler (1 to 3 years), early childhood (3 to 6 years), school age (6 to 12 years), and adolescent periods. At each stage, development in physical, cognitive, language, affective, and social domains is described, as well as special topics applicable to that age group. Interactions between physical illness or hospitalization and developmental status are highlighted. Important aspects of family functioning and development are covered in the last two sections of the chapter.

WHY STUDY DEVELOPMENT?

Within the context of the biopsychosocial model, knowledge of the normal development of children and adolescents provides an essential framework for the understanding of adult development and of both child and adult psychopathology. Developmental factors may influence the pathogenesis and symptoms of mental illness at any age. Knowledge of the developmental process also facilitates the medical care of young persons and adults and their families by making understandable their phase-specific emotional reactions to illness at each stage of the lifecycle.

Different Views of Development

There are two fundamental ways of discussing development. One may take a *cross-sectional view*, describing all aspects of a particular stage, or describe each developmental domain *longitudinally*, using one or more theoretical perspectives. This chapter takes the cross-sectional option in an attempt to integrate the various developmental theories and capabilities at each developmental stage, because this is the way patients present in the clinical setting.

What Is Normality?

Although this may seem like a question with an obvious answer, there are widely discrepant definitions of what constitutes "normality." The term may be used to describe data that fit a normal or gaussian frequency distribution, with a symmetrical distribution of scores and a mean that coincides with the median. In this case, the mean plus or minus two standard deviations encloses 95% of the contents. The term "normal" is then applied to individuals who score within this 95% range on a particular measure. For example, "normal" height and weight are typically determined in this way. A related use of the term "normal" refers to a statistical norm or average which, of course, is tied to the original population from which the data were gathered.

Alternatively, "normal" may refer to what is socially or culturally acceptable (to a particular group). Cultural aspects of normality and psychopathology are discussed in Chapter 4 by Dr. Brown and colleagues. "Normal" may also be used to describe individual-specific response patterns (i.e., what is normal or usual for a given person), in an attempt to distinguish unusual but stable characteristics from those that represent a change or deviation.

"Normal" may also be used to mean healthy, without pathology, or ideal. In the context of preventive medicine and psychiatry, normality implies that the individual or group carries no excess risk of future disease or psychopathology.

Development has many aspects, including physical, cognitive, and emotional, with finer subdivisions in each of these three areas. It is important not only to assess in which areas a person's development is normal or abnormal, but also to evaluate the evenness or synchrony of development across different domains.

Developmental Models

This chapter presents multiple theories of development, because at present no single theory is sufficiently comprehensive. Multiple perspectives, all with some degree of inherent value, must be invoked to provide an integrated and balanced view of the many factors that affect human development.

Each developmental theory identifies stages that unfold in an orderly progression, each phase building on the previous one, becoming more complex and differentiated, and then launching the next phase. Developmental theories identify the maximum expectable capabilities at each stage. A profile can be constructed for each person, noting progress compared to expected norms in each developmental area. In both normal children and in those with psychopathology, development may progress at different rates in different areas. For an individual, development rarely proceeds at a constant rate. Periods of apparent stagnation alternate with rapid growth. There are even times when regression to an earlier stage of development is not only normal, but facilitates subsequent growth.

Psychoanalytic, object relations, and behavioral and learning theories of development are described in Section II of this text, and psychosocial (Eriksonian) theory is discussed in Chapter 10. Current knowledge about the biological underpinnings of behavior is summarized in Section IV of this text.

This chapter focuses primarily on observable developmental milestones or landmarks, physiological and neurological aspects of development, cognitive development, and interactions between the child and the family as development proceeds. Findings from clinical observations and research in developmental psychology are applied to the child, adolescent, and family as they are likely to present in the medical setting.

Temperament

Temperament, the "how" or style of behavior, is a concept that cuts across developmental stages. The concept was developed by Thomas and Chess (1986) from the findings of their New York Longitudinal Study, which followed 133 children from 85 middle-class families from infancy through young adulthood. The nine relatively stable dimensions or traits identified in infancy are listed in Table 8–1.

Many of the children studied were found to demonstrate clusters of these variables. (See Table 8–2.) The *easy* child is a delight to parents and has a relatively low risk of emotional or behavior problems. *Difficult* children are at the highest risk (70%) of developing behavior problems. In the New York Longitudinal Study, difficult children were 10% of the total sample, but constituted 23% of the children with behavior problems. Children characterized as *slow to warm up* are also at risk, but the risk can be significantly reduced by sensitive management by parents and teachers.

A crucial predictor of outcome is the temperamental match or "goodness of fit" between the child and the parents' own temperament, expectations, and child-rearing style. Parent-child interactions, cultural expectations, and the child's own characteristics (e.g., sex, IQ) can reinforce inborn temperamental characteristics or change them for the better or the worse. Anticipatory guidance to parents from pediatricians can facilitate understanding of and adaptation to children's individual differences.

Table 8–1 **Dimensions of Temperament**

1. Activity level
2. Rhythmicity (regularity and predictability of biological functions)
3. Approach or withdrawal to novel stimuli
4. Adaptability to environmental change
5. Intensity of reaction
6. Threshold of responsiveness (intensity of stimulation required to evoke a response)
7. Quality of mood (positive, neutral or negative)
8. Distractibility
9. Attention span and persistence

Table 8–2 **Temperamental Clusters**

EASY
Positive mood
Regular biological rhythms
Adaptable
Low intensity
Positive approach to novelty
DIFFICULT
Negative mood
Irregular biological rhythms
Slow to adapt
Intense reactions
Negative response to novelty
SLOW TO WARM UP
Negative responses to new stimuli
Mild intensity
Gradual adaptation after repeated contact

(Adapted from Thomas A, Chess S: Temperament in Clinical Practice. New York, Guilford Press, 1986)

Thomas and Chess's work has inspired additional research on the measurement and properties of temperament characteristics. Twin studies suggest a substantial genetic contribution to temperament and other personality variables. Children demonstrating "behavioral inhibition to the unfamiliar" have been studied extensively. At age 2 years, these children are extremely inhibited, quiet, shy, and fearful in unfamiliar situations. The majority tend to remain shy and socially avoidant at age 7. Consistently inhibited children have greater sympathetic reactivity than more outgoing children, as measured by heart rate acceleration and early-morning salivary cortisol levels. These children are at risk to develop anxiety disorders. Their parents have an increased prevalence of both childhood anxiety and adult anxiety disorders (Hirshfeld et al, 1992). In contrast, 2 year olds who are uninhibited tend to remain fearless and outgoing.

Developmental Milestones

Pediatrician Arnold Gesell and his colleagues at the Yale Clinic of Child Development made a major contribution to pediatrics and child development with their objective observation of behaviors and capabilities in large numbers of children at various ages. Their data identified "milestones" by which to measure the intactness of the child's abilities, resulting from the interaction between biological endowment and environment. Areas assessed include motor, personal-social, adaptive (use of motor abilities to interact with the environment), and language domains (Gesell et al, 1940). There is a range of normal for the age at which each milestone appears, and times presented in this chapter are averages. The Denver II (Fig. 8–1), a recent revision and restandardization of the widely used Denver Developmental Screening Test, graphically displays the age at which each milestone is attained by 25%, 50%, 75%, and 90% of normal infants and children (up to 6 years of age). This test can be easily used by a physician or nurse to estimate a child's developmental status and to determine whether additional evaluation is needed.

Piagetian Cognitive Development

Jean Piaget, a Swiss cognitive psychologist, became intrigued by the *wrong* answers given to questions on intelligence tests by children of different ages. He devoted his career to the study of *epistemology*, or how thought is transformed into a body of knowledge. Unlike Freud, whose theories were developed primarily by retrospective extrapolation from neurotic adults, Piaget's conception of cognitive development was based on the direct observation of his own three children, starting in their infancy. He viewed children as active participants in learning, rather than as passive recipients. He believed that intelligence and knowledge of the world must be discovered and structured by the child's own activities.

Piaget believed that four factors influence cognitive behavior:

1. Maturation of the nervous system.
2. Experience.
3. Social transmission of information, or teaching.
4. *Equilibration:* The innate tendency for mental growth to progress toward increasingly complex and stable levels of organization.

Piaget defined four major stages of cognitive development: *sensorimotor, preoperational, concrete operations*, and *formal operations*. These are not uniformly attained but appear within a rather wide range of ages (see Figs. 8–2 and 8–3). Each child's rate of development is determined by his or her intelligence and the above factors.

Certain definitions are essential to understanding Piaget (Piaget and Inhelder, 1969). A *scheme* is an organized pattern of behavior that is repeatable and generalizable (e.g., sucking, reaching for a mobile hanging in the crib). Development proceeds through certain processes that represent basic tendencies in human beings:

1. Active seeking of stimulation.
2. *Organization:* The tendency to arrange processes into coherent systems.
3. *Adaptation:* A dynamic process combining *assimilation* and *accommodation*.
   Assimilation: The tendency to use current schemes to deal with the environment, in both familiar and new situations.
   Accommodation: The modification of the child's cognitive structures in response to environmental pressures.
4. The need for action to precede intellect.

Despite his small and select database and methods that would be considered primitive by today's standards, Piaget's theories have been highly influential in the study of child development. Although subsequent research has found that children can solve problems much earlier, and developmental stages are far more flexible, less

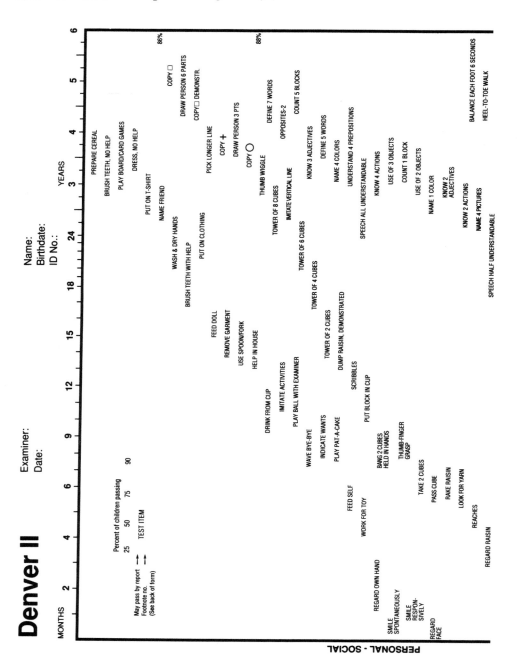

Figure 8–1. The Denver II.

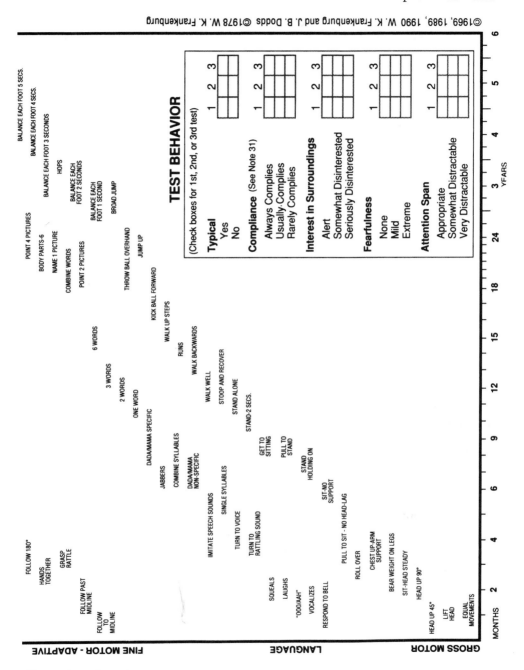

Figure 1 continued

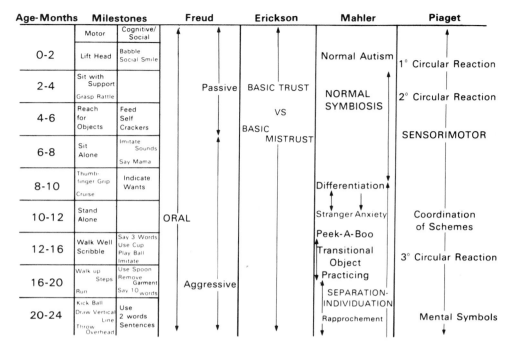

Age-Months	Milestones		Freud	Erickson	Mahler	Piaget
	Motor	Cognitive/Social				
0-2	Lift Head	Babble Social Smile			Normal Autism	1° Circular Reaction
2-4	Sit with Support Grasp Rattle		Passive	BASIC TRUST	NORMAL SYMBIOSIS	2° Circular Reaction
4-6	Reach for Objects	Feed Self Crackers		VS		SENSORIMOTOR
6-8	Sit Alone	Imitate Sounds Say Mama		BASIC MISTRUST		
8-10	Thumb-finger Grip Cruise	Indicate Wants			Differentiation	
10-12	Stand Alone		ORAL		Stranger Anxiety	Coordination of Schemes
12-16	Walk Well Scribble	Say 3 Words Use Cup Play Ball Imitate			Peek-A-Boo Transitional Object	3° Circular Reaction
16-20	Walk up Steps Run	Use Spoon Remove Garment Say 10 words	Aggressive		Practicing SEPARATION-INDIVIDUATION	
20-24	Kick Ball Draw Vertical Line Throw Overhead	Use 2 words Sentences			Rapprochement	Mental Symbols

Figure 8–2. *Correspondence of stages of development—birth to 2 years.*

discrete, and more responsive to context and affect than Piaget believed, his notion that thought and reasoning change qualitatively as well as quantitatively with development has remained important in our understanding of intellectual development.

Intelligence

Evaluation

The ability of "intelligence" testing in infancy to predict IQ test results at school age is controversial. Changes in IQ estimates can be attributed to both the remarkable resiliency of the central nervous system of the human infant and the marked differences in types of abilities able to be tested at different ages. At best, scores on specific tests in infancy account for 50% of the variation among children in specific cognitive and language abilities at age 2 years (Siegel, 1981). The accuracy of predicted IQ decreases as the time interval increases, in part because the caretaking environment can powerfully exacerbate or ameliorate early damage.

Mental retardation

Mental retardation is a condition of childhood onset defined by a score on a standardized intelligence test (see Table 8–3) that is significantly below average (i.e., IQ score below approximately 70), together with significant impairment in adaptive

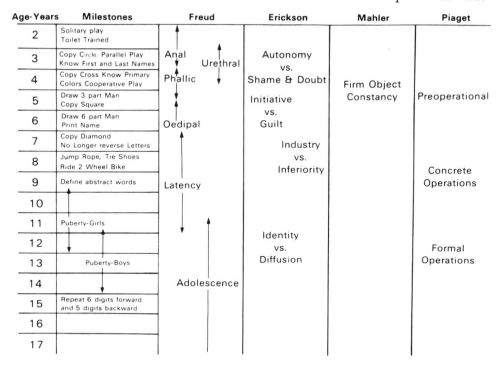

Figure 8–3. *Correspondence of stages of development—2 to 18 years.*

functioning (measured by a test such as the Vineland Adaptive Behavior Scales). It is important to remember that scores on standardized IQ tests can be significantly affected by cultural, motivational, and attentional factors.

Mental retardation has a wide variety of causes; the more common are listed in Table 8–4. Mild mental retardation (IQ from 50–55 to 70), by far the most common category, is not usually attributable to a known medical cause, but rather, to a combination of factors including inheritance from parents whose genetic endowment is below average, lack of cognitive stimulation, malnutrition of mother and child, inadequate prenatal and pediatric medical care, and environmental toxins such as lead. There is considerable diversity among retarded children, even when matched for IQ. Typical patterns of cognitive abilities, social and affective characteristics, and behavioral symptoms differ according to etiology (e.g., Down syndrome versus fragile-X syndrome) (Bregman and Hodapp, 1991). Among the mildly retarded, these characteristics, along with family resources and educational and vocational interventions, contribute more to adult adaptation than does IQ.

Primary prevention (reduction in the numbers of retarded children) includes efforts such as improved family planning and prenatal care, education of mothers, and larger societal efforts to reduce poverty. Immunization against rubella, genetic counseling, prenatal diagnosis through techniques such as ultrasound and amniocentesis,

Table 8–3 **Tests of Intelligence**

STANDARD IQ TESTS

Kaufman Assessment Battery for Children (K-ABC)
  Age 2½ to 12½ years
  Less dependent on culturally based information and schooling

Stanford-Binet Intelligence Scale (4th Edition)
  Age 2 years to adulthood
  Heavily language based

Wechsler Preschool and Primary Scale of Intelligence (WPPSI)   Age 4 to 6½ years
Wechsler Intelligence Scale for Children, 3rd Edition (WISC-III)   Age 6 to 16 years
Wechsler Adult Intelligence Scale-Revised (WAIS-R)   Age 16 years through adulthood

TESTS FOR SPECIALIZED USES

Bayley Scales of Infant Development-Revised
  Age 3 to 30 months
  Estimates cognitive developmental level in very young children

Leiter International Performance Scale
  Nonverbal test for use with children who are deaf, autistic, or do not speak English
  Not as well standardized as other IQ tests

Peabody Picture Vocabulary Test (PPVT-R)   Brief test of receptive language abilities, often used as screening test of IQ

Vineland Adaptive Behavior Scales
  Measure of behavioral capabilities, based on interview with primary caretaker
  Birth to adulthood
  Especially useful for developmentally handicapped individuals

and newborn screening for disorders such as phenylketonuria (PKU) can reduce the incidence of some of the more severe forms of mental retardation.

Secondary prevention focuses on early identification and intervention to reverse or minimize developmental delays. *Tertiary prevention*, minimizing complications and maximizing adaptive functioning, requires specialized treatment and rehabilitative services.

PRENATAL DEVELOPMENT

The prenatal period is an important one for both parents and fetus. The child's endowment depends on both genetic makeup and the prenatal environment. Subsequent influences include the timing and nature of the birth process, medical interventions, and later social, emotional, and physical factors in the environment of the child.

Table 8–4 **Significant Causes of Mental Retardation**

GENETIC FACTORS

Chromosomal abnormalities
Fragile-X syndrome
Down syndrome
Cri-du-chat syndrome
Many other rare, named syndromes
  Single gene abnormalities—inborn errors of metabolism
Phenylketonuria (PKU)*
Maple syrup urine disease*
Homocystinuria*
Tyrosinemia*
Galactosemia*
Hypothyroidism*
Lipid storage diseases
Glycogen storage diseases
Lesch-Nyhan syndrome
Wilson's disease
  Neurocutaneous disorders
Sturge-Weber syndrome
Tuberous sclerosis
von Recklinghausen's disease
Craniofacial anomalies
  Genetic endowment at the lower end of the distribution

PRENATAL FACTORS

Maternal chronic illness
Diabetes mellitus
Anemia
Emphysema
Hypertension
Malnutrition
  Maternal infection passed to fetus
Rubella (German measles)
Cytomegalic inclusion disease
Syphilis
Toxoplasmosis
Herpes simplex
AIDS
  Maternal ingestion of toxic substances
Alcohol
Narcotics
Cocaine

OBSTETRIC COMPLICATIONS

ACQUIRED COGNITIVE DEFICIT IN INFANCY OR CHILDHOOD

Severe malnutrition
Infection
  Encephalitis
  Meningitis
Head trauma
Lead intoxication
Asphyxia
Brain tumors

ENVIRONMENTAL AND SOCIOCULTURAL INFLUENCES

Note: Newborn screening techniques are available to permit early identification and treatment, which prevents or reduces sequelae of these disorders.

Risks to the Fetus

Prematurity

Causes of prematurity include multiple pregnancy, fetal abnormalities, and structural or endocrine abnormalities in the mother. Obstetricians and neonatologists are increasingly able to prevent or treat prematurity and its sequelae, such as respiratory distress syndrome and hemorrhage into the central nervous system.

Intrauterine Growth Retardation

Such babies are born small for their gestational age and may be delayed in other areas as well. Contributing factors include maternal malnutrition, drugs taken by the mother, placental abnormality, infection, and maternal disease such as hypertension.

Genetic Abnormality

Genetic counseling prior to pregnancy or use of new methods of prenatal diagnosis can reduce the incidence of babies born with a chromosomal aberration (e.g., Down syndrome) or inherited abnormality of a single gene (e.g., Tay-Sachs disease). Neonatal screening with subsequent dietary treatment has significantly reduced the sequelae of other genetic disorders, such as phenylketonuria (PKU).

Maternal Disease

Early and thorough prenatal care reduces the risk to the fetus by identification and medical management of maternal diabetes, hypertension, or other disorders.

Immunization of potential mothers protects babies from the often-devastating effects of maternal rubella infection. Intrauterine infection with the AIDS virus, transmitted across the placenta from an infected mother, is a rapidly increasing problem.

Adolescent Pregnancy

Infants of mothers less than 15 years old are at increased risk for low birth weight and neonatal death, in part because teenage mothers are less likely to obtain prenatal care. Injuries, illnesses, and sudden infant death syndrome (SIDS) have an increased incidence in the children of mothers less than 17 years old (McAnarney and Hendee, 1989).

Maternal Ingestion of Substances Harmful to the Fetus

Fetal alcohol syndrome (FAS) is characterized by varying degrees of prenatal and postnatal growth retardation, dysmorphic features, other physical malformations, below-normal intellect, and attentional and learning disabilities (Steinhausen and Spohr, 1986). At similar quantities of maternal alcohol consumption, FAS is more prevalent and more pronounced in children of lower socioeconomic status.

Cigarette smoking during pregnancy leads to increased risk for the child of hyperactivity, short attention span, impulsivity, hypersensitivity to sensory stimuli, and delays in the development of language and academic skills (Naeye, 1992).

Babies born to mothers addicted to narcotics have a low birth weight and show a neonatal abstinence syndrome consisting of extreme irritability, emotional lability, and intense reactions to environmental stimuli. Evidence is increasing of long-term effects on behavior and intelligence. As cocaine and "crack" abuse has reached epidemic proportions, the number of infants affected in utero continues to increase. The effect of cocaine is mediated primarily through lack of prenatal care, malnutrition, prematurity, intrauterine growth retardation, and microcephaly. Although "crack babies" are at high risk, the media have exaggerated their disabilities and made them appear more impaired and untreatable than they are. It is also crucial to recognize the effects of poverty and of inadequate parenting, rather than to attribute all of these children's problems to intrauterine "crack" exposure.

Emotional Factors

Emotional stress during pregnancy has been implicated in the genesis of birth defects and complications of pregnancy and delivery, as well as in later abnormalities. Animal data suggest a possible mechanism via alterations in levels of steroid hormones.

Complications in the Newborn Period

Sophisticated medical care in the newborn period can avert or moderate the harmful effects of birth injury, prematurity, hypoxia, hyperbilirubinemia, hypothyroidism, and infection.

Outcome

Although problems during pregnancy, birth, and the neonatal period may have physical, cognitive, and/or emotional sequelae, many high-risk infants, especially those with uncomplicated premature birth, improve with time and eventually demonstrate far less impairment than originally expected. Social risk factors such as single parents, poverty, and limited maternal education are powerful predictors of poor outcome. Early intervention with children, accompanied by family support services, can significantly improve outcome, even in infants with very low birth weight (less than 1.5 kg).

Communication

Even in utero the fetus's heart rate responds to chemical, auditory, and emotional stimuli to the mother and habituates to repeated exposure to these stimuli. At 7 months' gestation, the fetus perceives, discriminates, and responds to sounds.

Parental Response to Physical Illness or Handicap in the Newborn

The parents of an ill or handicapped infant are faced with the task of mourning the loss of their expected healthy child. The stages are similar to those following a death: anger, denial, and grief. (See also Chapters 10 and 14.) Parents must resign themselves to the loss of their fantasies of an ideal child and begin to adapt their expectations to the child's realistic potential.

Parents (and others) may view an infant's medical problems as a negative reflection on the parents. Parental guilt adds to the burden, especially for genetic diseases or complications that may be attributed (rightly or wrongly) to maternal behavior. The parents' anger, resentment, guilt, and/or denial may interfere with their ability to work with the pediatric team. Parents may find it difficult to relate to an infant with medical problems, especially if the baby's survival is in question.

Realistic additional caretaking and financial burdens may add stress to parents beyond their ability to cope. Parents with unresolved negative feelings, overwhelming stressors, insufficient emotional or material support, and/or inadequate understanding of the medical situation may be unable to comply with medical regimens after they take the baby home. Marriages may break down under the stress of the multiple demands of caring for a physically or mentally handicapped child. The importance of the primary physician in providing ongoing emotional support and assistance in obtaining appropriate services cannot be overemphasized.

INFANCY: THE FIRST YEAR

The neonate is much more competent than previously thought, although there is considerable variation among normal infants. Historically, the infant was viewed as passive. In the earliest psychoanalytic models, the child was seen as acted upon by instinctual drives. Classical behaviorists view the baby as a *tabula rasa*, shaped by external stimuli and contingencies or consequences. It is now recognized that babies are active participants in developing relationships and in influencing their environment. Heterogeneity in abilities and temperament leads to a variety of developmental paths.

Even in the first days of life, the newborn has considerable sensory, motor, intellectual, communicative, and affective abilities, which progress rapidly in the next 12 months (see Fig. 8–2).

Physical Development in Infancy

Neurologic

As neurons sprout multiple and branching dendrites, cortical synapses develop rapidly in the first year of life, to a number greater than that in adults. Excess synapses are subsequently "pruned" to reach adult numbers.

Newborns have remarkable sensory abilities. Visual fixation is possible within a few hours after birth. Infants seem to be genetically programmed to pay attention to complex patterns such as the human face. Infants less than 1 day old preferentially follow with their eyes and head a drawing that resembles a human face. By 2 days of age, infants look longer at their mothers' faces than those of unknown women. The 1-week-old infant can distinguish and prefers complex visual patterns and movement. Within the first month of life, the infant can use visual information to modulate motor responses such as reaching and grasping. Four-month-old babies are able to accommodate visually as well as an adult can.

Neonates can search with their eyes for the source of an interesting sound, especially speech. Within a week of birth, infants can distinguish their mother's voice and the smell of her breast milk from those of another woman. The pattern of the infant's sucking indicates a preference for sweet liquids.

The senses of proprioception, pressure, and touch are all functional at birth. Even premature infants are at least as sensitive to pain as adults. This evidence is ending the unfortunately common practice of performing circumcision or even major surgery on infants without anesthesia.

Gross Motor

At birth the neonate is unable to purposefully reach or grasp and has primitive motor reflexes. By 16 weeks of age, the infant can hold up his or her head. The child sits with support at 28 weeks, and sits alone, creeps, and pulls to stand at 40 weeks. Standing alone is achieved around 48 weeks. By 12 months of age, the ability to walk with support ("cruising") appears.

Sleep

Most infants sleep through the night (or at least do not fuss when they awaken) by 6 to 9 months of age. Up to half of all infants, however, have irregular sleep patterns and occasional or persistent night awakening throughout the first year.

Growth

The first year is a period of rapid physical growth, with an increase in weight of approximately 300%.

Cognitive Development in Infancy

Piaget's first stage, the *sensorimotor*, covers approximately the first 2 years of life. In the first 4 months of age, the infant demonstrates *primary circular reactions:* motor reflexes or habits centered upon his or her own body. These are initially quite simple (e.g., putting the thumb in the mouth and sucking), but become increasingly complex as the baby uses trial and error to attempt to repeat an interesting but accidental result. At this stage children are able to turn toward sounds, to engage in mutual imitation of sounds, and to visually follow a moving object.

Secondary circular reactions emerge in the 4-to-10 month old as schemes are extended to the external environment to reproduce interesting chance events (e.g., shaking the legs makes the crib mobile jiggle). The baby is able to follow the expected path of a moving object that disappears and to recognize an object, even if parts of it are hidden. By 10 to 12 months, babies begin purposefully to combine secondary schemes to reach a goal. At this age the infant can overcome simple obstacles, perceive a connection between events, and anticipate the next object in a familiar series. The child learns that a thing continues to exist even when out of sight (*object permanence*) and searches actively for an object that has disappeared. This progress is facilitated by the rapid enhancement of memory between 8 and 12 months of age.

Communication in Infancy

In the baby's first month of life, most parents learn to decipher their infant's cries as differentiated signals of fatigue, pain, hunger, fear, discomfort, anger, or wish for contact. In addition, babies engage in apparently noncommunicative crying that seems to serve the function of discharge of tension. This type of crying occurs at discrete, regular periods of the day, most often in the late afternoon and evening, for up to 2 to 3 hours. It can be distinguished from other crying, and the usual means of comfort are unsuccessful. It is most noticeable from 3 to 10 weeks, corresponding to "3-month colic." All normal babies demonstrate this type of crying to some extent, although there is wide variation in duration and intensity. Anticipatory guidance can help parents deal with the anxiety and tension these fussy periods cause, and avert the development of more serious problems.

The young child also has a repertoire of nonverbal techniques (e.g., smiling, reaching, looking toward or away from a person or object) for engaging with and eliciting behavior from adults.

Between 5 and 10 months, the infant begins to babble and to play with sounds, both alone and in interaction with an adult. At one year of age, most children use two or more words besides mama and dada and understand simple commands.

Affective Development in Infancy

Early Attachment
In the study of the development of the infant's relationship with the mother, it has become increasingly clear how powerfully the infant can influence adult behavior. The term *attachment* is used to describe the infant's behaviors, feelings, and cognitions directed toward the mother (or mothering figure). Attachment is an affectional or emotional tie formed between one person and another that endures over time and leads to seeking physical closeness to the important figure. Attachments are highly specific, although the infant may form an attachment to more than one person. Attachments are formed to both mother and father at about the same time. *Attachment behavior* promotes proximity or contact. Babies demonstrate this behavior toward both parents. When in distress, however, infants less than 2 years of age preferentially seek out the mother. The term *bonding* (unfortunately used rather indiscriminately) should be reserved for the parent's positive feelings and behaviors toward the infant.

John Bowlby and his colleague James Robertson became interested in attachment via their work with children separated from their parents by World War II, or for briefer periods by hospitalization or foster care. Bowlby (1969) drew from his own observations as well as from ethology (the study of the naturalistic behavior of animals), evolutionary theory, psychoanalysis, cognitive-developmental theory, and systems theory in his conceptualization of the purpose and mechanisms of attachment formation. He took a Darwinian view that the inborn behavioral systems characteristic of a species enhance survival, and proposed that the biological function of attachment behavior is protection from environmental danger because it ensures parental interest and proximity. In the human infant, he observed behaviors that are initially reflexive, such as following with the eyes, clinging, sucking, and smiling. These behaviors, maintained and promoted by cognitions and feelings, are used increasingly in a social interactive context with the parent.

As early as the first hours of life, the parents and child can engage in a reciprocal interaction that initiates the development of attachment. At 6 to 8 weeks of age, the infant selectively recognizes the mother's smile and smiles in response. This is the true *social smile*, and it produces a powerful affective response in the mother. The strength of these tendencies, their likely neurobiological underpinnings, and the remarkable adaptability of the human infant can be seen in blind babies, who show a specific smiling response to their mother's voice. Other infant behaviors that signify and strengthen attachment include crying, vocalizing, looking, greeting, and clinging, that are selectively directed at the mother (or other primary attachment figure).

Although the attachment process begins soon after birth, it is not instantaneous, but develops over time. In order to develop a stable attachment, the infant must have sufficient contact with a mothering person, the ability to distinguish the mother figure from other people, and at least the beginning of the conception that another person has an independent existence even when not present. Once the first attachment has formed, the infant can generalize to a small number of other people. Illness or handicap in the child, physical or emotional illness in the parent, or parental lack of sensitivity to the needs of the baby can all impair attachment formation. Abuse or neglect of the infant can prevent the formation of attachments, with catastrophic consequences for future personality development and the ability to form meaningful relationships.

The realization that attachment and bonding can begin immediately after birth has been influential in humanizing hospital maternity procedures, and in increasing opportunities for parental contact with premature and ill newborns. In many circles, however, there has been an unfortunate overemphasis on a "critical period," a very brief period of time immediately following birth after which formation of attachments and parenting ability are said to be impaired. This notion has added to the stresses on adoptive parents and parents of ill babies. Objective data do not support this "sensitive period" in the *first hours* of life or the necessity for extended immediate contact with the *neonate* in order to establish a secure affective relationship between the baby and either the mother or father.

Goldberg (1983) summarizes the evidence and its implications:

> Even among those who feel that early contact has been overrated, there are few who would argue that it is unimportant. Initial contacts are one phase in an ongoing process, and parents should be supported in this phase as well as others. Therefore, when not medically contraindicated, the opportunity for early interaction in the delivery or recovery room should be offered in order to make the experience of birth more humane, more positive, and more rewarding for parents.
>
> Second, individual differences in enthusiasm for immediate or even extended contact are normal. Insofar as possible, it is desirable to offer or allow contacts to occur when comfortable and convenient for the parents. The mother who wants or needs time to rest before holding her baby should not be made to feel that she is abnormal for not wanting to do so immediately. The mother who does not prefer rooming in or who does not keep the baby in her room as much as possible should also be made to feel comfortable with her decision.

Finally, the notion of early contact as critical rather than potentially beneficial needs to be dispelled. The emphasis on 'early bonding' has already created an expectation on the part of many parents that if they do not have this experience they have somehow failed and will never be fine parents (p 1379).

Erikson identified the establishment of *basic trust* as the primary affective task of this developmental period (see Chapter 10). This period also roughly corresponds to the Freudian *oral stage* of development described in Chapter 5.

Attachment Behavior and the Effects of Maternal Deprivation in Infancy

Mary Ainsworth pioneered in identifying and measuring attachment behaviors as indicators of the strength and security of attachment. She and others have found that insecure, anxious, or weak attachment may predict developmental problems later in childhood. A *securely attached* infant experiences separation anxiety when left by the mother. The baby seeks proximity and contact with the mother, especially when frightened or in a new situation. When with the mother, the child is able to play and to explore comfortably. When left, the infant protests or follows.

There are several types of *insecure attachment*, which are believed to have negative implications for the development of trust and healthy relationships, even into adulthood. A phenomenon Ainsworth called *anxious resistant attachment* is believed to be promoted by parental inconsistency. The parent is available and helpful at some times but not at others. There are frequent separations. Threats of abandonment are used to control the child, leading to feelings of uncertainty and excessive separation anxiety. Children demonstrating what Ainsworth calls *anxious avoidant attachment* expect to be rejected by others. This pattern is believed to result from constant rebuffs when the mother is approached for comfort or protection. This is most extreme in the case of severe abuse, neglect, or prolonged institutionalization. Mothers of insecurely attached infants have been observed to be less attuned to the baby's needs, often not giving assistance when needed, or intruding with help when the child does not need it. Others discourage the infant's efforts at exploration and autonomy. The pattern of attachment seen in the first year has been correlated with observations at ages 3½ and 6 years (Bowlby, 1988).

Attachment behavior is most discriminating between the ages of 6 and 12 months. By 10 months infants are capable of selective attachments to three or four people.

Stranger anxiety develops between 9 and 18 months, not only in response to strangers, but to anyone other than the mothering adult(s). At this age the infant can remember the mother's face, compare it with the stranger's, and realize the difference and the absence of the mother.

It is clear that the first year is a crucial time for forming the first attachment, and that afterwards the process is much more difficult. This has important implications for the care of young children who must be placed outside of the home.

Although some infants who are subjected to extreme stressors show remarkable resistance to developmental problems related to attachment, probably due to the child's genetic endowment and compensating factors in the family or support network, developmental trauma in this period may have lasting effects on the personality and vulnerability to childhood and adult psychiatric illness. Problems in developing secure attachments may be manifested clinically in later childhood, adolescence, and adulthood by persons who have difficulty in forming close, lasting, emotionally intimate relationships. Such persons may have "learned," from the inconsistency of the mother to anticipate rejection and the emotional distress and pain that accompanies it. Hence, closeness with other people may be viewed as an inherently risky emotional proposition where the threat of rejection or disappointment is always present. The anxiety resulting from expecting rejection or emotional abandonment may lead to a defensive posture of maintaining emotional distance and avoiding intimacy and commitment. In Chapter 11, Dr. van der Kolk discusses the scientific evidence for the lifelong consequences of developmental trauma during this stage of life.

Attachment behavior is exaggerated under stress from physical discomfort, fear, or separation from the mother. When separated from the mother, a baby older than 6 months of age shows a predictable sequence of emotions: first *protest*, with acute distress and crying; then misery and grief, or *despair;* followed by apparent apathy and disinterest, or *detachment* (Bowlby, 1975). Brief separations are benign, but as separations become longer, repeated, and/or accompanied by other stressors, the likelihood of emotional sequelae increases. Traumatic, prolonged separation can result in *anaclitic depression* (a state in which the child becomes withdrawn and relatively mute, and will not eat) or even death. Later sequelae may include an inability to form meaningful relationships or experience empathy for others, or the symptoms of post-traumatic stress disorder.

A favorite baby game, Peek-a-boo, demonstrates how the child's egocentric cognitive perspective (if I can't see something, it isn't there) is used in the practicing of separation from the parent. By covering and uncovering the eyes, the infant is making the adult come and go, thereby gaining control of the experience and of the anxiety about being left alone.

Many of the details of attachment theory need to be rethought in view of the current rarity of "traditional" families (two married parents, with the mother as full-time homemaker and the almost exclusive caretaker of the baby). One-year-old infants of mothers who work full-time or part-time in the first year of life are as likely to be securely attached to their mothers as infants whose mothers do not work outside the home (Zimmerman and Bernstein, 1983).

Rene Spitz's pioneering work on *hospitalism* and *anaclitic depression* identified the devastating effects on infants of separation from their mother when compounded by lack of stimulation (Spitz, 1945; 1946). Absence of a suitable mothering figure prevents or disrupts the formation of attachments. Severe maternal deprivation can lead to a decrease in intelligence, impaired ability to trust or to form meaningful interpersonal relationships, and even death. The syndrome of psychosocial *failure to thrive*, characterized by lack of growth despite adequate access to food, listlessness, and delayed cognitive, social, and motor development, has been attributed to insufficient or inappropriate mothering, although subtle physiologic factors often contribute.

Separation–Individuation
Mahler's model of the process of the infant's separation and individuation from the parent is covered in detail in Chapter 5 by Drs. Inderbitzen and James. Drs.

Wolman and Thompson, in Chapter 10, describe how the thematic paradigm of separation–individuation can be repeated throughout the life cycle. However, observational data about infant behavior and capabilities have called into question some of the details of this theory, particularly the stage of so-called normal autism.

The Transitional Object

By the end of first year, many children have chosen what Winnicott calls a *transitional object:* a toy, blanket, pillow or piece of clothing, usually soft, to which the child is very attached, and that is used for comfort, most often at times of separation or when going to sleep. It represents both the child and the mother. Whether or not a child has an identifiable transitional object has not been found to have prognostic significance.

Response of Child and Family to Physical Illness in Infancy

When infants less than 6 months old are hospitalized, they are most upset by change in the usual routine. It is helpful to have the parents provide as much of the care as possible, and to arrange for consistent nurses. For the older infant who has formed strong differential attachments, separation is traumatic, especially in the alien hospital environment and when accompanied by physical discomfort and frightening and painful medical procedures. Stranger anxiety adds to the baby's distress. The infant's immature cognitive development exacerbates the problem, because explanations are not understood. The constant presence of a parent is extremely important. In the absence of an attachment figure, the baby's thrashing, refusal to eat, and inability to sleep may have serious medical consequences. Fortunately, most pediatric hospital settings not only permit but encourage parents to room in while their young child is hospitalized.

Green and Solnit (1964) have described a *vulnerable child syndrome*, occurring after a child survives a potentially fatal illness. The family may have completed anticipatory mourning and have difficulty reintegrating the child. Alternatively, the child may subsequently be overprotected and underdisciplined, with resulting immaturity and difficulty with age-appropriate separation and development.

THE TODDLER: AGES ONE TO THREE (1–3)

Figures 8–2 and 8–3 summarize development in this period along multiple lines of development.

Physical Development of the Toddler

Gross Motor

By 30 months of age the child not only stands, but walks and runs with ease.

Fine Motor–Adaptive

During this period there is a rapid increase in fine motor abilities, such as using a crayon, and in eye-hand coordination.

Sleep

Parents are frequently concerned about their toddler's sleep habits. Among middle-class 1-to-3 year olds, daily sleep time averaged a total of 12 hours, including a 2-hour nap. In 1 week, 10% of the children reported a nightmare, and 7% experienced a *night terror (pavor nocturnus;* see later under Early Childhood). Twenty-one percent of 18-to-23 month olds awakened during the night. Thirty-one percent of the 24-to-29 month olds took more than 30 minutes to fall asleep on more than 3 nights in a week. Children aged 30 to 36 months were the most likely to have difficulty settling (16%) and to express fears of the dark (24%) (Crowell et al, 1987). Another survey of 1-to-3 year old children found that 42% resisted going to bed. Thirty-five percent woke and cried during the night (Johnson, 1991). The use of a nightlight is almost universal at this age.

Growth and Feeding

Young toddlers show increasing interest in feeding themselves, first with their fingers, then using utensils. The child's reduced nutritional needs, resulting from much slower physical growth than in the first year and compounded by increasing interest in activity and in the environment, lead to dramatic decreases in appetite. The parent who views this with alarm and focuses excessively on eating can promote a feeding problem. It is important to avoid turning mealtime into a power struggle. The child who consumes excessive quantities of milk or of "empty-calorie foods" can develop serious deficiencies in iron or other essential nutrients. Overindulgence in highly sweetened foods can result in obesity and/or tooth decay.

Toilet Training

Toilet training typically begins between ages 18 and 30 months. Prerequisites include the regularity of bowel and bladder function, the ability to sense bladder and rectal fullness, the ability to control the sphincter muscles, the psychological ability to delay, the wish to imitate adults and to please the parents, the ability to communicate the need to use the toilet, and the sufficient motor control to walk, stoop, stand, and remove clothing easily. A child reported to have been trained earlier than this is usually a very regular child whom the parent has learned to "catch," by putting him or her on the potty at predictable times of elimination. When toilet training is started too early, the resulting learning process is longer and often more difficult. Capitalizing on the child's wish to imitate adults and using rewards such as praise and small treats can facilitate learning in a positive manner. Punitive or threatening methods of training should not be used under any circumstances. Most children establish control of urination during the day by age 2½ and at night by age 3½ to 4 years. Approximately 10% of 6 year olds (predominantly boys) still wet the bed, however. Late attainment of nocturnal control tends to be familial. Almost all children have achieved bowel control by age 4.

Cognitive Development of the Toddler

Piaget's Stages

The *sensorimotor stage* continues. In the first half of the second year the *tertiary circular reaction* develops. This is the attempt to produce novelty for its own sake by extending existing schemes to a variety of objects. The *preoperational stage* begins in the third year (see section entitled "Early Childhood" for description).

Object permanence, the conviction that something continues to exist even when out of sight, solidifies around 18 to 20 months of age, but begins as early as age 4 months. Children understand this about people, especially their parents, before they understand it about things.

Milestones

Eighteen month olds can recognize themselves in mirrors and pictures. By the latter half of the second year, the child is able to retain and use mental symbols, a necessary precursor to the use of language.

Increased interest in the environment and ability to explore, in the absence of judgment or understanding of consequences, put toddlers at extremely high risk for accidents. Parents must ensure safety but avoid overly restricting the child's exploration or responding punitively to inadvertent damage of objects. Systematically "child-proofing" the house and using tactics that redirect the child into other activities can reduce both danger and parent-child power struggles.

Speech and Language Development of the Toddler

Over the first 6 months of this period, toddlers make extensive use of *jargon* (sounds that resemble speech, but are unintelligible). Most 2 year olds have a 300-word vocabulary, use phrases and two-word sentences, and can point to body parts when named. Around 30 months of age, most children can use pronouns correctly. In all children, comprehension precedes expressive abilities.

Private speech, which has a social intent but fails to communicate specific meaning, precedes true social speech. The child still has idiosyncratic meanings for some words. Toddlers often use pronouns without referents, as if the listener knew to whom the pronoun referred without being told.

Some *echolalia* (repetition of overheard words or phrases) is normal into the third year. Developmental dysfluency or repetition of words or phrases is normal between ages 2 and 4. This should be differentiated from *stuttering*, a symptom that includes blocking and repeating of sounds, with motor and subsequent emotional tension, and eventual severe anxiety about speech.

Although normal children vary widely in their rate and style of language acquisition, a hearing test and a language assessment are indicated if an 18 month old uses no words or just "mama" and "dada," and doesn't point to what he or she wants. An evaluation is warranted if a 2 year old is not putting two words together, has a vocabulary less than 20 words, has speech that is unintelligible to the parents, or does not understand commands or questions without gestures (Allen et al, 1988). Although a few normal children are simply late talkers, such a delay could be caused by deafness, aphasia, mental retardation, autistic disorder, or developmental language disorder. The Early Language Milestone Scale can be used by primary care practitioners to screen for speech and language delay (up to 48 months of age) (Coplan and Gleason, 1990). Hearing sensitivity can be tested using brain stem auditory evoked response audiometry on even the least cooperative child. Gross indications that the child hears sounds do not eliminate the possibility of a hearing impairment sufficient to limit the development of speech and language.

Affective Development of the Toddler

Object Relations

In the first half of the second year, a phenomenon that Emde and colleagues have called *social referencing* appears, in which the infant looks to the parent for emotional cues about a novel event.

Mahler's description of this period is discussed in detail in Chapter 5. To briefly recapitulate, as the *practicing subphase* continues (12 to 18 months), the toddler moves away from the parent to explore. The child returns frequently to the parent to "refuel" (to establish emotional contact and to refresh the internal image of the mother). A securely attached child is able to use the mother as a base from which to investigate the environment. In the *rapprochement subphase* (16 to 24 months), children's growing realization of their separateness, physical ability to move away from the parent, and their own helplessness leads to intense ambivalence about their attachment and dependency needs. Many toddlers increase clinging to parents, tantrums, thumb or finger sucking, and need for their transitional object. The child's third year sees *consolidation* and resolution, as the child becomes comfortable with brief separations. In later stages of development, such as adolescence and young adulthood, portions of the separation–individuation process may be repeated (see Chapter 10).

The third year is marked by the child's struggle for psychological autonomy and separateness from the parents. This may be seen in the form of negativity and tantrums as children practice making decisions and asserting themselves, but then become overwhelmed by feelings that they cannot yet express verbally. The middle of this year is the height of "the terrible twos." Although the duration and intensity vary greatly among children, some degree of negativism is essential in the child's development of a sense of independence and individuality. Children benefit from consistent, firm, but sympathetic limits. Tantrums should be ignored and *never* rewarded, to prevent transforming an expression of frustration into a device for manipulating adults. Whenever possible, direct confrontations should be avoided. It is helpful if parents can resist the temptation to interpret the toddler's obstinate behavior as a personal affront. Taking a punitive or rigidly controlling approach can be destructive to the child's development and to the parent-child relationship. The most effective means of handling defiant behavior is usually by brief periods of "time out" or in the case of tantrums, by ignoring them. (See Chapter 6 by Dr. Dorsett.) Physical punishment should not be used. Often, the adult can ease the process by presenting the child with choices, both of which are acceptable to the parent.

Emotions and Mechanisms of Defense

In the third year of life, a sense of empathy for others begins to emerge. The child also has a growing understanding of emotions and an ability to label them verbally. *Reaction formation* is a defense mechanism that typically appears in this period, as seen in children who have recently been toilet trained and become excessively upset by messiness. This defense is presumed to protect the child against wishes to urinate and defecate at will. The development of defense mechanisms is discussed in a psychoanalytic framework in Chapter 5.

Fears

The toddler's lack of experience, small size, and helplessness compared to adults foster the development of fears such as of loud noises, animals, the dark, and separation from parents. Fears of the bathtub or toilet are common, exacerbated by toddlers' inability to judge relative sizes and determine that they could *not* actually fit down the drain.

Gender-Related Issues

Core morphologic or gender identity is the usually unshakable conviction of being a male or a female, which develops through a complex interaction of physiological and environmental factors (Money, 1987). It can be seen around 18 months, or even earlier, and is often established by 24 to 30 months. Absolute integration of gender identity can be expected by age 3. While psychological and sociocultural factors play an important role in shaping gender identity, for most persons, biological gender determines psychological identity as a male or female.

As discussed in the preceding chapter by Drs. Becker and Hunter, in utero, sexual differentiation proceeds in the female direction in the absence of masculinizing hormones (androgens). Androgens alter the development of the central nervous system as well as of the genitalia. Normally, all of the child's gender-related characteristics are consistent: chromosomes, prenatal hormones, gonads (ovaries and testes), internal and external genitalia, postnatal hormones, and secondary sex characteristics (developing at puberty).

Cultural factors are extremely important in the development of *gender role behavior,* that is, behavior that is considered by society to be appropriate for one sex or another. Examples for children include tone of voice, physical mannerisms, gait, clothing, play activities, and playmates. Adults treat boys and girls differently from infancy (Shepherd-Look, 1982). Boys are picked up more as newborns, handled more roughly than girls, and more frequently engaged in rough-and-tumble play. Mothers talk more to girls than to boys. Adults offer different toys to boys and to girls, and by age 1 year, toy preference along stereotypical gender lines is established. Beginning in the second year, fathers pay significantly more attention to boys than to girls. By age 2, boys show a clear preference for their fathers over their mothers (Hodapp and Mueller, 1982). Differential treatment and expectations continue throughout the course of development. Extrafamilial influences are also important. Sex differences have been found in children's response to social reinforcement of specific behaviors. Girls respond to both male and female teachers and to other girls, but ignore reinforcement from boys. Boys, on the other hand, respond to reinforcement from male peers, but are unresponsive to reinforcement from girls or from teachers (Fagot, 1985). The peer group is a powerful determinant of gender role behavior, as are adult figures popularized by the media.

It has now been recognized that masculinity and femininity are not polar opposites, but orthogonal (independent) variables, each being found in varying amounts in both males and females. The interaction of physical and environmental factors in the development of gender identity and role behavior is complex. Some hints can be gleaned from the study of children with inconsistent gender-related factors. For example, girls whose mothers were treated with masculinizing progestogens during pregnancy are more likely to be tomboys, preferring intense outdoor play and male peers and avoiding doll play, but they are not more likely to become transsexual or homosexual.

Genetic females with congenital adrenal hyperplasia, a defect in cortisol synthesis that leads to prenatal and postnatal excess of androgenic hormone precursor, are born with masculinized external genitalia and normal female internal organs. Clear, early gender assignment with consistent medical and surgical treatment can result in stable gender identity as *either* a male or a female, depending on initial assignment. Reassignment attempts fail if carried out after 18 months to 3 years.

Androgen-insensitivity syndrome (testicular feminization) in XY genetic males is characterized by insensitivity of all body cells to testosterone, leading to female-appearing external genitalia. These children are usually reared as females. Histologically normal but nonfunctional testes are removed to avoid virilization and increased risk of malignancy. If the child is treated as a normal girl, she usually develops female gender identity, stereotypically feminine role behavior, and, in adolescence, sexual interest in males.

Tentative evidence from children prenatally exposed to treatment with estrogen and progestogen (to avoid loss of the pregnancy) shows behavioral demasculinization of males and increased feminization of females.

Social Development of Toddlers

Early in this period, children are curious about other children. The first half of the third year sees the development of *parallel play*, solitary unrelated play conducted in pairs. Over the next 6 months, children begin to engage in *associative play*, in pairs or small groups, doing the same thing side by side, but not really interacting. Toddler play is based on sensorimotor activity—opening and shutting, emptying and filling—with more interest in the process than the product.

Response to Illness and Hospitalization During the Toddler Phase

Hospitalized toddlers react primarily to separation from their parents. They may react by rejecting parents when they visit, being aggressive toward parent surrogates (e.g., nurses), regressing in toilet training, and/or refusing to eat. If parents are absent, children may develop depression, sleep disturbance, diarrhea, or vomiting. Fortunately, virtually all hospitals allow and encourage parents to stay with young children. The presence of a transitional object or other familiar items from home may be helpful.

Children with pre-existing problems in development or in the parent-child relationship have more sustained difficulty, although a child who is weakly attached may show less immediate distress on separation. A child who has been neglected may be indiscriminately eager for adult attention and stimulation.

Toddlers are also concerned about the intactness of their bodies, as seen in their great interest in stick-on bandages. Some children believe that body contents can leak out through a cut in the skin.

EARLY CHILDHOOD: AGES THREE TO SIX (3–6)

Physical Development in Early Childhood

Gross Motor

Most 3 year olds can stand on one foot, jump, run smoothly, and climb stairs using alternating feet. They are beginning to show hand preference and to be able to ride a tricycle. Four year olds should be able to ride a tricycle well, to climb on a jungle gym, and to throw a ball overhand. By age 5, balance is better, and the child should be able to skip smoothly.

Fine Motor–Adaptive

The 3 year old can build a tower of 9 or 10 blocks. By age 4, most children can button and lace, feed themselves neatly, pour from a pitcher, and dress and wash themselves. Drawing ability progresses from copying a circle (3 years), to copying a cross and drawing a simple man with head, eyes, and legs (4 years). The 5 year old can copy a square and a triangle and draw a recognizable man with basic body parts (eyes, nose, mouth, body, arms, legs, and feet). The 5 year old plans pictures in advance, and may include elaborate scenes or complex events.

Sleep

Many 3 year olds still take an afternoon nap, but give it up by age 4 or 5 years. A phenomenon that is often confused with nightmares is the *night terror* or *pavor nocturnus*. Unlike nightmares, which occur during rapid eye movement (REM) sleep, and are often remembered, the *night terror* occurs during the deep *non-REM* sleep stages 3 and 4. The child appears terrified, screaming, confused; has dilated pupils, sweating, rapid pulse, and hyperventilation; and does not respond to comforting. Once alert, the child rapidly returns to sleep. There is no memory of the episode in the morning. This phenomenon is most common in children ages 3 to 6 and does not indicate psychopathology. It is usually much more upsetting to parents than to the child!

Toilet Training

Most children are dry at night by the latter half of the fourth year. They are able to use the toilet independently in the daytime, at least in familiar places.

Cognitive Development in Early Childhood

Piaget's Stages

The *preoperational stage* of intellectual development extends from approximately 2 to 7 years of age, including both the toddler period and early childhood. The child learns to classify, to place objects in order (by trial and error), and to construct sets equivalent in number by matching one to one. Piaget believed that the preoperational child is unable to deal with more than one dimension (e.g., height and width) at a time, or to recognize that a person or thing conserves its identity when it undergoes minor variations in appearance. Problem solving is by trial and error, rather than by planned strategies.

The use of nonverbal mental symbols, followed by language, gives the child the ability to transcend space and time. This ability can be seen in the child's deferred imitation of actions, drawing of scenes clearly based on memory, and meaningful use of words. *Symbolic play* appears, consisting of pretend, or imaginative play with toys or dramatizing roles and stories in which toys and roles symbolize real objects and real persons.

Preoperational children are normally *egocentric*, relating everything to themselves. Piaget believed that the child was unaware of the point of view of the listener or even that the listener may have another point of view or different knowledge. More recent work has shown that 4 year olds do speak differently to adults than they do to 2 year olds, indicating an awareness of the listener's ability to understand. The 4 year old is able to show some understanding of another's perspective, if the task is carefully designed.

Children this age often have difficulty understanding cause and effect. Thinking tends to be *concrete*, with explanations often based on past experience, whether or not it is relevant. Reasoning is often *transductive* (attributing causality to juxtaposition in time or space) rather than *inductive* (from the particular to the general) or *deductive* (from the general to the particular). Piaget called this *phenomenalistic causality*.

Young children are *animistic*, believing that all events can be explained by the action of some humanlike agency or force that wills things to happen for its own purposes. Words and actions are not fully differentiated. *Magical thinking*, the belief that words, thoughts, and wishes can cause events in the external world, is typical of the child in the preoperational stage. Older children, or even adults, may regress to magical thinking under stress.

Four year olds have difficulty distinguishing truth from fiction. Even at age 7, strong wishes may distort the perception of reality. Adults may misinterpret this as deliberate lying. A child who desperately wishes he had not broken his mother's vase may actually convince himself that he did not. This phenomenon may be seen in older children and even adolescents who are cognitively or emotionally immature or under stress.

Moral development in the 3-to-6 year old is characterized by *moral realism:* the belief in immanent justice, and the inevitability of punishment. Physical misfortunes and accidents may be seen as direct punishment for wrongdoing (present at some time in all children, at least in thought). Piaget termed the morality of this stage *objective*, by which he meant that guilt is determined solely by the amount of damage, not the intent or motivation. A child who spills a whole bottle of ink while trying to help set the table is judged more guilty than a child who spills a drop of ink while playing with a pen that he has been forbidden to touch. Young children are absolute in their judgment of right and wrong. The *inability* to see simultaneous positive and negative aspects of the same person or event, considered pathological *splitting* in adults, is normal in early childhood (see Chapter 5).

Preoperational children do not know or follow rules of games, but insist that they do. They believe that rules are originated by a godlike absolute authority and are unchangeable. Children are more likely to follow parents' rules if they are highly identified with them (admire them, believe they take after them, and want to grow up to be like them). Hence, the ethical *examples* set by loving, fair, and honorable parents are *far more important* than the prohibitions and punishments imposed in an effort to train children in moral behavior.

Milestones

Four year olds have little understanding of past and future. By age 5, there is a better understanding of the concepts of yesterday and tomorrow, and an ability to carry over play activities from one day to the next. There is a beginning understanding of clock and calendar time. Five year olds can identify simple similarities among and differences between objects. Children at this age believe that death is reversible, like sleep.

Speech and Language in Early Childhood

Language permits the mastery of negative feelings by putting them into words instead of acting upon them, yielding improved impulse control and ability to delay gratification.

On average, vocabulary develops at the amazing rate of nine new words per day until the age of 6. Three year olds ask constant questions, just for the sake of talking. They play with words, and use and understand prepositions like in, on, and under. Four year olds' articulation is still somewhat immature, but their speech should be largely intelligible in context. Word play includes crude puns. Complex parts of speech, such as adverbs, and more difficult prepositions and conjunctions appear. By the age of 5 years, articulation should be clear and correct, answers to questions more succinct and relevant, and questions fewer, more direct, and more meaningful. Correct, finished sentences can be constructed, including hypothetical and conditional clauses. In this period, language development is ahead of the ability to understand concepts. Adults must be cautious not to assume that children understand more than they actually do.

Affective Development in Early Childhood

Object Relations

Mahler proposed that firm emotional *object constancy*, the ability to maintain a positive inner image of an important person despite the level of need or satisfaction, is established by around 36 months (see discussion of object relations theory in Chapter 5). The timing varies, however, depending on the child's previous experience and the character of the mother-child relationship. Under stress, previously attained object constancy can be temporarily lost.

Fears

Normal fears include the dark, animals, bodily harm, monsters, ghosts, and death. Cognitive development at this age does not permit the use of sophisticated psychological defenses to control anxiety in the face of perceived danger.

Gender-Related Issues

The learning of gender roles and societally determined gender role behavior starts in the toddler period. By age 3, children can identify tasks and possessions as masculine or feminine. Culturally determined gender role behaviors are so strong that they can override parental determination to encourage androgyny. Even kindergarten children know the sex-role stereotypes of Western culture, aspire to stereotypical sex-appropriate occupations, choose same-sex friends, and evaluate the work of same-sex adults and children more highly than those of the opposite sex. Each child has an individual balance of masculine and feminine characteristics, influenced by temperamental factors and parental modeling and expectations.

Cross-gender behavior is normal in boys until age 5 years. Cultural expectations for gender role behavior in girls are much more flexible, so tomboyish behavior is generally not considered abnormal at any age, unless it is accompanied by a rigid avoidance of all feminine clothes and activities. Boys are more aggressive than girls as early as age 2 years, continuing through adolescence.

Sexuality

Three year olds are aware of sex differences but are prone to primitive theories regarding sexuality and pregnancy. Boys are increasingly aware of sensations in the penis. The fear of loss of or damage to the genitals may be accentuated by viewing female genitals and by punitive threats made by parents attempting to stop a child from masturbating. Detumescence of the penis after an erection may reinforce fears of castration.

Belief in oral impregnation (encouraged by jokes about swallowed watermelon seeds turning into babies) may lead to irrational attitudes toward food. Children begin to demonstrate behavior that suggests fantasies about, observation of, or hearing sounds associated with parental sexual intercourse, which may be confused with some form of physical attack, fighting, or wrestling. Sex education geared to the level of the child's curiosity and understanding is important. Preoccupation with or detailed knowledge about sexual behavior suggests inappropriate exposure to sexual activity or even sexual abuse.

Imaginary Companions

Up to one-fifth of 3-to-6 year olds have an imaginary companion, a fantasy person or animal to whom the child gives a name, an appearance, and a character. Children may or may not tell their parents about their imaginary friends. The phenomenon is most often seen in creative children of above-average intelligence. At various times the companion serves as scapegoat, playmate, and protector. By 10 years of age, the imaginary companion is usually given up.

Dreams
Until about 5 years of age, the child believes that dreams are real events. Children frightened by their angry or aggressive feelings toward their parents may project them onto monsters, who then appear in nightmares.

Family Relationships
Toward the end of this period, children begin to recognize the discrepancy between reality and their idealized image of their parents. This leads to the "family romance," the fantasy that the child has other, real parents, who are far wiser, kinder, and more successful than those with whom he or she lives. This stage may be particularly difficult for adopted children and their parents.

Even those who do not accept Freudian developmental theory and the concept of the Oedipus complex (see Chapter 5), observe that many 3-to-6 year olds show exaggerated "romantic" behavior toward the parent of the opposite sex, coupled with disinterest in, or even rivalry with the parent of the same sex. As this stage passes, the child moves from a dyadic (one-to-one) preoccupation with the parent of the opposite sex to a more balanced relationship and identification with both parents, and a readiness to invest energy outside of the family into friendships and schoolwork.

Social Development in Early Childhood

Three year olds are able to play alone in parallel with another child for longer periods of time than is the toddler. Four year olds are more able to engage in *cooperative* or small group play. They are beginning to be able to share, but are often bossy and have difficulty understanding the feelings of other children. By age 5, most children can engage in the planning and execution of group projects and participate in elaborate dramatic play. Empathy and leadership begin to appear. Children who are friendly and helpful tend to be popular with peers, while aggressive and disruptive children are rejected. Rejection by peers is a powerful predictor of later psychopathology.

Play serves a critical defensive function, enabling children to regain a sense of control by playing out scenarios in which they have been passively acted upon (e.g., during a medical procedure) by taking an active role in the play. Libidinal and aggressive impulses can be discharged through symbolic or fantasy play. Play is also used to develop mastery of both skills and emotions and to prepare for adult roles. Play and recreation continue to fill a useful role throughout life.

Television

Preschool children watch an average of 3 to 4 hours of television per day, and in the vast majority of homes viewing is completely unsupervised. Research has shown that regular viewing of action/adventure programs leads to increased aggressive behavior in young children. Heavy television viewing also interferes with learning to read (Singer and Benton, 1989). The cognitive limitations of children in the Piagetian preoperational stage of development make it difficult for them to distinguish fantasy from reality, especially with the realistic special effects of today's television programs.

Starting School

The period from ages 3 to 6 is often called the preschool period, because the child who has been cared for at home by the parent(s) often has the first experience with major separation at entry to nursery school (age 3 or 4) or kindergarten (age 5). A temporary regression manifested by crying, clinging to the parent, wetting or soiling, refusal to eat, or sleep disturbance is not unusual. In an otherwise well-adjusted child, if the separation is handled sensitively by teacher and parent, the child soon returns to his or her previous level of functioning, or even makes a jump ahead. For children who have not mastered previous stages of separation–individuation, are temperamentally inclined to avoid new situations, or have parents reluctant to separate from them, the first signs of separation anxiety disorder or school phobia may be seen at this stage. Children whose prior exposure to peers has been limited may have more difficulty adjusting to the preschool experience. This is also the age at which oppositional defiant disorder or attention-deficit hyperactivity disorder may first become apparent, because the child is expected to function as a member of a group and follow rules, and is observed by the teacher, who has a wider experience with normative child behavior than the parents.

Response to Physical Illness

Separation from parents by hospitalization remains difficult, even for a child who is comfortably able to separate in other circumstances. Castration and mutilation anxiety and the belief in immanent justice increase the child's fears. When possible, preparation by simple explanations and a visit to the hospital may help. Regression is common, manifested by such behavior as whining, clinging, and loss of toilet training. Interestingly, even adults may regress and demonstrate similar types of immature childlike behavior under the strain of illness and hospitalization or another major life stress.

MIDDLE CHILDHOOD: AGES SIX TO TWELVE (6–12)

This period of development is often called *latency*, a term derived from the psychoanalytic developmental model. Most children attend elementary school during these years. The age of 7 (plus or minus 1 year) represents a significant developmental milestone in virtually all present and past cultures (Shapiro and Perry, 1976). This is the age at which the child is considered to be ready for formal schooling, apprenticeship, or more active learning of adult skills and roles. For example, the Roman Catholic Church has established the age of 7 as "the age of reason" and, therefore, the time for First Communion. Other religions and cultures have similar rituals to mark this developmental stage. The child's increasing cognitive and motor capacities allow for gradual independence from the family.

Physical Development in Middle Childhood

Neurologic

Changes in the child's abilities, interests, and role in society coincide with significant maturation of the central nervous system (Shapiro and Perry, 1976). By age 7, the brain has attained about 90% of its adult weight. The cerebral cortex is completely myelinated, and the electroencephalogram (EEG) is better synchronized, with a stable alpha wave pattern. Structural and functional changes at the microscopic level can be documented in the frontal lobe, perhaps facilitating verbal regulation of behavior. Children are able to perceive and to understand increasingly complex sensory stimuli. Their ability to integrate and to coordinate various sensory and motor capacities improves dramatically. They attain the ability to distinguish right from left, first in themselves, and then in others. Handedness is established around age 7, followed by dominance of one eye and one foot.

Gross Motor

Between the ages of 7 and 10, balance, equilibrium, control of large muscles, and timing improve dramatically. Children are able to learn a variety of sports, including skating, jumping rope, swimming, diving, riding a two-wheel bicycle, and the beginnings of team sports such as soccer.

Fine Motor–Adaptive

Small muscle control improves, and average 8 year olds can tie their shoes easily, wink, snap their fingers, and whistle. Games such as jacks are mastered. In drawings, the 8 year old can use perspective and correct body proportions.

Sleep

At age 8 years, sleep averages 10 hours, decreasing to 8 to 9 hours by age 10.

Growth and Pubertal Changes

At age 10, girls and boys are approximately equal in size and sexual maturity. Girls are the first to show subtle signs of puberty. The growth spurt begins at 9 or 10 years, with the growth rate peaking at 12. Hip rounding, nipple projection, waist accentuation, and early pubic hair follow the growth spurt. Puberty begins, on average, 2 years later in boys. A slight increase in the size of the penis and the testes, and the beginnings of pubic hair appear at age 10 or 11, with the growth spurt beginning at 11 or 12 years. Appetite tends to increase around age 10, especially in boys. (Pubertal development is also discussed in Chapter 7 by Drs. Becker and Hunter.)

Cognitive Development in Middle Childhood

Piaget's Stages

In the stage of *concrete operations* (7 to 11 years) the child acquires the ability to *decentrate*, that is, to consider more than one dimension simultaneously (e.g., height and width). Ability to take the perspective of another person improves. Children become able to reverse operations mentally, a skill essential to comfort with addition and subtraction. They develop the ability to *conserve*, first quantity (6 to 7 years), then weight (9 to 10 years), and finally volume (11 to 12 years). In other words, they come to understand that these properties of a substance are not changed by alterations in shape or size. Their explanations of conservation progress from negation or reversibility (you could just make it the way it was before), through identity (it's the same, none was added or taken away) to compensation or reciprocity (a short wide glass holds the same amount as a tall narrow one).

As moral development progresses, children are able to take motivation into account in judging right and wrong. Morality becomes *subjective*, as the child is increasingly able to understand the feelings of other people and the influence of their own actions on others.

Milestones

Perceptual-integrative abilities improve dramatically during this developmental period. School placement is crucial. If the work is too easy, it leads to boredom and poor study habits. If too hard, failure, loss of motivation, feelings of incompetence, and/or behavior problems result. Around 3% of school children are mentally retarded and need a special class or school. Approximately 10 to 25% of children are slow learners, with borderline or low normal IQ, 40 to 50% are average, 20 to 25% are bright or above average, and about 10% are gifted. Expectations vary from school to school. For example, a child with an average IQ may have difficulty getting good grades in a competitive suburban or private school. In general, girls tend to be better students than boys.

By age 7, accurate comprehension of time and calendar organization leads to a better understanding of the past and the future and an increased ability to delay gratification. Most 8 year olds are able to read for pleasure, but their ideas still exceed their writing ability. Nine year olds, typically in the 4th grade, should have an improved ability to set and to finish a task. Most find school enjoyable but may fear failure. Some previously immature children show a rapid growth in learning at this time. Alternatively, increased demands for using reading and math skills may uncover a learning disability that was not previously noticed.

Most 10 year olds memorize well but still have difficulty with abstraction. They can count forward indefinitely by ones, twos, fives, and tens, and backward by ones. They are also able to identify similarities and differences between objects, define concrete words, and add and subtract with ease.

By age 11, children should be able to interpret simple proverbs and perform multiplication and division. They are, however, usually unable to understand irony or sarcasm.

A more realistic concept of death is developing in children aged 10 to 11. Most understand that death is universal, especially those who have reached the Piagetian stage of concrete operations, but more than half of 4th graders do not yet clearly understand the irreversibility of death. Elementary-school-age children continue to view death as a punishment for bad behavior (White et al, 1978).

Five year olds literally think out loud, with a running description of their activities. By age 6 to 8, thinking becomes more covert or private, and takes on a self-regulatory and then problem-solving function. Private speech also takes on a role in academic performance. By age 10 or 12, children have developed *metacognitive* abilities (i.e., they understand something about what they know and how they learn), and are able to consciously develop strategies for learning. Impulsive children with learning, conduct, or attentional problems either do not develop these skills or do not use them when appropriate. Specific interventions have been developed to teach them, with variable degrees of success.

Affective Development in Middle Childhood

Superego and Conscience

New cognitive abilities permit better inhibition and control of drives, and postponement of action and gratification. Freudian developmental theory (described in Chapter 5) proposes that the *superego*, which emerges as the Oedipal crisis is resolved, is divided into the prohibiting and punitive *conscience*, and the *ego-ideal* or idealized model to which one aspires. The child identifies with the parents, and gives these identifications authority, facilitating obedience to parental instructions even without parental presence. Satisfying the ego-ideal leads to increased self-esteem, comfort, and well-being. Major discrepancy between the child's ego-ideal and actual abilities may lead to demoralization and low-self esteem, or to a defiant refusal to even attempt to succeed. Early in this period the newly developed superego is alternatively punitive and ineffective. Guilt may be handled by projection or by provoking punishment. When children misbehave, or believe that they have misbehaved, without parental awareness, they may then engage in further mischief until finally punished. A parent may say, "I don't understand it, Johnny was *asking* for it!" Under stress, children may be prone to regression, with loss of superego control. Emotions are often fluid, intense, and rapidly changing.

By ages 8 to 10, the superego is more firmly established, and the ego is stronger and more firmly consolidated. Children should be able to distinguish right from wrong and to be honest and truthful. Behavior is generally based on internalized values, rather than on seeking rewards or avoiding punishment. More mature obsessional defenses and sublimation can facilitate improved school performance. Normal compulsive traits are seen in the strong interest typical of this phase in establishing and organizing collections (e.g., stamps, rocks, dolls, baseball cards). If pronounced, these defenses, along with increased repression, may lead to a decrease in creativity and spontaneity.

Sexuality

Although this period has been termed latency in psychoanalytic developmental theory, it is only sexual wishes toward, and fantasies directly concerning *parents* that are typically latent. Sexual exploration, comparing of genitals, and group or mutual masturbation are common among boys. Prepubertal boys show a renewed interest in anal or fecal humor and in using sexual or excretory terms as expletives. Sex education begun in early childhood should be continued, although children of this age may not be willing to confess ignorance by asking questions. As puberty approaches, academic tasks may no longer provide adequate gratification and excitement or bind sufficient energy, and interest is transferred to sports and teen-age activities, and in dysfunctional social and family environments to "gangs."

Fears

Some fears, such as those related to body integrity, may be dealt with by counterphobic defenses and risk-taking behavior. Many children worry about their competence or appearance. Nightmares are usually related to daytime events, and children are easily calmed when awakened.

Social Development in Middle Childhood

Eight year olds should have a firm grasp of basic rules and an ability to cooperate well when playing games. By age 9 or 10, they should be able to both cooperate and compete, although games may still be interrupted by disagreements about the rules. By age 11 or 12, a legalistic fascination with making, changing, and negotiating rules emerges. An entire afternoon may be spent setting up teams, choosing leaders, making rules, and devising punishments for breaking rules (addressing all possible contingencies), without disappointment at never playing the actual game. Children come to understand that rules have been invented by human beings and are maintained by mutual consent. Rules may be altered if the change is fair and if all agree. Rules serve to promote social interaction, to define socially unacceptable behavior, and to strengthen the barrier against regression. Children who are generally helpful and who follow rules tend to be more popular with peers, although athletic and academic competence contribute more to popularity than they do for younger children. Bossy, aggressive, disruptive, hyperactive children (especially boys) are likely to be rejected by peers. Peer judgments tend to be long lasting, even after a child's behavior changes (for example, methylphenidate [Ritalin] treatment of a hyperactive boy improves his behavior but he is still unpopular).

Both boys and girls generally prefer single-sex groupings for play, sports, and social events. There is extreme peer pressure, especially on boys, for culturally appropriate gender role behavior and the exclusion of girls or even effeminate boys. Boys and girls both harbor rigid sexual stereotypes, even in families in which parents have equivalent roles at home and at work.

Girls have more intense friendships than boys do, with one or two peers, and may develop "crushes" on older adolescent or young adult women, who concretely represent their ego-ideal. These feelings should not be regarded as signs of homosexuality.

Compared to earlier stages, the school-age child is far more exposed to and influenced by the environment outside of the home. Childhood has its own subculture, passed from child to child by word of mouth, without adult intervention. This includes rhymes, chants, superstitions, rituals, jokes, riddles, and secret codes. Both boys and girls engage in hero worship of sports, music, television, or movie stars; coaches; or even teachers.

The ubiquitous sex and violence in the media exert a powerful influence. Viewing television violence has been demonstrated to increase aggression in children and adolescents (Pearl et al, 1982). Television, movies, and music videos probably provide a significant amount of sexual overstimulation and often present poor role models of precocious, promiscuous, or violent sexuality.

Informal groups and clubs are increasingly important, often with little purpose other than to include some children and exclude others. Organizations such as the

Boy Scouts and Girl Scouts are also popular. To be accepted by peers, children must learn to be loyal, to be able to compromise, to be good sports, and not to "tattle." Social competence and peer acceptance result from specific skills and characteristics, such as the ability to size up a social situation and adapt to it, to respond positively to approach by peers, and to take a gradual, indirect, process-oriented approach to social goals (Asher, 1983).

Unfortunately, group behavior is not always positive. Teasing is often cruel and persistent. Peer pressure may lead to dangerous or immoral behavior. Boys are especially vulnerable to dares or to suggestions of cowardice.

Even prior to adolescence, girls are acutely aware of cultural concepts of physical attractiveness. Many express unrealistic concern about obesity and try to diet, despite normal weight. In vulnerable girls, this may be accentuated at the beginning of puberty, with the normal increase in body fat, and may lead to the development of anorexia or bulimia nervosa.

Response to Physical Illness

School-age children usually tolerate acute illness and hospitalization relatively well, especially if they are prepared, parents visit daily for substantial periods, and preceding development was on course. Children this age may still have irrational explanations of illness. Oppositional or immature behavior is common. Unfortunately, nursing staff have limited tolerance for a child of this age who whines, cries, clings, or refuses to cooperate with medical procedures. Loss of recently acquired skills due to illness or injury is a major blow to the child. Chronic illness interferes increasingly with normal developmental tasks, especially those related to school and to peer relationships.

ADOLESCENCE

The major tasks of adolescence are the development of a secure personal and sexual identity, an occupational choice, and personal values. For many youth, prolonged education and the resulting economic dependence on the family extend the period of adolescent development well into their middle and late 20s.

Physical Development in Adolescence

Neurologic
Dendritic connections attain their adult level, which is a reduction from earlier proliferation. By age 14 the EEG shows mature alpha rhythms.

Endocrine
Puberty is the attainment of reproductive capacity. There is wide diversity in timing among youth of both sexes. On average, boys attain sexual maturity 2 years later than girls, typically at age 15 in girls and at age 17 in boys. Early maturation is generally an advantage for boys, but a disadvantage for girls. As a result of improved

nutrition and fewer serious childhood diseases, the average age of menarche in girls has declined from 15 to 16 years in the 1880s to 12 years. Combined with the prolongation of the adolescent stage for economic and educational reasons, the result is a long period of sexual maturity before it is culturally appropriate to marry and to start a new family.

Pubertal changes focus the adolescent's attention on his or her body. Many teenagers are extremely concerned about their physical appearance. Hormonal changes accompanying puberty, along with social and cultural factors, lead to an increased interest in sexuality and sexual experimentation. In addition, the pervasive sexuality in television, movies, music, and advertising may lead to overstimulation and pressure to engage in sexual activity before the teenager is sufficiently emotionally mature.

Cognitive Development in Adolescence

Piaget's Stages

At the level of *formal operations*, the youth is able to use abstract thought, to consider theoretical notions, and to devise hypotheses and ways of testing them. The late adolescent becomes able to understand metaphor and complex, abstract subjects such as algebra and calculus. A few children reach the stage of formal operations as early as the age of 12 years. It is attained by only 35% of 16-to-17 year olds. *Many adults never reach this stage, and have a limited ability to deal in a flexible and rational manner with such abstract concepts as religion, ethics, morality, philosophy, and politics.* Even when the stage of formal operations is attained, emotional pressure may cause temporary regression to functioning at the level of concrete operations.

Affective Development in Adolescence

Adolescent Turmoil

Adolescents in American society are beset by multiple stressors and pressures. The move from a smaller elementary school to a larger middle school or high school results in less supervision, more impersonal relationships with teachers, and a larger, more diverse peer group. Academic work is increasingly demanding, and there is a pressing need to make decisions regarding work or further education after high school.

Early psychoanalytic and Eriksonian theories propose that *adolescent turmoil* (psychological upheaval leading to significant disruption in personality organization, disequilibrium, and disturbances in mood and behavior) is not only ubiquitous but necessary for successful separation from parents and formation of adult identity. Studies conducted in the 1960s and 1970s by Offer and colleagues (Offer et al, 1981) of normal adolescents and those with a variety of emotional and physical illnesses found that serious emotional or behavioral problems are *not* normal in adolescents. Most teenagers cope reasonably effectively, without undue disruption of school or family life, with the tasks of adolescence. About 20% of youths experience tumult or diagnosable psychopathology in their teen years, most often those from less stable backgrounds and with more family conflict. About one-quarter of adolescents, most often those who experience few stressors and have parents who encourage independence, demonstrate essentially continuous growth and good interpersonal relationships. The remainder are characterized by developmental spurts alternating with periods of conflict. These youths, often "late bloomers," report more disagreements with their parents and more feelings of depression and anxiety.

It is normal, particularly in early adolescence, to experience a transient disturbance of self-esteem, increased feelings of anxiety and depression, and oversensitivity to shame and humiliation that do not reach a clinical level and are usually related to particular stressful situations. Interestingly, the 1970s cohort of adolescents surveyed by Offer and associates (1981) reported feeling less self-confident, controlled, and trusting of others than the teenagers studied in the 1960s.

Prior to adolescence, behavioral and emotional disorders are more common in boys than in girls. In adolescence, the girls catch up, and even exceed boys in the prevalence of eating disorders and depression.

Critical Developmental Challenges and Issues of Adolescence

Shapiro and Hertzig (1988) identify eight issues that must be resolved in the course of adolescent development:

1. Dependence on versus independence from the nuclear family.
2. Behavioral license versus intellectualized control.
3. Loyalty to family versus to peer group.
4. Normalizing function of sharing thoughts and feelings with peers versus need for privacy.
5. Idealization versus devaluation of peers and adults.
6. Formation of identity, role, and character.
7. Consolidation of sexual role and sexual object choice.
8. Reshuffling of defenses and consolidation of style of functioning.

Mechanisms of Defense

Adolescents may show a temporary increase in less mature mechanisms such as *projection, externalization, denial, reaction formation*, and *repression*, as well as development of the more advanced defenses of *rationalization, identification*, and *sublimation*. On balance, adolescents have an improved ability to use mature defenses, to tolerate frustration, and to delay gratification. (See Chapter 5 for more specific definitions of these defense mechanisms.)

Risk-Taking Behavior

Unfortunately, feelings of entitlement and the belief in their omnipotence and invulnerability common in adolescents may lead to dangerous experimentation and risk-taking behavior. The three leading causes of death in adolescents are accidents, homicide, and suicide. The 1990 national Youth Risk Behavior Survey found that almost one in five high school students had carried a gun, knife, or club at least once in the past month (Centers for Disease Control, 1991). Although adolescents cognitively understand the meaning of death, they do not accept that this is a real possibility for them. Some teenagers have a mental image of "surviving in fantasy," imagining how their parents and peers would react to their death, classically portrayed in Tom Sawyer's attendance at his own "funeral."

Adolescents commonly fluctuate between unrealistically positive and negative views of themselves. Compared to adults, they are more likely to attribute responsibility for their failures to others. They are generally able to take appropriate credit for success. In later adolescence, normal youth are able to give up their fantasies of omnipotence and recognize that some hardship is inevitable in life.

Adolescence is the critical period for initiation of drug abuse. First onset of drug use is rare among adults. Interference with normal developmental tasks puts young adolescent drug users at greatest risk for serious substance abuse and its medical, cognitive, and emotional sequelae. Youth who are rebellious, place a low value on achievement, are alienated from their parents, are influenced by peers with behavior problems, and live in a chaotic environment without clear discipline are at especially high risk. Experimentation with substances proceeds in a predictable sequence, beginning with tobacco and alcohol and progressing to marijuana. A smaller number of youth move on to abuse sedatives, stimulants, and psychedelics, with even fewer subsequently using cocaine or narcotics.

Tobacco use remains a major public health problem among adolescents, especially girls. In 1987, 16% of 8th graders and 26% of 10th graders surveyed reported smoking at least once in the past month (Centers for Disease Control, 1989). One-third of adolescents have used alcohol before 7th grade. In 1989, 26% of 8th graders and 38% of 10th graders surveyed reported having had five or more drinks on one occasion during the past 2 weeks (Centers for Disease Control, 1989). Five percent of teens drink alcohol daily. One-third of all adolescents surveyed report that most or all of their friends get drunk at least once a week (Johnston et al, 1986).

In 1987, 15% of 8th graders and 35% of 10th graders reported having used marijuana at least once (Centers for Disease Control, 1989).

Although overall rates of adolescent abuse of tranquilizers, amphetamines, hallucinogens, cocaine, and heroin have stabilized or declined, there is still cause for serious concern.

Sexuality

Masturbation is normal, and (especially in early adolescence) serves a generalized function of reducing anxiety and discharging tension. Teens often experiment with a variety of masturbation fantasies, and transient homosexual fantasies and activities are relatively common.

As noted in the preceding chapter, sexual activity in adolescence is becoming the norm rather than the exception. The 1990 school-based Youth Risk Behavior Survey found that 61% of males and 48% of females in grades 9 through 12 reported ever having had sexual intercourse. Of sexually active students, only 49% of males and 40% of females reported having used a condom during the most recent sexual intercourse (Centers for Disease Control, 1992). Risk factors for early sexual activity include lack of parental support and structure, less religious affiliation, early and frequent dating, and lack of educational ambition (McAnarney and Hendee, 1989). Adolescents who engage in unprotected and/or indiscriminate sexual activity run the risk not only of pregnancy but of AIDS and other sexually transmitted diseases. The United States has the highest rate of teenage pregnancy of any industrialized nation. In the 1980s, nearly one-quarter of all adolescent girls became pregnant by the time they were 18 years old, with about half of the pregnancies resulting in a live birth (Brooks-Gunn and Chase-Lansdale, 1991). The high physical, psychological, and socioeconomic morbidity for both mother and child create a major public health problem.

Although demonstration projects have been successful in decreasing the rate of teenage pregnancy in local areas (see Vincent et al, 1987), these proven strategies have not been widely implemented. The relationship with the pediatrician is often ruptured in adolescence, stemming from resistance from both physicians and teens. There is an urgent need for pediatricians and family physicians to become more comfortable with and skilled in providing anticipatory guidance, ongoing counseling, and medical care related to sexuality, birth control, and sexually transmitted diseases.

Adolescence is a particularly painful time for teenagers who are becoming aware that they have a gay or lesbian sexual identity. Adolescent peers are even more homophobic than adults, and are more likely to reject, tease, or even become physically aggressive toward schoolmates who are perceived or identified as homosexual. Parents are typically unsupportive and may even reject their child completely, extending the rejection to expulsion from home. Gay and lesbian adolescents are at increased risk for suicidal thoughts and attempts.

Family Relationships

The adolescent should experience gradual independence and autonomy from the nuclear family. There is a normal increase in parent-child arguing around the time of puberty. Young adolescents are increasingly critical of their parents, oppositional, and deliberately provocative. This may represent evolutionarily determined preparation for leaving home. In American culture, however, young adolescents are not emotionally or financially prepared to leave home, although they may be biologically ready.

Social Development of Adolescents

The psychiatrist Harry Stack Sullivan described early adolescent *chumship*, an intense friendship with a youth of the same sex. Adolescents are acutely interested in their peers. The need for absolute peer conformity is more important to early adolescents than it is later. There is a new interest in establishing heterosexual relationships.

Renewed egocentrism leads to the belief that others are similarly obsessed with the teenager's own behavior and appearance, leading to a feeling of being under constant scrutiny. Painful self-consciousness peaks in early adolescence.

Response to Physical Illness

Adolescents are increasingly able to take pride in being responsible for their own body and medical care. When ill or injured, their fears are more realistic than those of younger children. Loss of autonomy and privacy is especially painful for teenagers.

For chronically ill or handicapped adolescents, concern with physical appearance often leads to a view of their bodies, and therefore themselves, as defective. Low self-esteem may decrease adolescents' belief in their own ability to control their fate, resulting in hopelessness, impaired ability to resist peer pressure, and noncompliance with medical regimens.

Both individual adolescents and the peer group are intolerant of differences in appearance or behavior. Adolescents with a handicap or chronic illness may be embarrassed about their disease. Compliance with medical treatment may be avoided, because it exposes the teen as different. Peers may even encourage violating restrictions on diet or activities.

Chronically ill adolescents may use a variety of defense mechanisms, including denial, intellectualization, projection, displacement, regression, development of rituals, and identification with the aggressor (the physician). It is important to note, however, that psychopathology is not inevitable in chronically ill adolescents.

Possible contributing factors to medical noncompliance include the following: denial or lack of acceptance of the disorder, frustration with the outcome or nature of treatment, lack of knowledge or skills, miscommunication or lack of relationship with medical caregivers, rebellion against parents, inability to resist peer pressure, and psychopathology in the adolescent.

THE ROLE OF THE FAMILY IN DEVELOPMENT

Cultural Influences

While family systems theory and therapy are dealt with in detail in Chapter 9 by Dr. Fiore and colleagues and also discussed in the context of overall adult development by Drs. Wolman and Thompson in Chapter 10, the role of the family is briefly introduced here within a child and adolescent developmental context. Societal expectations of families and their members vary widely in different cultures. Even in our own country, regional and ethnic differences can be identified. The changing role of women, the increasing prevalence of divorce, and the growing number of two-career families have significantly changed roles and functions in many American families. However, certain tasks and functions must be carried out in some way by every healthy family or family group.

Family Tasks

Fleck (1966) has identified seven essential tasks for families with children:

1. To form and maintain a *marital coalition* between the adults that meets their emotional needs.
2. To form and maintain a *parental coalition* between the adults who function as parents to assure support and consistency when dealing with the children. In joint custody arrangements following divorce, maintenance of the parental coalition, despite dissolution

of the marital coalition, is essential for successful adaptation of the children.

3. To *nurture* the children, physically and emotionally.
4. To create and maintain appropriate *boundaries* between generations and individuals within the family and between the family and the community. Families may have difficulties if the boundaries are too strong and rigid or too weak and permeable.
5. To *enculturate* the younger generation, instilling the values of the family and the culture.
6. To promote *independence* and then emancipation of the children.
7. To deal with *crises*.

Insufficient material or psychological resources, parental psychopathology, and/ or severe stressors can interfere with a family's accomplishment of these tasks, resulting in developmental difficulties or even psychopathology in the child.

Parenting Styles

Research in child development has identified patterns of parenting that correlate with, although by no means inevitably lead to, certain outcomes in children (see Table 8–5).

Discipline characteristics that have been associated with aggressive and delinquent children include inconsistency, parental response based on the parent's own mood rather than the child's behavior, expression of dislike for the child, and lack of positive direction (Patterson, 1982).

Table 8–5 **Parenting Styles**

STYLE	CHARACTERISTICS	POSSIBLE OUTCOMES
Authoritarian	Firm rules and edicts No bargaining or discussion with children	Weak conscience Low self-esteem Social withdrawal Unhappiness
Indulgent–permissive	Few controls or restrictions Accept children's demands Unpredictable parental harshness	Low self-reliance Poor impulse control Aggression
Authoritative–reciprocal	Firm rules Shared decision making Discuss children's demands	Social responsibility Self-reliance Self-esteem Low aggression
Indifferent–neglectful	Uninvolved	Aggression Low self-esteem Low self-control Poor parent-child relationship

(Data from Rutter M, Cox A: Other family influences. In Rutter M, Hersov L (eds): Child and Adolescent Psychiatry: Modern Approaches, 2nd ed. Oxford, Blackwell Scientific Publications, 1985)

Stages of Family Development

The First Baby
Parents of an infant must integrate a new, very demanding and totally dependent person into their lives, which requires major readjustments in their previous relationship. Parenting of infants is accompanied by fatigue and anxiety. Fathers at times may jealously resent the attention given to the baby.

The Toddler
The child at this stage requires close supervision while he or she makes increasing demands for autonomy. Parents must be able to let the child go without pushing him or her away. Parents with a strong need to control may have great difficulty with the 2 year old.

The Child Aged 3 to 6 Years
As children pass through the Oedipal stage, they may be quite overtly seductive to the parent of the opposite sex. Parents may be flattered and respond in an overstimulating way, particularly if the relationship with the spouse is not emotionally or physically gratifying. The child's wish for an exclusive relationship with the opposite-sex parent may lead to jealousy and marital discord, if not understood and handled sensitively by the parents. Alternatively, parents may become guilty about their own fantasies elicited by the child's attentions, and become overly punitive or withdraw from the child. Parents who were sexually abused as children may be especially sensitive to these difficulties. The child may find a divorce particularly difficult at this time.

The School-Age Child
With the beginning of mandatory education, the child is no longer the exclusive possession of the parents. School and peers become increasingly important. Parents may view a teacher's complaints about their child as a criticism of their parenting ability. On the more positive side, parents now have more time and energy for their own interests. Previously isolated parents may benefit from participation in their child's school, church, or recreational activities.

The Adolescent
The family of an adolescent needs to provide more privacy and to tolerate the teenager's increasing autonomy. Parents should permit and encourage the degree of separation and independence that is appropriate for the youth's age and emotional development, and be able to understand and tolerate frequent shifts between apparent maturity and behavior typical of a much younger child. In many ways, it is reminiscent of parenting a toddler, but with a child who has much wider freedom of movement and is heavily influenced by peers. Parents must be flexible, and tread carefully between the dangers of holding too tightly and precipitously letting go.

Parents who find their loss of power and the adolescent's challenges to their authority intolerable may have difficulties with this stage of emancipation. Other parents may compete with their teenager in an effort to avoid recognition of their own aging. The most successful parents minimize power struggles and emphasize important rules and values, while being tolerant of many details of behavior, particularly in respect to clothing and hair styles. A style of collaborative negotiation and problem solving, begun prior to puberty, facilitates discipline and decision making.

Response to Physical Illness

Physical handicap or chronic or life-threatening illness places significant stress on both parents and siblings. Factors that may hamper a family's ability to function and to comply with medical regimens include an inability to encourage and to foster independence as the child matures; unresolved parental guilt, denial, anger, or fear; poor family communication skills; lack of an adequate family and social support system; insufficient financial resources; other stressors on family members; and problems originating in other family relationships (e.g., marital discord) being acted out in conflict over the child.

Working Parents

As changing societal expectations for women and economic necessity lead to ever-increasing numbers of working mothers, the issue of day care becomes more crucial. Mothers of young infants are the fastest growing segment of the labor market. In 1986, 7.8 million preschool children in the United States had mothers working outside the home (US Bureau of the Census, 1987). By 1989, half of all infants in the United States had employed mothers. An estimated 75% of all American mothers with children at home are in the work force (Zigler and Hall, 1988).

The effects of day care are difficult to study because of the inability to form appropriate control groups by randomly assigning children to care by their mother or various forms of day care. Mothers who choose (or are able) to stay home are different in many ways from those who are employed outside of the home. Many families with two working parents compensate for the mother's absence by increased involvement of the father in childrearing and by increased intensity of interaction with the child during the time the mother is in the home. Employed mothers place greater emphasis on independence training than do full-time homemakers. Families may experience more difficulties when the mother works more than 40 hours per week.

For young children, outcome is related to the amount of time spent in day care and the quality of the day care setting, especially the staff-to-child ratio and stability of caretakers. Other important factors are the mother's feelings about working and about her job, maternal stress, family financial status, parental absence, stability in the home, the quality of the child's attachment, and the child's temperament (Zigler and Hall, 1988). Children are *not* more likely to become primarily attached to the day care provider instead of the parent. There is no evidence of general maladjustment as a result of day care. Individual children vary in their response to day care. Some studies have found children who have been in group day care to be more social, assertive, and aggressive (especially boys). A few children may become more anxious when placed in a group day care setting. There are suggestions that children in out-of-home care prior to the age of 1 year are slightly more likely to show behavior in the laboratory (on the Ainsworth Strange Situation Test) characteristic of insecure attachment to their mothers, and to be more active, oppositional, and noncompliant at age 2. It is important to note that the findings from the Strange Situation Test may indicate greater independence or greater familiarity with unknown caretakers, rather than insecure attachment. Daughters may be more likely than sons to benefit from the greater independence and less stereotyped sex roles fostered by employed mothers.

School-age children who are on their own after school and during the summer when their parents work ("latchkey children") may be at risk for higher levels of fear and anxiety, as well as for poorer social skills, juvenile delinquency, and accidents (Zigler and Hall, 1988). The negative effects appear primarily when the child associates with peers during these times, and may be more related to variables leading to their self-care status (e.g., poverty, single working parent without a support network) than to the lack of adult supervision *per se*. Children who are immature or impulsive may have more difficulty.

Nontraditional Families

The "typical" nuclear family, including a husband and wife and their biological children, continues to decline in frequency. In 1988, only 60% of children were living with both biological parents. The number who will continue to do so throughout childhood and adolescence is even smaller. As noted above, the full-time mother is vanishing. Divorced parents and step-families are discussed in the next section of this chapter. Increasing numbers of children are born to single mothers.

Increasing attention has been paid to the children of gay and lesbian parents (Patterson, 1992). Most of these children were born in the context of a heterosexual relationship between the biological parents. Typically, divorce is associated with one or both parents' acknowledgment of a homosexual orientation, although some of these couples decide not to divorce even after a parent has come out. The gay or lesbian parent (alone or with a same-sex partner) may be custodial or not, or custody may be shared. More recently, children have been reared entirely by a gay or lesbian single parent or couple, following adoption or artificial insemination. Although courts and social agencies have been hostile to gay men and lesbians who seek parental rights, currently available research has not found any indications that homosexuality *per se* impairs parenting ability. There is no existing evidence that having a homosexual or even a transsexual parent leads to homosexuality, disturbance of gender identity or gender-role behavior, or psychopathology in the child. Interestingly, children being raised by lesbians are more likely to have contact with their fathers and with other adult males than are the children of divorced heterosexual women. Early adolescents have more difficulty learning for the first time of a parent's homosexual orientation than do younger children or older adolescents.

CHILDREN AT RISK

Attempts to understand and prevent pathology in children and adolescents have led to an interest in children who may be vulnerable. The risk or liability of a particular outcome is determined by a complex interaction of *diathesis* (negative genetic factors), environmental stressors, and assets or protective factors.

Divorce

The number of children affected by divorce continues to climb (see Chapter 9). The effects of a divorce differ between boys and girls, and at different developmental stages. The likelihood of a negative outcome is increased by the degree of family conflict preceding and following the divorce, as well as by associated stressors such as economic hardship, loss of extended family, need to move from familiar home, neighborhood and school, or decreased emotional support from an angry or grieving parent. Children commonly blame themselves for the divorce and internalize the experience as their failure to keep the parents together. Most children wish for their parents to be reunited, and many believe they have the responsibility and/or power to bring about a reconciliation. Adolescents are more likely to have difficulty following a divorce if they feel caught between hostile parents (Buchanan et al, 1991).

Most children of divorced parents spend a period of time in a single-parent home, but the frequency of remarriage is high. Marriage of a single parent with children creates what is known as a *reconstituted family*. An estimated one in every six American children under the age of 18 lives with a step-parent. The parents must simultaneously form new marital and parental coalitions while dealing with the behavior and emotional adjustment of children of various ages, who have their own feelings about the divorce and remarriage. Teenagers may be particularly resistant to developing a positive relationship with the step-parent. Children may fear being disloyal to the other parent if they accept a step-parent.

Children of Alcoholic Parents

Children whose parents drink excessively are at increased risk of abuse and neglect. Children of mothers who are "problem drinkers" are at twice the risk of serious physical injury as children of mothers who are nondrinkers. The risk is further increased if the father is also a moderate or heavy drinker (Bijur et al, 1992). A significant minority of children of alcoholic parents have behavioral problems, especially conduct problems, restlessness, inattention, poor academic performance, dropping out of school, and alcohol abuse, as well as emotional symptoms such as anxiety and depression. Probable mediating factors include marital conflict, divorce, disrupted family routine, inadequate parental nurturance and supervision, economic hardship, and modeling of maladaptive coping styles (West and Prinz, 1987). Genetic contributions (especially for conduct disorder in males), as well as the teratologic effects of a mother who drinks during pregnancy (see the section in this chapter on prenatal development) may add to the risk. Impairment is by no means inescapable, however, and many of these children and adolescents appear to cope reasonably well. Special self-help groups have evolved for adolescent children of alcoholics (Alateen) as well as for adults (ACOA).

Children of Mentally Ill Parents

Both genetic factors and the effect of mental illness on parenting skills and family environment increase risk. When abuse and neglect are present in a family with a mentally ill parent, the risk of child behavior problems increases. Children whose parents have a mood disorder have an increased (but not inevitable) incidence of depression and suicidality as well as nonspecific behavioral and emotional disturbance (LaRoche, 1989). Maternal depression results in impaired mothering skills and marital discord, both related to psychopathology in the children (Gelfand and Teti, 1990). Anxiety disorders are commonly shared by parents and children, probably due to a combination of genetic risk and learned behavior. Children of parents with major depression and/or panic disorder and agoraphobia have an increased frequency of "behavioral inhibition to the unfamiliar" (Rosenbaum et al, 1988), a marker for increased risk of subsequent anxiety disorder (Hirshfeld et al, 1992). Children of schizophrenic parents are more likely to demonstrate abnormalities in attention and information processing and poor social competence, even before emergence of any overt symptoms (Dworkin et al, 1991; Masten and Garmezy, 1985). They are at risk for a variety of psychopathology in addition to schizophrenia and related disorders.

Resilient Children and Adolescents

Graduated stressors or challenges that can be mastered may promote the development of flexible, diverse, and successful coping strategies and positive outcome. Children from high-risk groups who do not appear to suffer negative consequences have been called *resilient* or "invulnerable." There is great interest in elucidating how some children not only resist and cope with unusual stress but thrive and succeed despite adversity. Identified *protective factors* include a cohesive and emotionally supportive family environment as well as external support systems, such as caring extended family members or other adults, and/or institutional supports. Characteristics of resilient children include intelligence, hardiness, autonomy, positive social orientation, and self-esteem (Masten and Garmezy, 1985). Strong genetic endowment also probably plays a role in the ability of such children to survive and adapt to developmental stress and trauma.

Prevention and Early Intervention

Intervention programs for young children and their parents aim to counteract the effects of prenatal and neonatal insults, compounded by poverty and deprivation, which lead to impaired performance in school and, eventually in adult life. The most prominent example is Project Head Start, an ambitious preschool program for disadvantaged children aged 3 to 6, established with federal funding in 1965. While the Head Start program itself has been difficult to evaluate due to political controversy, wide disparity among local programs, and lack of appropriate control groups, long-term follow-up of children enrolled in preschool prevention and intervention projects finds that children show gains in IQ and other cognitive measures during the first year of the program, with cognitively structured curricula producing greater change than play-oriented programs. Some programs also produce improvement in adjustment to school and in social skills. Unless intervention, including parent involvement, continues after the child's entry into regular school, IQ declines to the lower 90s and below, especially in the most deprived children. Programs that focus simultaneously on parent and child, especially those beginning with 1 and 2 year olds, yield substantial gains in IQ for both the target child and younger siblings, which are maintained at least through the 1st grade. For the most severely intellectually and economically disadvantaged families, intensive and personalized family support programs that include day care, health care, nutrition, housing, advocacy for the family, and vocational training for parents are required if children are to show or to maintain improvement (Bronfenbrenner, 1974; Ryan, 1974). At long-term follow-up, success may be measured in maternal variables (employment, education, smaller family size) and such child measures as school attendance and reduced need for special education (Seitz et al, 1985).

SUMMARY

This chapter has been, of necessity, a dense, compressed, and abbreviated summary of the wealth of current theory and knowledge regarding human development from conception through adolescence. An understanding of the major concepts and principles of development stands the physician in good stead, no matter what the ultimate specialty choice. In all spheres, normal development proceeds in certain predictable sequences, although the rate varies considerably among healthy individuals. There is a constant reciprocal interaction between children and adolescents and their environment, with each shaping the other. Developmental outcome is not simple to predict, but is the result of multiple factors within the child, the family, the school, and the larger culture. Developmental considerations beyond adolescence and into early adulthood are discussed in Chapter 10.

ANNOTATED BIBLIOGRAPHY

Dulcan MK, Popper CW: Concise Guide to Child and Adolescent Psychiatry. Washington, DC, American Psychiatric Press, 1991

> A compact handbook on the evaluation and treatment of psychopathology in children and adolescents, targeted for students and residents beginning clinical work with children.

Ginsburg H, Opper S: Piaget's Theory of Intellectual Development: An Introduction. Englewood Cliffs, NJ, Prentice-Hall, 1969

> A brief, comprehensible summary of Piaget's work.

Konner M: Childhood. Boston, Little, Brown & Co, 1991.

> An easily readable narrative about child and family development in many different cultures, written by an anthropologist with medical training.

Levine MD, Carey WB, Crocker AC (eds): Developmental-Behavioral Pediatrics, 2nd ed. Philadelphia, WB Saunders, 1992

> A comprehensive text directed toward pediatricians. An excellent reference for medical and developmental problems in children.

Lewis M, Volkmar F: Clinical Aspects of Child and Adolescent Development, 3rd ed. Philadelphia, Lea & Febiger, 1990

> The best comprehensive summary of normal development. Written especially for medical students.

Minde K, Minde R: Infant Psychiatry: An Introductory Textbook. Beverly Hills, CA, Sage Publications, 1986

A handy paperback that covers the history of infancy, normal development, developmental and psychiatric assessment, and the management of common developmental problems and more serious psychiatric disorders in young children (birth to 3 years).

Wolman B (ed): Handbook of Developmental Psychology. Englewood Cliffs, NJ, Prentice-Hall, 1982

A detailed compendium of current research in developmental psychology. Chapters integrate and present implications of research findings.

REFERENCES

Asher SR: Social competence and peer status: Recent advances and future directions. Child Dev 54:1427–1434, 1983

Allen DA, Rapin I, Wiznitzer M: Communication disorders of preschool children: The physician's responsibility. Dev Behav Pediatr 9:164–170, 1988

Bijur PE, Kurzon M, Overpeck MD, et al: Parental alcohol use, problem drinking, and children's injuries. JAMA 267:3166–3171, 1992.

Bowlby J: Attachment. In Attachment and Loss, vol 2. New York, Basic Books, 1969

Bowlby J: Developmental psychiatry comes of age. Am J Psychiatry 145:1–10, 1988

Bowlby J: Separation: Anxiety and anger. In Attachment and Loss, vol 2. New York, Basic Books, 1975

Bregman JD, Hodapp RM: Current developments in the understanding of mental retardation, part I: Biological and phenomenological perspectives. J Am Acad Child Adolesc Psychiatry 30:707–719, 1991

Bronfenbrenner U: A Report on Longitudinal Evaluations of Preschool Programs, vol II: Is Early Intervention Effective? Washington, DC, Office of Human Development, USDHEW, 1974

Brooks-Gunn J, Chase-Lansdale PL: Children having children: Effects on the family system. Pediatr Ann 20:467–481, 1991

Buchanan CM, Maccoby EE, Dornsbusch SM: Caught between parents: Adolescents' experience in divorced homes. Child Dev 62:1008–1029, 1991

Centers for Disease Control: Results from the National Adolescent Student Health Survey. JAMA 261:2025, 2031, 1989

Centers for Disease Control: Weapon-carrying among high school students. JAMA 266:2342, 1991

Centers for Disease Control: Sexual behavior among high school students. JAMA 267:628, 1992

Coplan J, Gleason JR: Quantifying language development from birth to 3 years using the Early Language Milestone Scale. Pediatrics 86:963–971, 1990

Crowell J, Keener M, Ginsburg N, et al: Sleep habits in toddlers 18 to 36 months old. J Am Acad Child Adolesc Psychiatry 26:510–515, 1987

Dworkin RH, Bernstein G, Kaplansky LM, et al: Social competence and positive and negative symptoms: A longitudinal study of children and adolescents at risk for schizophrenia and affective disorder. Am J Psychiatry 148:1182–1188, 1991

Fagot BI: Beyond the reinforcement principle: Another step toward understanding sex role development. Dev Psychology 21:1097–1104, 1985

Fleck S: An approach to family pathology. Compr Psychiatry 7:307–320, 1966

Gelfand DM, Teti DM: The effects of maternal depression on children. Clin Psych Rev 10:329–353, 1990

Gesell A, Halverson HM, Thompson H: The First Five Years of Life: A Guide to the Study of the Preschool Child. New York, Harper & Row, 1940

Goldberg S: Parent-infant bonding: Another look. Child Dev 54:1355–1382, 1983

Green M, Solnit AJ: Reactions to the threatened loss of a child: A vulnerable child syndrome. Pediatrics 34:58–66, 1964

Hirshfeld DR, Rosenbaum JF, Biederman J, et al: Stable behavioral inhibition and its association with anxiety disorder. J Am Acad Child Adolesc Psychiatry 31:103–111, 1992

Hodapp RM, Mueller E: Early social development, In Wolman B (ed): Handbook of Developmental Psychology. Englewood Cliffs, NJ, Prentice-Hall, 1982

Johnson CM: Infant and toddler sleep: A telephone survey of parents in one community. Dev Behav Pediatr 12:108–114, 1991

Johnston LD, O'Malley PM, Bachman JG: Drug Use Among American High School Students, College Students and Other Young Adults. Washington, DC, US DHHS, 1986

LaRoche C: Children of parents with major affective disorders: A review of the past 5 years. Psychiatric Clin N Am 12:919–933, 1989

Masten AS, Garmezy N: Risk, vulnerability, and protective factors in developmental psychopathology. In Lahey BB, Kazdin AE (eds): Advances in Clinical Child Psychology, vol 8. New York, Plenum Press, 1985

McAnarney ER, Hendee WR: Adolescent pregnancy and its consequences. JAMA 262:74–82, 1989

Money J: Sin, sickness, or status: Homosexual gender identity and psychoneuroendocrinology. Am Psychol 42:384–399, 1987

Naeye RL: Cognitive and behavioral abnormalities in children whose mothers smoked cigarettes during pregnancy. J Dev Behav Pediatr 13:425–428, 1992

Offer D, Ostrov E, Howard KI: The Adolescent: A Psychological Self-Portrait. New York, Basic Books, 1981

Patterson CJ: Children of lesbian and gay parents. Child Dev 63:1025–1042, 1992

Patterson GR: Coercive Family Process. Eugene, OR, Castalia, 1982

Pearl D, Bouthilet L, Lazar J (eds): Television and Behavior: Ten Years of Scientific Progress and Implications for the Eighties. Washington, DC, US Government Printing Office, 1982

Piaget J, Inhelder B: The Psychology of the Child. New York, Basic Books, 1969

Rosenbaum JF, Biederman J, Gersten M, et al: Behavioral inhibition in children of parents with panic disorder and agoraphobia. Arch Gen Psychiatry, 45:463–470, 1988

Ryan S: A Report on Longitudinal Evaluations of Preschool Programs, vol I: Longitudinal Evaluations. Washington, DC, Office of Human Development, USDHEW, 1974

Seitz V, Rosenbaum LK, Apfel NH: Effects of family support intervention: A ten-year follow-up. Child Dev 56:376–391, 1985

Shapiro T, Hertzig M: Normal child and adolescent development. In Talbott JA, Hales RE, Yudofsky SC (eds): American Psychiatric Press Textbook of Psychiatry. Washington, DC, American Psychiatric Press, 1988

Shapiro T, Perry R: Latency revisited: The age 7 plus or minus 1. Psychoanal Study Child 31:79–105, 1976

Shepherd-Look DL: Sex differentiation and the development of sex roles. In Wolman B (ed): Handbook of Developmental Psychology. Englewood Cliffs, NJ, Prentice-Hall, 1982

Siegel LS: Infant tests as predictors of cognitive and language development at two years. Child Dev 53:545–557, 1981

Singer DG, Benton W: Caution: Television may by hazardous to a child's mental health. Dev Behav Pediatr 10:259–261, 1989

Spitz RA: Hospitalism: An inquiry into the genesis of psychiatric conditions in early childhood. Psychoanal Study Child 1:53–74, 1945

Spitz RA: Anaclitic depression. Psychoanal Study Child 2:313–342, 1946

Steinhausen H-C, Spohr H-L: Fetal alcohol syndrome. In Lahey BB, Kazdin AE (eds): Advances in Clinical Child Psychology, vol 9. New York, Plenum Press, 1986

Thomas A, Chess S: Temperament in Clinical Practice. New York, Guilford Press, 1986

US Bureau of the Census, Statistical Abstract of the United States: 1987. Washington, DC, US Government Printing Office, 1987

Vincent ML, Clearie AF, Schluchter MD: Reducing adolescent pregnancy through school and community-based education. JAMA 257:3382–3386, 1987

West MO, Prinz RJ: Parental alcoholism and childhood psychopathology. Psychol Bull 102:204–218, 1987

White R, Elsom B, Prawat R: Children's conceptions of death. Child Dev 49:307–310, 1978

Zigler E, Hall NW: Day care and its effect on children: An overview for pediatric health professionals. Dev Behav Pediatr 9:38–46, 1988

Zimmerman IL, Bernstein M: Parental work patterns in alternative families: Influence on child development. Am J Orthopsychiatry 53:418–425, 1983

9

The Family in Human Development and Medical Practice

Joan Fiore, Alan Stoudemire, and Nancy Kriseman

Of what relevance is the family for medical illness and medical health? Why devote an entire chapter to looking at the relationship between a person's family and his or her health status? A basic assumption of this text is that human problems, whether they be psychiatric or physical, are biopsychosocial systems problems, as discussed by Drs. Cohen-Cole and Levinson in Chapter 2. There are no psychosocial problems without biological elements, and no biological problems without psychosocial ramifications. Every patient's problems include the interaction of psychological, interpersonal, biological, and societal factors. The question for the physician is how to intervene in the most efficient and humane way. When considering the interpersonal aspect of this biopsychosocial system, the most influential and relevant one is often that of the family.

THE BIOPSYCHOSOCIAL MODEL

George Engel (1977), an internist with psychoanalytic training, is credited with popularizing the term "biopsychosocial" (see also Chapter 14 by Dr. Green). This model conceptualizes a hierarchical interdependent relationship between the biological, psychological, individual, family, and community systems. The dynamic interaction between these different levels of integration reflects the belief from a systems perspective that a change in any one level results in corresponding changes in other levels. In this context, this chapter focuses on how the family system interacts with other factors in affecting the course and outcome of medical illness.

THE FAMILY AS SOURCE
OF HEALTH BELIEFS

There are a number of ways in which the family may influence the course and outcome of medical conditions. *The first is that the family is unquestionably the primary source of many health beliefs and behaviors.* Any discussion about health-related behaviors requires discussion about the family, since it is in the family that health habits are learned (Doherty and Baird, 1983; McDaniel et al, 1990). As the Surgeon General's Report on Health Promotion and Disease Prevention attests, "Of the ten leading causes of death in the United States, at least seven could be substantially reduced if persons at risk improved just five habits: diet, smoking, lack of exercise, alcohol abuse, and use of antihypertensive medication" (US Department of Health, Education and Welfare, 1979, p 14). If the medical problem requiring treatment involves any of these factors, evaluating and involving the family in the treatment plan will almost always be more effective than treating the patient individually.

Moreover, understanding how the family is constructed and functions enables the physician to identify family members who have critical leverage in facilitating the patient complying with medical advice. For example, the grandmother may be the person who is in charge of deciding whether someone in the family is "allowed" to be "ill," whether they should see a physician, and whether the physician's advice is followed. In other words, *a second way in which families are an important element in medical care is that the family can be either a valuable resource and source of support or an obstruction to treatment.* Physicians can only *recommend* treatment. The recommended treatment may not be carried out if key family members do not support it. While communicating with influential or "powerful" parental family members is obviously important in the case of children, it is also essential in the case of adults. If a man has cardiac disease and his wife continues to cook french fries and fried eggs for him, the chances that his heart disease will improve are decreased in comparison to a spouse who encourages him to eat raw vegetables and to participate in an exercise routine.

Stress may also be an important factor in a person's health, and families can be a source of stress as well as a buffer to stress (see Chapter 3). As families progress through their natural cycles, at each point of transition, the family and its individual members may become increasingly stressed. (A more detailed exploration of the family life cycle is discussed later in this chapter.) As discussed in Chapters 2 and 3, Holmes and Rahe (1967) developed a life event scale and explored the relationship between stressful life events and illness. Since that time, many studies have investigated this relationship. For example, Meyer and Haggerty (1962) reported that chronic stress was related to higher rates of streptococcal pharyngitis and that 30% of strep infections in their populations were preceded by a stressful family event. Beautreis, Fergusson, and Shannon (1982) performed a prospective study looking at the correlation between life events and childhood morbidity. In this study of over 1,000 preschoolers, they found that family life events were strongly correlated with subsequent visits to the physician and hospital admissions for a wide range of conditions. They showed that if children came from families wherein more than 12 life events had occurred during the 4-year study period, they were six times more likely to be hospitalized than children who had undergone fewer life events during this 4-year period.

Many studies have investigated the relationship between family stress and illness. Certainly, the death of a spouse is a stressful life event. Kraus and Lillienfield (1959) found that young widowers had ten times the normal death rate for many illnesses. Other researchers have found, by studying animals and humans, that stress may lead to immunosuppression and an increase in illness (Ader, 1981; Calabrese et al, 1987). (See Chapter 3 by Drs. Walker and Katon and Chapter 11 by Dr. van der Kolk.)

SOCIAL SUPPORT AND ILLNESS

Research on stress and illness has led to a large body of research in another area—social support and illness. Two studies found that older individuals with poorer social supports had two to three times the death rate of those with good social support (Blazer, 1982; Zuckerman et al, 1984). Women with low family and social supports and who are also highly stressed have higher rates of obstetrical complications. There have, however, been a number of other studies that have not found a connection between social support and health behavior. A study by Fiore et al (1985) found that what was most important in health outcome was not so much the *positive* support provided by family members as what they called the *negative* support provided by family members (i.e., the degree to which family members were critical or did not provide support when it was needed). Negative support was related to a higher incidence of medical and psychiatric problems in family caregivers to Alzheimer's patients. In a randomized, controlled study, Moresky et al (1983) highlighted a significant effect of family involvement on hypertension compliance and overall mortality. These researchers studied the impact of three different educational interventions—brief individual counseling, instructing the spouse or significant other during a home visit, and small patient group sessions—on the outcome variables of keeping appointments, weight control, and medication compliance. The best outcomes were observed (overall compliance, reduction in blood pressure, and overall mortality) when the spouse was involved in family education.

IMPACT OF THE FAMILY
ON CHRONIC ILLNESS

There have been increasing numbers of studies on the influence of the family on chronic illness, including research on asthma, renal failure, heart disease, and cancer. Research into the relationship between the family and the course of diabetes has shown a significant correlation between family functioning and disease outcome. Several studies have demonstrated that overall family dysfunction is strongly correlated with poor diabetic control (Grey et al, 1980; Koski and Kumento, 1977; Orr et al, 1983). Clear family organization has been associated with good metabolic control (Shouval et al, 1982). In contrast, research by White et al (1984) showed many dysfunctional psychosocial factors such as absent fathers, poor living conditions, chronic family conflict, inadequate parental functioning, and lack of family involvement increased the likelihood of poorly controlled diabetes. Low family cohesion and high conflict correlate with poor diabetic control (Anderson et al, 1981). Parental indifference results in poor diabetic control and depression in the diabetic child (Khurana and White, 1970). In essence, then, an emotionally distant or disengaged family in which there is inadequate supervision and parental support may result in noncompliance with insulin and diet and, hence, in poor diabetic control.

THE ILLNESS AS ESSENTIAL
TO FAMILY FUNCTIONING

Paradoxically, *somatic symptoms may actually serve an adaptive function within the family and may be maintained by family patterns*. An illness may not have started from psychological factors, but the illness may eventually become an integral part of how the family operates. Failure to address family issues perpetuate the physiological problem. These patterns were addressed by Minuchin and his colleagues at the Philadelphia Child Guidance Clinic (1978) who studied poorly controlled diabetic children from families with high cohesion that they called "enmeshed." What these investigators found was that children from enmeshed families were having recurrent episodes of diabetic ketoacidosis despite their adherence to diet and insulin. When hospitalized, and thus removed from their families, these diabetic children were easily managed. It would seem that stress and emotional arousal within the family was directly affecting the child's blood sugar. Physiological responses of diabetic children to a stressful family interview were also studied (Baker et al, 1975). During the interview, the children had a rapid rise in free fatty acids that persisted beyond the interview. The parents of these children exhibited an initial rise in free fatty acid levels, which then fell to normal when the diabetic child entered the room. This research group hypothesized that in psychosomatic families, parental conflict is detoured or diffused through the chronically ill child, and the resulting stress leads to exacerbation of the illness. Minuchin and his colleagues discovered a specific pattern of interaction characterized by *enmeshment, overprotectiveness, rigidity*, and *conflict avoidance* in families with a psychosomatic member when they examined children with severe asthma and anorexia nervosa. At this point, an introduction to the case of "Johnny" may be helpful.

A CASE STUDY

Johnny is a 19-year-old diabetic. He was diagnosed with juvenile diabetes at age 12, and he has maintained himself on insulin and diet in a very stable way for the last 7 years. He presents at the doctor's office because in the last couple of months, he reports having had an episode approximately once a week in which he passes out and needs significant amounts of sugar to bring him out of it. This is highly unusual for him. He reports that he has continued to watch his exercise and diet, has taken his insulin regularly, and does not understand why he is having these dangerous episodes. After a thorough investigation of the biomedi-

cal parameters of his illness, the physician came up empty-handed, unable to identify any significant medical changes, and it was evident on testing that nothing was particularly different. Therefore, he began to investigate what was happening in Johnny's life, particularly within the family. He discovered that Johnny had started college a year and a half earlier. He had been accepted at some excellent universities far from home but had turned down scholarships at these places and chosen a local junior college instead. He told the physician that he tends to go home each weekend and spend time with his parents and misses them if he's away from them for too long. Upon further questioning by the physician about the status of his parents, the physician discovered that Johnny is an only child and that his parents have been married for 23 years. According to Johnny, his parents have never gotten along very well, although the conflict is fairly "underground." At this point, the physician begins to hypothesize that perhaps Johnny's family is in the life-cycle stage in which children are on the verge of emotional emancipation, and the family is having adjustment problems as a result. There is also evidence that Johnny's relationships to his parents may be enmeshed and rigid (since he is not leaving home) and that his parents appear to avoid conflict. The case of Johnny will be continued later in the chapter.

SOMATIZATION DISORDER, HYPOCHONDRIASIS, AND THE FAMILY

Another spectrum of disorders that is very likely to have become embedded in the family context and part of the family's operation is the entire range of disorders known as the somatoform disorders, which include hypochondriasis and somatization disorder. These problems are often the nemesis of the primary care physician: While frustrating the best effort of the physician, they may also drive medical costs upward and contribute to the patient's and family's feelings of being misunderstood. These disorders involve situations in which individuals present with many *physical* symptoms that cannot be explained on medical grounds. Such individuals often do not have the capacity to differentiate between emotional and physical experience. (The concept of "somatothymic language" has been developed to describe the use of physical complaints to express emotional or psychological distress (Stoudemire, 1991).) A study by Cummings and Vanden Bos (1981) found that as many as 60% of all primary care patients present with somatic complaints that are actually an expression of psychosocial distress. These patients require reassurance and time from medical providers that they are often hesitant to give. Another study (DeGruy et al, 1987) reported that patients with a diagnosis of somatization disorder had a 50% higher rate of office visits, 50% higher charges, charts that were nearly twice as thick as the average chart, and significantly more diagnoses than a control sample. These are the patients who may have expensive, potentially dangerous and unnecessary procedures and treatments. They often have a history of numerous hospitalizations, generate great cost to the healthcare system, and cause significant distress to the physician who is repeatedly faced with their complaints. Stoudemire (1991) suggests that physicians often have difficulty recognizing or understanding the somatothymic language of the patient, possibly leading to misdiagnosis and frustration with the poor outcomes that usually result.

Trying to treat the somatizing patient with a purely biomedical approach is likely to do nothing but make the problem worse, and treating them on a strictly individual basis is likely to miss much essential information. Here again, understanding the role that the somatization plays in the family system and the ways in which the family maintains the patient's problems are efficient and effective for treating this disorder. The somatoform disorders are discussed in detail by Folks and colleagues (1994) in the companion volume to this text, *Clinical Psychiatry for Medical Students* (Stoudemire, 1994).

THE FAMILY AND THE STAGES OF CHRONIC ILLNESS

John Rolland (1987), a family psychiatrist, has described how the specific *developmental phase* of an illness should be addressed to understand what situation the patient and his or her family is actually facing. He proposes a model for examining the different phases and types of illnesses, rather than separating illnesses across biological criteria, to gain a better understanding of the likely problems that the individual and family are going to face in managing the illness. Rolland distinguishes between the *crisis phase*, the *chronic phase*, and the *terminal phase* of illness and states that families have different tasks for each of these phases.

1. *Crisis Phase.* During the crisis phase, the family knows that something is wrong and tends to pull together to cope with the symptoms in the medical system. To deal effectively with this phase, families must reorganize temporarily to meet the immediate needs. They must begin to address the task of accepting the illness, creating a meaning for the illness, and dealing with uncertainty. This is a time when families need to pull together during the acute stage of an illness; they manage this phase relatively better or worse depending upon their ability to do so.
2. *Chronic Phase.* During the chronic phase, which may be fairly static or have acute exacerbations and remissions, depending upon the type of illness, the patient and the family need to accept the permanent change, grieve for the pre-illness identity and must negotiate new roles for chronic care. In Rolland's words, "Families try to live a normal life in abnormal conditions."
3. *Terminal Phase.* For chronic illnesses that result in death, the terminal phase, of course, occurs when death is clearly inevitable.

Beyond looking at the three developmental phases of illness, Rolland has also characterized illnesses based upon their onset, course, outcome, and degree of incapacitation. For example, the onset of an illness may either be *acute*, like a stroke, or *gradual*, as in Alzheimer's disease. A family that can muster its resources very quickly may manage an acute onset well. In a family that is unable to do this, however, the management of an illness with a more gradual onset may be more successful.

The course of the chronic illness may be *progressive, constant,* or *relapsing and episodic*. Alzheimer's disease can be considered progressive, although it is to some extent relapsing. The aftermath of a head injury is relatively constant. Asthma is an example of a relapsing illness. Obviously, the necessity for a family to arrive at a new set of roles to manage the chronic course of constant illness symptoms is very different from the kind of requirements placed on a family with a relapsing, episodic illness. In some ways, this is perhaps the most difficult type of illness for a family to manage because the illness "comes and goes" and the roles need to shift accordingly. For example, a Crohn's disease patient might manage personal affairs and do well when the illness is in remission but then may become quite incapacitated at another point in time, thus creating the necessity for other people to step in and take over the role. This patient and family may find it very difficult to continuously relinquish and take on the same role, and flexibility will be essential. Rolland refers to *outcome* to mean whether it is expected that the disease will shorten the lifespan or result in death. In this case, the family must anticipatorily grieve what is inevitable. Finally, *incapacitation*, according to Rolland, reflects the degree of disability. An illness is either incapacitating, such as Parkinson's, or relatively nonincapacitating, such as hypertension (refer to Table 9–1).

In order to understand the kinds of requirements and tasks that are required of a patient and the family, it may be far more effective for the physician to conceptualize according to this typology than it is to think in terms that are purely biomedical categories, such as "cardiac" or "neurologic." With this typology, it is easier to see where families may get stuck based upon the kinds of demands placed upon them and weighed against the sorts of resources they can bring to bear.

The first part of this chapter has focused on the important role of the family in the context of medical illness. In the second half of this chapter we focus on basic conceptual and practical aspects of family systems theory and explore the functions of the family in more detail.

WHAT IS A FAMILY?

Defining the family in the late twentieth century is not an easy task. The family has changed dramatically over the past century and will probably continue to change in the next. For the purposes of this chapter, "family" defines a group of people who are related to each other either biologically, emotionally, or legally. Usually, the physician is interested in the people who live together in a family or those who have important emotional connections. While many people today would continue to define the family as "Mom, Dad, the kids, the dog, and the station wagon," many others would just as likely be inclined to describe a remarried family, a single-parent family, a divorced family without children, a gay or lesbian family, or several people living together in a communal sense who are supportive of each other.

Table 9–1 **Categorization of Chronic Illness by Psychosocial Type**

	INCAPACITATING		NONINCAPACITATING	
	Acute	**Gradual**	**Acute**	**Gradual**
Fatal				
Progressive		Lung cancer with CNS metastases AIDS Bone marrow failure Amyotrophic lateral sclerosis	Acute leukemia Pancreatic cancer Metastatic breast cancer Malignant melanoma Lung cancer Liver cancer, etc.	Cystic fibrosis
Relapsing			Cancers in remission	
Shortened life span, possibly fatal				
Progressive		Emphysema Alzheimer's disease Multi-infarct dementia Multiple sclerosis (late) Chronic alcoholism Huntington's chorea Scleroderma		Juvenile diabetes Malignant hypertension Insulin-dependent, adult-onset diabetes
Relapsing	Angina	Early multiple sclerosis Episodic alcholism	Sickle cell disease Hemophilia	Systemic lupus erythematosus
Constant	Stroke Moderate/severe myocardial infarction	Phenylketonuria (PKU) and other inborn errors of metabolism	Mild myocardial infarction Cardiac arrhythmia	Hemodialysis-treated renal failure Hodgkin's disease

Nonfatal Progressive		Parkinson's disease Rheumatoid arthritis Osteoarthritis		Noninsulin-dependent, adult-onset diabetes
Relapsing	Lumbosacral disc disease		Kidney stones Gout Migraine Seasonal allergy Asthma Epilepsy	Peptic ulcer Ulcerative colitis Chronic bronchitis Other inflammatory bowel diseases Psoriasis
Constant	Congenital malformations Spinal cord injury Acute blindness Acute deafness Survived severe trauma and burns Posthypoxic syndrome	Nonprogressive mental retardation Cerebral palsy	Benign arrhythmia Congenital heart disease	Malabsorption syndromes Hyperthyroidism/hypothyroidism Pernicious anemia Controlled hypertension Controlled glaucoma

(Reprinted with permission from Rolland J: Toward a psychosocial typology of chronic and life-threatening illness. Fam Syst Med 2:245–62, 1984.)

The statistics are clear about the changing structure of the typical American family (US Bureau of the Census, 1986). While marriage continues to be a near universal experience, people are waiting longer to get married. The average age is about 23 years for women and 25 years for men. Most couples continue to have children (90%), but they are waiting longer to have them and are having fewer than people did in previous generations. The divorce rate continues to be around 50% for first marriages and 60% for second marriages. The classic nuclear family of father and nonworking mother with children accounts for only slightly more than 8% of American families, while two-income, single-parent, step-family, and childless couples make up the majority of all families today.

Single-parent families are increasing, with about 27% of all families with children having only one parent present, 90% of whom, of course, are women. Of all births, 22% are to unmarried women, (60% of black children and 15% of white children are born to single mothers). Not only are single-parent families becoming more prevalent but, even when both parents are present, the dual-career couple has become the norm. Consequently, children are often being raised by day care centers. People are also living longer, with an average age of about 78 years for women and 74 years for men.

THE FAMILY AS SYSTEM

With fragmentation of the so-called traditional family, high divorce rates, and rapidly changing cultural norms for family life, it is no surprise that various therapies to assist in family crises and family dysfunction have proliferated since the end of the second World War. The family therapy movement began in the 1950s in various parts of the country by a number of clinicians, most of whom were psychiatrists, and who felt that the focus on the individual by psychoanalysts was inadequate to explain or treat the problems they were seeing. While a number of different theories have emerged since the 1950s in the field of family therapy, all have in common the conceptualization of the family as a system. In other words, the family is thought of as more than the sum of its parts. Knowing each member individually does not really predict what happens when all family members come together. The concept of system is one that implies that a change or stress in one part of the system, in one member of the family, affects and is affected by other members of the family.

Families are conceptualized as having *repeated interactional patterns* that regulate the members' behavior. These patterns are regulated by rules—some overt, but most covert—about the way the family is to handle decisions, celebrate holidays, interact with each other, show affection, deal with conflict, etc. In other words, who talks to whom about what, in what way, and when, are vital pieces of information in understanding how the family operates as a system. The regular transactional patterns that occur in a family maintain the roles of family members. In addition, the family acts to achieve *balance*, or *homeostasis*, in its relationships. The repetitious, circular, predictable transaction patterns are what reveal this balance. When the family is confronted by pressure to change, if the system is flexible it will accommodate and reach a new equilibrium. However, if the family is too rigid—if change seems like too great a threat—each family member will exert more effort to maintain the status quo, the homeostasis. By implication, therefore, change in one family member means change for all family members, and all family members are part of the solution as well as of the problem.

THE FAMILY LIFECYCLE

Many family therapists choose to think of the family lifecycle as an overarching developmental model by which to view normal family processes. Carter and McGoldrick (1980) have synthesized much of the thinking on the family lifecycle and its relevance for normal family interaction. These authors conceptualize the family lifecycle as a *series* of *relatively stable plateaus* and more *stressful transitions*. The transitions tend to be related to significant *entrances* and *exits* by family members into and from the system and tend to require second-order changes, while the more stable periods tend to be made up of *first-order changes*. First-order change is defined as the kind of changes that happen every day, changes which require increases or decreases in mastery or adaptation. In other words, children who know how to ride a bicycle from their house to their neighbor's house at some point learn how to ride the bike from their house to school: They have undergone a first-order change. This is a change in mastery or adaptation only. *Second-order changes*, on the other hand, are changes that imply *transformations* of status and meaning. A person becomes something *new*, gains a different *identity*. Going from being not married to being married, or going from not being a parent to being a parent is a significant shift in one's identity and status within the family and requires major role readjustments on the part of all family members. (See Chapter 10 on Adult Development by Drs. Wolman and Thompson.)

Jay Haley (1973) clearly states in his book, *Uncommon Therapy*, his belief that family stress is highest at these transition points from one stage to the next, and that symptoms (physical or psychological) are most likely to appear in a family member when there is an interruption or dislocation in the natural unfolding of the family life cycle. Of course, families that are more rigid are more likely to "get stuck" and have difficulty moving through these transition points to the next phase. Even in relatively healthy families, the experience of moving from one stage to the next is often one of feeling strange, of having a sense that the predictability of events has been lost. Individual family members may feel sad or confused, anxious or betrayed, and there is a clear sense of discontinuity. As loyalties realign, affections change, and roles are reassigned. For example, in a family in which members have always spent Christmas holidays together, an expectation develops that all holidays will involve the entire family. However, the oldest child marries, begins to have children, and decides that she no longer wants to spend Christmas Day with her family of origin. This may be considered a betrayal by other family members, who now have to decide what they will do with their very changed holiday: The family member who for 30-odd years has been there is now absent and is demonstrating loyalty to her nuclear family. In fact, this is simply a normal lifecycle development for the individual who has decided to make Christmas a time with her own family. In the family that is too rigid and cannot adjust to individual needs of its members as they move through their own lifecycles, however, one can imagine the enormous family pulls not to shake up the structure as it has come to be expected.

The stages of the family lifecycle, as conceptualized by Carter and McGoldrick (1980) are illustrated in Table 9–2. In this table one can see six stages of the life cycle in the left-hand column. In the center column, the emotional process that needs to occur as each stage is transited are outlined. In the right-hand column, the second-order changes in family status that are required to proceed from one developmental stage to the next are specified. Like all stage theories, an inadequate resolution of any stage leads to greater difficulty negotiating later stages.

One can see that Carter and McGoldrick have started with the *Between-Families, Unattached Young Adult* stage. This is sometimes thought of as a particularly important stage, as a key time of individuation. This is a time to formulate life goals and to become a self away from one's family of origin before joining with someone else to form a new family system. The more adequately young adults *differentiate* from the emotional processes of their family of origin, the less likely it is that they will have trouble later in their marriage and in raising their own children. (Separation-individuation theory is discussed in Chapter 5 by Drs. Inderbitzen and James.)

The second stage, the *Joining of Families Through Marriage*, should not occur unless the first stage has been adequately accomplished. If an individual chooses to marry as a means of separating from the family (to please the family, or to spite the family), the likelihood of a primary loyalty to the new family forming for the right reasons is decreased. It is at this juncture that many mother-in-law jokes occur: "I'm going to run home to mother," or "I'll never be as good as your mother, I will never cook as well as she does," or jokes about the mother-in-law's interference in the couple's life. All of these jokes are indications of the adjustments required at this stage for adequate transition.

The *Family with Young Children* is the next stage. Again, to the extent that the previous stages have not been adequately accomplished, problems are likely to show up when young children enter the situation. It is often at this point that people first realize that they have not successfully separated from their families of origin as they become highly reactive to their parents' comments on their own parenting.

Carter and McGoldrick describe *Adolescence*, the next stage, as something that happens to a whole family, not just to an individual child. They talk about how family boundaries, having remained fairly stable around the family for 12 or 13 years, are suddenly required to become far more *elastic* or *flexible* so that adolescents can "come and go" as they need to. Adolescence represents a second, more advanced stage of separation-individuation from the teenager.

Stage five, that of *Launching Children and Moving On* is a very long stage of the family life cycle, and it requires a great deal of familial flexibility. This is the stage in which many children become symptomatic. If a child has played an important part in the marital system, it will be hard for those parents to "let" that child go, since the parents would then have to renegotiate fundamental aspects of their marriage. Consequently, children may find many conscious and even unconscious ways to avoid leaving home, such as having multiple physical ailments. Alternately, parents, because

Table 9–2 **Stages of the Family Lifecycle**

FAMILY LIFECYCLE STAGE	EMOTIONAL PROCESS OF TRANSITION KEY PRINCIPLES	SECOND-ORDER CHANGES IN FAMILY STATUS REQUIRED TO PROCEED DEVELOPMENTALLY
1. Between families: the unattached young adult	Accepting parent–offspring separation	a. Differentiation of self in relation to family of origin b. Development of intimate peer relationships c. Establishment of self in work
2. The joining of families through marriage: the newly married couple	Commitment to new system	a. Formation of marital system b. Realignment of relationships with extended families and friends to include spouse
3. The family with young children	Accepting new members into the system	a. Adjusting marital system to make space for children b. Taking on parenting roles c. Realignment of relationships with extended family to include parenting and grandparenting roles
4. The family with adolescents	Increasing flexibility of family boundaries to include children's independence	a. Shifting of parent–child relationships to permit adolescent to move in and out of system b. Refocus on midlife marital and career issues c. Beginning shift toward concerns for older generation
5. Launching children and moving on	Accepting a multitude of exits from and entries into the family system	a. Renegotiation of marital system as a dyad b. Development of adult-to-adult relationships between grown children and their parents c. Realignment of relationships to include in-laws and grandchildren d. Dealing with disabilities and death of parents (grandparents)
6. The family in later life	Accepting the shifting of generational roles	a. Maintaining own and/or couple functioning and interests in face of physiologic decline; exploration of new familial and social role options b. Support for a more central role for middle generation c. Making room in the system for the wisdom and experience of the elderly; supporting the older generation without overfunctioning for them d. Dealing with loss of spouse, siblings and other peers and preparation for own death; life review and integration

From Carter EA and McGoldrick M: *The Family Life Cycle.* New York, Gardner Press, 1980 of their *dependency on the children*, may sabotage efforts of their children to leave home by a variety of means, such as keeping the children financially dependent on them or by provoking guilt in the children for leaving.

The final stage, the *Family in Later Life*, again requires the shifting of roles. Very often, members of the middle (or "sandwich") generation become parents to the older generation. At a time when people are waiting longer to marry and to have children, this middle generation often becomes maximally stressed when they have to take care of both children at home and aging parents. In earlier times, when people were bearing children at a younger age, the children were "launched" and had moved on by the time the middle generation needed to care for the older generation.

A final note on the family lifecycle is that many families have major disjunctures in the lifecycle due to divorce, remarriage, the choice of a homosexual partner, the decision to parent without a partner, etc. These transitions require their own tasks of adjustment and second-order changes, making the lifecycle all the more complex and challenging.

FAMILY STRUCTURE

Another major model of family system theory was developed by Salvador Minuchin. Minuchin and his colleagues (Minuchin and Fishman, 1982) are credited with an in-depth analysis and understanding of the importance of the family *structure* for healthy adaptation. Minuchin conceptualizes the family as a *larger system* which is made up of *smaller subsystems*. A *subsystem* is any grouping within the family of two or more members that is organized around some common function. For example, the marital subsystem is organized around issues of the marriage. The parental subsystem is organized around issues of parenting. Siblings make up yet another subsystem organized around what it means to be peers of unequal power.

Each of these subsystems needs a certain amount of autonomy and independence for its members to develop—in other words, a lack of interference from outside (i.e., the couple needs privacy in discussing their sex life). At the same time, members of the subsystems need to be accessible to some degree. For example, a common question of parents is, "When do I interfere in my children's fighting?" Of course, the answer is somewhere between interfering all the time (in which case the children would never learn how to negotiate with each other and solve their own issues) and never interfering at all (and letting them become seriously abusive to each other). This necessary balance would be true of all subsystems.

Minuchin labels the specific rules about who participates under what circumstances within the individual subsystems as *boundaries*. Boundaries are something that an outside observer (such as a therapist or physician) infers as that line between people within the subsystem and people outside of the subsystem. It is important that the boundaries around subsystems be clear and understandable and reflect the "business" of those subsystems. For example, it should be clear that the husband and wife subsystem has a boundary around issues of their sexuality, and that the children do not become involved in that aspect of their parents' lives. This boundary would be violated if a mother confided in her daughter about her problems in sexual relationship with her husband.

The quality of relationships within subsystems varies on a bipolar scale from *disengaged* at one extreme, to *enmeshed* at the other. By enmeshed, Minuchin means *overinvolved*. Evidence of enmeshment in relationships is family members who speak for each other, think for each other, who are very interpersonally reactive to each other. This is the family in which the mother says, "Put on this sweater—you're cold," when in actuality she is cold herself. Family relationships that are *enmeshed* are ones in which the slightest distress or discomfort on the part of a member of the relationship causes immediate and intense response on the part of other family members. Enmeshed subsystems reflect emotional connectedness and relatedness at the expense of autonomy at one extreme. At the other extreme are disengaged relationships—relationships that are very detached and distant. These are relationships in which autonomy is at the expense of any kind of connectedness or loyalty to other members of the relationship. Only with a major stress does anyone respond. Neither of these extremes is ideal. The ideal is something in between. An enmeshed family may experience very profound distress and disorganization during an illness or death due to the excessive connectedness and the incapacity of individual family members to function autonomously. In contrast, when there is illness or death in a family in which the connections are disengaged, there will not be enough reaction and there perhaps will be neglect of a seriously impaired family member.

In Minuchin's view of the more *adaptive* family, there are a clear hierarchy and lines of authority. In other words, there is a clear *executive parenting subsystem* around which there are clear boundaries. Someone is in charge, and it is clear who and in what circumstances. In addition, the primary connections and primary loyalties are within generations; there are no crossgenerational coalitions (refer to diagram). Mom and daughter do not team up against dad (Fig. 9–1A). Where a husband has a tighter relationship with his mother than his wife (Fig. 9–1B), a child acts as a "go-between" for parents and has more connectedness with each of the parents than they have with each other (Fig. 9–1C). These would all be examples of crossgenerational coalitions, where the primary connection is between members of different generations *versus* between members of the same generation. Obviously, referring back to the family life cycle, if unattached young adults do not significantly differentiate from their family of origin and form strong interpersonal relationships to individuals outside the family system, they may run the risk of having a stronger coalition with a parent from their original family than with their partner or spouse. This could be problematic and probably be passed along to the next generation by having a stronger relationship with a child than with the marital partner.

Another characteristic of the healthy family is evidenced when individual members are assuming age-appropriate responsibilities and are receiving age-appropriate privileges. In some families, children are made to grow up too fast, either because their parents are not parenting adequately or because the whole family is under-resourced, and the child may have responsibilities beyond what is age appropriate. In turn, the privileges may not match the level of responsibility, and the child may be resentful. This is the situation of the "parentified" child and is also a frequent characteristic of families in which there is child abuse. Often, these are families in which the parent

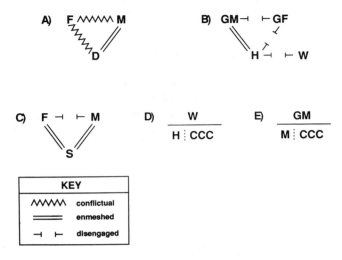

Figure 9–1. *Five Family Genograms based on Salvador Minuchin's family system theory.*

leaves a child with far more responsibility than they can manage, the child fails at accomplishing the responsibility, and then the parents beats them, judging the child to be misbehaving. Alternately, the child may have the privileges of an adult when he can only manage those of a teenager.

Another way in which age-appropriate responsibilities may not be assumed is in a family in which a parent acts like a child. An example is an irresponsible, alcoholic husband who takes none of the responsibility at home and does not predictably bring in money or take care of the family, yet has all the privileges of an adult (see Fig. 9–1D). Thus, he can use the family facilities, watch TV, and order the children (CCC in the genogram) around. Again, this is a case of responsibilities and privileges that are not in line with what a healthy person would be doing according to age.

Another case is a family in which a young, single mother winds up being like a child herself when her own mother continues to "parent" her as before (Fig. 9–1E). In all of these cases, there are problems in which boundaries are not clear enough, in which there may be problems of crossgenerational coalitions, in which the hierarchies may be upside down, and in which the members of the family are not being supported to grow and develop at the rate that they should.

An essential characteristic in families who tend to function better than others is that they are *flexible.* All families are confronted with many stresses, both from the outside (e.g., a job loss, a move, a war) and the inside (e.g., lifecycle changes and demands). A family that is flexible can readjust roles and alignments to compensate for the stresses and changes required. A rigid family, however, finds it particularly difficult to make the kinds of changes necessary for adaptation. It is in these families that a member is likely to become symptomatic, either medically or psychiatrically (Table 9–3).

Table 9–3 **Key Concepts of Structural Family Theory**

The family is a *system* made up of subsystems.
Boundaries around subsystems define who participates and in what
  ways; boundaries should be clear and appropriate.
Relationships vary from *enmeshed* to *disengaged;* healthier relationships
  tend to be somewhere in between the two.
Primary loyalties are within generations, not crossgenerational
Family members have age-appropriate privileges and responsibilities in
  healthy families.
Healthy families are *flexible*, not rigid.

SYMPTOM FUNCTION IN THE FAMILY SYSTEM

By observing the preferred transactional patterns in the family, one can deduce the structure of the family and assess whether the family structure is "out of line" with what is most healthy. Also, by observing the transactional patterns, one needs to answer the question, "What function is the symptom serving in the family system?" The best way to make that assessment is by a clear interpersonal analysis of the transactional patterns that precede and follow the symptom occurrence. Also, what were the relationships between family members before the symptoms occurred historically, and what has happened since the person has become symptomatic?

For example, a child presents to the physician with a case of intractable asthma. Upon finding out when the asthma attack happened, who was home, who did what, and what happened as a result of it, different possible pictures could emerge, depending upon the different function the asthmatic symptoms may be serving in the family. In one case, it may be that the child was home alone with Mom on a Friday night and Dad was out with the guys playing poker. This is a family in which the husband and the wife have a quite distant relationship, and the father is unavailable to the family. When this child has an asthma attack, however, the mother immediately calls the father, and he comes home. After the asthma attack has resolved, the father stays home for the rest of the evening with the mother and child, and they watch TV together. In contrast, it may be that the child's asthma attacks tend to occur when the father *is* home and that whenever the father approaches the child about something he expects of her or about something she did not do, she tends to begin to wheeze, at which point the father backs off. This may be a family in which the father's anger is an issue and in which the mother also has an issue with the father's anger. The child's asthma attacks, in a sense, are a way of keeping the father's anger more under control.

In each of these families, what presents is a child with asthma that is increasing in frequency. However, the solution to the problem, aside from medications, would be very different in each of these cases. In the first case, one would want to look at the situation between the husband and the wife to see if there is some way that the father can become more available to his wife and child around issues other than asthma attacks. In the second situation, one would want to deal with the issue of the father's anger, each family member's response to it, and find a more adaptive way of managing it than for the child to have asthma attacks to keep it under control.

Minuchin and his colleagues also have done a great deal of work and research with families who have a member with a psychosomatic problem. "The structure of the family is one that includes an overemphasis on nurturing roles. The family seems to function best when someone is sick. The characteristics of such families include overprotection, enmeshment, or overinvolvement of family members with each other and inability to resolve conflicts, a tremendous concern for the maintenance of peace or avoidance of conflict, and an extreme rigidity" (Minuchin and Fishman 1982, p 60).

FAMILY OF ORIGIN OR BOWENIAN FAMILY THERAPY

Murray Bowen, M.D., another well-known family therapist, conceptualized the family as an emotional unit of which the individual was a part. He is particularly noted for three concepts, which are helpful in understanding family functioning: (1) *Scale of Differentiation*, (2) *Triangles*, and (3) *Multigenerational Transmission Process* (Table 9–4). Bowen believed that family dysfunction was more likely to occur when family members were less emotionally differentiated from each other, and hence, the family was continually having to adapt to high levels of chronic anxiety. People with higher degrees of emotional differentiation were theorized to suffer from less chronic anxiety and could, therefore, tolerate greater amounts of acute stress before they became symptomatic. Bowen proposed that individuals who are less differentiated in relationship to their families have more anxiety about independence and the assumption of responsibility for themselves. As a result, some individuals never really "leave home" (emotionally, at least), while others pretend to separate but experience severe anxiety in the process, and subsequently produce families with problems similar to those of the family from which they came.

1. *Scale of Differentiation.* Bowen conceptualized the scale of differentiation to capture his notion that people vary considerably (from 0 to 100, low to high) in how differentiated or separated they are from their family of origin. The more differentiated indi-

---

Table 9–4 **Key Concepts of Family of Origin Theory**

Differentiation reflects an individual's ability to remain herself or himself while connected to others.

The more differentiated an individual is, the less likely he or she will be to continue a legacy of family problems into the next generation.

Triangulated relationships and communications reflect efforts on the part of the members to reduce anxiety in a twosome.

Triangles, particularly rigid, chronic, and generationally repeating triangles, occur in families in which a member is likely to be symptomatic.

Triangles and family issues tend to repeat across generations.

viduals are, the greater the "degree to which they are able to distinguish between the feeling process and the intellectual process," and the more their ability to choose between being guided by thoughts or feelings at any given moment (Kerr and Bowen 1988, p 97). This statement should not be construed to mean that an obsessive-compulsive personality is more differentiated than an emotionally aware and expressive person. Bowen is most concerned with "emotional reactivity" which is experienced more frequently the lower one is on the scale of differentiation. An illustration of emotional reactivity would be the experience of going home for a family visit fully determined to behave in a mature way, only to find oneself engaged in "the thousandth reenactment" of a problematic interaction with one's mother that had been repeated since age 12.

Bowen and Kerr describe individuals at a low level of differentiation (0 to 25) as emotionally needy and highly reactive to others. Much of their energy is focused on "loving" or "being loved." They find it difficult to make statements such as, "I believe...", "I am...", "I will do...". People with a moderate level of differentiation (25 to 50) are much more adaptive and can tolerate more stress and life change than people at the lower end of the scale, but they are still excessively reactive to emotional disharmony and to the opinions of others. They tend to be very focused on creating a good impression and on seeking approval. Individuals with a moderately high level of differentiation (50 to 75) have more choice to flexibly move back and forth between intimate emotional closeness and goal-directed activity.

Bowen and Kerr also described that rare individual who is highly differentiated (75 to 100):

[He is] sure of his beliefs and convictions; he is not dogmatic or fixed in his thinking. Capable of hearing and evaluating the viewpoints of others, he can discard old beliefs in favor of new. He can listen without reacting and can communicate without antagonizing others. He is secure within himself; his functioning is not affected by praise or criticism. He can respect the identity of another without becoming critical or emotionally involved in order to modify the life course of another. Able to assume total responsibility for self and sure of responsibility *to* others, he does not become overly responsible *for* others. He is realistically aware of his dependence on his fellow man and is free to enjoy relationships. He does not have a 'need' for others that can impair functioning, and others do not feel 'used.' Tolerant and respectful of differences, he is not prone to engage in polarized debates. He is realistic in his assessment of self and others and not preoccupied with his place in the hierarchy. Expectations of self and others are also realistic. Intense feelings are well tolerated, so he does not act automatically to alleviate them. His level of chronic anxiety is very low, and he can adapt to most stresses without developing symptoms. (1988, p 107)

2. *Triangles.* Another major concept of Bowen's family therapy is the idea of triangles. Bowen described the triangle as the smallest stable relationship system. Within a given family system in periods of emotional stability, the triangle is made up of a comfortable twosome and a less-comfortable third outsider. When anxiety in the system increases, the outsider or third person becomes more involved, often decreasing the tension between the twosome and spreading the anxiety through three relationships. A typical sequence of triangulation might be when Person A becomes an uncomfortable insider and pulls in the outsider, C, by complaining about the other insider, B. As C responds by taking sides with A, C and A will feel close, and B will be the new outsider. For example, a wife starts to feel angry at her husband but wants to avoid conflict with him. So she complains about him to her eldest daughter, who sympathizes. Mother and daughter feel close. Husband is now outside, but the husband and wife, while distant, are at least not in overt conflict. Of course, husband and wife will never resolve anything, either. Moreover, the confidante daughter will likely be left with the angry feelings and will get into conflict with her father for her mother. *The more healthy a family, the more its members can deal with their tensions directly in dyads without triangulating third parties into the conflict.* The less differentiated a family, the more repeated and multiple interlocking triangles occur.

A common family triangle is when two family members feel close by talking about, by scapegoating, or by agreeing that they do not like a third person. In this case, the two people can feel as if they are close to each other when in actuality if they had to deal directly with each other, they would have very little in common and perhaps a good deal of conflict. Another example of triangulating in a family is when communications about someone is upset or feelings about another are sent through a third party rather than given directly, so that much of the information about the other's feelings is hearsay.

A physician can easily be the unsuspecting third in a triangle. If the physician sides with a member of the family and sees the situation as having "good guys and bad guys" rather than equally participating players, the physician will inadvertently maintain the dysfunction in the family, since triangles decrease the experience of stress but also ensure that nothing will change. More often than not, introducing a third party into the triangle, whether it be a physician or a child, ensures that the anxiety-producing issues will not be resolved and that *more distance* will result between the original twosome than would have been possible without the triangle.

3. *Multigenerational Transmission Process.* Triangles within family systems tend to repeat themselves over generations, and people tend to evolve into fixed roles and alliances within the family system. Thus, knowledge that families in conflict tend to form triangles as a way to manage their anxiety and that these triangles tend to be passed down across generations can be helpful in planning family intervention and in understanding why certain family members may become symptomatic. In other words, when one views a family's history and looks for repetitive patterns, one may find eldest daughters who are mothers' confidantes; mothers and sons who are overinvolved and father-husbands are disengaged, generation after generation; eldest sons who follow in their father's footsteps, while second sons tend to be symptomatic in one way or another. All of these are examples of the multigenerational transmission process in which families pass on the legacy of the previous generation.

Returning now to the diabetic patient, Johnny, discussed earlier in this chapter, it is clear that as an only child, Johnny, when 18, should have been free to leave home and attend a distant university but instead chose to stay close to home and to visit home more frequently than most 19-year-olds would do. This may indicate the family is stuck at the life cycle stage of Launching Children and Moving On. However, this does not explain the recent exacerbation of Johnny's symptoms, in that his leaving for college occurred a year-and-a-half ago. When the physician inquired about recent events in the family, Johnny uncomfortably disclosed that while his parents had never particularly gotten along very well before, in the last few months, things had gotten significantly worse. His father had disclosed to his mother and to Johnny that he had tested HIV-positive and had homosexual relationships. It was shortly after this that Johnny's diabetes began to become more brittle. Without question, this type of family stress could exacerbate Johnny's health problems.

One could say, looking at this case from a linear perspective, that simply the shock of hearing about his father's medical and personal status was sufficient explanation for his worsening diabetes. However, it still made sense, given the seriousness of both the father's problems and Johnny's problems, that the physician meet with the entire family and try to achieve some understanding of the status of the family and what the family planned to do. The physician asked the entire family to come in, and at this point did a genogram (see next section) and discovered the following:

A CASE STUDY

Mr. B, Johnny's father, age 45, is an only child. He reports a very close relationship with his now 75-year-old mother, who knows nothing of any of the current situation. Mrs. B reports that Mr. B will never tell her about the situation because Mr. B's mother believes he is perfect and never does anything wrong. Mr. B reports a pleasant but distant relationship with his 80-year-old father, who is still living. Mrs. B reports herself to be the middle of five girls of a farm family where very little attention was paid to her and where she was mostly "lost in the shuffle." She reports a mildly conflictual relationship with her mother and a definitely more close and involved relationship with her father. She disagrees with Mr. B's mother significantly that Mr. B can do no wrong, but she believes that both Johnny and her father probably fit that category. When Mr. and Mrs. B speak of Johnny, they speak of an extremely well-behaved, compliant, and obedient child who has grown into a young man. They both report that they depend on him in many ways. Mr. B reports that Johnny is his confidante and his best friend, and he doesn't know what he would do without him. Mrs. B reports that Johnny has always been very close to her and is her helpmate, assisting her around the home with tasks that her husband will not perform (see Fig. 9–2).

As we look at this family, we see that Johnny is *triangulated* in his parents' marriage. He is overinvolved with both parents, has acted as a *parentified child* and essentially parented, cared for, and worried about them for many years. These are examples of crossgenerational alliances and lack of an adequate executive subsystem. Mr. and Mrs. B have experienced a distant, conflictual relationship in those years although the conflict has been covert. This is typical in psychosomatic families. The *triangles repeat over time* of an overinvolved son and his mother. Both Mr. and Mrs. B overinvolvement and idealization of an opposite-sex parent, leaving them in a position of difficulty in negotiating the family lifecycle stage of unattached young adult

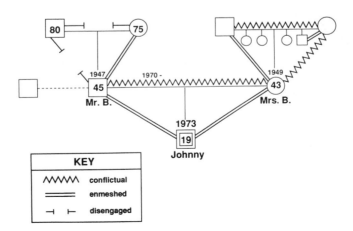

Figure 9–2. *Johnny's Family Genogram.*

transiting to predominant loyalty to the marital partner. Both of these individuals seem more connected to their family of origin and to their son than they do to each other, reflecting significant crossgenerational coalitions. The triangular patterns repeat down through the generations of distant relationships between same-generation parental/marital subsystems and crossgenerational overinvolvement between parents and children. (*Multigenerational transmission process*).

In terms of *age-appropriate tasks and responsibilities*, Johnny has clearly had more responsibility for a long time than a child his age should have, and this continues into the present, when he continues to stay close to home to make sure that his parents do not separate. What is significant here is that Johnny has received very little parenting from his parents. His father describes him as a best friend, and his mother describes him as a substitute spouse. When addressing Johnny's diabetic symptoms, it is clear that the focus on his symptoms may be the only place his parents can come together in agreement and do any form of parenting. Each time Johnny has a diabetic incident, the parents pull together and both arrive to help him. This sort of team effort and parenting effort are rare exceptions in the life of Johnny. This sort of pattern indicates the *function* Johnny's diabetes incidents may come to serve for him and his parents.

GENOGRAMS

In analyzing family systems, a practical way to start that is useful in the medical setting is a genogram. A genogram (a drawing of the family tree or pedigree) is a primary way in which physicians and family therapists alike can quickly come to see some of the issues discussed thus far. A genogram shows what stage of the lifecycle the family is in and helps identify some of the multigenerational transmission effects that may be occurring, illustrates the triangles in the family and repetitive patterns over time, and shows any crossgenerational coalitions and alliances and some of the significant family life events. Generally, the genogram affords significant information about a family dating back at least three generations. The genogram not only provides significant interpersonal and medical history, but also can improve communication between a patient and a physician. Patients tend to feel that their physician is concerned about them when the physician takes a thorough genogram and conducts a physical and psychosocial history (Gerson and McGoldrick, 1985). These authors point out that critical medical information can be "flagged" on the genogram and current medical problems can be seen immediately within the larger familial and historic perspective. Gerson and McGoldrick note that the genogram can help the physician "anticipate illness behavior" by recognizing current behavior or patterns of illness in the family system, as well as help to identify resources for enhancing compliance in the family system. The genogram documents life events and pinpoints stressors that affect treatment. It provides a better understanding of the biopsychosocial functioning of the patient within the family system. In certain cases, the genogram may help to uncover symptom patterns early in the detection of a problem, or in some cases, prevent or anticipate an illness by identifying patients at risk. The following three items are the most significant things a physician should look for in inspecting a genogram: (1) repetitive patterns of behavior in the family system (suicide, alcoholism, divorce), (2) coincidences of dates (e.g., death of a family member coinciding with a presenting symptom in another family member, anniversary reactions), and (3) impact of untimely life events (e.g., unexpected deaths or separations) (Gerson and McGoldrick 1985).

Information Needed for a Genogram

I. Facts.
  A. Dates of birth, marriage, separation, divorce, illness, hospital-izations, retirement, death.
  B. Sibling position.
  C. Profession and education.
  D. Patient's place of birth and current residence.
  E. Religious affiliation.
II. Historic Information.
  A. Important family events.
  B. At least two to three generations of family history.
  C. Messages, rules, or expectations that have been passed down from one generation to the next.
III. Relationships and Roles.
  A. Are there family members who do not speak to each other?
  B. How often are they in contact with one another?
  C. Are there any family members who are extremely close or distant, enmeshed or disengaged?
  D. How differentiated are family members? In particular, spouses, adult children and their parents?
  E. Are there marital conflicts?
  F. Who is the most and least supportive to the patient?
  G. Who seems to have the most or the least power and control?
IV. Questions About Family Functioning.
  A. Are there any current serious family problems?
    1. Medical or psychiatric?
    2. Sexual abuse, incest?
    3. Drugs, alcoholism?
    4. Financial or legal?
  B. Work History.
    1. Have there been recent job changes, such as unemploy-ment, retirement, or relocation?
    2. Are there financial stresses?
    3. How has the family coped with stress in the past?

FAMILY ASSESSMENT: SUMMARY

The following is a summation of the essential points outlined previously in this chapter. By obtaining answers to these questions, the physician can get an idea of how the symptoms presenting in the office may be functioning within the family context, and assist in constructing a genogram as outlined above. Reflect on the following:

I. What is the structure of the family?
  A. What are the alliances, coalitions, subsystems and boundaries? Are the boundaries clear?
  B. To what extent are family members enmeshed or disengaged?
II. How do the presenting symptoms make sense from a systemic perspective?
  A. In other words, what function is the symptomatic behavior serving in the system? This includes how the symptomatic behavior may be operating from a multigenerational perspective as well as operating in the current system.
  B. How are the symptoms being maintained? What are the interactional patterns that keep them going? In other words, what is the process of who talks to whom, when, about what, in what circumstances? How are family members involved in maintaining the symptoms?
  C. What are the relevant triangles? To what extent are there triangular patterns interlocking and repeating over the generations?
III. Why is the family presenting now?
  A. What is the family life context? What are the stresses, such as money, death, moving, etc. What are the supports and resources (e.g., extended family, community support services, day care, etc.)?
  B. At what stage is the family in its lifecycle? Are individuals being given age-appropriate responsibilities and privileges? Is the family getting stuck at a point of transition in which individual members of the family are needing developmental shifts, entrances into or exits from the family?
IV. How flexible is the family? How difficult is it to alter the alliances and boundaries? How much resistance is met when this is attempted?

CLINICAL "RED FLAGS"

At this point, while it is clear how to assess a family, the question of how to find the time to do it remains. Of course, this thorough an examination of the psychosocial features of every case that presents is not feasible, desirable, or economical. There are certain "red flags," however, for which one should look as a way of determining whether it will ultimately be more efficient and worthwhile to investigate the psychosocial aspects of the individual's medical problems. These red flags are as follows (Doherty and Baird, 1983):

  1. An illness that is not responding in a typical way to the typical treatment.

2. An illness such as asthma or diabetes that was previously under good control but that has suddenly become more difficult to manage or increased in frequency.

3. Atypical headaches of long-standing duration and other unexplained pain complaints.

4. Chronic anxiety and many office visits over several years for multiple and diffuse complaints without significant evidence of organic disease.

5. A primary complaint of chronic fatigue which, of course, may be indicative of depression.

6. Insomnia—also a possible reflection of anxiety or depression.

7. Multiple physical complaints of a nonspecific nature.

8. Complaints of nonspecific allergies.

9. In children: enuresis or encopresis, poor appetite, poor sleep patterns, hyperactivity, poor school performance or behavior problems.

10. Family history of serious chronic psychosocial problems, such as chemical dependency, chronic depression and anxiety, child or spousal abuse, or eating disorders.

Whenever a patient presents with any of these red flags, a more efficient and effective treatment is likely to result if a thorough psychosocial evaluation and assessment of the family situation is performed.

WHEN TO REFER AND WHEN TO TREAT

Depending upon whether the physician has some degree of time and resources, knowledge, and ability to treat the problem, the following are the types of problems that tend to be the most appropriate for primary care counseling by a physician. There are three major categories (Doherty and Baird, 1983):

1. *Family Transition Problems.* These are problems that reflect adjustment difficulties when families are responding to external stresses or undergoing stresses associated with the lifecycle changes mentioned earlier in the chapter. For example, the family may be experiencing marital distress due to the fact that the husband just lost his job. The family resources may be taxed when a cousin comes to live with the family. For such transition problems, supportive counseling, an understanding ear, and some solid advice can go a long way.

2. *Other Problems of Recent Origin.* When problems are recent and have occurred only once (e.g., a first-time depression, new acting-out behavior by a child, a new physical symptom with no evident medical basis), the physician is in an ideal position to assess what is happening in the family and to give some suggestions for the family to follow. When psychosocial problems have not become

firmly entrenched or rooted in a rigid family system, families may respond well to suggestion and support.

3. *Many Illness-Related Problems.* When a patient presents with a medical problem, he or she may not be willing to address the psychosocial factors occurring. The patient may, however, be willing to address them within the context of focusing on the medical situation. The physician, of course, is in an ideal position to hear the medical problems in a psychosocial context.

When what appear to be mild psychosocial problems do not respond to primary care help, the physician would be wise to refer for psychiatric consultation. In addition, other types of problems that make patients good candidates for referral are any which are serious, chronic problems. The following are good examples:

1. Chronic depression and anxiety.
2. Alcohol and drug dependency (including dependence on or abuse of prescribed medication such as benzodiazepines and analgesics).
3. Chronic family dysfunctional patterns. (For example, when the family history indicates repetitive patterns over time of long-standing difficulties, it is unlikely that the family has enough flexibility to respond to simple suggestions and support.)
4. Serious acute family symptoms, particularly child abuse, spousal abuse, and incest. These types of dangerous situations are likely to be beyond the scope of a physician's expertise and time.

HOW TO REFER

To ensure effective follow-up of the physician's suggestion for referral, it is important to follow a number of guidelines. Even psychiatric referrals made to patients who ask for psychiatric referrals have a relatively low rate of follow-through. Certainly, a family therapy referral to someone who is presenting with medical problems will likely have an even lower rate of follow-through. Doherty and Baird (1983) have suggested the following guidelines:

1. Have names and phone numbers of your referral sources immediately available.
2. Give patients a realistic idea about what the therapy will entail (including cost), whether it will be short term or long term.
3. It is often helpful to have patients make the appointment with the therapist before leaving the physician's office.
4. Ask patients to acknowledge when the referral has been successfully completed. Of course, this suggests that the matter is serious.
5. Check with patients on how the therapy is going. Ask if they are pleased and if the therapy is helping with their problems.

6. Ask the therapist to keep the physician informed about the main therapeutic strategies and the progress of the therapy so that the relationship can be supported by the physician. During the early part of therapy when the family is under more stress, a family member may present with physical symptoms and a complaint that family life has been worse since beginning therapy. If the therapist has informed the physician about what is going on, the physician will not assume that the therapy is ineffective.

It is important that the physician appear confident and enthusiastic about the value of family therapy. It is helpful if the physician knows the therapist personally and can reassure patients that the types of problems with which they are presenting are relatively common, understandable, and often helped by family therapy. The physician needs to reassure patients that he or she will continue to follow them for their physical symptoms and any underlying medical problems and general health care. Returning to the case of Johnny:

It was clear from talking with Johnny's family, discussed earlier, that his parents had maintained a chronically dysfunctional marriage for a very long time and that Johnny had been in a position of being helpmate to each of them. It was of great concern to the physician that this recent crisis was causing Johnny's diabetes to be out of control, a control that had been maintained well for many years (one of the red flags). It was clear that because of the long-standing family dysfunction and now life-threatening nature of Johnny's current problem, the situation was beyond the physician's level of expertise. He spent much time working with the family, supporting them and convincing them that, for Johnny's sake as well as their own, they needed to get help in figuring out how to negotiate this new crisis and to find ways in which the couple could deal with their feelings about each other, thus freeing Johnny to live his own life without having to worry about theirs. A referral was made in the office for family therapy, and the family set up their appointment in the presence of Johnny's physician. The physician requested that the family keep in touch to relate the progress they were making in family therapy and said that he would continue to treat the physical symptoms of Johnny's diabetes. He was hopeful that his collaboration with the family therapist would result in Johnny's being able to disengage from the family enough to get his diabetes back under control.

ANNOTATED BIBLIOGRAPHY

Doherty WJ, Baird MA: Family Therapy and Family Medicine. New York, Guilford Press, 1983

This is a well-written and comprehensive book that examines the relationships between family medicine and family therapy, with particular emphasis on the application of family systems concepts to medical practice. One author is a physician and the other, a psychologist. Both of their perspectives are brought to bear and integrated in their discussions of how to treat patients and their families in a medical system, management of treatment issues of noncompliance, and clinical "red flags."

Gerson R, McGoldrick M: Genograms in Family Assessment. New York, WW Norton, 1985

This is a short, well-written, and interesting book that provides a "how-to" approach to construction and use of the genogram. The authors describe what is relevant information, how to interview for it, and how to think about and understand the information acquired. This book would be very helpful for a physician wishing to use genograms in practice.

McDaniel S, Campbell T, Seaburn SB: Family-Oriented Primary Care: A Manual for Medical Providers. New York, Springer-Verlag, 1990

An outstanding, well-written, and easy-to-read book that provides information on the biopsychosocial assessment of the patient in the context of the family, how a physician should conduct a family conference, and how to take a family-oriented approach to a number of specific medical problems. This is a particularly fine book for physicians as it provides a helpful, clear, and simply-stated protocol at the end of each chapter.

McDaniel S, Hepworth J, Doherty WJ: Medical Family Therapy. New York, Basic Books, 1992

This book is the first of its kind—a book dedicated to defining a specialty in family therapy that focuses specifically on its application to medical problems. It also specifically addresses issues for the family therapist working in medical settings. As such, it is particularly useful to medical family therapists but also provides much well-researched and documented information on the interface between medical symptoms and family systems, and between the medical profession and the profession of family systems therapists.

REFERENCES

Ader R (ed): Psychoneuroimmunology. New York, Academic Press, 1981

Anderson BJ, Miller JP, Auslander WF et al: Family characteristics of diabetic adolescents: Relationship to metabolic control. Diab Care 4:586–594, 1931

Baker L, Minuchin S, Milman L, et al: Psychosomatic aspects of juvenile diabetes mellitus: A progress report. Mod Prob Paediatr 12:332–343, 1975

Beautrais AL, Ferguson DM, Shannon FT: Life events and childhood morbidity: A prospective study. Pediatrics 70:935–940, 1982

Blazer DG: Social support and mortality in an elderly community population. Am J Epidemiol 115:684–694, 1982

Bowen M: Family Therapy in Clinical Practice. New York, Jason Aronson Press, 1978

Calabrese JR, Kling MA, Gold PW: Alterations in immunocompetence during stress, bereavement, and depression: Focus on neuroendocrine regulation, Am J Psychiatry 144:1123–1134, 1987

Carter EA, McGoldrick M: The family life cycle and family therapy: An overview. In Carter EA, McGoldrick M (eds), The Family Life Cycle: A Framework for Family Therapy. New York, Gardner Press, 1980

Cummings N, VandenBos G: The twenty-year Kaiser-Permanente experience with psychotherapy and medical utilization: Implications for national health policy and national health insurance. Health Pol Q 1:159–175, 1981

DeGruy F, Columbia L, Dickinson P: Somatization disorder in a family practice. J Fam Practice 25:45–51, 1987

Doherty WJ, Baird MA: Family Therapy and Family Medicine. New York, Guilford Press, 1983

Engel GL: The need for a new medical model: A challenge for biomedicine. Science 196:129–136, 1977

Fiore J, Becker J, Coppel, DB: Social network interactions: A buffer or a stress? Am J Comm Psychol 11:423–439, 1983

Gerson R, McGoldrick M: Genograms in Family Assessment. New York, WW Norton, 1985

Grey MJ, Genel M, Tamborlane WV: Psychosocial adjustment of latency-age diabetics: Determinants and relationship to control. Pediatrics 65:69–73, 1980

Haley J: Uncommon therapy: The Psychiatric Techniques of Milton H. Erikson, New York, WW Norton, 1973

Holmes TH, Rahe RH: The social readjustment scale. J Psychosom Res 39:413–431, 1967

Kerr ME, Bowen M: Family Evaluation. New York. WW Norton, 1988

Khurana R, White P: Attitudes of the diabetic child and his parents toward his illness. Postgrad Med 48:72–76, 1970

Koski ML, Kumento A: The interrelationship between diabetic control and family life. Ped Adolesc Endocrinol 3:41–45, 1977

Kraus AS, Lillenfeld AM: Some epidemiological aspects of high mortality rate in the young widowed group. J Chronic Dis 10:207–217, 1959

McDaniel S, Campbell TL, Seaburn SB: Family-Oriented Primary Care: A Manual for Medical Providers. New York, Springer-Verlag, 1990

McDaniel SH, Hepworth J, Doherty WJ: Medical Family Therapy. New York, Basic Books, 1992

Meyer RJ, Haggerty RJ: Streptococcal infections in families: Factors altering individual susceptibility. Pediatrics 29:539–549, 1962

Minuchin S, Rosman BL, Baker L: Psychosomatic Families. Cambridge, Harvard University Press, 1978

Moresky DE, Levine DM, Green LW et al: Five-year blood pressure control and mortality following health education for hypertensive patients. Am J Public Health 73:153–162, 1983

Minuchin S, Fishman HC: Family Therapy Techniques. Cambridge, Harvard University Press, 1982

Orr DP, Golden MP, Myers G et al: Characteristics of adolescents with poorly controlled diabetes referred to a tertiary care center. Diab Care 6:170–175, 1983

Rolland J: Chronic illness and the life cycle: A conceptual framework, Fam Proc 26:203–221, 1987

Rolland J: Toward a psychosocial typology of chronic and life-threatening illness. Fam Syst Med 2:245–262, 1984

Shouval R, Ber R, Galatzer A: Family social climate and the health status and social adaptation of diabetic youth. Ped Adolesc Endocrinol 10:89–93, 1982

Stoudemire A: Somatothymia, I and II. Acad Psychosom Med 32:365–381, 1991

US Bureau of the Census: Current Population Survey, No. 406. Washington, DC, US Government Printing Office, 1986

US Department of Health, Education and Welfare: Healthy People: The Surgeon General's Report on Health Promotion and Disease Prevention. DHEW (PHS) Publication No. 79–55071, Public Health Service. Washington, DC, US Government Printing Office, 1979

White K, Kolman ML, Wexler P, et al: Unstable diabetes and unstable families: A psychosocial evaluation of diabetic children with recurrent ketoacidosis. Pediatrics 73:749–755, 1984

Zuckerman DM, Kasl SV, Osterfeld AM: Psychosocial predictors of mortality among the elderly poor: The role of religion, well-being, and social contact. Am J Epidemiol 119:410–423, 1984

Alan Stoudemire (ed). *Human Behavior: An Introduction for Medical Students,*
Second Edition. Copyright © 1994, 1990 by J. B. Lippincott Company.

10 *Adult and Later-Life Development*

Thomas Wolman and Troy L. Thompson II

There is a saying that it "takes a lifetime" to develop into a complete human being. The irony of this remark lies in our "having to give it up just when we have finished the job." However, a healthy lifecycle is, in large part, synonymous with growth and development, and someone who has ceased growing has, in a sense, stopped living optimally. Therefore, one may define mental health as the capacity to adapt to the various developmental tasks that a person encounters over the life span. However, adult development has been one of the most understudied areas of human behavior and, therefore, receives special attention in this text.

The purpose of this chapter is to discuss the adult lifecycle in a manner that is relevant and practical to physicians in the practice of medicine. The events of the adult lifecycle are related to health and illness, particularly focusing on the vulnerable transition points (e.g., choices about marriage, parenthood) where problems are more likely to occur. Bereavement, dying, and death are also discussed in the context of the adult lifecycle.

THE LIFECYCLE

Personal development is the unique path that each person takes through that sequence of milestones called the lifecycle. The lifecycle is a universal template whose features appear to remain generally constant for all people, cultures, and eras. Stages of infancy, childhood, adolescence, courtship, adulthood, marriage, parenting, and old age are universal, and all have phase-specific developmental challenges and opportunities. Traditionally, knowledge about the usual lifecycle patterns has resided in the folk wisdom of each culture. Great literature of all eras, from the Bible to Shakespeare to modern authors, has reflected this knowledge.

In recent times, people have often looked to physicians for advice about problems encountered in lifecycle phases. Until recently, however, physicians were hampered in their patient education and counseling in these areas due to spotty and unsystematized research and knowledge of the specific biological, psychological, and social complexities of each developmental phase. At the turn of the century, even childhood was *terra incognita* as far as systematic and scientifically based knowledge of development was concerned. Freud (1958) and his followers began the exploration of childhood stages of psychological development, and interest in this area has greatly expanded. In the 1960s, researchers, like Mahler (1975), produced the first detailed glimpse into the first 2 years of life. (See Chapter 8 by Dr. Dulcan and Chapter 5 by Drs. Inderbitzen and James) Adolescence also became the subject of much interest, thanks to the pioneering work of psychoanalytic clinicians and researchers like Anna Freud. Nevertheless, Erik Erikson (1963) in his "eight ages of man" paradigm (which is discussed later in this chapter) was the first to view the total lifecycle as a continuum (Table 10–1).

As was mentioned earlier, study of the lifecycle has been skewed toward the early years, mostly encapsulated by infancy on one hand and adolescence on the other. In part, this is a legacy of Freud's hypothesis that the personality is largely "fixed" by the age of 6. Yet, recent autobiographic studies of Freud himself (Anzieu, 1986) underscore the importance of his own midlife crisis in setting him on a course toward the discovery of psychoanalysis. This "distortion toward the young" has been partly overcome by recent studies of aging and adult development (Colarusso and Nemiroff, 1981; Gould, 1972; Levinson et al, 1978; Vaillant, 1977). However, more

Table 10–1 **Erikson's Psychological Stages of the Lifecycle**

	USUAL AGE RANGE	FUNDAMENTAL ISSUES	ROUGH EQUIVALENT	STRENGTHS BASED ON FAVORABLE OUTCOME RATIOS
Stage 1	0–18 mo	Basic trust vs mistrust	Infancy	Drive and hope
Stage 2	18 mo–3½ yr	Autonomy vs shame and doubt	Toddler stage	Self-control and will-power
Stage 3	3½ yr–5 yr	Initiative vs guilt	Oedipal stage	Direction and purpose
Stage 4	5 yr–12 yr	Industry vs inferiority	Latency	Method and competence
Stage 5	12 yr–20 yr	Identity vs role confusion	Adolescence	Devotion and fidelity
Stage 6	20 yr–35 yr	Intimacy vs isolation	Young adulthood	Affiliation and love
Stage 7	35 yr–65 yr	Generativity vs stagnation	Maturity	Production and care
Stage 8	65 yr and up	Ego integrity vs despair	Old age	Reconciliation and sense of integrity

(Adapted from Erikson EH: Childhood and Society, New York, WW Norton, 1963)

research is needed in many developmental areas and processes. For example, differences between males and females, heterosexuals and homosexuals, socioeconomic groups, and many other groups would be important information to use in patient care.

NEW DEVELOPMENTAL CONCEPTS

The Triad of Stage, Transition, and Normative Crisis

Life change may unfold through a typical sequence of preparation (a transitional period), rapid change (such as may occur with a normal developmental step or normative crisis), consolidation (the achievement of a new life stage), and "plateauing." Such a formula helps to organize an approach to the lifecycle, provided it is not taken too literally. For example, adolescence (or any other period) may be viewed in part as a *normative crisis*, as a *transition*, and as a *stage*. One of the important discoveries of recent years is that healthy psychological change and development may proceed on different paths and at variable rates (Table 10–2).

Table 10–2 **Psychological Developmental Concepts**

CONCEPT	BRIEF DEFINITION	EXAMPLES
Transition	Bridge or junction between successive stages	Late adolescence Courtship Midlife transition
"Limbo state"	A "sticking" point in development, usually at the transition between two stages	Pseudo-adulthood (prolonged adolescence) Prolonged courtship
Rite of passage	Social ritual that facilitates a transition	Graduation Marriage Funerals
Normative crisis	Period of rapid change and/or turmoil that strains person's adaptive capacity	Childbirth Midlife crisis Marital crisis
"Normal illness"	Hybrid state with features of both an illness and a normative crisis	Pregnancy Maternal preoccupation Bereavement
Stage	Period of consolidation of skills and capacities	Early adulthood Mature adulthood
Plateau	Period of developmental stability	Adulthood up to midlife
Developmental lines	Independent course of development of a particular skill or capacity	Love Work Play
Delay/precocity	Variations in the timing of developmental lines	Precocious adulthood "Late bloomer"
Regression	Temporary retrograde vector in development	Revival of adolescence or childhood attitudes and behaviors in midlife
Repetition	Reworking and reliving all or part of previous stage(s)	The second separation-individuation crisis of young adulthood/late adolescence

Stages

Most research on the human lifecycle, from Erikson onward, divides the developmental continuum into discrete *stages*. Each stage is characterized by its own specific tasks, conflicts, and viewpoints. Some stages, such as those of childhood, maturity, and old age, are universal; others, such as those of the age 30 and age 40 transition, are more culture dependent. Stages indicate periods of relative developmental stability in which considerable time is spent on age-specific tasks; these are periods of *consolidation of skills* rather than of rapid change.

Transitions

A more specialized period of transition is needed to bridge the wide gulf between the demands of successive stages (Levinson et al, 1978). People require time to get used to new demands, challenges, and outlooks. At the same time, they need the time to consider what to relish and what to relinquish from earlier periods. Most people make a transition of a different type every evening as they prepare themselves for sleep. Reverie and hypnagogic imagery are transitional states between conscious thinking and sleep and dreaming.

Transitional states are like vehicles that carry the person from one stage to another. Rites of passage (or rituals), such as cadaver dissection and dog laboratories for medical students and internship for house staff officers, perform the same function in a social context (Van Gennep, 1960). They help to concretize the change, giving it a sort of external scaffolding and making it feel more real to the participants. In addition, transitional states act to allay the anxiety of the person and of the group, for whom change always represents some degree of threat.

The Normative Crisis

The rate of change may vary considerably throughout life and almost everyone is familiar with the experience of overwhelming changes that strain their capacity to adapt. One can define a normative crisis as any period in the lifecycle whose chief characteristic is *turmoil*. This turmoil can result from external factors, such as illness or misfortune, or it can result from internal conflicts between opposing alternatives: self versus others, freedom versus bondage, and living versus dying. In many "crises," childbirth for example, external and internal factors coexist.

The Normative Crisis in Health and Illness

In our culture, individuals sometimes tend to define a normative crisis as a symptom of an illness. In the past, physicians have contributed to this trend, most notably in their attitudes toward pregnancy. An important task of today's physicians is in helping their patients reinterpret what is normative versus what is truly pathological. At times, this may mean some physicians' revision of some of their attitudes toward developmental blocks, obstacles, plateaus, doldrums, and even reversals.

It may even be a good exercise to try to reinterpret the "obviously" pathologic as if it were a normative crisis. Doing so serves to place the illness inside the more manageable framework of the lifecycle, thus allowing greater adaptation and assimilation of what seems alien. For example, symptoms of anxiety in young adults may be interpreted in the context of some expected difficulties in leaving the parental home.

Promiscuity in a middle-aged man may be a sign of the midlife crisis. Some mild depression in parents would be considered normal after their children's departure for college (the so-called empty nest syndrome).

On the other hand, the physician also needs to be knowledgeable about particularly vulnerable points in the lifecycle—those points that can more easily trigger actual illness. The transitional periods are particularly important in this regard: Adolescence has been frequently associated with the onset of schizophrenia and the midlife period with severe depression. Transitions can sometimes become prolonged into "limbo states," where people languish indefinitely, postponing the process of further growth.

Lines

Development is not a unilateral process. It is less like a single, uniform mass, and more like an army advancing along a broad front in a series of uneven "columns" or "lines." Each developmental line (love, work, play) acts like an independent unit and proceeds at its own pace (Freud, 1963). Consequently, any line(s) may be considerably out of phase with others. The same person can be advancing rapidly in some areas, retreating in others, and remaining stationary in still others.

Timing

This implies that development proceeds according to a person's own timetable. There is a certain fixed order to the stages and general age ranges for each, but these must not be interpreted too literally. There is an innate rhythm to each person's development which, unless extreme, should usually not be hurried or imposed upon by external factors. Each new stage is a challenge and a potential obstacle. It is best to reject fixed notions of the course of development as largely illusory. *Normal development is not synonymous with uniform forward progress; nor does it reach a peak at some predetermined point, followed by a rapid downhill course or shift toward another stage.*

There is considerable variation in rate of normal development. *Delay* and *precocity* (precocious behavior) are typical examples. Normative bias may prompt one to ask what is wrong in all cases of delay. But, in many cases, delay is simply a function of the unique rhythm of that person's growth curve. Folk wisdom recognizes this in the expression "late bloomer." For example, some people have a desire to "settle down" and have children in their 20s; others may not have this focus until their 30s, and still others may not resolve the issue about whether to have children until their 40s.

Similarly, there is a tendency to view precocity as superiority. Yet, cases are known in which precocity is followed by later failure. Precocity may mean that a particular stage or line of development has been shortchanged and needs to be reworked at a future time. The child who functions with adult maturity may be masking childhood needs that will resurface in some form at a later date.

Regression

During development, the person may appear to take "two steps forward and then one step backward" (i.e., regress in some area). *Regression refers to the revival of earlier and more childlike behavior and coping strategies in response to stress.* It is an expected feature of most normative crises and transitions. For example, most people are familiar with the child who begins to act more like a baby after the arrival of a new sibling. Yet, they sometimes forget that parents tend to regress under the same circumstances. The father, for example, may be secretly nursing a jealous grudge against the new baby for monopolizing his wife's attention, as he also may have done *vis-à-vis* his own mother when one of his younger siblings was born. The mother may also have increased dependency needs to be cared for and nurtured herself as she nurtures her own baby.

Repetition

People tend to underestimate the extent to which repetition is built into the lifecycle. Also, periodic "lulls and plateaus" may be as intrinsic to the lifecycle as rapid spurts of development. But, to the person caught in one of these doldrums, the reality is that "he or she is not getting anywhere." Only careful assessment can determine whether the complaint indicates a normal degree of pause or if it represents a "sticking point" requiring intervention.

One adaptive aspect of repetition is the opportunity it affords to rework tasks and conflicts of earlier eras, particularly those of separation-individuation. In optimal cases, this amounts to a second chance at development through greater mastery of previously highly conflicted issues. Psychotherapy attempts to facilitate this "second chance." Because it is stressful to talk about and, thereby, partially reexperience and focus upon conflicted issues, psychotherapy generally is also associated with some transient regression.

Transitional periods, in a sense, look backward as well as forward, in a kind of Janus, or double-faced, posture. *Transitions reflect the developmental need to reassess, rethink, reexperience, and rework the past,* while planning for the future. Only in retrospect can one generally see the positive aspects of a lull or get a new perspective on a period of rapid life change that seemed to be a blur at the time. Perhaps this is why adult stages of development have been relatively neglected until recently. Most of those doing scholarly research on the lifecycle are immersed themselves in a middle-age, life-stage plateau, and it is generally much more difficult to look carefully and critically at one's self than at others.

Erikson's Eight Ages of Man

Erik Erikson's model of human development (Erikson, 1963) laid the foundation for later lifecycle studies. Erikson divided the lifecycle into eight discrete, well-defined stages. Each stage is characterized by a specific task, usually a fundamental one that affects multiple life sectors. His "eight ages of man" (see Table 10–1) shows an underlying order in the lifecycle in a simple format, and its simplicity makes it a valuable tool for organizing life experience. For example, the first stage, *basic trust*, applies to all human relationships, self-confidence, and even religious faith. The pairing of each task fulfillment with its potential failure, or problems remaining within it, circumscribes a range of possible outcomes.

Each stage is a link in the chain of life. This has been called the *epigenetic* approach (i.e., the initiation and success of a new stage is partly dependent on the degree of successful negotiation of previous stages). The image of the chain empha- sizes the continuity of life. *Failure* is defined as development of a weak link or a break in the chain. Consequently, it implies that childhood lays the foundation for adulthood. However, success with basic mastery of childhood stages carries proportionately more weight in determining the probability of later successful development. Also, failure or major problems early on tend to be less reversible and to cause broader-ranging difficulties than problems that develop later in life.

The merits of Erikson's approach also determine its limitations. It is a sketch of development, not a detailed blueprint. His divisions are too broad to do total justice to the subtleties of an individual's life. They also may be too uniform to suggest the markedly different paths, lines of development, and rates of change that frequently occur in people's lives. The adult stages also seem relatively meager in number and in substance. Occupation, for example, is not mentioned at all. Many of these "deficien- cies" can be mitigated by viewing the adult stages as *midpoints* of the multiple other stages of development. By taking into account all related stages, each adult stage appears more comprehensive. Each adult stage also takes on added significance when it is viewed in the light of the quest for an individual's personal identity.

Identity and the Lifecycle

Erikson (1959) saw the lifecycle as a lifelong quest to achieve a coherent *personal identity*. By identity, he meant an inner sense of "sameness" or developing continuity of a "solid core sense of your goals and values" in the midst of change. Erikson was the first to affirm the importance of a sense of identity for success and happiness as a human being. A stable sense of identity is both a prerequisite for and an outcome of successful development. But even with a strong foundation in the early years, the sense of a stable personal identity can never be taken for granted. It is always a precarious achievement, liable to be upset or even overturned by the vicissitudes of change, such as a personal illness or external circumstances. Every normative crisis threatens to disrupt the ongoing sense of identity. The successful negotiation of adult stages requires extensive psychological reworking, adaptation, and integration. Every- one is periodically challenged to rework, revise, and reorient former ideas of whom he or she was, is, and wants to become; those who are able to do so as needed and to adapt accordingly have the highest degree of mental health and happiness. (The develop- ment of personal identity in the context of overall family development is also dis- cussed by Dr. Fiore in Chapter 9.)

The childhood stages contribute to people's first sketch of their own identity and sense of self. *Basic trust* gives children the conviction that they belong in this world and have a right to exist in their own right. It forms the fundamental basis of how one responds to others and expects others to respond. The stage of *autonomy* works in the other direction by helping the child learn that it is acceptable at times to say "no" to others' wishes and demands, and that, in part, *people define themselves by what they oppose as well as by what they value and support*. The stage of *initiative* fixes the first blueprint of identity through the activities with which each person selects to be involved, and often relates to the parental ideals. *Industry* helps to consolidate and expand the new sense of self by learning that hard work tends to pay off and that identification with a peer group is important, both by being supportive and pleasurable.

The transition to young adulthood (Erikson's stage of *identity consolidation versus role diffusion*) poses the first major challenge to identity for some people. The range and intensity of life changes during young adulthood may peak and severely strain the established psychological structure. Also, the biological vulnerability to onset of schizophrenia appears to peak in late adolescence and the early 20s. Therefore, during this time a person becomes more vulnerable to more severe breakdowns in identity, including the extreme of psychosis. But given some measure of success in the early stages, the person may be able to tolerate or postpone aspects of the chaos of multiple changes long enough for reintegrative psychological forces to "catch up." Erikson calls the postponement of adult commitments to allow more time to rethink and gradually address changes a *moratorium.*

Early adulthood initiates the process of forging a new adult identity from the fragments of adolescent flux. Accomplishing this goal often amounts to a major reorientation, a revolution, if you will, in the self-concept. The new structure must reconcile the competing claims of dependency, craving for autonomy, sexuality, and body image changes. Old attachments will have to be relinquished or preserved with modifications. New commitments have to be entered into, at first tentatively, and later definitively in the stage of intimacy.

The stage of *generativity* ushers in a further modification and expansion of adult identity. The life space widens to include the next generation; there is an identification with the parental role in the broadest sense. Individuals redefine their own contributions as a "passing of the torch" to their potential heirs. The need for bold self-assertion usually lessens. Occasionally, this new orientation is incorporated into a "mission" or life's work that results in an increased focus and enhanced productivity, optimally produced from a playful creativity and a renewed partnership with others. In the full sense, generativity connotes a confluence of love, work, play, and identity.

The completion of one's identity is the task of late life, and Erikson labeled this the stage of *ego integrity versus despair.* Integrity implies a feeling of self-worth associated with a final self-reconciliation. Seeing one's life as a whole highlights a person's achievements as well as disappointments and failures. Integrity is based on an awareness of the limits of any human life, and it is often hard to face these limits and to let go of one's omnipotence once and for all. But this final work of "delimitation" can also bring about a sense of underlying meaning, order, and uniqueness to the person's life. A process of reworking issues associated with each earlier stage occurs during each life stage in the context of the demands, opportunities, and limitations of the new stage, including the ultimate limitation of death (see Table 10–2).

THE STAGES OF ADULTHOOD

The Transition to Adulthood

After the initial period of adolescent flux, young people initiate their first tentative movement toward adulthood (Table 10–3). The transitional identity of student or apprentice teaches them the background skills, without committing them

Table 10–3 **Some Postinfancy Aspects of Psychologic Stages in the Lifecycle**

STAGE	TRANSITIONAL ISSUES	RITE OF PASSAGE	SYMPTOMS OF CRISIS	PATHOLOGIC OUTCOME
Transitions before adulthood	Novice, student, apprentice	School matriculation	School or work phobia	Agoraphobia
Consolidation of adulthood	New title	Graduation	Repeated career changes	"Pseudo-adult"
Courtship	Experimentation	Dating, "trial marriage"	Premature or delayed commitment	Schizoid character, precocious adult
Transition to marriage	"Contract" with spouse	Marriage ceremony	Boredom or constant warfare	Separation or divorce
Pregnancy	Physical changes, "new space"	Baby "shower," childbirth education classes	Hypochondriasis, detachment	Denial or pseudocyesis
Childbirth	Pregnancy	Labor and delivery	Excessive anxiety: prepartum and during labor	Postpartum depression
Parenting	Primary maternal preoccupation, "holding"	Naming ceremony	Marital unrest, developmental delay in child	Parental deprivation or overstimulation of child
Midlife transition	Mourning, loss of youth	"40th birthday," midlife crisis	Withdrawal, sudden life change	Depression, substance abuse
Transition to old age	Repository of cultural values	Retirement, illness, death of spouse and friends	Regression, "King Lear" complex	Depression, pseudodementia

to full responsibility (Levinson et al, 1978; Levinson and Goodeneh, 1985). In this guise, they can allow themselves the freedom to be experimental—to try out various roles. Such playful exploration is normative for a transitional stage and does not necessarily imply a lack of ability to focus and of perseverance.

The tasks of young adults are consistent with their transitional role of "novice" or learner. Several of these tasks merit consideration:

1. The relationship to the parents must undergo substantial modification. The old childhood dependence on the parents must be given up and replaced by a more mature partnership with them. One is not free to make strong future attachments while old ones are still totally in place. Moreover, one cannot feel truly independent while holding on to the idea that a parental figure will always be there to help put things right. Such magical expectations undermine the motivation to accept personal responsibility and to develop adult initiative.

2. The identity of "student" or "novice" serves as a helpful transition to mature mutuality (i.e., two adults interacting as each other's equals). The relationship of mentor to pupil includes some of the old parent–child dependent qualities. Some of the issues can be seen in the personal and professional development of medical students. Medical students understandably often complain of their passive position in the learning process: the long lectures, the hours of memorizing, the examinations—in short, their relative lack of control and initiative. On the other hand, the professor or mentor hopefully helps to model a more active and independent stance. Students may be progressively more encouraged to take their own positions and ask their own questions, such as in small group discussions, to develop their own approaches to situations, to design their own projects, and to be responsible for their own learning.

3. Identification with the mentor both fuels and modifies young people's idealism. In this context, they elaborate this identification into dreams for their future and later into more articulated adult aspirations (Levinson et al, 1978). Idealism helps to bridge the gap between childhood fantasies and adult hopes and aspirations. Early childhood fantasies are modified and, in part, incorporated into the new adult identity. Continuity is thus maintained between past and future. Keeping this in mind guards against the tendency of some adults to discourage or dismiss youthful idealism merely because it is unrealistic or rebellious in tone.

4. Studenthood is more specifically the transition to an occupation. It is a time of intense preparatory learning, during which students are protected from the full weight of responsibility for their performance. They can "try out" the work under supervision and in progressively larger doses. Normally, there is an atmosphere of tolerance of student's needs to experiment with different styles,

techniques, and roles, regardless of the inconsistencies these shifts may appear to entail. Possibly more disruptive, but still under the rubric of experimentation, is the tendency to go from one job to another, or one passionate interest to another.

5. The same bent for experimentation often rules the attempts to establish intimate relationships. There may be a prolonged period of "playing the field" or a series of "trial relationships." It must be borne in mind that success and happiness in relationships requires a period of learning as well. The peer group, as well as knowledge and fantasies about what the parents' early relationship was like, may provide the equivalence of mentorship in this area. Notions about the ideal mate must be tested against reality. Views about sexuality and love must be explored in the "laboratory" of a real relationship.

"Sticking Points" and Failures in Early Adult Development

Problems in early adulthood are often associated with delay in initiating adult tasks, and by far the most frequent cause for these delays is the failure to relinquish and separate from the parents. Such failures are often brought to the attention of the physician in the form of anxiety or depressive symptoms. College students in their first year away from home are virtually all grappling to some degree with separation-individuation issues. This process recapitulates many aspects of separation-individuation discussed in Chapter 5 and Chapter 8 that is part of early childhood development. For example, a student's "school phobia" may screen a more profound yearning for the parental home and grief and mourning over losing the daily contact and support from their parents, siblings, and home. The physician can often be helpful in bringing out the underlying depression and grief, and in helping students adjust to their separation from home. Sometimes a period of regression is necessary, during which the student may move back home for a while; frequent but brief trips back and forth from school to home also can be recommended to permit emotional "refueling" to decrease the strain of abrupt separation and allow more time for the individuation process to progress.

The young person who fails entirely to leave home may present physicians with a somewhat more difficult problem. Such persons may also have failed to initiate dating or job seeking. Their school phobia may have worsened into agoraphobia. Paradoxically, an escalation of their symptoms may also signal the alarm they increasingly feel in being isolated and removed from the mainstream of others their age. Often, it is the parents who bring these young people to medical attention out of concern that the symptom is exacerbating and perpetuating the young person's dependency, which, of course, it is designed to do. The literal fact of living at home is less important than the inner emotional attachment to the parents. An occasional young person can be living in the parental home past the age of 30 and still possess a clear sense of personal independence. In contrast, others may live thousands of miles away, yet be very tied to their parents and locked in unresolved, conflicted relationships with them. In the latter case, geographic distance becomes an attempted substitute for the emotional distance that cannot be achieved by other means.

The "Pseudo-Adult"

At times, the attachment to the parents, and to the world of childhood in general, leads to a kind of temporal dissociation, instead of to delay. Such persons feel that they can "have their cake and eat it, too." They may fabricate an adult "false self," while still maintaining their true internal identity as a child who never grows up. This condition has been dubbed the Peter Pan syndrome (Kiley, 1983), from the popular childhood story of a mythical boy who never had to grow up. In terms of the lifecycle, the pseudo-adult is stuck in a limbo—a "never, neverland," if you will—between childhood and adulthood. This syndrome often first becomes apparent in individuals in their 30s.

A CASE STUDY

Mr. N, a charming and moderately successful artist in his mid-30s, presented to a psychiatrist with symptoms of dissatisfaction with his marriage. Although talented, he had a formidable psychological block against advancing his career. His Peter Pan identity allowed him to work well under conditions of play, but he rebelled when it came to keeping a regular work schedule and to attending to the bookkeeping and business aspects of his work. He loved to think up new ideas but hated the work necessary to implement them. The same basic problem plagued him in his marriage: He could not stand the idea of having to work and compromise with his spouse to resolve the inevitable conflicts associated with a long-term, intimate relationship. In effect, he was going through the motions of being an adult without putting his heart and soul into it. And yet, he found that he could easily fool others with his act; many marveled at his "togetherness." This reinforced his secret wish to have it both ways: success in the adult world without ever having to grow up.

Precocious Adulthood

For some, the problem is not one of attachment, but rather of precocious autonomy and independence. As children, these persons typically detached themselves from dependence on their parents at a relatively young age. In some instances, they may have resorted to "self-parenting" as a result of parental deprivation, including having parents who were not able to play joyfully with the child to teach the child the pleasure of relationships and that fun and playing are not just for kids. Others may have had workaholic parents and felt deprived of a parent's loving and playful attention. In other cases, they may have been allocated the role of "parental child" and been delegated the task of taking care of younger siblings, grandparents, or others. But regardless of etiology, their precocity would seem to obviate any need for a transition to adulthood—they are already there. What is missing in them is their childhood "roots." They are often perceived by others as highly competent and responsible, but at the same time as stilted and as lifeless as robots. Their resemblance to automatons is based on an early identification with an ideal of total self-reliance and a lack of ability to be relaxed and playful.

Some of these individuals exhibit a pressured and almost manic pursuit of their goals and ideals, to the exclusion of any reflection or self-awareness. So immersed are they in life's externals that their inner life is stillborn; they never developed an appreciation of relaxation and playfulness as a catalytic aspect of being creatively alive. They often become the adult workaholic, who perpetuates this pattern by treating their own children as they were treated when they themselves were small. This flight into constant activity may carry them along for a surprising length of time, but they are at risk of a traumatic midlife crisis, including ultimate alienation from their children and friends, and an old age filled with loneliness, regret, and despair.

Others with this type of precocity develop a schizoid indifference to interpersonal life. One such patient presented at the age of 34 with the chief complaint of never having been physical or emotionally intimate with a single person, man or woman. In a way, he was bothered more by what other people thought about this than by personal distress, yet he had some degree of awareness that an important sector of life that is meaningful and enjoyable for many others was passing him by.

The Consolidation of Adulthood

In favorable circumstances, young adults reach a point when they can say, "Now I am a man (or woman)" (Blos, 1967). This stage of consolidation of adult personal and occupational identity usually occurs around the age of 30 (Vaillant, 1977) and may be associated with the so-called age 30 crisis (Gould, 1972). (This was typified by the crises of the characters of the recent television program, "thirtysomething.") It may have gradually evolved out of a variety of components, or it may have "crystallized" with some degree of abruptness. In some cases, the crisis does not come without some measure of inner struggle over the new "fixity" of adulthood, its associated commitments, and the loss of other options.

Recently, the term consolidation has become almost synonymous with the consolidation of occupational or professional identity; this is due, in part, to the central role that work plays in modern life (Simons, 1985). Increasingly, some have come to see work not as something they *do* but as something they *are*. For many, it has become more of "a calling" than "a job." Conversely, people whose work is "only a job" may feel a need to find their "real life's work." People who are failures at their work are sometimes considered failures in life. Accordingly, work has become a kind of microcosm of life. In addition to income, some look to work to provide them their sense of status, self-esteem, productivity, creative outlet, as well as social life, friendly collaborations, and even their "subculture" (the corporate or professional culture). Many workaholic physicians fall into this category. Retirement, especially if forced, may be a major stress for such individuals.

The rite of passage into true adulthood sometimes involves a type of graduation or certification *ritual;* this confers upon students a new title or name, which formalizes their new identity as well as cancels their old student identity. While important in this regard, graduation has also become more of a public recognition of a *fait accompli*. It is intended to give official, public recognition to what has already been accomplished, sometimes largely in private.

Medical students may provide an example in this regard. If one asks medical students at the beginning of their second or third year how they prefer to be addressed, the majority will answer, "as a medical student, Mr., Ms., and so forth." If one asks them the same question again in the fourth year, many will say "Student Doctor" and some will say "Doctor." At some point in the fourth year, the student will start "living up" to that title. They will start thinking and acting much more like a physician than like an earlier-year medical student. And the moment these students start making their own patient care decisions, the less they will need others to tell them what to do, and they will begin to look on others more as consultants. Their newfound feelings of basic competence as a physician may produce a sense of euphoria and power. At this time they can begin to expand their sense of their work to include a sense of playfulness and relaxation at appropriate times and a sense of mastery.

A CASE STUDY

Dr. G, a young resident physician, presented to a psychiatrist with complaints of extreme anxiety over the performance of medical procedures. Lately, he had started to ask consultants to do this type of work for him. He felt so ashamed over this state of affairs that he actively considered abandoning his medical career. After a period of psychotherapeutic work, Dr. G related this fear to the image of a punishing father. His father had often been quite critical of and detached from him, while his mother had been more understanding and supportive. He vividly recalled making rounds with his father, who was a veterinarian, and witnessing the castration of numerous farm animals. In effect, he had integrated the "maternal" aspects of being a doctor, but not the "paternal," as those were represented in his family. He was a responsible physician who cared for his patients and worked hard on their behalf. But his inability to integrate the degree of "intrusiveness and aggressiveness" that is needed to complete some medical tasks into his image of himself was holding up his adult consolidation as a comprehensive physician. The resolution of his "age 30 crisis" involved some rapprochement between aspects of both parents.

The Triad of Courtship, Marriage, and Marital Crisis

Courtship

Courtship is part of the transition to a committed partnership, often signified by marriage, in the same sense that student status is part of the transition to an adult occupation. In the former, the focus is "pair identity," while in the latter, it is an individual matter. Temporally, the stages of early adulthood and courtship usually parallel each other, and issues of intimacy occupy both. In courtship, its achievement is defined as the formation of a couple.

In American culture, dating functions as a rite of passage into the courtship stage. Its main function is to bring the young person into contact with the pool of possible marital partners. Young adults sometimes express the wish to bypass this process, complaining of the artificiality of the rituals involved. Nevertheless, some artificiality is a facet of all rituals and must be borne to some degree. The absence of dating in an adult's life history is virtually always significant. It may signal a delay in the courtship phase, or it may indicate that those stages were skipped, as in premature marriage.

Recently, it has become more common to have what was the stereotyped "honeymoon" precede the marriage. "Trial marriage" or "living together" has become an accepted part of courtship in most Western industrial societies. Optimally, living together might function as a laboratory for the exploration of what the realities of marriage would be for the couple. In practice, however, this does not always occur. When the "honeymoon" precedes the marriage, there is sometimes postponement of consideration of the more contractual aspects of couplehood until after marriage.

Recently, courtship in American society, sometimes progresses into a kind of "limbo" that does not lead to the transition to marriage. For some couples, courtship may then become a prolonged honeymoon or an indefinite extension of dating. Other couples choose to live together like roommates, out of convenience or friendship, keeping their romantic liaisons outside the relationship. A tendency to progressively split the romantic from the contractual aspects of the couple may continue into or develop in some marriages, sometimes resulting in stress and possibly divorce, despite years of preparatory living together, in some cases.

Marriage

Naturally, the psychological formation of a "couple" does not always coincide with the marriage ceremony. Some couples form a solid partnership well in advance of their marriage, other couples do not crystallize until some time after their marriage, and still others are effectively "divorced" before they are married. Nevertheless, most couples go through some type of postcourtship transition to the married state.

Marriage takes for granted a certain degree of personal maturity in both partners. Ideally, each of them should be capable of seeing the other as a whole, separate person with his or her own life and viewpoints. Each must be able to tolerate the good and the bad in the other, as reflected in the phrase "for better or for worse" that is frequently used in marital vows. And each must be able to empathize with (and not be overly threatened or annoyed by) the other's positions, even when they conflict with his or her own. In short, the partners will hopefully have acquired a sense of their own identity and self-worth as separate persons and the capacity to appreciate the same characteristics in others.

But some couples start married life before the partners have consolidated their own adult identities, and they may unconsciously decide to continue some model of infantile or adolescent dependence on each other. This kind of symbiosis can be mutually reinforcing in a way that may prevent an evolution of the relationship to more mature levels. Other couples feel so threatened by the new level of intimacy of their married state that their precarious coalition is vulnerable to decompose into two warring individuals.

Both the symbiotic couple and the "warring couple" lack clear boundaries between the partners. In the symbiotic couple, the partners function as "auxiliaries" for undeveloped aspects of each other. The warring couples are so threatened by defusion of boundaries that they must resort to opposition to reinforce and clarify those boundaries. The more exaggerated the differences in their positions, the easier it is to see and to grasp their separate identities. The partners in the latter type of couple may have too much privacy, just as in the symbiotic type the partners may not have enough, to facilitate further growth. Neither type possesses the basis for a mature partnership between equals.

One solution to these problems may be contained in the marriage ceremony itself, which is a rite of passage to transform two separate people into a new couple. The device that unites the pair is a simple contract. It is important to emphasize that *marriage is a formal arrangement imposed on the couple by society*. The contractual features are evident in several ways. First, there are *legalistic* trappings: the official representative of society (e.g., priest, rabbi, judge), the exchange of explicit vows, the presence of witnesses, and the finality of a signed document. Second, there is the almost arbitrary conventionality of the *quid pro quo* formula: one thing in return for another.

Discussion concerning the marital "contract" offers the couple a framework for holding together and for not just being an individual. We can look on it as a piece of scaffolding that can be discarded once the partnership is in place. In this sense, it is a transitional "vehicle" between the individual and the couple—a connecting link between the individual agendas. With the contractual *quid pro quo* in hand, the partners can begin to negotiate agreements over the entire range of their shared lives, including family finances, sexual etiquette, conflict resolution, allocation of privacy— even who sleeps on which side of the bed.

An especially thorny issue may be the question of the household division of labor. Traditionally, this matter was decided along the lines of stereotyped sexual roles. Now the couple must first decide where they stand on the sex role continuum before task allocation per se. Some successful marriages opt for a complete reversal of traditional sex roles, while others stay with the more traditional arrangement; still others occupy a middle ground.

At some point in the process of working out these issues, the partners may recognize a renewed sense of mutuality based on working together as equals. They may see that working together validates their separateness at the same time that it draws them closer together. The partnership is now the property of the couple and no longer something imposed by society. The framework of the contract helped them to discover a new mode of creative collaboration in which their different perspectives may play off each other with creative and novel results. Several of these may be an enriched sexual experience, a readiness for new ventures, and a vital miniculture of shared history and values.

Marital Crisis

It is quite common for physicians to encounter patients whose hidden or overt agenda is a marital crisis or a failing marriage. The patient may want the physician's permission to exit a moribund marriage. Or he or she may want the spouse to be "treated"—in other words, "brought into line." Or it may be the spouse who wants the patient "treated." The clue to the underlying situation is often revealed when, inevitably, the spouse is drawn into the discussions. If physicians fail to see the hidden agenda, they may unwittingly develop an unfruitful alliance with the patient that supports a bad marriage. (Family systems theory, family therapy techniques, and the physician's role in the referral process are also discussed in Chapter 9.)

We have discussed several ways in which the transition to the married state may result in turmoil for the couple; the forces of individuation may threaten to tear apart a fragile alliance. A crisis may occur whenever new conditions place excessive strain on the old arrangements, so a crisis will be most likely during a transitional period, such as childbirth, parenting, and the "empty nest syndrome." A crisis is more likely if the development of the marriage is out of synchrony with that of the partners. Many marriages have lasted 7 to 10 years before one or both of the partners has reached maturity as adults and become established in occupations or professions. When individuals go beyond their spouse's sphere of understanding and experience, they may begin to feel bored and constrained within an outmoded arrangement. For example, occupational success can throw the previous "contract" out of kilter.

A crisis may be preceded by a prodromal period during which signs of trouble are ignored. The increasing turmoil may make itself felt as tension and fighting—or the reverse: excessive calm, boredom, and withdrawal. Sometimes a full-blown crisis is necessary as a "wake-up call" that something is wrong. When this is recognized, the partners may be able to spell out their dissatisfactions to each other and begin a process of reformulation of their marriage contract.

However, such a reconciliation process is often complicated by the tendency toward regression that marks any crisis. In the context of the couple, this usually means a return to "nonpair" ways of relating. The prototypic example is a reversion to mutual blaming. In the first round of many marital squabbles, each partner wants to blame the other for the problem. Instead of viewing the problem in pair terms, he or she sees it primarily as the other person's responsibility. Frequently, there follows an escalation of blaming during which the pair revives many of their past conflicts and shortcomings.

Couples who already have an established pattern of fighting may be especially vulnerable at this point. Such a couple is usually unable to resolve a major crisis without professional help, because they have great difficulty recovering their "pair perspective." Spouse abuse is an ominous sign of such a deteriorating situation in "fighting" couples. If they can recover their couple perspective, they face the task of reassessing and then restructuring their marriage. They may have to renegotiate the old agreements from scratch. At best, they will have to substantially modify past agreements.

Although marital crises often occur at fairly specific points in the adult lifecycle, such as after childbirth, at midlife, and during the "empty nest" phase, it would be erroneous to view the developmental line of most marriages as a long period of stagnation due to latent conflict followed by an explosive climax. There is a unique evolution of every latent conflict. But in a healthy marriage there is usually a dynamic sequence of growth, plateauing, stagnation, reassessment, and new growth. The time frame for some of these phases may be years, months, or occasionally, just weeks.

The Role of Counseling and Psychotherapy

Even a normative crisis may carry significant risks. For example, the high rate of divorce (about half of all marriages) reflects the inherent instability associated with marital crises as much as it does the pathological aspects of a marriage and the changing mores of society. Thus, it is quite natural and wise for an individual or a couple to look for outside professional help when they see no other way out of their difficulties. When the couple can no longer mediate effectively between themselves, society can provide them with an outside mediator. The external mediator is, in a sense, a new version of society's official representative who married them in the first place. This role can be filled by any person in authority: a religious leader, physician (ultimately, often a psychiatrist), other mental health counselor, or even lawyers and a divorce court judge.

If the couple has never really learned how to negotiate, the psychiatrist or other psychotherapist may begin teaching them this art. One entire style of marriage therapy—aptly called "contract therapy"—does just this (Sholevar, 1981). However, with most couples, it is more a question of restarting a stalled negotiation. The first step may be a search for a new area of compromise. Each partner may need help in articulating his or her position, or in refraining from attack and counterattack. Most of all, they need encouragement to keep talking. In acting as a mediator, the psychotherapist must be careful to remain in the middle. The partners will usually try to draw him or her to their side as an ally, or to do their talking for them. (This phenomenon is also known as "triangulation" and is discussed in Chapter 9.) The psychotherapist gently deflects all such invitations away from himself or herself and back into discussion between the partners. Similarly, the psychotherapist discourages them from using other people, including children and in-laws, for the same purpose. The psychotherapist thus tries to stabilize the couple's coalition by decreasing use of outside coalitions that may undermine it.

Alternatives to Traditional Marriage and Parenting

The previous section discussed the fact that collaborative partnerships are not an invariable outcome of marriage. Many marriages endure despite the absence of any true alliance. And many viable partnerships develop outside the confines of traditional marriages into stable, long-term relationships. Also, nonmarital types of collaborative partnerships in our society include working partnerships, the psychotherapeutic alliance between therapist and patient, and community and religious networks.

Hence, there is some justification for the reverse assumption, namely that the establishment of a collaborative partnership produces a "marriage." Increasingly, our society has come to recognize a relationship as "binding" when there is public evidence of the existence of a partnership. This broader definition might include common-law marriages and homosexual marriages. In this context, "marriage" is a metaphor for any dedicated, supraindividual relationship. However, the "other party" to this relationship is not necessarily limited to one special person. Emotionally, a person may feel "married" to a collection of persons, a group/organization, a life's work, a political cause, or even God, as exemplified in some religious rituals and communities.

Parenting may sometimes also supply the raison d'être for such a "marriage." In examining the wide variations in parenting at all levels of society, many family studies have demonstrated the importance of collaboration for family development. They have defined collaboration according to three criteria: (1) A division of parental function between the role of a "mother"- and a "father"-type figure, (2) some degree of recognition and representation of differences in the parental roles, and (3) a barrier against crossgenerational alliances, and of incest, in particular (Sholevar, 1981). (See also Chapter 9.)

According to these criteria, many situations that were previously considered exceptions to the traditional model of parenting may prove quite capable of raising healthy families. Many successful families make effective use of surrogate parents, and in single-parent families, the role of surrogate may be played by a grandparent, uncle/ aunt, or friend. Other families distribute the roles of mother and father among several people; this method is present in the Israeli kibbutz and is typical of extended families and of postdivorce merged families. In homosexual parenting arrangements, the parental roles are divided between persons of the same sex. Such arrangements may be successful and usually there will be some differentiation between the two parent's roles. A third method uses the new institutions of day care, professional baby-sitters, and neighborhood networks to provide "auxiliary parents." It is common for single-parent families to call on all three methods at various times and settings. Even in so-called "matriarchal" families, the place of the "missing" parent is often occupied by a symbolic figure, such as a socially positive influence (e.g., the local minister, principal) or, unfortunately at times, an antisocial figure (e.g., neighborhood criminal, drug dealer).

It is this view of marriage (i.e., the formation of a collaborative partnership)—and this point cannot be emphasized too strongly—that constitutes the true developmental task. However, there are some persons for whom traditional marriage is contraindicated for a variety of reasons. For instance, the prototypic unmarried professional person may find deep satisfaction in dedication to (and partially feel "married" to) career, patients, clients, students, etc. and thereby arrive via a different path to "generativity" and a healthy validation of his or her self-worth.

Childlessness

The "ticking of the biological clock" is more than just a cliché. For many women it is a major crisis that influences their decisions about work and marriage. It is not unusual for single women in their late 30s (or older) to feel a sense of panic over childbearing issues. They may seek out a man who will agree to have children and use this as a major criterion for marrying him. They may consider becoming a single parent through artificial insemination, adoption, or other means. Other women may wrestle with a sense of guilt or question their own female identity if they decide they do not want children.

Some couples consciously decide not to have children, and there are a multitude of reasons for such a decision. As long as the decision is mutual, the couple may work out a deeply satisfying relationship in which other activities occupy the time and energy commitment that children would have filled.

However, problems may arise when one partner wants a child or when both wish to become parents but the couple is infertile. Both situations may lead to tremendous discord and possible divorce. The second situation may represent a growing problem in the United States. As many as 20% of couples who wish to conceive cannot do so, and women who have waited to have children sometimes find they are infertile, sometimes possibly due to age-associated physiological changes. Couples who cannot conceive may spend enormous time and money at infertility clinics and may subsequently turn to adoption. Many individuals and couples who want children do not succeed in having them, and the divorce rate is quite high in these couples.

The Triad of Pregnancy, Childbirth, and Parenting

Pregnancy

Nature usually offers expectant parents a 9-month "grace period" before the travails of childbirth and parenting begin. Pregnancy gives the couple time to make room for a new person in their lives and to realign their relationship and duties accordingly. Conception has the secondary meaning of a "new idea"—the idea of a child and new family member. Conception brings the idea of a child to life in the minds of the parents. The child becomes a subject of fantasy in both mother and father. The specific content of the fantasy will indicate to some degree the hopes, wishes, and fears concerning the new arrival.

The gradual physical changes in the mother-to-be give another support to the creation of a new "space" in the family. At first, they are the only evidence of the "reality" of the child. Most mothers cannot ignore what is happening to their own body, but the father is, of course, somewhat more removed from that process. He can avoid a tendency toward denial by actively discussing with the mother what she is feeling and by feeling the abdominal area for signs of fetal movement (quickening).

Bodily changes also direct the mother's attention inward to a growing identification with the living child inside her (Bibring et al, 1961; Winnicott, 1965). It is normal for her to become relatively more preoccupied with herself during pregnancy, to the relative neglect of externals. Her early attachment to the new baby is dependent on her undergoing this "normal illness," known as primary maternal preoccupation. The father can help by making arrangements and taking on some duties so that mother need not be overly distracted from this state of mind. In recent years, some women have gone to the other extreme in believing all expectant mothers should continue with their lives as if nothing new were happening until actual labor begins.

Mothers who cannot enter this preparatory state of mind to some degree often have trouble forming a strong initial bond to their infant. In contrast, there are mothers who become excessively caught up in bodily sensations to the point of hypochondriasis. Fathers may also identify with the mother and become anxious; some develop a wide range of physical symptoms (e.g., nausea) and bodily changes (e.g., weight gain) during the pregnancy—this is called the *couvade syndrome*. One can see that pregnancy creates some very real demands on the mother's and father's sense of adult identity. The new space for the child may be experienced as a kind of incursion. Mothers and fathers with a poorly formed sense of themselves and with strong ambivalence about parenthood may be more vulnerable to some forms of postpartum depression and other psychiatric reactions.

For both parents, the baby in the womb is a metaphor for a new growing space in their lives and marriage. The first fantasies about the baby are often elaborated into plans for the future. Usually an infant's room is decorated and furnished. Some account is taken of the parent's feelings about one sex or the other. Universal fears about the health of the child and mother are usually aired, a process that helps to make the responsibility of parenting more concrete. The preparation also involves the choice of names for the baby. The name selection helps create a new place in the family network that hopefully will someday be filled by a healthy human being. The names selected (e.g., the meaning of the names, history of the names in the family and new parents' lives) can indicate a great deal about the hopes, expectations, and even concerns regarding the baby. Sometimes the naming is celebrated in a *bris* or other ceremony shortly after birth.

Childbirth and Early Postpartum Period

The first challenge is posed by the tendency of labor pains to cause some degree of anxiety and sometimes even panic in the mother and father. Extreme pain of any kind signals the possibility of catastrophy for the organism (Simons, 1985). Somehow, a context must be found in which this pain is perceived as normative and indicative of work being done. In a sense, childbirth classes facilitate making labor and delivery a rite of passage into parenthood. One of their main goals is to remove the alarm that accompanies labor pain by reinterpreting it in a new context. Toward this end, childbirth classes teach basic physiology, as well as specific techniques for labor pain management and place labor and delivery at the end point of the preparation process started in pregnancy. They stimulate the couple's anticipatory planning for the future in tandem with the working through of anxiety. They help lay the foundation for parenting by encouraging the couple to act as a team. Giving the father the role of "coach" helps to counter his sense of helplessness in the face of his wife's labor-related activities and possible suffering. The multiple-couple, group context of these classes provides support as well as a circle of initiates on the threshold of parenthood.

However, it is important that the ideological underpinnings of these classes not foster magic expectations. Some pain is still a fact of life for most deliveries; however, it is important to educate the parents-to-be that epidural injections and other techniques can assure that discomfort remains at a mild and manageable level. The expectant mother should also be told to ask for analgesia when the pain begins to become unpleasant, rather than unbearable so that less overall medication will be able to control it. Not all fathers can deal with the actual birth and that should be sensitively monitored and respected. Most couples know instinctively what goes beyond the limits of their endurance and that should be assessed and honored by the physician.

Even with 9 months of active preparation, childbirth is virtually always a normative crisis in the lives of the new parents. This is because the rate of change in their lives due to childbirth and the immediate postpartum period is tremendous. The experience often leaves couples in a state of at least mild emotional shock and physical exhaustion, and it is not uncommon for new parents to experience feelings of depersonalization, derealization, and a distortion of time sense. At times, the shock can be masked or delayed by feelings of exhilaration after a healthy birth. Weeks or even months may go by before the full reality of the event begins to sink in. During this phase of normal "letdown," the new parents may start to recognize the automaticity of their responses and the postponement of their affective reactions until well after the fact. Indeed, these patterns of automatic behavior and postponement of responses often continues well into the first year.

This period may be particularly difficult for the woman who has the perception due to recent social pressures that she should "do it all," must "do it all" for financial reasons, or wants to "do it all" simultaneously for other reasons. These women may have to come to terms with how they will function as a new mother, a wife, and previously full-time member of the work force. Some women have compromised by saying "I can do it all but do not want to do it all at the same time." During this period, some women cut back to part-time or no work outside the home, if finances permit, citing that their children will only be young and have the opportunity for positive early experiences with them once and that the work world will always exist. Still others return to full-time work outside the home almost immediately and make arrangements for child care.

Parenting

The skills of parenting lean heavily on the established partnership of the couple and on the individual health and background of each parent, including the experiences each had with his or her parents. The demands of a new baby challenge the couple to improve their teamwork even further. Usually, this involves some modification and reallocation of roles and tasks. However, the new task orientation may present a danger to the intimacy of the couple and make previous marital problems worse. The partners may be tempted to communicate through issues involving the new "third party," instead of with each other directly; therefore, parents may need to work to preserve and protect their private relationship in the service of teamwork. They thus ensure from the start that parenting will not undermine the marriage that supports it. Some couples use parenting as a way of hiding or avoiding facing the issues in a bad marriage, and those couples are most vulnerable to emotional problems (e.g., "the empty nest syndrome"—when the children leave home) and to divorce at that time.

The couple's teamwork forms the basis of a "holding environment" for the new baby (Winnicott, 1965). Holding refers in a general way to all their efforts to adapt to the baby's needs, both psychological and physiological. It takes into account the literal holding of the child, as well as the monitoring of the early physical environment, of which the establishment of a stable home life is an important part. Also important is the protection of the child from stimuli and outside impingements that are beyond the child's capacity to assimilate. The earliest holding environment builds on the mother's growing empathy with her infant, itself founded on primary maternal preoccupation. The father's primary parental role in the beginning is to "hold" the mother and child "couple" so they can devote themselves much of the time to each other. This requires maturity and sensitivity in the father and, for some of this purpose, he may need to act as a substitute mother, thus allowing the mother some time to recover her "individual" identity.

Beyond the stage of facilitating intimacy between the mother and child, the father helps the child to later begin separating emotionally from the mother (Greenspan, 1982). In this new role, he can allow himself to be seen as someone different from the mother, who represents a limit or even sometimes an interference on the mother–child relationship. Yet, in the same guise, he is also supporting the child's **growing** independence.

With the passage of time, these roles may be freely distributed between the parents. Some role reversals may help to solidify the partnership by defusing stress. For example, it permits the parents to alternate in the role of disciplinarian. Doing this supports the idea that discipline is a joint effort, rather than the duty of one parent alone.

Raising children places a variety of stresses on the parental partnership. Even if both parents have achieved emotional adulthood, which is often not the case, they will be prone to some regression during the absolute dependency stage of a newborn. Such extreme dependency may evoke a range of reactions, from stoic counterdependency (the feeling they do not need help from anyone else) to childish resentment. After weathering this phase, they must adjust to strains in the opposite direction when the child begins to separate. With the onset of the rapprochement crisis (Mahler, 1972), at about 21 months of age, children alternate between intense clinging to and pushing away of the parents. Unless this is understood as a normal developmental struggle, this is often enough to drive the family into a minicrisis.

The holding environment must continue to be strong and flexible enough to assimilate later developments such as sibling rivalry, children learning to try to play one parent against the other, and adolescent rebellion. The parents must resist any action that threatens to drive a wedge between them, such as taking sides repeatedly in a "sibling war."

Nothing poses a greater challenge to parental teamwork than "acting out" by their children. Temper tantrums or an adolescent's breaking of curfew both require the setting of limits. Discipline is limit setting in action. The idea is not so much to punish as it is to contain behavior that threatens the holding environment. Children usually react positively to thoughtful limit setting that is explained because they accurately interpret it as a sign of love and concern and reflective of parental interest in facilitating the children's learning to set healthy limits for themselves.

As noted in Chapter 6 by Dr. Dorsett, discipline should not be confused with punishment. Physical or corporal punishment is ultimately ineffective in developing an internal sense of right and wrong and is indicative of parental ignorance about effective methods of disciplining. Physical punishment basically molds behavior around fear of retaliation, teaches children to hurt others (including possibly their future children) when they do not like what they do, and motivates children to focus on avoiding being caught. A goal of healthy development is to enable children to internalize self-regulatory behavior, appreciate the effects of their actions on others, develop empathy and consideration for the feelings of others, and solidify the substrate of a moral, ethical, and social conscience. Therefore, corporal or physical punishment should be condemned by physicians, and parents should be educated and counseled about other methods of limit setting and disciplining, such as brief periods of time out and withdrawal of rewards. These issues are discussed in detail by Dr. Dorsett in Chapter 6 as well as by Dr. Dulcan in Chapter 8.

By challenging the parents to strengthen their internal cohesion as a couple, children act as a catalyst to further adult development. The experience of being a parent emphasizes to adults the importance of reliability and consistency, which are essential to any position of responsibility. It also affords parents an opportunity to reexperience and rework some of their childhood stages as well. Thus, parents retain a vital connection with the world of childhood at the very time when they are detaching themselves further from it.

The Single Parent

The single parent (usually female) often faces additional challenges in parenting because he or she may not have a partner with whom to share the burdens of parenting. Some choose to be single parents. Others may feel this situation was forced upon them by divorce or an unplanned pregnancy. These differences often have an impact on how they see their role as a parent and how they view their children. Minor crises can more frequently become major issues. What does the single parent do with the sick child when he or she needs to go to work? What about their needs for adult companionship when their primary relationship and time involvement is with one or more children?

Many single parents meet these challenges with success but few do so without additional stress. Those who do well find ways to get their own needs met without sacrificing the needs of their children, including creative solutions in terms of support networks and alternative childcare arrangements.

Those who do less well may become bitter and resentful toward their children and may view them as adult surrogates (i.e., may overburden the children with their adult concerns and needs). They may also find it difficult to let their children become independent if the children have been their main source of emotional support. Others may be so overwhelmed by life stresses that they have little emotional support and guidance to offer their children.

The Effects of Divorce

Children often react to their parents as a couple in two contradictory ways. On the one hand, they want to drive a wedge between the parents to try to dominate and to control them. On the other hand, they have a deep need to get or keep their parents together in a productive relationship. These trends represent opposite attitudes toward the fact of dependency for children.

When parents divorce, the partial wish to split up the parental couple becomes a reality. Therefore, it should come as no surprise when many children see themselves as the cause of the separation and react with guilt. This may be so painful to children that they may attempt to deny the reality of the divorce. Or, if they accept the threat as real, they may engage in frantic reparative efforts to get the parents back together. Some may try to become "perfect" children and not share their concerns and stresses with their parents, thereby possibly short-circuiting some of their own developments and an open, honest relationship with their parents. If the parents themselves are vascillating on the issue of separation, children may discover that they alone are holding their parents together; such a sense of responsibility may only add to their burden of guilt, fear, and anger.

Divorce is almost always traumatic to some degree to children and parents. Naturally, the child's capacity to cope is influenced by the family context. If the marriage has a violent battleground or has been a cold, barren desert, divorce may be anticipated with something approaching relief. In some cases, the parents' capacity for parental collaboration may improve when living apart. In any case, the outcome is likely to depend on the parents' being able to sustain some degree of collaboration. The use of a child as a pawn in the parents' "games," sometimes played out in a courtroom, jeopardizes the holding environment needed for children's development. Some form of escape into premature independence by the child may be the only way out of such an intolerable situation. Some form of psychotherapy for parents and children is often indicated to minimize the deleterious effects of divorce on both.

The Midlife Transition

Some time between the ages of 35 and 55, most adults realize that they have reached the midpoint of their lifespan, and this realization often has a special psychological significance. Beyond the midpoint one can no longer say that most of one's life lies ahead. The end is now visible, as well as the beginning. It may be like stepping outside of the stream of life and seeing its horizon for the first time. From this perspective, one may grasp life as a whole, along with its boundaries and limits. The confrontation with these limits may form the basis of a thorough readjustment of the adult self.

Before the midpoint of life, many adults are basking in the mild euphoria of "consolidation." They are often continuing to make steady progress toward their professional and personal goals and are so immersed in various engagements that little time is taken for introspection. Indeed, they may wish to postpone any such self-assessment indefinitely. It is much easier to be carried along on the tide of youthful dreams than to realize one will not live forever.

It often takes some life crisis or trauma before this mild illusory state is interrupted. New realities make their appearance in midlife: signs of physical aging, including the onset of menopause in women and the first diminution of sexual desire in some men, the "sandwiching" produced by the simultaneous responsibilities for their children and for their aging parents, and plateauing of advancement at work. Not infrequently, a first major medical illness, such as a myocardial infarction, begins to drive home the idea that death is inevitable, or the reality may dawn when a peer dies in the prime of life.

Some experience of disillusionment of more youthful fantasies seems to be necessary in making the transition to mature adulthood. Coming face to face with these "narcissistic blows" may help people to give up the universal fantasy of unlimited possibilities (Jaques, 1965; Kernberg, 1980; Viorst, 1986). They may be motivated to undergo a comprehensive life review, in which the past and present are reassessed (Levinson et al, 1978). Each aspect of life will have to be measured against the new limits associated with the confrontation of one's own mortality. The ultimate goal of this quest is a new integration of self, in which a number of conflicting polarities—love-hate, self-other, male-female, success-failure—are partially reconciled (Levinson et al, 1978; Levinson and Goodeneh, 1985; Settlage et al, 1988). Although largely internal, such a readjustment is bound to influence relationships with others. Some have formulated this change as one of new "tragic" awareness replacing an older romanticism (Schafer, 1970).

The term midlife crisis is sometimes used to describe a block or maladaptive response to the midlife transition. For example, Mr. C presented to a psychiatrist with apprehension about an extramarital affair. In many ways, Mr. C's feelings about the affair resembled his passionate attachment to flying an airplane, an experience he described as "better than sex." Flying represented his last stand against the limits of earthbound life. Up in the sky, nothing could stop him, nothing could pull him down, nothing could get in his way. The controls were in his hands. He was quite oblivious initially to the fact that his marriage was already in a "nosedive" and that he could "crash" if he was not careful.

Bereavement

Loss plays a necessary role in every life transition. Every step forward in development implies the letting go of an important piece of one's past life. Thus, every developmental gain requires the working through of reactions to some loss, both real and imagined (Viorst, 1986). However, it may be helpful to distinguish between reaction to loss, which is a function of all transitions, and the more specific reaction to the loss of a person to whom one has been attached, referred to in this chapter as bereavement. In overcoming any major loss—whether it be of a spouse, parent, child, relative, or even a body part—the person must commit his psychological resources in part to the task of reviewing and reliving his lost relationship (Freud, 1958). Such a task is necessarily somewhat painful and also may be painstaking, protracted, and time consuming. Therefore, bereavement may be viewed as a largely self-limited psychological process that unfolds through a series of stages from initiation to resolution.

The initial reaction to sudden loss is often some form of denial. People are likely to react to any catastrophic event with exclamations like "No, it can't be," or "You've got to be kidding." Some people react to loss with an almost total absence of emotion. They are the ones on whom others may initially rely for support and, for example, the smooth execution of funeral arrangements. For many, the apparent absence of emotion is due to shock or psychic numbing. They may continue to go about their business in a kind of altered state of consciousness, as if on autopilot. In any case, the effect of such denial is that their actual grief experience is postponed or never reached.

Everyone recognizes the signs of true grieving, which is characterized by an intense emotionality that includes admixtures of sadness, tearfulness, and sometimes rage. Grieving people are usually preoccupied with their feelings and inner experiences. Quasihallucinatory phenomena, such as hearing the voice of the departed relative or believing they saw the person in a fleeting manner, are considered within the normal range of acute bereavement. Many of these feelings are worked through and reexperienced in private, because our society sometimes discourages public displays of grief.

An important task in grief is the coming to terms with *ambivalence;* every meaningful relationship has some mixed feelings of caring and frustration. Bereavement tends to exaggerate normal ambivalence but may short-circuit the working through of negative feelings by such injunctions as considering it wrong "to speak ill of the dead." Hence, some degree of guilt feelings is a normal aftermath of grief. For example, bereaved persons may chastise themselves for even tiny sins of omission such as some slight or error years ago, not being present at the moment of death, not trying some experimental treatment, or not prolonging an inevitable death through every conceivable mechanical medical means.

Some bereaved people may feel that any degree of ambivalence is unacceptable. They may tend to split their ambivalence by *overidealizing* the image of the lost person and by setting up scapegoats, whom they can blame for their loss. It is not uncommon in recent years for physicians to increasingly be placed in this role, particularly if he or she has been guilty of some perceived error or oversight in management of the case. Many malpractice suits have their origin in this emotionally charged response; such a legal battle may prolong or prevent resolution of grief and mourning. In the ordinary course of events, however, the bereaved are able to pull together their feelings of love and hate concerning the lost individual into a more integrated, internalized picture. If they can begin to see the lost person for what she or he was, both good and bad, they often find they can cherish her or his memory in a more meaningful and realistic way.

This task concluded, the stage is set for the final detachment from the lost person, and the resultant freeing up of emotional energy for new emotional investments. Such detachment is facilitated by the reality testing that takes place every time the bereaved person falls back into the illusion that the dead person is still alive, and then must remember that he or she is no longer to be found. Some have particular difficulty accepting the finality of such losses, and some of these people are particularly attracted to stories that JFK, Elvis Presley, and others are still secretly alive. Only with such gradual detachment can one truly "bury the dead" and go on with the business of living. For people whose grieving has been incomplete, the dead still "live" in another world or as ghosts, which haunt the survivor, refusing to let him go.

The whole grieving process is also marked by rites of passage that include funerals, eulogies, vigils, fasts, condolence rituals, wakes, and burial rites (Van Gennep, 1960). The erosion and weakening of some public mourning rituals may place a greater burden on the person's private means and resources. Wherever possible, public mourning provides a valuable support for many individuals' solitary efforts. For example, viewing the body may help some persons to accept the death as an undeniable reality (Simons, 1985). A funeral also helps the bereaved to remember the dead and to begin to relinquish their attachments in the presence of a group of others who also had attachments to the deceased. It emphasizes the continuity of life (the community of mourners and their link with the transcendent) as it dramatizes its transience.

To an extent, public mourning sometimes has been transferred from religious to medical settings. The physician now may often take the role formerly occupied by the clergy. Within this setting, the physician can be of great help in assisting the bereaved. Physicians can use their position and skills to guide bereaved people through the stages of grief. Simply by allowing patients and family members to openly grieve, physicians lend support to the legitimacy of grief, a legitimacy that is sometimes undermined by society's at times phobic attitude toward bereavement in general. More specifically, the physician's presence works to counteract bereaved individuals' fears that something is wrong with them ("Doctor, am I depressed?") and their guilt that they are overreacting emotionally.

Thus, bereavement is treated as a kind of "normal illness," analogous to puberty, pregnancy, menopause, and so forth. As a potential illness in the strict sense, it is up to the physician to diagnose and treat pathologic complications of grief and mourning. In pathological bereavement, one or more features of the grieving process become exaggerated and/or fixated at one stage. Common examples include absent grief, chronic bereavement, excessive guilt, and the loss of reality (psychosis). These and associated conditions, such as depression, mania and psychosomatic illness, may be triggered by the stress of grief and must be treated in their own right because, once triggered, these conditions tend to take on "a life of their own," regardless of what initially triggered them.

Psychotherapy for the bereaved can serve as a catalyst to the grieving process and as a means of unearthing blocks in the search for a healthier degree of resolution. The extent to which psychotherapy deals with issues of "stillborn" or inadequately resolved grief reactions has probably been underestimated. For example, a 33-year-old cabinetmaker consulted a psychiatrist for frequent outbreaks of panic and depression. In the course of psychotherapy, he revealed that his father had died about 10 years ago, suddenly and unexpectedly. For several years preceding his death, the patient had noticed a certain reserve in his otherwise cordial relations with his father. Now, it seemed as if a cruel fate had made any considerations of experiencing his sad feelings as irrelevant. Instead of grieving in the manner of his distraught mother, he said to himself, "Now you are the man of the family, so you better act like one," which to him meant to be a stoic. Ever since then, he had resolved to suppress all evidence of emotion and to "face reality" in a cool, detached manner. His recent decision to start psychotherapy was his way of keeping the appointment with this postponed grief and of owning up to it for the first time; this enabled him to begin to integrate this into his overall sense of his life experiences.

A CASE STUDY

Mrs. B, a 62-year-old woman, was brought to see a psychiatrist by her son and daughter. They were concerned that she had "not gone on with her life" after the death of her husband 6 years earlier and of her mother 2 years later. Her children observed that she had become more bitter, withdrawn, and covertly angry at them for "not understanding what she is going through." In psychotherapy, the patient was able to talk about her sense of self-sacrifice and her feeling that she had devoted her life to her husband and mother, who had then deserted her. Her fear was that if she gave up her "grief" she would lose the last remnants of the people who gave her life meaning. The work of psychotherapy with this patient was multifaceted. She needed support for her role as a "giver to others." At the same time she needed to begin to deal with her ambivalence about the demands placed on her by her husband and mother and her anger at those demands and at them for leaving her. She also needed encouragement to make new attachments in which she was again able to see herself as important and helpful to others.

The Transition to Late Life

Society's recent, more enlightened attitudes toward late life may sometimes tend to obscure its realities. An older person might say with a sense of humor that old age is not exactly what he or she had in mind. The sacrifices of this life stage in terms of illness, physical decline, and the death of loved ones are very real. Yet, many older persons respond to these losses as challenges to imbue their lives with new depth of meaning. One sign of increasing recognition of this challenge, as well as of many older person's capacity to meet it, is the resurgence of interest in psychotherapy and psychoanalysis for the elderly.

A major task of old age is to enhance and maintain a sense of inner emotional integrity in the face of increasing external threats. Throughout the lifecycle, the sense of identity is often propped up by a variety of external supports, including an attractive and healthy body, a social network and family, some authority in the workplace, and demonstrable productivity. Even a generally healthy person in the prime of life may suffer from identity defusion when deprived of these supports, such as may occur during a hospitalization, in prison, or other prolonged separations from family and friends. Such stresses call on a person's inner resources in combating depersonalization and identity confusion.

Luckily, one does not usually have to endure such trials all at once in the transition to old age, and each potential threat to a person's emotional integrity may be met and conquered using a variety of techniques. Among these are a search for new external supports, experiments with new methods of self-validation, and psychotherapy. These developmental issues are often discussed under the headings of retirement and the challenge to establish a sense of integrity.

The relinquishing of power and authority must stimulate a search for new sources of productivity and creativity (Levinson and Goodeneh, 1985); retirement often marks this transition. Less tied to the demands of the workplace, the older person may become more free to explore new interests and to deepen old ones. Adult education presents a popular means to this end. Besides opening the way to new undertakings and often to new friends, learning can serve as a basis for self-study or just be pursued as a pleasurable end in itself.

A renewed student status may reflect a basic change in older people's engagement with the world. Regardless of the specific activity, they may reengage society from a different angle. What they have to offer others, whether as grandparent, teacher, employee, or adviser, is the sum of the wisdom gained from their experiences. They are experienced experts on the human lifecycle and a vital link with the traditions of the past. Therefore, one social role for the elderly is to embody those traditions and to serve as a kind of custodian and transmitter of cultural values and history.

What the elderly may lose in actuality, they often can regain in symbolic forms; however, they may need to get used to the idea of being a "figurehead"—at least to some degree. Yet, even when they have to delegate many things, they may still have worth as the embodiment of societal, business, professional, and family values. This is where society's general attitude—veneration or vilification of their elderly members—makes a difference; symbolism works better if society lends weight to it. Ironically, its effectiveness may be most visible in the political arena, where older persons have sometimes been able to parlay this role of elder statesman into increased power and influence.

The older age transition usually requires the construction of new social networks to replace the previous ones, which were centered in the nuclear family and the workplace. Grandparenting may offer a new connectedness to family members. New peer relationships are made possible by the increasing numbers of people surviving into old age and the proliferation of institutions that focus on the needs of senior citizens.

However, not everyone succeeds in this readjustment. Some are seduced into a fantasy that retirement means an end to work, growth, and development. Of course, such beliefs often produce a self-fulfilling prophecy. These are the people who may go through a "honeymoon" phase after retirement, followed by disenchantment. Others approach retirement with great reluctance, often refusing to give up the reins of power and authority. And some express their ambivalence by making a show of handing over the responsibility, while still holding on to the ultimate authority, as occurs in *King Lear*. Some inner opposition to the "passing of scepter" is probably inevitable; however, a pronounced or prolonged conflict in this area is an indication for a psychiatric consultation and psychotherapy.

A CASE STUDY

Mr. H, a 65-year-old hospital administrator, consulted a psychiatrist with the complaint of excessive anger at the prospect of being replaced by a younger person. He noted that his whole life had been a search for new challenges that would confirm his identity as an effective person. What made stepping down particularly distasteful was the fact that, in his eyes, the replacement lacked even the basic qualifications for his position. Yet despite this lack of respect, he felt guilty at begrudging a "child" figure the chance to make good. Verbalizing these feelings helped him overcome this obstacle to his retirement and to go on with his life in a fulfilling manner and to be able to collaborate in a supportive and constructive manner with his successor during a transition period.

The Battle for Integrity

Isolation remains the most common threat to the sense of integrity of older persons. The elderly are especially vulnerable to the stimulus deprivation that results from decreasing sensory acuity (e.g., vision, hearing, smell, taste). As inner resources decline, the importance of external supports increases. Surrounded by familiar people and objects, even a person with mild-to-moderate visual and hearing impairment and dementia may be able to maintain a sense of positive personal identity for a long time. Physicians may be helpful in correcting or partly reversing the insidious combination of the effects of aging and by teaching compensatory mechanisms for those disabilities. Physicians also may be helpful by being aware of the loss of external supports, such as lower income, illness or death of a spouse, and family relocation. Physicians can support the family of an ill or demented older person by providing education and referral to assistance groups in the management of the home environment. In addition to medical treatment, such measures include recommending frequent family and friend visits; regular orientation to time, place, and person; a routine daily schedule; family photographs on the wall; the use of a nightlight; and being updated on current events through television news, newspapers and new magazines, and magazines and books focusing on their career and hobby interests.

In more optimal circumstances, older people may feel challenged to view sickness and death as a test of their personal integrity and inner resources. The near-universality of some type of illness in the elderly may make illness a kind of "normative crisis" that the elderly recognize as a rite of passage into old age. By finding ways of overcoming the passivity and the helplessness often associated with a major illness, the elderly may learn to see illness and even death as experiences that underscore their basic humanity; the major "battle" between integrity and despair is often fought in this arena.

Religion often provides solace and comfort to its believers, and this coping mechanism may shield medically ill individuals from depression, possibly by counter-balancing feelings of inadequacy and improve feelings of being in control. Religious affiliations may also facilitate the individual's social support network (Koenig et al, 1992).

Death and Dying

The approach of death may paradoxically open up new avenues for feelings of inner continuity. When the future is foreclosed, there may be a greater intensity to the present moment and a greater depth of self-awareness. At the end of their lifecycle, individuals may feel nearer to the beginning, nearer to the cycle of the generations of which they are a part. Having come full circle, the end of life may be approached with a heightened sense of mystery and an enriched interest in the transcendent, often expressed through an increased involvement with religious concerns and other larger social issues.

However, the encounter with one's own impending death is obviously unique among life's transitions. The idea of death, especially when it will occur before the expected end of the lifespan, is anticipated by most people as a very emotionally traumatic event, whose impact often exceeds even that of bereavement. (For the purposes of this section, the dying patient will be assumed to be conscious and aware; situations when this is not the case are addressed more under the section on Bereavement.) The disturbing quality of impending death is often due to three kinds of factors. First, death represents a threat to the part of our minds which seeks to place us in control of our destiny. At one time or another, almost everyone harbors the fantasy and wish of immortality and we find it difficult, even as adults, to grasp the idea of our own nonexistence.

Second, death stirs up primitive fears and fantasies in us, which may transform death into a horrifying specter, like the ghosts and monsters of our childhood. The ghouls, vampires, and other varieties of the dead who turn out to be "undead" personify these fears and are the characters of the "slasher movies" so popular with some adolescents. The image of the dead returning to take revenge on the living, implied by the adage mentioned in the section on Bereavement "not to speak ill of the dead," is but one of many fantasies reflecting archaic vestiges of thoughts about death from childhood. Death evokes, almost universally, a series of infantile emotional danger situations (Freud, 1923), including loss of the self and of the loved person (or "object"), loss of the object's love, castration and other forms of physical mutilation, and abandonment by parental caretakers (often symbolized as God) or fate.

Third, Western culture of the past 100 years has produced a massive denial of death. This is not meant to imply that some degree of denial of one's own death is inherently abnormal. In a study of the Hiroshima survivors, Robert Jay Lifton (1967) showed how an excessive exposure to death may undermine and destroy much of the meaningfulness of life. And a certain degree of adaptive denial may actually improve life expectancy in male patients with myocardial infarction (Levenson et al, 1984). This same denial-based attitude of "nothing bad can happen to me" undoubtedly proves helpful to some soldiers in the heat of battle and lethal to others. However, the effect of *societal* denial is to place death *outside* the realm of the normal lifecycle and thus to try to exclude it from everyday awareness. How else can it appear then, except as an alien and unwelcome intruder?

However, death was not always viewed as such an extraordinary event in Western society (Ariès 1973). During the Middle Ages, many people met their deaths with a sense of resignation and acceptance. Part of this attitude was probably due to the near-universality of religious faith and frequent exposure to death on a day-to-day basis. But another part of it often arose from the belief that death was not some extraordinary event, but rather an expected, if unwelcome, "guest" in this life. In the arts of that era, death was often personified as a mysterious stranger with whom one could have a conversation. Such a "dialogue with death" is dramatized in Ingmar Bergman's film, *The Seventh Seal*, in which the protagonist plays a game of chess with Death.

The revived interest in death and dying in medical settings, partly catalyzed by the studies of Elizabeth Kübler-Ross (1969) in the 1960s, led to a rediscovery of the latter attitude. Kübler-Ross conceived of the encounter with death as a developmental process not unlike other life transitions. Indeed, Leo Tolstoy (1981), in his classic short novel, *The Death of Ivan Ilych*, demonstrated that the encounter with death in a 45-year-old man contained most of the elements of a midlife crisis. In that novel, Ivan's encounter with death involves a lengthy and painful task of self-reassessment and realignment. It is interesting that the acceptance of death-related tasks described by Kübler-Ross—denial and isolation, anger, bargaining, depression, and acceptance—are roughly analogous to the stages of bereavement. This should not be surprising, since much of the pain of loss in bereavement is due to the emotional investment in the lost person, which makes it similar to the loss of one's self.

The first death of a patient is often a memorable event in the professional life of medical students, and it puts to the test one's attitudes toward death. That first death may reveal that they, too, were motivated in part to become physicians by altruistic "rescue fantasies" (a somewhat heroically tinged desire to correct the wrongs of the world, including illness, disability, and death), which they have measured primarily by the saving of life. Subsequently, some physicians align with society's recent prevailing attitude of denial, which is sometimes translated as "life at any cost." Most, however, will hopefully expand their definition of medical "success" to include helping dying patients and their families come to terms with and to achieve a dignified death.

Physicians' attitudes toward death are often also revealed in the way in which they approach the task of informing their patients of a terminal prognosis. Sensitive handling of this juncture can go a long way toward helping patients face their own death with more equanimity. A goal of the physician is to respect and enhance the patient's freedom to define this task in his or her own way. To reach this objective, the physician must avoid any pre-established or "prescribed" policy in this regard. Physicians who never inform their patients of their specific medical situation as well as those who, sometimes bluntly, inform *all* of their terminal patients of all the details, are both interfering with freedom of choice for some patients.

Some patients indicate through their speech and behaviors that they do not want to know the specific prognosis of their illness. Some patients may not even want to know their diagnosis, or if they do, will prefer to discuss it in vague terms (i.e., a growth or tumor, rather than a malignancy or cancer). These patients seldom ask the physician, "Am I going to die?" or "How long do I have to live?" While this attitude certainly shows some denial, it also indicates a certain choice of how to approach death. These patients, in effect, approach death as an invisible horizon, always just beyond their range of vision. They remain fully focused on the practical tasks of improving their situation and often wish for some palliative improvement and discovery of a miracle cure, which allows them to maintain their denial, to live with more hope, and to bolster their optimism. Lest one judge this attitude as naive or representative of unrealistic denial, it is well to remember that this degree of denial comes close to the normal day-to-day attitude of healthy individuals toward their own death, which is just as inevitable as that of the dying person. The point is that the physician is not in a position to know *beforehand* what path will be chosen by an individual patient.

Extreme denial may place a burden on the patient's family and business by resulting in lack of preparation of a will and of other planning for the future. Sometimes, a patient can be persuaded to make a will and to see to related matters in the name of "covering all contingencies." A will commits individuals to the serious consideration of their own death and its consequences for others. Physicians usually are able to determine when patients are ready to discuss this task. Some patients will ask the physician directly whether they are going to die from their condition and how much time they probably have left. At this point, the physician, besides answering this question, can offer to assist the patient in the tasks that lie ahead.

For many, death in the abstract is not the main source of anxiety. There are, of course, individuals who tend to brood and ruminate over the meaning of death. But when faced with the actuality of one's death, the concerns and fears are usually more mundane and circumscribed, hence also more manageable for the physician. Such patients may want reassurance, not that the physician will save them, but that he or she will stay with them as an ally, partner, and consultant right to the end. Often, the dying patient's most haunting fear is of being left alone. In the same vein, patients may want reassurance from their physician that they will not allow the patient to be overwhelmed by pain and physical suffering.

Several of these points are illustrated in the following hospital consultation:

A CASE STUDY

The staff of a medical-surgical unit suggested the surgeon request a psychiatric consultation on Mr. R, a 50-year-old man with terminal metastatic breast cancer. Mr. R was aware of his diagnosis and prognosis and was tearful and despondent at times. However, the staff was mainly concerned about oddities in Mr. R's behavior. For the past few weeks he had been asking his wife to bring him huge quantities of his favorite, nutritious foods (many dating back to his childhood), which he ate with relish several times a day. In addition, he had told the nurses that he sometimes felt as though they were trying to poison him through the intravenous (IV) lines.

After talking with the patient, the consulting psychiatrist began to see these behaviors and concerns as due to partial psychological regression. For most of the time Mr. R. acted like a mature man trying to work through his feelings about his impending death. His tearfulness was mostly due to the mourning process he was going through for the life he had to give up. In this area his reality testing was relatively intact, and the meals he was eating became like a kind of "last supper." In order to deal with the inescapable ending of his life, Mr. R had shrunk his temporal horizon to encompass only his next meal. Instead of thinking of the frightening future, he would instead substitute the prospect of his next meal, which he could anticipate with pleasure.

Mr. R was relating to his caregivers—his wife and the staff nurses (both male and female)—as all-powerful "mother" figures who held the power of life and death over him. He simultaneously felt as though they could keep him alive with magical, life-saving food, or they could kill him with poison introduced into his IV line. The latter fantasy was amplified by the fact that his pain was being controlled by fairly large doses of analgesia which also somewhat blunted his rational thought processes. Thus, according to this fantasy, it was they—the "mothers" (to whom he could relate)—who decided his fate and not the inevitable progression of his disease.

In the case of Mr. R, the psychiatrist only had to support and encourage the staff to accept the patient's unique approach to death. The psychiatrist encouraged Mr. R to speak openly about his feelings and, at the same time, tolerated his partial regressions without criticism. Discussion with the staff also helped them to take a more permissive attitude toward the regressions and to see his tearfulness as evidence of an ongoing mourning process.

In the course of this developmental process, many patients come to conceive of their relationship to death in terms of some overriding metaphor. Death may be conceived of as a fight that has been lost, a journey, a culminating closure of one's life, a return to the beginning of the lifecycle (mentioned in the section on old age), a profound rest that is akin to sleep, and even as a reward. Interestingly, many patients come to think of death as a transition of sorts, different only in degree from other life transitions. One patient, for example, dreamed about his death as a move from his old house to a new one; in the process of this move, the old house was completely divested of all its furniture and decorations, leaving it bare and empty—a mere shell or skeleton.

Perhaps the one aspect of psychological death work that sets it apart from other developmental tasks is the obvious need for a more thoroughgoing divestment from all of life's attachments. The dying person must, in effect, bid farewell to every person and thing which has held meaning in his or her life; and finally, one must bid farewell to something that almost everyone is quite attached to, namely one's "self."

As has been alluded to earlier, it cannot be emphasized enough that the most fundamental fear of patients is not necessarily death itself, but the fear of being alone, abandoned, and helpless *in the process of dying*. In this respect, the physician may play a powerful supportive role for the patient with terminal illness in a number of ways.

First, the physician should reassure patients that they will not be abandoned and that the physician will be available to them "no matter what happens." This assurance of help and support markedly decreases fears of dying alone. Physicians who withdraw from patients because they cannot emotionally tolerate the idea of death, or who react to the patient's terminal illness as a failure of their own to "save" the patient, are abandoning not only the patient but one of the most essential duties and obligations of being a physician. Emotional withdrawal and avoidance of the dying patient by the physician may derive from a variety of factors: the physician's own fear of death, discomfort with dealing with the emotional pain of bereavement, or, as noted above, a sense of helplessness and failure in the physician. It is important, therefore, for physicians to be aware of their own feelings toward death and the dying process and possess the ability to self-analyze their own avoidance or detachment from patients if this occurs in the context of terminal illness.

The second major fear of patients is the fear of feeling helpless in the process of dying. Again, physicians may provide comforting reassurance that everything will be done to assist patients in their care to ensure as much autonomy as possible, and that they will be allowed to participate in any medical decisions regarding their care.

Finally, physicians may provide powerful reassurance that the patient will not be allowed to be in significant pain. Terminal illness is not the situation in which to demonstrate conservatism in the use of narcotics, and patients should be reassured that adequate, if not generous, pain relief will be provided for them, as needed.

Hence, far from being helpless, the physician may provide powerful emotional and practical intervention in the care of dying patients and their families.

Choice in Adult Development: The Transitions in Adult Development as Crossroads

In the patient examples used in this chapter, each individual was confronted with a fateful choice: Mr. N, the artist in his mid-30s, had to decide whether to continue as an artist or to pursue a more business-oriented career; Dr. G, the resident physician, found himself at a crossroads of his professional life—he had to decide between continuing his career as a primary caregiver or switching to a consulting practice; and Mr. H, the 65-year-old hospital administrator, eventually chose a constructive path of retirement over the options of holding on to his job or seeking another position, which had previously been his typical life pattern.

In these patient examples, decisions in the lifecycle about relationships (e.g., marriage, parenthood, divorce) are as important as those involving job and career. Mr. N and Dr. G were both considering separating from their wives. In the case of Mr. N, who had a 5-year-old son, this choice was also about being a part-time or full-time father. In the course of treatment, the 34-year-old schizoid man finally took the plunge and successfully asked and took a woman on a date. His decision was, in part, a conscious effort to break out of his self-imposed prison of isolation. And finally, Mr. C, the man who loved to fly, found himself caught between his devotion to his wife of 20 years and his recent infatuation for an attractive female colleague. For Mr. C, the hardest task was acknowledging that he had to make a choice, that it was either one or the other. As he put it to his psychiatrist; "I know I can't have my cake and eat it, too."

Ultimately, however, it is not just a question of "this job or that job," or this relationship or that relationship, but of this or that life path. The individual must choose among various "life-lines." Committing oneself to one choice often means changing the direction of an entire life, and in some cases, altering one's destiny and sense of identity. From this viewpoint, adult transitions involve more than just a change from one stage to another. They also may be viewed as crossroads in the lifecycle, an opportunity for choice against the background of inevitable biologic and psychosocial change.

The range of choices in adult life are wide, but most midlife and later choices do not necessarily involve dramatic changes in behavior. In fact, radical changes in lifestyle in the midlife transition, for example, are more the exception than the rule. Some individuals do, however, make major changes in midlife, such as career shifts, geographic relocations, divorce, remarriage, becoming a parent again, and step-parenting. For others, the changes may be more symbolic and on a smaller scale, such as the resolution to change one's eating, smoking, and drinking habits, to get a regular physician and physical checkup, to start attending church and visiting family more often, to take a different kind of vacation, and to take an adult education course or develop a hobby in an area unrelated to professional concerns. Some important choices may involve no changes whatsoever in outward behavior, and it is important to remember that the act of choosing does not require change for the sake of change. An individual may opt to "stay the course," or, in other words, continue in her or his habitual modes of behavior. As the result of a process of reflection and the exercise of choice, the option of no change may be as valid as any other.

It may initially seem strange, however, to have "refocusing on life choices" as part of the lifecycle stage, which also includes accepting the absolute inevitability of death. Yet even in the face of death, a wide range of human choice is not lacking, including the option of rejecting or accepting the finality of death; that is, Kübler-Ross's stages do not imply universal progression leading inevitably to "acceptance." Many patients, without denying their own deaths, consciously choose to fight against death to the end. After all, such a combative stance follows a well-established tradition in Western society, summed up in the famous line about death from a Dylan Thomas poem, "Rage,

rage against the dying of the light." On the other hand, the alternative of "acceptance" should not be viewed as passive capitulation. In true "acceptance," the individual reaches a position where he or she, in effect, "chooses" to die, as if dying were somehow their decision (although to some degree the "when and how" may be). For such a patient, death may be thereby changed from an impersonal event into "my death." As implied in the section in this chapter on Death and Dying, reaching such a position with a sense of equanimity and grace is an extraordinary human accomplishment.

In later life, some individuals feel robbed of an idealized life they fantasize they would have had "if only they had made different choices." They are part of the group of adults who feel that their lives have been the product of situations and forces outside of their control. The midlife and late-life transition offers many of these people real or symbolic second chances. However, some adults are blocked from doing so by an ideology that "failure is my fate," which they have developed to justify their condition. These individuals may present to a psychiatrist or other physician with a complaint like "nothing ever goes right for me," "I'm jinxed," or so forth. They tend to portray themselves as fortune's plaything, and not uncommonly, as the victim of bad luck and fate. Therefore, they may consciously and unconsciously minimize the influence of their choices in shaping their lives. One patient, for example, when discussing several important life situations, including her decision to enter psychotherapy, said "I had no choice."

Indeed, psychotherapy for adults, including the elderly, may be looked upon as a kind of laboratory for the making of choices. Psychotherapy patients learn to reconsider past situations as the result of choices unwittingly made or evaded. This change in perspective may help them to redefine the present and the future as inherently open to influence. The next step is making new choices and dealing with their consequences, both external and internal. It is for this reason that some adults make use of at least brief psychotherapy at several times during their development and view it as an invaluable aid in their efforts to more successfully negotiate adult transitions.

ACKNOWLEDGMENT

The authors thank Susan Shelton, MD, for reviewing this chapter and for many contributions to the sections on childlessness and on the single parent.

ANNOTATED BIBLIOGRAPHY

Colarusso C, Nemiroff R: Adult Development. New York, Plenum Press, 1981

> This standard work presents a problem-oriented approach to the main stages of adult development.

Colarusso CA: Child and Adult Development: A Psychoanalytic Introduction for Clinicians. New York, Plenum Press, 1992

> This is a good introduction to psychodynamic and psychoanalytic theories and concepts of development; it is written in a clear, engaging, and clinically relevant manner.

Erikson EH: Childhood and Society. New York, WW Norton, 1963

This classic on adult development contains the "eight ages of man" schema, which has served as a foundation for much subsequent research in the field.

Gould RL: Transformations. New York, Simon & Schuster, 1978

Gould's paradigm of adult development stresses transitional stages such as the "age 30 transition."

Levinson DJ, Darrow CM, Klein EB et al: The Seasons of a Man's Life. New York, Alfred A Knopf, 1978

Based on more than a decade of rigorous research on the stages of adult development, this work achieved a fresh perspective on adulthood by viewing it as a series of transitions.

Mahler MS, Pine F, Bergman A: The Psychological Birth of the Human Infant. New York, International Universities Press, 1975

The product of many years of observational study on mothers and their infants, this classic work offered a new developmental schema for the first 3 years of life, based on the notion of separation-individuation. It originated the idea of a normative crisis—the so-called rapprochement crisis—at the age of about 21 months.

Vaillant G: Adaptation to Life. Boston, Little, Brown & Co, 1977

This book discusses the results of a large prospective study of male college students in which psychologic traits were correlated with measures of physical and psychologic health over several decades.

Viorst J: Necessary Losses. New York, Ballantine Books, 1986

Viorst elaborates the thesis that each advance to a new developmental stage is associated, to a greater or lesser extent, with the loss of an emotionally invested portion of previous stages.

Winnicott DW: The Maturational Processes and the Facilitating Environment. New York, International Universities Press, 1965

Winnicott's concepts of the "holding environment," "primary maternal preoccupation," and "the good-enough mother" are useful in appreciating the tasks of parenting.

REFERENCES

Anzieu D: Freud's Self-Analysis. Madison, CT, International Universities Press, 1986

Bibring GL, Dwyer TF, Huntington DS et al: A study of the psychological processes in pregnancy and of the earliest mother-child relationship. Psychoanal Study Child 16:9–24, 1961

Blos P: The second individuation process of adolescence. Psychoanal Study Child 22:162–186, 1967

Colarusso C, Nemiroff R: Adult Development. New York, Plenum Press, 1981

Erikson EH: Identity and the lifecycle (monograph). Psychological Issues, vol 1, no 1. New York, International Universities Press, 1959

Erikson EH: Childhood and Society. New York, WW Norton, 1963

Freud A: The concept of developmental lines. Psychoanal Study Child 8:245–265, 1963

Freud S: Mourning and melancholia. 1917. In Strachey J (ed): The Standard Edition of the Complete Psychological Works, vol 14. London, Hogarth Press, 1958

Freud S: Three essays on the theory of sexuality. 1905. In Strachey J (ed): The Standard Edition of the Complete Psychological Works, vol 7. London, Hogarth Press, 1958

Gould RL: The phases of adult life: A study in developmental psychology. Am J Psychiatry 129:521–531, 1972

Greenspan S: "The second other": The role of the father in early personality formation and the dyadic–phallic phase of development. In Cath S, Gurwitt A, Ross JM (eds): Father and Child. Boston, Little, Brown & Co, 1982

Jaques E: Death and the mid-life crisis. Int J Psychoanal 46:502–514, 1965

Kernberg O: Internal World and External Reality Object Relations Theory Applied. New York, Jason Aronson, 1980

Kiley D: The Peter Pan Syndrome. New York, Dodd, Mead, 1983

Koenig HG, Cohen HJ, Blazer DG et al: Religious coping and depression among elderly, hospitalized medically ill men. Am J Psychiatry 149:1693–1700, 1992

Kübler-Ross E: On Death and Dying. New York, Macmillan, 1969

Levenson JL, Kay R, Monteferrante J et al: Denial predicts favorable outcome in unstable angina pectoris. Psychosom Med 46:25–32, 1984

Levinson DJ, Darrow CM, Klein EB et al: The Seasons of a Man's Life. New York, Alfred A Knopf, 1978

Levinson DJ, Gooodeneh WE: The life cycle. In Kaplan HI, Sadock BJ (eds): Comprehensive Textbook of Psychiatry. Baltimore, Williams & Wilkins, 1985

Lifton RJ: Death in Life: Survivors of Hiroshima. New York, Simon and Schuster, 1967

Mahler MS: The rapprochement subphase of the separation–individuation process. Psychoanal Q 41:487–506, 1972

Mahler MS, Pine F, Bergman A: The Psychological Birth of the Human Infant. New York, International Universities Press, 1975

Schafer R: The psychoanalytic vision of reality. Int J Psychoanal 51:279–297, 1970

Settlage CF, Curtis J, Lozoff M et al: Conceptualizing adult development. J Am Psychoanal Assn 36:347–369, 1988

Sholevar P (ed): The Handbook of Marriage and Marital Therapy. Jamaica, NY, SP Medical and Scientific Books, 1981

Simons RC (ed): Understanding Human Behavior in Health and Illness. Baltimore, Williams & Wilkins, 1985

Tolstoy L: The Death of Ivan Ilych. New York, Bantam Books, 1981

Vaillant G: Adaptation to Life. Boston, Little, Brown & Co, 1977

Van Gennep A: The Rites of Passage. Chicago, University of Chicago Press, 1960

Viorst J: Necessary Losses. New York, Ballantine Books, 1986

Winnicott DW: The Maturational Processes and the Facilitation Environment. New York, International Universities Press, 1965

Alan Stoudemire (ed). *Human Behavior: An Introduction for Medical Students,*
Second Edition. Copyright © 1994, 1990 by J. B. Lippincott Company.

11

The Behavioral and Psychobiological Effects of Developmental Trauma

Bessel A. van der Kolk

Section II and the preceding chapters in this section on human development have laid the groundwork for considering the possible consequences of developmental stresses for human behavior and vulnerability to psychiatric illness. A growing body of psychiatric research has confirmed that certain types of adverse stresses, losses, and deprivations within the family system may cause abnormalities in psychological development with lifelong effects on the individual's personality, susceptibility to stressful events in later life, and vulnerability to certain types of mental illness. Moreover, the long-term *neurobiological* effects of developmental stress have also begun to be elucidated. These findings, some of which will be summarized here, provide an excellent model to integrate biological, psychological, and social theories of human behavior and mental illness. This chapter provides an overview of some of this evidence from a psychobiological perspective. This chapter also provides an entrée and transition to Section IV of this text, which considers in some detail neurobiological aspects of behavior.

It has been an unfortunate tradition in medicine and psychiatry to separate mental illness into "organic" *or* "functional" problems. This dichotomy implies that the origins and cure of mental problems are *either* biologically *or* psychologically determined. These assumptions are based on the existence of a body–mind dichotomy: that nature and nurture act on different parts of the mind, and that biological and psychological processes can somehow be segregated into two disconnected determinants of behavior. Human beings, however, are biological organisms that develop within an interpersonal and social context; much of the maturation of the central nervous system (CNS) occurs after birth.

In the past few decades, research has clarified the interaction between social environment and ongoing neurobiological development (Edelman, 1987; Kandel and Schwartz, 1985). Contemporary science has started to elucidate how *the most ordinary everyday events—sensory stimulation, deprivation, and learning—have biological consequences, causing disruptions of synaptic connections under some circumstances and activation of neural connections under others.* While genetic and embryonal processes determine the basic structure of the brain, *the pattern of interconnections between neurons depends largely on experience,* particularly during the first decade of life. The degree of impact of environmental events on the CNS and, therefore, on behavior varies with age.

It is thus no longer scientifically justifiable to make clear distinctions between psychological and biological processes; rather we need to define our understanding of the degree to which genetic, developmental, toxic, and social factors converge to result in certain clinical syndromes. Both psychopharmacological and psychotherapeutic interventions must work by acting on the CNS and thus, on the connections between nerve cells. This general approach is consistent with a biopsychosocial model of understanding human behavior both in normal development and psychopathological states. The following discussion presents evidence that provides scientific confirmation of this integrated model.

THE PSYCHOBIOLOGY OF ATTACHMENT AND SEPARATION

Nobody grows up and lives in isolation. We all have been shaped by and continually are affected by our social surroundings. This process starts with the mother–infant bond and continues with ever-wider interpersonal and cultural forces. Human attachment starts as a vital biological function, without which survival is not possible (Bowlby, 1969, 1973). Human beings by nature seem to be *monotropic* i.e., they tend to form specific relationships and preferences for particular people. By being attached to familiar caregivers as children, and a predictable environment and moral values as adults, people are assured of a "safe base" from which they can explore their inner and outer world. Secure caregiving experiences in infancy set the stage for the development of a capacity for safe, meaningful interpersonal relationships and for trust.

The importance of *bonding* in the process of human development has been previously mentioned by Dr. Dulcan in Chapter 8. Forced separations of the maternal-infant bond in developing primates lends to predictable behavioral "deprivation syndromes" similar to the phenomenon of *"anaclitic depression"* observed in human infants deprived of maternal contact (see Chapter 8). Separation studies with infant macaques has demonstrated—as in human infants—three characteristic phases of this distress response. These phases are (1) agitation-protest, (2) withdrawal/despair, and (3) total detachment. These affective reactions serve as a model for human bereavement as well as for clinical depression. Moreover, strong evidence suggests that early disruption and separations at critical phases of infant and childhood contribute to vulnerability to development of depression in later adult life.

If monkey infants are severely deprived, they demonstrate prominent self-directed behaviors such as biting, sucking, rocking and self-hugging. The infants "fail to thrive" and show evidence of suppression of the immune system. In infant rhesus monkeys that are socially isolated for a period of a year, resocialization may be difficult if not impossible since one of the characteristic signs of deprivation is hostile reactivity to the intrusion of others. While female monkeys that have been socially isolated are extremely difficult to mate with males, some may nevertheless become pregnant, but usually show abnormal mothering such as neglect and indifference toward their offspring (Zumpe and Michael, 1990). This behavior has been interpreted to suggest that failure to form normal bonds early in life leads to problems in forming interpersonal bonds in later life (Zumpe and Michael, 1990).

Mammals have developed highly complex ways of maintaining attachment bonds between caregivers and their offspring. The separation cry of infants induces adults to respond to provide safety, nurturance, and social (i.e., pleasurable) stimulation. Nonhuman primates express attachment bonds mainly with physical contact such as clinging. Humans have evolved to be able to supplement such behavior with language to maintain relationships. MacLean (1985) considers human verbal communication to be an evolutionary development from the infantile attachment cry of infants. He sees the human capacity to maintain attachment bonds over space and time by means of verbal communication as one of the principal reasons for the human ascendancy in the animal kingdom. This capacity also has a dark side: "when mammalians opted for a family way of life, they set the stage for the most distressful forms of suffering, a condition that, for us, makes being a mammal so painful, and that is having to endure separation and isolation from loved ones, and, in the end, the utter desolation of death" (MacLean, 1985).

Anxiety and Social Deprivation

When primate infants cannot find their caregivers, they emit a separation cry; these protest signals are aimed at bringing the primary attachment figure back, and they cease upon the adult's return. Failure of the caregiver to return results in withdrawal, grief, and mourning. If, after prolonged protest or mourning, no reunion or resolution follows, primates develop a detached stance, in which they turn away from mutually gratifying social interactions. Starting with Harlow's work (Harlow and Harlow, 1971), a long series of studies have demonstrated the remarkable similarities between the response of *nonhuman primates* to separation from mothers and peers and those of *human infants* and children. Harlow's isolated monkeys always sought the presence of mother surrogates in preference over food. In monkeys, social isolation for various periods during the first year of life produced grossly abnormal social and sexual behavior. Young monkeys who are separated from their mothers respond with self-stimulation such as huddling, self-clasping, self-sucking, and biting. This is accompanied by social withdrawal and unpredictable aggression. These primates do not learn to discriminate such social stimuli as facial expressions, because they lack the early experience of the synchrony between mother and child and its associated expressions.

Spitz (1945), as mentioned in Chapter 8, first described how essential interpersonal stimulation is for normal growth and development in infants. He compared children raised in a foundling home for abandoned children with those raised in a nursing home attached to a women's prison. In both places the children were clean and well cared for. However, the prisoners showered the children with physical affection for brief periods each day, while in the foundling home the children were hardly touched by anybody, except for the most perfunctory contact around feeding and changing. They even were unable to observe each other from their cribs. They led lives of severe sensory deprivation. After 1 year, the foundling home children, who suffered from a deficiency of nurturing maternal contact, developed a socially acquired immunodeficiency syndrome, and severe depressions that made them unresponsive to human interaction.

The Relevance of Critical Periods and the Persistence of Latent Effects

The effects of social deprivation in primates can be partially reversed by reunion with peers and adult caregivers, and by integration in a social structure (Kraemer, 1986; Reite, 1987; Reite and Field, 1985). Both the age at which the separation trauma occurs and individual genetic vulnerability affect the extent of long-term damage. After an initial period of marked aggression against their newly acquired peers, previously isolated monkeys slowly develop appropriate behavior when they are put back in a social setting. Kraemer and his colleagues have shown that by 3 to 4 years they are nearly indistinguishable from their socially reared counterparts. *However, this normal adaptation can be lost under stress, or after being given psychostimulants or alcohol.* These stimuli cause these formerly deprived monkeys to respond either with social withdrawal or with indiscriminate aggression. Even monkeys that recover in other respects may have persistent deficits in sexual behavior and continue to misperceive social cues, for example, failing to withdraw after a threat by a dominant animal. The increased alcohol consumption seen in the previously isolated monkeys, compared with normal controls, indicates that, in addition to the genetic vulnerability to substance abuse, there is a neurobiological linkage between early social attachment mechanisms, social stressors, and vulnerability to alcohol abuse and addiction.

Early Experience Contributes to Physiological Reactivity

Field (1987) has shown that normal play and exploratory activity in children requires the presence of a familiar attachment figure who modulates their physiological arousal by providing a balance between soothing and stimulation. In the absence of the mother, infants experience extremes of under- and overarousal that are physiologically disorganizing. Unresponsive or abusive caregivers may cause chronic hyperarousal states, which have a long-term effect on the child's ability to modulate strong emotions. These changes persist over time, even though under ordinary conditions there are no readily observable behavioral concomitants of this biological alteration.

Field (1987) notes: "On a continuum from low to high physiologic arousal there is an optimal level for every organism. The shape of an individual's optimal stimulation curve depends, in part, on their early life experiences."

The response to social isolation or stress also depends on age. Children under the age of 12 months admitted for elective surgery generally have little trouble with either separation from, or reunion with their parents. They hardly differentiate between their mothers and strangers; the only sign that something is wrong is that they may be unusually quiet. Hospitalized children over 2 years of age usually respond anxiously or angrily to strangers, and they are often demanding and clinging with their mothers. Upon return home, they tend to cling tenaciously to their mothers and are very distressed when left alone.

Increased Attachment in the Face of Danger

Both children and adults seek increased attachment in the face of external danger. This occurs even when the threat emanates from the attachment object itself; thus, attachment increases even when a caregiver no longer provides effective protection and nurturance (Rajecki et al, 1978). Children are most vulnerable to such pathological attachments, because they have much fewer choices than do adults about whom to turn to for protection. Thus, while only conditions of captivity make adults turn to tormentors for attachment, abused children, as a rule, display anxious attachment and exceptional loyalty to their abusing parents.

Freud already noted that one of the earliest indications that a child will later become neurotic can be seen in an insatiable demand for his or her parent's affections. This is, of course, another way of describing a child who shows excessive anxiety about separation and loss of love (see Chapter 3 by Drs. Walker and Katon).

What makes children vulnerable to such excessive separation anxiety? At least five factors now have been identified:

1. Kagan and associates (1987) have demonstrated the large *temperamental differences* between children, which show up behaviorally as shyness, neophobia, and clinging, and neuroendocrinologically as increased catecholamine and blunted cortisol responses to environmental stimuli.

2. Safety of the attachment bond. Children who are abused and neglected are afraid of new stimuli, unable to change sets, and physiologically hyperreactive. They tend to vacillate between being anxious and withdrawn socially, and being hyperaggressive and insensitive to other children's needs. This syndrome has been noted in children with prior experiences with sudden parental separations and loss, abuse, and confusion about boundaries and roles within the family, such as occurs in parental drug and alcohol abuse, suicidal threats, and incest (Cicchetti, 1984; van der Kolk, 1987).

3. Intactness of the central nervous system (CNS). Mentally retarded or intoxicated children and adults and those with other

neurologic syndromes are much more likely to react to separation and change with anxiety or aggression.

4. "Spoiling." An excess of gratification interferes with the development of mastery and trust in one's inner capacities to solve problems. Not learning the pleasures of mastering difficult problems leads to excessive worry, fear of not being able to face new challenges, and clinging to parents and other authority figures.

5. Excessive threats of separation and abandonment by parents. One study showed that 27% of parents used threats of abandonment as a method of discipline. Many studies have shown that offspring from such parents are prone to chronic anger and anxiety.

Separation Anxiety and Hostility

Separation anxiety, abandonment, and abuse activate hostility. Separation from mother, parental rejection of children, and lack of acknowledgment of legitimate grievances by loved ones and authority figures in adults all give rise to anger. Studies of neglected and abused children have demonstrated a tendency to grow up angry and disturbed (Burgess et al, 1987; Lewis et al, 1979). Separated children play violent games with dolls representing parental figures. Hostility tends to subside after reunion or acknowledgment. Bowlby has called this a situation in which a person's need for security competes with anger at abandonment. He points out that anger initially serves as an attempt to reestablish a broken connection. When this fails, many people do to others what has been done to them. This "identification with the aggressor" allows feelings of helplessness to be replaced with invulnerability and omnipotence. Reenactment of victimization is a major cause of violence in society. Abuse and victimization of children have been linked with the development of drug abuse, juvenile delinquency, and adult criminal behavior.

Identification with the aggressor may also lead to self-destructive behavior. Many abused children engage in headbanging, biting, burning, and cutting. There are, very frequently, childhood sexual abuse histories in adults who engage in various forms of self-harm later in life, particularly cutting and self-starving. Their self-destructive acts clearly are a repetition, both on a behavioral, and possibly on a biological level, of encounters with hostile caretakers during the first years of life.

When abused and neglected children grow up, and the possibility of intimacy arises, the expectation of a recurrence of loss and betrayal is likely to be accompanied by inappropriate hostility and anxiety. Thus, hostility and anxiety go hand in hand; they may be turned against the self, against others, or they may be expressed indirectly and manifest themselves in psychosomatic symptoms, where hostility and helplessness are reexperienced both by the patient and his caregivers.

Numerous studies have documented the relationship between early loss of safe attachment and later psychiatric illness. However, studies of refugees and other traumatized children regularly uncover a multiplicity of creative solutions and the development of particular gifts that allow many people to transcend horrendous early life experiences, at least to survive, though often in a world of impoverished interpersonal attachments.

Aggression

Several environmental variables have been identified that predispose to violent behavior in animals and include overheating, crowding, and uncomfortable living conditions (Lewis, 1992). Isolation of otherwise gentle animals during critical developmental phases can contribute to aggressive behavior. Deprivation of infants tends to predispose to developmental delays, depressive reactions, severe impairment in peer relationships, and aggressive behavior.

Strong learning factors influence the development of aggression, and a wealth of experimental data indicate that aggressive behavior can be learned. When children who display aggressive behavior are punished severely, the behaviors tend to continue. However, the presence of the punishing parent often results in avoidance strategies in displaying the aggressive behavior. Severe physical punishment of children also predisposes to aggressive delinquency. One of the most powerful causes of aggression in both animals and humans appears to be the repeated infliction of pain (Berkowitz, 1984). Abused children are much more aggressive and hypervigilant than nonabused children.

Studies in both animals and humans indicate that aggressive behavior is mediated by biological factors. In animal models, exposure to prenatal androgen is essential for the development of aggressive behavior in a variety of species—including primates. Animals whose brains are androgen-sensitive during early development respond more aggressively to stimuli that cause surges in testosterone secretion. In primates, levels of circulating androgens respond to experiences of dominance or defeat, and one classic study showed that testosterone levels fell by as much as 80% in a previously dominant male who was "bested" by a competitor (Rose, Holaday, Bernstein, 1971).

Certain neurotransmitter systems are also involved in the expression and modulation of aggression. Aggression in animals can be included and facilitated by administering noradrenergic drugs or their precursors. Dopamine depletion leads to decreases in aggressive behavior. The most consistent relationship between aggressive behavior and a neurotransmitter system in humans has been with serotonin—since diminished levels of serotonin have been associated with self-injurious and violent behaviors.

Lewis postulates that maltreatment of children alters the neurophysiology of the brain, diminishing the concentration in the brain of substances such as serotonin, which modulate aggressive behavior as well as facilitating the production of substances such as dopamine and testosterone, which lead the individual—who may be already hypervigilant and paranoid by being exposed to an abusive environment—to respond with aggression. As noted by Lewis, "Whatever increases impulsivity and irritability, engenders hypervigilance and paranoia, diminishes judgment and verbal competence, and curtails the ability to recognize one's own pain and the pain of others, also enhances the tendency towards violence. Abusive, neglectful caretaking does all of these things" (Lewis, 1992, pp 388–389). Clearly, the expression of these behaviors is modulated by the neurobiological factors noted above. Other data also indicates that sensitization of the brain may occur in very early development, influencing the tendency toward aggression that may become an inextricable personality characteristic. (The neurobiology of aggression is also discussed in Chapter 12 by Dr. Pedersen and associates.)

Information Processing and Memory Storage

Memories of past experiences determine a person's interpretation of contemporary life events. These memories are not necessarily conscious (i.e., encoded as verbal memory traces). Developmental psychologists have identified three modes of information processing: *enactive, iconic*, and *symbolic/linguistic* (Kihlstrom, 1984). These three modes of representation closely parallel Piaget's notions of sensorimotor, preoperational, and operational thinking, which reflect stages of development of the CNS (Piaget, 1973). Over the course of development there is a shift from sensorimotor (motoric action), to perceptual representations (iconic), to symbolic and linguistic modes of organization of mental experience. During periods of stress, people often return to processing events mainly on a visceral or motoric level (i.e., with somatic sensations or with action). Severe stress leaves people in a state of "unspeakable terror." Words do not allow for meaningful constructs. The terror overwhelms and cannot be integrated. In those cases, the experience is organized on a sensorimotor or iconic level—as anxiety attacks, nightmares, visceral sensations, or as fight/flight/freeze reactions (van der Kolk, 1987).

Children are particularly vulnerable to physiological disorganization in the face of stress, and they rely principally on their caregivers for modulation of arousal. The development of cognitive schemes that help to give meaning to current life experiences is crucial for learning how to interpret and thus modulate physiological arousal in the face of threat: cognitive schemata serve as a buffer against being overwhelmed. Thus, the cognitive preparedness (development) of a person interacts with the degree of physiological arousal to determine the capacity to organize potentially disturbing experiences. Frightening experiences can be stored in memory in a somatosensory mode without linguistic representation (i.e., conscious awareness). These experiences then are "remembered" as anxiety attacks and panic disorders, which result in increased clinging and neophobia.

Recent research on state-dependent learning sheds some light on why children are more likely to process stress on a somatosensory level rather than in conscious, verbal, memory (Jacobs and Nadel, 1985). The hippocampus, which serves a mapping function for locating memories for experiences in space and time, does not fully mature until the third or fourth year of life. However, the maturation of the *taxon system*, which subserves memories related to the quality (feel and sound) of things, occurs much earlier. Thus, in the first few years of life only the quality of events, but not their context, can be remembered. During subsequent development, the locale system remains vulnerable to disruption. Stress interferes with the functioning of the hippocampally based locale system and potentiates the taxon system (i.e., it leads to context-free fearful associations that are hard to locate in space and time). The hippocampus is rich in corticosteroid receptors, which are selectively activated during stress. *Severe or prolonged stress, with its accompanying increase in corticosteroid levels can result in a suppression of hippocampal functioning and thus amnesia for traumatic experiences.* Lacking localization in space and time, they are encoded in sensorimotor form and, therefore, cannot be easily translated into the symbolic language necessary for conscious linguistic retrieval (Squire, 1987).

Forgotten Memories Return under Stress

Learning is state-dependent. Information can only be retrieved in a state similar to the one in which the memory was encoded. State dependency can be roughly related to arousal levels and, thus, is affected by a large variety of stimuli that affect a person's mental state (e.g., both psychostimulants and depressants, meditative states, and situations of terror). Reactivation of past learning is relatively automatic. *Contextual stimuli* directly evoke stored memories without conscious awareness of the transition (Squire, 1987). The more similar the contextual stimuli are to conditions prevailing at the time of the original storage of memories, the more likely the probability of retrieval. *In practice, this means that feeling states are reactivated when a person is exposed to situations similar to the ones that occurred at the time that the original memory was stored.* This is true for both positive and negative experiences. Strains of music or smells may cause one to return to a happy frame of mind associated with past experience, but, similarly, when people who grew up in violent homes, and who as adults behave competently, are exposed to a threatening situation, they reexperience themselves as terrified children and may behave accordingly (van der Kolk, 1988).

These observations have implications for psychotherapy, because an essential feature of explorative psychotherapies is the necessity of "reliving" in memory and feeling traumatic experiences as part of the healing process. It is through the reactivation of emotionally traumatic affective (feeling) states and the memories associated with them that the person is freed up from these disabling influences on personality and interpersonal relationships. Distortions and problems in interpersonal relationships that have their roots in difficult developmental experiences are addressed in this reconstitutive process. The emotional "working through" occurs within a new intellectual and maturational framework, which the person now is able to use to reinterpret past experience.

Stress causes a return to earlier behavior patterns throughout the animal kingdom. In a state of low arousal, animals tend to be curious and seek novelty. When hyperaroused, they will seek the familiar, regardless of the rewards that follow. Because novel stimuli themselves cause arousal, an animal in a state of high arousal will avoid mildly novel stimuli even if it would reduce exposure to pain. Thus, highly stressed animals will return to a familiar, electrified box, in preference to an unfamiliar, but physically safe environment. The similarity between this behavior and that of people who seem unable to extricate themselves from painful relationships is obvious (Mitchell et al, 1985).

THE SOCIAL ENVIRONMENT AND CNS DEVELOPMENT: THE THEORY OF NEURONAL GROUP SELECTION

The work of Kandel, Edelman, and others has begun to shed some light on the way in which the CNS uses experience to form the unique structures that characterizes each person in his or her complexity. Edelman (1987) has pointed out that the task of the CNS is to "carry on adaptive perceptual categorization in an unlabeled world . . . that cannot be prefigured for an organism." After birth, a person's neural structure is basically in place, and the focus of development "now turns to modifications in the strengths of the synapses between neuronal groups, so the connections that are modified are between these groups, rather than between specific cells." The initial arrangement into groups is known as the primary repertoire; further experience is responsible for the creation of a secondary repertoire, which is involved in the subsequent behavior of the organism. The connections between the neuronal groups that are created in the secondary repertoire enable a person to "get around in the world." From Edelman's point of view, "the brain is a selective system more akin in its working to evolution than to computation or information processing." Both sensors and effectors are involved in this process of group selection. Action is fundamental to perception. Both sensory sheets and motor ensembles must operate together to produce perceptual categorization. Edelman believes that categorization (i.e., the way in which the mind imposes structures on a world which has no inherent labels) is the most fundamental of mental activities. Thus, he views memory as "the enhanced capacity to categorize and generalize associatively, not the storage of features, not objects as a list." In this model, learning consists of altering "the linkage of global mappings to hedonic centers through synaptic changes in classification couples. Such changes yield a categorization of complexes of adaptive value under conditions of expectancy."

Affiliation and the Brain

The leap from Edelman's theory of group selection to mental states is considerable. However, there now is considerable speculation that what is remembered best are not facts, things, or even faces, but what is known as the *taxon system*, the feelings and quality of experience. As Minsky (1980) puts it, "So we shall view memories as entities that predispose the mind to deal with new situations in old, remembered ways—specifically, as entities that reset the states of parts of the nervous system. Then they can cause that nervous system to be 'disposed' to behave as though it remembers. This is why I put 'dispositions' ahead of 'propositions.' "

Harlow and his successors have conclusively demonstrated that secure attachment is not merely a psychological event; it is essential for the development of core neurobiological functions in the primate brain. Early attachment patterns determine, to a large degree, how a child categorizes his interpersonal world. *Early disruption of the social attachment bond causes long-lasting psychobiological changes that reduce the capacity to cope with stress, interfere with learning and motivation, and disturb parenting processes, causing a similar vulnerability in the next generation* (van der Kolk, 1987).

Research in the past few decades has established that the limbic system guides the emotions that stimulate the behavior necessary for self-preservation and survival of the species. The limbic system is largely responsible for such complex behaviors as feeding, fighting, fleeing, and reproduction. Studies of people with temporal lobe epilepsy show that the limbic system is also responsible for free-floating feelings of what is real, true, and meaningful (Kling and Steklis, 1976). While neocortical activity is not necessarily involved in attachment behaviors, destruction of various parts of the limbic system in nonhuman primates abolishes social behavior, including care of the young. In young animals it also abolishes play, which is necessary to learn to experiment with peer attachments and social collaboration.

Neuroanatomical Correlates of Affiliative Behavior

The relationship of affiliative behaviors and specific anatomical areas in the brain is still speculative. However, brain lesion studies in nonhuman primates provide some indications that bonding, nurturance, and social cohesion are severely affected by ablations of the limbic system. Lesions of the amygdala, the cingulate cortex, the anterior temporal pole, and the prefrontal cortex all cause dramatic deficits in social behavior, such as nest building, nursing, and retrieval of the young. Cingulectomized animals treat others as if they were inanimate—walking over them and sitting on them. This does not lead to fights because they avoid even aggressive contact with others (Kling and Steklis, 1976). In human beings, cingulotomy has been used to treat obsessive–compulsive disorder and other emotional disturbances related to conflicts about social relationships.

Kling's electrical recording studies from the amygdala suggest that the amygdala responds to an external stimulus with an intensity proportional to its "emotional" significance. Kling believes that the intensity of the discharge may determine the extent of the projection field from the amygdala to the hypothalamus, brain stem, and possibly, cortical structures. Thus, temporal lobe lesions decrease facilitatory inputs and diminish amygdaloid activity. This reduces the capacity to make differential responses to specific stimuli and thus impairs affiliative behavior.

The human brain exhibits powerful capabilities for adaptation and plasticity. While the fundamental neuroanatomical structure of the brain is determined by the genome it is not fully configured by genomic factors (Spinelli, 1990). Full configuration of the brain is influenced by external stimuli and information from the environment (Schwartz and Goldman-Rakic, 1990). The influence of environmental stimuli on both the neuroanatomical and neurophysiological functions and structure of the brain is discussed in some detail by Dr. Pedersen and associates in Chapter 12. It is should be emphasized in passing here, however, that during certain critical development periods the configuration of the brain is determined by environmental stimuli and social experience, and that the capabilities for neuronal plasticity and configuration is greatest in higher animal species, particularly humans (Spinelli, 1990). While this plastic ability of the human brain facilitates the greatest degree of adaptability, it also lends the developing infant to be the most vulnerable to the influences of caretakers who, as Spinelli has noted, have the responsibility to "deliver the best configuration sequence," and that "the caretaker is unavoidably a *brain shaper* who has a very large impact in determining the future learning predispositions and potential of the infant" (Spinelli, 1990, p 81).

There are critical periods of development after which the CNS loses its plasticity and damage becomes irreversible. In the first year of life, there appears to be considerable *plasticity* of the nervous system. One study found that neonate rhesus macaques who sustained bilateral ablations of the amygdala and were returned to their mothers 6 to 12 hours later grew up no different from normal controls. In nonhuman primates, social affiliative bonds remain relatively intact after prefrontal and temporal cortical ablation during the first two years of life, provided that there is adequate mothering. However, monkeys with either prefrontal or amygdaloid lesions are even more responsive to the effects of maternal deprivation than are intact monkeys.

Psychophysiological and Biochemical Responses to Separation

In most young mammals, dependency on adult caregivers is so strong that mere separation from the mother, even without external danger, causes distress in infants. Pups of many species show a physiological response to removal from the mother, which includes a drop in temperature, cardiac and respiratory depression, and behavioral arousal. Even brief separations in squirrel monkeys cause highly elevated plasma cortisol levels; repeated maternal separations lead to chronic elevations of plasma cortisol (Reite and Field, 1985). Increased cortisol leads to elevated tryptophan hydroxylase, which, in turn, results in a decrease in serotonin, the neurotransmitter most implicated in the modulation of affect and aggression. Kraemer and McKinney (1986) have demonstrated that monkeys with early separation experiences have low resting cerebrospinal fluid (CSF) catecholamine levels, but extreme norepinephrine responses to social stressors and to amphetamines. These changes in serotonin, adrenal gland catecholamine synthesizing enzymes, plasma cortisol, and immunoresistance are not minor, and they persist over time. The opiate system seems to play an important role in mediating affiliative behavior. Minute amounts of morphine abolish the separation call in infants, as well as maternal protection of their pups. The areas of the brain with the highest binding for mu-like opiate receptors are precisely those that have been found to be involved in the maintenance of social bonding. There is some evidence that social isolation directly affects the number or sensitivity of brain opiate receptors, at least during critical stages of development (Panksepp, 1982).

The precise behavioral results of these neurochemical changes are difficult to determine. Because any given behavior is undoubtedly influenced by a large variety of interacting neurochemical systems, any attempt to establish connections between a particular neurotransmitter and a specific type of behavior is bound to result in an oversimplification.

The Social Environment as Mediator of Brain Development

In contemporary psychiatry, much research has been done to elucidate the relationship between subtle, implicitly genetic, brain abnormalities and human psychopathology. However, studies on nonhuman primates indicate that the CNS of neonates are plastic enough to permit compensation for some gross brain abnormalities in early life, provided that parental care is adequate. On the other hand, animal studies show that mothers of damaged and unresponsive offspring tend to show an aversion to close physical contact with their infants and show little emotional expressiveness.

Nonhuman primate data, however, indicate that early social deprivation itself can be the cause of lasting changes in neuronal functioning. David Hubel (1978) was the first to suggest that "it seems conceivable that early starvation of social interaction, such as contact with mother, may lead to mental disturbances that have their counterpart in actual structural abnormalities of the brain." There are intriguing similarities between the behavioral effects of maternal neglect on monkeys and those of ablations of the amygdala and the cingulate cortex. Both monkeys who have been amygdalectomized and those who were socially isolated or abused as infants develop an attentional deficit, with distractability and difficulty in performing complex tasks and both tend to neglect or abuse their own offspring.

There are no morphologic studies yet to indicate that the behavioral sequelae of amygdalectomy and early social deprivation are, in fact, based on the same structural abnormalities. However, it is striking that the effects of social deprivation are most pronounced during critical periods in a monkey's life. These critical periods may coincide with the myelinization of those parts of the nervous system that are related to bonding and affiliative behavior. *Thus, it is conceivable that early social deprivation causes lasting damage to brain structures concerned with affiliation and bonding.* This would be analogous to the irreversible damage from sensory deprivation during critical periods that has been observed in the visual system.

TRAUMA AND PSYCHIATRIC ILLNESS

In recent years, there have been consistent reports that at least 50% of psychiatric inpatients have a childhood history of severe chronic physical and/or sexual abuse (Carmen et al, 1984). While the variety of current psychological symptoms and maladaptive behaviors obscure the etiologic role of the childhood traumatic stressors, most of these patients continue to show such symptoms as physiological hyperreactivity, a subjective sense of loss of control, chronic passivity alternating with uncontrolled violence against the self or others, and sleep disturbances. Data from these studies indicate that the hallmark of psychiatric patients with chronic childhood trauma is the multiplicity of clinical presentations that they exhibit over time, the variety of diagnoses that are given, and the number of different medications received.

In order to gain a greater understanding of the spectrum of trauma-related psychiatric disorders, much work remains to been done to map out the differential effects of environmental trauma on people with different temperaments at varying stages of development. The biphasic protest/despair response to abandonment and fear in childhood could be related to hyperactivity or underactivity of neurotransmitter systems.

Norepinephrine, dopamine, serotonin, and the endogenous opioid and endocrine systems are all involved in the protest/despair response. This illustrates how complex the interactions between biological abnormalities and behavior are; depending on the age at which the trauma occurred, the nature of social support, predisposing biological factors, and the nature and severity of the trauma, childhood trauma can manifest itself in many ways: as somatic sensations in the form of anxiety and panic, as behavioral reenactments of aspects of the trauma, or integrated into the totality of a person's personality organization, in which violence against self or others has become a way of life. As people mature they become less vulnerable to gross disruptions in their environment.

SUMMARY: ENVIRONMENT, GENETICS, AND HUMAN DEVELOPMENT

Contemporary psychiatry has justifiably paid much attention to both the neurologic and genetic concomitants of mental disorders. While numerous studies have found intriguing leads toward a greater understanding of the biology of such psychiatric disorders as schizophrenia, mood (affective) disorders, phobias, and attention deficit hyperactivity disorder, there often has been an implicit assumption that abnormal biological conditions must be genetically transmitted and encoded in DNA. However, the social environment can have profound effects on neurobiological maturation. The precise relationship between early experiences and subsequent psychopathology remains as elusive as that between DNA and mental illness. However, given the fact that secure social attachment bonds during infancy are essential for normal development in humans, and loss, abuse, and neglect are often devastating, it is obvious that understanding the psychobiological effects of early disruptions in attachment bonds and the subsequent development of psychopathology is one of the great challenges of contemporary psychiatry. Section IV of this text discusses in some detail derivatives of this psychobiologic approach to understanding human behavior from neurobiologic and genetic perspectives.

ANNOTATED BIBLIOGRAPHY

Bowlby J: Attachment and Loss, vol 1: Attachment. New York, Basic Books, 1969

Bowlby J. Attachment and Loss, vol 2: Separation. New York, Basic Books, 1973

> Bowlby's monumental but very readable work integrates current knowledge about the development of attachment and affectional bonds and the consequences of their disruption at various stages throughout the lifecycle.

Edelman GM: Neural Darwinism: The Theory of Neuronal Group Selection. New York, Basic Books, 1987

> This challenging work makes a major contribution toward explaining the evolution of neuronal solutions to information processing tasks. Its wide-ranging theory integrates knowledge from a range of neurosciences, from molecular genetics to evolutionary and developmental biology and the newly emerging field of cognitive science.

Kandel ER, Schwartz JH: Principles of Neural Science. New York, Elsevier, 1985

> This work addresses in depth and with a grand vision the questions of how life events are translated into neuronal changes and interconnections, and how mind and body are embedded in the same basic matrix.

Rajecki DW, Lamb ME, Obmascher P: Toward a general theory of infantile attachment: A comparative review of aspects of the social bond. Behav Brain Sci 3:417–464, 1978

This lengthy article reviews and integrates current knowledge about the ethology of attachment throughout the animal kingdom and the role of external events on imprinting, bonding, and individuation.

Reite M, Field T (eds): The Psychobiology of Attachment and Separation. Orlando, Academic Press, 1985

A comprehensive and detailed review of the scientific data of the neurobiologic and behavioral ramifications of early separation and attachment. This challenging book reviews the current status of our knowledge about the psychobiology of attachment and separation primarily in nonhuman primates. Its data about the specificity of the attachment bond, the long-term psychobiological effects of early trauma, and the development of the limbic system in the context of environmental stimuli are particularly noteworthy.

van der Kolk B: Psychological Trauma. Washington, DC, American Psychiatric Press, 1987

This book attempts to integrate current knowledge about the developmental, psychodynamic, cognitive, and biological aspects of human traumatization and discusses the need for a treatment approach that integrates all these dimensions when treating children and adults who have been traumatized.

REFERENCES

Berkowitz L: Physical pain and the inclination to aggression. In Flannelly KJ, Blanchard RJ, Blanchard DC (eds): Biological Perspectives on Aggression. New York, Liss, 1984, pp 27–47

Bowlby J: Attachment and Loss, vol 1: Attachment. New York, Basic Books, 1969

Bowlby J. Attachment and Loss, vol 2: Separation. New York, Basic Books, 1973

Burgess AW, Hartmann CR, McCormack A: Abused to abuser: Antecedents of socially deviant behavior. Am J Psychiatry 144:1431–1436, 1987

Carmen EH, Reiker PP, Mills T: Victims of violence and psychiatric illness. Am J Psychiatry 141:378–379, 1984

Cicchetti D: The emergence of developmental psychopathology. Child Dev 55:1–7, 1984

Edelman GM: Neural Darwinism: The Theory of Neuronal Group Selection. New York, Basic Books, 1987

Field T: Interaction and attachment in normal and atypical infants. J Consult Clin Psychol 55:1–7, 1987

Harlow HF, Harlow MK: Psychopathology in monkeys. In Kimmel HD (ed): Experimental Psychopathology. New York, Academic Press, 1971

Hubel D: Effects of deprivation on the visual cortex of cat and monkey. Harvey Lect 72:1–51, 1978

Jacobs WJ, Nadel L: Stress-induced recovery of fears and phobias. Psychol Rev 92:512–531, 1985

Kagan J, Reznick S, Snidman N: The physiology and psychology of behavioral inhibition in children. Child Dev 58:1459–1473, 1987

Kandel ER, Schwartz JH: Principles of Neural Science. New York, Elsevier, 1985

Kihlstrom JF: Conscious, subconscious, unconscious: A cognitive perspective. In Bowers KS, Meichenbaum D (eds): The Unconscious Reconsidered. New York, John Wiley, 1984

Kling A, Steklis HD: A neural substrate for affiliative behavior in non-human primates. Brain Behav Evol 13:216–238, 1976

Kraemer GW: Causes of changes in brain noradrenaline systems and later effects on responses to social stressors in rhesus monkeys: The cascade hypothesis. In Antidepressants and Receptor Function (Ciba Foundation Symposium 123). Chichester, Wiley, 1986

Lewis D, Shanok SS, Pincus JH et al: Violent juvenile delinquents: Psychiatric, neurological, psychological and abuse factors. J Child Psychiatry 18:307–319, 1979

Lewis DO: From abuse to violence: Psychophysiological consequences of maltreatment. J Am Acad Child Adolesc Psychiatry 31:383–391, 1992

MacLean PD: Brain evolution relating to family, play, and the separation call. Arch Gen Psychiatry 42:505–417, 1985

Minsky M: K-lines. A theory of memory. Cog Science 4:117–133, 1980

Mitchell D, Osborne EW, O'Boyle MW: Habituation under stress: Shocked mice show non-associative learning in a T-maze. Behav Neural Biol 43:212–217, 1985

Panksepp J: Toward a general psychobiological theory of emotions. Behav Brain Sci 5:407–468, 1982

Piaget J: Structuralism. New York, Basic Books, 1973

Rajecki DW, Lamb ME, Obmascher P: Toward a general theory of infantile attachment: A comparative review of aspects of the social bond. Behav Brain Sci 3:417–464, 1978

Reite M: Some additional influences shaping the development of behavior. Child Dev 58:596–600, 1987

Reite M, Field T (eds): The Psychobiology of Attachment and Separation. Orlando, Academic Press, 1985

Rose R, Holaday J, Bernstein I: Plasma testosterone, dominance rank, and aggressive behavior in male rhesus monkeys. Nature 231:366–368, 1971

Schwartz ML, Goldman-Rakic P: Development and plasticity of the primate cerebral cortex. Clin Perinatology 17:83–102, 1990

Spinelli DN: Plasticity triggering experiences, nature, and the dual genesis of brain structure and function. Clin Perinatology 17:77–83, 1990

Spitz R: Hospitalism: An inquiry into the genesis of psychiatric conditions in early childhood. Psychoanal Study Child 1:53–74, 1945

Squire LR: Memory and the Brain. New York, Oxford University Press, 1987

van der Kolk B: Psychological Trauma. Washington, DC, American Psychiatric Press, 1987

van der Kolk BA: The trauma spectrum: The interaction of biological and social events in the genesis of the trauma response. J Traumatic Stress 1:273–290, 1988

Zumpe D, Michael RP: Ethology and human behavior. In Stoudemire A (ed): Human Behavior: An Introduction for Medical Students, 1st ed. Philadelphia, Lippincott, 1990, pp 241–260

IV Biological Basis of Behavior

Alan Stoudemire (ed). *Human Behavior: An Introduction for Medical Students,*
Second Edition. Copyright © 1994, 1990 by J. B. Lippincott Company.

12 *Neurobiological Aspects of Behavior*

Cort A. Pedersen,
Robert N. Golden, John M. Petitto,
Dwight L. Evans,
and John J. Haggerty, Jr.

Enormous *advances* in neuroscientific research in recent years have provided the basis for exciting insights into the biological basis of behavior and invigorated the search for the biochemical and genetic basis for the major psychiatric disorders. This chapter will present an overview of the major neural networks and primary neurochemical systems that underlie complex behavior. The basic neurochemical systems will be reviewed (norepinephrine, serotonin, acetylcholine, dopamine, and so forth) as well as the major neuroendocrine systems. The neurobiology of learning and memory will be reviewed as well as basic neurobiologic aspects of behaviors such as reproductive behavior, consumptive behavior, aggression, and stress responses. Finally, a brief overview of sleep architecture and physiology will be presented.

MAJOR COMPONENTS OF BEHAVIOR AND THEIR NEURAL CORRELATES

Behavior may be understood as the product of integrated activity of a number of interacting brain systems. Among these systems are mechanisms that monitor internal and external sensory input, focus and maintain attention to significant stimuli, and arouse other brain regions involved in behavioral response patterns. For example, if an external stimulus (e.g., food) harmonizes with an internal drive state (e.g., hunger) a specific behavioral motivational system (e.g., feeding) activates goal-directed motor sequences. If the "reward" (i.e., food) is achieved, the internal drive state is tempo-

347

rarily satisfied and the motivated behavior (i.e., food seeking and eating) ceases. Conversely, aversive stimuli (e.g., predator, unfamiliar object) will activate avoidant or aggressive defensive systems and initiate motor sequences, such as fight-or-flight, freezing, or a generally cautious approach. If the resulting behavioral response decreases the danger associated with the situation, avoidant or aggressive motivation will usually subside.

Activation of the brain's motivational system is also accompanied by arousal of endocrine and autonomic responses. Affective or mood-related systems also influence the intensity and quality of behavioral responses and, in higher animals and humans, generate a range of subjective experiences known as emotion.

The basic characteristics of rewarding or aversive stimuli determine the degree of affective arousal in the organism. Frustration in achieving the goals associated with motivated or avoidant behavior also mobilizes affective responses. As discussed by Dr. Dorsett in Chapter 6, learning modifies behavior by allowing stimuli that might be otherwise neutral (conditioned stimuli) to become associated with rewarding or aversive stimuli (unconditioned stimuli). Through the learning process, conditioned stimuli become capable of activating arousal and attention mechanisms as well as motivational and affective systems. Thus, behavior is shaped by the following basic processes: arousal and attention, motivation, affect, motor performance, and learning. While much of the brain is involved to some extent in each of these components of behavior, certain brain areas and neural circuits are known to specialize in special areas. We will discuss the neuroanatomy, interconnecting pathways, and functions of brain regions that are involved in the activation and execution of behavior, specifically the reticular activating system, the hypothalamus, the limbic system, the association cortices, and the basal ganglia.

The Reticular Activating System

A diffuse network of neurons with widespread connections runs along the entire length of the midline brainstem. This system, referred to as the *reticular formation,* has long been known to influence level of consciousness (Kandel and Schwartz, 1991). We will describe later in the section on neurotransmitters ascending monoamine-containing pathways, which originate in the midbrain and ascend to forebrain structures. Neuronal cell bodies giving rise to these noradrenergic, dopaminergic and serotonergic projections are located within the reticular formation. Reticular monoaminergic pathways influence the processing of sensory information at higher brain centers as well as at the level of the dorsal horn of the spinal cord where primary sensory neurons connect with the central nervous system (CNS). They also regulate behavioral arousal and control levels of awareness. In particular, noradrenergic pathways ascending from the locus ceruleus, a pontine nucleus, play a key role in establishing and maintaining focused attention on significant stimuli. Monoaminergic pathways ascending from the reticular formation project to many other regions of the CNS including areas involved in initiation of motivated behaviors, affect, organization of motor output, and learning. *Thus, arousal and attention systems, originating in the midline brainstem, activate the neural substrates of other components of behavior.*

The Hypothalamus

The hypothalamus is a midline structure at the base of the brain beneath the thalamus and attached to the pituitary gland below by the infundibulum (Fig. 12–1A). Anteriorly, it is bordered by the preoptic area, the optic chiasm and the lamina terminalis; posteriorly, it extends to the caudal margins of the mammillary bodies. In humans, the hypothalamus is relatively small, constituting less than 1% of the entire brain. Despite its modest size the hypothalamus contains a large number of neural circuits that regulate the internal environment and coordinate autonomic, endocrine, and behavioral systems that maintain homeostasis. Critical physiological parameters such as temperature, osmolarity, blood pressure, and glucose concentrations are monitored by specialized neurons within the hypothalamus. Other neurons are equipped with receptors that detect levels of reproductive or stress hormones.

The hypothalamus is divided by neuroanatomical convention in the anterior–posterior dimension into anterior, middle, and posterior regions and in the lateral-medial dimension into the lateral, medial, and periventricular regions (Figs. 12–1B and C). The descending column of the fornix separates the lateral and medial regions of the hypothalamus. The most well-defined nuclei of the hypothalamus are found in the medial region: the *preoptic* and *supraoptic* nuclei in the anterior region; the

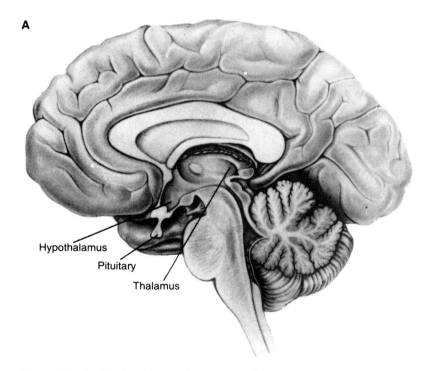

A

Hypothalamus

Pituitary

Thalamus

Figure 12–1. *The location and structure of the hypothalamus.*
A. *Medial view showing the relationship of the hypothalamus to the pituitary and thalamus.*

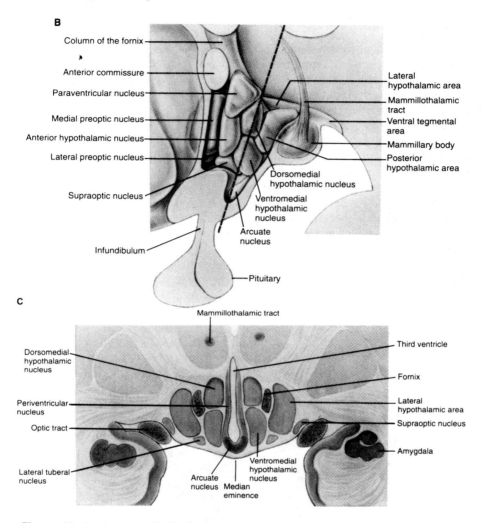

B

Column of the fornix

Anterior commissure

Paraventricular nucleus

Medial preoptic nucleus

Anterior hypothalamic nucleus

Lateral preoptic nucleus

Supraoptic nucleus

Infundibulum

Lateral hypothalamic area

Mammillothalamic tract

Ventral tegmental area

Mammillary body

Posterior hypothalamic area

Dorsomedial hypothalamic nucleus

Ventromedial hypothalamic nucleus

Arcuate nucleus

Pituitary

C

Mammillothalamic tract

Dorsomedial hypothalamic nucleus

Periventricular nucleus

Optic tract

Lateral tuberal nucleus

Third ventricle

Fornix

Lateral hypothalamic area

Supraoptic nucleus

Amygdala

Ventromedial hypothalamic nucleus

Arcuate nucleus

Median eminence

Figure 12–1. (continued) **B**. *Medial view showing positions of the main hypothalamic nuclei. Some nuclei are visible only in the frontal view in part C.* **C**. *Frontal view of the hypothalamus (section along plane shown in part B). (Reproduced with permission from Kandel ER, Schwartz JH, Jessell TM (eds): Principles of Neural Science. New York, Elsevier, 1991.)*

paraventricular, dorsomedial and *ventromedial* nuclei in the medial region, and the *posterior* nucleus and *mammillary bodies* in the posterior region. The lateral region of the hypothalamus contains a number of ascending and descending pathways that connect rostrally with the forebrain. The largest of these is the *medial forebrain bundle* (MFB), which contains important fiber tracts that originate from aminergic neurons in the midbrain and project to neocortical regions. The periventricular region is composed of the portions of the hypothalamus immediately adjacent to the third ventricle. The basal parts of the medial and periventricular regions contain the *tuberal nuclei* in primates and the *arcuate nuclei* in subprimate species. The hypothalamus is interconnected with more rostral structures by fibers that course through the fornix, the mammillothalamic tract, and the stria terminalis. Connections with more caudal structures are made through the MFB, the mammillotegmental pathway and the dorsal longitudinal fasciculus (Fig. 12–2).

Drive states originate within motivational systems located in the preoptic-hypothalamic area (Kandel and Schwartz, 1991). Some drive states (e.g., thirst, hunger, desire for warmth) result from changes in homeostasis of the internal physiologic milieu. Indeed, specialized cells that monitor certain parameters of the internal state (osmolarity, glucose concentrations, temperature) may be directly involved in activating drive states. Sex-specific motivated behaviors (e.g. mating, parenting, social aggression) are dependent upon reproductive hormone conditions and the availability of appropriate external stimuli (e.g., receptive females, newborns). As discussed earlier, threatening or painful conditions elicit avoidant, defensive, or submissive

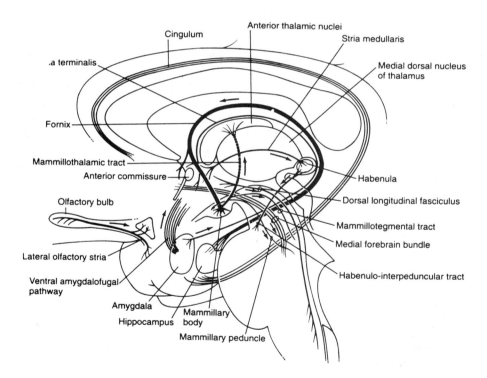

Figure 12–2. *Interconnections of the deep-lying structures included in the limbic system. The predominant direction of flow of neural activity in each tract is indicated by an arrow, but the designated tracts typically have bidirectional activity. (Reproduced with permission from Kandel ER, Schwartz JH, Jessell TM (eds): Principles of Neural Science. New York, Elsevier, 1991.)*

behaviors depending on the nature of the aversive situation. Output from motivational systems descends along the midline or through the MFB to the brain stem where connections are made with pathways that control specific motor sequences. Beginning with the work of Olds and Milner in 1954, numerous investigators have found that electrical stimulation at some locations within the hypothalamus and associated structures (the limbic system and the MFB) acts as a potent reward. *Animals with electrodes in these regions stimulate themselves at very high rates for long periods of time even if they are in no drive state (i.e., not hungry, thirsty, sexually aroused, and so forth).* These findings have obvious significance for understanding the neurobiological basis of addiction. Stimulation at other hypothalamic sites elicit escape, aggressive or submissive behavior. Dopaminergic pathways, especially the mesolimbic pathway, are important in maintaining electrical self-stimulation and may have a more general role in the mediation of reward.

The *paraventricular* nucleus exemplifies the multifunctional role of the hypothalamus as a whole and many of its nuclei. Neurons in the paraventricular nucleus fall into three distinct groups: those projecting to the posterior pituitary, those projecting to the median eminence, and those projecting to extrahypothalamic sites in the limbic system or the brainstem. Many of the later terminate in nuclei that regulate the autonomic nervous system. Neurons in the paraventricular nucleus, as well as throughout the mediobasal hypothalamus, synthesize and secrete into the portal hypophyseal vasculature the substances (for the most part small peptides) that promote or inhibit release of anterior pituitary hormones. Many of these hypothalamic neurons project to other brain sites where the release of peptides alter behavior. It is fascinating that the endocrine and behavioral effects of peptides are often harmonious. For example, luteinizing hormone-releasing hormone promotes both ovulation (by releasing luteinizing hormone from the anterior pituitary gland) and sexual behavior (by stimulating neurons in the ventromedial nucleus and the medial preoptic area of the hypothalamus) while corticotropin-releasing hormone stimulates both adrenal activation as well as various behavioral responses to stress by acting at, respectively, the anterior pituitary and specific brain sites.

The Limbic System

As stated above, the hypothalamus appears to be the center of coordination of autonomic, endocrine, and behavioral aspects of affect and emotion (Kandel and Schwartz, 1985). *Ablation of the hypothalamus almost totally eliminates affective responses to stimuli.* The *parahippocampal* gyrus (including the underlying hippocampal formation), the cingulate gyrus, and the subcallosal gyrus encircle the underlying hypothalamus and midbrain (Fig. 12–3). These structures, which are considered to be phylogenetically primitive cortex, were first referred to as the limbic lobe by Paul Broca in the last century. In 1937, James Papez speculated that the limbic lobe may provide circuits through which emotional impulses arising within the hypothalamus could reach the cerebral cortex and, reciprocally, the cerebral cortex could modulate emotional states at the hypothalamic level (the Papez circuit). Additionally, the limbic lobe was also thought to play a primary role in processing and integrating cognitive perceptions originating in the cerebral cortex and instinctive impulses emerging from

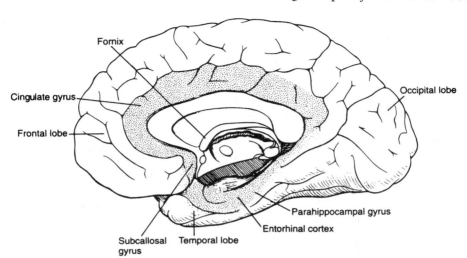

Figure 12–3. *This medial view of the brain shows the limbic lobe, which consists of primitive cortical tissue (stippled area) that encircles the upper brain stem. Also included in the limbic lobe are the underlying cortical structures (hippocampus and dentate gyrus). (Reproduced with permission from Kandel ER, Schwartz JH, Jessell TM (eds): Principles of Neural Science. New York, Elsevier, 1991.)*

the hypothalamus. Papez specifically proposed that information from the hypothalamus was conveyed from the mammillary bodies to the anterior thalamic nucleus along the mammillothalamic tract, and then to the cingulate gyrus, where integration with information from the cerebral cortex would occur. Cortical influences would then be transmitted from the cingulate gyrus to the hippocampal formation and from there along the fornix to the mammillary bodies (Fig. 12–4). Further processing of information would take place at each junction in this circuit.

Paul MacLean later suggested that other structures (Fig. 12–4) should be included in the limbic system first proposed by Papez. These included the *amygdala*, the *septum*, the *nucleus accumbens* (part of the striatum in the basal ganglia), portions of the *hypothalamus anterior to the mammillary bodies* and the *orbitofrontal cortex* (part of the prefrontal and limbic association cortices).

Rostral structures within the limbic system have various modulating effects on the behavioral, autonomic, and endocrine output of the hypothalamus. For instance, in some species, lesions of the amygdala produce a placid state with muted affective responses. On the other hand, lesions of the septum produce increased irritability and exaggerated rage responses to aversive stimuli. In primates, lesions of the orbitofrontal cortex, which connects with underlying limbic structures, *eliminate* normal levels of aggression and affective responsiveness, while electrical stimulation in this region has opposite effects.

Neuroanatomical studies have largely confirmed the speculations of Papez and MacLean about the organization of the limbic system and have described substantial

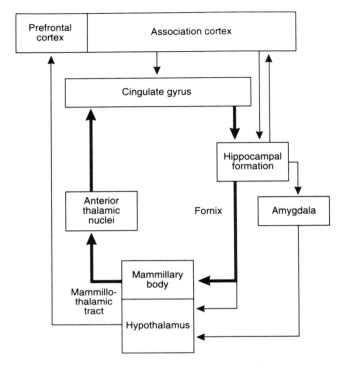

Figure 12–4. *The neural circuitry of the limbic system that probably mediates emotion. The circuit originally proposed by Papez is indicated by thick lines; additional connections later proposed by MacLean are indicated by fine lines. (Reproduced with permission from Kandel ER, Schwartz JH, Jessell TM (eds): Principles of Neural Science. New York, Elsevier, 1991.)*

interconnections between the hippocampal formation, amygdala, and the overlying neocortex. The association cortices project to the entorhinal cortex which, in turn, projects along the perforant path through another area of cortex called the *subiculum* to the hippocampal formation. The subiculum, which gives rise to the efferent fibers in the fornix that innervate the hypothalamus, has extensive reciprocal connections with other brain areas, including the neocortex. The subiculum has been favored during evolution and has achieved its greatest relative size in humans. The amygdala contains a number of distinct nuclei that are reciprocally connected to the hippocampal formation, neocortex, thalamus and the hypothalamus. One of the two major projections from the amygdala, the stria terminalis, innervates the bed nucleus of the stria terminalis, the nucleus accumbens, and the hypothalamus. The other major efferent projection, the ventral amygdalofugal pathway, innervates the rostral cingulate gyrus, the dorsal medial nucleus of thalamus, and the hypothalamus (see Fig. 12–2).

The Association Cortices

During phylogeny the cerebral cortex increased enormously in size relative to other brain structures. The most impressive expansion has taken place in higher order motor and sensory cortex and association cortex (Fig. 12–5). There are three association cortices; the *prefrontal association cortex*, the *parietal–temporal–occipital association cortex*, and the *limbic association cortex*. Information from sensory organs projects initially to primary sensory cortices and then to higher-order sensory cortices where more complex analysis of sensation occurs. Each higher-order sensory cortex in turn, projects to one, two, or all three association cortices. The association cortices integrate multimodal sensory information and initiate and execute a number of higher functions. The major functions of the association cortices are summarized in Table 12–1.

The *prefrontal association cortex*, which is quite sizeable in higher primates and humans, appears to be involved in thinking through potential future outcomes and selecting plans of action (executive functions). This cortex occupies the rostral and inferior portion of the frontal lobe just anterior to the premotor and primary motor cortex. The frontal association cortex is composed of two main subregions, the prefrontal association cortex proper, which is located on the dorsolateral surface of the frontal lobe, and the orbitofrontal cortex, which is located on the medial and ventral surface of the frontal lobe. The orbitofrontal cortex is also part of the limbic association cortex and the limbic system.

The prefrontal association cortex of the monkey is subdivided into the principal sulcus and the superior and inferior prefrontal convexities (Fig. 12–6A). *The princi-*

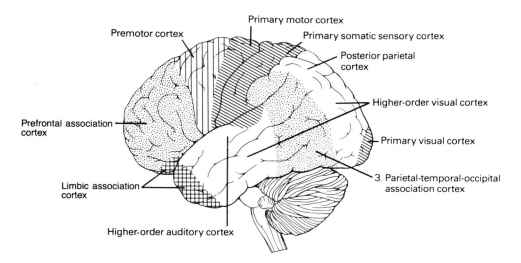

Figure 12–5. *A drawing of the lateral surface of the human brain on which are illustrated the locations of the primary sensory and motor cortices, the higher-order sensory and motor cortices, and the three association cortices. (Reproduced with permission from Kandel ER, Schwartz JH, Jessell TM (eds): Principles of Neural Science. New York, Elsevier, 1991.)*

Table 12-1 **Major Functions of the Association Cortices**

PREFRONTAL	PARIETAL–TEMPORAL–OCCIPITAL	LIMBIC
Abstract thinking	Integration of multimodal sensory information	Emotional behavior, including aggression (orbitofrontal cortex and cingulate gyrus)
Working memory Planning	Perception of spatial relationships Understanding the meaning of words and syntax (dominant side) and nonsyntactic aspects of spoken language (nondominant side)	Memory storage (temporal lobe)
Appropriate delay of responses		

pal sulcus is critical to the successful performance of any task that requires retention of spatial information over time. Early studies showed that monkeys with discrete lesions of the principal sulcus were unable to remember into which of two containers a morsel of food had been placed 5 or more seconds previously. Further investigation has established that lesions of the principal sulcus do not produce a generalized deficit of short-term memory but rather a specific deficit in *working memory*, i.e., the ability to temporarily retain information that is being used to plan future action (Goldman-Rakic, 1990). Lesions of the *inferior prefrontal convexity* disrupt a monkey's ability to perform any task involving delayed response, not just tasks that are spatial in nature. Lesions of an area of cortex adjacent to the principal sulcus called the arcuate concavity interfere with a monkey's ability to choose a specific motor response to a particular sensory cue. Thus, discrete portions of the prefrontal association cortex appear to subserve retention of specific sets of sensory information while the appropriate motor response is selected. The prefrontal association cortex sends projections primarily to other association cortices and to the premotor cortex.

The prefrontal cortex has been the focus of much recent speculation about the biology of schizophrenia. Neuropsychological tests reveal that schizophrenic patients have difficulty performing tasks requiring some of the delayed responses that depend upon the prefrontal association cortex. Mesocortical dopaminergic projections, disturbances of which are thought to occur in schizophrenia, terminate in the prefrontal cortex. Indeed, dopamine depletion in this area interferes with delayed responses. New imaging techniques show that schizophrenics do not exhibit the rise in blood flow or glucose uptake in the frontal lobes that occurs in normal subjects when they perform tasks that require prefrontal functions. (See Chapter 5 by Drs. Ninan and Mance in the clinical text that accompanies this volume.)

The *parietal-temporal-occipital association cortex*, which is located at the juncture between the three cerebral lobes for which it is named, is surrounded by and highly interconnected with higher order somatic, visual, and auditory cortices. The primary functions of this association cortex is to integrate multimodal sensory information to create a three-dimensional representation of the external environment. This task appears to be shared with the prefrontal association cortex because regions

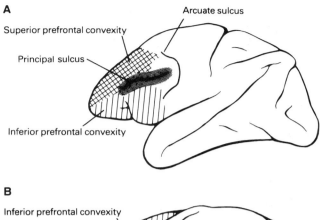

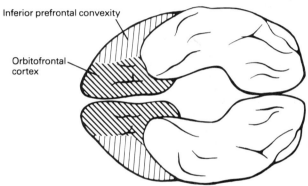

Figure 12–6. *Drawings of the basic subdivisions of the frontal association cortex of the monkey from the lateral view (A) and the ventral view (B). The orbitofrontal cortex is a subdivision of the limbic association cortex. (Reproduced with permission from Kandel ER, Schwartz JH, Jessell TM (eds): Principles of Neural Science. New York, Elsevier, 1991.)*

in both cortices, which are involved in processing spatial information, are interconnected and project to the same targets. Damage to the parietal–temporal–occipital association cortex can produce *severe distortions in body image* and *perception of spatial relationships*. Damage to the *dominant* (usually left) side of this association area often results in *aphasia*, the inability to understand spoken or written language, and *agnosia*, the inability to recognize objects. Patients with lesions of the *nondominant* (usually right) side of this association cortex frequently exhibit *deficits in understanding and utilizing nonsyntactic aspects of spoken language such as the meaning conveyed by the tone, pitch, rhythm, and timing of words.*

The limbic association cortex is composed of two regions, the orbitofrontal cortex (Fig. 12–6B) and the cingulate gyrus, which are involved in emotional behavior and the *anterior and inferior pole of the temporal lobe*, which is primarily involved in memory *storage*. As mentioned in the description of the limbic system, ablation of the orbitofrontal cortex in monkeys was noted earlier in this century to markedly diminish aggressiveness and emotional responsivity. Because of these striking results in animals, prefrontal lobotomies or transection of pathways connecting the frontal lobes to other parts of the brain were performed in human patients who suffered from severe mental illnesses associated with high levels of agitation and dangerous aggressiveness. While many of these patients became significantly calmer after surgery, a number of undesirable side effects also became apparent such as alterations in personality including loss of initiative and drive, disinhibition of behavior and speech, and impaired judgment. Neuropsychological testing also revealed that patients who had undergone these types of psychosurgery had difficulty changing strategies when switching from one mental task to another.

The *temporal lobe* portion of the limbic association cortex is involved in the acquisition and retention of long-term *memory*. This will be described in more detail later in the section on Learning and Memory. There is some regional specificity within this portion of the limbic lobe concerning where memories involving specific sensory modalities are stored. For example, memories of visual stimuli tend to be stored in the inferior temporal lobe nearer higher order visual cortex, while memories of auditory stimuli are selectively stored in the superior temporal lobe region of the limbic association cortex which is adjacent to higher order auditory cortex. The left (dominant) temporal lobe specializes in verbal and linguistic memory, while the right nondominant temporal lobe specializes in memory for spatial and temporal patterns of sensory input. The temporal lobe portion of the limbic association area probably plays a role in emotional responses as well. Stimulation of this area has been reported to produce a variety of emotions. Intensification of emotional feelings are often seen in patients suffering from temporal lobe epilepsy.

The Basal Ganglia

The essence of behavior is purposeful movement. Motor neurons arising in the anterior horn of the spinal cord or cranial nuclei are controlled directly or indirectly by cerebrospinal or cerebrobulbar neurons that originate in the motor cortex. The motor output of this system is regulated by the premotor and prefrontal cortex, the cerebellum and the basal ganglia (Kandel and Schwartz, 1991). Voluntary movement requires a plan of action (motor plan), which is formulated in the premotor and prefrontal cortices. The cerebellum compares descending motor control signals with sensory signals resulting from motor action and then adjusts the motor signals at the level of the motor cortex and brainstem motor nuclei. In addition to processing motor information the basal ganglia play a critical role in integrating information about motivational and emotional state into the motor planning process.

The basal ganglia are composed of five large subcortical nuclei: the caudate nucleus, the putamen, the globus pallidus, the subthalamic nucleus, and the substantia nigra. The globus pallidus (also called the pallidum) consists of an external and internal segment. The substantia nigra is also subdivided into the pars reticulata caudally and the more rostral, dark-stained pars compacta where dopamine-synthesizing cell bodies are located. Almost all of the input to the basal ganglia comes directly or indirectly from the cerebral cortex and their output is routed through the thalamus

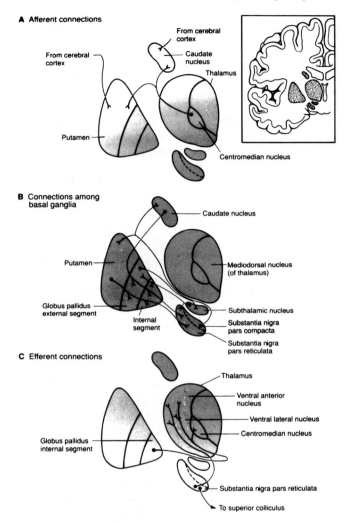

Figure 12–7. *The major connections of the basal ganglia.* **A**. *The caudate nucleus and putamen receive almost all afferent input to the basal ganglia.* **B**. *The connections between the nuclei of the basal ganglia are topographically organized.* **C**. *Efferents from the basal ganglia connect principally with the thalamus. (Reproduced with permission from Kandel ER, Schwartz JH, Jessell TM (eds): Principles of Neural Science. New York, Elsevier, 1991.)*

back to the portions of the cerebral cortex involved in motor control (i.e., the prefrontal, premotor, supplementary motor, and primary motor cortices). While this system plays a major role in controlling motor aspects of voluntary behavior, it is also involved in cognition and emotion.

The caudate nucleus and putamen, which together are called the neostriatum (most commonly referred to as the striatum), receive all of the input to the basal ganglia (Fig. 12–7A). These two structures develop from the same telencephalic tissue, are composed of similar neurons, and are fused anteriorly. Every region of the cerebral cortex projects to the striatum; these projections are topographically organized. The different portions of the striatum specialize in aspects of behavior controlled by the regions of cortex from which they receive projections. Thus, the *putamen* is primarily involved in motor control, the *caudate* regulates eye movements and some cognitive functions, and the *ventral striatum*, which is linked to the limbic system, modulates emotion. The striatum also receives topographically organized input from the intralaminar nuclei of the thalamus. The motor cortex exerts strong control over the basal ganglia through its projection to the centromedian nucleus of the thalamus which in turn projects to the putamen. The ventral striatum (which contains the nucleus accumbens, a portion of the limbic system) receives the important mesolimbic dopaminergic projection from the ventral tegmental area that transmits motivational and emotional information originating from the hypothalamus and limbic system to the basal ganglia. Aberrant dopaminergic neurotransmission in this pathway has been implicated in psychotic disorders such as schizophrenia (Deutch, 1992).

There are several pathways interconnecting the basal ganglia (Fig. 12–7B). The caudate and the putamen project to the external and internal segments of the globus pallidus and to the pars reticulata portion of the substantia nigra. The external segment of the pallidum projects to the subthalamic nucleus which projects back to the external and internal segments of the globus pallidus as well as to the substantia nigra pars reticulata. The motor and premotor cortices exert additional influence on the basal ganglia through direct connections with the subthalamic nucleus. The substantia nigra pars compacta sends an important dopaminergic projection to both portions of the neostriatum.

Outputs from the basal ganglia (Fig. 12–7C) originate from the internal segment of the globus pallidus and the substantia nigra pars reticulata and project to three nuclei in the thalamus: the ventral lateral, ventral anterior, and mediodorsal nuclei. The internal segment of the globus pallidus also projects to the centromedian nucleus of the thalamus. These thalamic nuclei project to the motor cortex, supplementary motor cortex, premotor cortex, and the prefrontal cortex.

Neural projections from the cerebral cortex to the striatum release the excitatory neurotransmitter *glutamate*, which activates both a direct and an indirect pathway through the basal ganglia (Figure 12–8). The direct pathway originates in the striatum and terminates in the internal segment of the pallidum and the substantia nigra pars reticulata. GABA and substance P are the neurotransmitters released by this pathway; they inhibit activity of the GABAergic projections from the output nuclei of the basal ganglia to the thalamus. Cortical activation of the striatum increases the inhibitory signals to the output nuclei of the basal ganglia which, in turn, diminishes inhibitory transmission to the thalamic nuclei. Movement is facilitated when disinhibited thalamic projections activate premotor and supplementary motor cortex projections to the motor cortex, the brain stem, and the spinal cord.

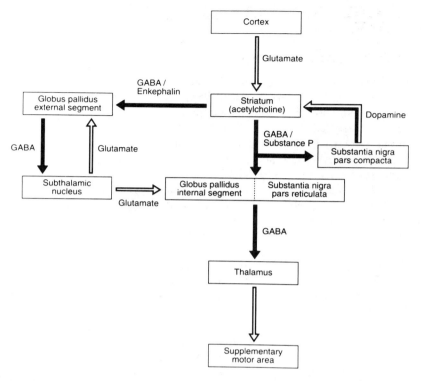

Figure 12–8. *This figure summarizes current knowledge about neuro-transmitters released by afferent, efferent and internuclear pathways of the basal ganglia. The direct and indirect routes through the basal gan-glia are also illustrated. (Black arrows represent inhibitory pathways; white arrows represent excitatory pathways.) (Reproduced with permission from Kandel ER, Schwartz JH, Jessell TM (eds): Principles of Neural Science. New York, Elsevier, 1991.)*

Activation of the indirect pathway through the basal ganglia has the end result of inhibiting movement. The first link in this pathway is a projection from the striatum to the external segment of the globus pallidus mediated by GABA and enkephalin that inhibits an inhibitory GABAergic projection to the subthalamic nucleus. This pro-duces increased activity of an excitatory glutamate-mediated link to the output nuclei of the basal ganglia, which increases inhibition of thalamic projections to motor areas of the cortex. The dopaminergic projection from the substantia nigra to the striatum excites the direct pathway but decreases activity in the indirect pathway. The result of both effects is to facilitate cortical initiation of movement.

The direct and indirect pathways through the basal ganglia appear to counter-balance each other. Deterioration, such as occurs in the nigrostriatal dopamine neurons in Parkinson's disease, or trauma in the basal ganglia may lead to imbalance between these pathways and impairment of movement (as well as cognition and emotion) of one type or another depending upon the location of the disturbance.

NEUROCHEMICAL DETERMINANTS OF BEHAVIOR

"Classic" Neurotransmitters

The Discovery of Neurotransmission

Although scientific interest and curiosity about the nervous system date back to antiquity, the concept of biochemical compounds acting as the mediators of neural transmission is less than 100 years old. In the late 19th century, a number of investigators demonstrated that adrenal extracts could produce physiological effects that were strikingly similar to those seen following stimulation of sympathetic nerves; adrenaline (epinephrine) was subsequently identified as the active compound in these extracts. In 1904, Langely demonstrated that pilocarpine could mimic the effects of parasympathetic nerve stimulation. The next year, Elliot pulled together these observations in formulating a hypothesis of chemical neurotransmission. Elliott proposed that nerve endings might release small amounts of a chemical substance, such as adrenaline, which might then act on effector sites (Elliot et al, 1977).

The initial proof of the hypothesis of neurochemical transmission focused on acetylcholine (ACH). Dixon, in 1907, reexamined the physiological effects of muscarine and argued that parasympathetic nerves release a muscarinelike compound. Over the next decade, Dale and colleagues performed a series of studies that led them to conclude that ACH was involved in parasympathetic neurotransmission. Dale proposed that the parasympathetic nerve fibers should be described as "cholinergic," and that ACH and similar compounds should be called "parasympathomimetic." Then, in 1921, Loewi performed a series of elegant experiments on isolated frog hearts connected by perfusion media; he found that vagus nerve stimulation of innervated heart produced a compound, which he called "vagusstoff," which slowed the second, denervated heart. Vagusstoff was found to be acetylcholine (Elliot et al, 1977).

During the same year of Loewi's classic experiments, Cannon and Uridil isolated "sympathin," a compound that was released following stimulation of sympathetic nerves. Later studies showed that sympathin was released by all sympathetic nerves. In 1946, Von Euler identified norepinephrine as the "sympathin" neurotransmitter of the sympathetic nervous system (Elliot et al, 1977).

Table 12-2 **Criteria for a Neurotransmitter**

1. Neurons contain the substance.
2. Neurons synthesize the substance.
3. Neurons release the substance upon depolarization.
4. The substance is physiologically active on neurons.
5. The postsynaptic physiologic response to the substance is identical to that of the neurotransmitter released by neurons.

(Adapted from Coyle JT: Neuroscience and psychiatry. In Talbott JA, Hales RE, Yudofsky SC (eds): Textbook of Psychiatry. Washington, DC, American Psychiatric Press, 1988)

Table 12-3 **Criteria for Linking a Neurotransmitter to a Behavior**

1. The neurotransmitter must be present in the central nervous system.
2. Precursors and enzymatic machinery for synthesis and degradation must be present in association with the transmitter.
3. A characteristic pattern of transmitter release should occur in relation to the behavior.
4. Elicitation of the characteristic transmitter release pattern should evoke the behavior.
5. Destruction of the involved neuronal system should both deplete the transmitter and abolish normal control of that behavior.
6. Increases or decreases in transmitter activity should have opposing behavioral effects.

(Reis DJ: Considerations of some specific behaviors or disease. J Psychiatr Res 11:145–148, 1974)

As interest in neurotransmission grew, a number of criteria were established for determining whether a particular substance is, in fact, a neurotransmitter (Table 12–2). It is quite difficult to demonstrate for a given substance that all of these criteria have been met. Thus, we often refer to "putative" neurotransmitters, because most, but not all, of these criteria have been met for a number of substances.

We briefly review here the physiology of some of the "classic" neurotransmitters. We have selected those that seem to be most relevant and most extensively studied in reference to normal and pathologic human behavior. How does one, however, establish a link between a neurotransmitter and behavior? This is an exceedingly complex challenge, because the study of both neurotransmission and of behavior is difficult. Nonetheless, Reis (1974) has provided useful guidelines for establishing a connection between these complex phenomena (Table 12–3).

Representative "Classic" Neurotransmitters

Norepinephrine. Historically, the catecholamine norepinephrine (NE) has been viewed as a stress-related hormone. Hans Selye described the critical role it plays in

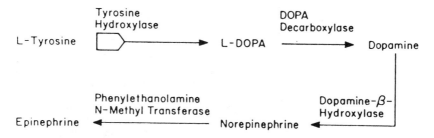

Figure 12–9. *The biosynthetic pathway for catecholamines. Tyrosine hydroxylase is activated by phosphorylation by protein kinases and the synthesis of phenylethanolamine-N-methyl transferase depends on glucocorticoids. (Reproduced with permission from Coyle JT: Neuroscience and psychiatry. In Talbott JA, Hales RE, Yudofsky SC (eds): Textbook of Psychiatry. Washington, DC, American Psychiatric Press, 1988.)*

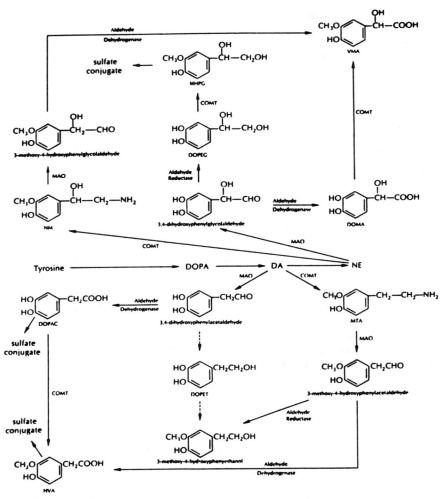

Figure 12–10. *Dopamine and norepinephrine metabolism. The following ab-breviations are used: DOPA, dihydroxyphenylalanine; DA, dopamine; NE, norepinephrine; DOMA, 3,4-dihydroxymandelic acid; DOPAC, 3,4-dihydroxy-phenylacetic acid; DOPEG, 3,4-dihydroxyphenylglycol; DO-PET, 3,4-dihydrox-yphenylethanol; MOPET, 3-methoxy-4-hydroxyphenylethanol; MHPG, 3-methoxy-4-hydroxy-phenylglycol; HVA, homovanillic acid; VMA, 3-methoxy-4-hydroxy-mande-lic acid; NM, normetanephrine; MTA, 3-methoxytyramine; MAO, monoamine oxi-dase; COMT, catechol-O-methyl transferase; Dashed arrows indicate steps that have not been firmly established. (Reproduced with permission from Cooper JR, Bloom FE, Roth RH (eds): The Biochemical Basis of Neuropharmacology. New York, Oxford, 1991.)*

orchestrating the physiological response to stress. Cannon identified NE and epinephrine (EPI) as key components in the mobilization of the organism for a fight–flight response to stimuli that are perceived as threatening.

The metabolic pathways involved in the synthesis of NE, as well as the other catecholamines dopamine (DA) and EPI, are shown in Figure 12–9. The amino acid tyrosine is taken up into the neuronal cell body where it becomes the basic "building block" for catecholamine synthesis. The rate-limiting step involves hydroxylation by the enzyme tyrosine hydroxylase. Catabolism of the catecholamines is accomplished by several enzymes acting in an extensive pathway. Monoamine oxidase (MAO) is the enzyme that is principally involved in the intraneuronal degradation of catecholamines, where it catalyzes the oxidative deamination of NE. Catechol-O-methyltransferase (COMT) plays a similar role in the extraneuronal catabolism of NE and the other catecholamines. The O-methylated products of COMT catabolism also become substrates for further degradation by MAO. MHPG (3-methoxy-4-hydroxy-phenylglycol) is a major metabolite of NE (Cooper et al, 1991). Figure 12–10 summarizes the metabolism of NE and DA.

In humans, noradrenergic neurons are organized into anatomically and functionally discrete nuclei in the upper brainstem. Two of the most important are the locus ceruleus, which projects extensively within the CNS (Figs. 12–11 and 12–12), and the nucleus of the tractus solitarius, which projects to the brain stem and the peripheral autonomic nervous system. Noradrenergic neurons are also organized into ganglia in the peripheral sympathetic nervous system.

Neurotransmission in noradrenergic systems is representative of synaptic transmission for the biogenic amines (NE, EPI, DA serotonin). When NE, which is stored in presynaptic vesicles, is released, it diffuses across the synaptic cleft and interacts with postsynaptic receptors (Figs. 12–13 and 12–14). This leads to a cascade of events, by a "second messenger" system involving activation of adenylate cyclase and cyclic AMP formation (Fig. 12–15), which ultimately produce excitation (or inhibition) of the postsynaptic neuron (Hyman, 1988).

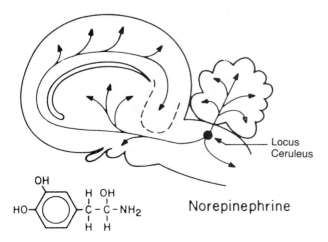

Locus
Ceruleus

Norepinephrine

Figure 12–11. *The primary projections of the noradrenergic locus ceruleus. (Reproduced with permission from Coyle JT: Neuroscience and psychiatry. In Talbott JA, Hales RE, Yudofsky SC (eds): Textbook of Psychiatry. Washington, DC, American Psychiatric Press, 1988.)*

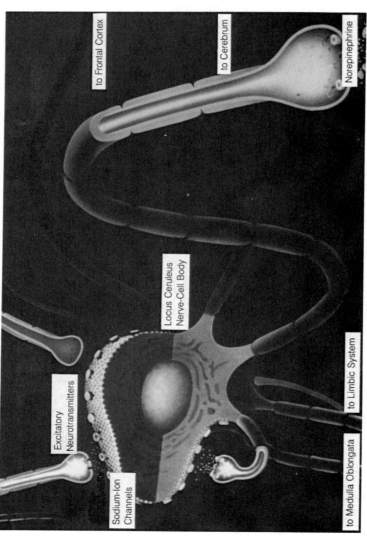

Figure 12–12. *Noradrenergic cell bodies in the locus ceruleus project to other critical brain regions, including the limbic system and the medulla oblongata. (Used with permission of the Upjohn Company.)*

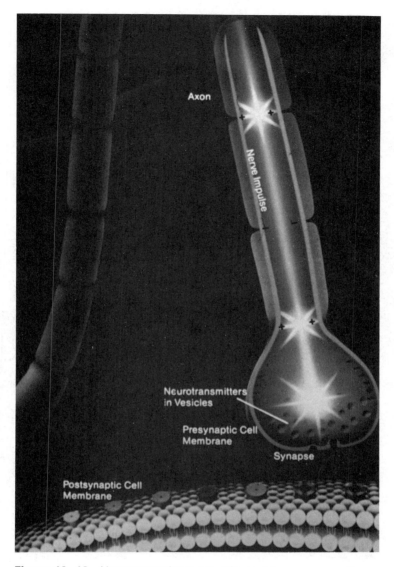

Figure 12–13. *Neurotransmitters are released from presynaptic storage vesicles and diffuse across the synaptic cleft, where they interact with the postsynaptic cell membrane. (Used with permission of the Upjohn Company.)*

Noradrenergic receptors are classified, and subclassified, based on their characteristic responsivity to different agonists (Table 12–4). Thus, for *alpha₁-adrenergic* receptors, the pharmacologic potency (i.e., amount of drug required to produce a particular effect) of agonists can be "rank ordered" as EPI > NE > isoproterenol

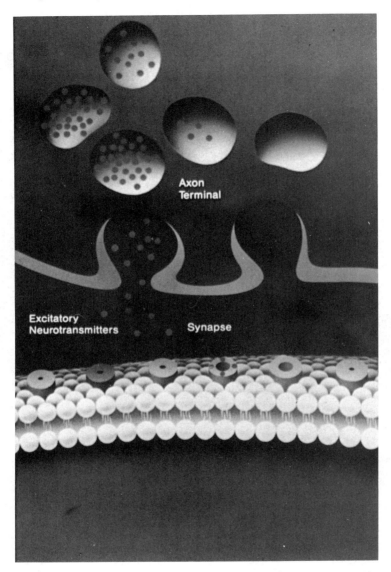

Figure 12–14. *Neurotransmitters, when released from storage vesicles in the presynaptic axon terminal, bind to those postsynaptic receptors that offer the best "fit." (Used with permission of the Upjohn Company.)*

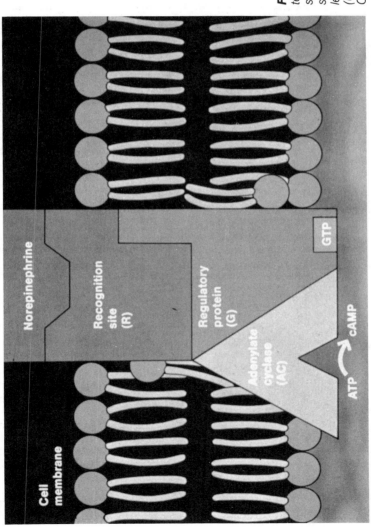

Figure 12–15. *After the neurotransmitter norepinephrine binds to its receptor site on the postsynaptic membrane, it sets into play a cascade of events, leading to the formation of cyclic AMP. (Used with permission of the Upjohn Company.)*

Table 12-4 **Drug and Neurotransmitter Receptors Relevant to Psychopharmacology**

RECEPTOR TYPE	CHARACTERISTICS
Adrenergic	
Alpha$_1$	Located postsynaptically in both sympathetic nervous system and brain (where it is found on both neurons and blood vessels). Produces vasoconstriction. Agonist potency: EPI>NE>ISO.
Alpha$_2$	Mostly presynaptic autoreceptor (in sympathetic terminals, locus ceruleus) but also postsynaptic (e.g., in pituitary: mediates growth hormone release). Agonist potency: NE = EPI>ISO. Clonidine is selective agonist; yohimbine is selective antagonist.
Beta$_1$	Localized in heart>lung; found regionally in brain. Stimulates heart. Agonist potency: ISO>EPI = NE. Practolol is selective antagonist.
Beta$_2$	Localized in lung>heart; found in brain, glia>neurons. Produces bronchodilation, vasodilation. Agonist potency: ISO!EPI>NE. Salbutamol, terbutaline are selective agonists.
	Classification still controversial.
Serotonin (5-HT)	Four subtypes:
5-HT$_1$ 5-HT$_{1A}$	Found in gut and dorsal raphe nucleus in various species. Appears to mediate contraction in gut, neuronal inhibition in brain. Spiperone is antagonist; the anxiolytic, buspirone, is partial antagonist.
5-HT$_{1B}$	Found in cortex and sympathetic nervous system. Mediates contraction of smooth muscle and neuronal inhibition.
5-HT$_{1C}$	Found in stomach; mediates contraction.
5-HT$_2$	Found in brain, platelets, gut, uterus. Down-regulated by antidepressant treatment. Mediates "serotonin syndrome." Methysergide, cyproheptadine, and ketanserine are antagonists.
5-HT$_3$	Linked to ligand-gated ion channels.
5-HT$_4$	Linked to stimulation of adenylyl cyclase.
Dopamine	All known dopamine receptors to date are members of the G-protein superfamily. They fall into two general classes based on pharmacologic functional, and molecular characteristics.
D$_1$-like	Two genes are known that code for two receptors: D$_1$ (or alternately D$_{1a}$) and D$_5$ (or alternately D$_{1b}$). The former exists in much higher density than the latter. Significant pharmacological and functional differences are only speculative.
	The members of this subfamily are linked to stimulatory G protein-mediated events such as stimulation of cAMP synthesis.
	Selective antagonists include drugs chemically similar to SCH23390 (phenyltetrahydrobenzazepines). While D$_1$-like receptors also bind many traditional antipsychotics (like haloperidol or chlorpromazine), they have low affinity for raclopride, sulpiride, and other benzamides.
D$_2$-like	At least three genes code for four different receptors: D$_{2long}$ and D$_{2short}$, D$_3$, and D$_4$. Of these, the D$_{2long}$ is expressed at the highest levels. The D$_3$ and D$_4$ may occur somewhat selectively in limbic and cortical areas.
	The members of this subfamily are linked to inhibitory G protein-mediated events such as inhibition of cAMP synthesis.
	They bind traditional antipsychotics (butyrophenones like haloperidol, phenothiazines, like chlorpromazine, etc.), but have selectivity for substituted benzamides like raclopride or sulpiride.

(continued)

Table 12-4 *(continued)*

RECEPTOR TYPE	CHARACTERISTICS
D₂-like (continued)	Clozapine appears to have some selectivity for the D_4 receptor, suggesting an important role for this receptor in the unique antipsychotic action of this drug. Significant pharmacologic and functional differences between these subtypes have not been conclusively resolved.
Muscarinic Cholinergic	Antagonized by atropine-like drugs, but also by tricyclic antidepressants, many antihistamines, and low-potency neuroleptics, resulting in side effects. Loss of muscarinic cholinergic transmission in Alzheimer's disease may be partly responsible for cognitive decline. Two types generally recognized pharmacologically, but four types predicted by cloning.
M_1	Located in sympathetic ganglia, frontal cortex, corpus striatum, hippocampus.
M_2	Located in brain stem, cerebellum, heart. Recently shown to open a K^+ channel by a G protein-linked mechanism causing hyperpolarization and, therefore, bradycardia.
GABA	Two types:
GABA$_A$	Mediates classic inhibitory transmission in higher brain centers. (Glycine serves this purpose in the brain stem and spinal cord.) Thus, receptors found on majority of neurons in forebrain. The receptor also contains binding sites for benzodiazepines and barbiturates. Binding of these drugs increases the affinity of the receptor for GABA. Muscimol is a selective agonist; bicuculline (proconvulsant) is an antagonist.
GABA$_B$	Works through G proteins, not Cl^- channel (nonclassic effect). Baclofen is selective agonist.
Opiate	At least three types; naloxone is an antagonist at all types with affinity: $m{\rightarrow}d{\rightarrow}k$.
mu (*m*)	Localized in periaqueductal gray, thalamus, substantia gelatinosa of spinal cord, and other regions. Mediates analgesia and indifference to pain, miosis, and respiratory depression. Morphine and related opiate alkaloids are exogenous agonists; beta-endorphin and the enkephalins are endogenous agonists.
delta (*d*)	Highest density in limbic system. Mediates analgesia, hypotension, and miosis. Enkephalins are endogenous agonists. No selective agonists in clinical use because only peptide agonists known.
kappa (*k*)	Located in deep cortical layers. Mediates sedating analgesia, miosis. Benzomorphan drugs (e.g., ketamine, pentazocine) selective agonists. Dynorphins are the endogenous agonists.

Note: Where possible, clinically relevant agonists and antagonists are listed. The most selective agonists and antagonists are often not clinically important.
Abbreviations: Epi = epinephrine, NE = norepinephrine, ISO = isoproterenol.
(Reproduced with permission from Hyman SE: Recent developments in neurobiology. Psychosomatics 29:157, 1988)

(ISO); for *alpha₂-receptors*, the rank order of agonist potency is NE = EPI > ISO; the rank order of agonist potencies for *beta₁*- and *beta₂-adrenergic* receptors is ISO > EPI = NE and ISO > EPI > NE, respectively.

Alpha₁ receptors are found postsynaptically in both the sympathetic nervous system and the brain. Alpha₂ receptors are often located presynaptically, in the locus ceruleus and in sympathetic terminals, where they are thought to function as auto-receptors that modulate output by serving as homeostatic regulators; they are also found postsynaptically in certain sites, such as the pituitary gland, where they play a role in regulating growth hormone release. Beta$_1$ receptors are found regionally in the brain, and beta$_2$ receptors are located on glial and neural tissues in the brain.

Electrophysiologists have advanced the concept that NE serves as an "orchestrator" or modulator of other signals in the CNS. In the cerebellum, for example, NE released following locus ceruleus stimulation decreases the spontaneous firing of Purkinje cells, thereby increasing the relative signal generated by exogenous stimuli. Thus, NE increases the "signal-to-noise" ratio in that area of the brain, thereby increasing reactivity to stimuli. In a similar way, projections from the locus ceruleus to other areas in the brain, such as the hypothalamus and cortex, may enhance responsiveness to exogenous stimuli (Golden and Potter, 1986).

Historically, NE has played a pivotal role in the development of biologic theories relating to the pathogenesis of mood disorders such as depression. Two decades ago, the original formulations of the "catecholamine hypothesis of depression" identified decreased functional activity of central NE systems as an etiologic mechanism in the development of depressive illness (Bunney and Davis, 1965; Schildkraut, 1965). More recently, with our growing appreciation for the complex dynamic regulatory mechanisms of neurotransmitter control, researchers have emphasized relatively subtle forms of NE systems dysregulation rather than absolute deficiencies (Golden and Potter, 1986).

More recently, the role of the locus ceruleus and the NE system has received attention as being involved in the pathogenesis of panic disorder, a severe anxiety disorder often accompanied by agoraphobia. Although the exact mechanisms are not clear, it is believed that some sort of disruption or dysregulation in the locus ceruleus/NE system results in a flooding of the CNS with anxiety and a plethora of secondary physiological and psychological symptoms.

Serotonin. Serotonin, or 5-hydroxytryptamine (5-HT), plays a critical role in the regulation of such diverse functions as sleep, temperature homeostasis, pain sensitivity, appetite, neuroendocrine secretions, and mood regulation. Many of these functions are felt to be regulated, in part, by 5-HT input to the hypothalamus. Cell bodies of 5-HT containing neurons are localized in a series of nuclei in the upper pons and lower midbrain, called the raphe nuclei. Axons ascending from the raphe project to almost all brain regions (Fig. 12–16). Serotonin within these cell bodies is formed from the amino acid tryptophan, which is an "essential" amino acid in that dietary intake regulates its availability. Tryptophan is taken up into 5-HT neurons by active transport across the blood–brain barrier. The enzyme tryptophan hydroxylase catalyzes the rate-limiting step of hydroxylating tryptophan into 5-hydroxytryptophan, which is then decarboxylated to form 5-HT.

As with NE (see above), 5-HT is inactivated by reuptake into the presynaptic nerve terminal following its release and interaction with postsynaptic receptors. There it is oxidized by MAO to form 5-hydroxy-indoleacetic acid (5-HIAA), which is released into the cerebrospinal fluid (CSF) and eventually excreted in urine. Figure

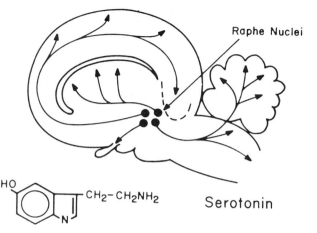

Figure 12–16. *The pathways of the raphe serotonergic neurons. (Reproduced with permission from Coyle JT: Neuroscience and psychiatry. In Talbott JA, Hales RE, Yudofsky SC (eds): Textbook of Psychiatry. Washington, DC, American Psychiatric Press, 1988.)*

12–17 summarizes the metabolic pathways involved in the synthesis and metabolism of 5-HT.

5-HT receptors are also classified based on agonist affinity; the classification is currently an area of extensive investigation and is somewhat controversial (see Table 12–4). 5-HT$_{1A}$ receptors are found in the gut and in the dorsal raphe nucleus in some species. These receptors appear to mediate contraction in the gut and neuronal inhibition in the brain. The anxiolytic medication buspirone is a partial 5-HT$_{1A}$ agonist. 5-HT$_{1B}$ receptors are found in the cortex and in the sympathetic nervous system; they mediate smooth muscle contraction and neuronal inhibition. 5-HT$_{1C}$ receptors mediate contraction in the stomach. 5-HT$_2$ receptors are localized in the brain, platelets, gut, and uterus. Several antidepressant medications have been found to down-regulate (i.e., decrease the density and responsivity of) these receptors. 5-HT$_3$ receptors have recently been described (Hyman, 1988), and 5-HT$_3$ antagonists (e.g., ondansetron) have proven useful in treating the nausea and vomiting associated with cancer chemotherapy. In addition, 5-HT$_4$ receptors have now been identified; their functional significance is currently under investigation.

At about the same time that American researchers were developing the catecholamine hypothesis of depression (see above), British scientists began to emphasize the role that 5-HT might play in depressive illness (Coppen et al, 1965). Prange and associates (1974) synthesized these two bodies of data in formulating the "permissive hypothesis" of affective illness: A decrease in the functional activity of central 5-HT systems could permit the development of depressive illness when coupled with a deficiency in central NE, while the coexistence of decreased 5-HT and increased NE could lead to the emergence of mania. Recently, a number of investigators, using various pharmacologic "challenge tests" have identified 5-HT dysregulation in depressed patients as measured by altered neurohormonal response to 5-HT agonists. 5-HT has also been implicated in the pathogenesis of many other major psychiatric syndromes, including schizophrenia, personality disorders, obsessive-

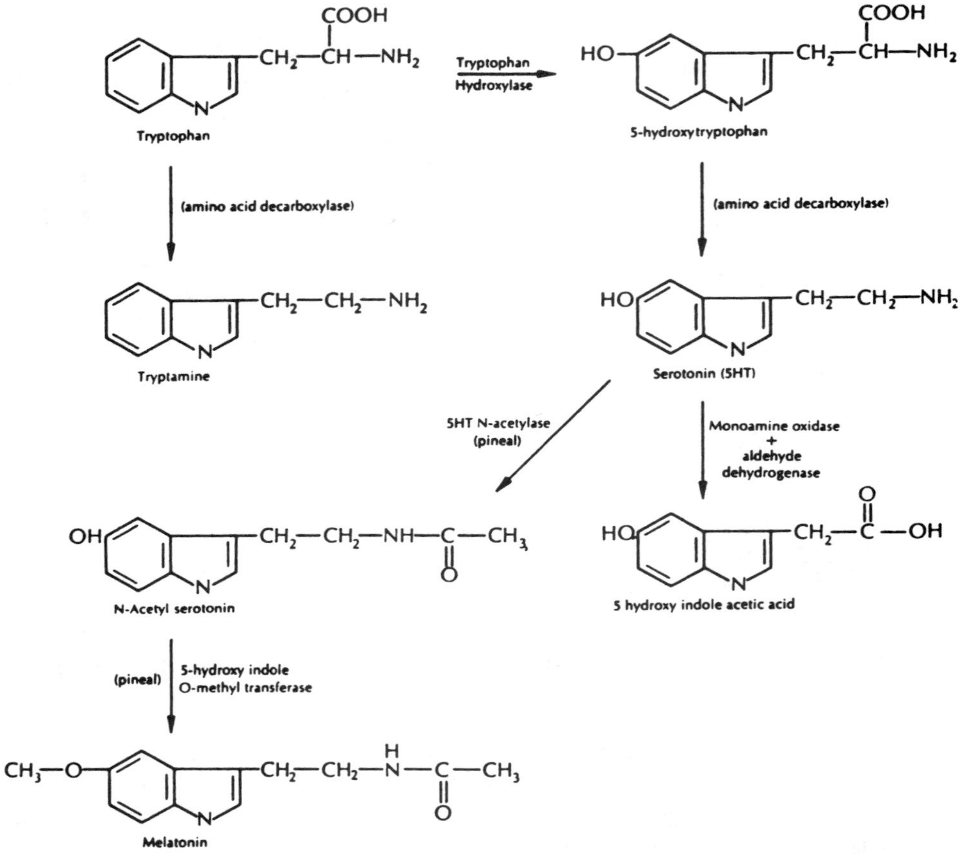

Figure 12–17. *The metabolic pathways available for the synthesis and metabolism of serotonin. (Reproduced with permission from Cooper JR, Bloom FE, Roth RH (eds): The Biochemical Basis of Neuropharmacology. New York, Oxford, 1991.)*

compulsive disorder, anxiety disorders, alcoholism, and chronic pain syndromes (Coccaro and Murphy, 1990).

   Dopamine. Dopamine (DA), like NE, is a catecholamine neurotransmitter synthesized from the amino acid tyrosine (see Fig. 12–9) and metabolized by MAO and COMT. As shown in Table 12–4, dopamine receptors can be subdivided into two families: D_1-like and D_2-like. Such a classification was originally derived on pharmacologic grounds, but has been expanded by recent molecular biological studies. As described in Table 12–4, there are clear pharmacological and functional differences between the two subfamilies. The current trends in the field suggest that new generations of drugs (ones having binding selectivity for specific receptors forms and/ or unique functional properties) are likely to appear in the immediate future. Because of the role of dopamine receptors in therapy (and etiology?) of schizophrenia (*vide* *infra*) and neurological disorders, such new drugs are likely to have important clinical impact.

There are three major DA systems in the brain: the meso-cortico-limbic midbrain-forebrain system, the nigrostriatal system, and the tuberoinfundibular system (Fig. 12–18). The meso-cortico-limbic system is felt to play an important role in regulating mood and behavior. The nigrostriatal system is involved in the control of fine movement, and disruption of DA neurotransmission in this area by neuroleptic medication can lead to the emergence of "extrapyramidal" side effects (i.e., acute dystonia, parkinsonian symptoms, and akathisia). The tuberoinfundibular system primarily contains D_2 receptors; dopamine released into the hypothalmic–pituitary portal venous system regulates prolactin and growth hormone secretion (Hyman, 1988).

Most research exploring the relationship between DA and human psychopathology has focused on psychoses. The "dopamine hypothesis" of schizophrenia was derived, in part, from two observations: (1) clinically effective antipsychotic medications (e.g., phenothiazines, butyrophenones, reserpine, and so forth) share a common property of diminishing central DA neurotransmission; (2) amphetamine and other psychostimulants that enhance central dopaminergic activity have been associated with the emergence of psychotic syndromes that in some ways resemble schizophrenia. In addition, hypotheses have been developed that link alterations in central dopaminergic systems with mania and depression (Janowsky et al, 1988).

Acetylcholine. Although acetylcholine (ACH) was the first neurotransmitter to be discovered, until recently limitations in technology have slowed the pace of investigations of its role in CNS function (Janowsky et al, 1988). ACH is synthesized by choline acetyltransferase, using acetyl-coenzyme A and choline as substrates. Brain ACH formation is relatively dependent on bloodborne choline derived from dietary intake, because choline cannot be synthesized in the brain in adequate amounts.

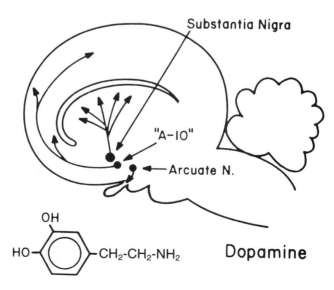

Figure 12–18. *The three major dopaminergic pathways. These include the nigrostriatal, the mesocorticolimbic (A-10), and the tuberoinfundibular pathway from the arcuate nucleus to the infundibulum. (Modified with permission from Coyle JT: Neuroscience and psychiatry. In Talbott JA, Hales RE, Yudofsky SC (eds): Textbook of Psychiatry. Washington, DC, American Psychiatric Press, 1988.)*

In the brain, there are nicotinic and muscarinic, pre- and postsynaptic receptors, as well as other cholinergic receptors that do not appear to belong to either of these classic types. Muscarinic receptors (see Table 12–4) are more plentiful in the brain than nicotimic receptors and play a more vital role in behavioral regulation. Unlike the catecholamine neurotransmitters, ACH inactivation following synaptic release does not depend on reuptake, but instead takes place by hydrolysis by either neuronal acetylcholinesterase or nonneuronal (glial) pseudocholinesterases.

The limbic system and the cerebral cortex, two brain systems that are felt to play major roles in the regulation of emotion in humans, receive considerable cholinergic innervation (Fig. 12–19). Thus, there is a theoretical basis for anticipating that ACH may play a role in the regulation of mood and in the pathogenesis of mood disorders. In 1972, Janowsky et al proposed a cholinergic-adrenergic balance hypothesis of affective illness, which postulated that affect (mood) may represent a balance between cholinergic and adrenergic neurotransmitter activity in the areas of the brain that regulate mood. Depressive illness could represent a disease state of relative cholinergic predominance, while mania could result from relative adrenergic predominance. Numerous animal studies, clinical observations, and human studies lend support to this theory, although contradictory data also exist (Janowsky et al, 1988).

Cholinergic projections to the cortex and hippocampus also play a critical role in cognition and its disorders (see section entitled Learning and Memory).

Gamma-Aminobutyric Acid. Gamma-aminobutyric acid (GABA) is synthesized from the amino acid glutamic acid through a decarboxylation reaction. Approximately 99% of all GABA in humans is found within the CNS, where it functions as an inhibitory neurotransmitter (Fig. 12–20).

There are at least two types of GABA receptors, $GABA_A$ and $GABA_B$ (see Table 12–4). The former is linked to the benzodiazepine receptor and chloride ion channel and thus has been linked to the development of and treatment of anxiety disorders.

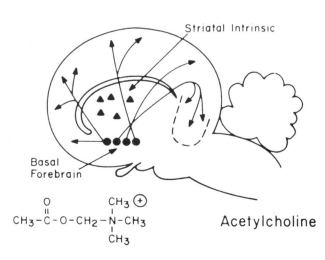

Striatal Intrinsic

Basal Forebrain

$$CH_3-\overset{\overset{\displaystyle O}{\|}}{C}-O-CH_2-\overset{\overset{\displaystyle CH_3}{|}}{\underset{\underset{\displaystyle CH_3}{|}}{N}}-CH_3 \quad \oplus$$

Acetylcholine

Figure 12–19. *The forebrain cholinergic neurons. Cholinergic neurons in the basal forebrain (including the nucleus basalis of Meynert, the diagonal band of Broca, and the medial septal nucleus) innervate the cerebral cortex, hippocampus, and limbic structures. The striatum contains local circuit cholinergic interneurons. (Reproduced with permission from Coyle JT: Neuroscience and psychiatry. In Talbott JA, Hales RE, Yudofsky SC (eds): Textbook of Psychiatry. Washington, DC, American Psychiatric Press, 1988.)*

Figure 12–20. *Major GABA-ergic pathways. The inhibitory neurotransmitter GABA (gamma-aminobutyric acid) is synthesized by local circuit stellate cells within the cerebral cortex, by the cerebellar Purkinje cells, and by striatonigral neurons. (Reproduced with permission from Coyle JT: Neuroscience and psychiatry. In Talbott JA, Hales RE, Yudofsky SC (eds): Textbook of Psychiatry. Washington, DC, American Psychiatric Press, 1988.)*

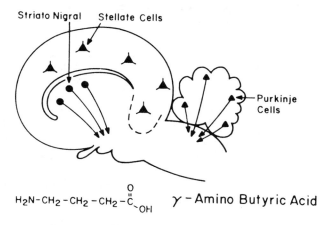

$$H_2N-CH_2-CH_2-CH_2-\overset{O}{\underset{OH}{C}} \quad \gamma - \text{Amino Butyric Acid}$$

The benzodiazepine receptor is believed to act synergistically with the GABA receptor to increase the affinity for the neurotransmitter. In addition to its association with anxiety disorders, GABA has been implicated in the pathogenesis of affective illness, such as depression, although the data related to GABAergic theories of affective disease are quite preliminary (Janowsky et al, 1988).

Neuropeptides

Neuropeptides are small proteins containing two to several dozen amino acids. They are, therefore, much larger than the "classic" small molecule neurotransmitters described above. The diversity of structure of neuropeptides is great. At least 50 are known and certainly many more will be found (Table 12–5). They occur in the CNS at concentrations far lower than classic small molecule neurotransmitters. Neuropeptides have a broad range of physiological and behavioral effects, which are exerted at concentrations three or more orders of magnitude lower than small molecule neurotransmitters. Neuropeptides also tend to have durations of effect considerably longer than classic neurotransmitters. These effects often persist well after proteolytic degradation of the neuropeptide.

Synthesis of neuropeptides is similar to that of other proteins (i.e., it involves translation of messenger RNA sequences on ribosomes; Coyle, 1988). This process occurs exclusively within the cell bodies and possibly dendrites of neurons. Translation usually produces a relatively large preprotein or precusor of the neuropeptide. Initial proteolytic cleavage of the precursor protein occurs in the endoplasmic reticulum and the Golgi apparatus. The final stages of posttranslational processing occur after the precursor and proteolytic enzymes are packaged into neurosecretory granules, which are then transported to neuron terminals for storage or release. Processing may include further proteolytic cleavage to produce shorter peptides as well as C-terminal amidation, N-terminal acetylation, cyclization of glutamate to form pyroglutamate, disulphide bond formation, glycosylation, phosphorylation, or sulfa-

Table 12-5 **Some Putative Neuropeptide Neurotransmitters**

ACTH	Interleukin-1
Angiotensin II	Leu-enkephalin
Atriopeptin	Luteinizing-hormone-releasing factor
Beta-endorphin	Met-enkephalin
Bombesin	N-acetyl aspartyl glutamate (NAAG)
Bradykinin	Neurotensin
Calcitonin gene-related peptide (CGRP)	Neuropeptide Y
Carnosine	Oxytocin
Cholecystokinin	Pancreostatin
Corticotropin-releasing factor (CRF)	Somatostatin
Dynorphin	Substance P
Galinin	Thyrotropin-releasing hormone (TRH)
Gastrin	Vasoactive intestinal peptide (VIP)
Glucagon	Vasopressin
Insulin	

tion. Precursor molecules in some neuropeptide-synthesizing neurons contain several amino acid sequences of the same neuropeptide. This allows the neurons to produce multiple copies of a particular neuropeptide and thereby multiply the signal produced by translation of the precursor molecule. Precursor molecules in neuropeptide-synthesizing neurons may also contain amino acid sequences of several different neuropeptides. Changes in the cleavage pattern in the precursor can produce different clusters of neuropeptides, each of which may have quite different effects.

Release of neuropeptides from presynaptic sites depends on Ca^{++} influx. Neuropeptides act at specific postsynaptic receptors either by stimulating changes in membrane conductance or by releasing second messengers. Thus, mechanisms of release and receptor activation within synapses are very similar in neuropeptides and small molecule neurotransmitters. Inactivation of neuropeptides appears to depend entirely on extracellular proteolysis. Unlike many small molecule neurotransmitters, presynaptic reuptake and recycling of neuropeptide molecules does not occur. Extracellular proteolysis may produce fragments that have physiological effects similar or quite different from the parent neuropeptide.

There has been much speculation about whether neuropeptides are true neurotransmitters or play a less specific neuromodulatory role. While no neuropeptide to date has been demonstrated to meet all of the exacting criteria required for neurotransmitter status (see Table 12–2), very likely many neuropeptides function as neurotransmitters. Neuromodulators are substances that are also released presynaptically but which act both locally and at more distant postsynaptic sites to diminish or amplify the effects of neurotransmitters. Neuromodulators may also influence the rate of release of neurotransmitters from presynaptic sites. Many neuropeptides have been localized within neurons containing small molecule neurotransmitters or other neuropeptides (Cooper et al, 1991). These observations suggest that neuropeptides may be coreleased with and serve as neuromodulators of small molecule or neuropeptide neurotransmitters. Neuropeptides very likely exert their effects well beyond the synapses into which they are released. Neuropeptide receptors are often located some distance from the terminal fields of neurons synthesizing those neuropeptides.

Endogenous opioids have received more investigative attention than any other family of neuropeptides. Approximately 18 separate opioid molecules have been described so far, among which beta-endorphin, leu-enkephalin, met-enkephalin, and dynorphin are of primary interest. All opioids arise from three major precursor molecules, pro-opiomelanocortin, pre-proenkephalin, and pre-prodynorphin, each of which is synthesized in a different population of neurons. The proteolytic cleavage products of pro-opiomelanocortin are summarized in Figure 12–21. Processing of opioid precursors varies with brain region. Enkephalin and dynorphin-containing neurons form discrete pathways in many regions of the CNS. Enkephalins are found in high concentration in the basal ganglia and are often colocalized in neurons with monoamines or other neuropeptides such as substance P. Beta-endorphin is synthesized primarily in neuron cell bodies in the arcuate nucleus from which project long ascending and descending pathways. A number of separate opiate receptor types have been described (see Table 12–4), and several classification schemes have been suggested. Individual opioid molecules have different affinities for each of these receptor types.

Many other families of neuropeptides are found within the CNS. Neuronal processes containing the posterior pituitary hormones, vasopressin and oxytocin, project from the paraventricular nucleus of the hypothalamus to many sites in the limbic system, brain stem, and spinal cord. In addition, nests of vasopressinergic neurons are located at a number of sites outside the hypothalamus. Many hypothalamic neuropeptides that regulate release of anterior pituitary hormones are also

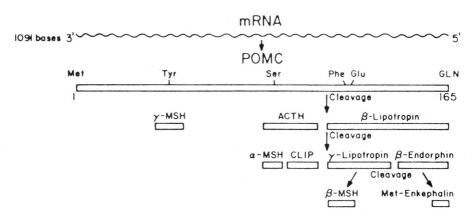

Figure 12–21. *Processing of proopiomelanocortin (POMC). The precursor protein, POMC, which contains 165 amino acids, is enzymatically cleaved to yield the physiologically active peptides indicated. Depending on the cellular localization (anterior pituitary, hypothalamus, midbrain nerve terminals), certain of these neuropeptides are expressed and others are not. (Reproduced with permission from Coyle JT: Neuroscience and psychiatry. In Talbott JA, Hales RE, Yudofsky SC (eds): Textbook of Psychiatry. Washington, DC, American Psychiatric Press, 1988.)*

synthesized and released in other regions of the brain. Among these are corticotropin-releasing factor, thyrotropin-releasing hormone, luteinizing hormone-releasing hormone, and somatostatin. Some peptides that were first localized in the gastrointestinal tract, such as cholecystokinin and vasoactive intestinal peptide, have also been identified in the brain. Neurotensin, first isolated from brain tissue, was subsequently found to be widely distributed in the gut. Summaries of physiological effects and brain localization of these and other neuropeptides can be found in Nemeroff and Dunn (1984).

Steroid Hormones

Although steroid hormones have profound effects on behavior and other brain functions, they are all synthesized in peripheral tissues. Gonadal steroids are synthesized primarily in the ovaries (estrogens and progestins) or the testes (androgens), although the adrenal cortex synthesizes significant amounts of sex steroids. The adrenal cortex is the primary site of glucocorticoid and mineralcorticoid synthesis. After secretion into the blood, steroid molecules are either tightly bound to specific steroid-binding globulins or less tightly bound to albumin. Steroids bound to albumin, much more so than steroids bound to specific binding globulins, readily dissociate, diffuse across the blood–brain barrier, and gain access to all regions of the CNS. Steroids also diffuse readily into the neuronal cytoplasm where they may undergo a variety of metabolic transformations (see discussion that follows).

Mechanisms of Effect

Mechanisms of possible steroid effects on neurons are summarized in Figure 12–22. Steroids appear to have their most profound and prolonged effects by altering genomic regulation of protein synthesis (Luttge, 1983). After diffusion into neuronal cytoplasm, steroids form noncovalent high-affinity attachments to macromolecules called cytoplasmic steroid receptors. Binding of cytoplasmic steroid receptors is quite specific in individual neurons, allowing genomic regulation of a target cell only by a particular type of steroid molecule even though other types of steroid molecules may enter that cell. Hormone–receptor complexes diffuse through pores in the nuclear membrane into the nucleoplasm where the complex interacts with nuclear "acceptors" and DNA, resulting in changes in synthesis of messenger RNA sequences coding for specific proteins. The steroid–receptor complex may then be processed so that the receptor is either recycled to the cytoplasm for reutilization or is catabolized and destroyed.

While genomic mechanisms of action have been most thoroughly studied, steroids may influence neurons in other ways. Steroids have short latency effects on postsynaptic electrical activity resulting from presynaptic neurotransmitter release. While steroids do not appear to have membrane-bound receptors like those of small molecule or peptide neurotransmitters, their affinity for the lipid-rich membrane environment may allow steroids to affect directly the physicochemical properties of neuronal cell membranes.

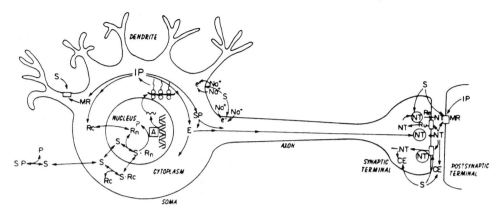

Figure 12–22. *Diagrammatic representation of various possible molecular and electrophysiologic actions of steroid hormones in mammalian brain neurons. In the extracellular space, cerebrospinal fluid, and blood, the steroid may exist in either the free (S) or carrier-protein bound (S · P) state. The free steroid enters the neuron either by diffusion or carrier-mediated transport, after which it may be metabolized or bind to a cytosolic receptor macromolecule (Rc) and diffuse as a steroid-receptor complex (S · Rc) to the nucleoplasm, or it may directly enter the nucleoplasm and then bind to the nuclear receptor (Rn). The intranuclear steroid-receptor complex (S · Rn) may then undergo a poorly understood "activation" process that facilitates its interaction with acceptor proteins (A) and DNA. This S · Rn · A interaction in the chromatin may, in turn, precipitate the production of specific mRNAs that code for the production of specific "induced proteins" (IP) and enzymes (E). Examples of IPs include structural proteins (SP) (e.g., tubulin), membrane receptor proteins (MR) (e.g., MRs for biogenic amines, acetylcholine, GABA, neuropeptides), cytoplasmic receptor proteins for steroids (Rc) (e.g., E_2 and P_4 receptors), and various anabolic and catabolic enzymes (CE) (e.g., ChAcT). Release (Re) and reuptake (Ru) of neurotransmitters (NT) may also be modulated by the direct actions of steroids. Last, steroids may interact directly with the neuronal soma or axonal plasma membrane to modulate the transmembrane diffusion or distribution of ions (e.g., Na^+) and thereby produce an electrophysiologic response (e^-) or alter the conduction velocity of a response. (Reproduced with permission from Luttge WG: Molecular mechanisms of steroid hormone actions in the brain. In Svare BB (ed): Hormones and Aggressive Behavior. New York, Plenum Press, 1983.)*

Location of Steroid Binding in the Brain

Neuronal cell bodies that bind specific steroids are located in discrete regions of the brain (Luine and McEwen, 1985; Luttge, 1983). Estrogen and androgen binding is located in the anterior and medial portions of the hypothalamus, the preoptic and septal areas, the amygdala, as well as midbrain sites such as the mesencephalic central gray. Implantation of gonadal steroids into these sites, but not into other brain sites, elicits hormonal and behavioral effects that are dependent on these steroids. Brain areas that bind gonadal steroids have been implicated in the regulation of reproductive behaviors (see section entitled Reproductive Behaviors: Sex and Mothering), other sexually differentiated behaviors, and gonadotropin release.

Progesterone-binding is localized in the same areas as estrogen binding with the exception of the amygdala. Synthesis of some progesterone receptors requires estrogen stimulation. Progesterone receptor concentration peaks between 24 and 48 hours after estrogen treatment. If progesterone levels rise simultaneously with estrogen levels, progesterone receptor proliferation does not occur.

The pattern of glucocorticoid binding within the brain is markedly different from the pattern of gonadal steroid binding. Glucocorticoid binding is most prominent in the hippocampus (in the pyramidal cells in the CA_1 and CA_2 fields of the horn of Ammon and the granule neurons of the dentate gyrus) and, to a lesser degree, in the septal area, the amygdala, and some areas of the cerebral cortex. Behavioral effects of glucocorticoids are exerted in these limbic brain areas.

Estrogen, androgen, and glucocorticoid-concentrating cells have also been found in the lower brainstem and in the spinal cord. Androgen or glucocorticoid-labeled cells predominate in some somatomotor cranial nerves and spinal cord regions, while estrogen-labeled cells predominate in some sensory cranial nerves and spinal cord regions.

Metabolism of Steroid Hormones

In the brain, regional differences in metabolism influence local availability of specific steroid molecules (Luttge, 1983). Estradiol (E_2) is the major estrogen secreted by the ovary as well as the most potent estrogen in neural and nonneural tissues. However, other estrogen species, estrone (E_1), estriol (E_3), as well as catechol estrogens (2-OH-E_2, 2-OH-E_1, 4-OH-E_2, 4-OH-E_1), are synthesized in peripheral and brain tissues. Many brain regions are capable of interconverting E_1, E_2, and E_3. The relative amount of each estrogen species resulting from interconversion differs with brain region. For instance, E_1 is relatively increased by metabolism of estrogen molecules in the posterior hypothalamus, while E_2 is the primary metabolic product in the anterior hypothalamus and the preoptic area. Estrogen metabolism in the hypothalamus, preoptic area, septum, and amgydala produces relatively more E_2, less E_3, and about the same amount of E_1 as does estrogen metabolism in the hippocampus and cortical regions. Catechol estrogens, which are synthesized primarily from E_2, are found in greater abundance in the hypothalmus than in cerebral cortex and increase markedly during proestrus in rats. Catechol estrogens, especially 4-OH-E_2, compete with E_2 for high-affinity binding to cytoplasmic estrogen receptors in brain tissue and are as potent as E_2 in inducing female sexual behavior and LH secretion. Catechol estrogens also have high affinity for some enzymes involved in small molecule neurotransmitter synthesis and catabolism (e.g., tyrosine hydroxylase, catecholamine-O-methyl-transferase, and others).

Progesterone (P_4) is the major progestin synthesized in peripheral tissues of mammals. However, other progestins, such as 20 alpha-OH-P_4, are also synthesized and penetrate the blood–brain barrier. The principal metabolic conversion of progestins in the brain is 5 alpha-reduction which is irreversible. P_4 is converted by 5 alpha-reductase to 5 alpha-DHP. Both P_4 and 20 alpha-OH-P_4 are preferred substrates over testosterone for 5 alpha-reductase, suggesting that progestins may inhibit 5 alpha-reduction of testosterone to DHT, a conversion that is important for some behavioral effects of testosterone.

Testosterone (T) is the primary androgen in mammals, although a number of other androgen molecules are also found in the circulation. Interconversion of T and androstenedione (AE) by 17 beta-oxidoreductase occurs in many brain regions. The 5 alpha-reduction of T to DHT, which is irreversible, occurs primarily in the hypothalamus. Some androgens are converted to estrogen by the enzyme aromatase (e.g., T or AE conversion to E_2 or E_1), while other androgens cannot be aromatized (e.g., DHT). Aromatase activity in the male rat brain is highest in the medial preoptic area, periventricular nucleus of the preoptic area, and the medial amygdala, while lower levels are found in the lateral preoptic area, mediobasal hypothalamus, and the lateral hypothalamus. Nonlimbic brain areas contain little if any aromatase activity.

Corticosterone is the primary circulating glucocorticoid in some mammals (e.g., rats), while cortisol predominates in other mammalian species (e.g., lower primates and humans). Other glucocorticoids, such as cortisone, are also found in blood. Reversible and irreversible metabolic conversion of glucocorticoids may occur in the brain. Interconversion of cortisol and cortisone and cortisol conversion to corticosterone have been reported. However, little, if any, conversion of corticosterone has been demonstrated. This may explain why, in some primates where the major circulating glucocorticoid is cortisol, corticosterone appears to be concentrated preferentially by nuclear receptors in a number of brain areas.

Regulatory Effects of Steroids

Steroid hormones affect synthesis, release, turnover, reuptake, catabolism, and receptor concentration of small molecule neurotransmitters. These effects differ with type of steroid and vary with brain region. While less studied, evidence to date suggests that synthesis, release, and receptor concentrations of several neuropeptides are also regulated by steroids. Steroids exert most of these effects by altering expression of genes coding for specific proteins. However, some neurons that respond to steroids with changes in neurotransmitter synthesis, release, or receptor concentration do not contain steroid receptors. These nongenomic effects may result from steroid alteration of cell membrane properties and ion permeability (McEwen, 1991).

Thyroid Hormone

The thyroid gland and its hormones constitute but one part of a larger regulatory system, the hypothalamic–pituitary–thyroid (HPT) axis. Key hormonal components of this system include the thyroid hormones thyroxine (T_4) and triiodothyronine (T_3), thyroid-stimulating hormone (TSH), and thyrotropin-releasing hormone (TRH). The thyroid hormones T_4 and T_3 are iodinated bi-mers of the amino acid, tyrosine. TSH, a glycoprotein synthesized in the pituitary gland, regulates the production of T_3 and T_4. TSH, in turn, is regulated by TRH, a tripeptide (pro-his-pro), which is synthesized by neurons in the hypothalamus, released in the median eminence, and delivered to the pituitary by the hypophyseal portal venous system. The activity of this system is also partially regulated by other extrathyroidal factors, such as thyroid-binding glob' .in, which serves as the main serum reservoir for thyroid hormone, and peripheral enzymes that convert T_4 either to T_3 or to its metabolically inactive form, reverse T_3.

Some hormonal components of the thyroidal system are found in virtually all animal species suggesting that it developed early in evolution and serves fairly basic biologic ends. By interacting with membrane as well as nuclear receptors, thyroid hormone affects a variety of cellular functions including energy utilization, enzymatic rates, and cell growth and division. While evolution appears to have adapted the HPT axis for multiple functions, its main job may be to modulate and coordinate overall metabolic activity. The ability to adjust cellular energy utilization to different circumstances such as growth, procreation, and seasonal change would provide obvious adaptational advantage. Thyroid hormone concentrations are more actively regulated in the brain than in other organ systems, suggesting that thyroid hormones may play additional specific roles in the coordination of behavior.

Since the turn of the century it has been known that deficiency or excess of thyroid hormone is associated with psychopathology. Severely hypothyroid adults are often depressed, demented, or psychotic. Hyperthyroid persons are typically anxious or appear to have agitated depressions. The components of the HPT axis are probably partially involved in a variety of behavior responses. Based on available data, we can identify three key areas in which HPT axis activity influences behavioral adaptation: regulation of nervous system development, augmentation of catecholaminergic stress response, and modulation of biological rhythms.

Nervous System Development

Thyroid hormone has a nerve growth factor-like effect on neurons in the CNS. Dendritic and axonal growth is enhanced by thyroid hormone and is impaired in thyroid deficiency states. There appears to be a developmental window, occurring perinatally in most species, during which thyroid hormone availability is absolutely essential for brain maturation (Sokoloff, 1967). In humans, deprivation of thyroid hormone prenatally or in early infancy leads to the severe and irreversible form of retardation known as cretinism. The HPT axis probably also facilitates neuronal maintenance and repair in the mature organism. Administration of TRH appears to stimulate cell growth and enhance recovery of function following brain and spinal cord trauma. Although the adult CNS is more tolerant of thyroid deficiency than that of the infant, prolonged thyroid deficiency states may cause irreversible cognitive decline in adult humans.

Stress Responses

Thyroid hormone augments the firing of beta-adrenergic neurons. This is mediated by a facilitating interaction at postsynaptic beta-adrenergic receptors (Whybrow and Prange, 1981). Thus, the HPT axis may help mediate the increase in catecholaminergic neurotransmission that is an essential component of the general stress response (see section entitled Stress and Behavior) perhaps by way of a centrally induced neurohormone cascade involving TRH, TSH, and thyroid hormone. The HPT axis, in turn, can be directly tuned up or down by the sympathetic nervous system, which innervates the HPT axis at several levels. The ability of the HPT axis to enhance beta-adrenergic neurotransmission may be an important factor in recovery from the mood disorder depression, which appears to be associated with deficient or inefficient catecholaminergic neurotransmission. A slight increase in the tone of the thyroid axis may be able to compensate, at least partially, for such a deficiency (Whybrow and Prange, 1981). This concept is strongly supported by the observation that T_3 administration has been reported to augment response to antidepressant medication in some patients. Conversely, one of the earliest and most consistent neuroendocrine findings is that 20% to 30% of depressed patients exhibit a diminished TSH response to exogenously administered TRH. Prange has postulated these findings to be the consequence of prolonged reliance in depressed persons on the ability of the HPT axis to compensate for deficient catecholaminergic neurotransmission; tachyphylaxis develops at the pituitary level to chronic TRH overdrive.

Modulation of Biological Rhythms

As with other hormonal systems, HPT axis activity fluctuates diurnally and possibly seasonally. However, there is also evidence that HPT axis activity itself regulates the length of biological rhythms (Schull et al, 1988). TRH mediates the change from hibernation to the active state in some species. In mice, the thyroid changes the length of motor activity cycles. The extent to which the HPT axis affects normal biological rhythms in humans is unknown. However, there is evidence for HPT axis abnormalities in bipolar affective disorder, a disease state in which mood and activity cycle at an abnormal rate and to an excessive degree. In particular, an association has been observed between hypothyroidism and rapid cycling bipolar disorder. Administration of thyroid hormone will stabilize cycling in a portion of these patients.

It can be seen from the preceding overview that there has been a dramatic and rapid expansion in our understanding of the neurobiology of behavior and an emerging body of data in elucidating the biochemical basis for not only normal behavior but several of the major mental disorders as well. In the next section, the neurochemical basis of certain specific behaviors such as learning, memory, reproductive activity, feeding, and aggression are discussed.

THE NEUROBIOLOGY OF SPECIFIC BEHAVIORS

Learning and Memory

An impressive array of cognitive abilities enables humans to analyze situations, review past experiences, consider options, anticipate developments, and rehearse future actions. Therefore, human behavior depends on and is the result of a great deal of cognitive activity within the brain before overt, observable behavior occurs. Despite the critical nature of cognitive function in the shaping of human behavior, exploration of the biologic basis of most cognitive functions is in its infancy. Many cognitive abilities do not appear to be localized. In brain-damaged persons, impairment of cognitive functions such as attention, concentration, calculation, inductive and deductive logic has been related to the total amount of cortical damage but has not been associated with damage in specific areas. Some brain regions, however, have been implicated in particular cognitive tasks. As discussed earlier, the frontal lobes, for instance, play a key role in abstract thinking and planning. The neurobiological basis of most cognitive functions is unknown. However, progress has been achieved in our understanding of the mechanism of learning and memory.

The Components and Dimensions of Learning and Memory

Learning is the capacity to change behavior in response to experience. Memory is the retained record of experience and is composed of a short-term and a long-term phase. (See Table 12–6 for a summary of the phases of memory formation and the types of memory that are discussed later.) Short-term memory, lasting seconds to minutes, is probably based on a sustained pattern of activity of the primary sensory neural substrate stimulated by the new experience. Distraction by other stimuli, which disrupts the pattern of activity of the primary sensory neural substrate, results in loss of the new information stored in short-term memory. Acquisition of long-term memory requires persistent physical change either in the primary sensory neural substrate activated by the new information or physical change in cerebral cortex where information is stored after processing in the hippocampus (see later). Changes in neural structures underlying acquisition of long-term memory depend on protein synthesis. After initial acquisition, long-term memories require a period of *consolidation* before they can no longer be abolished by pharmacologic or electroconvulsive means. Consolidation of long-term memory requires a few hours to a few days in animals. Electroconvulsive therapy in psychiatric patients produces loss of some memories acquired as much as 3 years prior to treatment (Squire, 1987). This observation suggests that complete consolidation of memory in humans can require long periods of time. *Retrieval* of memories from long-term storage operates by mechanisms that differ from those mediating acquisition of memory. Retrieval does not involve information processing in the hippocampus nor does it depend on protein synthesis.

Recent investigations of the amnestic syndrome in humans, which results from a variety of neurologic insults, have provided new insights into the complexities of long-term memory. The amnestic syndrome is characterized by impaired acquisition of memories without accompanying sensory, motor, or other neurologic deficits. Amnesics have intact short-term memory and have no problem retrieving information

Table 12-6 **Types of Memory and Phases of Long-Term Memory**

TYPES OF MEMORY	CHARACTERISTICS
Short-term	Seconds to minutes in duration, probably mediated by sustained neural electrical activity.
Long-term	
Procedural	Involves retention of information about motor or cognitive sequences; does not depend upon the hippocampus.
Declarative	Depends upon the hippocampus; impaired in amnesics.
Semantic	Involves retention of information about abstract concepts or events.
Episodic	Involves retention of information about personal experiences.
PHASES OF LONG-TERM MEMORY	
Acquisition ⎤	Protein synthesis is necessary.
Consolidation ⎟	
Retrieval ⎦	Protein synthesis is not necessary.

stored in long-term memory prior to the neurologic insult. Moreover, cognitive functions other than acquisition of memories (e.g., concentration, calculation, logic, and so forth) remain intact.

Detailed investigation of which types of information can and cannot be learned by amnesics suggests the existence of different types of long-term memory mechanisms (Squire, 1987). *Procedural memory* involves acquiring knowledge of motor or cognitive sequences (e.g., tying knots, solving puzzles, and so forth). *Semantic memory* is the retention of abstract knowledge or events in time (e.g., the chemical composition of water or the assassination of President Kennedy). *Episodic memory* is the recollection of personal experiences (e.g., one's last visit to the doctor). *Semantic and episodic memory together are termed declarative memory.* It is generally agreed that amnesics can acquire procedural memory but are impaired in acquiring declarative memory. This produces the interesting situation in which amnesics can increase their retention of procedural information with training but have no memory of having learned and, in fact, have no awareness of their increased knowledge. There is debate about the extent of the deficit in acquiring declarative memory in amnesics. Some argue that episodic memory is specifically eliminated in the amnestic syndrome while semantic memory capability persists. Others argue that acquisition of both episodic and semantic memory is impaired. Careful neuropsychological studies should resolve this controversy. Because amnesics have discrete impairment of declarative but not procedural memory these separate types of memory are probably acquired by different mechanisms.

Studies of the effects of priming on memory retrieval in amnesics also suggest that different mechanisms underlie procedural and declarative memory (Squire, 1987). Amnesics are very poor at free recall of lists of words. However, when given the first three letters of words they have previously seen, amnesics are able to complete accurately the spelling of many words. If normal subjects are given a list of words and instructed to focus on features of the words other than their meaning (such as counting vowels), subsequent recall is also poor. However, when given the first three letters of those words, recall is much improved, demonstrating a learning effect very similar to that seen in amnesics. These results suggest that amnesics can learn but cannot store information based on meaning or category. Declarative memory, which is impaired in amnesics, may, therefore, involve processing and storage of information based on meaning and category, while procedural memory, which is intact in amnesics, involves processing and storage based on the more concrete and literal aspects of information.

Localization of Learning and Memory

Where does acquisition of memory occur? Where is memory stored? The answers to these questions depend on the complexity of learning that occurs.

Habituation, the decline and extinction of a response with repeated presentations of a particular stimulus, is the simplest type of learning. *Sensitization* is another simple learning process involving the enhancement of responses following a strong noxious stimulus. *Classical conditioning* is a more complex learning task involving the association of a conditioned and unconditioned stimulus. Classical conditioning always requires that the conditioned stimulus precede the unconditioned stimulus in time, and that only a brief period of time elapse between the conditioned and unconditioned stimulus. (See Chapter 6 by Dr. Dorsett.) The neurobiological basis of simple learning has been investigated in a number of animal models.

The marine snail *Aplysia californica* has a respiratory organ, the gill, and a spoutlike organ, the siphon, which is used to discharge sea water and body waste. Light tactile stimulation of the siphon causes a reflexive withdrawal of the gill and siphon. With repeated moderate tactile stimulation of the siphon, the withdrawal reflex habituates. On the other hand, strong noxious stimulation, such as electroshock of the tail of *Aplysia*, produces a subsequent increase, or sensitization, of the gill and siphon withdrawal reflex. A single aversive stimulus produces short-term sensitization while repeated aversive stimuli produce long-term sensitization. The gill and siphon withdrawal reflex can also be classically conditioned.

The mechanisms underlying habituation, short-term and long-term sensitization, and classic conditioning of the gill and siphon withdrawal reflex in *Aplysia* have been studied in great detail (Kandel and Schwartz, 1991). The nervous system of *Aplysia* is relatively uncomplicated. The neural circuit mediating the gill and siphon withdrawal reflex consists of sensory neurons directly synapsing on motor neurons that effect the response. Although action potentials are generated in sensory neurons by each stimulation, release of neurotransmitter from the presynaptic processes of sensory neurons decreases with repeated tactile stimulation. As a result, synaptic transmission declines until the motor neuron is no longer activated. Electroshock of the tail of *Aplysia* activates pathways that converge on and stimulate the presynaptic processes of sensory neurons involved in the gill and siphon withdrawal reflex. Subsequently, more neurotransmitter is released from the sensory neuron in response to tactile stimulation of the gill, resulting in increased activation of motor neurons. Intracellular mechanisms underlying sensitization of the gill and siphon withdrawal reflex are summarized in Figure 12–23. Short-term sensitization is based upon covalent modification of preexisting proteins while long-term sensitization involves synthesis of new proteins as is illustrated in Figure 12–24. If light tactile stimulation is consistently given just prior to tail shock, *Aplysia* become conditioned to withdraw the gill and siphon vigorously in response to tactile stimulation alone. Pairing of the conditioned and unconditioned stimulus in this manner selectively increases neurotransmitter release from the presynaptic processes of sensory neurons by a mechanism that is explained in Figure 12–25.

Brain mechanisms underlying classic conditioning have also been studied in other animal models. In the rabbit, a brief puff of air directed at the cornea reliably produces an eyeblink response. This reflex can be conditioned by pairing a brief tone just before the puff of air. In pigeons, foot shock reliably produces an increase in heart rate. When bright illumination of the visual field is repeatedly presented prior to foot shock, heart rate acceleration becomes conditioned to the light stimulus. Classic conditioning in both of these cases does not depend at all on the cerebral cortex or other forebrain structures but rather occurs within discrete areas of the lower brain where neurons conveying sensory information converge on neurons activating motor or autonomic outputs (Squire, 1987). The studies described above collectively suggest that acquisition and storage of simple learning tasks are located entirely within the direct or nearly direct connections between sensory neurons and neurons mediating relevant responses.

Complex learning occurs by mechanisms that differ from those subserving simple learning. Midtemporal brain structures, especially the hippocampus, are essential for acquisition of complex memory (Squire, 1987). Lesions in this area eliminate the ability of animals to learn complex conditioning and operant tasks successfully. Examination of the brain of deceased amnesics invariably reveals damage to the midline temporal lobe area. Connections between the hippocampus and the cerebral cortex may be essential for processing and storing complex information. For instance, in the human and lower primate brain, the frontal association cortex (which connects with the hippocampus), the sulcus principalis, and the inferior prefrontal convexity play a critical role in sorting information in time. After processing, complex information is probably stored within the cortical areas that were involved in the processing. The importance of the cerebral cortex in the storage of complex memories is suggested by two lines of evidence. First, lesions that are restricted to the cortex interfere with the acquisition of complex learning. The size of the lesion, more so than the location, appears to be related to the degree of impairment. Second, repeated learning trials have been observed to produce hypertrophy within cortical regions that are known to process the types of sensory and motor information involved in the execution of the learned response (Squire, 1987).

In a manner analogous to simple and complex learning in animals, procedural and declarative memory in humans may depend on different neural substrates. Procedural memory may be acquired and stored within subcortical connections between neurons conveying sensory information and neurons activating responses. However, acquisition of declarative memory may require initial sorting, categorizing, organizing, and so forth that can only be accomplished with an intact midthalamic–hippocampal apparatus interacting with the cerebral cortex. When this apparatus is damaged, as in the amnestic syndrome, impairment or complete loss of the ability to acquire declarative memory occurs.

The Neurochemical Basis of Learning and Memory

Cholinergic pathways in the brain play a role in the acquisition and retrieval of memories (Decker and McGaugh, 1991; Fibiger, 1991). Muscarinic neurotransmission facilitates initial acquisition of learning tasks but inhibits retrieval of memories from about 5 to 14 days after training. However, around 28 days after training, muscarinic neurotransmission facilitates memory retrieval. These observations suggest that memory consolidation is composed of a number of successive phases, each mediated by differing cholinergic mechanisms. Brain regions involved in learning, such as the hippocampus and the frontal cortex, are heavily innervated by cholinergic pathways. Dementia of the Alzheimer's type has been associated with loss of cholinergic neurons in the nucleus basalis of Meynert, the major source of cholinergic projections to the cortex. Noradrenergic neurotransmission enhances learning primarily by increasing attention. Several neuropeptides affect learning and memory. ACTH or vasopressin administration after a learning trial facilitates retention of learned avoidance behavior. Oxytocin, on the other hand, inhibits retention of learned avoidance behavior. Learning and memory effects of vasopressin and oxytocin are mediated within the dentate

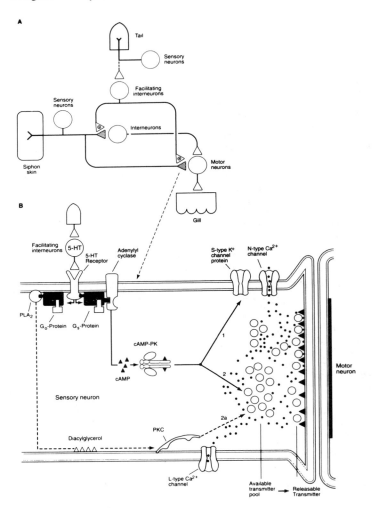

Figure 12–23. *Presynaptic facilitation is a factor in sensitization of the gill-withdrawal reflex in Aplysia.*
A. *Sensitization is produced by applying a noxious stimulus to another part of the body, such as the tail. Stimuli to the tail activate sensory neurons that excite facilitating interneurons. The facilitating cells, some of which use serotonin (5-hydroxy-tryptamine, or 5-HT) as their transmitter (indicated by dense core vesicles in the terminal of the facilitating neuron) in turn end on the synaptic terminals of the sensory neurons from the siphon skin, where they enhance transmitter release by means of presynaptic facilitation.*
B. *Postulated biochemical steps of presynaptic facilitation in the sensory neuron. The action of serotonin and other facilitating transmitters leads to enhanced transmitter release by modulating a number of steps in the release process; one of these is the closure of a special class of K^+ channels, which causes*

gyrus of the hippocampus, the dorsal septum, and the midbrain dorsal raphe nucleus. ACTH effects are exerted primarily in the caudal thalamus (Squire, 1987).

Reproductive Behaviors: Sex and Mothering

Sexual interest is obviously a major influence on behavior in animals and humans. Perhaps less appreciated as a behavioral motivator is the drive of parents, especially mothers, to nurture and protect their offspring. Maternal behavior, along with female and male sexual behavior, are classified as reproductive behaviors because they result in propagation of species and they are under the control of reproductive hormones.

Components and Dimensions of Reproductive Behaviors

Female sexual behavior includes proceptive behavior, which elicits sexual advances from males, and receptive behavior, which facilitates attempts by males to copulate. In the presence of sexually active males, female rats signal their receptivity to mating by hopping, darting, wiggling their ears, and proffering their backsides. During copulation, tactile stimuli from the male elicit adjustment in the female's body

---

*a consequent increase in Ca^{2+} influx through a (N-type) Ca^{2+} channel. Serotonin produces these actions by binding to a receptor that engages a G-protein, which increases the activity of adenylyl cyclase. The adenylyl cyclase converts ATP to cyclic AMP, thereby increasing the level of cyclic AMP in the terminal of the sensory neuron. The cAMP activates the cAMP-dependent protein kinase by attaching to its regulatory sub-unit, which releases its active catalytic sub-unit. The catalytic subunit then phosphorylates the K^+ channel (either directly or by acting on a regulatory protein associated with it), thereby changing the conformation of the channel and decreasing the K^+ current (**pathway 1**). This prolongs the action potential, increases the influx of Ca^{2+}, and thus augments transmitter release.*

*In addition to broadening the action potential (pathway 1), serotonin also leads to an increase in the availability of transmitter by mobilizing vesicles from a transmitter pool to the releasable pool at the active zone (**pathway 2**). This second pathway concerned with mobilization of transmitter vesicles reflects the joint action of the cAMP-dependent protein kinase and protein kinase C, a second kinase activated by 5-HT (**dotted line and pathway 2a**). Protein kinase C (PKC) is activated by 5-HT acting through another G-protein that activates a phospholipase that in turn stimulates diacylglycerol in the membrane. Diacylglycerol activates protein kinase C. (Reproduced with permission from Kandel ER, Schwartz JH, Jessell TM (eds): Principles of Neural Science. New York, Elsevier, 1991.)*

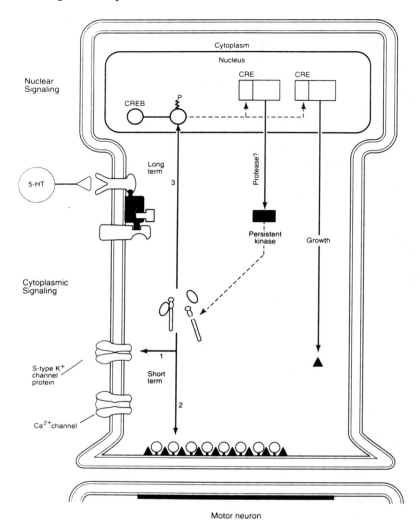

Figure 12–24. *Schematic outline of the two major sets of changes in the sensory neurons of the gill-withdrawal reflex that accompany long-term memory for sensitization in* Aplysia: *persistent phosphorylation and structural changes. Serotonin (5-HT), a transmitter released by facilitatory neurons, acts on a sensory neuron to initiate both the short-term and the long-term facilitation that contribute to the memory processes.*

  Short-term facilitation *(lasting minutes to hours), involves covalent modification of preexisting proteins (pathways 1 and 2). Serotonin acts on a transmembrane serotonin receptor to activate a GTP-binding protein that stimulates the amplifier, the enzyme adenylyl cyclase, to convert ATP to the second messenger cAMP. In turn, cAMP activates protein kinase A, which phosphorylates and covalently modifies a number of target proteins. These include closing a K^+ channel (pathway 1) as well as steps involved in transmitter availability and re-*

position that enhances penetration by the male. For example, a receptive female rat arches its back into an exaggerated lordosis posture and moves its tail to one side. Brain pathways mediating sensory signals that trigger lordosis are summarized in Figure 12–26.

Female sexual behavior is exhibited in most species only during a brief period of the ovarian cycle near the time of ovulation when fertilization is possible. Cyclic changes in estrogen and progesterone levels that stimulate ovulation also initiate female sexual behavior. In the absence of ovarian steroids, for instance after ovariectomy, sexual behavior ceases in animals and some, but not all, women.

Male sexual behavior includes penile erections, repeated intromissions, and ejaculation. In addition to proceptive behaviors, rodent males are attracted to receptive females by the odor of vaginal secretions. Primate males are attracted by the swelling and changes in pigmentation of the females' external genitalia that occur near ovulation. The initiation of male sexual activity depends on testosterone. Sexually experienced males of subprimate species undergo a gradual decline in sexual behavior after castration. However, men and primates sometimes experience no loss of sexual interest or potency after castration.

Maternal behavior is composed of a number of integrated activities that result in the cleaning, feeding, and protection of offspring. The specific behaviors vary widely between species. Nursing is also associated in a number of species with increased food intake, enhanced aggressiveness, and diminished fearful and avoidant responses to aversive stimuli. The initiation of maternal behavior after parturition depends, in most subprimate mammals, on the rise in estrogen and fall in progesterone occurring in late pregnancy. In primates and humans, early social experience is critical in preparing females to provide effective mothering behavior.

---

lease *(pathway 2). The duration of these modifications represents the retention or storage of a component of the short-term memory.*

Long-term facilitation *(lasting one or more days) involves the synthesis of new proteins. The switch for this inductive mechanism is initiated by the protein kinase A, which is thought to translocate to the nucleus where it is thought to phosphorylate one or more transcriptional activators that bind to Cyclic AMP Regulatory Elements (CRE) located in the upstream region of cAMP-inducible genes (pathway 3). The transcriptional activators, thought to belong to the protein family of Cyclic AMP Response Element Binding (CREB) proteins, activate two classes of effector genes that encode two classes of proteins. (β and v). Inhibiting protein synthesis during learning blocks the expression of these sets of induced proteins. These two sets of proteins have distinct functions. One set of proteins (β), one of which perhaps is a specific protease, leads to a down-regulation of the regulatory subunit. This results in persistent activity of kinase A, leading to persistent phosphorylation of the substrate proteins of pathways 1 and 2. The second set of proteins (v) is important for the growth of new synaptic connections. (Reproduced with permission from Kandel ER, Schwartz JH, Jessell TM (eds): Principles of Neural Science. New York, Elsevier, 1991).*

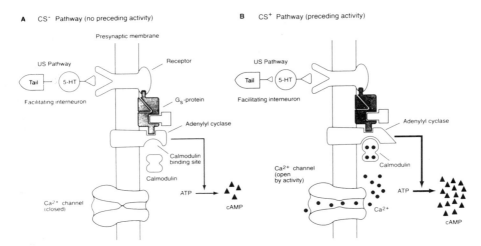

Figure 12–25. *A molecular model of the synaptic action underlying classical conditioning. The model is based on the hypothesis that activity in the sensory neurons of the conditioned stimulus (CS) pathway prior to the presentation of the unconditional stimulus (US) permits an influx of Ca^{2+} that enhances the activity of Ca^{2+}-dependent adenylyl cyclase.*
A. *In the unpaired pathway (CS) the sensory neuron is not active prior to presentation of the CS, so its Ca^{2+} channels are closed at the time the US input arrives.* **B**. *In the paired pathway (CS^+) the sensory neuron is active prior to the CS and thus its Ca^{2+} channels are open when the US input arrives. Increased intracellular Ca^{2+} binds to calmodulin, which in turn binds to adenylyl cyclase, which undergoes a conformational change as a result. This change enhances the ability of the adenylyl cyclase to synthesize cAMP in response to serotonin released by the US. The greater amount of cAMP activates more cAMP-dependent protein kinase, and leads to a substantially greater amount of transmitter release than would occur normally (without paired activity). (Reproduced with permission from Kandel ER, Schwartz JH, Jessell TM (eds): Principles of Neural Science. New York, Elsevier, 1991.)*

Brain Sites Implicated in the Regulation of Reproductive Behaviors

Brain mechanisms have been more thoroughly investigated for female sexual receptivity than for other reproductive behaviors (Pfaff and Schwartz-Giblin, 1988). Pathways initiating receptive posturing in rats project from the anterior and ventromedial hypothalamus to midbrain structures such as the mesencephalic central gray. This apparatus regulates descending multisynaptic pathways that control motor neurons innervating muscle groups involved in lordosis (see Fig. 12–26). The medial preoptic area and the septum exert a tonic inhibitory effect on receptive behavior that is probably mediated by pathways that descend to the midbrain. Estrogen facilitates receptive posturing by suppressing the inhibitory influence of the medial preoptic area and increasing the facilitating influence of the ventromedial and anterior hypothalamus. Estrogen also enhances female sexual behavior by stimulating synthesis of progesterone receptors. Tactile stimulation essential to the activation of the lordosis

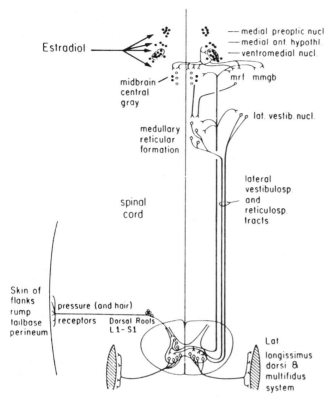

Estradiol

— medial preoptic nucl
— medial ant hypothl.
— ventromedial nucl

midbrain
central
gray

mrf   mmgb

lat. vestib. nucl.

medullary
reticular
formation

lateral
vestibulosp.
and
reticulosp.
tracts

spinal
cord

Skin of
flanks
rump
tailbase
perineum

pressure (and hair)
receptors   Dorsal Roots
L 1-S1

Lat
longissimus
dorsi &
multifidus
system

Figure 12-26. *Schematic representation of the minimal neural circuit for lordosis behavior in the female rat. Estradiol effects are mediated at estrogen-binding neurons in the hypothalamus and the central gray. Ascending spinal fibers conveying sensory information necessary for induction of lordosis travel in the anterolateral columns of the spinal cord. mmgb = medial division of the medial geniculate body; mrf = dorsal mesencephalic reticular formation. (Reproduced with permission from Pfaff D, Modianos D: Neural Mechanisms of Female Reproductive Behavior in Adler N, Pfaff D, Goy RW (eds): Handbook of Behavioral Neurobiology, Vol 7: Reproduction. pp 423–493. New York, Plenum Press, 1985.)*

reflex ascends through the anterolateral columns of the spinal cord. If permissive ovarian steroid conditions are present, this sensory information activates the hypothalmic–midbrain apparatus that initiates the lordosis posture. Other than dependence on ovarian steroids, very little is known about the mechanisms of proceptive behavior.

Male sexual behavior is initiated within pathways that originate in the medial preoptic area (Sachs and Meisel, 1988). Testosterone acts throughout the preoptic-anterior hypothalmic area to stimulate male copulatory behavior. Depending on the species, male reproductive behavior depends on conversion of testosterone to one or several metabolites: androstenedione, dihydrotestosterone, other androgens, or estrogen. Inputs from limbic brain structures influence male motivation to copulate. For instance, lesions of the temporal lobe that include the basolateral nucleus of the amygdala produce hypersexuality in monkeys and cats. On the other hand, lesions of the corticomedial nucleus of the amygdala in rodents depress male sexual behavior probably by interrupting olfactory inputs indicating female reproductive state.

Maternal behavior is mediated by pathways that originate in the medial preoptic area, project laterally, and then descend through the medial forebrain bundle to rostral midbrain structures such as the ventral tegmental area (Numan, 1988).

Estrogen acts in the medial preoptic area to initiate mothering. Limbic structures such as the hippocampus and septum play a more prominent role in the regulation of maternal behavior than in other reproductive behaviors.

The Neurochemical Basis of Reproductive Behaviors

A large number of drugs that affect classic neurotransmitter systems have been tested for their effects on reproductive behaviors, especially sexual behaviors (Meyerson et al, 1985; Pedersen and Prange, 1987). Serotonergic neurotransmission inhibits both female and male sexual behavior. Selective destruction of serotonergic neurons in the hypothalamus increases receptive behavior. Peripheral drug treatments that enhance dopaminergic neurotransmission increase proceptive behaviors (the mobile component of female sexual behavior), decrease receptive posturing (the immobile component of female sexual behavior), and increase male mounting behavior. However, in the medial preoptic area and the ventromedial nucleus, dopamine agonists increase while dopamine antagonists decrease receptive posturing, suggesting that dopamine may have different effects in separate brain regions involved in female sexual behavior. Destruction of noradrenergic pathways that descend to the spinal cord suppresses proceptive and receptive behavior as well as components of male sexual behavior. The ascending ventral noradrenergic bundle is critical to receptive but not proceptive female sexual behavior. Peripheral treatment with different adrenergic drugs has a variety of effects on sexual behavior that do not fit into a coherent mechanistic scheme, probably because adrenergic pathways play different roles in different brain regions. Muscarinic cholinergic neurotransmission in the hypothalamus facilitates receptive behavior.

The neuropeptide, luteinizing hormone-releasing hormone (LH-RH), stimulates female receptivity and male copulatory behavior. In females, LH-RH acts in the medial preoptic area, ventromedial nucleus of the hypothalamus, and the central gray area of the midbrain. In males, LH-RH exerts its effects in the medial preoptic area. Administration of LH-RH in humans has been reported to increase sexual interest in some persons but not others. Endogenous opioids (beta-endorphin, enkephalins) inhibit female and male sexual behavior, observations that are consistent with the effects of narcotics in humans. Central administration of other peptides derived from proopiomelanocortin (ACTH, MSH) induce repeated erections, ejaculations, and copulatory movements and may enhance receptive behavior. Oxytocin also acts in the brain to increase receptivity and penile erections and may prolong the postejaculatory refractory period (Pedersen and Prange, 1987).

Maternal behavior has been subjected to much less neuropharmacologic investigation than sexual behavior. Peripheral administration of dopamine antagonists block maternal behavior. Adrenergic as well as muscarinic neurotransmission may be critical for the initiation but not the maintenance of maternal behavior. Increased aggression and food intake as well as decreased avoidance behavior during lactation could reflect increased central GABAergic neurotransmission. Morphine potently blocks both the initiation and maintenance of maternal behavior. Central release of oxytocin contributes to the initiation of maternal behavior (Pedersen and Prange, 1987).

Consumptive Behavior

Feeding behavior can be broken down into several discrete functions: initiation of feeding, food selection and maintenance of eating, and satiety. The first two are coordinated by neural structures located with the hypothalamus, especially the paraventricular nucleus. Satiety is mediated by a combination of central and peripheral mechanisms. The manner in which specific neurotransmitter systems interact varies with function, as indicated in Table 12-7. Other subcortical structures such as brainstem motor nuclei, the nigrostriatal tract, and sympathetic pathways play a role in carrying out the eating impulse by mediating stereotyped ingestive behaviors such as chewing and swallowing. In humans, it is clear that cortical structures can exert considerable influence over appetitive behavior, to the point of completely overriding hunger. The mechanisms by which this occurs are not yet well understood (Halmi et al, 1987).

The initiation of feeding is evoked in part by decreases in serum glucose concentration. Noradrenergic neurons have a strong facilitating influence on the initiation of feeding, perhaps mediated through inhibition of corticotropin-releasing factor, which has a powerful anorexic effect. Neuropeptide Y and opioids also initiate eating. Glucocorticoids facilitate eating and may regulate feeding (Morley, 1987).

Maintenance of homeostasis requires that an organism be able to select those nutrients that best fit current metabolic needs. The mechanisms involved in food choice are closely linked with reward centers in the hypothalamus. Dopaminergic neurons play a prominent role in the pleasurable reinforcement of food choice and in the maintenance of eating. Endorphins also influence food choice and, in particular, increase the consumption of fat. Noradrenergic stimulation increases fat and carbohydrate intake, while serotonergic stimulation decreases carbohydrate choice (Morley, 1987).

Satiety is initiated in the gut in part by food-triggered secretion of the gastrointestinal peptides cholecystokinin (CCK), satietin, and bombesin. Gut peptides exert their effects on feeding through afferent neuronal connections between the gastrointestinal tract and the CNS. For example, CCK satiety signals are transmitted to the brain through the vagus nerve. However, injection of CCK into the paraventicular nucleus also induces satiety, suggesting that direct peptide regulation of central ingestive systems may also occur (Morley, 1987).

Table 12-7 **Neurohormonal Regulation of Eating Behavior**

	NE	5HT	DA	END	CCK	NPY	INS	SAT	CRF
Initiation of feeding	I	–	–	D (P,I)	D	I	I	D	D
Food choice									
CHO	I	D	–	–	–	I	–	–	–
Fat	I	–	–	I	–	–	–	–	–
Pleasure	–	–	I	–	–	–	–	–	–
Satiety	–	I	–	–	I	–	–	I	–

Abbreviations: End = Endorphin,   Ins = Insulin,   Sat = Satietin,   D = Decrease,   I = Increase,   – = No difference,
P = Peripheral administration.

Aggression

Aggression occurs in a number of distinct behavioral contexts. In animals and humans, aggression is one component of a larger repertoire of social behaviors, the goals of which are reproductive success as well as acquisition and protection of resources, territory, and status. Aggression is also one of a number of behavioral responses to aversive situations other than social conflict. Unfortunately, excessive, maladaptive violence directed toward others or self occurs in the form of assault, murder, or suicide. This section will focus primarily on the neurobiology of social aggression but will also review our limited understanding of pathologic violence. The neurobiology of behavioral responses to stress is reviewed in the next section of this chapter. Rodent studies have provided insight into brain mechanisms that regulate social aggression while primate studies have elucidated situational and hormonal determinants that may be of particular relevance to humans.

Social Aggression in Rodents

Adult rodents do not, as a rule, live in groups but rather establish individual territories. Aggressive behaviors are a part of a larger set of social behaviors including offensive attack, defensive attack, submission, and behaviors that establish territory such as patrolling and scent-marking with urine or other specialized secretions. Adult rodents, particularly males, attack same-sex intruders in their territory. Aggression is most likely when there is competition for desirable goals (e.g., copulation). When attacked in another's territory, rodents respond either with defensive behavior if the animals have not previously encountered each other or submissive behavior if prior confrontations have established territorial rights. Encounters between adult con-specifics of opposite sex stimulate increased marking behavior in both sexes and, in nonpregnant, nonlactating females, submissive behavior. Reproductive and other motivated behaviors are strongly influenced by social situation and territorial considerations. For instance, males copulate more frequently in areas that they have previously marked.

Offense, defense, and submission in rodents each involves distinct postures and motor sequences, and is mediated by different neural circuitry (Svare, 1983). Offensive attack includes repeated series of bites and kicks directed at the flanks of the opponent launched from a stereotypical aggressive posture. Defense involves lunging and biting directed at the face of the attacker. Submissive behavior is characterized by ultrasonic vocalizations and stereotyped posturing. Offense is mediated by the preoptic area and the lateral hypothalamus; defense and submission are under the control of the midbrain central gray and tegmentum. Projections to the midbrain from the ventromedial nucleus of the hypothalamus suppress defense and enhance submission. Limbic brain regions (e.g., septum, amygdala), which analyze olfactory and other sensory cues, are essential for the interpretation of social situations. Projections from the limbic brain to the preoptic area, hypothalamus, and midbrain regulate both the initiation and direction of aggressive and submissive behavior. Note the similarity in neural circuitry mediating aggression and sexual behaviors (see section entitled Reproductive Behaviors: Sex and Mothering).

Gonadal steroids regulate aggression and other dimensions of social behavior by acting on the neural apparatus outlined above (Coe and Levine, 1983; Sheard, 1987;

Svare, 1983). Sexual differentiation of the nervous system determines the pattern of aggressive and social behavior during development and adulthood. Male juveniles engage in more rough-and-tumble play with age-mates than female juveniles. Adult males display higher rates of aggression, especially offensive behavior, in virtually all mammalian species. Testosterone and its metabolites facilitate offense toward other males but, in the presence of estrogen-treated females or their odors, suppress offense and increase patrolling and marking. In females, estrogen decreases offense toward all types of opponents but increases patrolling and marking behavior in the presence of testosterone-treated males or their odors. Progesterone enhances estrogen effects. During pregnancy and lactation, rodent females display much more offensive and defensive behavior and will readily attack males that approach their nests. Aggression in rat mothers appears to be under the same ovarian steroid control as other components of maternal behavior (see section entitled Reproductive Behaviors: Sex and Mothering).

Neurotransmitter regulation of social aggression has been extensively studied in rodents (Eichelman, 1990; Svare, 1983). Noradrenergic and dopaminergic neurotransmission are essential for offensive behavior but play a less critical role in defense. Serotonin also facilitates offensive attack, while serotonergic antagonists increase submissive, defensive, and escape behaviors. Social aggression is inhibited by muscarinic antagonists and nicotinic agonists. Opioids also diminish aggression. Defeat in social confrontations produces analgesia, which is also opioid-mediated.

Social Aggression in Primates

Primates tend to live in groups in which each individual establishes a position in a dominance hierarchy. Outright physical assault is rare. Rather, individuals, especially males, establish and maintain their social rank by means of behavioral displays that vary with species. Aggression between males is much greater when sexually receptive or estrogen-treated females are introduced into the group. Display behavior increases dramatically at puberty in male primates, concomitant with the rise in testosterone levels. Adult aggression in male primates depends both on prenatal testosterone exposure during sexual differentiation and on increased testosterone secretion during sexual maturation. However, once established, the adult pattern of aggression is not necessarily dependent on testosterone. Testosterone levels in men do not correlate well with measures of aggression. Castration of adult primates often has no effect on dominance rank. Similarly, castration of sex offenders or excessively violent men frequently has no ameliorating behavioral effect (Coe and Levine, 1983).

While hormones play a limited role in initiating aggression in adult primates, success or failure in achieving dominance within a group has a powerful effect on the hypothalamic–pituitary–gonal (HPG) and hypothalamic–pituitary–adrenal (HPA) axes (Coe and Levine, 1983; Sheard, 1987; Svare, 1983). A dominance hierarchy is rapidly established after formation of a new group. Individual testosterone and cortisol levels prior to new group formation fail to correlate with subsequent dominance rank. However, testosterone levels rise considerably in dominant males but fall in subordinate males shortly after formation of new groups. Cortisol levels increase both in dominant and subordinate males after group formation. The influence of dominance rank on HPG and HPA activity of males is more pronounced when females are included in new groups. Testosterone and, to some extent, cortisol levels rise earlier and to higher levels during the mating season in dominant than in subordinate males. Elevated testosterone may be related to the much greater reproductive success of dominant male primates. Competition influences activity of the HPG axis in humans as well. Triumph during tennis matches and other competitive situations increases testosterone levels while defeat lowers levels. (See Chapter 11).

HUMAN AGGRESSION AND SUICIDE

Aggressive acts of violence, directed at others or at one's self, are a major public health problem in this country. Initially, violence and suicide were studied from sociological and psychological perspectives, but beginning in the 1960s, researchers have applied increasingly sophisticated technologies to the study of the neurobiologic bases of these behaviors.

Clinical Neurobiology of Aggression

Several neurotransmitters have been studied in clinical investigations exploring the neurobiological correlates of aggression. The most compelling data implicate the indoleamine serotonin in the pathophysiology of impulsive aggression. Low levels of the serotonin metabolite, 5-hydroxyindoleacetic acid (5-HIAA), have been found in the cerebrospinal fluid of diverse groups of subjects with histories of violent aggression, including military recruits and prisoners with selected personality disorders; violent offenders, including murderers and arsonists; and children with disruptive behavior disorders (see Golden et al, 1991 for a review). Other peripheral measures of serotonergic function, including studies of platelet serotonin content, platelet serotonin reuptake, and whole blood serotonin content, have also supported the hypothesis that dysregulation in serotonin function is correlated with aggressive behavior. Finally, Coccaro and colleagues (1989) have shown that the hormonal response to the serotonin releasing agent fenfluramine is reduced in patients with aggressive/impulsive behavior, compared to healthy controls. Together, these data suggest that aggression is associated with dysfunction in serotonin neurotransmission in the brain.

Other neurotransmitters have also been implicated in the pathophysiology of aggression. One report found a significant positive correlation between cerebrospinal fluid concentrations of the norepinephrine metabolite 3-methoxy-4-hydroxyphenylglycol and a life history of significant aggressive behavior. Another study reported increased levels of the amphetamine-like compound phenylethylamine in aggressive prisoners (Eichelman, 1990).

Numerous pharmacological interventions have been used in efforts to control violent, aggressive behavior. Benzodiazepines have been reported to be effective in treating aggressive outbursts in both nonpsychotic and psychotic patients; there are, however, a few reports of paradoxical "disinhibition," leading to increased aggression, in a small number of patients (Eichelman, 1990). Dopamine receptor antagonists have also been extensively applied to the control of aggressive behavior, with several encouraging reports of the reduction of aggression in psychotic patients (Leventhal and Brodie, 1981). Dopamine antagonists have also been used to treat nonpsychotic subjects with aggressive behaviors, including demented patients, and children with mental retardation or conduct disorder. Drugs which block beta-adrenergic receptors, including propranolol and nadolol, may ameliorate aggressive behavior in children with brain disease and adults with rage outbursts (Eichelman, 1990).

Serotonin and Suicide

As with aggression, abnormalities in serotonergic function have been linked to suicide. Postmortem studies of brain tissue from suicide victims have found abnormalities in various aspects of serotonergic systems, including concentrations of serotonin and 5-HIAA, 5-HT$_2$ receptor binding sites, and ^{3}H-imipramine binding sites, which are closely related to the 5-HT uptake site. Clinical studies of suicide attempters have reported diminished cerebrospinal fluid concentrations of serotonin and 5-HIAA, as well as decreased levels of the dopamine metabolite homovanillic acid. Peripheral measures of serotonin function, including platelet serotonin uptake and 5-HT$_2$ binding sites, and neuroendocrine responses to serotonergic agonists, have also been reported to be abnormal in patients who have attempted suicide (Golden et al, 1991). Recognizing that there are probably multiple determinants of suicidal behavior, it nonetheless appears that abnormal serotonergic function may be linked to self-destructive acts in many instances.

Stress and Behavior

Certain theoretical and practical aspects of stress as it affects vulnerability to physical illness (particularly the immune system) were introduced in Chapter 3 by Drs. Walker and Katon. The neurobiological mechanisms involved in stress responses are discussed here in more detail, particularly the neuroendocrine system.

The environment often subjects animals and humans to aversive stimuli and situations (stressors). Stress is the internal response to aversive conditions, which includes situationally specific patterns of hormone release, central neuroendocrine change, and autonomic activation. Stressors also elicit behavioral responses, which vary widely with the type and magnitude of aversive stimulus. Hormonal and neuroendocrine components of the stress response act within the brain to stimulate appropriate behavioral responses to specific stressors.

Behavioral Responses to Stressors

Stressful conditions can be grouped under three general categories, which will be discussed later (Field et al, 1985). Specific behavioral responses as well as endocrine and autonomic responses differ with type of stressful condition. The first category is composed of *stressors for which the organism has readily available effective coping responses*, which may include escape, offensive or defensive attack, or other proactive behaviors that allow the organism to diminish or master the aversive situation. Under these conditions, cardiac output, heart rate, blood pressure, and vasodilation in skeletal muscle all increase. The second category is composed of *stressors for which the organism has no active coping option*. Under these conditions, organisms become hypervigilant but immobile, adopting either a frozen or submissive posture. Peripheral resistance and blood pressure rise while heart rate and blood flow through skeletal muscle decrease. The third category of stressors includes *unfamiliar, novel, or uncertain stimuli or situations*. Reactions to such conditions include initial hypervigilance and immobility followed by cautious exploration interspersed with behaviors that are thought to be manifestations of anxiety (e.g., self-grooming in animals; tapping, clearing the throat, pacing, and so forth in humans). Cardiovascular responses to novelty are initially (during the immobile hypervigilant phase) similar to those occurring when active coping strategies are not available, but, as the organism begins to explore and emote, the cardiovascular response shifts to that associated with active coping. The sudden onset of high-intensity aversive stimulation often elicits an initial immobile, hypervigilant response with attendant cardiovascular changes even if active coping strategies are readily available. *Repeated exposure to aversive conditions that cannot be controlled produces a state of "learned helplessness" in which the organism will passively endure stressors even when coping options become available.* Aversive stimuli also inhibit reproductive, eating, drinking, and other motivated behaviors.

Exposure to stressors early in development profoundly affects behavior and stress responses in adulthood. Male offspring of rodent mothers that were stressed during pregnancy are both demasculinized and feminized; female offspring are little affected. For instance, as adults, these males display much reduced mounting and increased lordosis behavior (Ward and Ward, 1985). Prenatal stress alters catecholamine levels in a number of brain sites. In humans, prenatal stress has been associated with behavioral, psychiatric, and sexual identity problems. Separation of infants from their mothers also has lifelong effects on behavioral, endocrine, and autonomic responses to stressors (Field et al, 1985; Reite and Field, 1985). (See Chapter 11 by Dr. van der Kolk.) Repeated brief periods of separation and handling of rat pups result in improved modulation of stress responses in adulthood. However, prolonged isolation of infant rhesus monkeys produces exaggerated stress responses in adulthood that resemble clinical depression in humans. Thus, stability in the face of stressors in adulthood may be enhanced by short periods of early maternal separation but impaired by excessive parental deprivation. Approximately 15% of human infants display exaggerated fear of unfamiliar objects and situations. Fearful infants had higher levels of cortisol and norepinephrine as well as elevated heart rates compared with other infants (Kagan et al, 1987). Early differences in individual temperament may also influence adult patterns of stress response.

Neuroendocrine Components of the Stress Response and Their Behavioral Effects

The hypothalamic–pituitary–adrenal (HPA) axis is particularly responsive to stressors. As established by the pioneering work of Selye, vigorous release of adrenal glucocorticoids and pituitary ACTH is a prominent feature of the stress response. Levels of beta-endorphin, which is coreleased with ACTH from the anterior pituitary, also rise in response to stressors. Norepinephrine and epinephrine release from the adrenal medulla is the other component of the classic stress response (Johnson et al, 1992).

Early stress researchers conceptualized HPA axis activation and catecholamine release as a general, nonspecific response to all types of stressors. However, more recent studies demonstrate that the pattern of release of peripheral neuroendocrine components of the stress response varies under differing stressful conditions (Field et al, 1985). Release of ACTH and adrenal glucocorticoids are most dramatic when organisms are confronted with aversive stimuli that are unfamiliar or for which they have no readily apparent coping mechanism. Epinephrine release is also relatively greater than norepinephrine release under these more psychologically stressful conditions.

Hypothalamic neuropeptides that are secreted into the hypophyseal portal system regulate the activity of the HPA axis by modulating the release of ACTH from the anterior pituitary. The most potent of these is corticotropin-releasing factor (CRF). However, vasopressin and oxytocin amplify CRF stimulation of ACTH release. The degree to which vasopressin and oxytocin are released into portal blood varies under different stressful conditions. Neural pathways containing CRF, vasopressin, oxytocin as well as beta-endorphin, enkephalins, and ACTH fragments are widely distributed within the brain. Stressors very likely stimulate central release of these neuropeptides. Indeed, various kinds of stressors decrease concentrations of opioids and CRF and increase opioid binding in some brain regions. Turnover and synthesis of norepinephrine, epinephrine, and serotonin all increase in a number of brain regions in response to acute stressors. Exposure to prolonged uncontrollable stress has been associated with depletion of total brain norepinephrine (Field et al, 1985).

Neuroendocrine components of the HPA axis influence behavioral responses to stressors. Glucocorticoids increase immobility and submissive behavior. ACTH, on the other hand, increases attack, as will exploratory behavior (Svare, 1983). Self-grooming behavior is activated by ACTH, vasopressin, oxytocin, beta-endorphin, and CRF. ACTH, vasopressin, and oxytocin all influence acquisition of avoidance behavior (see section entitled Learning and Memory) suggesting that they may be crucial in gaining familiarity with novel stimuli, remembering aversive aspects of situations, and learning coping strategies. Stress inhibition of some behaviors may also be mediated by central neuroendocrine components of the HPA axis. Glucocorticoids, CRF, vasopressin, and beta-endorphin all inhibit sexual behavior, while CRF and beta-endorphin also antagonize food consumption. Central noradrenergic pathways play a key role in focusing attention and arousing appropriate behavioral responses to acute stressors. Depletion of brain norepinephrine resulting from exposure to repeated uncontrollable stress may contribute to the behavioral suppression associated with learned helplessness (Field et al, 1985).

Psychoneuroimmunology

The CNS modulation of systemic homeostatic processes such as blood pressure regulation has been recognized for a number of years. Only recently, however, has the two-way flow of information between the CNS and immune system been appreciated. As previously mentioned in Chapter 3, much new data over the past decade demonstrates that the CNS may play an important role in the modulation of aspects of immune function (for review see Ader, Felten, and Cohen, 1991). Numerous preclinical studies indicate that certain forms of stress may result in alterations in aspects of immune function. Pioneering studies by Ader, Cohen and coworkers at the University of Rochester provide some of the most powerful illustrations of the interrelationships between the CNS, behavior and the immune function. For example, as already described in Chapter 3, by pairing saccharin (a conditioned stimulus) with an immunosuppressant cyclophosphamide (an unconditioned stimulus) mice were behaviorally conditioned so that later exposure to saccharin alone resulted in immunosuppression and altered the course of murine systemic lupus erythematosus (Ader and Cohen, 1982). Of particular relevance to psychological trauma and psychiatric illness are recent animal studies by Lysle and colleagues (1990) showing that conditioned environmental stimuli (inherently nonaversive stimuli) previously paired with an aversive event (footshock stress) can themselves induce pronounced immunosuppression. (Other neurobiologic effects of developmental trauma are discussed in Chapter 11 by Dr. van der Kolk.)

The CNS pathways involved in the neural mediation of immune function are the focus of ongoing investigations (Ader, Felten, and Cohen, 1991). Experimental evidence indicates that the hypothalamic–pituitary–adrenal (HPA) and sympathetic autonomic nervous system (SNS) are the two primary immunomodulatory pathways subserved by the CNS. Although the specific central circuitry has not yet been elucidated, basic studies suggest that the neural modulation of immune activity involves limbic forebrain and cortical regions. These brain structures are intimately associated with the control of affective and emotional processes as well as the modulation of the activity of the HPA axis and descending sympathetic autonomic pathways which innervate immune organs (e.g., spleen).

The molecular basis of the bidirectional flow of information between the immune and nervous systems is highlighted by evidence that these systems share identical or closely related chemical signals and receptors. For example, some lymphocyte subsets possess receptors for catecholamines (e.g., β-adrenergic receptors) and neuropeptides (e.g., endorphins and enkephalins). Stimulated lymphocytes also produce peptides such as ACTH and β-endorphin, which have important behavioral and other physiological effects. Analogous to the discovery years earlier that digestive system peptides such as CCK and VIP were present in the CNS, cytokines (e.g., interleukin-1) and their receptors are now being identified in the brain and their role as neuromodulators and growth factors is of great interest.

In the classic study discussed in Chapter 3, Spiegel et al (1989) examined prospectively the effects of weekly supportive group therapy on survival time in a randomized, 10-year follow-up study of patients with metastatic breast cancer. It is noteworthy that these researchers actually hypothesized that this psychotherapeutic intervention would improve quality of life, but would not influence the course of the disease. Contrary to their hypothesis, they found that breast cancer patients who took part in weekly supportive group therapy lived twice as long as matched breast cancer patients who received the same cancer treatment interventions but did not participate in group therapy. Other clinical studies designed to replicate this finding and examine the related neural-immune interactions of this behavioral intervention are under way. Overall, clinical studies attempting to correlate immunologic changes with psychiatric disorders have been ambiguous. Although some cross-sectional clinical studies have correlated changes in psychological or psychiatric conditions such as bereavement and major depression with changes in certain measures of cellular immune function, the long-term clinical relevance of this research is unknown (Perkins et al, 1991). It is important to underscore that although there has been much popular enthusiasm about the notion that stress or depression may influence the development of physical illness, it is critical for clinicians to bear in mind that there is no substantive, reproducible evidence supporting such a relationship in patients with depression or other psychiatric disorders.

Sleep

Sleep is a fundamental, complex, and essential behavior. Sleep was regarded as a homogeneous, passive experience until 1935, when Loomis and colleagues described distinct states of sleep that could be identified by specific electroencephalogram (EEG) patterns. By the mid-1950s, scientists had observed that bursts of conjugate rapid eye movements (REM) appear periodically during sleep; these REM sleep periods were subsequently linked to dreaming. In the past 3 decades, increasingly sophisticated technology has allowed us to decipher more of the mysteries of the experience we call "sleep." Yet even today, many medical school physiology courses virtually ignore the biology of sleep, when in fact, the cardiovascular, respiratory, and neurochemical physiology of sleeping humans differs in many ways from the waking physiology that is usually taught.

Sleep Architecture

As Hauri (1982) has pointed out, sleep is an active, complex state, similar to a building with various components; thus, the expression "sleep architecture" is used to describe the stages and cycles of sleep and their interrelationships. The different stages of sleep are defined by distinct patterns of brain electrical activity and by distinct behavioral and physiological states.

Sleep Stages. Sleep can be divided into two broad categories: rapid-eye-movement (REM) and non-rapid-eye-movement (NREM) sleep. NREM sleep can be further subcategorized into four stages. Stages 1, 2, 3, and 4 can be conceptualized as representing a progression from very light to very deep sleep, with concurrent EEG changes from fast (high-frequency) low-amplitude waves to slow (low-frequency) high-amplitude patterns (Fig. 12–27).

Stage 1 consists of the transition from wakefulness to sleep. In normal sleepers, it lasts from 30 seconds to 7 minutes. During this stage, reactivity to external stimuli is blunted, thinking becomes less "reality oriented," and short dreams may develop as thoughts begin to drift. Many people will report that they felt that they were awake during this stage.

Stage 2 sleep is heralded by the onset of "sleep spindles" on the EEG (i.e., bursts of 12- to 14-Hz activity lasting 0.5 to 2 seconds) and "K-complexes" (i.e., sudden, high-amplitude bipolar spikes; see Fig. 12–27). By convention, sleep researchers define the onset of sleep by the appearance of the first sleep spindle or K-complex. Mentation during stage 2 consists of short, fragmented, mundane thoughts, and most people who are awakened during stage 2 will acknowledge that they were asleep and will not remember any dreams, although they may recall fragments of thoughts.

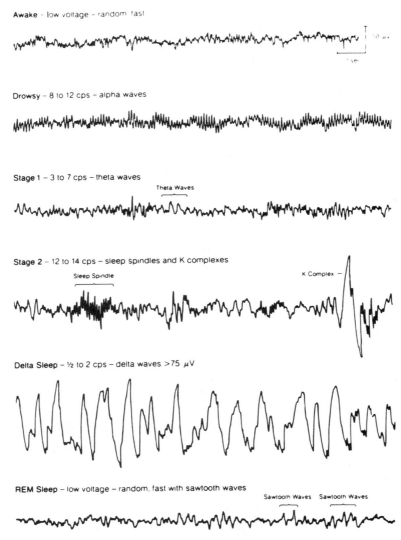

Figure 12-27. *Stages of human sleep. (Reproduced with permission from Hauri P: The Sleep Disorders. Kalamazoo, The Upjohn Co., 1982.)*

Stage 3 and stage 4 sleep, collectively referred to as delta sleep, is characterized by slow, 0.5- to 2-Hz, high-amplitude waves on the EEG (see Fig. 12–27). Delta sleep can be thought of as "deep," or "heavy" sleep.

REM sleep derives its label from the periodic vertical and horizontal darting eye movements that are observed in this stage. The EEG during REM sleep presents a picture of low-voltage, mixed-frequency waves that resemble the pattern of stage 1 sleep except for the additional presence of sawtooth waves (see Fig. 12–27). When people are awakened during REM sleep, they will recall dreams about 80% of the time, while only 5% of NREM awakenings are associated with complete dream recollection.

Sleep Cycles. During normal sleep, sleep stages do not occur at random; a pattern of progression can be described for a normal *sleep cycle* (Fig. 12–28). A healthy young adult typically moves from an awake state into a period of NREM sleep. After a brief period (e.g., 5 to 10 minutes) of relaxed, drowsy wakefulness, the sleeper passes through a brief 1- to 5-minute period of stage 1 sleep, then descends into deeper stage 2 sleep. Thirty minutes into the sleep process, the sleeper enters delta (stage 3 to stage 4) sleep, which then lasts about 30 to 60 minutes. Typically, the sleeper then "ascends" back to stage 2, during which a brief, first REM period is experienced. Following this initial REM period, the sleeper returns to stage 2, and the second "sleep cycle" is begun. Thus, the first sleep cycle lasts about 90 minutes, with a brief REM period occurring 70 to 90 minutes after the initiation of sleep.

The typical healthy young adult sleeper will pass through four to six sleep cycles over the course of the night, and as Figure 12–28 shows, these cycles are not identical. Following the first cycle described above, subsequent cycles show progressively less delta sleep. REM periods become progressively longer over the course of the night.

Sleep and the Lifecycle

The normal process of aging is accompanied by changes in the sleep cycle. In fact, age is the single most powerful determinant of a person's sleep physiology. Total sleep time and the total nightly amount of time spent in each of the sleep stages are age-dependent. In general, total sleep time is greatest in infancy, decreases during childhood, and remains relatively stable during the adult years until a late-life decline is seen. Sleep becomes more "fragmented" over the course of a lifetime; the amount of waking time and the number of awakenings after sleep onset increase (Hauri, 1982).

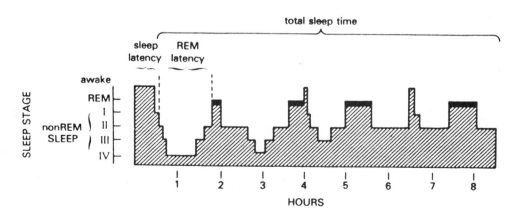

Figure 12–28. *Sequence of sleep stages in a healthy young adult. (Reproduced with permission from Mendelson WB: Human Sleep: Research and Clinical Care. New York, Plenum Press, 1987.)*

In addition to these general parameters, the proportion of the various sleep stages also changes with aging. The percentage of REM sleep is highest in infancy and childhood, decreases and levels off in adulthood, and then declines in the geriatric years. Stage 4 sleep is also highest in infancy, then progressively declines with age.

The incidence and types of sleep disturbances change over the lifecycle. In childhood, sleep problems tend to include principally night terrors, enuresis, and bedtime fears and anxiety. Adolescents often are chronically sleep deprived and have difficulty getting up in the morning. In the elderly, there is a marked increase in the occurrence of insomnia, as well as in the specific sleep disorders of sleep apnea and nocturnal myoclonus. The quality of insomnia itself seems to vary with age; the elderly are inclined to experience more frequent and longer nighttime awakenings or early awakenings, while young insomniacs more often complain of difficulty falling asleep. In general, these changes occur earlier in women than in men (Lacks, 1987).

Circadian Rhythms

The sleep–wake cycle requires about 24 hours to complete in most humans. Thus, it is an example of a *circadian* rhythm. Other important biological functions also follow a circadian rhythm in humans, including body temperature (which reaches a nadir during nighttime sleep and peaks during the day), certain endocrine systems, and some metabolic processes. There is considerable variation among people regarding the exact shape of some of these 24-hour oscillations. Scientists have suggested that people who seem to be "early birds" in terms of their preferred time of day for maximal performance may have different points of maximal efficiency for some of their circadian biological systems compared to "night owls."

When humans are placed in environments where there are no external time cues (e.g., a constantly lit, soundproof room with plenty of food but no clock), they still maintain a circadian rhythm. However, under these constant conditions, their sleep–wake cycles usually do not last exactly 24 hours. Most people settle into rhythms lasting between 24 and 28 hours, although sleep–wake cycles lasting as long as 50 hours have been observed under these conditions.

Neurobiology of Sleep

Nearly 100 years ago, Mauthner suggested that sleep induction was regulated by the area of the brain surrounding the third cranial nerve nuclei. A half century later, Bremer concluded that the junction between the diencephalon and the brain stem was crucial to sleep and wakefulness, based on his encephale isole and cerveau isole experiments (Hauri, 1982). Both Mauthner and Bremer viewed sleep as a "passive" process in which decreased cortical activation leads to a loss of wakefulness. It was later proposed that the reticular activating system plays a key role in maintaining arousal.

Other sleep researchers began to argue that sleep is a function of an active sleep-inducing center. Both stimulation and lesion experiments in animals, performed in the 1940s and 1950s, lent support to this view. Today, most sleep scientists have reconciled the "active" versus "passive" debate into an integrated theory.

Following transection at the midbrain, the forebrain above and the midbrain below both show wake–NREM sleep cycling, suggesting that there is no single center for NREM sleep. However, there are regions that do facilitate waking, including the ascending reticular activating system and the posterior hypothalamus, and regions that facilitate sleep (i.e., the basal forebrain, the area surrounding the solitary tract of the medulla, and possibly the dorsal raphe). Also, the superchiasmatic nucleus seems to serve as the major biological "clock" for most circadian rhythms and, thus, is also involved in the sleep–wake cycle.

Thus, it appears that there are two systems that regulate the sleep–wake cycle: a sleep-promoting system and a wakefulness-promoting system. For sleep onset to occur, activity in the more powerful arousal system must first passively decrease; following this, the less powerful sleep-promoting system can actively begin to play a role. Earlier, it had been suggested that serotonin controls NREM sleep, but currently it is recognized that the neurochemical control is much more complex. It appears that serotonin, acetylcholine, norepinephrine, as well as other neurotransmitters modulate the sleep–wake cycle in a complex, interactive manner.

In addition to the sleep–wake cycle, the REM–NREM cycle has been the subject of considerable study and debate. In the early 1960s, Jouvet (1965) reported the discovery of a REM-inducing system in the higher pons. More recently, Hobson and associates (Hobson et al, 1975) have developed a model in which two classes of neural systems control the REM–NREM cycle. An aminergic system, which includes serotonergic neurons in the dorsal raphe and noradrenergic neurons in the locus ceruleus and nucleus peribrachialis lateralis, discharges at its highest rate during wakefulness, progressively decreases its discharge rate during NREM sleep, and produces very low discharge rates during REM sleep. A cholinergic reticular system, located primarily in the mesencephalic, medullary, and pontine gigantocellular tegmental fields, demonstrate the opposite pattern of activity. Thus, according to the Hobson McCarley model, these two opposing systems continuously interact to produce the cycling between REM and NREM sleep. This model is not universally accepted, and this area remains an important focus of ongoing research.

SUMMARY

After 2 decades of breathtaking discovery, it is clear that we are now in the golden age of neuroscience. Much progress has been made in our understanding of the brain mechanisms involved in behavior. Most of this knowledge has been obtained through investigation of animal behavior. The challenge for the future is to achieve as much insight into the biological basis of human behavior. Fortunately, we are on the brink of a new era in which technical advances are opening the way for safe, noninvasive study of human brain function. For instance, the availability of an increasing number of radio-emitting substances allows quantification and precise localization of blood flow, glucose utilization, and binding of specific molecules in the living brain. These methods will permit identification of brain regions and neurochemical systems involved in human behavior, cognition, and emotion. New capabilities of this sort may revolutionize our ability to diagnose and treat behavioral and psychological disorders in humans.

ANNOTATED BIBLIOGRAPHY

Ader R (ed): Psychoneuroimmunology. New York, Academic Press, 1981

> This is an excellent and comprehensive review of an emerging area in psychiatry. The field of psychoneuroimmunology is supplanting older theoretical approaches of psychosomatic illness with a solid scientific basis, and this text provides the most comprehensive treatment of the subject to date.

Cooper JR, Bloom FE, Roth RH (eds): The Biochemical Basis of Neuropharmacology. New York, Oxford University Press, 6th ed, 1991

> A concise but superb review of neuropharmacology; a classic small text that is "must" reading for all medical students.

Coyle JT: Neuroscience and psychiatry. In Talbott JA, Hales RE, Yudofsky SC (eds): Textbook of Psychiatry. Washington, DC, American Psychiatric Press, 1988

> Basic concepts in neuroscience as they relate to clinical psychiatric disorders are reviewed in this well-written chapter.

Kandel ER, Schwartz JH, Jessell TM (eds): Principles of Neural Science. New York, Elsevier, 1991

> This is a masterful text that is remarkable for its clarity and depth; an extremely valuable resource for students interested in recent advances in the neurosciences.

Meltzer HY (ed): Psychopharmacology: The Third Generation of Progress. New York, Raven Press, 1987

> A compendium of the field of psychopharmacology and biochemical treatments for mental illness; excellent reference for research and in-depth reading.

REFERENCES

Ader R, Felten DL, Cohen N (eds): Psychoneuroimmunology. New York, Academic Press, 1991

Ader R, Cohen N: Behaviorally conditioned immunosuppression and murine systemic lupus erythematosus. Science 215:1534–1536, 1982

Bunney, WE Jr, Davis JM: Norepinephrine in depressive reactions: A review. Arch Gen Psychiatry 13:483–494, 1965

Coccaro EF, Murphy DL: Serotonin in Psychiatric Disorders. Washington, DC, American Psychiatric Association, 1990

Coccaro EF, Siever L, Klar HM, et al: Serotonergic studies in patients with affective and personality disorders: Correlates with suicidal and impulsive aggressive behavior. Arch Gen Psychiatry 46:587–599, 1989.

Coe CL, Levine S: Biology of aggression. Bull Am Acad Psychiatry Law 11:131–148, 1983

Cooper JR, Bloom FE, Roth RH (eds): The Biochemical Basis of Neuropharmacology, 6th ed. New York, Oxford University Press, 1991

Coppen A, Shaw D, Malleson A, et al: Changes in 5-hydroxytryptophan metabolism in depression. Br J Psychiatry 3:993–998, 1965

Coyle JT: Neuroscience and psychiatry. In Talbott JA, Hales RE, Yudofsky SC (eds): Textbook of Psychiatry. Washington, DC, American Psychiatric Press, 1988

Decker MW, McGaugh JL: The role of interactions between the cholinergic system and other neuromodulatory systems in learning and memory. Synapse 7:151–168, 1991

Deutch AY: The regulation of subcortical dopamine systems by the prefrontal cortex: Interactions of central dopamine systems and the pathogenesis of schizophrenia. J Neur Transmission (Supplementum) 36:61–89, 1992

Eichelman B: Neurochemical and psychopharmacologic aspects of aggressive behavior. In Meltzer HY (ed): Psychopharmacology: The Third Generation of Progress. New York, Raven Press, 1987

Eichelman BS: Neurochemical and psychopharmacologic aspects of aggressive behavior. Ann Rev Med 41:149–158, 1990

Elliot GR, Holman RB, Barchas JD: Neuroregulators and behavior. In Barchas JD, Berger PA, Ciaranello RD et al (eds): Psychopharmacology: From Theory to Practice. New York, Oxford University Press, 1977

Fibiger HC: Cholinergic mechanisms in learning, memory and dementia: A review of recent evidence. Trends Neuroscience 14:220–223, 1991

Field TM, McCabe PM, Schneiderman N (eds): Stress and Coping. Hillsdale, NJ, Lawrence Erlbaum Associates, 1985

Golden RN, Gilmore JH, Corrigan MH et al: Serotonin, suicide, and aggression: Clinical studies. J Clin Psychiatry 52 (Supplement):61–69, 1991.

Golden RN, Potter WZ: Neurochemical and neuroendocrine dysregulation in affective disorders. Psychiatr Clin North Am 9:313–327, 1986

Goldman-Rakic PS: Cellular and circuit basis of working memory in prefrontal cortex of nonhuman primates. Prog Brain Res 85:325–336, 1990

Halmi KA, Ackerman S, Gibbs J, et al: Basic biological overview of the eating disorders. In Meltzer HY (ed): Psychopharmacology: The Third Generation of Progress. New York, Raven Press, 1987

Hauri P: The Sleep Disorders. Kalamazoo, The Upjohn Co, 1982

Hobson JA, McCarley RW, Wyzinski PW: Sleep cycle oscillations: Reciprocal discharge by two brainstem neuronal groups. Science 18:55–58, 1975

Hyman SE: Recent developments in neurobiology. Psychosomatics 29:157–165, 254–263, 373–378, 1988

Janowsky DS, El-Yousef MF, Davis JM et al.: A cholinergic-adrenergic hypothesis of mania and depression. Lancet 2:6732–6735, 1972

Janowsky DS, Golden RN, Rapaport M et al: Neurochemistry of depression and mania. In Georgotas A, Cancro R (eds): Depression and Mania. New York, Elsevier, 1988

Johnson EO, Kamilaris TC, Chrousos GP et al: Mechanisms of stress: A dynamic overview of hormonal and behavioral homeostasis. Neuroscience Biobehav Rev 16:115–130, 1992

Jouvet M: Paradoxical sleep: A study of its nature and mechanisms. In Himwich WA, Schade JP (eds): Sleep Mechanisms: Progress in Brain Research. Amsterdam, Elsevier, 1965

Kagan J, Reznick JS, Snidman N: Temperamental variation in response to the unfamiliar. In Krasnegor NA, Blass EM, Hofer MA et al (eds): Perinatal Development: A Psychobiological Perspective. Orlando, Academic Press, 1987

Kandel ER, Schwartz JH (eds): Principles of Neural Science. New York, Elsevier, 1985

Lacks P: Behavioral Treatment for Persistent Insomnia. New York, Pergamon Press, 1987

Leventhal BL, Brodie HKH: The pharmacology of violence. In DA Hamburg, MB Trudeau (eds): Biobehavioral Aspects of Aggression. New York, Liss, 1981, pp 85–106

Luine VN, McEwen BS: Steroid hormone receptors in brain and pituitary: Topography and possible functions. In Adler N, Pfaff D, Goy RW (eds): Handbook of Behavioral Neurobiology, vol 7: Reproduction. New York, Plenum Press, 1985

Luttge WG: Molecular mechanisms of steroid hormone actions in the brain. In Svare BB (ed): Hormones and Aggressive Behavior. New York, Plenum Press, 1983

Lysle DT, Cunnick JE, Kucinski BJ, et al: Characterization of immune alterations induced by a conditioned aversive stimulus. Psychobiology 18:220–226, 1990

McEwen BS: Non-genomic and genomic effects of steroids on neural activity. Trends Pharmacol Sciences 12:141–147, 1991

Mendelson WB: Human Sleep: Research and Clinical Care. New York, Plenum Press, 1987

Meyerson BJ, Malmns CO, Everitt BJ: Neuropharmacology, neurotransmitters and sexual behavior in mammals. In Adler N, Pfaff D, Goy RW (eds): Handbook of Behavioral Neurobiology. New York, Plenum Press, 1985

Morley JE: Behavioral pharmacology for eating and drinking. In Meltzer HY (ed): Psychopharmacology: The Third Generation of Progress. New York, Raven Press, 1987

Nemeroff CB, Dunn AJ (eds): Peptides, Hormones, and Behavior. New York, SP Medical & Scientific Books, 1984

Numan M: Maternal behavior. In Knobil E, Neill JD et al (eds): The Physiology of Reproduction. New York, Raven Press, 1988

Pedersen CA, Prange AJ Jr: Effects of drugs and neuropeptides on sexual and maternal behavior in mammals. In Meltzer HY (ed): Psychopharmacology: The Third Generation of Progress. New York, Raven Press, 1987

Perkins DO, Leserman J, Gilmore JH et al: Stress, depression, and immunity: Research findings and clinical implications. In Plotnikoff N, Murgo A, Faith R et al (eds): Stress and Immunity. Boca Raton, CRC Press, 1991

Pfaff DW, Schwartz-Giblin S: Cellular mechanisms of female reproductive behaviors. In Knobil E, Neill JD et al (eds): The Physiology of Reproduction. New York, Raven Press, 1988

Prange AJ Jr, Wilson IC, Lynn CW et al: L-tryptophan in mania: contribution to a permissive hypothesis of affective disorders. Arch Gen Psychiatry 30:56–62, 1974

Reis DJ: Considerations of some specific behaviors or disease. J Psychiatr Res 11:145–148, 1974

Reite M, Field T (eds): The Psychobiology of Attachment and Separation. Orlando, Academic Press, 1985

Sachs BD, Meisel RL: The physiology of male sexual behavior. In Knobil E, Neill JD et al (eds): The Physiology of Reproduction. New York, Raven Press, 1988

Schildkraut J: The catecholamine hypothesis of affective disorders: A review of the supporting evidence. Am J Psychiatry 122:509–522, 1965

Schull J, McEachron L, Adler NT et al: Effects of thyroidectomy, parathyroidectomy and lithium on circadian wheelrunning in rats. Physiol Behav 42:33–39, 1988

Sheard MH: Aggressive and antisocial behavior. In Nemeroff CB, Loosen PT (eds): Handbook of Clinical Psychoneuroendocrinology. New York, Guilford Press, 1987

Sokoloff L: Action of thyroid hormones and cerebral development. Am J Dis Child 114:498, 1967

Spiegel D., Kraemer HC, Bloom JR et al: Effects of psychosocial treatment on survival of patients with metastatic breast cancer. Lancet 14:888–891, 1989

Squire LR: Memory and Brain. New York, Oxford University Press, 1987

Svare BB (ed): Hormones and Aggressive Behavior. New York, Plenum Press, 1983

Ward IL, Ward OB: Sexual behavior differentiation: effects of prenatal manipulations in rats. In Adler N, Pfaff D, Goy RW (eds): Handbook of Behavioral Neurobiology. New York, Plenum Press, 1988

Whybrow PC, Prange AJ Jr: A hypothesis of thyroid–catecholamine–receptor interaction. Arch Gen Psychiatry 38:106–113, 1981

Alan Stoudemire (ed). *Human Behavior: An Introduction for Medical Students,*
Second Edition. Copyright © 1994, 1990 by J. B. Lippincott Company.

13 *Behavioral Genetics*

Miron Baron

Major advances in population genetics, cytogenetics, biochemistry, and molecular biology have heightened the awareness that much of the variation in human behavior may be attributed to complex interactions among hereditary, social, developmental, and environmental factors. These observations are in keeping with the biopsychosocial model of understanding disease and illness. Attempts to quantify the relative contributions of genetic and environmental factors in behavior have led, by necessity, to an interdisciplinary framework of scientific thought, which has replaced previously held artificial dichotomies between biological and psychological or "nature *versus* nurture." In actuality, both interact to determine behavior and vulnerability to illness.

This interdisciplinary framework is consistent with the thesis that has been repeated throughout this text—that human behavior should be understood from multiple perspectives: psychological, biological, and sociological. This chapter reviews methods of genetic investigation as they bear on studies of human behavior and mental illness. Areas to be discussed include the classic methods of family, twin, and adoption studies; pedigree analysis; the study of biological susceptibility traits and chromosomal markers; and the basic techniques of molecular biology. The implications of recent research for current trends in behavioral and psychiatric genetics are also discussed.

*Supported by a Research Scientist Award MH00176 from the National Institute of Mental Health.

413

METHODS OF GENETIC INVESTIGATION

Family, Twin, and Adoption Studies

These strategies constitute the most traditional approach to behavioral genetics. *Family risk studies* attempt to determine the rate of a disorder or trait among the relatives of identified index cases who are themselves affected with the condition. For the most part, family risk studies focus on first-degree relatives, but more distant relatives can be considered as well. Because many behavioral disorders have variable age at onset, the observed familial rates must be adjusted by age. The *age correction procedure* yields expectancy rates or morbidity risks. The risk figures for the various groups of relatives can be compared with the expectancy rates for normal controls or the general population to determine the degree to which the condition being studied has a familial component.

Prediction studies are a variant of the family risk study. Prediction studies are concerned with the identification of behavioral or biological precursors of the disorder in subjects who are at high risk for the disorder in question by virtue of their being related to specific family constellations, for example, the children of one or two affected parents. These studies are prospective by nature and require a longitudinal approach.

Family risk studies can provide empirical risks for given conditions but are inconclusive with respect to the genetic versus environmental contribution to the observed familial patterns. By contrast, twin and adoption studies offer a way of separating genetic and environmental influences. The use of twins in genetic research is commonly based on comparing the *concordance rate* (when both twins of a pair are affected they are said to be concordant) in monozygotic (or identical) and dizygotic (fraternal) twins. Because monozygotic twins share all their genes whereas dizygotic genes share only 50% of their genetic endowment, a higher concordance rate in the former is taken as evidence that genetic factors are important in etiology. From the concordance rates it is possible to derive the *heritability*, which is a measure of the proportion of the genetic component in the overall familial resemblance. The concordance rate is somewhat dependent on the method of computation. Higher concordances result from the use of the proband method whereby pairs are counted twice if each twin has an ill proband ascertained independently. In contrast, the pair method considers every pair only once. The probandwise concordance (using the proband method) is more widely used, because it can be compared with the population risk.

Adoption studies are based on three principal designs: (1) The *adoptees family method* determines the risk for a given condition to the biological and adoptive parents of index cases versus controls. A higher risk among the biological relatives of the index cases compared with the control group points to the importance of genetic factors in the development of the disorder. A higher risk to the adoptive relatives of index cases indicates that rearing influences contribute to etiology. (2) The *adoptees study method* is concerned with the adopted-away children of affected parents. A higher risk for the disorder in this group of adoptees compared with a matched control group indicates that heredity plays an important role in the development of the disorder. (3) The *crossfostering method* compares adoptees who have an affected biological parent (but whose adoptive parents are normal) with adoptees whose biological parents are normal but who are reared by an adoptive parent who is affected with the condition under study. Knowledge of the risk for the disorder in the two groups of adoptees is useful in evaluating the relative contributions of heredity and rearing influences. These three designs are summarized in Table 13–1.

Questions of ascertainment (case selection), adequate controls, phenotypic classification (e.g., diagnosis), and zygosity (twin studies) require careful consideration in these research strategies. These and related issues are discussed in greater detail by Rosenthal (1970) and Emery (1976).

Pedigree Analysis

The studies described in the preceding section can point to the presence of genetic factors in etiology. However, they do not address the question of the underlying genetic mechanisms. Specifically, the mode of genetic transmission remains unknown. Discerning the mode of inheritance can strengthen the genetic evidence and can be useful both in the design and interpretation of genetic investigations (e.g., genetic linkage studies, see later) and in genetic counseling.

The search for mode of inheritance can be conducted through the use of statistical models that test the fit of specific genetic hypotheses to observed familial patterns. The method most commonly used for hypothesis testing is based on maximum likelihood, with "likelihood" referring to the probability of observing a given data set under a specific hypothesis (Thompson, 1986).

Most behavioral disorders do not have a clear single gene inheritance that conforms to mendelian laws. The deviation from classic mendelian inheritance has led to the introduction of concepts such as *reduced or incomplete penetrance,*

Table 13-1 **Adoption Studies**

TYPE	DESIGN	INTERPRETATION
Adoptees family method	Compares the risk for a given condition among the biologic and adoptive parents of index cases (groups I and II, respectively) and matched controls.	A higher risk to group I compared with the control group indicates that heredity contributes significantly to the condition studied. An increased risk to group II points to the importance of rearing influences.
Adoptees study method	Determines the risk for a given condition in the adopted-away children of affected parents (group III) versus matched controls.	An increased risk to group III points to the importance of genetic factors.
Crossfostering method	Compares adoptees whose adoptive parents are normal, but who have an affected biologic parent (group IV) with adoptees whose adoptive parents are affected, but whose biologic parents are normal (group V).	A higher risk to group IV compared with group V supports the role of heredity and minimizes the role of environment. An increased risk to group V indicates that the environment plays an important role in the disorder studied.

phenocopies or sporadic cases, and multifactorial–polygenic effects. *Reduced penetrance* refers to the incomplete manifestation of the trait in persons who have the genotype, and is usually ascribed to an interaction with other genes or to nongenetic factors. *Phenocopies* are persons who do not carry the genotype but who nevertheless manifest the trait, a phenomenon commonly attributed to other genetic or nongenetic causes. *Multifactorial–polygenic* effects result from a large number of underlying genes and other factors that contribute to the person's liability to a given trait.

The most commonly employed genetic formulations are the single major locus (or gene) (SML) and multifactorial–polygenic (MFP) models. The SML model stipulates that the transmission of a trait or disorder can be explained entirely by a single gene with two alleles resulting in three genotypes, two homozygous states and a heterozygous condition. Several subhypotheses can be tested under the SML model, such as dominant (where one dose of the abnormal allele may bring about the disorder) and recessive (where a double dose of the allele is required) modes of inheritance, as well as contributions from the environment. The parameters of the model are the frequency of the allele, the genotypic means of the three genotypes, the threshold (a point on a liability scale beyond which the penetrance is 100%), and a measure of environmental variance.

The MFP model invokes multiple genes and random environmental factors (each of small and additive effects) that contribute to phenotypic expression. The model incorporates such features as the liability of the general population and that of affected persons, and a threshold (a point on a liability scale above which all persons are affected and below which all are normal); the threshold corresponds to the genetic–environmental load that is sufficient to bring about the phenotype. Nongenetic factors such as cultural influences that are transmitted between generations, and environmental factors that are not transmissible can also be incorporated in the models.

Other models that are thought to address more fully the complex transmission pattern of some behavioral disorders have been devised. These include (1) the "mixed" model that combines single gene transmission, a polygenic background, and environmental effects; (2) the two-locus model that postulates two separate genes with varying degrees of interaction; (3) SML models with more than two alleles; and (4) a polygenic model with graduated effects across the different loci.

One should note that the results of pedigree analysis must always be interpreted with due attention to methodological issues such as etiologic heterogeneity, epistasis (the interaction between genes), reduced fertility, and assortative mating (the tendency of persons with like behavioral dispositions to marry and to reproduce).

Susceptibility Traits and Gene Markers

Pedigree analysis aims to examine the fit of a given data set to a particular genetic model; however, in the absence of additional information on inherited biological traits or chromosomal markers, statistical formulations cannot uncover the underlying genetic abnormality.

Biological susceptibility traits derive from etiologic or pathophysiological hypotheses. They span diverse fields such as biochemistry, neurophysiology, and neuroanatomy, and are thought to be part of the pathway from the genotype to phenotype.

Potential susceptibility traits include neurotransmitter enzymes, receptor proteins, and metabolites; attentional and electroencephalographic measures; and indices on brain scanning such as with positron emission tomography (PET). To qualify as a genetic susceptibility trait, the biological characteristic must be *heritable and state independent* (stable over time, regardless of clinical state); in addition, it should *segregate* with the disorder in families of affected probands (Rieder and Gershon, 1978). Although the specific mode of inheritance need not be known, traits of interest can be incorporated in genetic models that examine the underlying genetics of both the behavioral disorder and the biological trait.

Gene markers refer to chromosomal loci with known genomic position. They can be assigned to two general categories: (1) classic or conventional markers such as leukocyte antigens (HLA system), red blood cells antigens (i.e., blood groups), serum proteins, and observable traits such as color blindness; and (2) the new generation of DNA markers, namely, inherited variations that are detectable by molecular genetic techniques (see below).

The relation of gene markers to a trait or disorder can be determined by linkage analysis (Ott, 1991). Genetic linkage refers to the tendency of chromosomal loci to be coinherited. The distance between loci can be inferred from the recombination frequency (recombination is an exchange of material between homologous chromosomes during meiosis leading to a rearrangement of alleles in the offspring generation). The closer the loci are to each other, the less likely is recombination to occur between them. The odds ratio (the ratio between the probability of there being linkage at a given recombination frequency and that of there being no linkage), more commonly known as the lod score (the logarithm of odds), serves as the principal statistical measure of linkage.

By definition, gene markers have a mendelian mode of inheritance. Unlike susceptibility traits, they need not stem from etiological or pathophysiological hypotheses of the disorder being studied. By virtue of their coinheritance with the gene for the disorder they point to its presence and approximate chromosomal location. The most efficient approach to the study of linkage markers requires extended pedigrees with large sibships and high density of illness. An alternative approach, known as the *sibpair method,* is concerned with pairs of affected siblings and does not require multigeneration family pedigrees. An extended version of this approach, known as the affected pedigree member method, includes other relative pairs as well. Gene markers can also be studied for association with a given trait in the general population; such an association can imply a causal link between the marker locus and the trait.

The demonstration of linkage with gene markers is interpreted as proof of single gene inheritance in the informative pedigrees and can also provide external validation for behavioral assessments. In addition, the study of inherited biological traits and chromosomal markers can offer a means of addressing the important question of etiologic heterogeneity. For example, linkage or association of a trait with different gene markers in different family pedigrees or populations would suggest the presence of several independent genetic forms.

Molecular Biology

Perhaps the single most important development in human genetics in recent years involves the application of molecular biology techniques. The insights gleaned by these methods can be briefly summarized as follows. First, the new technology can reveal numerous DNA variations that span the entire human genome. In conjunction with linkage analysis, these DNA markers can lead to the chromosomal localization of the genes responsible for many inherited conditions. DNA markers have already been used to map the abnormal genes in several human disorders, such as Huntington's disease, Duchenne muscular dystrophy, X-linked mental retardation, and familial forms of Alzheimer's disease. Second, the structure and function of the abnormal genes can be determined. This, in turn, can shed light on the underlying molecular mechanisms. A case in point is Duchenne muscular dystrophy where the gene has been characterized and its protein product identified. Third, the molecular biology approach can increase the precision of genetic diagnosis and might lead to improved preventive and treatment measures. The chromosomal mapping and the gene defects for some neurobehavioral disorders are summarized in Table 13–2.

DNA markers have evolved in stages. The first-generation markers, also known as restriction-fragment-length polymorphisms (RFLPs), are detected by a method known as Southern hybridization whereby a DNA molecule digested by restriction enzymes (endonucleases) is hybridized to a genetic probe specific for the DNA segment suspected to be variant. The resultant pattern of DNA fragments that contain complementary genetic information can then be displayed by autoradiography and

Table 13-2 **Genetic Mapping of Neurobehavioral Disorders**

DISORDER	CHROMOSOMAL LOCATION	GENE DEFECT	REFERENCE
Tay-Sachs	15q22-25	Hexosaminidase (α chain)	Gilbert et al, 1975
Duchenne	Xp21	Deletions Dystrophin	Murray et al, 1982 Hoffman et al, 1987
Huntington's	4p16	Unknown	Gusella et al, 1983
Lesch-Nyhan	Xq27	HPRT	Nussbaum et al, 1983
Wilson's	13q14	Unknown	Frydman et al, 1985
Neurofibromatosis	17cen	Unknown	Barker et al, 1987
Bipolar disorder (manic-depression)	Xq27-28?	Unknown	Baron et al, 1987 Mendlewicz et al, 1987
Alzheimer's	21q21	Unknown	St. George-Hyslop et al, 1987
	19q13	Unknown	Pericak-Vance et al, 1991
	14q24	Unknown	Schellenberg et al, 1992

Note: q,p: the long and the short arms of the chromosome, respectively; cen: the centromere; preceding these notations are the chromosome numbers; following the q,p notations are the numbers of the chromosomal bands.

tested for linkage with presumed genes for a given disorder. Localization of the gene to a specific chromosomal region can be inferred from prior evidence that the marker is on a particular chromosome, or by physical methods such as somatic cell hybridization.

RFLPs are being supplanted by the more abundant and more polymorphic mini- and microsatellite markers, which are largely detected by a molecular method known as polymerase chain reaction (PCR).

As noted earlier, a linked marker merely points to the approximate chromosomal location of the gene of interest but is not likely to contain it. Several molecular genetic methods have been developed to bridge the distance between the marker and the putative disease gene. These include chromosome "walking" and "jumping" and pulsed-field gradient electrophoresis. Once the DNA segment containing the gene has been identified and its structure (nucleotide sequence) has been determined, both the messenger RNA and the associated protein product can be characterized according to the principles of transcription and translation. Conversely, knowledge of the gene product can lead to the identification of the gene itself. Namely, the DNA sequence corresponding to the nucleotide code of the protein can be synthesized, cloned, and used as a probe to screen for the DNA segment that includes the relevant gene. This method has been used successfully to identify the genes for the hormones insulin and erythropoietin, coagulation factor VIII, and the globin chains, among other protein-encoding genes. In behavioral disorders, such genes, also known as candidate genes, include genomic regions that code for neurotransmitter receptors and enzymes.

The availability of tightly linked DNA markers or gene-specific probes can provide powerful and accurate tools for genetic diagnosis of a given trait or disorder. These tools can also be used for risk prediction (and thereby genetic counseling) by the detection of carriers of abnormal alleles. Inherited disorders where these methods are being applied include sickle-cell disease, thalassemia, phenylketonuria, and Lesch-Nyhan syndrome. The characterization of genes and their products can lead to specific drugs of a therapeutic or preventive nature; in some instances (e.g., insulin, erythropoietin, and the antihemophilic factor VIII), the product itself can be used for treatment purposes. Eventually, the replacement of defective genes with normal clones could be contemplated. The clinical applications of molecular biology techniques to some medical disorders are listed in Table 13–3.

The principles that underlie the new DNA technology and its implications for psychiatry are reviewed in detail elsewhere (Gurling, 1985; Martin, 1987; Baron and Rainer, 1988).

Phenotypic Classification

An accurate definition of the phenotype is crucial in behavioral genetics. The current emphasis on structured, criterion-based approaches to the assessment of behavior has improved reliability and consensus between investigators and practitioners. "Ill" versus "well" dichotomies largely depend on descriptive diagnostic practices in the absence of external validating measures. The question of external validity pertains to the likely heterogeneity both within and among diagnostic categories. Additional information, such as biochemical measures, can aid in refining behav-

Table 13-3 **Clinical Applications of Molecular Biology Techniques**

	APPLICATION	
DISORDER	**Risk Prediction**	**Treatment***
Sickle cell anemia	+	
Thalassemia	+	
Phenylketonuria	+	
Lesch-Nyhan	+	
Cystic fibrosis	+	
Diabetes mellitus		+ (Insulin)
Hemophilia	+	+ (Coagulation factor VIII)

*Therapeutic products produced by molecular biology techniques.

ioral and psychiatric nosology and lead to the demarcation of homogeneous sub-groups, which, in turn, may enhance the prospects of genetic studies. Conversely, data on biological vulnerability traits, linked genetic markers, and differential familial loading can aid in the classification of behavioral conditions by circumventing the uncertainties inherent in descriptive diagnostic phenomenology, which is largely based on behavioral signs and symptoms.

Genes and Environment

Although the main emphasis in this review is on the genotypic determination of inherited conditions, *the environment can play an important role in the pathway from genotype to phenotype.* The environment shapes and modifies the transmission and expression of the genetic makeup, at all levels, from the cellular to the behavioral. This regulation may be in the form of activation or suppression of the underlying genetic mechanisms.

The contribution of the environment to phenotypic expression in most behavioral disorders can be readily evidenced by the incomplete concordance in identical monozygotic twins. To some extent, this contribution can be quantified by statistical measures, such as heritability, and the incorporation of reduced penetrance, sporadic cases or phenocopies, multifactorial influences, and other types of environmental variance in the genetic analysis of pedigrees. The study of biologic inherited traits may provide a more definitive approach to the elucidation of gene–environment interaction. For example, if a specific environmental factor operates in conjunction with the underlying genotypic makeup, this factor will more likely be present in the affected than in the unaffected relatives when the illness in both groups of subjects is linked to a particular genetic marker. A complementary approach, which falls under the rubric of high-risk paradigms, would be to study prospectively putative environmental factors in persons who carry the genetic marker and are therefore at risk for developing the disorder.

PSYCHIATRIC GENETICS

Major Disorders

Family, Twin, and Adoption Studies

The major mental disorders, schizophrenia and bipolar disorder (manic–depressive illness), occupy center stage in psychiatric genetics because both conditions run in families. In recent well-designed studies, the morbidity risk for schizophrenia in first-degree relatives of schizophrenic patients is 3% to 6% as compared with 0.2% to 0.6% in the general population. The corresponding rates for bipolar disorder in the general population are 4% to 9% and 0.2% to 0.5%, respectively. (When major depression, also known as unipolar major depressive disorder and thought to be a milder manifestation of the bipolar genotype in families of bipolar patients, is included in the bipolar "spectrum," the risk to first-degree relatives of bipolar probands is 13% to 35% versus 5% to 8% in the general population.) The variable rates among studies are attributable in part to different diagnostic practices and other methodological issues, such as sampling scheme. For example, the rate at which schizophrenia is diagnosed can vary severalfold depending on how narrow or how broad the criteria are (Baron, Gruen, Kane et al, 1985). Similarly, the familial rate of major depressive disorder can be reduced considerably by requiring "impairment incapacitation" as an essential inclusion criterion (Gershon et al, 1982). It is of interest, however, that, despite the varied methodology, the relative risk (the ratio of the risk to patients' relatives to the risk to relatives of normal controls) is high (approximately 10 to 20 for schizophrenia; 17 to 20 for bipolar disorder), indicating significant familial aggregation. When major depression is considered independently of bipolar disorder, the risk to first-degree relatives of patients with major depression is 11% to 18% compared with 5% to 6% in controls; the relative risk is 2 to 3. Thus, the evidence for familial clustering is not as impressive as that for schizophrenia and bipolar disorder but is nevertheless significant. The results overall support earlier family studies dating to the beginning of the century. Morbidity risk data on schizophrenia and mood disorders are presented in Table 13–4.

Twin studies have consistently shown higher concordance in both mood disorders and schizophrenia rates in monozygotic than in dizygotic twins, consistent with a genetic hypothesis. The ratio of monozygotic versus dizygotic concordance rates is approximately 4 to 1 for schizophrenia and bipolar disorder, although the absolute rates vary among studies. The heritability estimates based on these data are 30% to 50% and 60% to 80% for schizophrenia and bipolar disorder, respectively. As with the family risk data, the evidence for a genetic component in major depression is not as strong; the monozygotic:dizygotic ratio in concordance rates is only 2 to 1. It is noteworthy that an appreciable proportion of the monozygotic twin pairs are discordant for schizophrenia and bipolar disorder (approximately 50% and 20%, respectively), pointing to the important role of environmental factors in the pathogenesis of these disorders.

Using both the adoptees family method and the adoptees study method, adoption studies have reinforced the notion that genetic factors play an important role in schizophrenia and major mood disorders. In addition, a crossfostering study has

Table 13-4 **Morbidity Risk for Schizophrenia and Mood Disorders**

DISORDER	MORBIDITY RISK IN FIRST-DEGREE RELATIVES (%)	MORBIDITY RISK IN RELATIVES OF CONTROLS (%)	RELATIVE RISK	REFERENCE*
Schizophrenia	5.8	0.6	9.7	Baron et al, 1985
	3.7	0.2	18.5	Kendler et al, 1985
Bipolar disorder†	3.9	0.2	19.5	Tsuang et al, 1980
	4.5(8.6)	0.0 (0.5)	(17.2)	Gershon et al, 1982
	3.9(8.1)	No data		Andreasen et al, 1987
Major depression	11.0	4.8	2.3	Tsuang et al, 1980
	17.5	5.9	3.0	Weissman et al, 1984
	22.8	No data		Andreasen et al, 1987

*The studies cited fulfill modern criteria for genetic-family investigations. They represent four large-scale research efforts: the Iowa 500 (Tsuang et al, 1980; Kendler et al, 1985); the New York-Columbia University Study (Baron et al, 1985); the NIMH Study (Gershon et al, 1982); the New Haven-Yale University Study (Weissman et al, 1984); and the NIMH Collaborative Study (Andreasen et al, 1987).
†Bipolar disorder has two variants: bipolar I, the more severe illness form (depressive and manic episodes), and bipolar II (depression and hypomania). The figures in parentheses are the combined morbid risks for bipolar I and bipolar II disorders; the other risk figures are for bipolar I disorder.

shown that the adopted-away offspring of schizophrenic parents are at increased risk for the illness compared with the adopted-away offspring of nonschizophrenic parents. The adopted-away offspring of normal biological parents reared by schizophrenic parents showed no increase in the risk for schizophrenia. This study has been interpreted as evidence against a strong environmental component in the etiology of schizophrenia.

Taken together, family, twin, and adoption studies support the role of heredity in the major psychoses. A spectrum of conditions thought to be related to the "core" disorders have also been considered in the genetic framework. For example, some forms of schizoaffective illness (a mixed pattern of schizophrenic and affective symptoms), schizotypal, and paranoid personality disorders are believed to belong in the schizophrenia spectrum, whereas other subtypes of schizoaffective disorder and some forms of alcoholism, sociopathy, anxiety, eating disorders, and minor disorders with affective coloring such as cyclothymia may be related to the affective spectrum. These studies are reviewed in detail elsewhere (Andreasen et al, 1987; Baron et al, 1985; Gershon et al, 1982; Gottesman and Shields, 1982; Kendler et al, 1985; Weissman et al, 1984).

Pedigree Analysis

Numerous applications of genetic models to family data have been reported, including the SML and MFP models and variations thereof. Despite the advances in statistical genetics, the analysis of clinical genetic data has not led to consistent results. Based on these studies, the mode of inheritance of either schizophrenia or major mood disorders remains elusive. The inconsistency among studies has been attributed to variations in the methods for data collection (sampling scheme, diagnosis) and analysis (mathematical formulations) and to the likely heterogeneous nature of these disorders. The prevailing wisdom is that the analysis of familial patterns using statistical genetic techniques in not likely to unravel the underlying genetic mechanism without the added benefit of biological susceptibility traits and chromosomal markers. Detailed reviews of this topic are provided by Baron (1986) and by Goldin and Gershon (1983).

Biological Susceptibility Traits and Gene Markers

A large array of biologic variables, including biogenic amine enzymes and metabolites, neuroreceptor sensitivity, neuromuscular function, immune response, attentional and electrophysiological measures, and brain morphology have been examined as potential vulnerability traits for schizophrenia and mood disorders. As has been noted in recent reviews of this area (Baron, 1986), some of these traits, such as attentional (Continuous Performance Test and eye tracking), neurophysiological (auditory evoked response), and brain morphology measures (brain ventricular size) appear promising, but the data are as yet not adequate to arrive at firm conclusions. In bipolar affective disorder (manic depression), alterations of the GABA (CSF GABA and GABA-transaminase) and cholinergic (muscarinic receptor sensitivity) systems show promise as elaborate potential susceptibility traits. For example, induction of REM sleep by the muscarinic agonist arecoline has been claimed to distinguish euthymic bipolar patients from controls, and is concordant in monozygotic twins, suggesting genetic control of this trait. The information available to support this theory fully is incomplete (Goldin and Gershon, 1983). Based on the available evidence, none of the proposed biologic traits qualifies as a major factor in the genetic susceptibility to the major psychoses.

Potential breakthroughs in this area may come about by means of linkage studies with chromosomal markers. Baron and associates (1987) reported close linkage of bipolar affective illness to the X chromosome markers color blindness and glucose-6-phosphate dehydrogenase (G6PD) activity, thus supporting earlier suggestions that a gene on the distal long arm of the X chromosome plays a role in a subset of bipolar disorder (see Baron et al, 1981; Risch and Baron, 1982). Subsequently, Mendlewicz and associates (1987) provided further supportive evidence for the X-linkage hypothesis by demonstrating linkage between bipolar illness and a DNA marker associated with the factor IX (F9) locus on the long arm of the X chromosome. Another group of investigators (Egeland et al, 1987) reported linkage between two DNA markers on the short arm of chromosome 11, the Harvey-ras (HRAS1) and insulin loci, and bipolar illness in an Old Order Amish pedigree. A similar strategy was applied to schizophrenia where linkage was reported between the illness and DNA markers on chromosome 5 (Sherrington et al, 1988); this linkage study used as an indicator an earlier report on a cytogenetic abnormality, a balanced translocation between chromosomes 5 and 1 in a family segregating schizophrenia (Bassett et al, 1988). Unfortunately, subsequent studies have failed to replicate these findings (see Baron et al, 1990 for review). Moreover, the addition of new genetic and clinical information has led to diminished evidence of linkage in these pedigrees (Kelsoe et al, 1989; Mankoo et al, 1991; Baron et al, 1993). These apparent false starts (especially the chromosomes 11 and 5 findings; some of the X-linkage data remain intriguing pending further investigation) can be traced to methodological uncertainties and other limitations in studying complex diseases (Baron et al, 1990; Baron, 1992). The search for genetic mechanisms that underlie the major psychoses continues using improved molecular biology techniques and analytical paradigms.

Other Mental Conditions

Other psychiatric disorders with possible genetic components include certain types of dementia, alcoholism, behavioral conditions associated with chromosome anomalies, and nonpsychotic states such as panic, eating disorders (bulimia nervosa and anorexia nervosa), agoraphobia, somatization disorder (Briquet's syndrome) and some of the personality disorders, and several neuropsychiatric disorders.

Linkage studies with DNA markers have shown the chromosomal sites for three neuropsychiatric conditions with neurologic and behavioral features: Huntington's disease (chromosome 4), Lesch-Nyhan disorder (the X chromosome), and familial forms of Alzheimer's disease (chromosomes 21, 19, and 14). Huntington's and familial Alzheimer's disease follow a dominant mode of inheritance whereas Lesch-Nyhan syndrome is inherited as an X-linked recessive trait.

Alcoholism appears to have a genetic component as evidenced by family, twin, and adoption studies, but the mode of inheritance has not been established. The role of genetic factors seems clearer in males than in females. Environmental factors have also been invoked. In some instances, alcoholism is thought to be related to affective disorder and antisocial personality, but the precise relation is unclear. It is of interest that familial alcoholics are distinguishable from the nonfamilial cases with respect to the severity of alcohol-related problems (more severe), onset of physical dependence (earlier), and treatment outcome (poorer). The two groups of alcoholics also differ on some physiologic and endocrine measures. These findings point to the heterogeneous nature of this condition. A recent study reported an association of the D_2 dopamine receptor gene and alcoholism (Blum et al, 1990), but conflicting results and methodological uncertainties have rendered this finding controversial (Conneally, 1991).

Chromosome anomalies marked by behavioral features chiefly involve the sex chromosomes. These are Klinefelter's syndrome (XXY karyotype) and the XYY aberration. The behavioral manifestations in Klinefelter's syndrome can range from mild personality changes to delinquency to psychosis-like behavior. The XYY anomaly seems to occur more often than expected among delinquent and criminally inclined persons who show episodic violence and other forms of aggression and impulsive behavior. The interaction between the extra sex chromosome and other factors in the development of these behavioral conditions is not well understood.

Genetic contributions to panic disorder, eating disorders, agoraphobia, obsessive-compulsive disorder, somatization disorder, and schizotypal, borderline, and antisocial personality disorders have been surmised from family, twin, and adoption studies, although these studies are not as comprehensive as those carried out on the major psychoses. In some studies, the familial pattern of panic disorder is consistent with single gene inheritance. Panic disorder, eating disorders, agoraphobia, borderline personality disorder, and antisocial personality disorder appear to share a comorbidity with mood disorders, whereas schizotypal personality disorder is thought to be part of the schizophrenia spectrum. Obsessive-compulsive disorder may have a genetic link to Tourette's syndrome. The biological and genetic basis of these conditions and their possible relation to the major psychiatric disorders require further elucidation.

The genetics of the disorders reviewed in this section are discussed further by Rainer (1985). Morbidity risk data on some of these disorders are presented in Table 13–5.

The Genetics of Personality

Although the focus of interest in behavior genetics, especially within the framework of psychiatry, has been on psychopathology, personality is an increasingly important area of inquiry. Most of the evidence on the role of heredity in shaping personality stems from twin studies. In Loehlin and Nichols's (1976) pioneering study, a wide array of personality traits measured in identical versus fraternal twins were shown to have substantial heritabilities of about 50%. No effect of shared environment was detected. In a study of identical twins reared apart, Bouchard and McGue (1981) confirmed the high heritability rates for personality traits and showed that the correlations for identical twins reared apart and those reared together were very much alike, indicating that the contribution of common environment to the similarity between twins reared together is fairly small compared with genetic influences. Of interest are the findings that genes also seem to influence social attitudes and that some environmental influences are genetically mediated.

Taken together, these studies suggest that genes play a major role in determining personality traits. Compared with the person's genetic endowment, the common environment appears to exert a negligible influence on personality. The results are somewhat reminiscent of the substantial heritability shown for various cognitive abilities as measured in IQ tests. The similarity carries over to the controversy that such findings evoke, partly owing to potential social and political implications. In the absence of a clear biological substrate, questions of the nature and interpretation of

Table 13-5 **Morbidity Risk for Some Psychiatric Disorders**

DISORDER	MORBIDITY RISK IN FIRST-DEGREE RELATIVES (%)	MORBIDITY RISK IN RELATIVES OF CONTROLS (%)	RELATIVE RISK	REFERENCE
Alcoholism	16.1	1.6	10.1	Pitts and Winokur, 1966
Panic disorder	17.3	1.8	9.6	Crowe, 1985
Anorexia nervosa	2.3	0.5	4.6	Strober et al, 1985
Agoraphobia	11.6	4.2	2.8	Crowe, 1985
Briquet's syndrome (somatization disorder)	7.7	2.5	3.1	Cloninger et al, 1986

personality measurement scales, prenatal and perinatal factors, and gene–environment interaction will continue to arouse debate and stimulate further investigation in this complex area. This subject matter is discussed in greater detail by Loehlin and Nichols (1976) and by Plomin and Daniels (1987).

IMPLICATIONS

The burgeoning field of human genetics has yielded important insights into several conditions affecting behavior. Applications of the classic genetic methodologies involving family, twin, and adoption studies underscore the role of heredity in various behavioral manifestations ranging from personality traits to severe psychopathology. Studies with biologic susceptibility traits and genetic linkage markers, in conjunction with molecular biology techniques, hold great promise for elucidation of etiology and pathophysiology, identification and characterization of abnormal genes, refinement of phenotypic classification, disentangling gene–environment interaction, risk prediction, and, eventually, improved prevention and treatment measures.

ANNOTATED BIBLIOGRAPHY

Baron M, Endicott J, Ott J: Genetic linkage in mental illness: limitations and prospects. Br J Psychiatry 157:645–655, 1990

> Reviews methodological issues in genetic linkage strategies, with special reference to psychiatric disorders.

Baron M, Rainer JD: Molecular genetics and human disease: Implications for modern psychiatric research and practice. Br J Psychiatry 152:741–753, 1988

> Reviews the principles and potential applications of molecular biology techniques in medicine and psychiatry.

Emery EH: Methodology in Medical Genetics 2nd ed. New York, Churchill Livingstone, 1986

> Reviews statistical methods and research designs in medical genetics.

Goldin LR, Gershon ES: Association and linkage studies of genetic marker loci in major psychiatric disorders. Psychiatr Dev 4:387–418, 1983

> Reviews strategies and findings in studies of schizophrenia and affective disorders using genetic linkage markers and biologic susceptibility traits.

Rainer JD: Genetics and Psychiatry. In Kaplan HI, Sadock BJ (eds): Comprehensive Textbook of Psychiatry, 5th ed. Baltimore, Williams & Wilkins, 1989

> Overall review of genetic theories and findings in psychiatry.

Rosenthal D: Genetic Theory and Abnormal Behavior. New York, McGraw-Hill, 1970

> Reviews classic research designs and methodologies in psychiatric genetics.

REFERENCES

Andreasen NC, Rice J, Endicott J et al: Familial rates of affective disorder: A report from the National Institute of Mental Health Collaborative Study. Arch Gen Psychiatry 44:461–469, 1987

Barker D, Wright E, Nguyen L et al: Gene for von Recklinghausen neurofibromatosis is in the pericentromeric region of chromosome 17. Science 236:1100–1102, 1987

Baron M: Genetics of schizophrenia. I. Familial patterns and mode of inheritance. Biol Psychiatry 21:1051–1066, 1986

Baron M: Genetics of schizophrenia. II. Vulnerability traits and gene markers. Biol Psychiatry 21:1189–1121, 1986

Baron M, Endicott J, Ott J: Genetic linkage in mental illness: Limitations and prospects. Br J Psychiatry 157:645–655, 1990

Baron M, Freimer NF, Risch N et al: Diminished support for linkage between manic depressive illness and X-chromosomes markers in Israeli pedigrees. Nat Genet, 3:49–55, 1993

Baron M, Gruen R, Kane J et al: Modern genetic criteria and the genetics of schizophrenia. Am J Psychiatry 142:697–701, 1985b

Baron M, Gruen R, Rainer JD et al: A family study of schizophrenia and normal control probands: Implications for the spectrum concept of schizophrenia. Am J Psychiatry 142:447–454, 1985

Baron M, Rainer JD: Molecular genetics and human disease: Implications for modern psychiatric research and practice. Br J Psychiatry 152:741–753, 1988

Baron M, Rainer JD: Risch N: X-linkage in bipolar affective illness: Perspectives on genetic heterogeneity, pedigree analysis and the X-chromosome map. J Affective Disord 3:141–157, 1981

Baron M, Risch N, Hamburger R et al: Genetic linkage between X-chromosome markers and bipolar affective illness. Nature 326:289–292, 1987

Bassett AS, McGillivray BC, Jones BD et al: Partial trisomy chromosome 5 cosegregating with schizophrenia. Lancet 8589:799–801, 1988

Blum K, Noble EP, Sheridan PJ et al: Allelic association of human dopamine D_2 receptor gene in alcoholism. JAMA 263:2055–2060, 1990

Bouchard TJ Jr, McGue M: Familial studies of intelligence: A review. Science 212:1055–1059, 1981

Conneally PM: Association between the D_2 dopamine receptor gene and alcoholism: A continuing controversy. Arch Gen Psychiatry 48:664–666, 1991

Cloninger CR, Martin RL, Guze SB et al: A prospective follow-up and family study of somatization in men and women. Am J Psychiatry 143:873–878, 1986

Crowe RR: The genetics of panic disorder and agoraphobia. Psychiatr Dev 2:171–186, 1985

Egeland JA, Gerhard DS, Pauls DL et al: Bipolar affective disorder linked to DNA markers on chromosome 11. Nature 325:783–787, 1987

Emery EH: Methodology in Medical Genetics. New York, Churchill Livingstone, 1976

Frydman M, Bonne-Tamir B, Farrer L et al: Assignment of the gene for Wilson's disease to chromosome 13: Linkage to the esterase D locus. Proc Natl Acad Sci USA 82:1819–1821, 1985

Gershon ES, Hamovit J, Guroff JJ et al: A family study of schizoaffective, bipolar I, bipolar II, unipolar, and normal control probands. Arch Gen Psychiatry 39:1157–1167, 1982

Gilbert F, Kucherlapati R, Creagan RP et al: Tay-Sachs and Sandhoff's diseases: The assignment of genes for hexosaminidases A and B to individual human chromosomes. Proc Natl Acad Sci USA 72:263–267, 1975

Goldin LR, Gershon ES: Association and linkage studies of genetics marker loci in major psychiatric disorders. Psychiatric Dev 4:387–418, 1983

Gottesman II, Shields J: Schizophrenia: The Epigenetic Puzzle. Cambridge, Cambridge University Press, 1982

Gurling HMD: Application of molecular biology to mental illness. Analysis of genomic DNA and brain mRNA. Psychiatric Dev 3:257–273, 1985

Gusella JF, Wexler NS, Conneally PM et al: A polymorphic DNA marker genetically linked to Huntington's disease. Nature 306:234–238, 1983

Hoffman EP, Brown RH, Kunkel LM: Dystrophin: The protein product of the Duchenne muscular dystrophy lucus. Cell 51:919–928, 1987

Kelsoe JR, Gings EI, Egeland JA et al: Reevaluation of the linkage relationship between chromosome 11_p loci and the gene for bipolar affective disorder in the Old Order Amish. Nature 342:238–243, 1989

Kendler KS, Gruenberg AM, Tsuang MT: Psychiatric illness in first-degree relatives of schizophrenic and surgical control patients. Arch Gen Psychiatry 42:770–779, 1985

Loehlin JC, Nichols RC: Heredity, Environment and Personality. Austin, University of Texas Press, 1976

Mankoo B, Sherrington R, Brynjoltsson J et al: New microsatellite polymorphisms provide a highly polymorphic map of chromosome 5 bands 911.2–913.3 for linkage analysis of Icelandic and English families affected by schizophrenia. Psychiatr Genet 2:17, 1991

Martin JB: Molecular genetics: Applications to the clinical neurosciences. Science 238:765–772, 1987

Mendlewicz J, Simon P, Sevy S et al: Polymorphic DNA marker on X-chromosome and manic depression. Lancet 8544:1230–1232, 1987

Murray JM, Davies KE, Harper PS et al: Linkage relationship of a cloned DNA sequence on the short arm of the X chromosome to Duchenne muscular dystrophy. Nature 300:69–71, 1982

Nussbaum R, Brennand J, Chinault C et al: Molecular analysis of the hypoxanthine phosphoribosyltransferase locus. In Caskey CT, White RL (eds): Recombinant DNA Application to Human Disease, pp 81–90. New York, Cold Spring Harbor Laboratory, 1983

Ott J: Analysis of Human Genetic Linkage. Baltimore, The Johns Hopkins University Press, 1985

Pericak-Vance MA, Bebout JL, Gaskell PC Jr et al: Linkage studies in familial Alzheimer's disease: Evidence for chromosome 19 linkage. Am J Hum Genet 48:1034–1050, 1991

Pitts FN, Winokur G: Affective disorder. VII. Alcoholism and affective disorder. J Psychiatr Res 4:37–50, 1966

Plomin R, Daniels D: Why are children in the same family so different from one another? Behav Brain Sci 10:1–60, 1987

Rainer JD: Genetics and psychiatry. In Kaplan HI, Sadock BJ (eds): Comprehensive Textbook of Psychiatry, 4th ed. Baltimore, Williams & Wilkins, 1985

Rieder RO, Gershon ES: Genetic strategies in biological psychiatry. Arch Gen Psychiatry 35:866–873, 1978

Risch N, Baron M: X-linkage and genetic heterogeneity in bipolar-related major affective illness: Reanalysis of linkage data. Ann Hum Genet 46:153–166, 1982

Rosenthal D: Genetic Theory and Abnormal Behavior. New York, McGraw-Hill, 1970

St. George-Hyslop PH, Tanzi RE, Polinsky RJ et al: The genetic defect causing familial Alzheimer's disease maps on chromosomal 21. Science 235:885–889, 1987

Schellenberg GD, Bird TD, Wijsman EM et al: Genetic linkage evidence for a familial Alzheimer's disease locus on chromosome 14. Science 258:668–671, 1992

Sherrington R, Brynjolfsson J, Petursson H et al: Localization of a susceptibility locus for schizophrenia on chromosome 5. Nature 336:164–167, 1988

Strober M, Morell W, Burroughs J et al: A controlled family study of anorexia nervosa. J Psychiatr Res 19:239–246, 1985

Thompson EA: Pedigree Analysis in Human Genetics. Baltimore, John Hopkins University Press, 1986

Tsuang MT, Winokur G, Crowe R: Morbidity risks of schizophrenia and affective disorders among first degree relatives of patients with schizophrenia, mania, depression and surgical conditions. Br J Psychiatry 137:497–504, 1980

Weissman MM, Gershon ES, Kidd KK et al: Psychiatric disorders in the relatives of probands with affective disorders: The Yale University-National Institute of Mental Health Collaborative Study. Arch Gen Psychiatry 41:13–21, 1984

V Clinical Applications

14 Supportive Psychological Care of the Medically Ill: A Synthesis of the Biopsychosocial Approach in Medical Care

Stephen A. Green

This entire text has been a prodrome to this concluding chapter, which addresses how a knowledge of human behavior contributes to the compassionate psychological and emotional care of patients again, focusing on the critical importance of the doctor–patient relationship. In addition, the basic themes of the biopsychosocial model introduced by Drs. Cohen-Cole and Levinson are discussed again in light of the multiple perspectives that have been presented in previous chapters as well as the model's practical application in patient care.

THE DOCTOR–PATIENT RELATIONSHIP AND THE BIOPSYCHOSOCIAL MODEL

The interaction between physician and patient is too often an impersonal, mechanistic encounter due to their shared cause-and-effect mindset concerning the diagnosis and treatment of specific symptoms. Medical practice has long been considered an exercise of determining etiology, prescribing the indicated therapeutic regimen, and monitoring the patient's response, a perspective that highlights intellectual problem solving while neglecting central emotional factors that influence the course of an illness. This approach is based on the biomedical model, discussed in Chapters 1 and 2, which is a parochial viewpoint rooted in the oversimplification and misinterpretation of the theories of René Descartes involving mind–body duality.

A strictly biomedical model compromises patient care by supporting the inaccurate belief in a mind–body dichotomy and perpetuating the simplistic notion that complex pathophysiological phenomena are ultimately explained by a single principle (Engel, 1977). For example, it defines peptic ulcer disease as the anatomical end product of gastric hypersecretion, implying that definitive treatment consists solely of appropriate medication and dietary restrictions. Undoubtedly, these are necessary measures; however, they may be no more than palliative if medical interventions fail to address specific psychosocial issues affecting and affected by the patient's ulcer. The biomedical model promotes "the physician's preoccupation with the body and disease and the corresponding neglect of the patient as a person," and it fails to consider "how the patient behaves and what he reports about himself and his life [because] it does not include the patient and his attributes as a person, a human being" (Engel, 1980). In sum, the biomedical model suggests that treating one's specific physical pathology is synonymous with treating the patient, which ignores the fundamental truth that all illness simultaneously affects the mind and the body.

Every patient must be seen as a singular human being if medical care is to be appropriate and effective. This requires application of the biopsychosocial model, a theoretic construct that assesses a person within the distinctive context of supports and stressors affecting his or her daily functioning. As discussed in Chapters 1, 2, and 3, an understanding of the interplay among each patient's medical disorder, intra-psychic life, and the positive and negative impact of their external environment is important for several reasons.

First, the genesis and exacerbation of an illness (Rahe, 1973), even mechanisms of sudden death (Engel, 1968; Reich et al, 1981), are affected by numerous psychoso-cial factors. Second, as discussed in Chapters 3, 11, and 12, extensive scientific research has demonstrated mind–body interactions in specific physiological, endo-crinological, and immunological processes, as well as in generalized stress reactions. Third, one's willingness and ability to cooperate in prescribed care is often affected by myriad nonphysical factors, including intrapsychic issues (Lipowski, 1975) and socio-cultural norms (Zola, 1963). Finally, physical illness itself can precipitate a variety of abnormal psychological states that adversely influence the disease process, or reach a degree of severity so intense that they become more threatening to patients than their original medical disorder (Green, 1985).

The preceding discussion demonstrates that optimal medical treatment re-quires the biopsychosocial treatment approach, which Engel (1980) conceptualizes by interposing the patient between two hierarchies that combine to form an overall hierarchy of natural systems (Fig. 14–1). The person is at the same time at the highest level of an organismic hierarchy, which ranges from subatomic particles through the nervous system, and the lowest stratum of a social hierarchy, which ranges from a two-person system to the biosphere. These two hierarchies are in a dynamic equilibrium, because every system (e.g., cells or two-person) within each hierarchy is a distinctive whole that is simultaneously interrelated with every other system. Consequently, disturbances at any system level can alter any other system level; through feedback controls, they may modify or aggravate the system originally affected. Engel presents a clinical case to illustrate the workings of this medical model, which, as discussed next, is ultimately based on the clinician's appreciation of the meaning of illness to an individual patient.

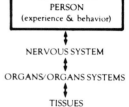

BIOSPHERE
↕
SOCIETY-NATION
↕
CULTURE-SUBCULTURE
↕
COMMUNITY
↕
FAMILY
↕
TWO-PERSON
↕

PERSON
(experience & behavior)

↕
NERVOUS SYSTEM
↕
ORGANS/ORGANS SYSTEMS
↕
TISSUES
↕
CELLS
↕
ORGANELLES
↕
MOLECULES
↕
ATOMS
↕
SUBATOMIC PARTICLES

Figure 14–1. *Hierarchy of natural systems. (Reprinted with permission from Engel G: The clinical application of the biopsychosocial model. Am J Psychiatr 137:535–544, 1980).*

ILLNESS DYNAMICS

The biopsychosocial model demonstrates that nonphysical issues are part and parcel of the disease process and can transform the same organic pathology into vastly different illnesses in different patients. Consider that premise in terms of the following two men who suffered similar myocardial damage from a heart attack. Their histories highlight the many psychosocial factors that influenced when and to what degree they became ill, as well as their response to treatment and ultimate prognosis.

TWO CASE STUDIES

Mr. A, a 40-year-old widower, is a midlevel manager diligently working his way up the corporate ladder while supporting three young children. In addition to family responsibilities and professional obligations, he devotes considerable time to a flourishing relationship with a coworker he hopes to marry. His past history is significant for the unexpected death of his mother from a cerebrovascular accident when he was 13 years old.

In contrast, Mr. B is a 63-year-old executive vice-president on the threshold of retirement, a husband of 40 years eagerly anticipating more leisure time with his wife and grown family. He has consistently enjoyed good health; his only major medical event, a cholecystectomy, was a scheduled procedure that caused minimal disruption to his life. Although Mr. B's father died at the age of 70 of metastatic carcinoma, his mother, siblings, wife, and children are all in good health.

After surviving the immediate threat of death from a myocardial infarction, each man exhibited a unique reaction to his damaged myocardium. Mr. A's initial anxiety was progressively supplanted by a growing sense of helplessness. The death of his mother at an early age had generally sensitized him to loss, and specifically affected his psychological development by enhancing dependent yearnings. Moreover, because she died of a cardiovascular illness, he more closely associated his heart disease with her sudden demise. He also identified with his children's concerns, as he had experienced the same anxiety that comes from recognizing that one's future is largely dependent on the welfare of a single parent. Significant feelings of anger and depression arose when he considered the impact of his illness on the course of his career and the developing relationship with his girlfriend. All these factors contributed to a heightened affective response to his heart attack, making it more difficult to resolve those intense feelings and fostering an increasing helplessness and dependency on those around him.

Mr. B, on the other hand, was also angered and depressed by his bad luck, but basically because it occurred at a stage of life primarily reserved for relaxation. However, the intensity of his feelings was tempered by the knowledge that his family was grown, that his loving spouse had consistently provided reassurance and support when needed, that he had already realized his professional ambitions, and that he was financially secure. For these reasons, Mr. B more easily worked through the emotions stirred by his physical impairment and quickly returned to his premorbid level of functioning.

Although these patients suffered the exact same anatomical and physiological pathology, each reacted to the period of ill health in a highly distinctive fashion due to the impact of idiosyncratic psychological and social issues. Mr. A's heart attack precipitated a considerable emotional upheaval, marked by anxiety, depression, and helplessness, because it reawakened traumatic memories and painful feelings related to his mother's death, and he experienced it as a significant threat to many important aspects of his current life. Although some concerns were more imagined than real, they interfered with his ability to accurately assess and, consequently, to accept the effect of an uncomplicated heart attack on his daily existence.

The relationship among one's biological status (e.g., genetic constitution and physical pathology), emotional makeup, and the supports and stresses of a social matrix constitutes that person's *illness dynamics* (Green, 1985). This idiosyncratic standard, which represents the patient's understanding of a specific disease during a particular period of life, is portrayed schematically in Figure 14–2. The shaded area defines the distinctive interrelationship between the conscious and unconscious psychosocial factors affecting and affected by a patient's biological status (Table 14–1), which predisposes to certain diseases and protects against others. Illness dynamics incline one to assess all illness-related information in light of singular values, wishes, needs, and fears, *ultimately causing the patient to perceive, assess, and defend against the loss of health in a highly subjective manner.* As demonstrated by the preceding case histories, this may significantly affect the patient's ability to cope with disease.

Both Mr. A and Mr. B shared the common pathology of an uncomplicated myocardial infarction; however, the most significant biological component of Mr. A's illness dynamics was his mother's genetic endowment. The affected organ system also bore special meaning, raising doubts that he would have sufficient strength and stamina to devote to a rising career or to meet the emotional—and sexual—demands of a second marriage. Mr. A's excessive dependency was an important psychological component of his illness response, a probable legacy of the early loss of his mother that was intensified by the death of his wife. And his stage in the life cycle contributed to his significant depression because the heart attack occurred at a time when persons are more focused on the challenges and joys of life than on the fear of death. The predominant social determinants of Mr. A's illness dynamics concerned family relationships. His heart disease had considerable effect on his young children, whose welfare depended on his wage-earning ability; this lack of flexibility in the family system placed greater stress on him to recuperate rapidly and completely. All of these issues were in contrast to the impact of a heart attack on Mr. B's life. His physical resilience, psychological strength, and the supports of his social network combined to help him readily negotiate this period of ill health.

These patients' distinctive illness dynamics, illustrated in Figure 14–3, greatly influenced their ability to cope with heart disease *by affecting a grief process that normally accompanies loss of health.* Emotionally processing an episode of illness, reaching an accommodation with the diverse and powerful

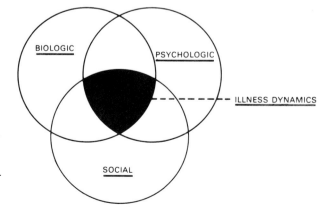

Figure 14–2. *Illness dynamics. (Reprinted with permission from Green S: Mind and Body: The Psychology of Physical Illness. Washington, DC, American Psychiatric Press, 1985).*

Table 14–1 **Major Components of Illness Dynamics**

Biological

Nature, severity, and time course of disease
Affected organ system, body part, or body function
Baseline physiological functioning and physical resilience
Genetic endowment

Psychological

Maturity of ego functioning and object relationships
Personality type
Stage in the life cycle
Interpersonal aspects of the therapeutic relationship (e.g., counter-
  transference of healthcare providers)
Previous psychiatric history
Effect of past history on attitudes toward treatment (e.g., postoperative
  complications)

Social

Dynamics of family relationships
Family attitudes toward illness
Level of interpersonal functioning (e.g., educational and occupational
  achievements; ability to form and maintain friendships)
Cultural attitudes

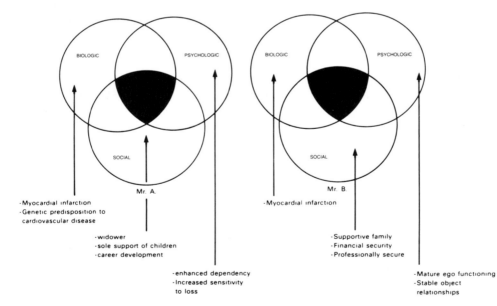

Figure 14–3. *Comparative illness dynamics. (Reprinted with permission from Green S: Mind and Body: The Psychology of Physical Illness. Washington, DC, American Psychiatric Press, 1985).*

feelings that accompany it, is a prerequisite for return to healthy functioning. As discussed next, the working through of these emotions, in order to prevent them from intruding on one's daily responsibilities and interpersonal relationships, is analogous to grieving for a loved one.

THE GRIEF PROCESS AND ILLNESS

Illness is universally experienced as a loss, namely the loss of health, because it decreases one's degree of autonomy. Illness imposes restrictions on people that may be transient and mild (e.g., immobilization of a sprained joint) or chronic and severe (e.g., hemiparesis following a cerebrovascular accident). Although feelings of loss are most intense when a serious health problem permanently and profoundly alters one's physical status, they also occur with minor ailments. The bedridden patient suffering a febrile viral syndrome often feels anxious, frustrated, and depressed about the inability to pursue his or her daily activities and responsibilities. Illness also precipitates a sense of loss due to its various symbolic meanings. The concrete demonstration of physical vulnerability deprives one of infantile invulnerability, while idiosyncratic reactions to disease cause patients to experience more specific losses, such as Mr. A's conviction (founded on his mother's medical history) that his heart attack inevitably signaled an early death.

Whether illness has a predominantly symbolic or concrete effect, it precipitates a predictable psychological reaction—namely, a grief reaction during which patients mourn the loss of their previous healthier functioning. The process is identical to bereavement, causing an outpouring of varied and shifting emotions as patients acknowledge their current state of health and contrast it with a premorbid level. Grieving entails recognition of the good and bad associated with a particular loss, which prompts a series of feeling states—*denial, anxiety, anger*, and *depression*— that a person must progress through before resolving those emotions and coming to terms with a temporary or permanent health impairment. The emotional response to a myocardial infarction illustrates this process.

Although well aware that severe precordial pain may signal an evolving heart attack, patients often attempt to deny that reality by minimizing the symptom or explaining it away as indigestion, myalgia, or bronchitis. That denial recedes as persisting angina underscores the medical reality and precipitates a host of intense feelings. There is immediate anxiety about the prospect of dying, the discomfort of acute treatment, and the need to abdicate considerable responsibility and autonomy to anonymous caretakers.

Anxiety persists into the recuperative period due to concern about long-range effects of the illness (e.g., dietary and physical limitations), although anger becomes the predominant feeling once patients feel secure that they will survive the medical emergency. During this phase of illness, patients direct their resentments globally, as well as toward specific targets. They curse the gods for their bad luck, while blaming specific family members, friends, and medical personnel for real and imagined transgressions and omissions that promoted ill health. As the anger abates, patients may experience a growing depression, characterized by emotional, behavioral, and cognitive changes that reflect their extreme preoccupation with real and potential losses brought on by the heart attack. In the short term, all aspects of their lives (e.g., family, professional, and social commitments) must assume secondary importance to health concerns. Patients also mourn longer-term losses caused by their diseased myocardium, such as restricted physical activities because of persistent angina.

The grief process proceeds toward closure as patients begin to achieve a realistic perspective concerning the consequences of illness. This entails acknowledgment of all limitations imposed by the disease, and of one's physical vulnerabilities and ultimate mortality. "Working through," or attempting to resolve those issues, is a dynamic process that allows reestablishment of the emotional equilibrium that characterized premorbid functioning, illustrated by Mr. B. Patients unable to resolve feelings precipitated by loss may develop one of several syndromes that characterize pathologic grief reactions (Brown and Stoudemire, 1983). These may take the form of a mood disturbance (e.g., the heightened anxiety and depression that complicated Mr. A's recuperation and persisted even after his physical recovery), a behavioral disturbance (e.g., compulsive eating or substance dependence), or impaired interpersonal relationships. As discussed in preceding chapters, there may also be neurobiological correlates to the inability to work through feelings precipitated by ill health. Severe stress, such as physical illness and other circumstances involving loss of control, influences the neurochemistry by endogenous opioids, catecholamines, indoleamines, and pituitary functioning. Dr. van der Kolk in Chapter 11 suggests that these changes promote heightened anxiety, difficulties modulating aggression, and depression—affective disturbances characteristic of unresolved grief—that may represent adult responses to the effects of earlier trauma and stress. Similarly, immunologic and neuroendocrinological data highlight the correlation between grief and discrete physiological changes (Irwin et al, 1987). Consequently, a patient's ability to come to terms with the loss of health is a comprehensive psychobiological response. One's illness dynamics facilitate or impede this grief process; in the latter circumstance, the person is likely to develop one of the following pathological reactions.

ABNORMAL ILLNESS RESPONSES

Persons unable to acknowledge and put into perspective the disturbing feelings brought on by disease are prone to abnormal illness responses, which significantly detract from physical and/or mental health. In these circumstances, individuals may deny their feelings or, more often, strongly experience one emotion while significantly minimizing all others. In essence, the patient becomes mired in one stage of the grief process, promoting a preoccupation with feelings characteristic of that phase, thereby preventing resolution of the varied emotions precipitated by loss of health; the situation is analogous to pathological grief. Because of the interdependence between emotional and somatic functioning, abnormal illness responses often aggravate medical conditions (e.g., increased cardiac irritability due to heightened anxiety following a heart attack), often promoting psychological and biological distress more disabling than the initial illness. The most common abnormal illness responses include the following.

The Denial Response

Denial is a common defense mechanism that enables one to reject cognitive and emotional aspects of anxiety-provoking unpleasant external reality. Despite this function, denial usually serves an adaptive role (Vailliant, 1977), such as facilitating continued functioning by moderating the impact of an overwhelming stressor that might otherwise threaten one's psychological health (e.g., the massive anxiety that precedes battle or other potentially life-threatening situations). Denial becomes maladaptive only when it is exclusively defensive, causing significant distortions in the assessment and acceptance of life's realities. For example, persons who never recognize their contribution to their recurrent failed relationships will probably perpetuate the pattern and increasingly become isolated as life progresses.

Pathological denial may be present throughout the course of a medical or surgical illness. A common example of denial during an acute medical emergency is seen in cardiac patients who dismiss severe precordial pain as heartburn. Persistent denial is often reflected in noncompliance with a therapeutic regimen, which may commence immediately after a medical crisis (e.g., refusal to maintain bedrest while recuperating from a myocardial infarction) and continue throughout a chronic illness (e.g., continued smoking in a patient with chronic obstructive pulmonary disease). Denial is seen in terminal patients who refuse to acknowledge impending death. In sum, denial, if extreme, may interfere with accurate diagnosis, impede definitive treatment, and, consequently, perpetuate the disease state.

The Anxiety Response

Anxiety is an adaptive feeling that signals danger, prompting one toward purposeful action. The fight–flight behavior of animals confronted by a predator illustrates how this affect spurs self-protective behavior. In relation to illness, anxiety promotes preventive behaviors (e.g., scheduled immunizations, healthy diet) and timely medical attention following the onset of symptoms. And its persistence during an episode of ill health, secondary to patients' concern about a multitude of diverse issues (e.g., the discomfort of diagnostic and therapeutic procedures, long-term limitations to daily functioning), further motivates compliance with treatment. However, anxiety can become excessive, prompting an irrational preoccupation with health issues that evolves into a pathological illness response.

Anxiety is maladaptive when the concern it causes the person exceeds its protective function. In this circumstance, patients may become hypersensitive to all aspects of an illness (e.g., ruminating about casual remarks passed by caretakers, obsessing to the point of indecision about therapeutic options). Such absorption with one's physical status greatly detracts from all other aspects of life, progressively displacing former pleasures with a debilitating angst. Paradoxically, this also interferes with medical care. Heightened anxiety compromises objectivity and, consequently, one's ability to provide an accurate history, tolerate diagnostic procedures (e.g., colonoscopy, an MRI scan), or even cooperate in a routine physical examination. Should such pervasive apprehension progress into a chronic anxiety, the patient is then burdened with an unpleasant, counterproductive affective state, in addition to the limitations caused by his or her physical pathology. Finally, continued demands for reassurance from friends, family, and healthcare personnel may progressively alienate those support systems. The anxiety response compromises diverse aspects of medical treatment and, consequently, diminishes the patient's potential for returning to premorbid or optimal functioning.

The Anger Response

All medical and surgical patients become frustrated, resentful, or overtly hostile about their plight, and vent those feelings in several directions. The anger is directed globally and specifically. Patients may curse the fates, God, the unfairness of life, or, alternatively, castigate themselves for being ill whether or not such self-criticism is warranted (e.g., cirrhosis secondary to alcohol abuse) or unreasonable (e.g., the result of an uncontrollable infectious disease). They may lash out at family members and friends for varied reasons—condemning ancestors for passing on a defective gene, blaming friends or family for causing exacerbations of an illness (e.g., the impact of marital discord on labile hypertension), or basically resenting the reality of heightened dependency on people in their social network who enjoy continued good health. Medical personnel are often primary and direct targets for patients' hostility because of the restrictions they impose (e.g., constraints on diet and physical activity), the discomfort they may cause (e.g., performing painful diagnostic procedures, prescribing medications with unpleasant side effects), the limitations of the profession (e.g., inability to cure many diseases), and their role as bearers of grim news about patients' welfare and mortality.

Patients who fail to work through these angry feelings may develop an illness response that is often characterized by severe interpersonal conflicts. They engage in overt and covert struggles with the people in their lives, which fosters a progressive isolation from necessary support and undermines their medical care. Patients may angrily refuse to submit to important diagnostic tests, comply with rehabilitative programs, or take prescribed medications; these behaviors frustrate family members, control caretakers, and also reflect a self-directed anger because all these actions are ultimately detrimental to the patient. Struggles may also occur in subtle, unstated ways, by passive–aggressive behaviors (e.g., failing to adhere to a prescribed diet or medication regimen), which afford the pleasure of secret control over persons. In this manner, the anger response progressively transforms the patient's supportive alliances into adversarial relationships, with widespread negative effects on treatment and day-to-day life.

The Depression Response

This illness response is characterized by the common cognitive, affective, and behavioral signs and symptoms that constitute a clinical depression. These include changes in mood, most commonly a sustained sadness with tearfulness and anhedonia (loss of pleasure and interest in life), although irritability and agitation may also be present. The patient also manifests physiological sequelae of depression, which span the spectrum from the usual neurovegetative complaints (e.g., insomnia, anorexia, fatigue, decreased sexual drive) to somatic disturbances of any organ system (Lindemann, 1944). The most prominent behavioral manifestation of this illness response is a change in established daily patterns, which most often takes the form of generalized withdrawal from one's environment. Patients can manifest more specific behaviors, such as neglecting professional responsibilities or avoiding family interactions, reactions influenced by the particular illness and/or its treatment (e.g., one may be inclined to retreat from social commitments, and to rely more on family support following a disfiguring surgical procedure). Behavioral changes also include radical departures from usual routines of life, such as quitting a satisfying job, preciptiously moving, or ending a long-term marriage. Finally, diminished self-esteem is a prominent feature of this illness response. Already stressed by the effects of a physical impairment that may prevent one from returning to a healthy premorbid level of functioning, the psychological reaction to that reality can provoke a negativistic spiral of self-criticism and self-reproach that ultimately leaves the patient feeling helpless and worthless. Each of these four areas of objective and subjective signs and symptoms can vary in intensity, with the result that the depression response may range from a relatively mild adjustment disorder to a major depression.

The depression response detracts from medical care by direct effects on patients and its impact on their relationships with healthcare personnel. Diverse psychophysiological symptoms are often mistaken as primary manifestations of serious underlying medical illness, which complicates accurate diagnosis and, consequently, treatment. The differentiation becomes even more difficult when depression causes such withdrawal that the patient is unwilling or unable to provide an adequate medical history or report objective and subjective responses to a therapeutic regimen. Depression also interferes with normative healing processes by debilitating neurovegetative symptoms (e.g., anorexia), a diminished immunological response (Stein et al, 1985), the passive abandonment of a will to live (Engel, 1968), or even purposeful self-destructive behaviors (Slaby and Glicksman, 1985). In sum, depression may become so severe that it becomes a greater threat to one's welfare and survival than the original underlying physical pathology.

The Dependency Response

As discussed in Chapter 5, behavioral regression is common to all illness, the result of factors endemic to patients (e.g., general preoccupation with one's illness, restrictions caused by specific symptoms) and external issues (e.g., limitations of a structured hospital routine, constraints of the treatment regimen, like a controlled diet). Such adaptive regression forms the basis of effective medical care; reversion to more passive behaviors, characteristic of early developmental stages, allows a patient the comfort and familiarity of diminished responsibility while simultaneously enabling caretakers to assume a necessary degree of control over the treatment. Diminished autonomy also serves the defensive purpose of helping a patient deal with distressing emotions by assigning accountability for one's welfare to others and readily accepting their concern and support.

As previously mentioned in Chapter 2, Parsons (1951) discusses these aspects of regression in his description of the dynamics of the *sick role*, emphasizing the *collaborative* nature of medical treatment. He outlines the usual course of enhanced dependency on healthcare personnel during the early stages of illness, but emphasizes the importance of patients assuming increased responsibility for their welfare as they progress toward wellness. For example, the stable postmyocardial infarction patient is expected to adhere to a prescribed diet and exercise regimen, important steps toward recovery and maintenance of healthy, independent functioning. Some persons, however, are so gratified by the ministrations of others they refuse to cooperate in their treatment. Warmed by the concern and constant attention of healthcare providers and, consequently, disinclined to strive for the autonomy of premorbid life, they abdicate increasing responsibility to family, friends, and caretakers. This can lead to an increasing dependency that may ultimately culminate in a semihelplessness that endangers one's physical and emotional well-being.

Treatment noncompliance is a common manifestation of excessive dependency, as patients haphazardly adhere to prescribed therapies (e.g., a medication regimen, physical rehabilitation following a traumatic injury). Although the motivation for such behavior may be purposeful or unconscious, it yields the same end point: prolonged dependence on healthcare personnel who must then compensate for the patient's self-neglect by providing an even greater degree of care. At a minimum, this slows one's return to optimal functioning; at worst, it aggravates the illness by intensifying its pathophysiological effects.

Individuals' interpersonal relationships also suffer when illness spawns excessive dependency. Established family patterns must adapt to the patient's prolonged regression, sometimes causing considerable disruption to relatives who now tend to matters usually managed by the patient. Growing resentments may, in turn, detract from their supportive efforts. A parallel situation occurs when healthcare providers develop a negative reaction to so-called hateful patients (Groves, 1978), fostering conscious or unconscious neglect of their care. The dependency response signals the evolution of an individual into a professional patient who is more concerned with being cared for than with achieving an optimal level of coping. When physicians fail to recognize this illness response, which may be hidden by a patient's stated desire to get well quickly, there is greater risk that the collaborative doctor–patient relationship will steadily degenerate into an adversarial association harmful to both parties.

THE DOCTOR–PATIENT RELATIONSHIP IN THE PSYCHOLOGICAL CARE OF THE MEDICALLY ILL

Psychotherapy, in general, can be broadly classified as *supportive* (anxiety-suppressing) or *introspective* (anxiety-provoking). The former (anxiety-suppressing psychotherapy) seeks to preserve the patient's psychological status quo; the latter (anxiety-provoking psychotherapy) attempts to heighten insight by obliging the patient to explore painful memories and emotional experiences.

Introspective therapy is usually required with medically ill patients if they manifest symptoms of a *pathological* illness response. Treatment is then administered by a psychiatrist or other mental health professional specifically trained to help patients work through abnormal affective states (Green, 1985). More often, however, psychotherapeutic care of the medically ill patient is initially *supportive*. Usually effected by primary caretakers (e.g., nonpsychiatrist physicians, nursing staff, rehabilitation therapists), it is designed to help patients identify and ventilate the intense feelings precipitated by ill health, thereby enabling them to contain emotional distress within limits that were acceptable premorbidly. As discussed by Frank (1961) in his classic study concerning the process of healing, this type of treatment is highly dependent on the personal influence exerted by caretakers. For example, a positive relationship can yield favorable effects even with *symbolic* interventions, such as the administration of an inert medication. Alexander and French (1946) specifically exploit the doctor–patient interaction in this manner by the technique of manipulating the transference during psychotherapy (see Chapter 5).

Whether supportive or introspective psychotherapeutic treatment is indicated, patients' comprehensive medical care derives from an accurate appreciation of their emotional condition caused by their ill health in addition to a thorough knowledge of their underlying physical disease. The biopsychosocial approach, which acknowledges the inextricable link between mind and body, requires an understanding of patients' illness dynamics and the application of standard psychotherapeutic principles to medical management (Reichard, 1964; Kahana and Bibring, 1964). A necessary requirement for this treatment approach is *empathic* communication between patients and their caretakers.

As mentioned by Dr. Shelton in Chapter 1, the concept of *empathy* involves a process that enables clinicians to appreciate the conscious and unconscious internal experiences of patients, that is, the capacity "to think and feel oneself into the inner life of another person" (Kohut, 1984). A somewhat intuitive capacity, empathy is a response to emotional signals from patients, such as their facial expressions, level of motor activity, speech patterns, and content of mental productions. These emotional signs from the patient evoke intrapsychic responses in their caretakers. The responses of the caretakers, in turn, are influenced by their own emotional makeup (Buie, 1981), autonomic reactions (Basch, 1983), and associated memories and overall personality style. In this manner a physician can experience the patient's emotional states by "oscillating" between the role of observer and participant (Book, 1988), which Jaffe (1986) describes as alternately "thinking *with* the patient and then *about* the patient." This process involves transiently identifying with the patient, that is, imagining what it would be like to be in his or her situation, then "pulling back" as an understanding and now objective yet empathic observer.

A CASE STUDY

Dr. L entered Mr. M's hospital room and saw a young teenager lying on top of the bedsheets, his right leg supported by a series of pillows and heavily bandaged around the knee. Dr. L immediately felt a sinking feel-

ing in his stomach, then found himself recalling a serious childhood ac-
cident of his own that had required an extended hospitalization. Mr. M
trembled slightly as he greeted Dr. L, attributing it to the air condition-
ing which had given him a chill, then grimaced in pain as he propped
himself up in bed. When asked how he was feeling, Mr. M reported that
he was being "treated like a rock star" by "a hundred people taking care
of me." Although Dr. L did not have the patient's obvious physical pain,
he felt he understood Mr. L's anxiety and helplessness and could also
understand his wish that a multitude of caretakers minister to all his
needs.

The physician's emotional reaction to this patient derived primarily from the
young man's signals of emotional and physical distress, data that afforded an accurate
appreciation of Mr. M's affective and cognitive condition. He felt empathy for the
frightened young man, but this empathy nevertheless did not necessarily benefit the
patient until it was used positively. Empathy does not lead to an empathic interaction
until observations by clinicians are communicated in a genuine manner to the patient
(Bachrach, 1976). This requires conveying to the patient an understanding of his or
her internal emotional states in a manner that causes the patient to feel that the
physician is emotionally "with them" (Book, 1988).

Mr. M's ability to maintain a facade of artificial cheerfulness quickly
faltered as he began describing the details of his injury. The victim of a
hit-and-run driver, he had suffered considerable trauma to his knee that
required extensive reconstruction and a regimen of rehabilitative ther-
apy, the extent of which would be determined by the success of his sur-
gery. His agitation steadily increased during the interview, until he
abruptly stopped speaking "because I'm tired and want to crash for a
while." Dr. L agreed that rest was a good idea, and suggested that he re-
turn later. Shortly before leaving, Dr. L recalled how the conversation
brought back memories of his own hospitalization for a concussion when
he was 15. He remembered feeling frightened by the strangeness of the
hospital and the uncertainty of his prognosis, and guessed that Mr. M
might have similar feelings. As Dr. L reflected to the patient how he
might be feeling in this situation, the young man sensed the physician's
empathy and invited Dr. L to stay "a little longer," then ventilated
myriad thoughts and feelings about his injury. He concluded with the
prediction that he'd be "jogging again by Christmas."

As the case illustrates, empathy is only therapeutic when "accurate reception
[is] complemented by accurate feedback" (Keefe, 1976). This results in "empathic
communication" (Miller, 1989), an affective experience similar to the good feeling that
follows discussion of a problem with a close friend and leaves one feeling better due to
the sense of being heard and understood. A measure of the existence and benefit of
this type of interaction between Dr. L and his patient was Mr. M's emotional catharsis,

which greatly diminished his anxiety and concluded with a positive and probably realistic hope of running again.

Cohen-Cole's (1986) discussion of common supportive technical interventions used with the medically ill (briefly referred to in Chapter 2 in this text), and Buckley's (1986) exploration of their theoretical basis, highlights the role of empathy in psychotherapy. In general, physicians should present themselves as available and concerned, which requires "giving of self" as a real person as opposed to being neutral, objective, and analytic. They should use a personable, conversational tone to offer advice and reassurance (e.g., commenting on the patient's response to a treatment regimen), praise when warranted (e.g., when the patient progresses in a rehabilitative program), and didactic instruction about the illness (e.g., identifying normal emotional and behavioral aspects of the sick role). They should consistently attempt to involve patients in the treatment (e.g., inviting input into decisions concerning therapeutic options) in order to strengthen the working alliance. This overall posture helps limit patients' behavioral regression by retaining focus on the here-and-now, improves their compromised ego functioning by supporting usual defense mechanisms, and enhances self-esteem by acknowledging inherent strengths and therapeutic gains.

Hollis's (1964) description of the supportive approach also underscores the importance of empathic communication. He discusses four categories of intervention: (1) sustaining procedures (e.g., demonstration of a desire to help), (2) procedures of direct influence (e.g., offering suggestions and advice), (3) facilitation of catharsis (e.g., sanctioning the expression of emotions), and (4) guidance concerning the day-to-day implications of illness (e.g., urging the return to work or a change in one's living situation).

Finally, effective psychological care of medical patients ultimately depends on the ability of physicians to maintain perspective on their *own* emotions. Frequent exposure to severely ill individuals may cause considerable distress to physicians frustrated by their patients' marginal improvement or continued decline. Clinicians' heightened anxiety or mounting depression may cause them to unconsciously deny their own physical and emotional needs, grow increasingly emotionally distant by spending less time with the patient or becoming increasingly aloof, or generally neglect a patient's psychological needs by simply ignoring signs and symptoms of emotional distress.

One of the true personal arts of medicine is the ability to retain the capacity for empathy for patients, to sense when patients need an empathic response and to respond in a timely manner. This shifting back and forth from the more objective, technical, and analytic functions of being a physician to that of being a supportive empathic therapist is a skill that is difficult to achieve and maintain. It is nevertheless, *the* essential quality of being a physician.

An empathic approach in the context of a biopsychosocial frame of reference is " . . . to treat the whole patient and not merely characterize the nature of an illness and impede biologic deterioration" (Slaby and Glicksman, 1985). Excellent, integrated, and compassionate treatment of each patient as a unique individual is the ultimate goal of the compleat physician—and the goal of this text.

ANNOTATED BIBLIOGRAPHY

Engel G: The need for a new medical model: A challenge for biomedicine. Science 196:129–136, 1977

> In this article, Engel carefully articulates the shortcomings of the biomedical model, which he feels leaves no room within its framework for the social, psychological, and behavioral dimensions of illness. He demonstrates a need for the biopsychosocial approach as a "blueprint for research, a framework for teaching, and a design for action in the real world of health care."

Engel G: The clinical application of the biopsychosocial model. Am J Psychiatry 137:535–544, 1980

> An excellent complement to the above, this article uses the biopsychosocial model to describe the impact of an acute myocardial infarction on a middle-aged man. It explores the effect of relevant psychosocial issues (e.g., the role of family members, healthcare providers, and coworkers) on the onset, treatment, and course of his illness.

Frank J: Persuasion and Healing. Baltimore, Johns Hopkins University Press, 1961

> In this classic study of psychotherapy, the author explores the relationship between healer and sufferer, stressing the fundamental importance of the clinician's personal influence. Frank's observations concerning general attitudes and specific procedures that facilitate communication with patients constitute the basis of all forms of psychotherapy, including the supportive care of the medically ill.

Green S: Mind and Body: The Psychology of Physical Illness. Washington, DC, American Psychiatric Press, 1985

> This text expands on the basic principles discussed in this chapter, including the clinical applications of the biopsychosocial model and psychodynamic factors in the doctor–patient relationship.

Lipowski Z: Psychiatry of somatic disease: Epidemiology, pathogenesis, classification. Compr Psychiatry 16:105–124, 1975

> In this comprehensive article, the author presents a wealth of information concerning the linkage between psychiatric and physical illness. It is particularly notable for discussion of psychological responses to disease and injury, and the psychosocial determinants influencing those responses.

Lindemann E: Symptomatology and management of acute grief. Am J Psychiatry 101:141–146, 1944

> This landmark paper discusses the psychological and widespread psychophysiological manifestations of acute grief. Although subsequent investigations of bereavement modify Lindemann's initial conclusions (e.g., Rynearson E: Psychotherapy of pathologic grief: Revisions and limitations. Psychiatr Clin North Am 10:487–500, 1987), the work remains a standard in the field.

Parsons T: The Social System. Glencoe, IL, The Free Press, 1951

> Part of this lengthy sociologic text is devoted to study of medical practice, including a sophisticated discussion of the dynamics of the sick role. Emphasizing the collaborative nature of medical care, Parsons details distinctive roles for patient and clinician during the various stages of illness. Of particular importance is his description of the changing levels of dependency and autonomy required of the patient by different aspects of the treatment.

REFERENCES

Alexander F, French T: Psychoanalytic Therapy. New York, Ronald Press, 1946

Bachrach H: Empathy: We know what we mean, but what do we measure? Arch Gen Psychiatry 33:35–38, 1976

Basch M: Empathic understanding: A review of the concept and some theoretical considerations. J Am Psychoanal Assoc 31:101–125, 1983

Book H: Empathy: Misconceptions and misuses in psychotherapy. Am J Psychiatry 145:420–424, 1988

Brown J, Stoudemire GA: Normal and pathological grief. JAMA 250:378–382, 1983

Buckley P: A neglected treatment. Psych Ann 16:515–521, 1986

Buie D: Empathy: Its nature and limitations. J Am Psychoanal Assoc 29:281–307, 1981

Cohen-Cole S, Bird J: Interviewing the cardiac patient II: A practical guide for helping patients cope with their emotions. Qual Life Cardiovasc Care 3:53–65, 1986

Collenda C: Training in empathy (letter). Am J Psychiatry 146:125–126, 1989

Engel G: A life-setting conducive to illness: The giving-up–given-up complex. Ann Intern Med 69:293–298, 1968

Engel G: The need for a new medical model: A challenge for biomedicine. Science 196:129–136, 1977

Engel G: The clinical application of the biopsychosocial model. Am J Psychiatry 137:535–544, 1980

Frank J: Persuasion and Healing. Baltimore, Johns Hopkins University Press, 1961

Green S: Mind and Body: The Psychology of Physical Illness. Washington, DC, American Psychiatric Press, 1985

Greenson R: Empathy and its vicissitudes. Int J Psychiatry 41:418–424, 1960

Groves J: Taking care of the hateful patient. N Engl J Med 298:883–887, 1978

Hollis F: Casework: A Psychosocial Therapy. New York, Random House, 1964

Irwin M, Daniels M, Weiner H: Immune and neorendocrine changes during bereavement. Psychiatr Clin N Am 10:449–466, 1987

Jaffe D: Empathy, counteridentification, countertransference: A review, with some personal perspectives on the "analytic instrument." Psychoanal Q 55:215–243, 1986

Kahana R, Bibring G: Personality types in medical management. In Zinberg N (ed): Psychiatry and Medical Practice in a General Hospital. New York, International Universities Press, 1964

Keefe T: Empathy: The critical skill. Social Work 21:10–14, 1976

Kohut H: How Does Analysis Cure? Chicago, University of Chicago Press, 1984, p 82

Lindemann E: Symptomatology and management of acute grief. Am J Psychiatry 101:141–146, 1944

Lipowski Z: Psychiatry of somatic disease: Epidemiology, pathogenesis, classification. Compr Psychiatry 16:105–124, 1975

Miller I: The therapeutic empathic communication (TEC) process. Am J Psychother 43:531–545, 1989

Parsons T: The Social System. Glencoe, IL, The Free Press, 1951

Rahe R: Subjects' recent life changes and their near-future illness reports. Ann Clin Res 4:1–16, 1973

Reich P, DeSilva R, Lown B et al: Acute psychological disturbances preceding life-threatening ventricular arrhythmias. JAMA 246:233–235, 1981

Reichard J: Teaching principles of medical psychology to medical house officers: Methods and problems. In Zinberg N (ed): Psychiatry and Medical Practice in a General Hospital. New York, International Universities Press, 1964

Slaby A, Glicksman A: Adapting to Life-Threatening Illness. New York, Praeger, 1985

Stein M, Keller S, Schleifer S: Stress and immunomodulation: The role of depression and neuroendocrine function. J Immunol 135 (Suppl 2):827–833, 1985

Vailliant G: Adaptation to Life. Boston, Little, Brown, & Co, 1977

Winston A, Pinsker H, McCullough L: A review of supportive psychotherapy. Hosp Comm Psychiatry 37:1105–1114, 1986

Zola I: Socio-cultural factors in the seeking of medical aid: A progress report. Transcult Psychiatr Res 14:62–65, 1963

Index